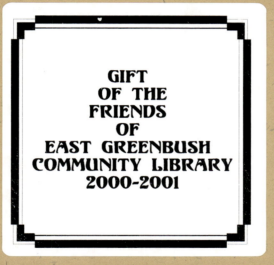

The Historical Encyclopedia of

WORLD SLAVERY

VOLUME I
A-K

The Historical Encyclopedia of
WORLD SLAVERY

VOLUME I
A-K

Junius P. Rodriguez
General Editor

ABC-CLIO

Santa Barbara, California
Denver, Colorado
Oxford, England

Library of Congress Cataloging-in-Publication Data

The Historical encyclopedia of world slavery / Junius P. Rodriguez,
    general editor.
        p.   cm.
    Includes bibliographical references and index.
    ISBN 0-87436-885-5 (alk. paper)
    1. Slavery—Encyclopedias. I. Rodriguez, Junius P.
    HT861.H57 1997
    306.3'62'03—dc21   97-42839

02 01 00   10 9 8 7 6 5 4 3

ABC-CLIO, Inc.
130 Cremona Drive, P.O. Box 1911
Santa Barbara, California 93116-1911

This book is printed on acid-free paper ♾.
Manufactured in the United States of America

⧼CONTENTS⧽

The Historical Encyclopedia of
WORLD SLAVERY

❧CONTRIBUTORS❧

Valerie Abrahamsen
Jamaica Plain, Massachusetts

Tunde Adeleke
Loyola University
New Orleans, Louisiana

Funso Afolayan
University of New Hampshire
Durham, New Hampshire

Carlos Aguirre
University of Oregon
Eugene, Oregon

J. Michael Allen
University of Auckland
New Zealand

Richard B. Allen
Champaign, Illinois

Randal S. Allison
College Station, Texas

Donald Altschiller
Boston University
Boston, Massachusetts

Thanet Aphornsuvan
Thammsat University
Thailand

Andrea M. Atkin
Wake Forest University
Winston-Salem, North Carolina

Edward E. Baptist
University of Pennsylvania
Philadelphia, Pennsylvania

Robert Berkhofer
Harvard University
Cambridge, Massachusetts

Matt C. Bischoff
Tucson, Arizona

Jackie R. Booker
South Carolina State University
Orangeburg, South Carolina

Daniel L. Boxberger
Western Washington University
Bellingham, Washington

Kevin Brady
Drew University
Madison, New Jersey

Kimberly Henke Breuer
Vanderbilt University
Nashville, Tennessee

Stefan Brink
Uppsala University
Sweden

Christopher L. Brown
Institute of Early American History
  and Culture
Williamsburg, Virginia

Ron D. Bryant
Kentucky Historical Society
Frankfort, Kentucky

Carlos Buitrago Ortíz
University of Puerto Rico
San Juan, Puerto Rico

Keith Byerman
Indiana State University
Terre Haute, Indiana

Joseph P. Byrne
North Georgia College and State
  University
Dahlonega, Georgia

Sydney J. Caddel
Colorado Springs, Colorado

John Callow
Lancaster University
United Kingdom

Stephanie M. H. Camp
University of Pennsylvania
Philadelphia, Pennsylvania

Robert W. Cape, Jr.
Austin College
Sherman, Texas

Jesper Carlsen
Odense University
Denmark

Vincent Carretta
University of Maryland–College Park
College Park, Maryland

Brian Catlos
University of Toronto
Canada

Mark Cave
Williams Research Center
New Orleans, Louisiana

Bill Cecil-Fronsman
Washburn University
Topeka, Kansas

Craige Champion
Allegheny College
Meadville, Pennsylvania

Mark W. Chavalas
University of Wisconsin–La Crosse
La Crosse, Wisconsin

Anthony Q. Cheeseboro
Southern Illinois University–
  Edwardsville
Edwardsville, Illinois

Constance J. S. Chen
University of California–Los Angeles
Los Angeles, California

William L. Chew III
Vesalius College, Vrije Universiteit
Belgium

Boyd Childress
Auburn University
Auburn, Alabama

Tim Clarkson
University of Manchester
United Kingdom

David M. Cobin
Hamline University
St. Paul, Minnesota

Philip R. P. Coelho
Ball State University
Muncie, Indiana

Jim Comer
Bowling Green, Ohio

Jerry W. Cooney
University of Louisville (ret.)
Castle Rock, Washington

Mary-Ellen Cummings
Auburn University
Auburn, Alabama

Enrico Dal Lago
University College, London
United Kingdom

Russ Davidson
University of New Mexico
Albuquerque, New Mexico

Brian Dirck
University of Kansas
Lawrence, Kansas

Leland Donald
University of Victoria
Canada

Laurent Dubois
University of Michigan
Ann Arbor, Michigan

Elizabeth Dubrulle
Colonial Society of Massachusetts
Boston, Massachusetts

Francis A. Dutra
University of California–Santa Barbara
Santa Barbara, California

Jonathan Earle
Princeton University
Princeton, New Jersey

Eric Ehrenreich
Madison, Wisconsin

Eckhard Eichler
University of Heidelberg
Germany

Maureen G. Elgersman
Clark Atlanta University
Atlanta, Georgia

Patience Essah
Auburn University
Auburn, Alabama

Raingard Eßer
London School of Economics and
*   Political Science*
United Kingdom

David L. Ferch
Sierra College
Rocklin, California

Paloma Fernández-Pérez
University of Barcelona
Spain

Peter S. Field
Tennessee Technological University
Cookeville, Tennessee

Robert Fikes, Jr.
San Diego State University
San Diego, California

Roy E. Finkenbine
University of Detroit–Mercy
Detroit, Michigan

Jerise Fogel
University of Illinois at Urbana-
*   Champaign*
Urbana, Illinois

William H. Foster III
Cornell University
Ithaca, New York

Baltasar Fra-Molinero
Bates College
Lewiston, Maine

DoVeanna S. Fulton
University of Minnesota
Minneapolis, Minnesota

Gwilym Games
Lancaster University
United Kingdom

Larry Gara
Wilmington College
Wilmington, Ohio

John D. Garrigus
Jacksonville University
Jacksonville, Florida

Joseph Goldenberg
Virginia State University
Petersburg, Virginia

Henry H. Goldman
University of Phoenix
Phoenix, Arizona

Marquetta L. Goodwine
Afrikan Kultural Arts Network
Brooklyn, New York

Larry Gragg
University of Missouri–Rolla
Rolla, Missouri

John Grenier
Lafayette, Colorado

Lynne Guitar
Vanderbilt University
Nashville, Tennessee

Mark T. Gustafson
Calvin College
Grand Rapids, Michigan

Sally E. Hadden
Florida State University
Tallahassee, Florida

Bertil Haggman
Helsingborg, Sweden

Ian Hancock
University of Texas–Austin
Austin, Texas

Judith E. Harper
Canton, Massachusetts

J. Albert Harrill
DePaul University
Chicago, Illinois

Jane Hathaway
Ohio State University
Columbus, Ohio

David Hay
Pontifical Institute of Medieval Studies
Toronto, Canada

Edward F. Heite
Camden, Delaware

Louise Heite
Seydisfjord, Iceland

Sharon Roger Hepburn
Radford University
Radford, Virginia

Wallace Hettle
University of Northern Iowa
Cedar Falls, Iowa

Gary L. Hewitt
Grinnell College
Grinnell, Iowa

Birgitte Holten
University of Copenhagen
Denmark

Timothy S. Huebner
Rhodes College
Memphis, Tennessee

T. K. Hunter
Columbia University
New York, New York

Anthony A. Iaccarino
University of California–Los Angeles
Los Angeles, California

Fidel Iglesias
Eastern Kentucky University
Richmond, Kentucky

Au'Ra Muhammad Abdullah Ilahi
Universal Islamic School
Chicago, Illinois

Alexander Ingle
Boston University
Boston, Massachusetts

Timothy Insoll
St. John's College, Cambridge University
United Kingdom

Eric R. Jackson
Northern Kentucky University
Highland Heights, Kentucky

David A. Johnson
Texas A & M University
College Station, Texas

James Jupp
Australian National University
Canberra, Australia

Laura Croghan Kamoie
College of William and Mary
Williamsburg, Virginia

Kenneth G. Kelly
Northern Arizona University
Flagstaff, Arizona

Jeffrey R. Kerr-Ritchie
Wesleyan University
Middletown, Connecticut

Barbara J. Keys
Harvard University
Cambridge, Massachusetts

Patricia A. Kilroe
University of Wisconsin–Milwaukee
Milwaukee, Wisconsin

Hyong-In Kim
Seoul, South Korea

Stewart R. King
Johns Hopkins University
Baltimore, Maryland

Martin A. Klein
University of Toronto
Canada

Wim Klooster
Harvard University
Cambridge, Massachusetts

Robert S. Kramer
St. Norbert College
De Pere, Wisconsin

Diane Kriger
University of Toronto
Canada

Thomas W. Krise
U.S. Air Force Academy
Colorado Springs, Colorado

Sharon Landers
Franklin, Tennessee

Tom Lansford
Old Dominion University
Norfolk, Virginia

Benjamin N. Lawrance
Stanford University
Stanford, California

Lori Lee
University of Texas–Arlington
Arlington, Texas

Kurt E. Leichtle
University of Wisconsin–River Falls
River Falls, Wisconsin

David J. Libby
University of Mississippi
Oxford, Mississippi

David B. Malone
Wheaton College
Wheaton, Illinois

Maurice Major
Bernice Pauahi Bishop Museum
Honolulu, Hawaii

Eric Martin
Northeastern University
Boston, Massachusetts

Charles H. McArver, Jr.
Woodberry Forest School
Woodberry Forest, Virginia

Dwight A. McBride
University of Pittsburgh
Pittsburgh, Pennsylvania

Bryan McCann
Yale University
New Haven, Connecticut

Jerry D. McCoy
Eureka College
Eureka, Illinous

Robert A. McGuire
University of Akron
Akron, Ohio

Scott A. Merriman
Northern Kentucky University
Highland Heights, Kentucky

Debra Meyers
University of Rochester
Rochester, New York

Suzanne Miers
Ohio University
Athens, Ohio

Mary Jo Miles
Wayne State University
Detroit, Michigan

Chandra Miller
Boston National Historical Park
Boston, Massachusetts

Dennis J. Mitchell
Jackson State University
Jackson, Mississippi

Andrew P. Morriss
Case Western Reserve University
Cleveland, Ohio

Bruce L. Mouser
University of Wisconsin–LaCrosse
La Crosse, Wisconsin

Doug Munro
University of the South Pacific
Fiji

Julie R. Nelson
Iowa State University
Ames, Iowa

Caryn E. Neumann
Ohio State University
Columbus, Ohio

Elsa A. Nystrom
Kennesaw State University
Marietta, Georgia

Onaiwu W. Ogbomo
Allegheny College
Meadville, Pennsylvania

Jeff Pardue
University of Waterloo
Canada

Craig S. Pascoe
University of Tennessee
Knoxville, Tennessee

Diana Paton
Yale University
New Haven, Connecticut

Wesley Phelan
Eureka College
Eureka, Illinois

Julieanne Phillips
University of Dayton
Dayton, Ohio

Michael Phillips
University of Texas–Austin
Austin, Texas

Jan Pilditch
University of Waikato
New Zealand

David Pleasant
Brooklyn, New York

Federico Poole
Naples, Italy

Johannes Postma
Mankato State University
Mankato, Minnesota

James M. Prichard
Kentucky State Archives
Frankfort, Kentucky

John W. Pulis
Adelphi University
Garden City, New York

Karen Racine
Tulane University
New Orleans, Louisiana

Richard Raiswell
University of Toronto
Canada

James H. Rasheed
Muslim Teachers' College
Richmond, Virginia

Lindy J. Rawling
University of California–Santa Barbara
Santa Barbara, California

Douglas S. Reed
Georgetown University
Washington, D.C.

Richard A. Reiman
South Georgia College
Douglas, Georgia

Eric Reinders
University of Colorado–Boulder
Boulder, Colorado

Nora Reyes Costilla
El Colegio de Mexico
Mexico

James D. Rice
Central Washington University
Ellensburg, Washington

Claire Robertson
Ohio State University
Columbus, Ohio

Patricia Romero
Towson State University
Towson, Maryland

Barbara Ryan
Michigan Society of Fellows
Ann Arbor, Michigan

Robin Sabino
Auburn University
Auburn, Alabama

Frank A. Salamone
Iona College
New Rochelle, New York

Richard W. Sanders
Eureka College
Eureka, Illinois

L. Natalie Sandomirsky
Southern Connecticut State University
New Haven, Connecticut

Walter Scheidel
Darwin College, Cambridge University
United Kingdom

Arnold Schmidt
California State University–Stanislaus
Stanislaus, California

Elizabeth Schoales
University of Toronto
Canada

Jeanne Schock
University of Toronto
Canada

Angelie Sens
University of Utrecht
The Netherlands

Juan Manuel de la Serna
Universidad Nacional
  Autónoma de Mexico

John F. Shean
University of Wisconsin–Madison
Madison, Wisconsin

Talaat Shehata
Miami University
Oxford, Ohio

Jason H. Silverman
Winthrop University
Rock Hill, South Carolina

Malik Simba
California State University–Fresno
Fresno, California

Frederick J. Simonelli
Mount St. Mary's College
Los Angeles, California

James L. Sledge III
Truett-McConnell College
Cleveland, Georgia

Dale Edwyna Smith
Washington University
St. Louis, Missouri

John David Smith
North Carolina State University
Raleigh, North Carolina

Chunghee Sarah Soh
San Francisco State University
San Francisco, California

John Stauffer
Yale University
New Haven, Connecticut

William O. Stephens
Creighton University
Omaha, Nebraska

Michael C. Stone
Hartwick College
Oneonta, New York

Susan A. Stussy
Kansas City, Kansas

Harold D. Tallant
Georgetown College
Georgetown, Kentucky

H. Micheal Tarver
McNeese State University
Lake Charles, Louisiana

Luana Tavernier
Florence, Italy

Anthony Tibbles
Merseyside Maritime Museum
Liverpool, United Kingdom

Anthony Todman
St. John's University
Jamaica, New York

Víctor Torres-Vélez
University of Puerto Rico
San Juan, Puerto Rico

Hélène N. Turkewicz-Sanko
John Carroll University
Cleveland, Ohio

Terrence M. Vaughan
National Park Service
Boston, Massachusetts

Albert Wachtel
Pitzer College
Claremont, California

Peter Wallenstein
Virginia Polytechnic Institute
  and State University
Blacksburg, Virginia

Nagueyalti Warren
Emory University
Atlanta, Georgia

Mary Ellen Wilson
Middle Georgia College
Cochran, Georgia

Yolandea Wood
Colorado Springs, Colorado

Nigel Worden
University of Cape Town
South Africa

Judith T. Wozniak
Cleveland State University
Cleveland, Ohio

John J. Zaborney
University of Maine
Orono, Maine

Robert J. Zalimas, Jr.
Ohio State University
Columbus, Ohio

Joseph W. Zarzynski
U.S. Schooner Alligator Project
Wilton, New York

~INTRODUCTION~
Slavery in Human History

The institution of slavery in all of its varied forms is one of the most idiosyncratic practices found in all of human history. Throughout time, practically all of the world's civilizations and cultures have experienced some type of slavery, and peoples both ancient and modern in societies ranging from the simplest to the most complex have coped with the practice and with the many manifestations of its legacy. In a seemingly dichotomous world, the presence of slavery has occasionally served to fashion a meaning for freedom by defining such an attribute through its negation. So manifest is slavery to the whole of human history that it is difficult to try to understand the modern world without considering one of the most perplexing elements of the human condition. Making sense of slavery, and all of its associated elements and consequences, encompasses much of human history.

Over the years, historians, sociologists, anthropologists, economists, psychologists, and many others have all struggled to find a rational explanation of slavery's origins, its purpose, and its essential place in the human experience. Variations, both subtle and pronounced, characterize the meaning of the word "slavery," and it evokes discordant images throughout history. Although no single explanation exists that is suitable as a global definition of the institution, certain characteristics are commonly found in those societies that have practiced slavery. These attributes help to structure an institutional matrix of bondage that has existed in society from the dawn of civilization to the modern age.

Certain characteristics are basic to an understanding of the institution of slavery. First, most slave societies tended to dehumanize the individual by considering the slave to be property that is owned by another. Even though each polity often legislated the level of mobility that was afforded the slave, he or she remained bound as legal property that could be bought, sold, or traded at the whim of another. Second, slaves were generally objectified as lesser beings by legal codes which maintained that the commercial rights and prerogatives of owners or masters were superior to any natural rights that the slave might possess. In such a system, a slave's level of production was deemed to be far more important than his or her actual person or identity, and accordingly, the slave was essentially an economic creature. Third, most slave societies tended to marginalize the slave by enslaving only people who might be considered as separate from the community—especially criminals, foreigners, and war captives. These individuals endured what some scholars have described as "social death" as they owed their very survival to the magnanimous mercy of their captors. Within such a society, there were no rights or privileges that applied to the once-spared. Essentially, slavery was perceived as a benevolent act.

One feature that seems common among most slave societies was the understanding that enslavement was not something done to one's own people. Although voluntary slavery was permissible in many societies, it was usually restricted only to those situations that involved the repayment of a debt. Early slave societies did not use race or ethnicity as a determinant in who would be enslaved, but they did recognize the value of group identity and would not generally submit one of their own to involuntary enslavement. For example, though they were ethnically similar as Greeks, it was permissible for Spartans to hold the Messenians in a form of virtual slavery as Helots. Although the Peloponnesus (peninsula in southern Greece) was a relatively small place, group identity prevailed and helped to determine societal norms.

Most societies did not deny all rights to the slave. In most legal codes, the slave was protected from the most extreme physical abuse that an owner or overseer might inflict. Yet statutes alone could not protect most slaves from harm, and societies often maintained fluid definitions of what constituted necessary and proper action when disciplining an unruly slave. Societies also maintained differing attitudes toward the slave's right to marry and live in a family setting. Although some slave societies stressed the beneficent results that family living produced (i.e., slaves were more productive and less likely to escape), other cultures had no respect for slave kinship and some went so far as to control the slave's sexuality and reproductive abilities for the owner's pleasure or economic benefit. Slaves enjoyed some rights within all slave societies, but the distribution of justice was certainly not fair and impartial, and even in the most enlightened settings, the liberties afforded to slaves were always more theoretical than real as the rights of property owners superseded the rights of the property.

It is not known precisely how or when slavery

began. The most ancient of civilizations all appear to have had some form of slavery present in their earliest years. Slave laborers worked the fertile fields along the Tigris and Euphrates Rivers in Mesopotamia; they also toiled along the Nile in Egypt during the Old Kingdom period; and slaves worked in the budding civilizations of India and China that formed in the Indus and Yangtze (Chang) River valleys, in the forests and savannas in the earliest of African civilizations, and even in the Americas, where pre-Columbian indigenous peoples maintained social structures that included a class of slaves. Thus, we are presented with a paradox. In the societies that represent the birth of civilization—the cultural transformation from primitive to modern—we find the transfer and continuation of an ancient practice that has had a sweeping influence on modernity. Culturally advanced peoples have incorporated slavery into their social systems over time, and history has had to reckon with the consequences.

In all societies where slavery has existed it has become a part of the manifest culture of that particular setting. As a cultural phenomenon, slavery has always been directly influenced by the various cultural attributes that exist in each society where it appears. The interaction between slavery and the political, social, economic, religious, intellectual, and aesthetic spheres of cultural life creates the primary attributes that distinguish one form of slavery from another. For just as the cultural dimensions influence slavery, so too does slavery influence each respective sphere. Thus, even in two societies that seem culturally similar, subtle variations might still be detected in the ways that slavery operates in each.

In ancient societies, slavery was accepted as being part of the natural social order. As an economic tool that could distribute labor and institutionalize wealth, its validity and purpose were unquestioned. Neither governments nor organized religions made any attempt in the earliest societies to intervene on behalf of the enslaved to mitigate the circumstances of their bondage. No systematic movement toward abolition ever existed in ancient societies because slavery was not viewed as an issue of public morality. Accordingly, it is difficult for the modern world to comprehend the values and the structures that legitimized such a system.

Slavery in the Ancient World

In the earliest societies of the Near East, slavery assumed much of the form that it would have throughout history. In the societies of Mesopotamia, slavery generally existed in one of two basic forms. Some viewed slavery as a type of punishment that might be imposed upon one who had transgressed the laws or customs of the polity, or perhaps one who had taken up arms against the community in warfare and in so doing, had become an enemy of the state. Others

thought the institution had a more utilitarian purpose. For them, slavery was a way of organizing laborers to perform much needed responsibilities that were critical to the welfare of the entire community. An important characteristic common to both views was that slavery did not utilize race or ethnicity to distinguish between the slaveowner and the bondsman or bondswoman. Slaves were culturally indistinguishable from free people. Although one Sumerian pictograph represents the idea of a slave as a "male of foreign land," the conflicts that ensued between ethnically similar neighbors produced a class of slaves who were not dissimilar to their masters.

The Code of Hammurabi, issued in the eighteenth century B.C., demonstrates that the ancient Babylonians understood the complex nature of the institution of slavery and passed laws to regulate the practice. Even though the code regarded the slave as merchandise, it contained significant humanitarian terms that recognized basic rights owing to the slave. Male slaves could marry freewomen, own property, and in some cases purchase their own freedom, but the code continued to view them as chattel rather than as human beings. In formulating these legal distinctions, the Code of Hammurabi and subsequent law codes that addressed the issue fashioned a spectrum of various status levels ranging from one of abject powerlessness to one of supreme control. Thus, the slave occupied an indistinct status that often varied according to individual circumstance and location. In the Hittite Code, which was in effect from the seventeenth to the fourteenth centuries B.C., the slave was recognized as a human being, but the inferior status of the enslaved was more manifest.

Certain ancient civilizations practiced forms of slavery in which the slave's status was not very different from that of the slaveowning class. In such societies an institutional process of manumission (formal emancipation) usually existed to facilitate the transition from slave status to freedom. Among the Hebrew people it was understood that a slave of Hebrew origin became free after six years of servitude. By combining notions of adoption with their practices of enslavement, many West African societies incorporated practices that allowed slaves and their progeny an opportunity to live in freedom after manumission. Yet, even with the existence of these customs, the condition enjoyed by the formerly enslaved was not comparable to the modern Western notion of personal freedom. Most scholars agree that that notion was born several centuries later in the city-states of classical Greece.

Ancient Egypt was the early civilization that was generally the least dependent upon the economic value of slave labor. In Egypt, the existence of a large regimented population and a limited amount of agricultural land under royal ownership precluded the need for large-scale agricultural slavery in the valley of the Nile. War captives who became slaves tended to be employed on temple estates, in government quarries, or on certain state construction projects. Egyptian society also included a significant number of individuals who submitted themselves voluntarily into slavery as a result of indebtedness until the practice was ended in the eighth century B.C. One indication of the relative social worth of the slave as compared to the slaveowner was the practice of murdering slaves so they might accompany their deceased owners into the afterlife.

Slavery existed in some form or another in all of the earliest civilizations, but that does not suggest that these ancient societies had a dichotomous social order that pitted the free against the unfree. The spectrum of status that existed in the ancient world was generally fluid as one's social identity and hierarchical significance depended upon the degree of liberty that one was allowed to enjoy. Cultural variations developed, and certain forms of intermediate status—e.g., Babylonian *mushkēnum*, and Indian Sudras—became a part of the social identity that existed within distinct cultures.

All early civilizations practiced slavery, but none can be accurately described as a slave society. In none of these cultures did slaves constitute a majority of the population—in fact, in most of them, the percentage of slaves within the society was comparatively small. Accordingly, the economic value of the labor performed by slaves in the ancient world was generally insignificant, and thus economic determinism alone cannot be used as a rationale to justify the perpetuation of slavery within ancient cultures. Apparently the value of slavery as a social institution that absorbed the outsider into a culture was justification enough to perpetuate its existence. The concept of "social death" produced a sense of societal order that in a cost-benefit analysis can be viewed as basic to the establishment of civil societies.

Slavery in Classical Societies

It was in the civilizations that developed in Greece and Rome that the world's first true slave societies came into existence. Perplexing as it may be, the same societies that are credited with formulating some of humankind's most stellar accomplishments in philosophy and the arts and sciences were also the first peoples to elevate slavery to an institutional level that had not been attained in more primitive societies. In short, "the glory that was Greece and the grandeur that was Rome" stemmed largely from slave-based economies that utilized human capital to an unprecedented extent.

The evolution of slavery in ancient Greece is particular noteworthy because many Western notions of freedom and liberty developed in the milieu of defining and institutionalizing slavery. Ironically, contemporary notions equating slavery with tyranny stem from this era in which liberty was defined by its negation and the birthright of freedom came to be cherished by all—except slaves. Also significant in this context is the realization that for centuries, apologists for slavery used classical Greece as a shining example of the achievements that were attainable in a society in which slavery was a natural part. For these reasons, a clear understanding of slavery as it existed in the classical age is critically important if one hopes to comprehend the legacy of slavery and its nature in the modern world.

The Greeks used philosophy to rationalize their acceptance of slavery. Plato did not oppose slavery as an institution, but he did not look favorably upon the practice of Greeks' enslaving fellow Greeks. Aristotle echoed this concern, but believing that Greeks were superior to foreigners, he felt that it was quite logical and proper for superiors to rule over inferiors. Aristotle also viewed slaves as instruments that could be used by their betters to perform unsavory tasks in society, which would thus allow the superior Greek citizens to have a greater amount of leisure in which to pursue more sophisticated cultural attainments.

The society that formed in the autonomous Greek city-states was heavily dependent upon slave laborers. The Homeric epics indicate that slavery existed in Greece in the earliest years (c. twelfth century B.C.), but these references also indicate there was no organized trade in slaves at that time. During the late archaic period (eighth to sixth centuries B.C.), substantial numbers of Athenians held in bondage as debt-slaves worked the agricultural holdings of their fellow citizens. So pervasive was this social practice that by the sixth century B.C., it had produced a political crisis in Athenian life, and only substantial reform of the institution could remedy the situation.

Large numbers of poor Athenian farmers worked as sharecroppers on the lands of aristocratic citizens, and increasingly farmers, their wives, and their children were being enslaved as debtors because of an inability to produce the shares demanded by their landlords. Hoping to avert a crisis, in 594 B.C. the Athenian lawgiver Solon freed all Athenian slaves and outlawed the practice of enslavement for nonpayment of debts. Thereafter, Athens was a slave-based society, but the enslaved had to be foreign-born noncitizens—generally, captives of war. Athenian participation in the Persian Wars provided a ready source of war captives, and as Athens entered the classical period (fifth to third centuries B.C.), perhaps one-third to one-half of the population of Athens consisted of slaves. In the second century B.C., the Greek historian Polybius described slaves as being among "the necessities of life" and considered them as being comparable to cattle.

Although transformations in slavery certainly

changed Athenian society—making Athens a more cosmopolitan city-state—the institution of slavery also had a profound impact throughout the Greek world. In the seventh century B.C., the Spartans conquered neighboring Messenians and subjugated the population there to a state of virtual enslavement as Helots. After several decades, the Messenians rose in revolt and tried to end the Spartan overlordship. The 30-year rebellion was fierce, and though the Spartans eventually were able to overcome the formidable Messenian challenge, Sparta learned the true cost of maintaining a slave society. Vigilance was the key to self-preservation, and Sparta developed into a garrison state based on rigid militaristic lines so it might be constantly prepared for the potential onslaught of another slave-inspired rebellion. Sparta, in adopting this posture of having a perpetual war economy, reflected the truism that both master and slave are enslaved by the institution of slavery. Once again, the meanings of freedom and liberty were defined by their negation.

Sparta eventually fought and defeated Athens in the Peloponnesian War (431–404 B.C.) that hastened the end of the Golden Age in Greece. Practically all the Greek city-states were left in a weakened condition by the prolonged intensity of this conflict, and the entire peninsula was unable to avert the invasion by the Macedonians that culminated in the Battle of Chaeronea in 338 B.C. Philip II of Macedonia, the father of Alexander the Great, freed most, but not all, of the Greek slaves. The institution of slavery continued in a somewhat modified form in the Hellenistic world as Alexander the Great extended Greek customs and practices throughout his far-flung empire of conquest. Reliance upon slavery declined during the Hellenistic age, partly because of the moderating influence of the Stoic philosophy, which condemned slavery and war, but also because the economic prosperity of the times made it cheaper to hire free laborers and pay them wages than to purchase and maintain slaves.

Slavery was an uncommon institution when the city of Rome was developing along the banks of the Tiber River, but that would change as Rome emerged victorious from several wars of conquest. Rome and the North African city of Carthage vied for control of Sicily and the right to navigate the Mediterranean freely, and the two eventually fought a series of three Punic Wars. Rome emerged victorious from these conflicts and became the sole power in the Mediterranean world, but the economic and social tensions that accompanied these victories would lead to the eventual undoing of the Roman Republic. As a result of the wars of conquest and the many captives accrued in the process, Rome became a slave society.

Although the Roman Republic existed initially as a community of small independent farmers, wars of conquest gave the Romans an abundance of slaves that eclipsed the levels of previous civilizations. The decision to employ these slaves in agricultural pursuits had the effect of reordering or restructuring Roman society. With slaves increasingly being used to perform agricultural labor in the countryside, many Roman farmers found employment in the military. As the armies swelled, additional wars of conquest produced even more captives and the expansion of slavery continued. As the economy became increasingly based upon estate slavery, many independent farmers lost their landholdings, moved to the urban centers, and essentially became wards of the state. A decline in civic virtue, caused in large part by the massive development of a slave system, was one of the factors that helped precipitate the collapse of the Roman Republic.

The slave system that developed in the Roman Republic was unparalleled in antiquity. Military conquests in Syria, Galatia, Gaul, and North Africa produced numerous war captives, and thousands of slaves labored on the large estates (latifundia) in the Roman countryside under the tacit control of a few very wealthy owners. These owners had virtually limitless power over their vast number of slaves since the Romans viewed absolute authority as an equalizing force that would help prevent any type of unrest among the slave population. Yet rather than preserving public order, cruelty and mistreatment occasionally caused significant numbers of slaves to rise in concert to overthrow their owners' control. Servile rebellion was one of the few avenues available to slaves to demonstrate their humanity. The revolt Spartacus led from 73 to 71 B.C. is probably the best known of these uprisings. For Romans, the ever-present fear of slave revolt was one of the unanticipated consequences of their military success and subsequent rise to greatness. Even though they recognized the possibility that every slave within the republic was a potential insurgent, the Romans were also confident that their legions could suppress any insurrection that might arise.

Political destabilization and declining public morality were two of the major forces that destroyed the Roman Republic, but even as the republic faded and Rome moved toward imperial administration, the institution of slavery remained relatively unscathed. Aristocratic Romans had become accustomed to a lifestyle of excessive luxury that was made possible largely by a dependence upon slave labor, and few were willing to alter or challenge the institution that had created the socioeconomic status they enjoyed. As the Roman Empire extended its boundaries, slavery continued to flourish.

The Romans believed that manual labor was a sign of lowliness and should be performed only by slaves, but as the empire expanded, the Roman attitude toward labor became much more inclusive. In the early years of the Roman Empire, slaves occupied many of the white-collar and blue-collar jobs in Roman society, and thus some of them were able to attain positions of great wealth, power, and prestige. Many slaves held significant positions in business and in government bureaus during the first century of the Principate (27 B.C.–A.D. 180). Slaves constituted as much as 30 percent of the population in the early years of the Principate, but the number of Roman slaves gradually declined as many were legally converted to *coloni* (serfs) and it became increasingly difficult for the Romans to find new sources of outsiders to enslave.

The advent of Christianity did not have a significant impact upon the practice of slavery in the Roman world. Like the Jewish tradition from which it developed, Christianity questioned neither the morality nor the legitimacy of the institution of slavery. The teachings of Jesus included no official condemnation of slavery, and both the Old and the New Testaments of the Bible contain passages that reflect an acceptance of the social and political conditions of the times—including an acceptance of slavery as it existed. Perhaps the most significant influence of Christianity upon slavery was the message of hope that was found in the otherworldly focus of this new faith. Regardless of how horrid the conditions of the temporal life might be, Christianity offered the promise that great rewards awaited the true believer in an eternal life within the kingdom of God. Although the writings of Paul and other early fathers of the church reflect a sense of pity for the slave, their works condemn neither the institution of slavery nor the slaveowner.

Slavery in the Medieval World

The 1,000-year period that followed the collapse of the Roman Empire in the west was a formative period in the historical evolution of slavery. The Byzantine Empire, which perpetuated a sense of Roman rule in the east, maintained significant reliance upon a slave system until the thirteenth century, while at this same time, Western Europe developed into a feudal society that maintained an economic system based upon manorialism and the use of serfs and slaves as agricultural laborers. The rise of Islam and its rapid expansion during the seventh and eighth centuries generated new slave-based societies in the Near East, parts of Africa, and Europe. This era also witnessed the extension of the institution of slavery into the Crimea and modern Russia.

Especially significant during this era was the formation of sophisticated kingdoms in western Africa's Sudan region. The respective states of Ghana, Mali, and Songhai developed into societies that practiced slavery, and each maintained commercial ties with European and Near Eastern cultures through trans-Saharan trade routes. Items traded in this fashion included gold, ivory, salt, and also slaves. Additional trade in

Zanj slaves from eastern Africa to the region of modern-day Iraq also occurred during this era. Significant numbers of Zanj slaves who were assigned to clearing salt flats for use as agricultural lands rose in revolt during the ninth century.

Some twentieth-century scholars have argued that the medieval era marks a significant point in the historical evolution of labor as slavery gave way to serfdom and serfdom, in turn, developed into wage labor. Certain Marxist scholars who share this opinion would posit that wage labor is nothing more than a transitional phase that will eventually give way to the revival of a primitive form of communism similar to what is found in a state of nature. Accordingly, much of the scholarship regarding slavery in the medieval era, particularly in Western Europe, tends to pit conflicting economic communities—the free and the less-than-free—against one another in a classic proto-Marxist struggle for social and economic viability.

It appears that the practice of slavery that survived in Western Europe after the fall of the Roman Empire was more harsh than earlier forms of slavery. Several barbarian law codes treat the slave on the same level as livestock, and the most basic elements of human rights were not acknowledged by these codes. The practice of slavery survived for several centuries during the Middle Ages, and England's Domesday Book indicates that large numbers of slaves still existed when that census was taken in 1086. Various political and economic forces within Europe combined to make slavery practically nonexistent within Western Europe by the eleventh century, but sporadic Viking and Magyar raids continued to enslave those who were unfortunate enough to be taken as captives. Large numbers of Irish, in particular, were enslaved in this fashion during the medieval period.

Perhaps the most significant development in the history of world slavery during the medieval period was the rise of Islam. Although both Judaism and Christianity acknowledged the institution of slavery and neither faith sought to condemn the practice, Islam was the first of the major world faiths to take a limited type of abolitionist stance regarding certain aspects of the institution. The Qur'an specifically prohibits the enslavement of Muslims by fellow Muslims, and though this prohibition was not always enforced, its articulation was a powerful indication that slavery was a less-than-palatable practice and one that should not be imposed upon coreligionists. In later centuries, some people would argue that Christians also adopted this prohibition as a de facto custom, although such a view was perhaps more an aspiration than actually practiced.

Even more spectacular than the rise of Islam was the rapidity with which the new faith spread throughout the Near East, across North Africa, into the sub-Saharan Sudan, and into Europe. Within less than a century after its founding, Islam had become a dominant force in much of the Mediterranean-centered world, and the religious rivalries that ensued often included familiar practices of warfare—the taking of captives and their subsequent enslavement. Both Christians and Muslims developed their own notions of the meaning of a "just war," and each faith developed its own rules of engagement that permitted the taking of captives and the enslavement of the same under certain conditions. In later centuries, the desire of Europeans to find Christian allies who might join the fight against Islam encouraged the early expeditions that explored the African coastline searching for the mythical Prester John and his legendary Christian warriors.

Many within western Africa's sudanic kingdoms accepted Islam when it was introduced by trans-Saharan traders in the eighth century. Initially transmitted orally, before the Qur'an was standardized into a written text, Islam spread rapidly in a culture that had a historical affinity for the oral tradition. Many of the leaders of the West African kingdoms converted to Islam, and in so doing, large numbers of their subject peoples were also converted. The new faith seemed especially common among the merchants and traders who maintained a more cosmopolitan outlook through international trade with associates in other regions. In the kingdoms of West Africa, Islam always maintained its strongest support among the cultural elite, and the religion was primarily urban-based. Muslim theology was compatible with many indigenous religious practices of West African societies, and the promise of equality in the larger Muslim community was appealing to many.

Certain dynastic Muslim states such as the Ummayyad caliphate, the Abbasid caliphate, and eventually the Ottoman Empire arose in the Near East as slave-based societies. Household slavery tended to be a more common practice in this setting than dependence upon agricultural slavery. Frequently, slave women were imported to serve as concubines of the wealthy, and some private harems were quite large. Emasculated male slaves were purchased to guard these harems from intruders. Only about 10 percent of these eunuchs survived the crude form of castration that was generally performed before they were transported to their final destination as slaves, but among those who did survive, many found favor at the court and attained positions of power and prestige. Over the centuries, Christian children were enslaved and trained to serve as Janissary soldiers—an elite fighting corps that served the Ottoman rulers.

Christian Europeans maintained a strained relationship of prolonged hostility with the Islamic states, and occasionally the feelings of ill will escalated into warfare. Both groups viewed this type of religious conflict, or holy war, as a justification for enslaving captives. During the Crusades, Christians enslaved large numbers of Muslims who were captured in battle, and Muslim pirates countered by enslaving large numbers of Christians captured in commercial raiding expeditions. Even the Byzantine city of Constantinople, which was a major commercial center and a transshipment point for slaves, was attacked by the European warriors during the Fourth Crusade.

On the Iberian Peninsula, where Islamic forces first entered Western Europe in 711, Christian warriors mounted a campaign of reconquest that survived intermittently for seven centuries until Muslim forces were finally removed from Spain in 1492. During the Reconquista, the Spanish captured and enslaved the Moors (North African Muslims) as new territories were liberated by advancing forces. The practice that developed during this extensive campaign against the Muslims—granting privileges (encomienda rights) to certain Christian warriors (adelantados) who reestablished Spanish control—was the same system that was later modified and employed to subjugate indigenous populations in the Americas.

Africa and the Slave Trade

Until the mid-fifteenth century, slavery had been practiced extensively in various cultures and settings, but it had never been affiliated with race or ethnicity. Enslavement was simply the custom that befell people who had been defeated in conflict and were captives of war. In a theoretical sense, it was a humanitarian gesture that prevented the wholesale execution of captives, but that notion began to change as European navigators explored the coastline of West Africa and large-scale commerce in a human commodity began to develop.

As in other societies, slavery had existed in Africa since antiquity, but the African variety of slavery was indeed different from that found in other settings. Generally, African societies did not consider slaves to be personal property, and slavery was seldom viewed as a permanent condition. The rights of the slave were usually protected by local tribal law and custom, and avenues generally existed through which a slave could purchase freedom for himself or for his family members. These practices and customs were challenged as increasing numbers of European expeditions reached the African coastline and a harsher system of slavery was imposed upon the peoples of western Africa.

Seeking adventure and wealth, and emboldened by innovations in sailing technology, Portuguese navigators began a gradual process of exploring the West African coastline shortly after the conquest of the port of Ceuta in modern-day Morocco in 1415. By the 1440s, sailors had reached Cape Verde on the coast of modern-day Senegal and were able to exchange trade goods for several Africans who were shipped back to Portugal and sold into slavery. What began as a trickle soon became a veritable torrent as Europeans realized there was an almost limitless supply of Africans who lived to the south of the Sahara. The recognition that these Africans were either pagans who practiced indigenous religions or perhaps Muslims tended to legitimize their enslavement in the eyes of many European Christians. Papal pronouncements soon declared that any African who was captured for the purpose of enslavement might be properly viewed as a foe who was taken in an act of just war. Other papal pronouncements would later expand upon this notion and declare that the enslavement of the African was an act of Christian benevolence aimed at the slave's moral uplift.

Initially, the Africans who were transported as slaves by the Portuguese were taken to Spain or Portugal, where some became household servants but most were transported to sugar-producing islands in the Mediterranean or off the African coast where they labored as agricultural slaves. Transported beyond their homeland and exposed to new European diseases for which they lacked any natural immunity, African slaves labored in the fields of Majorca, Sicily, the Azores, and São Tomé. The demand for slaves in these locations was limited by the amount of land that was under cultivation, but once Columbus reached the Americas and the full potential for exploiting the new territories there was realized, the need for African slaves increased and the levels of the trade intensified.

As Europeans began to appreciate the need for African slaves on a larger scale, internal problems in West Africa destabilized the region and contributed to the intensity of the slave trade. Civil strife between the various peoples who constituted West Africa's vast Songhai Empire created an atmosphere of instability that only exacerbated development of the transatlantic slave trade. Even worse, the introduction of trade goods that could be employed as armaments of war perpetuated the internal strife, and a vicious cycle of extended hostility ensued. A near-constant state of warfare produced many captives of war, and Europeans were more than willing to exchange trade goods for these captured Africans.

Slavery in the Caribbean

Initially, Europeans followed the advice of conquerors like Hernán Cortés who suggested that the Americas contained a sufficient population of native peoples who might be enslaved to do the bidding of their European masters. The Spanish sought to plunder the riches of the Americas and believed that the indigenous peoples could be made unwilling accomplices in this endeavor. The combined effects of intensive forced labor and the introduction of Euro-

pean diseases decimated the ranks of the native peoples as thousands died from the burden that was placed upon them by the Spanish. Those who could escape did so, and the Spanish soon realized that attempting to enslave these people was impractical.

At the same time, religious leaders like Bartolomé de Las Casas began to appeal to the Spanish authorities on behalf of the enslaved native populations, urging that the Spanish rely instead upon African slavery as a solution to the perennial colonial labor shortages. Las Casas, known thereafter as "the apostle of the Indies," would later recant his suggestion of using African slavery, but the Spanish and the other European powers that established colonies in the Caribbean basin continued to rely upon an extensive use of enslaved African labor. The trade would last for four centuries and would influence permanently the character and definition of slavery in the modern world.

The transition in the Spanish Caribbean from enslaving indigenous peoples to the enslavement of Africans was complicated by the geopolitical realities of the early-sixteenth century. In 1493, shortly after Columbus's first expedition to the Americas, Pope Alexander VI issued a papal bull that fixed a line of demarcation dividing the Atlantic world between Spanish and Portuguese interests. The following year, this practice was made a part of the European diplomatic arrangement through the Treaty of Tordesillas, which drew a line 370 leagues west of the Cape Verde Islands that divided all eastern (Portuguese) regions from all western (Spanish) areas. If the Spanish wanted to maintain the pretense of honoring this arrangement, and thereby assure their sole right to claim the Caribbean basin and much of South America, they would have to devise a system of importing slaves from Africa—a region that fell entirely within the Portuguese sphere.

The solution that was developed was the Spanish crown's practice of offering an *asiento* (contract) to Portugal, and later to other European powers, to transport African captives as slaves for use in the Spanish colonial possessions. This practice maintained the spirit of the Treaty of Tordesillas, and it afforded the Portuguese, or whichever nation held the right, a lucrative contract that offered the possibility of substantial profits. Over the centuries, the *asiento* belonged to different nations as it became a valuable prize of war that occasionally fell into the hands of the victors during treaty negotiations. For those nations that held the contract for significant periods—especially the Portuguese, the Dutch, and the English— slave trading became a systematic practice in which efficiency and profitability tended to overshadow the inhumanity of the practice.

An elaborate system to capture, trade, and transport Africans across the Atlantic as slaves developed in the sixteenth century and continued to function until the rise of the Atlantic abolitionist movement forced an end to the practice in the early-nineteenth century. Estimates suggest that as many as 11 million slaves may have been transported across the Atlantic over four centuries in what came to be called the Middle Passage. Although Africans were certainly victimized by this system, many African kingdoms and states trafficked in slaves and assisted the European and American slavers who plied the West African coast searching for captured Africans to complete their cargoes. For much of the seventeenth and eighteenth centuries, a "triangular trade" existed between ports in New England, West Africa, and the Caribbean. This commerce had the effect of providing enslaved Africans to the labor-starved colonies of the Americas in exchange for trade goods from the New World.

European (and later American) slave traders maintained a limited presence along the western coastline of Africa, occupying factories, barracoons, or commercial forts where the actual trading and exchange of slaves took place. Tropical diseases took their toll on the unacclimated slavers who visited the region, and those Europeans and Americans who were drawn to the area by an interest in the slave trade seldom ventured into the African interior. Africans who were captives of war or who were victims of raids into the interior conducted by other Africans were brought to the coastal locations where they were exchanged for trade goods.

As the demand for slaves in the Americas grew and the interior raids became increasingly frequent and more intense, captives were taken from distant inland villages and forced to march to the coast where they were sold. Large numbers of Africans died in the process, and the effects of depopulation upon the African continent resulting both from death in captivity and from enslavement was enormous. Additionally, the nearly constant practice of conducting slave raids and the wars that ensued between rival peoples had a terribly destabilizing effect upon Africa.

Many Africans who were transported across the Atlantic Ocean as slaves would later attest that the Middle Passage was the most horrible aspect of their enslavement. Large numbers of Africans were tightly packed in an often less-than-seaworthy vessel and forced to endure an ocean crossing that might range from three weeks to two months in length depending upon the route taken and the fortune of the winds. During these crossings, the male slaves were generally kept in chains so as to reduce the possibility of an uprising at sea. The vessels were overcrowded, fresh water and sufficient food supplies were seldom adequate for the voyage, disease and occasional epidemics were rampant on the vessels, and not surprisingly, large numbers of enslaved Africans died during the Atlantic crossing.

Those Africans who survived the voyage found themselves put in the slave markets of the Caribbean basin where they were purchased at auction and introduced to the intensive labor of agricultural slavery. Newly recruited Africans who were unseasoned as slaves were not highly valued upon their introduction to the Caribbean because the anticipated mortality rate among this group was excessively high. The market value of those slaves who survived the rigors of disease, acclimation, and work increased as they were recognized as being seasoned and more apt to survive an extended period of enslavement in the Caribbean.

Large-scale importation of Africans as slaves into the Caribbean coincided with the "sugar revolution" that occurred in the seventeenth century. As sugar cultivation spread from the Portuguese colony of Brazil to Suriname and islands such as Jamaica, Cuba, and Barbados, sugar's profitability and its reliance upon labor-intensive planting and harvesting techniques created an almost insatiable demand for slave laborers in these locations. Owners of vast sugar plantations reaped huge profits from the labor of African slaves who worked their estates, and the potential for immense earnings fashioned a cycle in which the destinies of sugar and slavery became inextricably intertwined.

The Enlightenment and the Atlantic Abolitionist Movement

It was not until Europeans entered the eighteenth century's age of the Enlightenment that slavery came to be questioned as an institution that denied human dignity and was, therefore, a practice that should be abolished. This view was not one that was immediately accepted by the countries involved in the slave trade, and it would take more than a century of agitation before the humanitarian impulse, buttressed by legislative action, would initiate a movement that aimed at abolishing the African slave trade and, eventually, slavery itself.

While intellectuals debated the merits of abolition, the institution of slavery became entrenched in the Americas as sugar cultivation spread, the cultivation of tobacco, rice, indigo, and cotton expanded, and the importation of Africans continued unabated. By the early-seventeenth century, the practice of using enslaved Africans as slave laborers was common throughout the Caribbean basin, Brazil, and northern portions of South America, and after a Dutch trading vessel introduced 20 Africans into Virginia in August 1619, the practice of slavery developed within a generation in the English colonies on the North American mainland. The moral imperative against the practice notwithstanding, slavery continued to spread because it was perceived by many people to be a profitable venture.

Although the first Africans introduced into the Virginia colony were brought there as indentured servants rather than as slaves, it seems that they and their descendants were being held in perpetual bondage as early as the 1640s. By the late-seventeenth century, slavery was the legally sanctioned and commonly accepted status of Africans throughout the colonies in British North America. The perception of slavery as a matter of racial distinctiveness is one that developed more strongly in the English colonial experience than in Iberian-influenced societies. Whereas the Spanish and the Portuguese had experienced several centuries of Muslim domination and had developed cultures in which domestic slavery was common, the English had no comparable experiences upon which to draw, and thus their attitudes toward race evolved differently. Certainly the English attitude toward race was a factor in some areas in the gradual transformation from using large numbers of white indentured servants as laborers to a total dependence upon using imported Africans or Caribbean-born blacks as slave labor.

In the same age in which slavery was becoming institutionalized in the Americas, the abolitionist message began to be voiced by some people who abhorred the practice of slavery. Antislavery ideology in early modern Europe can be traced back to the works of the French jurist Jean Bodin (1530–1596), who criticized the practice of slavery as immoral and viewed it as counterproductive in that it excluded individuals from complete membership in civil society. Similar stirrings of abolitionist thought could be found in Elizabethan England when in the Cartwright decision (1569), court justices decreed that "England was too pure an air for slaves to breathe in."

Abolitionist sentiments grew throughout the eighteenth century as the writers of the Enlightenment were almost unanimous in their condemnation of slavery, and such ideas helped to inspire the French Revolution and the revolution in Saint Domingue (modern Haiti) that sounded the death knell for slavery in the French Caribbean. In the English colonies in North America, the Society of Friends (Quakers) was the first group to advocate publicly the abolition of slavery, and support for that position would galvanize during the generation of the American Revolution.

When Thomas Jefferson penned the Declaration of Independence in 1776, few people failed to see the troubling irony when Jefferson, a slaveowner, wrote "that all Men are created equal . . . [and] are endowed by their Creator with . . . Life, Liberty, and the Pursuit of Happiness." Even more perplexing perhaps was the practice of equating England's onerous rule over the North American colonies with the practice of slavery. Jefferson and the other American Founders considered revolution to be an appropriate response if it were to throw off the oppressive yoke of tyranny (or slavery), but only the most extreme would have argued that slaves held in bondage had the same right to revolt since they too were "created equal" and maintained liberty as a natural right until it was stolen from them by enslavement.

Decisions regarding the future status of slavery in the United States that were made when the American Revolution ended had profound implications for the institution and strongly influenced the direction and the practices that the antislavery movement would follow in the nineteenth century. In many respects, the U.S. attempt to be half slave and half free made eventual emancipation almost inevitable, though the timing and the circumstances of that decision were yet to be decided.

Seven Northern states (Pennsylvania, Rhode Island, Massachusetts, Connecticut, New Jersey, New York, and New Hampshire) each devised strategies to end the practice of slavery within their borders, but for those states, emancipating their slaves was neither an economic nor a social hardship. In Virginia, Maryland, Delaware, North Carolina, South Carolina, and Georgia, the practice of slavery continued, and the U.S. Constitution, which was written in 1787 and was ratified and took effect in 1789, gave legal standing and judicial protection to the institution. Because of these decisions, the notion of emancipating the slaves in the United States had the potential makings of a constitutional crisis, and political leaders generally sought legislative consensus through compromise solutions to postpone a crisis over the issue.

Much of the credit for the rising antislavery attitude in the Atlantic world during the late-eighteenth century was owing to the tireless efforts of abolitionists who agitated against the African slave trade in the British Parliament. After many unsuccessful attempts, leaders like William Wilberforce and Thomas Clarkson were finally able to gain parliamentary approval in 1807 of a measure that outlawed the African slave trade within the British colonial sphere as of January 1, 1808, the search and seizure of suspected slaving vessels on the high seas, and provided funding for the liberation of captured slaves. The U.S. Congress also enacted a measure in March 1807 that prohibited the importation of slaves into the country after January 1, 1808. Supporters of both the British and the U.S. measures believed that cutting off the supply of new slaves by prohibiting importation and working actively to end the effective trade were important steps that would doom the institution of slavery to certain death. When this assessment failed to materialize, both the British and the U.S. governments pursued alternative routes to ending the practice of slavery.

By the late-eighteenth century, the English economy was being transformed by the effects of the Industrial Revolution. English investors made huge capital investments to construct factories, develop canal projects, and create other transportation infrastructure networks to assist the establishment of new commercial ventures. Ironically, much of the "old money" that supported this new spirit of enterprise had been earned through profits from the trade in sugar and slaves. The abolition of slavery was one part of the social and economic transformation that occurred as an older order based upon a colonial mercantilist system gave way to a new industrialized, capitalistic society. To many people, the transition from dependence upon slave labor to that of wage labor was essential if the new order were to maximize workplace efficiency and generate the profits that a manufacturing-based economy could produce. Accordingly, shortly after the British Parliament passed the Reform Act of 1832, which restructured archaic political structures according to a more modern model, Parliament also enacted the Emancipation Act of 1833, which promised an end to slavery within the British Empire by 1838.

In the United States, the abolitionist campaign followed a different track than the British model. Late-eighteenth abolitionists like the Quaker John Woolman believed that persuasion and human reasoning were sufficient tools to inspire slaveowners to manumit their slaves, but the effectiveness of such campaigns was localized and limited. In the 1830s, a new and more assertive attitude became common among many abolitionists after William Lloyd Garrison began publishing the *Liberator* in 1831, in which he demanded an end to all attempts at compromising on the issue of slavery. Calls for unconditional emancipation polarized attitudes between the nonslaveholding states of the North and the slaveholding South. In addition, as the United States expanded to the west in the era of "manifest destiny," the issue of whether or not slavery should be allowed in the newly acquired territories became the primary political question in the United States during the antebellum period.

The Kansas-Nebraska Act (1854), which included the political decision to allow the question of slavery's expansion to be decided by popular referendum, encouraged many abolitionists to adopt a more direct approach in the crusade against slavery. The Republican Party, a political party founded in 1854 upon the principle that the further expansion of slavery should be halted, represented a new tactic in the abolitionists' methodology as the divisive issue of slavery continued to dominate the national debate. Republican candidate Abraham Lincoln's election in 1860 as president of the United States was the signal to several slaveholding states that their "peculiar institution" would soon be in jeopardy, and the decision that those states made to secede from the Union precipitated a constitutional crisis that threatened not only the future of slavery in the United States but the future of the United States itself.

The U.S. Civil War (1861–1865) is an important conflict in world history in that it was one of the first truly modern wars, but its relationship to the issue of slavery is also noteworthy. Although the issue of slavery was certainly not the only issue responsible for causing the Civil War, its importance as a contributing factor cannot be denied. As the war progressed, Lincoln's wartime aims increasingly became connected to the issue of emancipation. In September 1862, Lincoln issued a draft of the Emancipation Proclamation that took effect on January 1, 1863, and freed slaves in areas that were still in rebellion against the U.S. government as of that date. Eventually the passage of the Thirteenth Amendment to the U.S. Constitution in 1865 legally abolished the practice of slavery in the United States.

Though a joint effort of the governments of the United States and Great Britain to abolish the African slave trade persisted through the nineteenth century, attempts to monitor African coastal waters with naval patrols could not always be totally effective, and some slaving vessels still managed to get through. The African captives aboard the slaving vessels that were seized were generally taken to either Liberia or Sierra Leone on the West African coast, two states that had been established as homelands for repatriated former slaves who had served as slaves in the United States or in the British colonies. Some vessels were able to elude capture and continued to transport slaves to the United States during the antebellum era. In the postwar period, they transported captive Africans to Cuba and to Brazil where the practice of slavery continued for another generation beyond the end of the U.S. Civil War.

The abolition of slavery in the Americas did not herald the end of Africa's experience with slavery. Throughout the many years of the slave trade, many African states had come to specialize in the taking of captives and exchanging them for trade goods. Some local leaders had become quite wealthy through this practice, and the custom of slavery within Africa and the domestic slave trade that was required to perpetuate it were quite common in many parts of Africa during the nineteenth century. English abolitionists such as Sir Thomas Fowell Buxton organized groups like the Society for the Extinction of the Slave Trade and for the Civilization of Africa to combat these practices by introducing the establishment of new settlements in Africa that encouraged agriculture so legitimate commerce might replace the necessity for trading in slaves. Inspired by a spirit of trusteeship, much of the missionary activity in nineteenth-century Africa was aimed at ending slave-trading practices, and a major component of the new imperialism that inspired the "scramble for Africa" in the 1880s was the moral imperative to end the practice of slavery on the African continent.

Slavery in the Modern World

If the institution of slavery were something that only ancient peoples had practiced, the custom would be nothing more than a historical curiosity in the modern world, but that is not the lesson that history teaches us. Modern postindustrial peoples have managed to practice various forms of slavery in the twentieth century, and it is quite probable that the practice continues even today among some of the world's developing nations as certain forms of debt-peonage, pseudo-adoption, concubinage, contract labor, child labor, servile forms of marriage, and more traditional forms of enslavement persist. Thus, the study of slavery reveals that its practice is ubiquitous—regardless of the progress that has been made in human history, the practice of enslaving fellow human beings has not disappeared entirely from history.

Slavery still existed in parts of Africa and Asia at the start of the twentieth century. In China, the imperial government officially abolished the practice of slavery in 1906. The Korean government had abolished slavery in reforms of 1894, but it was commonly accepted that the institution of slavery survived in Korea until 1930. A vigorous domestic trade in slaves continued in parts of Africa until the end of World War I in 1918, and following the end of that conflict, the League of Nations took upon itself the international obligation to bring about an end to slavery in those areas where the practice continued to exist.

During the years of World War II (1939–1945), barbarous new practices of slavery were applied in both major theaters of the conflict. In Europe, the Nazi regime instituted a systematic campaign in which Jews and other "undesirables" were assigned to forced-labor camps where they labored unceasingly until their death. In this genocidal system, the slave was viewed as nothing more than a consumable resource whose labor could be used for the benefit of the state. Millions died in the forced-labor camps and the extermination camps that were a part of Hitler's "final solution."

In the Pacific theater, another form of slavery appeared during the years of World War II. The Japanese government regularly recruited young women to serve as comfort women, or sexual slaves, to satisfy the carnal needs of Japanese servicemen who were stationed in Korea and China. These young women were raped repeatedly and suffered the dual humiliation of being enslaved by the Japanese and of being shunned for bringing shame upon their families. Even 50 years after the end of the war, the issue of the comfort women remains a contentious diplomatic issue between the governments of both Koreas and Japan.

In the years since World War II, the United Nations has worked to abolish the practice of slavery in the modern world. The United Nations Universal Declaration of Human Rights, enacted in 1948, proclaimed both the immorality and the illegality of slavery in all its forms. Subsequent UN conventions in 1949, 1953, and 1956 reaffirmed earlier protocols attesting that slavery was illegal and member states agreed to these statements. Even at the end of the twentieth century, the UN Working Group on Contemporary Forms of Slavery still carefully monitors reports that surface about incidents of contemporary slavery, and investigations are ongoing. In addition, several private organizations—like Anti-Slavery International and the American Anti-Slavery Group—monitor reports concerning cases of contemporary slavery from around the world and try to publicize these events to draw the world's attention to what remains a perplexing issue.

Epilogue

In his work *Hecuba* (c. 425 B.C.), the Greek dramatist Euripides described slavery as "that thing of evil, by its nature evil, forcing submission from a man to what no man can yield." Much of both ancient and modern human history contains a record of slavery and its legacy for civilized societies, but the lessons of the past have not prohibited the sporadic reappearance of "that thing of evil" in our world. The effects of slavery certainly touch the human psyche, but a complete understanding of the practice still eludes total comprehension. The practice of slavery appears to be a societal character flaw that waxes and wanes—a recessive historical gene that can reappear almost without warning. As a result, we must study about slavery to learn more about ourselves and our world.

Human history marvels at the accomplishments of previous civilizations, but the art, architecture, philosophy, law, science, and literature that have been bequeathed to the modern world from the ancients are only a part of this brilliant cultural inheritance. How nations have struggled through the centuries with war, slavery, and other issues of social justice is also important as we try to comprehend an essential meaning for the human condition. Though slavery remains an enigma and its demons burden us still, the institution of slavery is an indelible part of our history.

—*Junius P. Rodriguez*

☙ACKNOWLEDGMENTS☙

It would have been certainly impossible to produce this encyclopedia without the assistance of many individuals, and I owe a tremendous debt of gratitude to all who helped to make it a reality. I wish to thank the members of the Board of Consulting Editors, who offered their expertise when this project was only an idea and continued to offer their advice and encouragement as the idea developed. I also would like to thank the many scholars from around the world who contributed. Without their efforts in planning, researching, and writing the articles, this work would have been impossible, and I cannot thank them sufficiently for their dedication to the task and for their professionalism. It has been a pleasure to work with these individuals, and I feel that I have gained many new friends as a result of the process.

I am also indebted to the staff of ABC-CLIO for their patience and counsel over the past two years. Todd Hallman, Acquisitions Editor, has worked with me from the conception of this project, and his assistance has been invaluable. Susan McRory, Managing Editor, has overseen the project and has helped to make hundreds of disparate articles come together into final form. Without Megan Schoeck's copyediting, the work would bear the scars of too many of my imperfections. I appreciate her keen eye and perceptive queries, which helped fashion the material into a better book. I also appreciate the efforts of Liz Kincaid, who handled the details of obtaining the illustrations.

I treasure the understanding and support of my colleagues and my students, and they have helped me cope with the stress of looming deadlines and have shared my joy in meeting the same—generally. Your encouragement and support along the way have meant much to me, and I will always remember your kindness. I would also like to thank the Eureka College Faculty Status and Development Committee, which offered financial assistance to fund postage and duplicating costs when this project was just beginning.

I owe a special debt of gratitude to several student assistants who worked with me as this volume developed. Sarah Lunt Ewart, Shannon Wettach, Byron Painter, Nathan Meyer, Ryan Tompkins, and David Steinbeck all did an admirable job in helping make this encyclopedia a reality. Each of them had a hand in its development, and I thank them for their efforts. Marsha VanEtten and Joy Kinder offered secretarial assistance and helped make sure that important mailings went out on time. Lynne Rudasill, Paul Lister, Ann Shoemaker, Peg Toliver, Ginny McCoy, Eldrick Smith, and Kathy Whitson all pitched in to help when various glitches appeared, and I appreciate their assistance.

I am proud to have been associated with the development of this encyclopedia and take responsibility for its inevitable shortcomings. I hope that the work will be valuable to students and researchers alike and that this labor of love will serve as a valuable reference tool for years to come.

Junius P. Rodriguez
May 30, 1997

MAPS

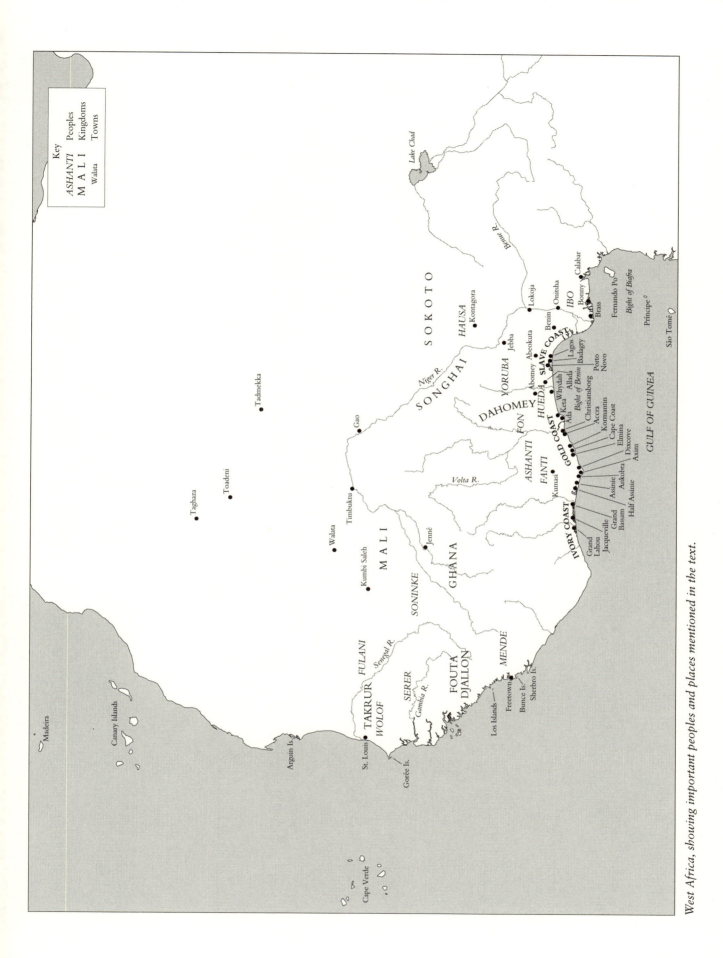

Madeira

Canary Islands

Arguin Is.

St. Louis

Gorée Is.

Cape Verde

TAKRUR
WOLOF
SERER
FULANI
Senegal R.
Gambia R.
FOUTA
DJALLON
MENDE

Los Islands
Freetown
Bunce Is.
Sherbro Is.

SONINKE

GHANA

MALI

Kumbi Saleh
Walata
Jenné
Timbuktu
Taghaza
Toadeni
Tadmekka
Gao

Volta R.
Niger R.

SONGHAI

SOKOTO

HAUSA
Kontagora
Jebba
Lokoja
Benin
Onitsha
IBO
Calabar
Bonny
Brass
Fernando Po
Bight of Biafra
Principe
São Tomé

YORUBA
Abeokuta
Lagos
Badagry
Porto Novo
Allada
Bight of Benin

DAHOMEY
Abomey
FON
HUEDA
Whydah
Keta
Ada
SLAVE COAST

ASHANTI
FANTI
Kumasi

GOLD COAST
Accra
Christiansborg
Kormantin
Cape Coast
Elmina
Dixcove
Axum

IVORY COAST
Grand
Lahou
Jacqueville
Grand
Bassam
Assinie
Ankobra
Half Assine

GULF OF GUINEA

Lake Chad

Benue R.

West Africa, showing important peoples and places mentioned in the text.

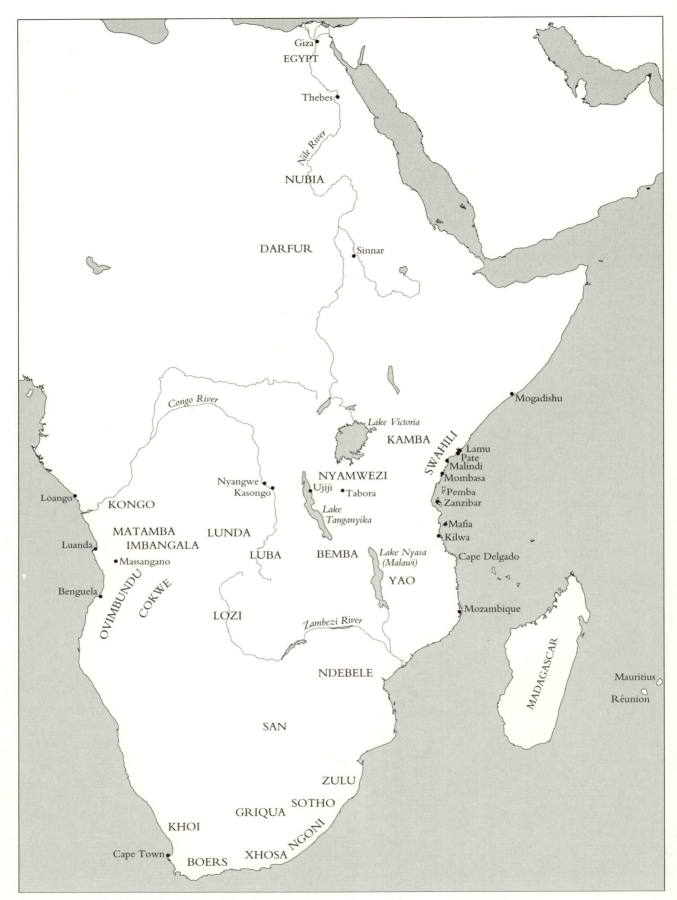

Eastern, Central, and Southern Africa, showing important peoples and places mentioned in the text.

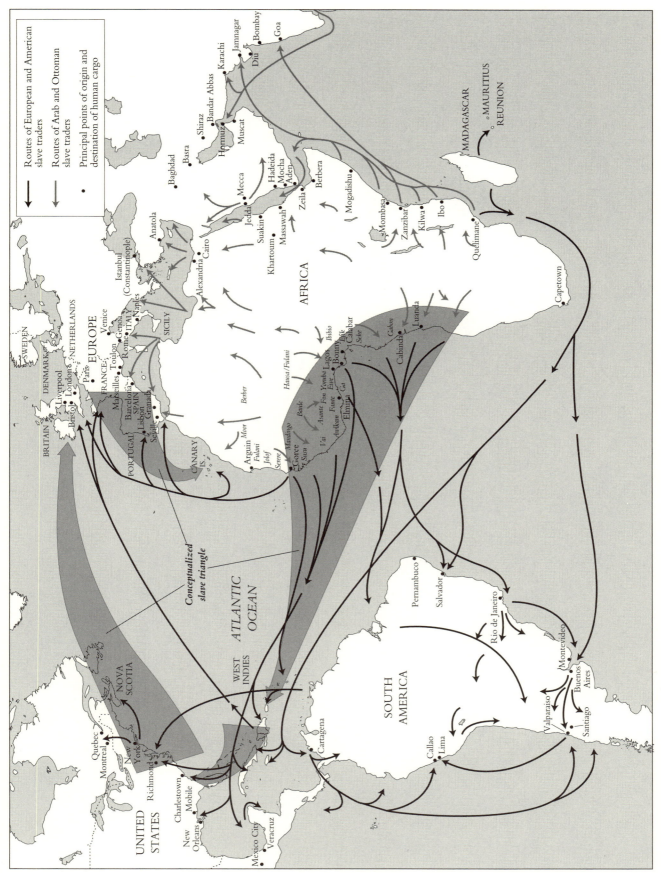

The African Diaspora. Courtesy of Joseph E. Harris.

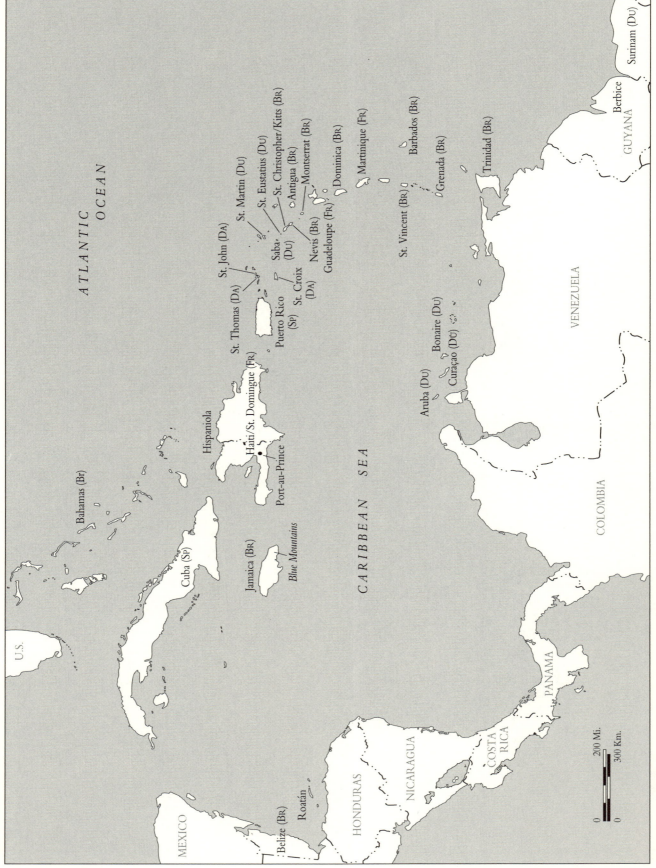

U.S.

MEXICO

Belize (BR)

Roatán

HONDURAS

NICARAGUA

COSTA
RICA

PANAMA

ATLANTIC

OCEAN

Bahamas (BR)

Cuba (SP)

Jamaica (BR)

Blue Mountains

St. Thomas (DA)

St. John (DA)

St. Martin (DU)

St. Eustatius (DU)

St. Christopher/Kitts (BR)

Antigua (BR)

Montserrat (BR)

Dominica (BR)

Martinique (FR)

Barbados (BR)

Grenada (BR)

Trinidad (BR)

Saba
(DU)

Nevis (BR)

Guadeloupe (FR)

St. Vincent (BR)

Puerto Rico
(SP)

St. Croix
(DA)

Hispaniola

Haiti/St. Domingue (FR)

Port-au-Prince

CARIBBEAN SEA

Aruba (DU)

Bonaire (DU)

Curaçao (DU)

VENEZUELA

COLOMBIA

GUYANA

Berbice

Surinam (DU)

200 Mi.

300 Km.

0

0

The Caribbean, late eighteenth century (present-day boundaries of countries in Central and South America shown for reference).

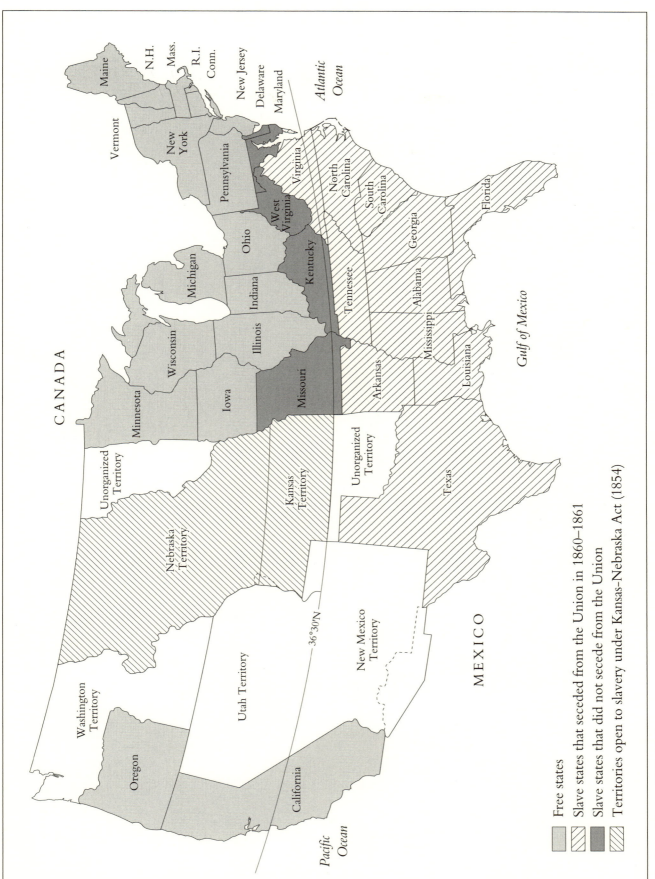

CANADA

Maine

N.H.

Mass.

R.I.

Conn.

New Jersey

Delaware

Maryland

Vermont

New York

Pennsylvania

West Virginia

Ohio

Michigan

Indiana

Illinois

Wisconsin

Minnesota

Iowa

Missouri

Kentucky

Virginia

North Carolina

South Carolina

Georgia

Tennessee

Alabama

Mississippi

Arkansas

Louisiana

Florida

Atlantic Ocean

Gulf of Mexico

Unorganized Territory

Kansas Territory

Nebraska Territory

Unorganized Territory

Texas

36°30'N

Washington Territory

Utah Territory

New Mexico Territory

MEXICO

Oregon

California

Pacific Ocean

Free states

Slave states that seceded from the Union in 1860–1861

Slave states that did not secede from the Union

Territories open to slavery under Kansas–Nebraska Act (1854)

The United States, 1860–1861.

The Historical Encyclopedia of

WORLD SLAVERY

VOLUME I
A-K

A

ABLEMAN V. BOOTH
(1859)

Sherman M. Booth, the editor of a small antislavery newspaper, became the subject of several related legal cases resulting from the recapture (and subsequent escape) of a fugitive slave named Joshua Glover. The Supreme Court case (62 U.S. 506), decided in March 1859, followed in the wake of multiple cases flowing out of the conflict between the Wisconsin state courts and the federal courts (including *In re Booth* 3 Wis. 1 [1854], *U.S. v. Rycraft* 27 F. Cas. 918 [1854], *U.S. ex rel. Garland v. Morris* 26 F. Cas. 1318 [1854], and *In re Booth and Rycraft* 3 Wis 157 [1855]).

Joshua Glover had fled his Missouri owner and re-settled in Racine, Wisconsin. His owner, Benjamin Garland, found him in 1854 and tried to recapture him, using the Fugitive Slave Act of 1850, by having a federal commissioner issue a warrant for Glover's arrest. When Glover was imprisoned in Milwaukee, abolitionist forces surrounded the Milwaukee jail, and clamored for his release. Racine's mayor issued a warrant for Garland's arrest for having kidnapped Glover. Meanwhile, a mob attacked the Milwaukee jail and freed Glover, who promptly fled to Canada. The supposed leaders of the mob, Booth and John Rycraft, were arrested and charged for their role in allegedly rescuing Glover.

As a result of differing attitudes toward runaway slaves, conflict between the Wisconsin state and U.S. federal courts was almost inevitable. Booth and Rycraft were convicted in federal trials for assisting a fugitive slave and appealed to the state court for relief. The Wisconsin Supreme Court decided, in *In re Booth and Rycraft*, that the 1850 Fugitive Slave Act was unconstitutional, and ordered the release of both men from jail. The state court's decision was appealed to the U.S. Supreme Court, which decided in *Ableman v. Booth* that federal courts could not be overruled by state courts: to do so "would subvert the very foundations of this Government." The case also upheld the constitutionality of the Fugitive Slave Act of 1850, which had been a portion of the Compromise of 1850, saying that, in Chief Justice Roger B. Taney's words, "in all its provisions" the law was "fully authorized by the Constitution."

The Wisconsin court decision was part of a broader trend in which Northern state courts obstructed the recapture of runaway slaves. Earlier cases, like *Prigg v. Pennsylvania* (1842), had relied upon state-sponsored personal liberty laws, which placed stringent requirements upon any person attempting to claim a fugitive slave. Combat between state and federal courts mirrored the increasing sectional tension felt in the late antebellum period. During the conflict, the Wisconsin Supreme Court went so far as to instruct its clerk not to send a copy of the *Ableman v. Booth* case to the U.S. Supreme Court, as had been requested after it pronounced the Fugitive Slave Act unconstitutional. Acts like this went far toward damaging relations between the North and the South in the period immediately preceding the Civil War, and only the Civil War resolved the differing interpretations between state and federal courts over the constitutionality of the Fugitive Slave Act of 1850.

—*Sally E. Hadden*

See also
Abolition, United States; *Dred Scott v. Sandford; Jones v. Van Zandt; Prigg v. Pennsylvania;* Taney, Roger B.; U.S. Constitution

For Further Reading
Cover, Robert. 1975. *Justice Accused: Antislavery and the Judicial Process*. New Haven, CT: Yale University Press; Finkelman, Paul. 1981. *An Imperfect Union: Slavery, Federalism, and Comity*. Chapel Hill, NC: University of North Carolina Press; Swisher, Carl. 1974. *History of the Supreme Court of the United States: The Taney Period, 1836–1864*. New York: Macmillan; Wiecek, William E. 1978. "Slavery and Abolition before the United States Supreme Court, 1820–1860." *Journal of American History* 65: 34–59.

ABOLITION, AFRICA

The abolition of slavery in Africa came from the same nations that had purchased most of the slaves. In 1807, the British made the slave trade illegal for British subjects. The Danes had abolished their trade in 1802, and the Dutch followed in 1814. Having denied British subjects the profits of trading in slaves, Britain proceeded to deny them to its rivals. Under British pressure, various European nations agreed to prohibit the slave trade and to allow the British navy to search their ships.

Starting with Zanzibar in 1822, Britain also signed treaties with various African states to restrict slave exports. For a half century, the Royal Navy tried to stop the export of slaves, and some French and U.S. ships also cruised West African waters. Between them, they freed about 160,000 slaves, only 5 percent of those exported from Africa. Almost all of them were freed by the British and taken to Freetown in Sierra Leone.

Slavery itself was abolished in the British Empire in 1833 and in the French colonies in 1848. These acts affected small areas—for the British, Cape Colony, and for the French, the islands of St.-Louis and Gorée off the coast of Senegal and a handful of posts in and around Senegambia (the basin of the Senegal and Gambia Rivers)—but abolition still threatened colonial interests.

Cape farmers were dependent on coerced labor and used various subterfuges to get it. Elsewhere, slave labor was producing most of the commodities Europeans bought. African states near European colonies feared loss of their slaves, and Europeans feared the threat to their commerce and hopes of expansion. They moved to prevent flight, often closing their doors to refugees or turning them back over to the jurisdiction of their masters. As European colonies absorbed new areas on the African mainland, they tried to prevent the application of antislavery laws there. The most common method was to make the new areas protectorates that were nominally ruled by traditional chiefs under traditional law. These chiefs were usually large slaveholders.

By contrast, in the home countries, hostility to slavery was growing stronger. In 1888, a Catholic antislavery movement was created in both France and Africa by the energetic Charles-Martial-Allemand Lavigerie, cardinal primate of Africa and archbishop of Carthage. By that time, the budgets of most European nations were controlled by elected parliaments, and nations that sought expansion could not imagine doing so if slavery were abolished. The only cheap way to rule conquered areas in Africa was through African chiefs. Armies were purchased in the slave market, and soldiers were often rewarded with booty—the most common being women and children.

The most important limitation on slave systems was the constant flight of slaves and their efforts to either create a new life or to return to their earlier home. Increasingly, as European Christian missions spread out over Africa, slaves found that mission stations would provide them with a refuge. Missionaries also described for European readers the horrors of the slave trade within Africa. Under pressure from the home countries, hesitant actions were taken. In 1861,

Lagos was annexed by Britain to end slavery there, and in 1873, Britain induced Zanzibar to ban the slave trade. In 1874, slavery was abolished on the Gold Coast. Pressure from France forced stricter enforcement of French law in Senegal, and from 1883 on, any slave finding his or her way to an area directly administered by France was free.

In 1890, the European powers agreed at Brussels to ban the export of slaves from Africa and to take action against the slave trade within Africa. King Leopold of Belgium and other colonizers used the horrors of the slave trade to justify further conquest, though most conquerors did not at first do anything about the trade. They did generally abolish enslavement and end the large-scale trade in slaves, and African slaves were often able to exploit the defeat of their masters to flee.

Gradually, under pressure from public opinion at home, many colonies took further action. A French general, Alfred-Amédée Dodds, sought to break the power of Dahomey by encouraging slaves to flee, and in 1897, the status of slave was abolished in Zanzibar. Most early efforts at abolition used the Indian formula, which meant the state simply refused to recognize the rights of masters of slaves. This was the policy adopted in 1903 when French West Africa proclaimed a new law code. In 1905, the French abolished any transaction in people, and in the same year, slaves began leaving their masters. Over six or seven years, as many as a million slaves left their masters to return to their earlier homes or to seek work in the towns and other areas where work was available.

The British tended to be cautious about abolition. After conquering northern Nigeria, Frederick Lugard prohibited enslavement and the trade in slaves there, but he feared that emancipation would lead to lawlessness and a decline in food production. Slaves were required to purchase their freedom, and fugitives were denied mobility and access to land. Many British colonies did nothing about slavery, but the Sudan was the most sympathetic toward it, even tolerating a clandestine slave trade. Often, as in French Africa, it was the slaves who took the initiative. In Italian Somalia, a reluctant act of abolition proclaimed under pressure from home was followed by a massive departure from slave plantations. The Germans pursued a piecemeal abolition process in East Africa, and in 1905, they proclaimed the freedom of all slaves born after 1890. Less than 10 percent of them sought liberty papers, but by 1914, most slaves had left their masters.

International publicity about slaves exported from Angola to the cocoa plantations of São Tomé led Portugal to abolish the practice in 1910. Scandals in the Belgian Congo (Congo, formerly Zaire) led Belgium to abolish slavery there in 1910 as well. In the 1920s, reports of slave raiding along the Ethiopian borderlands led the League of Nations to create the Temporary Slavery Commission in 1924 and to pass the Slavery Convention of 1926, which bound signatories to suppress slavery in all its forms. Inquiries by the League of Nations forced Ethiopia and Liberia to take action and also embarrassed Britain, a prime mover in League efforts. In 1928, slavery was abolished in Sierra Leone; in the 1930s, Sudan took more resolute action against the slave trade; and in 1936, Nigeria abolished slavery.

Many of the people who had been born in slavery chose to remain where they were. For them, freedom was a complex process of renegotiating relationships. The crucial questions for slaves involved control over their work and family lives. They wanted to work for themselves, negotiate their own marriages, and have the right to bequeath and inherit. Former masters were most successful in controlling former slaves in places where the colonial regime recognized them as owners of the land. Formal slavery remained only in some Saharan regions, where colonial regimes ignored their own legislation.

—*Martin A. Klein*

See also
African Squadron; League of Nations; Lugard, Frederick John Dealtry; Transition from Slave Labor to Free Labor, Africa
For Further Reading
Cooper, Frederick. 1980. *From Slaves to Squatters: Plantation Labor and Agriculture in Zanzibar and Coastal Kenya, 1890–1925.* New Haven, CT: Yale University Press; Klein, Martin, ed. 1993. *Breaking the Chains: Slavery, Bondage, and Emancipation in Modern Africa and Asia.* Madison: University of Wisconsin Press; Lovejoy, Paul, and Jan Hogendorn. 1993. *Slow Death for Slavery: The Course of Abolition in North Nigeria, 1897–1936.* Cambridge: Cambridge University Press; Miers, Suzanne, and Richard Roberts, eds. 1989. *The End of Slavery in Africa.* Madison: University of Wisconsin Press.

ABOLITION, BRITISH EMPIRE

Although it is true that what might be called abolitionist sentiment has been around for as long as slavery itself, as an institutionalized movement abolitionism in England did not get under way before the 1780s. The first abolitionist organization was founded in London by Quakers in 1783. The Meeting for Sufferings, at the urging of its Philadelphia Quaker counterpart, established a Committee on the Slave Trade, and in the summer of 1783, the Quakers first petitioned Parliament to declare the slave trade illegal.

That petition was not, however, the first such motion made in Parliament, for in 1776, one member of Parliament, David Hartley, had asserted that slavery was "contrary to the laws of God and the rights of man" (Davis, 1966). Hartley's effort was unsuccessful, but it prepared the way for subsequent united political action. Although some very powerful public figures (like Thomas Clarkson, William Wilberforce, and Granville Sharp) were also interested in abolition, it can still be said that the Quakers provided much of the initial force—political and financial—for what was to become the abolitionist movement in England.

The English antislavery movement meant different things during the decades of its existence from the 1780s to the 1830s and beyond. Early abolitionist activism targeted the slave trade instead of slavery itself as the primary evil to be resisted. The logic of such thinking assumed that slavery was an evil institution primarily because of the human horrors and the moral degradation associated with it. The argument went that if the supply of slaves were halted, then the value of the slave would be increased and the planters in the British colonies would be obliged to treat slaves more humanely.

The advocates associated with that particular arm of the early abolitionist movement were often known as ameliorationists, but that does not mean that all the early abolitionists were ameliorationists. Some, from the very beginning of the movement, favored emancipation—earning for themselves the appellation "emancipationists." But even most early emancipationists understood the need for a more graduated political approach to the end of slavery. In the decades following the cessation of the slave trade in 1807, however, the antislavery movement became increasingly emancipationist.

Early debates over slavery were waged in both moral and economic terms. Planters argued that they needed a ready supply of slave labor in the colonies to ensure that they would be able to provide England with much needed raw materials. In addition, if they were to remain competitive with the French, Spanish, and others in the trading markets, British planters could not emancipate their slaves and still maintain competitive trading prices unless emancipation were universal and all nations decided to emancipate their slaves at once. The abolitionists, seizing upon the rhetorical strategy of this logic, countered with their own view, which was that slavery was actually opposed to the national interest. If the slaves were emancipated and liberated, then they would be happier and more productive. By creating out of former slaves a working class of wage earners, you would create a broader consumer base for the consumption of goods in the colonies.

Although there were many flaws as to the economic

This popular antislavery drawing by an unknown artist appeared in an 1827 British publication.

viability of the abolitionists' argument, it, along with the tide of public opinion, did bring about the first major victory for the abolitionist movement when England passed a measure for the cessation of the slave trade in 1807. Many people had great faith that this measure would be enough to ameliorate the institution of slavery, perhaps even to the point that it would gradually and inevitably become extinct. With the slave trade now illegal in Britain, the Society for Effecting the Abolition of the Slave Trade, which had been founded in 1787, was replaced by the African Institution in 1807. That body had three goals: to see that new laws against the trade were properly enforced, to encourage legitimate trade with Africa, and to convince other countries to follow England's example by giving up the slave trade.

To its credit, the British government did make many efforts to negotiate agreements with other European nations to suppress the slave trade—being highly motivated to do so because the British knew that if they did not successfully negotiate such suppression agreements, they would be unable to remain competitive economically. The efforts were unsuccessful. The French, Spanish, and Portuguese all believed that while the British had made sure that their colonies were kept well stocked with slaves during the American Revolution, others had not. Therefore, it was only fair that these countries should have an opportunity to make up the difference before withdrawing from the slave trade. England rejected this argument and promised generous financial subsidies if the other countries would cooperate. This offer, too, was refused.

In addition to such setbacks, the abolitionists were increasingly aware of mounting evidence suggesting that the cessation of the trade was not having the desired effect of ameliorating the life of the slaves. Evidence of this kind led to the establishment of the Society for Mitigating and Gradually Abolishing Slavery throughout the British Dominions, or the Anti-Slavery

Society, in 1823. This group's membership was not very different from that of the African Institution, but its focus was. It demanded the adoption of measures to protect slaves from wanton mistreatment, together with a plan for gradual emancipation leading to complete freedom. By limiting itself to such proposals, it sought to enlist the support not only of radicals but of conservatives as well. Thomas Clarkson went on the road for the group and encouraged the establishing of local auxiliary bodies that would contribute to the work of the larger group. By 1826, there were 71 local chapters throughout England, with Quaker membership and support once again being in great evidence.

In the decade following 1823 the work and agitation of abolitionists, especially Thomas Fowell Buxton, caused Parliament to take certain legal actions to improve the lot and condition of slaves in the colonies. Although Parliament did not adopt the stricter measures submitted to them by the abolitionists, it did adopt certain diluted versions of those measures and passed them on to the colonial legislative bodies with the request that they be given the sanction of law at the earliest opportunity. These measures included giving slaves more of an opportunity for religious instruction, removing obstacles to manumission, keeping slave families together, regulating flogging more carefully, and discontinuing flogging altogether for women.

The measures caused a virtual standoff between Parliament and the colonial legislatures concerning who had jurisdiction over and best knew how to make decisions for the colonies. The colonial legislatures, especially the one in Jamaica, accused the government of taking the side of enemies of the colonies. Given this standoff between the colonies and the government, it became apparent to some members of the Anti-Slavery Society that they could not hope to accomplish even their goal of gradual emancipation through appeal to Parliament alone. Some members wanted to appeal more directly to the people of England through a grassroots effort and thus bring public opinion to bear on Parliament. There was some resistance to this method of action by more conservative members like Buxton, but even they were convinced that such efforts were not antithetical to their own.

In 1831, therefore, the Anti-Slavery Society established a subcommittee known as the Agency Committee. This committee hired a group of lecturers and sent them to speak in specific districts to rouse public sentiment and support for the cause. Its efforts were so successful that in summer 1832, it officially separated from the Anti-Slavery Society and became an independent organization.

In 1832, the antislavery campaign was aided by a concomitant struggle over parliamentary reform.

When Parliament reassembled in January 1833 after the December 1832 elections, abolitionists were delighted at the character of the new Parliament. It was evident that the abolitionists' efforts to support members who would be sympathetic to their cause had been successful. Through a series of political negotiations, Parliament passed the Emancipation Act on August 29, 1833, which emancipated all slaves in the British dominions. The law stipulated that a system of forced apprenticeship would last for five years (1834–1838) as a transition to complete emancipation, but by 1837, slavery had effectively ended throughout the British Empire.

After emancipation, abolitionists did not cease their activities altogether. Many continued, under the auspices of newly founded organizations, to attempt to ensure that the government made good on its bill of emancipation and to work toward universal abolition by their European neighbors and the United States.

—*Dwight A. McBride*

See also
The African Institution; Clarkson, Thomas; General Abolition Bill; Quakers; Sharp, Granville; Sierra Leone; Somersett Case; Wilberforce, William; *Zong* Case

For Further Reading
Davis, David Brion. 1966. *The Problem of Slavery in Western Culture*. New York: Oxford University Press; Higman, Barry W. 1984. *Slave Populations of the British Caribbean, 1807–1834*. Baltimore: Johns Hopkins University Press; Stephen, George. 1854. *Antislavery Recollections: In a Series of Letters Addressed to Mrs. Beecher Stowe, Written by Sir George Stephen, at Her Request*. London: Thomas Hatchard; Temperley, Howard. 1972. *British Antislavery, 1833–1870*. London: Longman.

ABOLITION, EAST ASIA

*I*n China and Korea, where slavery had existed from antiquity, the twelfth century became the dividing line for the decay of the institution. It was at that time that substantial agricultural innovations in China, largely involving the use of new kinds of fertilizer and hydraulic technology, brought about a revolutionary improvement of farming techniques.

The Southern Sung people invented a new manure-based fertilizer that doubled land productivity, as it enabled people to grow crops twice a year by planting rice in the spring and other grains in winter on the same land. New water reservoirs, made possible by the new technology, also expanded arable land to the mountainous area. As a result, the production of foodstuffs doubled, and farmers were able to plant commercial crops such as medical herbs, mulberry, and

cotton on the new land. These improvements developed the domestic market economy, and better nutrition and improved medical care increased the population. These overall changes took place in Korea about a century later after they occurred in China, and from the fifteenth to the sixteenth centuries, China and Korea experienced population explosions.

With the high population growth, the number of landless people increased, and they provided labor for the growing domestic economy. The small ratio of land to population weakened slavery, as the greater opportunities for employment enticed slaves to run away. When Choson, the last dynasty of Korea, exhibited the symptoms of a downward dynastic cycle after the Japanese invasion in 1592, and as the Qing dynasty in China did the same after the Opium War (1839–1842), the life of the commoners became hard and sank to slave conditions. Many Chinese were sold and shipped as coolies to Southeast Asia and North America.

Administrative measures tried to cope with the social problems. King Yongjo of Choson cut the slaves' tribute tax by half in 1736, yet the difference in the tax payment remained. In 1775, he finally exempted any tribute from female slaves, which made the slave's tax burden equal to that of commoners. Many travelers to China at the end of the nineteenth century witnessed that people usually treated slaves as hired laborers. By that time hardly any difference remained between the poor free and the slaves, except status, and the social groundwork for gradual emancipation had already been laid.

In 1801, the Korean royal family and the central government emancipated all the slaves working on their farms, and other government agencies then gradually began freeing their slaves. Finally, in 1895, the modernized Choson court, influenced by the Japanese government, totally abolished slavery. Also for the purpose of modernization, a Ching China imperial ordinance abolished slavery in 1910, starting with the following introduction: "In the prosperous times of the Three Ancient dynasties the buying and selling of human beings were unknown, though criminals were punished by being reduced to slavery. It was during the decline of the house of Ch'ou that the first talk of selling men and women was heard, and during the succeeding dynasties of Ch'in and Han the practice became established" (Williams, 1910).

East Asian slavery was nonracial, which worked to the advantage of the freed, as once freed, it was difficult for anyone else to trace one's origin. Dynamic changes in the political leadership and economy of the two nations shook the whole traditional social order of each, which also made tracing origins difficult. Japanese annexation, U.S. military rule, the establishment of a republic, and economic development have made it almost impossible for Koreans to trace slave posterity, and the same sort of situation occurred in China. After the establishment of socialist government, integration of slave descendants into mainstream society was complete.

—*Hyong-In Kim*

See also
China (Ancient, Late Imperial, Medieval); East Asia; Korea
For Further Reading
Doolittle, Justus. 1867. *Social Life of the Chinese.* New York: Harper's; Grey, John Henry. 1878. *China: A History of Laws, Manners, and Customs of the People.* London: Macmillan; Williams, E. T. 1910. "The Abolition of Slavery in the Chinese Empire." *American Journal of International Law* 4 (4): 794–805.

ABOLITION, ISLAMIC WORLD

The earliest written records of the Babylonians, Sumerians, and Egyptians attest that since human history began, slavery has existed in one form or another. It continued through the Greco-Roman period, and it is recognized and accepted in both the Old and the New Testaments. Both of those texts often indicate a slave's basic humanity, suggesting that the Lord may look compassionately on any or all slaveowners who heed the advice to treat their slaves justly. Both the Talmud and the Bible reminded the Jewish people to treat slaves decently since they themselves had been slaves in Egypt. Psalm 123 reminds slaveowners of God's mercy when they seek it and entreats them to similar action toward their slaves (or servants). Despite later developments in Islamic history, the seventh-century Muslim arrival introduced significant changes in the ancient institution of slavery, changes that had far-reaching effects. First, Muslims maintained the initial assumption of freedom for all humans under God, slaves or not. Accordingly, the evolving *sh'ariah* ("religious law") sought the eventual elimination of the institution by regulating the often harsh and callous preexisting practices of the older societies that their forces conquered. The enslavement of free people, by conquest or otherwise, was strictly forbidden. Later practices of Muslim societies—like Africa's Songhai Empire, Eurasia's Ottoman Empire, and other Islamic regions—were regarded as secular undertakings not having justifiable religious prescription in the Qur'an.

Even so, the institution of slavery was common in many Muslim states between the ninth and seventeenth centuries, and it saw its fruition and eventual decline with the last of the great Muslim states, the Ottoman Empire. Prior to slavery's abolition in the Islamic world, the Ottoman Empire had a unique non-European concept of state and society. Private landed property was almost nonexistent as the sultan was the hereditary owner of all the empire's agricultural land and he exploited it as he saw fit. Since there was no hereditary nobility, the concept of landholding was a rather tenuous and uncertain reality. The entire population was totally subservient to the sultan's needs. Slave corps occupied the highest ranks of the sultan's bureaucracy, and the government annually levied a "tax" of 1,000–3,000 male children on conquered Christian populations in the Balkans. Raised as Muslims in the empire, these enslaved children were trained to administer the bureaucracy and to fight in the military. The most talented slaves were swiftly promoted to the highest bureaucratic levels; others were recruited into the sultan's very efficient and much feared Janissary corps.

The system worked wonders for the sultan. As the empire continued acquiring new lands, he imposed the slave tax on an ever-increasing population. Also, conquered Christian peasants had a predetermined amount of their income appropriated by their new Muslim overlords. By 1570, many "transient" Muslim landowners were seeking to acquire permanent tutelage over their designated conquered property, and compared to the financial benefits gained from most conquered territories, converting their Christian subjects to Islam was of little significance. But the administration of the sultan's earlier territorial "rewards" to his troops for efficiency, loyalty, and steadfastness in battle against European armies proved logistically complex. Gradual and successful European military cohesion gathered against the government, the sultan's increasingly luxurious lifestyle, and diminishing morale within the Janissary ranks all slowed the advance of the Ottoman forces to the west.

With Britain's growing abolitionist sentiment—outlawing the slave trade by its own citizens in 1807 and abolishing slavery altogether in its colonies in 1833—the Ottoman slave trade gradually entered a critical period of reckoning. By the mid-nineteenth century, Austria, Russia, Holland, Spain, Portugal, and France had all signed treaties with Britain to eliminate the African slave trade. Consequently, the decline of the Atlantic trade, growing European influence in Ottoman domestic affairs, and increased pressure from the British Foreign Office and British naval vessels in the Bosporus Strait and the Black, Mediterranean, and Red Seas led to a gradual diminishment of the Ottoman trade. In 1830, an Ottoman *firman* (decree) emancipated Christian slaves who had maintained their religion, which primarily affected those Greek and other Christian slaves of the empire who had been accused of or actually participated in earlier seditious or rebellious acts against the state. The British won further concessions to eliminate the black slave trade in 1847. By 1855, new edicts had abolished Circassian and Georgian slave traffic, and in 1857, a major Ottoman *firman* abolished slavery throughout the empire with the exception of the Arabian peninsula. Anticipating a serious rebellion led by slave merchants in the Hejaz on that peninsula, which included the holy sites of Mecca and Medina where the prophet Muhammad was buried, the sultan and Ottoman authorities thus sought to forestall any secession of the land that legitimized their claims of authority over all Muslims within the empire.

By the early 1860s, military slavery had been abolished and only freemen could serve in the sultan's armies. Through state acquisition, followed by subsequent manumission, many former slaves served in the navy and army as freemen. The Egyptian viceroy Muhammad Ali had instituted this practice 50 years earlier, and his successors continued it. Placing many freed slaves in military units and bands, Ottoman Sultan Abdul-Hamid II hoped to train them in naval skills to prevent their reenslavement.

Between the twentieth century's two world wars, many of the newly independent states within the Islamic world legally eliminated slavery. The Iranian 1906 constitution had already officially forbidden it, and Saudi Arabia, with Egyptian-led pro-Nasserite and secular Arab nationalist sentiments running high in the late 1950s and early 1960s, ended the much maligned institution in 1962. After centuries of collusion with non-Muslim forces in a dark chapter of human history, inhabitants of the Muslim world were finally able to attempt living according to the highest ideals initially prescribed by their collective faith.

—*Talaat Shehata*

See also
Janissaries; Ottoman Empire
For Further Reading
Beachey, R. W. 1976. *The Slave Trade of Eastern Africa*. New York: Barnes and Noble; Davison, Roderic. 1963. *Reform in the Ottoman Empire 1856–76*. Princeton, NJ: Princeton University Press; Ochsenwald, William. 1980. "Muslim European Conflict in the Hijaz: The Slave Trade Controversy, 1840–1859." *Middle Eastern Studies* 16 (1): 115–126; Shaw, Stanford J. 1976. *History of the Ottoman Empire and Modern Turkey*. Cambridge: Cambridge University Press.

ABOLITION, LATIN AMERICA

The Latin American countries abolished slavery in different ways and in several stages. The methods varied from a slave revolt on Saint Domingue to a continuous occurrence of rebellion and *cimarronaje* ("runaway slaves") during the colonial period in practically all Latin American colonies. Escape was, perhaps, the most conspicuous way for slaves to free themselves and an individualized way to attack the hated system of slavery.

An essential element to understanding the abolition of slavery in Latin America is the ethnic composition of the countries, as Europeans, Creoles (of different blood mixtures), and Indians were the most common mixture (except for Haiti where the black population was dominant). It is commonly thought that because of intense *metizaje* ("miscegenation," or a mixing of the races") during the colonial period, African slavery was almost nonexistent in some areas. Another argument sustaining this idea is that legally, Hispanic American slaves could obtain their freedom through actions like buying it or receiving it from a master's will. Religion and the role played by the Catholic Church are elements that favored the liberation of individuals and might also be considered when studying particular manumission cases when more than one slave was involved.

Abolition and cultural assimilation developed early in the cities, and escaped slaves from rural areas— plantations and haciendas—organized themselves in *pueblos de cimarrones* ("runaway towns," *quilombos* in Brazil). Eventually, the *cimarrones* dealt with local authorities, who often recognized and legalized not only their free status but also their settlements as legal villages. Individual liberalization in rural areas followed similar patterns to those established in the cities, and in both cases, religious beliefs were important in the decision-making process.

The economic factor was also decisive in the abolition of slavery within specific industries, both urban and rural. By the late-eighteenth century, most of the few slaves remaining were concentrated in the declining sugar plantations. Thus, abolition became almost an economic necessity because the declining profits in sugar could not support the cost of maintaining a slave society. Slaves were kept as long as the economic situation allowed it in urban industries or *obrajes* ("textile factories"), where they were an important part of the specialized labor force. After the late-eighteenth century, judicial documents show that urban slaves frequently demanded and obtained their freedom through legal means. Liberation was the objective of nearly all of the legal processes involving slaves, whether the purpose was evident or not.

The closest legal precedent to the Latin American

abolition movement was the British decision to abolish the slave trade. Additionally, the Hidalgo rebellion in Mexico (1810), with its abolition decrees, contributed to a factual liberation in a revolutionary environment. The Cortes (city council) of Cádiz proposed an eight-point plan designed to bring about a gradual abolition of slavery, and it also emphasized particular concerns about a slave revolt. In contrast to the broad and extended process of Anglo-American abolition, the Latin American process was "generally contingent on the fate of colonial mobilization for national independence. The process on the American Continent extended over half a century until the 1860s" (Drescher, 1988).

Spain and its colonial administrators in Cuba and Puerto Rico encouraged support of their abolition plans by including elaborate provisions offering compensation to slaveowners (promises that were never accomplished). Despite an 1817 treaty signed between Spain and Britain to abolish the slave trade, the United States, acting as a counterweight to Britain's politics, continued to help introduce slave cargoes into Cuba until almost the end of the Ten Years War in 1878.

Abolition of the slave trade also played a significant role in the territorial conflicts involving Mexico, Cuba, the Republic of Texas, and Britain. In accordance with political principles, Mexico enacted a law abolishing slavery in 1823 and urged Cuba to follow a similar policy. Nevertheless, in an attempt to gain control over its vast territory, Mexico assumed a contradictory position by authorizing a settlement in Texas where slaves were admitted. In the struggle to keep its territories, Mexico finally signed a treaty with Great Britain in 1842 that legally ended the slave trade.

The liberation process of the Cuban slaves was "gradual and interactive," just as in other Spanish colonies. In 1870, a legal process of abolition was initiated with the Moret Law; the Peace of Zanjón, a treaty signed by Spaniards and Cuban revolutionaries in 1878, honored the freedom obtained by slaves who had fought in the war for Cuban independence from Spain; and by the late 1880s, an intense legal and illegal mobilization of abolitionist measures completed a long-expected demise of slavery.

The abolition of slavery in Brazil shared some of the characteristics of the gradual liberation of slaves in Hispanic America. In 1851, parliamentary legislation prohibited the slave trade; an 1871 act granted freedom to all slave children (free birth); and the emancipation laws of 1888 abolished slavery entirely. Serious and prolonged debates regarding abolition were held in Brazil, which was a significant difference from the experience of Hispanic America. During the Triple Alliance War (1865–1870), as Brazil, Argentina, and Uruguay fought Paraguay, the Brazilian army purchased slaves to fight against the Paraguayan army.

Surviving slave soldiers received their freedom and were integrated into Brazilian society.

Some Latin American anthropologists consider *mestizaje* a process of liberation and abolition. From this perspective, the liberation of slaves might have been initiated with the first mixed marriage. This interpretation ignores economic and political considerations, however, and those considerations are key elements if one is to achieve a thorough comprehension of the abolition process.

—*Juan M. de la Serna*

For Further Reading
Clementi, Hebe. 1974. *La abolición la esclavitud en América Latina*. Buenos Aires: Pleyade; Drescher, Seymour. 1988. "Brazilian Abolition in Comparative Perspective." *Hispanic American Historical Review* 68 (3): 429–460; Klein, Herbert. 1986. *African Slavery in Latin America and the Caribbean*. New York: Oxford University Press; Scott, Rebecca. 1985. *Slave Emancipation in Cuba: The Transition to Free Labor, 1860–1899*. Princeton, NJ: Princeton University Press.

ABOLITION, SCANDINAVIA

Denmark and Sweden were the only Scandinavian countries involved during the era of slavery and the slave trade. Norway and Iceland were part of the Danish realm, and prior to 1809, Finland was part of the Swedish realm but came under Russian rule from 1809 to 1917. Denmark, Norway, and Iceland were ruled from Copenhagen, and Sweden/Finland from Stockholm.

No organized abolitionist movement was created in Denmark or Sweden such as those that arose in France, Great Britain, and the United States. To a certain extent, this lack was because the two Scandinavian countries were relatively more backward; it was not until the late-eighteenth century that one could speak of a true public debate in Denmark and Sweden. Therefore, the early abolition of the slave trade and slavery in the Danish and Swedish colonies did not result from the work of organized pressure groups.

Although the question of slavery was being debated on the European continent and in Britain by the 1760s, the Danish debate did not begin until the 1780s. A Protestant priest, Peder Paludan, was the first to publish on the question when he asked for better treatment of black slaves in an open letter. The British probably influenced the growing debate in Denmark, but in the latter country, criticism of the slaves' plight did not result in demands for abolishing slavery.

In 1790, Paludan demanded the abolition of the slave trade. In 1788, the German-born Paul Erdmann

Isert published a collection of travel letters from Guinea and the West Indies, and in the early 1790s, he also demanded the abolition of the slave trade. When Denmark moved in 1792 to abolish the slave trade after 1803, becoming the first European colonial power to take such action, it was not as a result of organized pressure, though the public had been informed of the problem through the debate.

In Sweden, the slave trade was never a major issue. Sweden's experience with the slave trade covered only a short period in the seventeenth century; there was none during the eighteenth century. But slavery was an issue because of the Swedish colony of St. Barthélemy (St. Bart's) in the Caribbean. British influence, especially the agitation in the British Parliament against slavery, was important in Sweden. With a growing liberal influence and the interest of humanitarian organizations, there was increased pressure to abolish slavery in Sweden, and during Sweden's 1844–1845 parliamentary session, it was decided to free the slaves in the only Swedish colony by purchase.

—*Bertil Haggman*

For Further Reading
Højlund Knap, Henning. 1983. "Danskerne og slaveriet-negerslavedebatten i Danmark indtil 1792." In *Dansk kolonihistorie - indføring og studier*. Ed. Peter Hoxcer Jensen. Århus, Denmark: Forlaget HISTORIA; Norman, Hans. "När Sverige skulle bli kolonialmakt." *Populär historia* 14: 35–40.

ABOLITION, UNITED STATES

The abolition of slavery in the United States resulted from several ideological, religious, and psychological sources. Enlightenment ideals and the First Great Awakening (1720–1770) suggested a divine basis for human equality while John Locke's writings convinced most Americans that "the rights of man" were a natural birthright. Pennsylvania founded the first antislavery society in 1775, but abolition did not become a sectional issue until the nineteenth century. Even though Massachusetts, Pennsylvania, New York, and other Northern states had emancipated their slaves by 1800, some of the laws resulted from court opinion rather than legislation, and gradual emancipation typically applied. Southern states temporized as well, refusing emancipation but in some cases permitting slave enlistments (military enlistments that were rewarded with the slaves' freedom) and manumission.

Although many supporters of the American Revolution (like James Otis, Abigail Adams, and Thomas Jefferson) recognized the contradiction between slavery and the patriot struggle for rights, eighteenth-century antislavery thought possessed none of the moral urgency it achieved in the next century. Revolutionaries like Patrick Henry (who spoke of the "inconvenience" of laboring in the South without slaves) revealed that self-interest was one motivation for opposing black freedom, but the real reason abolition faltered was ideological.

Some philosophes granted blacks a theoretical equality of rights but not an equality of abilities. Jefferson surmised that blacks were equal in their capacity for moral sense but unequal in intelligence, creativity, courage, or imagination. Although supporting emancipation in theory, he believed slaves would have to be prepared over many decades before they could be safely freed. This view, which the historian Leon Litwack has shown was common among Northerners, helps explain why the most popular form of antislavery activity between 1800 and 1830 was the colonization movement. The American Colonization Society, chartered in 1816, declared that blacks were not innately equipped to assume the blessings of liberty other Americans enjoyed and therefore had to be persuaded voluntarily to find it in Africa, a sentiment Northern and Southern members alike (including Francis Scott Key, Henry Clay, John Marshall, and James Madison) evidently agreed with.

Confidence in human perfectibility, a cardinal tenet of nineteenth-century romanticism, increasingly rendered colonization, with its gradualist and pessimistic mind-set, untenable. The Second Great Awakening (1790s–1830s), by suggesting that a man's salvation lay in his and other men's hands, supplied a religious impetus to emancipation. But it was the organizing skill of a new generation of abolitionists, combined with their contentious personalities, that captured the attention of thousands. Without their flair for publicity (a gift that proved fatal for the editor Elijah P. Lovejoy), the wing of abolitionism identified with William Lloyd Garrison might have reflected its times without changing the political dynamics of the slavery issue.

In 1831, Garrison began publishing the *Liberator*, promising to be "as uncompromising as justice" and demanding the immediate destruction of slavery. He soon established the American Anti-Slavery Society, which had 200,000 members by 1839. No doubt Garrison's bid for support was helped by sectional polarization on the slavery issue, to which he was by no means the only contributor (alarmed by the Nat Turner rebellion, which coincidentally occurred the same year the *Liberator* appeared, some Southern states demanded that Garrison be silenced).

Garrison and other abolitionists were master publicists, declaring that the U.S. Constitution was a covenant with the devil, publishing tracts on the horrors of slavery, and playing on Victorian feelings about hearth and home by portraying slavery as an assault on the integrity of the family. Still, it was not until Harriet Beecher Stowe published *Uncle Tom's Cabin* (1852) that slavery became a national issue. Stowe's novel became the greatest publishing sensation in U.S. history, with 300,000 copies sold in the first year alone, and it created a national consensus that slavery was a problem that could not be ignored.

By that time, abolitionism had largely spent itself as a political force and thereafter played only a sporadic role in paving the way for the Thirteenth Amendment. The antislavery movement was always weakened by deep divisions within its ranks and plagued by an ugly racism, which kept surfacing as a divisive issue. Some abolitionists demanded that the North secede from a sinful South, a demand captured in the phrase, "no Union with slaveholders." But an alarmed Frederick Douglass protested that such a doctrine left the slaves defenseless to fight their own battles in their own ways.

Furthermore, as the historian Leonard Richards shows, antiabolition mobs were a frequent problem in many Northern cities, and the leadership of the mobs was drawn from the ranks of the best and the brightest of the local elites. Finally, those Northerners who did not have racism or status concerns as reasons for opposing abolition steered clear of the antislavery movement out of a conviction that it was a luxury neither the Union nor the Constitution could afford. Abraham Lincoln and most Republicans fell into this category.

When the antiabolitionists are considered, it is easy to see that the political influence of the antislavery movement can be exaggerated. Still, in 1859, the abolition movement once again took center stage as a sectional irritant when John Brown, financed in part by prominent abolitionists, launched an attack on the federal arsenal at Harpers Ferry, Virginia. Brown's mission was to provoke a slave rebellion to purge the nation's sin, but the unrepentant Northern reaction to Brown's misdeed and evidence of abolitionist involvement only accelerated the nation's slide toward war.

The abolitionist movement contributed much toward the creation of a political and moral crisis that needed to be faced and also toward compelling the nation to face that crisis. Once addressed, it was the U.S. political system and even more the Civil War—not the antislavery movement—that achieved the resolution of emancipation. The abolition movement was too entangled in the country's history of race to begin to separate the strands on its own. In the end, only the death of 600,000 men could accomplish that.

—*Richard A. Reiman*

See also
Brown, John; Douglass, Frederick; Garrison, William Lloyd; The *Liberator;* Manumission Laws; U.S.

Constitution; Women and the Antislavery Movement
For Further Reading
Filler, Louis. 1960. *The Crusade against Slavery.* New York: Harper; McFeely, William. 1991. *Frederick Douglass.* New York: Simon and Schuster; Perry, Lewis, and Michael Fellman, eds. 1979. *Antislavery Reconsidered: New Perspectives on the Abolitionists.* Baton Rouge: Louisiana State University Press; Quarles, Benjamin. 1991. *Black Abolitionists.* New York: Da Capo Press.

ABOLITIONIST CONFEDERATION

T he Abolitionist Confederation was founded in Rio de Janeiro, Brazil, in May 1883 by the newspaper *Gazeta da Tarde.* The paper was owned by José do Patrocínio, who was known for his inflammatory rhetoric and was the most requested agitator of the abolitionist movement. The Abolitionist Confederation became an important vehicle of the antislavery movement in Brazil as it united and reactivated abolitionist clubs in various cities, many of which had become almost extinct after the setback abolitionism suffered in 1881 when many abolitionist members of the legislature were not reelected.

The confederation had immediate success. In only three months it incorporated 17 clubs in six different provinces, including clubs at two military academies (in Rio de Janeiro and Pernambuco). The movement spread to institutions of higher education like the law school at São Paulo and the polytechnic academy in Rio de Janeiro where another known abolitionist, André Rebouças, held a chair.

The Abolitionist Confederation introduced an activist strain into the movement in Brazil. Its methods included public meetings, parades in the cities, inflammatory speeches, and funds for freeing slaves. The press became a main factor in the campaign, and there were many journalists among the most prominent abolitionists. In August 1883, the confederation's manifesto, a strongly worded document authored by Patrocínio and Rebouças, was read in the Pedro II theater in Rio to an audience of 2,000. In 1884, inspired by the spontaneous abolition of slavery in the province of Ceará in northern Brazil, members of the confederation tried in vain to convince slaveowners in Rio de Janeiro to emancipate their slaves.

The promulgation of the Sexagenarian Law (1885) was a setback to the movement. This law, which liberated elderly slaves, was a follow-up to the Law of the Free Womb (Lei do Ventre Livre) of 1871, which had declared the freedom of the newborn. The passing of both bills involved much political struggle since slaveowners considered any step a final legal concession. The laws hurt the abolition movement, for many people believed their implementation would be sufficient to end slavery—and thus the need for imminent emancipation could be postponed.

The impact of such thinking was that it made the abolitionists adopt illegal actions. Under the leadership of Antônio Bento, publisher of the newspaper *A Redempção* in São Paulo, and his followers (the *caiphazes*), slaves were persuaded to abandon the plantations and flee to Ceará or to the city of Santos. In the latter place, they constructed a huge *quilombo* (settlement of runaway slaves) on the hillsides overlooking the port. Bands of fugitive slaves also marched on the cities and caused so much fear of social unrest that they finally helped put an end to slavery in Brazil.

The Brazilian abolitionists contemplated more than just ending slavery. After Joaquim Nabuco published *O abolicionism* in 1883, many people believed that true abolition also involved educational and agrarian reform. The Liberal Party promoted these ideas, and the emperor looked on them positively, as such a policy would help to promote immigration. However, the initiatives were never implemented. Despite these apparent setbacks, slavery was abolished in Brazil in 1888.

—*Birgitte Holten*

See also
Brazilian Anti-Slavery Society; Lei Aurea; Nabuco de Araujo, Joaquim
For Further Reading
Bento, Antônio, ed. 1887. *A Redempção.* São Paulo; Conrad, Robert. 1972. *The Destruction of Brazilian Slavery.* Berkeley: University of California Press; Patrocínio, José do, ed. 1880–1888. *Gazeta da Tarde.* Rio de Janeiro; Toplin, Robert Brent. 1992. *The Abolition of Slavery in Brazil.* New York: Athenaeum.

ABOLITIONIST MOVEMENT
See **Atlantic Abolitionist Movement**

ADAMS, JOHN QUINCY (1767–1848)

The sixth president, son of the second president, and a statesman with a long and varied public service record, John Quincy Adams spent much of his postpresidential career opposing the institution of slavery in the United States in numerous ways, most notably as a congressman battling the proslavery gag rule and as an attorney arguing for Africans' rights in the *Amistad* case before the U.S. Supreme Court.

Adams was president from 1825 to 1829, but the real beginning of his public antislavery efforts came after he lost his bid for reelection in 1828. All his life, Adams had personally objected to slavery as immoral and repugnant to the republican tradition of the nation's Founding, but he also realized that the issue was explosive enough to splinter the Union. In 1820, while serving as secretary of state, Adams watched apprehensively as Congress resolved the controversy surrounding Missouri's admission to the Union by dividing the United States into free and slaveholding territories. Privately, Adams remarked, "If the Union must be dissolved, Slavery is precisely the question upon which it ought to break" (Richards, 1986).

Since he hoped to be president and knew that no candidate voicing such opinions could win an election, Adams kept his convictions to himself until after his term as president. At that time, Adams did not retire quietly to his Massachusetts farm. Instead, he did what no other ex-president has done: he went to Congress in 1831 and represented the Plymouth, Massachusetts, district in the House of Representatives for the last 17 years of his life. There, Adams battled the notorious gag rule.

The gag rule, an attempt to silence one means of antislavery sentiment, forbade the presentation of antislavery petitions, or written pleas for the demise of slavery signed by private citizens, to Congress. The antislavery petitioners were often women, free blacks, or even slaves, none of whom could vote and who used petitions to participate in political life. Therefore, the gag rule not only stifled debate, it barred segments of the population from access to the political process and violated the First Amendment right to petition.

On those grounds, Adams used his fabled eloquence and obstructionist tactics to attack the gag rule in the House of Representatives. Every week, he arrived at his desk with piles of antislavery petitions and rose to read them in spite of the insults, accusations, and censure other congressmen subjected him to. Adams prevailed, and in 1844 the gag rule was revoked.

Adams further supported the antislavery cause by serving as counsel for the defense in the *Amistad* case (1841), a critical antebellum Supreme Court case. On June 28, 1839, the Spanish ship *Amistad* sailed from Havana, Cuba, with a cargo of 54 Africans to be sold as slaves in Puerto Príncipe in east-central Cuba. Four nights later, the Africans freed themselves from their irons, mutinied, killed the ship's captain and cook, sent two crewmen overboard, and instructed two surviving crewmen to sail for Africa.

The crewmen had other ideas, and when the *Amistad* landed at Long Island, New York, on August 26, after being seized in the Atlantic by the U.S. Coast Guard, the Africans were jailed and charged with mutiny and murder. Meanwhile, the Spanish government had claimed them as its property and demanded their return. The case moved from district court to circuit court and arrived before the Supreme Court in late 1840.

Antislavery advocates took an interest in the case and convinced Adams to defend the *Amistad* Africans. Adams hesitated, partly because he had not practiced law in years and partly because he was afraid his own heated emotions about the case might prevent him from carrying out the defense in a cool, rational manner. In his diary, Adams worried about how to "defeat and expose the abominable conspiracy" against the *Amistad* Africans while simultaneously managing to "escape the imminent danger of . . . overheated zeal . . . and losing my self-possession" (Adams, 1874).

Adams addressed the Supreme Court for over four hours on February 24, 1841, and again on March 1, presenting arguments that ranged from the minute wording of shipping laws to the ideals of the Declaration of Independence. On March 9, 1841, not only did Chief Justice Roger B. Taney find the Africans innocent of murder and piracy, he also ruled that they were free and should be allowed to return to Africa. The Africans sailed for Sierra Leone in November 1841 to serve as missionaries.

The *Amistad* case won, Adams devoted his efforts to his congressional duties, which he continued for the rest of his life. Adams was at his desk in the House of Representatives on February 21, 1848, when he suffered a stroke. He died two days later.

—*Chandra Miller*

See also
Amistad Case
For Further Reading
Adams, Charles Francis. 1874. *Memoirs of John Quincy Adams Comprising Portions of His Diary from 1795 to 1848.* Philadelphia: Lippincott; Cable, Mary. 1971. *Black Odyssey: The Case of the Slave Ship Amistad.* New York: Viking Press; Miller, William Lee. 1996. *Arguing about Slavery: The Great Battle in the United States Congress.* New York: Knopf; Richards, Leonard L. 1986. *The Life and Times of Congressman John Quincy Adams.* New York: Oxford University Press.

AFONSO I OF KONGO
(R. 1506/7–C. 1545)

The second Christian ruler of the Kongo Kingdom, Afonso I, initiated a large-scale Portuguese slave trade but after 20 years unsuccessfully sought to end it. First called Nzinga Mbemba, this Kongolese prince was baptized and renamed Afonso by the Portuguese shortly after their contact with the kingdom in 1490. It was probably with Portuguese aid that Afonso defeated tribal and regional enemies and assumed the throne as manicongo, or regional ruler, over the Kongo and the tributary states of Loango, Ngola, and Matamba. He established a remarkable relationship with Portuguese King Manuel I, corresponding with him and his successors as "royal brother." Afonso was eager to adopt European technologies and customs, and to this end Manuel sent a *regimento,* or document, in 1512 outlining ways Africans might absorb late-feudal European political and social forms. In return, as was customary, Afonso offered the Portuguese representative 420 slaves, of whom he took 320. Later that year Afonso sent a mission of 12 nobles and his son to Rome to formalize relations with the papacy. A number of young Kongolese men also went to Portugal for formal education, though the Portuguese with whom they sailed seized many of them and passed them into slavery.

After a few years it was clear that slave-taking had become a social and political problem for the manicongo. Vassal and tributary chiefs and Portuguese slavers were regularly seizing the king's subjects and shipping them away via the offshore island of São Tomé, and because he was dependent on his vassals' cooperation and African allies, Afonso could not openly threaten this activity. Ruthless Portuguese colonists with powerful friends in Lisbon held São Tomé, and in the absence of a royal Portuguese liaison these rogues managed a lucrative monopoly that bypassed Afonso. Fernam de Mello, lord of São Tomé, received 28.75 percent of all slaves shipped from Kongolese territories, including those sent to Portugal in trade by the manicongo. Afonso received empty promises and assurances of support by the crown. It is estimated that the annual number of exported slaves at this time ranged between 5,000 and 10,000 persons. It was a trade regulated only by greed and the availability of cargo space in Portuguese ships.

On many occasions Afonso complained to his "royal brother" of the slavers' brutal practices, but to no avail. Finally, in 1526, Afonso attempted to stanch the flow of humanity from his kingdom. He wrote to John III of Portugal warning of the Kongo's depopulation and advising against both the trading and marketing of slaves in the kingdom. Vassal chiefs were to screen improperly seized slaves, and even though adverse political and economic effects rather than any humanitarian considerations prompted this fruitless initiative, the attempt is nonetheless notable.

Early on, Afonso had tried to use slaves as currency to acquire some of the advantages of European civilization for his kingdom. He requested Portuguese doctors, teachers, and priests, but increasing Portuguese disinterest and the rapacity of his own vassals and the slavers devalued his "currency" and wrecked his hopes for his people.

—*Joseph P. Byrne*

For Further Reading
Duffy, James. 1959. *Portuguese Africa.* Cambridge, MA: Harvard University Press; Hilton, Anne. 1985. *The Kingdom of Kongo.* Oxford: Clarendon Press; Mannix, Daniel, and Malcolm Cowley. 1965. *Black Cargoes: A History of the Atlantic Slave Trade 1518–1865.* New York: Viking; Thornton, John K. 1983. *The Kingdom of Kongo.* Madison: University of Wisconsin Press.

AFRICA

Many Africans were captured in the interior and transported to the coast to be sold to European traders there.

Slavery in Africa has a long history, predating European arrival by several centuries and lasting even into the twentieth century. Scholars consider slavery a "central institution in many parts of Africa" and know that Africa was the chief supplier of slaves for "ancient civilizations, [the] Islamic world, India and [the] Americas" (Lovejoy, 1983). A vigorous two-way slave trade between Africans and Arab peoples existed from initial contacts in the ninth century, a trade in which Africans both imported and exported human beings. Slavery was not considered a badge of inferiority, and many slaves were people of great skill and even of great learning.

Europeans arriving in West Africa discovered a well-developed, operational slave-trading system. The trans-Saharan slave trade started as part of the overall trade of salt and other minerals for food, food that was essential for survival in desert communities. Contrary to popular belief, this trade declined after Moroccans conquered the Songhai Empire, but the slave trade again increased when gold trading declined.

Portugal's Prince Henry (Henry the Navigator, 1394–1460) witnessed the slave trade's importance and its relationship to the gold trade during his participation in the conquest of the African city of Ceuta in 1415. One reason for Henry's interest in Africa was to reduce Morocco's control of the trans-Saharan trade in gold and slaves. Henry's idea was to reach Africa's western coast and eliminate the Moroccan middlemen. Toward that end he sponsored a series of sailing expeditions, using a new ship, the caravel, a smaller, less-expensive, but very seaworthy ship.

Most European slave transactions were conducted in a peaceful and orderly fashion, with negotiation being the rule rather than force. Initially, African rulers perceived the European slave trade as simply a continuation of the trade they conducted with Arabs. Arab trade routes had connected the Sahel region, the northern Sudan, and the eastern coast into an Islamic trade network from medieval times. Africans purchased salt, horses, cloth, glassware, and metalware from Arab traders, and in return, sub-Saharan Africa provided gold and slaves. These two items comprised 90 percent of Africa's exports, and ivory made up most of the balance in trade goods.

Although Arabs found uses for slaves—mostly females for domestic service—the Portuguese initially had to sell slaves within Africa, mainly to Moroccans. Slowly, the Portuguese began finding use for slave labor—mostly male—on their sugar plantations on the Cape Verde Islands, Madeira, São Tomé, and Príncipe. During the sixteenth century, they extended this trade to Portuguese possessions in the Americas.

The fact that African kingdoms participated in the slave trade is not surprising considering that slavery has had a long history in many world societies. Slavery had long been part of the normal order of things in many African societies, and African rulers deemed European interest in the trade comparable to Arab interest. Only when this trade became insatiable and replaced all other legitimate commerce, even providing guns for humans, did the slave trade inflict its destructive effects on Africa, particularly West Africa.

Scholars have formulated theories about the basis for slavery in West Africa among the Ashanti, the Yoruba, and the Bini, as well as the rulers of Dahomey. One anthropologist has noted that "essentially agricultural, all these societies manifest a considerable degree of specialization, from which are derived the arrangements for the exchange of goods that take the form principally of stated markets, wherein operations are carried on without the aid of a monetary system which, in pre-European days, was based on the cowry shell to facilitate the expression of values"

(Herskovits, 1958). This highly organized economic system produced a surplus, and that surplus supported a highly differentiated class system, including the institution of slavery. In Dahomey, plantation slavery existed while in other coastal West African systems it does not appear to have done so. Slavery in other coastal West African areas was part of the highly elaborate labor specialization of the distributive system. In other kingdoms, slavery appears to have been of the domestic sort, with many slaves being reserved for the ruler's use. Rulers could use these slaves to obtain European goods or for ritual sacrifice.

Each of the three stages of the slave trade (1350–1600, 1600–1800, and 1800–1900) was marked by slavery's spread over ever-larger geographic areas, slavery's increasing role in the economy of African polities, and transformation of the political and economic order (Lovejoy, 1983). Scholars note a strong link between gold production and trade and the slave trade, especially in five areas of important production—three in West Africa and two in East Africa. There was also, of course, a regional trade in luxuries that included slave trading.

Several interesting characteristics marked African slavery. Slavery was one of many types of dependency in Africa, and it was enmeshed in the kinship system, the dominant form of social organization in most African societies. In slavery's earliest forms, no separate slave class existed in Africa. Political influence in small-scale, kinship-based societies depended on the size of a person's kinship group. Many, if not most, of these societies allowed slaves to become full members of the kinship group. Alternately, they might be retained as dependents whose welfare was joined with that of their owners and a relevant kinship group. Slaves formed only one type of dependency group. Early African society was not based on slavery as a central institution, but as it grew more important many African societies became slave societies.

In contrast to Islamic slavery, which expanded slowly and essentially retained many traditional African features while adding the stamp of training in a universal religion, the beginning of the transatlantic slave trade marked an explosive growth in slave trading. This expansion caused major changes in those African societies that it touched. Slavery expanded to vast areas in a short time and it did so intensely. From 650 to 1600, approximately 3.5 million to 10 million people were removed from Africa by the slave trade. This is a considerable number, but it averages to transporting 5,000–10,000 people per year over six Saharan routes and two major East African ones. These figures should be contrasted with numbers taken from 1650 to the end of the Atlantic slave trade where estimates range from just over 11 million to more than 20 million.

Clearly, there was much money to be made in the trade, and many African polities became slave societies. Little could be gained economically or militarily by opposing European traders' desires, since their home countries often backed them. Some African rulers became so secure in their positions that they relaxed control of their court slaves. Sultan Bangassou, of what is now the Central African Republic, became so enriched by the slave trade and the support of Europeans involved in it that he raised the status and personal freedom of his court's slave women.

Scholarly studies make it clear that slavery's growth could just as easily have proceeded from internal or external factors or an interaction of both. Indicative of this fact are slavery studies conducted on the Julas and other similar Islamic commercial groups. The Julas inhabited an area of the western Sudan and had "a chain of villages worked by their slaves who provided them with provisions and served as carriers on their commercial expeditions." Village heads in these settlements formed a type of minor nobility in the region. The conclusion is that "the development of commerce and of social mobility based on commerce was intimately linked to the growth of slavery, for slaves in villages performing agricultural work or carrying goods in caravans or working in mines under private supervision were essential to private commercial development" (Thornton, 1992).

Slaves also measured the political elite's wealth. They could be used to generate private armies, rule client areas, or produce wealth through labor or investment. For example, Sudanese empires used slave armies and administrators to check the feudal nobility's power, and studies indicate that slavery also performed the same function in other African regions. In the case of the Congo, kings collected their slaves into a central area, Mbanza Kongo, and turned them into the capital needed to consolidate power. Many of these slaves owned estates, and their combined wealth enabled rulers to resist tendencies to fragment the area into smaller and weaker political units. Similarly, the nearby Ndongo kings used slaves as administrators to combat the power of independent-minded nobles.

Not surprisingly, Europeans entering Africa in the fifteenth and sixteenth centuries found a ready source for the slave trade. A thriving market for such transactions existed, and slaveowners, merchants, and state officials were the very people Europeans made contact with. The nature of African society was such that transferring rights in people was intimately bound with the legal construction of wealth and obligation. "This legal structure made slavery and slave marketing widespread and created secondary legal mechanisms for securing and regulating the sale of slaves, which Europeans could use as well as Africans" (Thornton, 1992).

The conclusion appears inescapable. A well-developed system of slavery and a slave trade existed before Europeans arrived in Africa, although the rapid increase of slave exports suggests the diversion of internal routes to external ones. According to one scholar: "The Atlantic slave trade and African participation in it had solid origins in African societies and legal systems. The institution of slavery was widespread in Africa and accepted in all the exporting regions, and the capture, purchase, transport, and sale of slaves was a regular feature of African society." Seemingly, "This preexisting social arrangement was thus as much responsible as any external force for the development of the Atlantic slave trade" (Thornton, 1992).

—*Frank A. Salamone*

See also
Abolition, Africa; Closing of the African Slave Trade; Historiography, African; Proslavery Argument, Africa; Salt Trade; Transition from Slave Labor to Free Labor, Africa; Women as Slaves, Africa

For Further Reading
Herskovits, Melville J. 1958. *The Myth of the Negro Past*. Boston: Beacon Press; Klein, A. Norman. 1994. "Slavery and Akan Origins." *Ethnohistory* 41: 627–656; Lovejoy, Paul E. 1983. *Transformations in Slavery*. Cambridge: Cambridge University Press; Thornton, John. 1992. *Africa and Africans in the Making of the Atlantic World, 1400–1680*. Cambridge: Cambridge University Press.

AFRICAN BURIAL GROUND

The African (sometimes Negro) Burial Ground is located in New York City's borough of Manhattan. The burial ground was used as a cemetery, primarily by colonial New York's African population, from approximately 1712 until 1798, and it is estimated that nearly 10,000–20,000 people were buried in the five–six acre site.

The African presence in New York began in 1626 when the Dutch West India Company imported 11 male slaves into what was then New Amsterdam. Attracting European settlers was difficult for the Dutch, and the manpower shortage was a critical issue that threatened profitability. As a response, slave importation increased, and by 1644, just before the Dutch ceded Manhattan to the British, 40 percent of the colony's total population consisted of enslaved Africans. By the end of British control in the mid-1770s, New York had the second-highest number of enslaved Africans of any English colonial settlement and the highest ratio of slaves to Europeans of any Northern settlement. Africans played a vital role in the foundation, building, and functioning of colonial New York.

New York City adopted a policy of mortuary segregation in November 1697, which forced blacks to find an alternative place to bury their dead. An area of common land outside the city limits was chosen for the burial ground. The first known reference to Africans burying their dead in this spot appears in a letter written by a chaplain, John Sharpe, in 1712. Soon after, the African Burial Ground began appearing on local maps and was identified in contemporary land surveys.

When the American Revolution ended, antislavery movements gained popularity in New York City. Slaveowners there offered little resistance to the movements, as the postwar immigration of white colonists from other places made it cheaper to hire labor than to own it. Emancipation was a gradual process that began in 1799 with passage of a state law freeing slaves over a period of time. The official emancipation day of New York slaves was July 4, 1827.

In 1798, a branch of the African Methodist Episcopal Church was founded in New York City by Peter Williams, a black tobacconist and a former church sexton. African New York residents and their descendants now had their own place of worship and a place to bury their dead on consecrated soil, thus ending the days when they were consigned to the African Burial Ground. An additional burial ground for African Americans was established on the Lower East Side at about the same time. In the late-eighteenth and early-nineteenth centuries, the city's population growth led to a northward expansion, and the land covering the African Burial Ground was divided into lots for commercial and residential development. By the late-nineteenth century, the African Burial Ground had been entirely paved or built over and all but forgotten, with the exception its being noted on a few historical maps and in some documents.

In December 1990, the federal government purchased land from the New York City to construct a 34-story office tower. The archaeological section of the site's environmental impact statement identified the area as a section of the African Burial Ground, but it was thought that any archaeological remains would have been destroyed by nineteenth- and twentieth-century construction. In May 1991, archaeological testing was begun to determine if there were any intact human remains left, and by July 1992, the remains of approximately 390 individuals, approximately 93 percent African and 7 percent European and Native American, had been excavated from a small section of the African Burial Ground, probably the earliest and largest collection of African American remains discovered.

The excavation provided unparalleled data for Howard University scholars, led by Dr. Michael Blakey, who took on the study of the remains. Artifacts recovered from the burials were relatively few and far between, probably reflecting the minimal economic standing of those who used the cemetery, and of the approximately 560 artifacts found, most were shroud pins. Aspects of traditional African cultures, like pennies placed on eyelids and seashells to return the dead symbolically back across the seas, were found in some of the burial sites. Some skeletons had filed teeth, which accords with a contemporary West African coming-of-age ritual. One adult female skeleton was found with beads and shells around the lower torso, probably the remnants of a decorated garment or piece of jewelry with clear antecedents in West African traditional adornment.

It is expected that further analysis of the remains will reveal aspects of the social and economic conditions that affected the health of the enslaved Africans and additional information about their African ethnic identity. Preliminary findings reveal that a high percentage of the individuals excavated were children, approximately 40 percent. Both child and adult skeletons reveal signs of malnutrition, disease, and the hard labor the individuals endured during life. The skeletons will be reinterred on site after a five-year research period. The African Burial Ground received National Historic Landmark status on April 19, 1993.

—*Lori Lee*

See also
Archaeological Record of the Slave Trade; New York
For Further Reading
Diehl, Lorraine. 1992. "Skeletons in the Closet: Uncovering the Rich History of the Slaves of New York." *New York* 25(39): 78–86; Harrington, Spencer. 1993. "Bones and Bureaucrats: New York City's Great Cemetery Imbroglio." *Archaeology* 2: 28–38; Scarupa, Harriet. 1995. "Learning from Ancestral Bones: New York's Exhumed African Past." *American Visions* (February/March): 18–21.

AFRICAN DIASPORA

African diaspora refers to the dispersal of people of sub-Saharan African descent throughout the world, primarily, though not exclusively, through various transoceanic slave-trading networks. The term first came into common use at the 1965 International Congress of African Historians held in Tanzania, but the African diaspora is a truly ancient phenomenon. Black Africans were present in all major civilizations of the classical Mediterranean: the Greco-Roman world and the ancient civilizations of Egypt, Arabia, and India all included significant populations from sub-Saharan Africa.

Although populations of Africans have existed outside of sub-Saharan Africa since the earliest periods of recorded time, the development of the African diaspora is largely a product of the postclassical and modern eras. After the spread of Islam and the reinvigoration of Indian Ocean trade networks, Africans began to be purchased in large numbers and were put to work in the Middle East as slaves. Evidence of numerous Africans being taken to the Middle East is found in historical incidents like the serious revolts that occurred on the part of African slaves in Iraq in the tenth century and the increasing numbers of African slaves employed as soldiers and sailors throughout the Middle East, especially in Egypt and the Gulf regions.

Also of future significance was the number of Africans who were introduced to the Iberian Peninsula as slaves during the period of Muslim rule there, 711–1492. Additionally, for a short period of the fifteenth century in the northern Indian province of Bengal, African soldiers gained considerable influence as political advisers to the local dynasty. In 1486, Sultan Shahzada, a eunuch, took power briefly, but in 1493, the native Indians regained power and expelled the African soldiers.

Although it is clear that Africans were present in both the Asian and the Western worlds, this article concentrates primarily on the development of the New World and European African diaspora. The reason for this emphasis lies in the Western diaspora's greater size and its much more distinctive cultural development and later impact on both the West and Africa.

The transatlantic slave trade was the vehicle that created the African diaspora in the Western world. The two nations that initiated the great period of Western expansion, Portugal and Spain, had been made aware of the existence of African slaves through the years of Moorish domination in Iberia. Once the Portuguese began exploring the African coastline under the direction of Prince Henry the Navigator early in the fifteenth century, they began to trade in African slaves, and the trade began to involve large numbers after the Portuguese reached the Senegal River in 1441. The first diaspora resulted from Portuguese incursions near the African mainland—in the island chains of Cape Verde and the separate islands of São Tomé and Príncipe. These islands were important because they were prototypes for the sugar plantations that later dominated the economic development of much of the Caribbean and Brazil.

Africans went to the Caribbean on Christopher Columbus's first voyage, serving in various roles ranging from navigator to servant. Despite the predominance of slavery as the common status of Africans in the New World prior to emancipation, it was never a universal condition, but by 1502, the Spanish had begun importing slaves specifically for work in the Caribbean, most of them on the sugar plantations that were being rapidly developed. The constant importation of slaves combined with the rapid decline of Native Americans owing to death and conflict with Europeans created the current demographic makeup of most of the Caribbean (outside of Cuba and Puerto Rico), which is overwhelmingly of African ancestry.

Many Africans were also introduced to the mainlands of Mexico and South America to perform various tasks. Many were engaged in the mining of silver and other precious metals in Peru and Mexico; others were involved in cattle herding and agricultural work. Numerous slaves worked in urban environments in assorted occupations, including ironworking, music, and domestic service.

During the 1600s, the English, French, and Dutch became more active in the New World. Although the tropical colonies of the northern European powers followed patterns already established by the Iberian nations, the English-speaking North American colonies saw the development of a different kind of African slave community. The introduction of Africans into British North America, which began in 1619 in Jamestown, Virginia, was different from the earlier slave regimes in the Caribbean since the overall proportion of slaves tended to be smaller, the slaves had less cultural autonomy, and the importation patterns tended to introduce both genders in roughly equal proportions.

Africans who were sent to the Americas came from many ethnic and religious backgrounds, but there are some general statements that can be made. Most came from Africa's western coast from the area between the Senegal and Zaire Rivers. The only major exception was the population of Mozambicans who were mainly settled on the plantations of Brazil.

Generally, the origin of Africans in a particular region of the Western Hemisphere depended on what country controlled the territory. In Haiti, for instance, at different times large numbers of slaves were from the Congo region of west-central Africa; at other times, Africans from the Dahomey (Benin) section of West Africa were common. In colonial South Carolina, many planters preferred slaves who were of Gullah or Angola (Zaire River basin) origin. Many of the Carolina slaves came from the upper Guinea coast region of what is modern-day Sierra Leone, Liberia, and Guinea.

Once these Africans were in the New World, the extent to which their culture remained identifiably African and the degree to which it was absorbed by the larger society also varied considerably. Generally speaking, those areas with higher concentrations of Africans tended to have more overt expressions of African culture. For instance, African styles of religious expression like Candomblé became commonplace in Brazil, and other regions like Haiti developed strong African-based religious traditions like vodun, or voodoo.

Even in areas where Africans did not compose the absolute majority, their religious and musical traditions often became the dominant modes of cultural expression. In Cuba, for example, many people who were ostensibly non-African adopted African-based religious practices like Santeria and claimed salsa, with its rhythmic concept, as their primary means of musical expression.

The question of African influence in the culture of the United States has often been more contentious. For many years, it was commonly accepted that direct African expression did not exist in the United States as it did in the Caribbean and Latin America. This interpretation of African American culture was most forcefully argued by E. Franklin Frazier, an African American sociologist who was active in the early- and mid-twentieth century. Gradually, through the efforts of writers like Zora Neale Hurston and academics like Melville Herskovits, the concept of African survivals in African American culture came to be acknowledged. According to this concept, certain African American practices—such as the use of call and response in church services, the use of particular designs in quilts, and the employment of particular rhythms in music—are indications of African influence that have simply been modified in the new surroundings.

Perhaps the most important aspect of the African diaspora has been its ideological impact on the greater African world. During the nineteenth and twentieth centuries, many of the great ideological movements of the African world originated in the diaspora, the most basic being the idea of blackness or African identity. In most traditional African societies there was no concept of blackness as a bond between morphologically similar people. There was only the idea of ethnic identity. The idea of blackness spread and eventually led to the concept of Pan-Africanism that was expressed in the writings of W. E. B. DuBois, Marcus Garvey, and George Padmore. Pan-Africanism is the idea of a common destiny and the need for fundamental unity among all people of African extraction, and it and similar ideas have had a great seminal effect on the writings and actions of African political activists like Nnamdi Azikiwe, Kwame Nkrumah, and Jomo Kenyatta.

—*Anthony Q. Cheeseboro*

See also
Candomblé; Drums; Gullah; Zanj Slave Revolts
For Further Reading
Conniff, Michael, and Thomas Davis. 1994. *Africans*

in the Americas. New York: St. Martin's; Fanon, Frantz. 1968. *The Wretched of the Earth.* New York: Grove Press; Gilroy, Paul. 1993. *The Black Atlantic.* Cambridge, MA: Harvard University Press; Harris, Joseph, ed. 1993. *Global Dimensions of the African Diaspora.* Washington, DC: Howard University Press.

THE AFRICAN INSTITUTION

Founded shortly after Britain abolished that country's slave trade in 1807, the African Institution was a semiofficial watchdog organization created to monitor enforcement of the new abolition laws. A moderate lobbying group, it utilized its members' personal connections and influence on high-level figures in Parliament and the British navy to ensure full compliance with the hard-won legislation.

The founding members of the African Institution, the child of both the Sierra Leone Company and Britain's evangelical movement, included Sierra Leone's former governor Zachary Macaulay, abolitionists Thomas Clarkson and James Stephen, and parliamentarian William Wilberforce. Other executive committee members were William Pitt, George Canning, Samuel Romilly, Henry Brougham, William Huskisson, Granville Sharp, Thomas Babington; the bishops of London, Durham, and Bath and Wells; and the Duke of Gloucester. Obviously a stellar group, the organization believed in all men's dignity and freedom regardless of skin color. Almost immediately after its first meeting on April 14, 1807, the African Institution initiated correspondence with its American counterparts, including the Pennsylvania Abolition Society (Benjamin Rush) and the New York Manumission Society (John Jay). Their mutual desire to share information and coordinate activities reveals the growing sophistication of interest-group politics on both sides of the ocean.

Throughout its 16-year history, the African Institution had five main goals: monitoring enforcement of abolition laws in Britain and abroad, disseminating accurate information about Africa and its people, advancing African knowledge by establishing written forms for African languages, introducing modern medical knowledge to Africa, and improving Africa's agricultural production. Members pressured the British government to lower tariffs on African goods to stimulate commercial alternatives to slave trading—cotton, ginger, wool, coffee, and palm oil were among the recommended products. Using information provided by correspondents and representatives in the major ports of Britain, West Africa, and the Caribbean, members proposed draft legislation to Parliament (for example, the Slave Trade Felony Act of 1811) and often intervened to force seizure of suspected slave ships. Perhaps the African Institution's most significant contribution to abolition was James Stephen's creation of a central slave registry, which was intended to document harsh treatment; it listed the name, dates, family members, and personal history of each captive African and helped expose to the British public slavery's human cost.

Unfortunately, the African Institution's success contained the seeds of its decline: its personality-driven, behind-the-scenes style worked well in the days immediately after the abolition of the slave trade in Britain, but it had become less effective by the 1820s, when more forceful and public roles were required for action. In 1823, the organization's members decided to push for full emancipation and replaced the outmoded African Institution with the Society for Mitigating and Gradually Abolishing the State of Slavery throughout the British Dominions, commonly shortened to the British Anti-Slavery Society. Still, the African Institution played a vital role in altering the attitudes toward slavery of both the British politicians and the British public in the crucial decades of the early-nineteenth century.

—*Karen Racine*

For Further Reading
Drescher, Seymour. 1977. *Econocide: British Slavery in the Era of Abolition.* Pittsburgh: University of Pittsburgh Press; Fladeland, Betty. 1972. *Men and Brothers: Anglo-American Antislavery Cooperation.* Urbana: University of Illinois Press; Hurwitz, Edith. 1973. *Politics and the Public Conscience: Slave Emancipation and the Abolitionist Movement in Britain.* London: Allen and Unwin; Turley, David. 1991. *The Culture of English Antislavery.* London: Routledge.

AFRICAN METHODIST EPISCOPAL CHURCH

The African Methodist Episcopal Church (generally called the AME) is the oldest black religious denomination in the United States and now comprises more than 8,000 churches in 29 countries with a membership exceeding 2.5 million people. The AME dates from 1787, and its history is testimony to the efforts of slaves in America to establish places of worship for themselves. The history also speaks of the virulent racism that often prevented white Christians from living their creed. In 1787, a small group of black Christians walked out of St. George Methodist Episcopal Church in Philadelphia, Pennsylvania, because newly imposed segregated practices made blacks sit in the balcony, away from white Christians. One November Sunday in 1787, Richard Allen and other black members of the congregation were being led to their segregated seats when the minister began praying. The group of blacks knelt to pray, but the usher tried to remove them from the area because it was reserved for whites. The indignant black men—Allen, Absalom Jones, Dorus Ginnings, and William White—walked out of the unwelcoming church.

By 1794, the former slave Richard Allen had founded his own church, Bethel AME Church in Philadelphia. Born a slave in 1760 in that same city, he was owned by Benjamin Chew, chief justice of the Commonwealth of Pennsylvania, a Quaker lawyer who later sold Allen to a man named Stokley Sturgis in Dover, Delaware. Richard Allen purchased his own freedom in 1780 for $2,000. He became a traveling preacher, returned to Philadelphia, and joined St. George's, where he was often permitted to preach an early morning service.

After leaving the sanctuary of St. George Methodist Episcopal Church, Richard Allen and his associates had a plan, one that led to the acquisition of property on which to establish their own church. In 1787, Allen purchased a plot of land from Mark Wilcox, a transaction that marks the oldest parcel of real estate owned continuously by black people in the United States. Future church buildings would be erected on this location at Sixth Street and Lombard. Allen also purchased an abandoned blacksmith shop for $35 from a man named Sims and hauled it to the newly acquired lot with a team of six horses. Dedicated as the first church on the site in July 1794, this building was named Bethel and today is known as Mother Bethel. Paternalistic meddling in Bethel Church's affairs by the leaders of St. George, who apparently saw their church as the mother church, was soon brought to an end. In 1796, Richard Allen solicited the help of Dr. Benjamin Rush, Robert Ralston, and attorney David Brown to secure a charter for Allen and his congregation. A special act of the Commonwealth of Pennsylvania's legislature was required to obtain such a charter, but Bethel became an independent organization and adopted the name African Methodist Episcopal Church.

For 11 years the congregation used the small church renovated from the blacksmith shop, but in 1805 a second church was erected. This new church was the site of the first AME convention held in April 1816. During this meeting, on April 11, 1816, Allen was ordained a bishop by his old friend Absalom Jones, now a priest in the Protestant Episcopal Church.

From its beginnings, the AME Church and its congregation have stood for liberty. The leader and founder was himself a man of character whose ideas were steeped in a desire for freedom, and he recognized slavery's threat to his own liberty. Therefore, on April 12, 1787, Allen established the Free African Society. Through the years of slavery in the United States, the AME Church was a voice for abolition, and Bethel was a way station on the Underground Railroad, a covert network for helping slaves escape from the American South. Bethel AME Church's basement sheltered many runaway slaves, and the congregation collected large sums of money to feed and clothe those seeking freedom. Prominent abolitionists, including Frederick Douglass, Lucretia Mott, William Still, Alfred Love, and William Forten, denounced slavery from the church's pulpit.

Bethel AME Church was the only institution for black Methodists in America until 1816. The example set by Allen and his congregation encouraged other black people who were suffering insults and rejections at the hands of white Christians, and in 1816, these black groups began to withdraw from other Methodist Episcopal churches. The question of a separate independent church was discussed at the April 1816 convention, and those attending resolved that black people wanting to unite with the African Methodists could do so regardless of their location. They would become one body known as the African Methodist Episcopal Church.

Today, the African Methodist Episcopal denomination thrives in the United States and has over 2,000 churches in Africa, Canada, England, and the Caribbean. The AME Church employs 90 people at its national headquarters in Washington, D.C., and manages a budget of $5.8 million. The AME Church spends 38 percent of its budget on education, and historically, it has stood at the forefront of providing education to former slaves, establishing Wilberforce University (1856) in Ohio; Edward Waters College (1866) in Jacksonville, Florida; Allen University (1870) in Columbia, South Carolina; Paul-Quinn College (1872) in Waco, Texas; and Morris Brown College (1881) in Atlanta, Georgia. The AME Church's role in the fight against slavery and in the effort to educate and raise the status of former slaves is perhaps surpassed only by the American Missionary Association, a group it worked closely with.

The AME Church's constitution and bylaws have not always reflected the egalitarian principles on which it was founded. Fortunately, some amendments have been made. On March 5, 1953, the official and legal name of the first church became Mother Bethel, and women were permitted to participate in the business of the corporation. On April 8, 1957, Mrs. Willie V. Simpkins was elected to the board of trustees, but to date, no woman has been elected bishop.

—*Nagueyalti Warren*

See also
Abolition, United States; Allen, Richard; American

Missionary Association; Jones, Absalom; Underground Railroad

For Further Reading

Allen, Richard. 1983. *The Life Experience and Gospel Labors of the Right Reverend Richard Allen Written by Himself.* Ed. George A. Singleton. Nashville, TN: Abingdon; George, Carol V. R. 1973. *Segregated Sabbaths: Richard Allen and the Emergence of Independent Black Churches 1760–1840.* New York: Oxford University Press; Payne, Daniel Alexander. 1891. *History of the African Methodist Episcopal Church.* Nashville, TN: Publishing House of the A.M.E. Sunday School Union; Williams, Leonard F. 1972. *Richard Allen and Mother Bethel: African Methodist Episcopal Church.* Philadelphia: Historical Commission of Mother Bethel A.M.E.

AFRICAN SQUADRON

The African Squadron, also known as the Anti-Slavery Squadron or the Preventive Squadron, was a division of the Royal Navy that patrolled the African coastline throughout most of the nineteenth century as part of Great Britain's campaign to suppress the transmarine slave trade. Largely in response to abolitionist pressure, the British government sent two ships in 1808 to enforce the abolition of its own slave trade. After the Napoleonic Wars, Britain began signing treaties outlawing slave trading with European powers, which, in principle, allowed for the mutual right of search and seizure of illegal slave ships from either country, with adjudication in an international court of mixed commission. If condemned, the arresting captain received prize money for each slave on board. In practice, however, only Britain possessed the means of enforcement—in fact, over 95 percent of all captures were made by the British.

Concentrating its efforts first on West Africa, the African Squadron (known as the West African Squadron from 1819 to 1869) initially had little effect. It consisted on average of six ships of poor quality, its task was to patrol 2,000 miles of coastline, and its officers worked under heavy restrictions regarding arrest. By the 1840s, however, many of these problems had been overcome. Almost all of the countries had agreed to stronger measures in the treaties, especially the so-called equipment clause, which allowed the squadron to arrest vessels without slaves aboard. Squadron officers also began making treaties that outlawed the slave trade with African leaders themselves. Furthermore, the number of patrol vessels increased dramatically after the late 1830s, peaking at 36 in 1845, and the first steamers were introduced in this period as well. The squadron increasingly pushed its patrols southward until by 1860, it was patrolling the eastern coast of Africa and continued to do so for the next 30 years.

Although initially popular, the African Squadron had several critics in Britain by the 1840s. Pacifists, liberal free traders, parsimonious members of Parliament, and even literary figures criticized the squadron as costly, useless, and/or an immoral use of force. Supporters of the squadron, however, included most abolitionists, led by Thomas Fowell Buxton; various West India interests, who worried about competition from foreign slave-grown produce; and West African merchants, who looked to the squadron for security. The debate in Britain came to a head in 1850, but William Hutt's motion to quit the patrols failed, and the idea was never proposed again. As might be expected, foreign governments were always cynical about the African Squadron, seeing it as another example of *machiavélisme anglais* ("English Machiavellianism") cloaked behind humanitarianism.

The African Squadron never threatened to extinguish the slave trade on its own, which was virtually impossible if only because of the amount of territory involved. David Eltis (1987) estimates that between 1811 and 1867, the squadron detained one in five slave ships and liberated perhaps 160,000 of the some 2.7 million slaves shipped from Africa in those years. Although the patrols probably increased the price of slaves, it was not until the slave-trading countries themselves adopted their own antislavery measures that their trades came to an end.

Nearly 2,000 British officers and crewmen died, mainly from disease, between 1825 and 1865, and the squadron cost an estimated £7.5 million between 1816 and 1867. Africans paid an even higher price. As arrests were made farther away from the court in Sierra Leone, increased transit times had a devastating effect on the slaves aboard the captured ships. For example, between 1819 and 1839, slaves on average suffered higher mortality rates on the journey from the Bight of Biafra to Sierra Leone (21 percent) than they did on the voyage to the Americas (10 percent).

Perhaps more significantly, the squadron also became an instrument of coercion, as illustrated in the Palmerston Act (1839) and Aberdeen Act (1845), which unilaterally sanctioned the arrest of Portuguese or Brazilian slavers. In Africa itself, the squadron greatly facilitated British control, sometimes directly through the use of force, as in the destruction of the Gallinas slave barracoons (temporary slave barracks) in 1840 and the bombardment and capture of Lagos in 1851. More often, however, the constant presence of such a large force gradually undermined the authority of the African leaders, and the squadron also actively helped supplant political instability with British consular control.

Like the slave trade itself, the African Squadron also had an enormous economic, social, and demographic impact on Africa, especially on its coastal regions. The ships could help shut down the trade in some regions, which might consequently foster its growth elsewhere. And whole populations of liberated Africans were created in places like Sierra Leone from a heterogeneous mix of peoples from all over the African continent.

—*Jeff Pardue*

See also
Barracoons; Closing of the African Slave Trade; Courts of Mixed Commission; Palmerston Act; Sierra Leone; Vienna, Congress of; Webster-Ashburton Treaty

For Further Reading
Eltis, David. 1987. *Economic Growth and the Ending of the Transatlantic Slave Trade.* Oxford: Oxford University Press; Howell, Raymond C. 1987. *The Royal Navy and the Slave Trade.* New York: St. Martin's; Lloyd, Christopher. 1949. *The Navy and the Slave Trade.* London: Longmans; Northrup, David. 1978. "African Mortality in the Suppression of the Slave Trade: The Case of the Bight of Biafra." *Journal of Interdisciplinary History* 9 (Summer): 47–64.

AGRICULTURAL LABOR IN THE PACIFIC ISLANDS

The Pacific islands were subject to a general pattern of eighteenth-century European exploration (sixteenth century in the far western Pacific), missionization within one or two generations, and the growth of commercialized agriculture in the mid-nineteenth century. Although natural products like sandalwood and bêche-de-mer (sea cucumbers) were extracted for the world market, true integration into the global economy began when large-scale commercial agriculture was begun by Euroamerican colonists; of the cash crops, sugar was king. For commercialized agriculture to be profitable, planters needed a supply of cheap, dependable labor, so a system of contract agricultural labor developed.

Although most early efforts at utilizing contract labor involved hiring indigenous islanders, plantation managers found that natives often had different work habits and tended to leave the plantation and return to their homes, so a search for foreign labor ensued. Labor recruiters visited cities and villages in southern and eastern Asia, the Philippines, the Madeira Islands, the Caribbean, Europe, and even the U.S. South in order to get young men to sign labor contracts that offered them a chance to earn a nest egg or to send money home but were essentially contracts for indentured labor. Rarely were entire families recruited. In

the Melanesian Islands in the South Pacific, laborers were frequently kidnapped and enslaved outright, in a practice known as "blackbirding," to provide the plantations in Queensland, Australia, with laborers.

Once in Australia or Hawaii or on Fiji and other plantation islands, contract laborers found themselves in a system in which their long workdays were compensated with money that could be spent only at the company-run store; they also found that saving money was hard. Absence from work was punished with fines and sometimes incarceration, and the *luna*, or field boss, usually was allowed to use whatever force he deemed necessary to coerce laborers into working hard. In effect, if not on paper, most contract laborers spent their plantation years as slaves.

As geopolitical and economic conditions shifted—as, for example, when friction between China and the United States caused plantation owners in Hawaii to have to seek new labor sources in Japan—many islands ended up with a variety of ethnic groups in their labor pool. Managers usually located the different groups in distinct settlements and used interethnic rivalry to spur the workers into working harder and to prevent any unified organization of labor interests. Work assignments linked ethnicity and ability. Euroamerican whites almost always owned and managed the businesses, and they employed other immigrant Europeans as field bosses and members of various Asian groups to cultivate, haul, and process the crops.

Ethnic division of labor and settlement served to maintain a system in which contract laborers remained tied to the plantation, signing new contracts every two or three years rather than returning home with savings as planned. One result of this tendency was the permanent introduction of diverse ethnic populations onto some islands that had previously been uniformly Polynesian. Once it was clear they would stay, contract laborers often sent home for "picture brides," women they did not know who were themselves not free to leave the contract-labor place once the marriage was arranged. Typically, these permanent immigrants, or their children, eventually began private businesses, established their own family farms, and otherwise escaped labor contracts if not the pervasive influence of plantation economies.

Although current islanders often identify with ancestral ethnic groups, many islands have developed a rich, mixed local culture, one that often celebrates plantation culture. In island groups such as Fiji and Hawaii, recent indigenous political movements have incorporated rejection of foreign cultural influences in their call for a return to sovereignty of the original inhabitants. These demands, however, are being met with resistance from the descendants of contracted labor immigrants as they, too, consider the islands to be home.

—*Maurice Major*

See also
Pacific Islander Labor in Australia; Transition from
Slave Labor to Free Labor, Polynesia
For Further Reading
Beechert, Edward. 1985. *Working in Hawaii: A Labor
History*. Honolulu: University of Hawaii Press; Scarr,
Deryck. 1968. *A Cruize in a Queensland Labour Vessel
to the South Seas*. Honolulu: University of Hawaii
Press; Takaki, Roland. 1983. *Pau Hana: Plantation Life
and Labor in Hawaii*. Honolulu: University of Hawaii
Press.

AGRICULTURAL SLAVERY

The connection between agriculture and slavery dates back nearly 5,000 years to the ancient civilizations of Mesopotamia, Greece, and Rome. The use of slaves to improve land and cultivate crops was, in fact, the earliest use of slave labor, and landholders needed workers to construct irrigation systems, plant seeds, raise livestock, and harvest crops. Slavery emerged to meet extensive labor shortages in areas where landholders sought wealth by growing a surplus of commercially profitable, labor-intensive crops such as rice, indigo, sugar, tobacco, and cotton. Although the use of slaves for agricultural pursuits took various forms in different regions and periods, beginning in antiquity and lasting until the late-nineteenth century, the landholders' desire for profits and free agricultural labor served as a common link between cultures over time.

The first known use of slaves for agricultural work was around 3000 B.C. in Mesopotamia (present-day Iraq) as Sumerians began to plant crops and to breed animals rather than gather food and hunt wild animals. Settled agricultural communities replaced the nomadic wandering of the hunter-gatherer peoples of previous civilizations, and Sumerians settled the bottomlands of Mesopotamia between two powerful rivers, the Tigris and the Euphrates. Growing food crops in the bottomlands proved challenging, however, because of the semiarid, subtropical climate. Inadequate rainfall made irrigation necessary, which in turn required a massive labor force to construct irrigation canals. The Mesopotamian rulers forced slaves to build sophisticated irrigation systems that brought water to the land in dry seasons and controlled the overabundant rainfall during wet seasons.

In the ancient world, the use of slaves in agriculture varied by region and time period. In Egypt, instead of slave labor, the peasants worked the land as serfs who were bound to the land. The serfs worked under a sharecropping system on landed estates. Slaves rarely worked in the fields; instead, Egyptians enslaved Semites, Nubians, and other captives for personal service

and a variety of other tasks. Slave labor was not essential to agricultural growth in Egypt.

In Greece prior to the eighth century B.C., families were self-sustaining, growing enough food to survive. Everyone worked, even in wealthy families. Labor needs were uncomplicated. Greeks lived on steep mountains in a rocky terrain better suited to small family-run farms. Families grew food crops such as grapes and olives that were not grown on a large scale but were carefully cultivated in small batches by skilled agricultural workers.

However, around the sixth century, after a series of wars, growers expanded their markets within the Mediterranean world, and the Greek economy became more complicated. Trade with other regions meant that farmers had to produce quality foodstuffs, including olive oil and wine. Peasant families were driven from the land as landholders created larger farms and purchased slaves to work the land. This development forever changed Greek agriculture. Slaves from western Asia and northern Africa flowed into Greece to work the land for the ruling class. By 350 B.C., slavery had evolved as the principal form of labor on Greek estates and larger farms, even as some families remained on smaller farms.

Although Sumerians, Egyptians, and Greeks all employed slaves as agricultural workers to varying degrees, it was the Romans who first developed full-scale plantation slavery in the second century B.C. Romans became slavers because the Punic Wars (264–146 B.C.) made the Romans rich in Carthaginian slaves, who had been used in agricultural work prior to the wars and were, therefore, skilled agricultural workers. Italy's climate was excellent for growing grains, grapes, olives, and fresh fruit, and the Carthaginian slaves brought knowledge and labor to bear on the natural abundance of the land. The combination of geography and slavery created conditions favorable to the rise of plantation agriculture, and the basic structure of later agricultural slavery emerged as captured slaves were put to work as farmers and herders.

As the number of captured slaves increased, the number of agricultural workers rose dramatically, and Roman landowners exploited slave labor to create large plantation estates. Trade routes in the Mediterranean were beginning to expand, and the more landowners could produce, the greater the profits. Slave labor thus became essential to the profitable existence of large-scale plantation agriculture. During the same period, the institution of slavery spread throughout the Mediterranean and beyond.

The development of plantation agriculture in Rome increased awareness about the profitability of food crops for landowners, but the end of the Roman Empire brought a temporary decline in slavery. It became expensive to house and feed slaves when peasant sharecroppers or tenant farmers might work the land instead. Following the classical period, most European regions adopted a feudal tenancy system whereby the mass of peasants worked the land for the landowner, a noble lord who, in turn, paid his allegiance to a sovereign. The landed classes took responsibility for protecting peasants from invasion and starvation; in return, peasants cultivated and improved the lands of the noble classes. Although technically not slaves, the peasants were bound to the land much as Egyptian serfs had been in ancient times.

The course of agricultural slavery in Africa followed a different path from that of classical Rome and Medieval Europe. In ancient Africa, the development of slavery and the slave trade itself had significant implications for agricultural pursuits. Africans enslaved other Africans captured as prisoners of war for countless centuries prior to the European slave trade of later centuries. As the historian John Hope Franklin has pointed out, slavery was widespread in Africa, and as an economic and social institution, it was as old as African society.

Africans considered agriculture so central to their way of life that land belonged to all community members. This belief had been passed down among African peoples from ancient times and did not lend itself to the development of plantation agriculture in Africa. Largely because of the geographical diversity of Africa, the people there specialized in growing a wide variety of food crops and in developing vast natural resources for economic ends. Palm oil, grains, minerals, iron, pepper, rice, coffee, and other agricultural foodstuffs flourished in certain African regions, and African agriculture was so diversified that, in time, areas became associated with specific products, including gold and ivory. Even African slaves were included in the list of valuable agricultural "products." Slaves were valued not only for their labor but also because they possessed agricultural skills.

By the fifteenth and sixteenth centuries, Portuguese and Spanish slavers understood the commercial value of enslaving Africans for agricultural work. Skilled at growing certain crops and accustomed to an agrarian life, Africans were, from the European point of view, ideal agricultural workers. Other factors also influenced the development of the modern slave trade. The rise of the modern nation-state, technological advances in shipbuilding and navigating, and the expansion of commercial markets combined to create conditions in which the African slave trade flourished. In addition, centuries of Christianity, the Italian Renaissance, and the new age of exploration led Europeans to believe in their "cultural superiority," which allowed them to justify slavery in spite of stated Christian and Renaissance ideals.

Once again, the demand for labor and a desire for profits led to agricultural slavery, but this time, to new levels of cruelty and profitability. The Roman antecedents of plantation slavery resurfaced during the age of exploration as Portuguese, Spanish, French, Dutch, and English explorers and colonizers sought to profit economically from natural resources and commercial agriculture by employing slave labor.

During the mid-sixteenth and seventeenth centuries, Brazil supplied almost all of Europe with sugar. Slaves were producing over 55 million pounds a year by 1600, and sugar brought tremendous wealth to those who invested slaves and money in the development of this single cash crop. The commercial success of the crop only increased investments and expanded the use of slavery throughout the Americas. By the seventeenth century, slaves were as valuable as gold, as their labor could produce enormous wealth. A lucrative slave trade emerged, and slavers shipped African slaves to the sugar plantations of Brazil and, later, to the Caribbean (or West Indies).

Sugar plantations operated under a complicated system. The Brazilian sugar plantation owner usually leased land to subcontractors, who used their own slaves to plant and harvest sugarcane (in other words, the plantation owner owned the land but not the slaves who worked the land). Slaves needed to be strong and healthy because growing and harvesting sugarcane was backbreaking work. Once the crop had been cultivated, slaves cut the sugarcane with broadswords and carried the cane to sugar mills located on the plantation. There, raw sugarcane was processed into an exportable product. Some large plantations produced over 120 tons a year. The sugar plantation owner and the subcontractor divided the profits, with the plantation owner taking a larger share.

When Brazilian profits fell off after 1650, the sugar industry shifted to the Caribbean where the Dutch followed a similar production process. By this time, the slave traders were also transporting slaves to North America. Sugar would not grow in the English colonies along the eastern Atlantic seaboard, for the climate was unsuitable, but in 1617, John Rolfe, an English colonist living in the Virginia settlement of Jamestown, created a superior kind of tobacco. Rolfe had experimented, crossing various tobacco species from the West Indies with the bitter tobacco leaf that was indigenous to Virginia, and developed a hybrid that had an excellent flavor and became a commercial success throughout Europe. Tobacco, like sugar, required intensive labor. With a commercially profitable crop and a high demand for cheap labor, the slave trade intensified, and African and West Indian slaves were imported by Virginians eager to realize high profits from their adopted land. Slavery in the English colonies had begun in earnest.

Other cash crops developed in the Southern colonies. In South Carolina, rice and indigo produced tremendous profits for plantation owners. Rice was particularly labor intensive, which created an urgent demand for African slave labor, and not just any African slave labor. Africans who lived in present-day Ghana near the Grain Coast possessed superior skills in cultivating rice, and it was they who, as slaves, brought riches to the plantation owners, who knew little or nothing about growing rice.

Important as rice cultivation was to South Carolina, cotton was to become the "sugar crop" of the United States. Initially, English colonists grew their own cotton, which they used to make homespun clothing. However, two events in the late-eighteenth century increased the production of cotton and transformed it into a commercially profitable, labor-intensive crop. First, the American Revolution impeded the flow of English cloth into the colonies, which created scarcity and demand among colonists, and after the Revolution, a growth in the number of textile mills in England increased the demand for raw cotton. Second, with Eli Whitney's invention of the cotton gin in 1793, a machine that successfully separated seeds from cotton fibers, cotton production soared first in South Carolina and Georgia and later in Alabama and Mississippi.

Cotton created an economic foundation for the new nation. The United States exported 60 percent of the world's cotton in 1840, and by 1860, cotton plantations were turning out about a billion pounds of cotton annually. The crop brought tremendous wealth to the plantation owners and gave the United States a profitable export. Ironically, the expansion of cotton also expanded agricultural slavery throughout the Southern United States. The demand for labor outweighed republican rhetoric, and the institution of slavery took root in the United States and agricultural slavery flourished on plantations throughout the South.

Agricultural slaves in the South did not, of course, think of themselves as economically profitable investments. For them, the experience meant harsh labor, separation from family members, whipping, and unsanitary living conditions. Field laborers were worked to death. Unlike Brazilian slavery, where large plantation owners owned the labor of slaves but not the slaves themselves, Southern plantation owners owned the slaves and thought of them as property. Nevertheless, African American slaves retained cultural traditions from Africa, and those traditions blended with new cultural experiences on large rice, tobacco, and cotton plantations. What may have been an economic arrangement for the plantation owner was a social reality for the African American slaves who labored in the fields, as it had been for slaves throughout human history.

—*Julie R. Nelson*

See also
Latifundia; Sugar Cultivation and Trade; Whitney, Eli

ALCAÇOVAS, TREATY OF

The Treaty of Alcaçovas (Spanish: Tratado de Alcaçobas-Trujillo; Portuguese: Tratado das Alcáçovas) refers to four separate treaties signed by representatives of the Spanish and Portuguese crowns in the city of Alcaçovas, Portugal, on September 4, 1479. Besides ending the war of succession over Isabella's ascension to the throne of Castile, the treaty also addressed matters like territorial concessions, spheres of influence, and the right of the signatories to punish piracy in their spheres of influence. Of these items, the territorial concessions and establishment of spheres of influence by the two Iberian powers proved to be of crucial importance. By the terms of the treaty, King Alfonso V of Portugal recognized Castile's claim to the Canary Islands while Queen Isabella of Castile and King Ferdinand of Aragon recognized Portugal's right of possession to the African mainland and the Azores, Cape Verde Islands, and Madeira. Thus, the Treaty of Alcaçovas drew a line of demarcation running along latitudinal lines, granting Portugal possession of all lands either found or conquered "from the Canary Islands down toward Guinea" (Article 8).

The Treaty of Alcaçovas was ratified by King Alfonso and Prince John on September 8, 1479, at Evora, Portugal, and by Queen Isabella and King Ferdinand on March 6, 1480, at Toledo. The treaty was then confirmed by Pope Sixtus IV by the Bull Æterni Regis on June 21, 1481. Because the treaty drew a line of demarcation dividing the world into north and south sections, another agreement was needed in 1493 after Christopher Columbus found islands in the West. Subsequently, the Treaty of Tordesillas (Tordesilhas), signed in 1494, divided the ocean lands into east-west sections.

The Portuguese had been active in African trade since the early-fifteenth century when Prince Henry the Navigator oversaw Portuguese expansion into African waters. As a consequence of the 1479 treaty, the Portuguese were able to establish a monopoly in African coastal trade and exploration, and one of the things the Portuguese would come to monopolize was the trading of African slaves, first in Europe and later in the Americas. Thus, a direct consequence of the Treaty of Alcaçovas, which removed any Spanish interference in the African theater, was the development of the Atlantic slave trade by the Portuguese with little early competition from the other European powers.

—*H. Micheal Tarver*

See also
Tordesillas, Treaty of
For Further Reading
Albuquerque, Luís de, ed. 1989. *Tratado de Tordesilhas*

e outros documentos. Lisbon: Publicações Alfa; Davenport, Frances, ed. 1967. *European Treaties Bearing on the History of the United States and Its Dependencies to 1648*. Gloucester, MA: Peter Smith; Hilgarth, J. 1978. *The Spanish Kingdoms, 1250–1516*. Oxford: Clarendon Press; de la Torre y del Cerro, Antonio, and Luis Suarez Fernandez, eds. 1952. *Documentos referentes a las relaciones con Portugal durante el reinado de los reyes cateds. 19* Valladolid: Consejo Superior de Investigaciones Cientificas.

ALLEN, RICHARD
(1760–1831)

Born a slave in Philadelphia, Richard Allen nurtured a moral and religious conviction throughout his life to combat slavery and oppression. Purchasing his freedom, he began a distinguished career as a minister, businessman, and community leader. Allen cofounded Philadelphia's Free African Society, the first autonomous organization of free blacks in the United States. He later became minister of Bethel African Methodist Episcopal Church and was the denomination's first consecrated bishop. His legacy and achievements include writing sermons and hymnals and drafting articles of governance for various civic organizations. In his work, Allen fought for racial equality, human rights, and economic independence for all black people.

Born on February 14, 1760, to slave parents owned by Philadelphia lawyer Benjamin Chew, Allen and his family were sold to Delaware farmer Stokley Sturgis in 1768. When he turned 17, he converted to Methodism, an event that coincided with Sturgis's selling some of his family members and their division. With Sturgis's permission, Allen joined the Methodist Society, and he later convinced Sturgis to convert to Methodism. Conversion led Sturgis to develop a moral opposition to slavery, and he agreed to allow Allen and his brother to purchase their freedom for £60, or $2,000. Allen had worked as a bricklayer, woodcutter, and wagon driver and purchased his freedom in 1780.

In his initial years of freedom, Allen began a six-year sojourn as an itinerant Methodist preacher. He traveled to Maryland, Delaware, Pennsylvania, and New Jersey preaching to black and white crowds. Although lacking formal education, Allen gained many skills during this time: reading, writing, and the mental and social attributes that would help him become a significant leader.

Richard Allen

In 1786, white Methodist ministers invited Allen to preach to the black membership of Philadelphia's Saint George Methodist Episcopal Church. The majority white congregation restricted the services blacks were allowed to attend and segregated the worship. Allen considered the possibility of establishing an all-black congregation, but the idea met with opposition from both blacks and whites. As a result, Allen and Absalom Jones founded the Free African Society on April 12, 1787, an organization that was dedicated to the abolition of slavery and racial hatred.

Later that year, Allen, Jones, and other black worshipers at St. George's were forced from their usual seats on the main floor and ordered to sit in the segregated gallery. They refused and left in unison, more determined than ever to establish their own house of worship. Services were held at the Free African Society while they searched for a new spiritual home, and on July 29, 1794, a converted blacksmith shop was officially dedicated Mother Bethel Church. It is the oldest piece of property in the United States continuously owned by blacks.

Mother Bethel soon became Philadelphia's largest black church, but white Methodists resisted Allen's efforts to establish an independent black Methodist organization. Allen was ordained a deacon in 1799 and became Bethel's pastor, but he was still subject to white Methodist elders' authority even though he held the tenuous and enviable position of a free black man. After years of struggle, Pennsylvania's Supreme Court granted Bethel independent status on January 1, 1816. Similar secessions occurred in New York, New Jersey, Delaware, and Maryland, and on April 7, 1816, 16 independent congregations met in Philadelphia to create the African Methodist Episcopal Church (AME). Allen was ordained an elder and consecrated as the church's first bishop on April 11, 1816.

Allen and the AME Church played a crucial role in black history. Frederick Douglass decried slavery from Mother Bethel's pulpit, and as an Underground Railroad station, the church provided protection to many fugitive Southern slaves. The AME Church fought for the rights of enslaved and free blacks, and Allen wrote an autobiography, sermons, and pamphlets denouncing slavery, the slave trade, racism, and oppression. He organized numerous conferences and conventions espousing the principles and virtues of social justice, economic development, and educational opportunity for blacks in the United States. He was recognized as the first black national leader. By 1830, the AME Church had members in Canada, Haiti, and West Africa. Current membership is estimated at 2.5 million, and there are 8,000 churches in 29 countries. Allen remained pastor of Bethel AME Church until his death on March 26, 1831.

—*Anthony Todman*

See also
African Methodist Episcopal Church; Jones, Absalom
For Further Reading
Barringer, James G. 1987. "The African Methodist Church: 200 Years of Service to the Community." *Crisis* 94 (June/July): 40–43; Murphy, Larry; J. Gordon Melton; and Gary L. Ward, eds. 1993. *Encyclopedia of African-American Religions*. New York: Garland; Nash, Gary B. 1989. "New Light on Richard Allen: The Early Years of Freedom." *William and Mary Quarterly* 46 (2): 332–340; Salzman, Jack; David Lionel Smith; and Cornel West, eds. 1996. *Encyclopedia of African-American Culture and History*. New York: Macmillan Library Reference.

ALLIGATOR *(WARSHIP)*

The U.S. schooner *Alligator* (1820–1822), the third U.S. naval vessel to bear the name, is one of the United States' most historic warships as it opened Liberia for settlement by free African Americans, patrolled West Africa's coastline to suppress the slave trade, and fought piracy in the West Indies. The ship was one of five small schooner-class vessels built during the Monroe administration that were designed for use in the shoal waters off Africa and in the Caribbean. It was 86 feet long and carried 12 cannon. The 198-ton vessel was laid down in the Boston Navy Yard on June 26, 1820, and was launched November 2, 1820.

Lt. Robert F. Stockton commanded the *Alligator* when it departed Boston in April 1821 as part of the African Squadron. The vessel had the dual mission of cruising off West Africa to seize slave vessels in support of the U.S. ban on the African slave trade and of aiding the American Colonization Society in securing African territory to return blacks to their ancestral lands.

After stopping briefly at Sierra Leone, the *Alligator*, which transported Dr. Eli Ayres of the American Colonization Society, arrived at Cape Mesurado, West Africa. After some difficulties, Stockton and Ayres met with a local chieftain named King Peter to purchase land for a colony, and in late 1821, they purchased a strip of land for the American Colonization Society in exchange for various quantities of muskets, nails, knives, umbrellas, hats, shoes, and other items. Approximately 130 miles long and 40 miles wide, the area was called Liberia, meaning "liberty." Monrovia, named after President Monroe, was the area's capital when Liberia became a republic in 1847.

The *Alligator* would be successful, too, during this voyage in capturing several slave vessels. The vessel returned to Boston in summer 1821; in October, the *Alligator*, again under Stockton's command, sailed for Africa once more. During this tour, the warship apprehended more slave ships, including the *Mariano Faliero*, a Portuguese vessel taken after a several-hour cannon duel.

In 1822, the *Alligator* was in the Caribbean to check piracy. After losing its commander, Lt. William H. Allen, during action against pirates in Cuba, the *Alligator* went aground in the Florida Keys on November 19, 1822. After efforts to get the ship off the reef failed, the crew set the vessel afire, destroying it so enemies could not capture it. Although it had a short career, this warship of "the era of good feelings" had a notable record. Most significant was its role in the founding of Liberia.

During the 1990s, a wrecked ship believed to be the *Alligator* became the focus of an archaeological study by the National Center for Shipwreck Research, the National Oceanic and Atmospheric Administration (NOAA), the Naval Historical Center, the state of Florida, and Bateaux Below, Inc., to list the *Alligator* on the National Register of Historic Places.

—*Joseph W. Zarzynski*

See also
African Squadron; American Colonization Society; Liberia
For Further Reading
Duke, Marvin L. 1974. "Robert F. Stockton: Early U.S. Naval Activities in Africa." *Shipmate* (December): 22–25; Mooney, James L., ed. 1991. *Dictionary of American Naval Fighting Ships*. Washington, DC: Naval Historical Center; Williams, Michael W., ed. 1993. *The African American Encyclopedia*. New York: Marshall Cavendish.

ALMAGRO, DIEGO DE (1475–1538)

Diego de Almagro, the son of Castilian peasant farmers from the village of Almagro, was a noted Spanish *encomendero* (a holder of *encomienda* rights; see *Encomienda* System), soldier, and explorer. After working as a servant of a Castilian court magistrate, he traveled to Panama with the 1514 expedition of Pedro Arias de Ávila. While in Panama, Almagro served in the military under various captains, and in the process, he acquired some property, slaves, and Indians. It was also in Panama that Almagro went into business with Francisco Pizarro, with Almagro handling the financial matters of their ventures. With little funds to equip an expedition for exploration of New World lands, Almagro and Pizarro created an uneven partnership and engaged in mining and farming, utilizing Indian labor.

In 1524, the men sold their farm and undertook a small expedition to search for reported kingdoms to the south of Panama. Because of damage to the ships, they were forced back to Panama, where they eventually met Hernando de Luque, who provided them with additional financial backing. A 1526 expedition also ran into difficulties and was forced back, but not before collecting exotic materials from South America as further evidence to support Spanish territorial claims. For each of these early voyages, Almagro recruited and utilized black slaves for manpower.

In 1528, Francisco Pizarro went to Spain to present his land claim to Emperor Charles V, and a year later the charge was signed by Charles's wife, the queen regent. By that instrument, Almagro was appointed governor of Tumbez, with a salary less than half of that assigned to Pizarro (who also received grand appointments and lands). Additionally, the crown authorized Pizarro to transport 50 slaves to Peru in provide additional manpower and skill for his expedition. The differences between the two men were resolved, and they continued their partnership in the conquest of Peru. Eventually, Almagro was granted the territory of New Toledo, which was located approximately 800 miles south of the equator. Almagro led an expedition into the region, which consists of modern-day Chile, but he found no great sources of gold and silver. Accompanying Almagro was a runaway slave from Mexico, Juan Valiente, who would later return to Chile and receive land and an *encomienda* for his service.

When the Inca revolted in Cuzco in 1533, Almagro returned to Peru from Chile to aid the Pizarro brothers Gonzalo and Hernando and took issue with them about the ownership of Cuzco. Almagro claimed Cuzco was situated inside New Toledo and thus claimed the city as his domain. This claim and his actions against the brothers of Francisco Pizarro would eventually lead to a civil war between Almagro and the Pizarros. Almagro was eventually defeated in this war, captured, and executed. Almagro's son, Diego, and his followers continued the war with the Pizarros, which resulted in the execution of Francisco Pizarro in 1541.

—*H. Micheal Tarver*

See also
Encomienda System
For Further Reading
Alvarez Argel, Luis Raul. 1964. *Don Diego de Almagro y el descubrimiento de Chile*. Santiago: Editorial Universitaria; Ballesteros Gaibrois, Manuel. 1987. *Diego de Almagro*. Madrid: Sociedad Estatal para la Ejecucion Programas del Quinto Centenario; Blazquez y Delgado-Aguilera, Antonio. 1898. *El adelantado Diego de Almagro*. Ciudad Real, Spain: Establicimiento Topografico Provincial.

AMERICAN ANTI-SLAVERY GROUP

The American Anti-Slavery Group (AASG), a human rights organization that publicizes the plight of black slaves in Mauritania and Sudan, was founded on March 20, 1993, in Washington, D.C., by Charles Jacobs, a U.S. management consultant; Mohamed Nacir Athie, an exiled Mauritanian diplomat; and David Chand, a black Christian from southern Sudan. Jacobs first learned about modern-day African slavery from an acquaintance who informed him that one could purchase a slave in Mauritania for $15. Soon after the AASG was founded, Jacobs contacted several African American civil rights organizations about this grave human rights situation, but his efforts initially elicited little interest. Finally, in 1995, the National Association for the Advancement of Colored People (NAACP) and the chairman of the Congressional Black Caucus strongly condemned the sale of African slaves in Mauritania and the Sudan.

The primary focus of the AASG is the plight of black slaves in Africa. According to Jacobs (U.S. House, 1996), his organization believes that "freedom in North and West Africa should be valued no less than freedom in South Africa . . . does freedom count for more in Johannesburg than in Nouakchott and Khartoum?" The organization has vigorously publicized the issue, and its work has been reported in the *New York Times* and the *Washington Post* as well as on the public broadcasting show *Tony Brown's Journal* and the NBC television newsmagazine *Dateline*.

In May 1995, the AASG helped to convene at Columbia University in New York City what was probably the first abolitionist conference in the United States in more than a century. Almost 200 people attended, including members from the southern Sudan, the Committee for Human Rights in Mauritania, and the New York chapter of the National Conference of Black Social Workers. After the conference, several activists formed other groups in New York, Chicago, Detroit, and other cities.

Samuel Cotton, a New York journalist, wrote a series of articles from February 28 to March 19, 1995, about the enslavement of black Africans in Arab-dominated countries for the now-defunct, Brooklyn-based, African American weekly the *City Sun*. These articles led the African American media to increase its coverage of the topic and thus generate more interest in the work of the AASG. Akbar Muhammad, of the Nation of Islam, soon attacked Cotton and the AASG, claiming the articles sought to demean Arabs and the Nation of Islam's activities on behalf of the Arab-dominated government of the Sudan.

In March 1996, Louis Farrakhan issued a challenge at a news conference in Washington, D.C.: "Where is the proof of black slaves?" Two journalists, Gregory Kane and Gilbert Lewthwaite, found the proof and wrote a major investigative series for the *Baltimore Sun* (June 16–18, 1996) about the sale of African children by Arab slave traders in the southern Sudan.

The U.S. House of Representatives Committee on International Relations held hearings on slavery in Mauritania and Sudan in March 1996, and representatives of the American Anti-Slavery Group and other organizations testified. The work of organizations like the American Anti-Slavery Group continues as long as reports of contemporary slavery continue to circulate. It is to be hoped that the work of AASG and other similar organizations will hasten the day when nations will be more forthcoming and slavery can be abolished.

—*Donald Altschiller*

For Further Reading
U.S. House. Committee on International Relations. 1996. *Slavery in Mauritania and Sudan.* Joint Hearings, March 13, 1996. Washington, DC: Government Printing Office.

AMERICAN COLONIZATION SOCIETY (1816–1963)

During the nineteenth century, the American Colonization Society (ACS) was the principal institution promoting the resettlement of black Americans to Africa as a solution to problems associated with slavery and race in the United States. The idea of colonization dated from the late-eighteenth-century work of Virginians like Thomas Jefferson, James Madison, and James Monroe. The British provided an early model for the ACS by establishing a refuge in Sierra Leone for poor blacks from London's slums in the 1780s. In the United States, Robert Finley, Ralph R. Gurley, Francis Scott Key, and Charles Fenton Mercer were especially important in promoting colonization.

The ACS was founded in 1816, and in 1822 the organization established the West African settlement of Liberia to receive colonists. By 1899, the ACS had settled 15,386 colonists in Liberia, a tiny portion of the African American population in the United States. Life initially was precarious in the colony, and before 1842, 41.3 percent of the colonists died within six

years of settling there. Those who survived dominated the surrounding Africans, and Liberia experienced long-standing class tensions between the descendants of the colonists and the original inhabitants of Liberia. The ACS played a significant role in governing the colony until 1847 when Liberia became an independent nation.

The society drew support from groups with remarkably diverse motives, and to prevent controversy among potential supporters, the ACS avoided the issue of slavery. The ACS officially endorsed only the idea of resettling free blacks, not slaves, in Africa. Despite the caution of the society's program, some opponents of slavery hoped the ACS would encourage the emancipation of slaves.

Several abolitionist leaders, including Arthur and Lewis Tappan, James G. Birney, and Gerrit Smith, were initially prominent colonizationists. They believed slaveholders would gladly emancipate their slaves if offered a plan for freeing their slaves without increasing the number of free blacks in America. Indeed, just over half of the African Americans colonized by the ACS before the Emancipation Proclamation of 1863 were slaves freed specifically for the purpose of colonization. The remainder of the colonists were free people. Ironically, many Southern colonizationists saw the ACS as a means for making slavery more secure, and they believed the colonization of free blacks would remove people who allegedly corrupted the morals of slaves and encouraged them to escape.

Many of the colonizationists, regardless of their views on slavery, believed that removing free blacks would promote national progress and safety. Because free blacks were denied equality with whites, it was claimed that free blacks lacked ambition, a work ethic, and other inducements to good behavior. They seethed with anger regarding their oppressed condition and posed an internal threat to the United States. Some colonizationists argued that removing free blacks to Africa would remove them from the ill effects of white prejudice. Blacks would be placed in an environment where they could exercise their talents and abilities, and some colonizationists hoped that blacks from the United States would plant Christianity in Africa.

Given the large diversity of motives for supporting colonization, it was a popular solution to racial problems in the United States. The ACS was endorsed by the U.S. Congress and a dozen state legislatures, several of which joined Congress in funding the ACS. Even bitter political enemies like Andrew Jackson and Henry Clay united to support the ACS.

The Americans who most strongly objected to colonization were African Americans. Even slaves who were offered freedom in exchange for colonization sometimes refused the offer. Seeing through the prejudice that undergirded the ACS, blacks were skeptical of the claims that colonization would improve their condition and were reluctant to leave their families and homes. The ACS typically had more funds available to send out colonists than they had persons willing to be colonized.

Some African Americans did believe that colonization provided a means of escaping prejudice and white domination. Shortly before the founding of the ACS, a black merchant and sea captain, Paul Cuffe, took a group of blacks to Africa. Alexander Crummell, Daniel Coker, Lott Cary, and Colin Teague were prominent blacks who migrated to Liberia as missionaries. Martin R. Delany, Henry Highland Garnet, and Lewis Woodson promoted emigration as a way for African Americans to assert control over their lives. Black colonizationists often had ambivalent attitudes toward the ACS. They were wary of its motives and suspicious of its control but jealous of its resources.

Support for the ACS peaked about 1832, when the society sent 796 emigrants to Liberia and there were 302 local and state branches of the ACS. After that year, the ACS faced serious defections. Repelled by racial prejudice and proslavery attitudes within the ACS, many former supporters of the society became abolitionists, favoring immediate emancipation without colonization. Their actions were galvanized by the pamphlet *Thoughts on African Colonization* (1832) written by the former colonizationist William Lloyd Garrison. In response, many proslavery colonizationists withdrew their support from the ACS as they became suspicious of a society that was the breeding ground for abolitionism.

During the financial panic of 1837, contributions to the ACS dried up and Americans took a critical look at the society's record. The ACS's plan seemed overly complex, expensive, and impractical, since comparatively few blacks had been settled in Liberia. The ACS continued to function after the abolition of slavery until 1963, but it had little public support after the U.S. Civil War and Reconstruction and worked mostly to promote Liberian and African American educational causes. When the society disbanded, its remaining funds went to the Phelps-Stokes Fund to help support African and African American education.

—*Harold D. Tallant*

See also
Garrison, William Lloyd; Liberia; Sierra Leone
For Further Reading
Campbell, Penelope. 1971. *Maryland in Africa: The Maryland State Colonization Society 1831–1857.* Urbana: University of Illinois Press; Miller, Floyd J. 1975. *The Search for a Black Nationality: Black Colonization and Emigration, 1787–1863.* Urbana: University of Illinois Press; Shick, Tom W. 1971. "A Quantitative Analysis of Liberian Colonization from 1820 to 1843 with Special Reference to Mortality." *Journal of African History* 12: 45–59; Staudenraus, Philip J. 1961. *The African Colonization Movement, 1816–1865.* New York: Columbia University Press.

AMERICAN FREEDMEN'S INQUIRY COMMISSION

Created in 1863 at the request of Massachusetts congressman Thomas D. Eliot, the American Freedman's Inquiry Commission began investigating how to give equality to the nation's 4 million ex-slaves after the U.S. Civil War. As one of the first committees of its kind, a four-member panel heard testimony from ex-slaves, former slave-owners, and others regarding the conditions faced by slaves and their probable needs in the postwar era. After months of testimony, the committee issued preliminary and final reports to Secretary of War Edwin M. Stanton.

With overwhelming evidence from a plethora of witnesses, commission members were unanimous in their conclusion: slavery had destroyed the slave family. The breakup of these families, the reports indicated, stood as a painful and lasting legacy of slavery.

As a result of these and other findings, the American Freedman's Inquiry Commission supported a preliminary effort to assist some slaves along the coast of South Carolina. Known as the Port Royal Experiment, this endeavor before the end of the Civil War led to a greater effort after the conflict.

After the end of the Civil War, and using the reports of the American Freedman's Inquiry Commission, Congress created the Bureau of Refugees, Freedmen, and Abandoned Lands, commonly known as the Freedmen's Bureau, on March 3, 1865. Between 1865 and 1872, the Freedmen's Bureau administered to the needs of 4 million ex-slaves in their transition from slavery to freedom.

—*Jackie R. Booker*

See also
Freedmen's Aid Societies; Port Royal Experiment; Transition from Slave Labor to Free Labor, North America
For Further Reading
Rose, Willie Lee. 1964. *Rehearsal for Reconstruction: The Port Royal Experiment.* New York: Bobbs-Merrill.

AMERICAN MISSIONARY ASSOCIATION

The American Missionary Association (AMA) is best known for its work in establishing educational institutions for freed slaves after the U.S. Civil War. But the AMA actually began years earlier in 1839 when a group of abolitionist members of the Homes Missionary Society organized a committee to give legal assistance to 54 Africans charged with mutiny on the *Amistad,* a schooner they had seized in American waters. Successful in their legal maneuver to aid the slaves, the group united with the Committee for West Indian Missions and the Western Evangelical Missionary Society to established the AMA in 1846. The group's purpose was to protest the inactivity of Northern churches against slavery.

This predominantly white abolitionist society, led by Arthur Tappan and later by his brother Lewis, was unique for its time and included African Americans as voting members and as members of the executive board. The first African Americans to serve were Theodore S. Wright, Samuel Ringgold Ward, James Pennington, and Charles Bennett Ray. Not only were the officers of the AMA an integrated group, they were also ministers or lay members of racially integrated congregations. The schools and colleges established by the AMA were not designated for African Americans only but were open to all without regard to race, gender, religion, or class. Berea College in Kentucky, founded in 1855, is one example. It enrolled its first African Americans in 1866 and maintained an integrated student body in the then-segregated South.

The abolitionist movement, often characterized as a political reform movement and secular in nature, was, in fact, a movement of "liberal Protestantism" and is a part of religious history. Even though many historians prefer to discuss the abolitionist movement led by William Lloyd Garrison as being nonreligious in nature, Clara DeBoer argues convincingly that Garrison was a "Christian abolitionist" (DeBoer, 1994). There were, nonetheless, significant differences between Garrison's American Anti-Slavery Society and the AMA.

In 1865, Garrison called for the dismantling of the American Anti-Slavery Society because he felt that with the end of the Civil War its mission had been accomplished. In the same year, however, the work of the AMA shifted into establishing schools and colleges in the South and providing teachers and education for the newly freed. Thus, Garrison and his group of so-called radicals had more limited goals than did the AMA and its group of evangelical abolitionists. Garrison's goal was the end of slavery; the AMA intended to eradicate racism, hatred, classism, greed, and all the sins that had produced slavery in the first place.

The AMA professed to stand on the tenets of pure Christianity in that it saw slavery as a fundamental sin. The goal of its members was to reform American Protestant Christianity and to eliminate caste based on race, class, or color. Their reform effort was larger than wiping out slavery. They believed that Southern Christianity affirmed a "diluted message that denied African Americans humanity" (DeBoer, 1994) and that this perverted message was necessary in order to maintain the institution of slavery. To tolerate slavery, the North also had to depart from the basic tenets of Christianity. Thus, the AMA, while political, was also religious because it recognized the limits of political action in changing the hearts and minds of people.

The AMA's mission was to "uplift" slaves from the morally degenerate South. According to AMA doctrine, slavery was a sin against God and humanity. It endangered the mortal souls of both slaveowners and slaves and poisoned all Southern institutions, including the home, church, and school. Thus, AMA members advocated a religious revival. Instead of using the speaker's podium and lecture circuit in their effort to abolish slavery and injustice, the AMA, under the direction of Lewis Tappan and George Whipple, organized churchmen in the war against prejudice and ignorance. The AMA was nonsectarian and ecumenical.

One of the first organizations to begin the work among the freed slaves, the AMA also worked on behalf of Japanese and Chinese immigrants on the West Coast of the United States, worked for and with Native Americans and poor whites in Appalachia, and established schools for Eskimos in Alaska. It sent teachers to Puerto Rico and maintained education there until public education was established, and it also opened schools for Mexican-Americans in New Mexico. In 1861, it was the first organization to send agents into the South. By 1864, there were 250 AMA missionaries in the Southern and border states, and by 1868, there were 532. These missionaries helped the newly freed African Americans acquire land, demand their political rights, establish schools and churches, and lobby for a system of public education.

The AMA worked assiduously during the years of Reconstruction to establish educational institutions for the freed slaves. Between 1866 and 1869, it opened Fisk University (1866) in Nashville, Tennessee; Atlanta University (1865) in Georgia; Talladega College (1867) in Talladega, Alabama; Straight (now Dillard University, 1869) in New Orleans, Louisiana; Tillotson (now Huston-Tillotson College, 1877) in Austin, Texas; LeMoyne (now LeMoyne-Owen College, 1870) in Memphis, Tennessee; Hampton Institute (1868) in Hampton, Virginia; Tougaloo College (1869) in Tougaloo, Mississippi, and assisted in the founding of Howard University in Washington, D.C., in 1867. The Southern schools for blacks started by the AMA were scoffed at and called unrealistic. However, many have become eminent institutions.

As Joe Richardson (1986) stated, the AMA had its shortcomings. Even as it gave valuable assistance to African Americans with respect to health, education, and welfare, it suffered from blatant paternalism, cultural imperialism, and perhaps an unrealistic belief that education could eradicate prejudice and racism. In light of its high and noble ideals and the contribution it made in the training of African American teachers, ministers, lawyers, and other leaders, its flaws seem but minor. The AMA disbanded in 1890 after institutional "Jim Crow" legislation made it increasingly difficult for the association to achieve its objectives.

—*Nagueyalti Warren*

For Further Reading
DeBoer, Clara Merritt. 1994. *Be Jubilant My Feet: African American Abolitionists in the American Missionary Association 1839–1861.* New York: Garland; DeBoer, Clara Merritt. 1995. *His Truth Is Marching On: African Americans Who Taught the Freedmen for the American Missionary Association 1861–1877.* New York: Garland; Richardson, Joe M. 1986. *Christian Reconstruction: The American Missionary Association and Southern Blacks, 1861–1890.* Athens: University of Georgia Press; Stanley, A. Knighton. 1979. *The Children Is Crying: Congregationalism among Black People.* New York: Pilgrim Press.

AMERICAN PARTY (KNOW-NOTHING PARTY)

A political party in the United States during the 1850s, the American Party, generally nicknamed the Know-Nothing Party, focused on the perceived threat that Roman Catholics and recent immigrants posed to political and cultural values in the United States. Some historians have argued that this political movement arose to divert the sectional tensions that were wrought by slavery.

The American Party was the political manifestation of a nativist movement that included numerous secret organizations such as the Order of the Star-Spangled Banner and the Order of United Americans. In the late 1840s and early 1850s, unprecedented numbers of European immigrants, primarily from Ireland and Germany, moved to the United States, and they brought with them new cultural traditions and greatly increased the nation's Roman Catholic population. As these immigrants became eligible to vote, many long-time residents, particularly in the northeastern states where this new immigration had its greatest impact, were concerned about their loss of cultural and political power. Urban laborers in particular felt threatened by the increased economic competition posed by the low-paid, unskilled immigrants.

Secret nativist organizations were organized to combat this "menace" by tougher immigration laws, longer residency requirements for citizenship, and a proscription on foreign-born citizens holding political office. Since most immigrants voted for Democratic candidates and the Whig Party was collapsing under the weight of sectional disputes over slavery, these nativist anti-Democrats created a new political organization, the American Party, and ran candidates successfully in several Northern states in the early 1850s.

The American Party also had political support in Southern states where former Whigs saw it as a natural political platform to continue opposing the Democratic Party. Many Southern Know-Nothings also hoped that anti-immigration sentiment could be used to divert political attention from the sectional issue of slavery. As long as the American Party was active only at the state and local levels, slavery posed few problems; Southern Know-Nothings could be proslavery and anti-Democratic while Northern Know-Nothings could be antislavery and anti-Democratic. Attempts at national political activity, however, proved to be problematic. Just as the Whig Party had discovered, national parties had to reconcile conflicting sectional stances on slavery, especially after the controversial Kansas-Nebraska Act (1854).

The American Party's national convention in 1855 was controlled by Southern delegates, who pushed for the adoption of a report endorsing the repeal of the Missouri Compromise (1820) and the passage of the Kansas-Nebraska Act, which opened western territories to the expansion of slavery. When the report was endorsed over staunch Northern opposition, the entire delegations of all the Northern states except New York bolted the convention and denounced this attempt to validate slavery's expansion. In 1856, Southerners again dominated the national meeting, which endorsed the Kansas-Nebraska Act and nominated former president Millard Fillmore for president.

Angered by this support of slavery, the bulk of the Northern Know-Nothings bolted the party and supported the Republican candidate, John C. Frémont. Although Fillmore and the American Party ran well throughout the country, garnering over 21 percent of the popular vote, they won only Maryland's electoral votes. Following this disaster, most Northern Know-Nothings rapidly abandoned the party for the Republican Party. In the South, the American Party continued to run state and local candidates in some areas, but it, too, collapsed within five years. Like the Whig Party it tried to replace, the American Party found it impossible to reconcile sectional differences over slavery.

—*James L. Sledge III*

For Further Reading
Beals, Carleton. 1960. *Brass-Knuckle Crusade: The Great Know-Nothing Conspiracy, 1820–1860*. New York: Hastings House; Holt, Michael F. 1992. *Political Parties and American Political Development from the Age of Jackson to the Age of Lincoln*. Baton Rouge: Louisiana State University Press; Leonard, Ira M., and Robert D. Parmet. 1971. *American Nativism, 1830–1860*. New York: Van Nostrand Reinhold; Maizlish, Stephen E. 1982. "The Meaning of Nativism and the Crisis of the Union; The Know Nothing Movement in the Antebellum North." In *Essays on American Antebellum Politics, 1840–1860*. Ed. Stephen E. Maizlish and John J. Kushma. College Station: Texas A & M University Press.

AMERICAN-CANADIAN RELATIONS

Between the American Revolution and the U.S. Civil War, the institution of slavery influenced relations between the United States and Canada. Slavery's continued existence in the former and its demise in the latter after 1793 gave rise to a situation that strained the relationship between the two countries; namely, the fact that thousands of runaway slaves from the United States sought refuge in Canadian territory.

The exact number of blacks who relocated in Canada (estimated at 30,000–45,000) is elusive as is the percentage of those who were fugitive slaves as opposed to free blacks. It is probable that most blacks who left the United States and resettled in Canada were fugitive slaves, and Canada's rejection of U.S. appeals to extradite such fugitives led to numerous attempts to resolve the issue diplomatically. Eventually, all attempts by Southern slaveholders to obtain a satisfactory solution to the fugitive slave problem—meaning the return of their property—met with failure.

As Canada's reputation as a haven for runaway slaves grew in the early-nineteenth century, so too did the pressure placed upon the U.S. and Canadian governments by slaveowners and abolitionists alike to implement government policies favorable to their cause. Southern slaveholders resented the lack of assistance from the U.S. government and the lack of cooperation from the British and Canadian governments in the return of fugitive slaves. Especially aggravating to slaveowners was the fact that Canadian courts consistently upheld the principle, espoused in the Upper Canadian Abolition Act (1793), that fugitive slaves who entered Canada were thereafter free.

The first official attempt by U.S. slaveholders to elicit aid in the recovery of fugitive slaves was made in 1819 when the owners of several slaves who had escaped from Tennessee to Canada urged the U.S. secretary of state to negotiate an arrangement whereby they could regain possession of their property. The official Canadian response was that the fugitives, by their residence in Canada, were free. This became the standard reply to such requests.

The U.S. House of Representatives resolved several times between 1821 and 1860 to engage in full-fledged diplomatic negotiations to draw up a treaty acceptable to slaveholders' interests, and successive U.S. ministers to Great Britain, including Richard Rush, Albert Gallatin, and James Barbour, were instructed to engage in negotiations for a favorable disposition of the issue. Each time, however, the British government refused to acquiesce to U.S. wishes.

Facing the continued failure of diplomatic endeavors to solve the problem of extraditing fugitive slaves, masters frequently took matters into their own hands. Some slaveowners traveled to Canada and attempted to regain their property forcibly. This type of activity, however, flagrantly violated Canadian kidnapping laws, and authorities in that country consistently protected fugitives. Slaveholders also continued to seek individual extradition orders in their quest to regain their property: most of those efforts, too, were unsuccessful.

Some slaveholders tried to extradite their runaway slaves under the pretext that the slaves faced criminal charges before Southern courts. This particular hope of recovering fugitives was based on an 1833 Canadian statute that provided for the surrender of fugitive criminals from foreign countries. Three test cases came from Kentucky, where, in the late 1830s, individual slaveowners requested the extraditions of runaways Thornton Blackburn, Solomon Mosely, and Jesse Happy.

In the first, Blackburn's master tried to have him extradited on the basis that Blackburn had participated in the mob that had effected his rescue, but the Canadian authorities denied the extradition request. Mosely had stolen his master's horse and ridden it to Buffalo, New York, where he sold the animal and escaped across the Niagara River into Canada. Extradition was requested on the basis that Mosely was a horse thief. Canadian officials agreed that the crime had been proved and ordered the extradition. Mosely, however, escaped from his jailers and was never returned to his master. Jesse Happy had also stolen his master's horse in the process of escaping and had also left the horse in the United States, but this owner later reclaimed the animal. In what is seen as the definitive ruling on extraditions arising from the 1833 Canadian statute, Canadian and British officials declared that extradition in Happy's case not be granted. The decision implied that any act a slave committed as part of his escape should be considered an act of self-defense rather than a felony.

The closest the countries came to resolving this

issue was in the Webster-Ashburton Treaty (1842). Article 10 of this treaty between the United States and Great Britain provided for the mutual surrender of fugitive criminals from both countries and Canada. Yet in the end, Canadian and British officials made it clear that a liberal interpretation of Article 10 would be followed when it came to fugitive slaves and that crimes which occurred as a result of a slave's escape were not considered to be the basis for extradition. Canada remained a haven for refugee slaves until slavery was abolished in the United States.

—*Sharon Roger Hepburn*

See also
Abolition, British Empire; Canada; Webster-Ashburton Treaty
For Further Reading
Lindsay, Arnett. 1920. "Diplomatic Relations between the United States and Great Britain Bearing on the Return of Negro Slaves, 1788–1828." *Journal of Negro History* 5: 261–278; Manning, William, ed. 1942. *Diplomatic Correspondence of the United States: Canadian Relations, 1794–1860.* Washington, DC: Carnegie Endowment for International Peace; Silverman, Jason. 1980. "Kentucky, Canada, and Extradition: The Jesse Happy Case." *Filson Club History* 54 (January): 50–60; Winks, Robin. 1971. *The Blacks in Canada: A History.* New Haven, CT: Yale University Press.

AMERINDIAN SLAVERY, GENERAL

Amerindian slavery can refer to the enslavement of Indians by European-Americans or to the enslavement of others by Indians—whether whites, African Americans, or other Indians. Written documentation of the enslavement of indigenous Americans by Europeans begins with Columbus's arrival in the West Indies in October 1492. The first slaves were taken so that they might learn Spanish and subsequently serve the explorers as interpreters. Within several years, the Spanish and Portuguese, and later French, English, and other Europeans, began establishing plantations to grow sugarcane, tobacco, and other crops in the Caribbean and elsewhere in the Americas. The Europeans forced the indigenous peoples to work the fields, and many Indians were also enslaved to mine gold and other metals. Thousands died from disease and cruel treatment.

Occasionally Spanish clergymen tried to protect the Indians. Friar Bartolomé de Las Casas went to Spain in 1515 to lobby the king on their behalf. Despite his efforts, however, and the declaration by the Spanish government that slavery was unjust and illegal, the condition of the Indians improved only slightly.

For the early European explorers—Spanish, English, Portuguese, French, and Dutch—the taking of Indian slaves was a routine part of any expedition. Some of the better-known individuals and the countries they explored for include John Cabot, England (1497); Gaspar Côrte-Real, Portugal (1500); Giovanni da Verrazano, France (1524); and Francisco Vásquez de Coronado and Hernando de Soto, Spain, in the early 1540s. Another Spaniard, Juan Ponce de Leon, sailed to Florida in 1513 and later to settle new lands and attempt to distribute the natives among the colonists according to the *encomienda* system, which meant a land grant that included the people to work it.

Unlike the Spanish government, the English government did not outlaw slavery, although opposition was occasionally expressed publicly. English enslavement of Indians increased following a 1622 Powhatan uprising in Virginia, which prompted the colonists to justify regarding the Indians as hostile. The French in Canada enslaved many Indians, called *panis*, apparently derived from the tribal name Pawnee, from whom many of their slaves were drawn. Indian slaves were also found on French plantations in Louisiana, although Africans outnumbered Indians there.

Indians enslaved by Europeans labored in the fields alongside African slaves or were exported to the West Indies, where they could not escape and return to their people. In the South, Indian slaves were also put to work hunting and fishing. In New England, they were employed in stock farming and domestic chores. Some Indian slaves were trained in a manual trade; this practice was objected to, however, as interfering with the immigration of craftsmen from Europe.

Perhaps the first nonnatives to be enslaved by North American Indians were Álvar Núñez Cabeza de Vaca, a Spaniard; Estevanico, an African; and three other survivors of the ill-fated Narváez expedition to Florida in 1527–1528. Cabeza de Vaca, the expedition's treasurer; Estevanico, a slave of the Spanish; and the others were put into a sort of informal slavery by Indians along the Texas Gulf coast. After six years, Cabeza de Vaca, Estevanico, and two of the other captives escaped; the fifth decided to remain with the Indians.

The number of white captives taken by Indians from the sixteenth through the nineteenth centuries is possibly in the tens of thousands. Indians took captives for several reasons, including retaliation for loss of land and tribal members, ransom, replacement of the ranks depleted by war or diseases introduced by whites, and for use as slaves. Becoming a slave, however, did not eliminate the possibility of being ransomed or adopted at a later date. In the seventeenth century, for example, numerous Jesuits, and French women, men, and children were enslaved by the Iroquois. Some of them were ransomed and freed by the Dutch.

Some form of slavery existed among the Indians be-

This sixteenth-century illustration by Robert de Bry depicts the Spanish enslaving the native peoples of the Americas.

fore Columbus's arrival. In precontact Mexico, for example, the Aztecs had a large population of slaves they called *tlacotin*. These slaves might have been foreigners who were war captives, criminals who needed to work off a debt, or simply people in debt who could make payment by volunteering themselves or another family member as a slave.

North of Mexico, early historical evidence of Indian slaveholding is found in the accounts of the Coronado and the de Soto expeditions. While Coronado was at the Southwestern pueblo of Cíbola in 1541, a chief from east of the Rio Grande led some of the Spanish to his own pueblo at Cicúye where there were two slaves, captives from the Plains to the northeast. One may have been of the Wichita tribe, the other Pawnee. The two slaves later guided the Spanish east to the Plains. Traveling through southeastern North America in 1540, de Soto reported that captives taken from enemy tribes in war were kept as slaves—women as concubines, men as laborers.

Indians captured other Indians from enemy tribes

for the same reasons they captured whites: they might be tortured and killed to avenge the death of kin; they might be adopted to replace family members who had died; they might prove of value when sold or ransomed; or they might be enslaved, in which case they were obliged to perform menial tasks and do the heavier labor. Among the Indians of the Northwest Coast, where material wealth had greater significance than elsewhere, slaves carried a relatively greater value and became a regular commodity.

Less common than the enslavement of war captives were the other causes for slavery. For example, some gamblers staked themselves as slaves when there was nothing else left to gamble; individuals were sold to whites by their own tribe as punishment for a serious offense, such as theft; or members of a family were sold for a period of temporary servitude in exchange for money or goods.

In the 1790s, the United States began a program to encourage Indians to adopt the lifestyle of the white culture. In the South, Indians who took plantation owners as their role models began to acquire African American slaves to work in their fields. These tribes included the Cherokee, Choctaw, Chickasaw, Creek, and Seminole, although the Seminole developed a tributary relationship with African Americans rather than viewing them as chattel. There was considerable internal controversy over slaveholding among Indians, since many of them saw it as being alien to their culture and therefore an abandonment of native heritage. In the treaties negotiated with the United States following the Civil War, the Indians of these tribes, called the Five Civilized Tribes, freed their slaves and agreed to make them citizens of their nations, although not every Indian nation accepted the latter provision.

—*Patricia A. Kilroe*

See also
Amerindian Slavery (Pacific Northwest, Plains, Southeast); Native American Peoples, Enslavement of; North American Indigenous Peoples, Slavery among; Seminole Indians

For Further Reading
Abel, Annie Heloise. 1992. *The American Indian as Slaveholder and Secessionist.* Lincoln: University of Nebraska Press; Debo, Angie. 1970. *A History of the Indians of the United States.* Norman: University of Oklahoma Press; Lauber, Almon Wheeler. 1969. *Indian Slavery in Colonial Times within the Present Limits of the United States.* New York: AMS Press; Perdue, Theda. 1996. "Slavery." In *Encyclopedia of North American Indians.* Ed. Frederick E. Hoxie. New York: Houghton Mifflin.

AMERINDIAN SLAVERY, MESOAMERICA

Upon arriving in Mesoamerica (parts of modern Mexico, Honduras, Guatemala, El Salvador, and Belize), Spaniards found highly stratified societies with social class divisions of nobility, middle groups, commoners, and slaves. Among the Aztec of Mexico's central valley, most of the population consisted of commoners, a category that included the *macehualtin* and the *mayeque.*

Macehualtin were common laborers, craftsmen, farmers, and fishermen, and they served in the military. They were organized into *calpulli* (wards or barrios) of towns and cities. They received the rights to use *calpulli* lands and elect a leader and council for their barrio, and in return, they were required to pay tribute to the *tlatoani,* or ruler, and to the *calpulli.* *Macehualtin* were fully enfranchised commoners in Aztec society, and they could leave one *calpulli* and

join another if they wished. The *mayeque* were akin to serfs. They were rural tenants residing on a noble's private land and owed tribute to that noble. They had no internal governing organization and could not leave the noble's land.

Commoners could also be *tlacotin,* or slaves. Slave status could only be acquired, not inherited. A person could sell himself, or another family member, into slavery for subsistence needs or to pay debts. During times of drought or famine, the number of people entering slavery increased. The government created slaves from those who failed to pay tribute or committed some crime, and excessive gambling losses also led many to slavery. Decisions to enter into slave status had to be witnessed by independent observers, and free status could be retrieved by paying a previously stipulated sum.

A new slave retained many personal rights, including the rights to marry and own property. Some slaves even owned other slaves. Slaves generally continued residing in their own households instead of those of their owners. Intransigent slaves could be sold in the marketplace, and if sold three times, they could be used for ceremonial sacrifice. The Aztec also made slaves of war captives, but these individuals were usually sacrificed shortly after capture.

The Maya of the Yucatan also had a highly stratified society at the time of Spanish contact. The *mazehualob,* a word derived from the Nahuatl *macehualtin,* referred to free common people living on the outskirts of towns and villages and holding communal rights, through lineage, to land. Unlike the Aztec, the Maya did not have a "serf" position, but they did have slaves, the *p'entacob.* Slavery could be hereditary, but Mayan law allowed for the redemption of children born into slavery, though orphans were often made slaves in return for their upkeep. Additionally, orphans, especially those of slave women, were often used as sacrificial offerings. Any orphans caught stealing were bound to the person they had robbed and could remain slaves for life unless they redeemed themselves.

The most common way to be enslaved was through warfare, since constant internecine regional strife meant large numbers of captives. High-status captives were usually sacrificed, but lower-ranked captives became the property of the soldier who captured them. The Maya usually sold male captives and retained women and children. These individuals remained slaves for life, and their status was hereditary. Early Spanish chroniclers noted a very widespread and prolific regional slave trade at the time of contact.

—*Kimberly Henke Breuer*

See also
Amerindian Slavery (General, Pacific Northwest, Plains, Southeast)

For Further Reading
Berdan, Frances. 1982. *The Aztecs of Central Mexico: An Imperial Society.* New York: Holt, Rinehart and Winston; Sharer, Robert J. 1994. *The Ancient Maya.* Stanford, CA: Stanford University Press.

AMERINDIAN SLAVERY, PACIFIC NORTHWEST

The Pacific Northwest culture area extends from southeastern Alaska to northern California and includes the coastal areas of present-day southeastern Alaska, British Columbia, Washington, Oregon, and northern California. Within this area the Native American cultures varied considerably in language, social organization, and religion, but even so, several distinguishing characteristics linked the Pacific Northwest cultures. These included reliance on seasonal runs of salmon and other maritime resources; large multifamily longhouses, which composed the core of the village; a dependence upon water transportation; and a hierarchical social organization, which in most tribes included a slave class.

Amerindian slavery in the Pacific Northwest was unusual in several respects. Slavery is generally associated with intensive agricultural production; it is unusual to find slavery practiced in foraging societies like those of the Pacific Northwest. Slaves there were sometimes treated as subordinate members of the family, being allowed to marry, pursue their own acquisition of wealth, and obtain spirit helpers. Some slaves successfully purchased their freedom by accumulating goods. Slavery in the Pacific Northwest was tied to the class distinctions and ranked social order that distinguished the Pacific Northwest Amerindian cultures.

At the time of initial contact with Europeans in the late 1700s, the Amerindians of the Pacific Northwest had a well-established network of trade extending north and south along the Pacific Coast and inland through several mountain routes. Many goods moved along these trade routes, and slaves were one item of wealth that was highly valued and used in trade by many Pacific Northwest tribes. In addition to obtaining slaves by trade, raids on neighboring tribes were also a means of acquiring slaves. The practice of slavery apparently accelerated in the early contact period in the late 1700s because of the introduction of new trade goods and increased trade opportunity, but by the mid-1800s, Pacific Northwest slavery was in decline and by 1900, it had disappeared entirely. The decline was the result of a variety of factors, including the influence of missionaries, increasing government control, and a reduced population owing to introduced infectious diseases.

It is difficult to estimate the pervasiveness of Pacific Northwest slavery in the precontact period. Among some tribes, it was entirely absent; among others, slaves very probably constituted nearly 25 percent of the population. Some tribes only traded slaves whereas others heavily depended upon slave labor. How slavery functioned in Pacific Northwest Amerindian societies varied widely.

Throughout the Pacific Northwest, slaves were considered to be property, and slaves had little control over their fate. Their owners held power over their lives, and slaves could be traded, sold, given away, or killed. Although slaves could acquire personal property, most of their labor was for the benefit of their owners. Slaves worked with their owners, engaging in subsistence activities like salmon fishing, and were also expected to do most of the menial household tasks, like gathering firewood.

Slaves possessing particular skills were highly valued. The actual value varied, but historical accounts list the value of slaves in dentalia, or tooth shells. Dentalia were used as a standard of exchange in the Pacific Northwest, and the exchange value of the shells depended upon the distance from the source of the shells on the west coast of Vancouver Island. For example, on Vancouver Island itself, a slave may have been purchased for five strings of dentalia, measuring the length from fingertip to fingertip of outstretched arms. In northern California, where dentalia were less common, one string purchased a slave.

Slaves were also important in the trade that developed with Europeans. Female slaves were prostituted, and European fur traders encouraged traffic in slaves and engaged in it themselves. Later, as settlement of Europeans and Euroamericans increased in the Pacific Northwest, slavery was actively discouraged and later outlawed by U.S. and Canadian legal systems.

Slave raids were the most common form of warfare in the Pacific Northwest, with some groups traveling several hundred miles to raid for slaves. The flow of slaves was from south to north; the Tlingit of southeastern Alaska and the Haida and Kwakiutl of north-central British Columbia raided the southern British Columbia and Puget Sound tribes. The Chinook at the mouth of the Columbia River obtained slaves from their interior neighbors and from tribes along the Oregon and northern California coasts.

—*Daniel L. Boxberger*

For Further Reading
Averkieva, Julia. 1941. *Slavery among the Indians of North America.* Moscow: USSR Academy of Sciences; Ruby, Robert H., and John A. Brown. 1993. *Indian Slavery in the Pacific Northwest.* Spokane, WA: Arthur H. Clark; Suttles, Wayne, ed. 1990. *Handbook of North American Indians: Northwest Coast.* Washington, DC: Smithsonian Institution.

AMERINDIAN SLAVERY, PLAINS

The Plains of North America extend from Texas to Canada and from the Mississippi River to the Rocky Mountains, and many different tribes representing several language families inhabited the area until the nineteenth century. Following contact with Europeans, the Indians of the Plains began to acquire horses and guns, which caused their way of life to shift as buffalo hunting became easier and therefore more important.

Slavery was known to Plains Indians both before the arrival of the Europeans and, increasingly, following contact. One of the earliest written accounts indicating that Plains tribes were engaged in some form of slavery in the precontact era is that of the Coronado expedition. While Francisco Vásquez de Coronado was at the Southwestern pueblo of Cíbola in 1541, a delegation headed by two chiefs arrived from the eastern Pueblo frontier. One of the chiefs conducted a party of the Spanish to his own pueblo of Cicúye, where there were two slaves who were captives from the Plains to the northeast. One was possibly of the Wichita tribe nation; the other, whose appearance prompted the Spanish to call him "the Turk," may have been Pawnee.

The two slaves later guided the Spanish east to the Plains. The Turk told them that to the northeast lay Quivira, a place of fabulous wealth. The place he led the Spanish to, however, was a small village in present-day Kansas. Because their expectations were not met, the Spanish killed the Turk. The Spanish also took many Indians as slaves during this expedition.

Indian capture of whites, Mexicans, and other Indians occurred on the Plains until well into the nineteenth century. Although it was not uncommon for captives to be put to work as slaves, that was not the only fate captives might meet—adoption or ransom, for example, were others. Perhaps best known among the later Indian captives is Sacagawea, famous for her role in guiding the Lewis and Clark expedition west from North Dakota in 1805. At age 10, Sacagawea had been captured by the Hidatsa from her tribe of origin, the Shoshoni. She was enslaved and later, at age 13, sold to a French-Canadian fur trader.

The Indian slave trade in the west increased enormously with European presence. The Europeans themselves conducted slaving expeditions, or they would encourage the Indians to raid their enemy tribes for captives, which they would then exchange for goods such as guns and ammunition. By the late 1600s, for example, the Apache had horses and guns and were raiding Caddoan villages. The Comanche, too, became known for extensive raiding; they may have been responsible for taking thousands of captives. The Sioux appear to also have trafficked in numerous captives.

Tribes to the east, such as the Ottawa and the Sauk, took captives from Plains tribes such as the Pawnee, Osage, Missouri, and Mandan. The Menominee did not usually take part in these distant expeditions, but they had Pawnee slaves which they bought from the Ottawa, Sauk, and others who had captured them. The Illinois also obtained slaves for barter from west of the Mississippi and, once again, among the chief sources for these slaves were the Pawnee. Indeed, among the French in Canada, all Indian slaves regardless of tribe were referred to as *panis*, apparently derived from "Pawnee."

Notable among the various European groups who participated in the slave trade involving Plains tribes were the French, many of whom were involved with the fur trade. French *coureurs de bois* (trappers) mingled with the Indians and traded for goods they could take to French or English settlements, including slaves obtained from tribes who had captured them in war. Even through dealing in slaves was unauthorized, the *coureurs de bois* carried on a thriving trade, obtaining pelts and slaves to sell at centers like Mobile, Alabama. They were especially active among the Osage, inciting them to raid the Pawnee and the Comanche for captives.

—*Patricia A. Kilroe*

See also
Amerindian Slavery, General; Native American Peoples, Enslavement of; North American Indigenous Peoples, Slavery among
For Further Reading
Axtell, James. 1992. *Beyond 1492*. New York: Oxford University Press; Debo, Angie. 1970. *A History of the Indians of the United States*. Norman: Oklahoma University Press; Lauber, Almon Wheeler. 1969. *Indian Slavery in Colonial Times within the Present Limits of the United States*. New York: AMS Press; Weatherford, Jack. 1991. *Native Roots: How the Indians Enriched America*. New York: Crown Publishers.

AMERINDIAN SLAVERY, SOUTHEAST

In 1540, Hernando de Soto, the first European to make an extensive expedition through the southeastern portion of North America, observed that captives taken in attacks upon enemies were often kept, with the children being adopted, the women made into concubines, and the men used as laborers—mutilated just enough to prevent escape. This form of slavery was in operation among groups of southeastern Indians before the arrival of Europeans, and capture from enemy tribes was the usual way that slaves were obtained. Among the Cherokee, a captive who was not ransomed, tortured to death (to avenge a clan member's killing), or adopted into the tribe was kept on the fringes of tribal society. These captives were called *atsi nahsa'i* ("one who is owned"). They were not kept to increase the wealth of their owners but instead worked alongside them at numerous tasks.

Trade between southeastern Indians and whites began not long after contact, with the latter seeking deerskins and captive Indians to be sold as slaves. The English traded knives, axes, clothing, guns, ammunition, and liquor for captives. Some captive Indians were put to work in the South, but many were sold and worked in the West Indies, New York, or New England. Charleston, South Carolina, founded in 1670, became the major slave market and port for the export of southeastern Indian captives. This slave trade had a devastating impact on Indian life in the late-seventeenth and early-eighteenth centuries, as tribes like the Choctaw, Chickasaw, and Cherokee turned on each other to meet the European demand for slaves and to satisfy their own eagerness for European goods.

Whereas in the precontact era the purpose of war among Indian tribes was to take an enemy to avenge the killing of a member of one's own clan, following contact, captives were taken for profit and vengeance. Indian slaves were worth less than Africans because the latter tended to survive better on plantations, but because of the availability of Indians, the demand for them continued. English traders not only bought Indian captives and encouraged tribes to engage in warfare to gain captives, but on occasion the traders themselves led a war party of natives against their enemies to raid for slaves. Efforts by the colonies to regulate the Indian slave trade were largely ineffectual.

The process of obtaining Indian slaves through trade was part of a competition for territory and commerce between the French and the English. Having a major tribe like the Chickasaw or the Choctaw as an ally was important, and whites did much to gain influence over these tribes. A tribe that refused to give allegiance to the English, for example, would become prey for English allies.

In the 1790s, the United States began a program to encourage Indians to adopt the lifestyle of the white culture, and southeastern Indians who modeled themselves after plantation owners began to acquire black slaves to cultivate crops and perform menial labor. Participating tribes included the Cherokee, Choctaw, Chickasaw, Creek, and Seminole, and those groups, because of their acculturation, came to be known as the Five Civilized Tribes. Even though they had demonstrated their ability to adapt to white society, during the 1830s and 1840s most of the thousands of members of the Five Civilized Tribes were removed from their homelands to Indian Territory in Oklahoma, which freed up their lands in the Southeast for white settlers.

Unlike the other four tribes, the Seminole had developed a tributary relationship with their black slaves rather than viewing them as chattel, and during the armed conflict between the Seminole and the United States over removal (1835–1842), these black Seminole fought alongside the Seminole Indians. When the defeated Seminole were removed to Indian Territory, they resisted the government's plan to settle them among the Creek because they feared that the Creek would enslave the blacks among them. Many took refuge in the Cherokee Nation, where the independent status of the black Seminole contributed to a rebellion by Cherokee slaves. The matter was resolved when the Seminole were granted a separate nation in Indian Territory in 1856.

Although only a few Indians owned slaves, those that did tended to be wealthy and to have a dominant political voice in their respective tribes. There was considerable internal controversy over slaveholding among Indians, however, because many saw it as being alien to their indigenous culture and therefore an abandonment of native heritage. Southern Indians fought on both sides in the U.S. Civil War, and in treaties negotiated with the United States following the war, the Indians freed their slaves and agreed to make them citizens of their nations, although not every nation accepted this latter provision.

—*Patricia A. Kilroe*

See also
Amerindian Slavery, General; Native American Peoples, Enslavement of; North American Indigenous Peoples, Slavery among; Seminole Indians

For Further Reading
Kehoe, Alice Beck. 1992. *North American Indians: A Comprehensive Account.* Englewood Cliffs, NJ: Prentice-Hall; Lauber, Almon Wheeler. 1969. *Indian Slavery in Colonial Times within the Present Limits of the United States.* New York: AMS Press; Perdue, Theda. 1996. "Slavery." In *Encyclopedia of North American Indians.* Ed. Frederick E. Hoxie. New York: Houghton Mifflin; Perdue, Theda. 1979. *Slavery and the Evolution of Cherokee Society, 1540–1866.* Knoxville: University of Tennessee Press.

AMISTAD CASE
(1841)

In July 1839, a slave mutiny occurred aboard the Spanish slaver *Amistad* off the Cuban coast. On June 28, 1839, the *Amistad*, commanded and owned by Ramón Ferrer, had departed

Havana for Puerto Príncipe in east-central Cuba with 6 crew members and 54 illegally imported African slaves belonging to José Ruiz and Pedro Montes. On the fourth night at sea, one of the slaves, Joseph Cinqué, led a mutiny in which the ship's captain and cook were killed. For 57 days, the *Amistad* skirted the eastern coast of the United States until August 26, when a U.S. Coast Guard brig commanded by Lt. Thomas Gedney seized it.

Gedney's seizure of the *Amistad* raised questions. First, did the *Amistad*'s cargo and slaves still belong to Ruiz and Montes? Second, what crimes had the slaves committed in mutinying, and by what means and where would they be punished for those crimes? Third, would the U.S. government return the *Amistad* and the "*Amistad* captives" to Spanish authorities under Pinckney's Treaty (1795), or would it free them according to Anglo-American agreements outlawing the slave trade?

The U.S. State Department recommended that the Spanish minister take custody of the *Amistad* and its cargo, but when the mutineers were indicted for piracy, Lewis Tappan and other abolitionists established the *Amistad* Committee to raise money for their defense. Committee attorneys prepared arguments that Ruiz and Montes had violated international law by purchasing slaves that had been smuggled illegally into Cuba.

On January 8, 1840, a U.S. district court ruled that all the slaves except one, Antonio, Ferrer's Creole cabin boy, were entitled to their freedom and that the United States should transport them to Africa. When the U.S. district attorney appealed the lower court's decision, former president John Quincy Adams agreed to serve as the slaves' counsel before the U.S. Supreme Court.

Adams presented the Africans' case in February 1841. On March 9, 1841, Justice Joseph Story affirmed the lower court's decision and granted the captives their freedom. In November 1841, the *Amistad* Committee, aided by Yale University's Divinity School, returned the 35 *Amistad* survivors to Africa. The committee naively expected the captives to promote Christianity and serve as positive examples for the American Colonization Society.

The *Amistad* case remained a contentious point in antebellum U.S.-Spanish relations. From 1844 until 1860, when Spain abandoned its claims in the *Amistad* case, every president suggested that the U.S. government should indemnify Spain and mentioned the *Amistad* case in state-of-the-union addresses. Ironically, two years after the Supreme Court had ruled on the *Amistad* case, the *Creole* case presented the U.S. State Department with a quandary similar to the one Spain had faced in the *Amistad* case.

—*John Grenier*

See also
Adams, John Quincy; American Colonization Society; Cinqué, Joseph; Illegal Slave Trade
For Further Reading
Cable, Mary. 1971. *Black Odyssey: The Case of the Slave Ship* Amistad. New York: Viking Press; Jones, Howard. 1987. *Mutiny on the* Amistad: *The Saga of a Slave Revolt and Its Impact on American Abolition, Law, and Diplomacy.* New York: Oxford University Press; McClendon, R. Earl. 1933. "The *Amistad* Claims: Inconsistencies of Policy." *Political Science Quarterly* 48: 386–412.

ANANSI STORIES

A genre of West African, Caribbean, and Gulf Coast stories focuses on the trickster figure Anansi, whose appearance changes alternately from animal to human depending upon the story. There is also a more generic classification of stories in the West Indies and the Caribbean in which the central figures and basic plots are similar to those of the Anansi stories. The tales, traditional stories drawn from the West African tradition, are widespread throughout the region. As a folktale genre in the Americas, African slaves transported them, and white settlers and native populations adopted them.

The key figure, Anansi, commonly typifies Anansi stories. There are numerous variations on Anansi's name, some resulting from transcribers' preferences and others preferred by local custom. Anancy appears with regular frequency and is close to the preferred spelling in scholarly discussion. Nancy also appears frequently in literature and is used with the same frequency as Anansi in oral performances. *Zayen*, from the French *araignée*, is used in Grenada and sometimes in Trinidad; *Zayen* translates into Spider when the tales are told in English. Rabbit is the most common figure in Barbados, Dominica, Montserrat, St. Kitts, and St. Lucia; in other places, Monkey is common. The figures Brer Rabbit and Brer Fox are familiar along the Gulf Coast and in the southern United States. In these regions, it is common to find more than one of the characters in a single story, each trying to outwit the other. Frequently, Anansi is accompanied by his sidekick, Tacuma, one of the few consistently African-derived characters in the stories. Tacuma, also Tucama, is probably derived from *Intikuma*, the Ashanti name for son of Anansi. Tacuma remains fairly constant, although Chickerber (on Nevis) and Terracooma (on Montserrat) appear as variations.

As an anthropomorphic figure, Anansi's appearance, and even gender, can change from story to story and sometimes within a story. Although typically a spider, Anansi can also appear as any number of animals or as a human. The name Anansi and the associated story genre probably derive from the Twi word *ananse* ("spider") and the Bambara *nansi* ("chameleon"). As a trickster story genre, Anansi in all variations is both good and bad, victor and victimized, loved and hated. Typically, Anansi's cleverness backfires, and he falls victim to his own plans. Quite often, he victimizes his friends and family, but occasionally they get the best of him if his own foolishness does not.

Anansi stories still have a special significance throughout the Caribbean and Gulf Coast regions today as well as in their West African home. Like many folktale genres, these stories serve a multiple function. At a basic level, they are entertaining—some in a very frank, and sometimes sexually explicit, way. The stories are also entertaining because of Anansi's cunning, deceit, and occasional wickedness. At this level, Anansi is entertaining because he is able to violate normal codes of behavior. On the other hand, Anansi stories also serve as warnings for small children and others who might transgress codes of behavior. As a perpetrator of bad behavior and lawlessness, Anansi is more often than not punished for his actions, either by his own tricks or by other characters in the story. By recounting Anansi's torments that result from his behavior, rules of proper and acceptable behavior are reinforced.

—*Randal S. Allison*

See also
Folktales; Trickster
For Further Reading
Abrahams, Roger D. 1983. *The Man-of-Words in the West Indies: Performance and the Emergence of Creole Culture*. Baltimore: Johns Hopkins University Press; Dance, Daryl C. 1985. *Folklore from Contemporary Jamaicans*. Knoxville: University of Tennessee Press; Roberts, Peter A. 1988. *West Indians and Their Language*. Cambridge: Cambridge University Press; Sherlock, Phillip Manderson. 1954. *Anansi the Spider Man*. Binghamton, NY: Vail-Ballou Press.

ANGOSTURA, CONGRESS OF (1819)

Situated along the Orinoco River in Venezuela, Angostura was the political and military headquarters for patriot forces during the later stages of the wars of independence in northern South America. Between February and December 1819, patriot leaders met in Angostura to debate the nature and form of a successor government to the Spanish colonial regime. In December 1819, that congress passed a law establishing a new Republic of Colombia. This state united the colonies that had constituted the former Viceroyalty of New Granada: the Captaincy-General of Venezuela, the New Kingdom of Granada, and the Presidency of Quito.

Among the issues that delegates confronted at the Congress of Angostura was slavery and its disposition within the soon-to-be-created republic, and the position delegates took on slavery reflected the complex interplay of forces underlying the question. Many of the Creole elite were fully opposed, morally and philosophically, to the institution, believing slavery and the slave trade were part of the oppressive legacy of Spanish colonial rule against which they had taken up arms and declared their independence. Thus, slavery could no more be defended than could autocracy.

Some local juntas, inspired equally by prorevolutionary and anti-Spanish sentiments, declared an end to the slave trade when the wars of independence began in 1810, and others followed suit by passing manumission laws. Although few patriot leaders favored slavery per se, some tempered their opposition out of economic necessity and a sense of social and political paternalism. In 1810, the Viceroyalty of New Granada's total population of approximately 3 million included 140,000 slaves, and most of them were concentrated in the plantation agriculture areas along the Venezuelan littoral or in western Colombia's mining regions. Slaveowners were therefore a powerful force in the colonial economy and an effective counterweight to the more outspoken antislavery element at the congress.

The situation the delegates faced was further complicated by the contingencies of war. Patriot forces needed the slaves in order to defeat the royalist armies and win independence, and slaves who enlisted and fought for the patriot cause were to be rewarded with freedom. Similarly squeezed, the commander of the Spanish expeditionary forces, Pablo Morillo, was authorized to offer the same inducement. In many districts, slaves simply took advantage of the breakdown of order to flee, and by the time of the Congress of Angostura, the phenomenon of runaway slaves was common in the area.

In his opening address to the Angostura assembly on February 15, 1819, Simón Bolívar, the leader of the patriot armies and the future president of Gran Colombia, called for the abolition of slavery. A former slaveowner himself, Bolívar had become convinced that slavery could not be justified in a society founded upon the principles of political democracy. When the Congress of Angostura opened, Bolívar was at the apex of his personal and political prestige, but the delegates rejected his call for complete abolition of slavery. Agreeing in principle that slavery was wrong and that slaves should be free, delegates opted for a more gradual approach.

Before closing in December, the congress took several specific actions. Slaves already free would remain so, and slaves who had served in the armed struggle against the Spanish forces would also gain their freedom. The remaining slaves would be freed within a fixed period of time. The existing ban on slave imports would remain effective, and a fine of 1,000 pesos would be levied for every new slave brought into the country. Finally, runaway slaves from other countries would be denied the right of asylum. None of these laws and actions decided by the delegates had any binding force. They were merely provisional, awaiting final consideration by the Congress of Cúcuta, whose business it would be to write and promulgate a constitution for the new republic.

—*Russ Davidson*

See also
Bolívar, Simón; Cúcuta, Congress of; Pétion, Alexandre Sabès
For Further Reading
Bushnell, David. 1970. *The Santander Regime in Gran Colombia*. Westport, CT: Greenwood Press; Henao, Jesús María, and Gerardo Arrubla. 1938. *History of Colombia*. Chapel Hill: University of North Carolina Press; Lombardi, John V. 1971. *The Decline and Abolition of Negro Slavery in Venezuela, 1820–1854*. Westport, CT: Greenwood Press.

ANTHONY, SUSAN BROWNELL (1820–1906)

Although Susan B. Anthony is best remembered for her leadership in the woman suffrage movement, she was also an ardent, active Garrisonian abolitionist and a radical egalitarian, rigorously committed to universal equality. Anthony grew up in a climate steeped in antislavery sentiment. Her father, Daniel Anthony, a Hicksite Quaker, espoused the liberal antislavery beliefs integral to that sect. After relocating to Rochester, New York, in 1846, the Anthony family became closely associated with a group of Hicksite Quakers involved in temperance, antislavery, and woman's rights reforms. Through the late 1840s and early 1850s, the Anthonys hosted gatherings that included abolitionist notables such as Frederick Douglass, William Henry Channing, Samuel J. May, William Lloyd Garrison, and Wendell Phillips.

Despite Anthony's regular attendance at antislavery meetings, her efforts to educate herself on abolitionist issues, and her longing to be a Garrisonian, she began her reform career working in the temperance movement in 1848. Even a week of antislavery lecturing with Abby Kelley Foster and Stephen Foster in upstate New York in 1851 did not dispel her notion that she lacked the knowledge and the oratorical skills required of Garrisonians.

In 1856, following many successes as a temperance and woman's rights organizer and lecturer, Anthony eagerly accepted a post as New York agent for the American Anti-Slavery Society. From this point on, she worked indefatigably for the abolitionist cause. For $10 a week plus expenses, she organized antislavery meetings throughout New York State and directed a large, constantly changing group of speakers.

Antiabolitionist sentiment increased steadily throughout the late 1850s, changing typically antagonistic crowds into violent, egg-throwing, knife-flashing mobs in 1860 and early 1861. Frequently abandoned by overstressed speakers, Anthony was often left alone to confront audiences with her vituperative rhetoric. Referring to the South as "the Hydra monster," she declared in one of her few surviving speeches from this period, "He sucks his lifeblood from the unpaid and unpitied toil of the slaves and can only die when those bleeding backs and breaking hearts are wrested from his gory lips" (Anthony, 1954).

In 1863, Anthony and her fellow-activist and friend Elizabeth Cady Stanton, both impatient with the non-participatory role of women in the Civil War, formed the Women's National Loyal League because of their conviction that an amendment to the Constitution was essential to guarantee the freedom of African Americans. Anthony, with Stanton's support, directed the project that collected and presented to Congress 400,000 signatures supporting a thirteenth amendment.

In the final months of the Civil War and after, Anthony recognized the urgent need to continue the struggle to secure civil and political rights for African American men and all women. In fact, she was one of the first abolitionists to insist that African Americans be given the right to vote. Following the suggestion of abolitionist and independent editor Theodore Tilton, both Anthony and Stanton were instrumental in leading the battle for universal suffrage by helping to form the American Equal Rights Association (AERA) in 1866.

Both women remained key players in the AERA until it became clear that their male abolitionist colleagues, in their scrambling to secure the right to vote for African American males through a fifteenth amendment, could not be persuaded to reconsider their decision to withdraw their decades-long commitment to woman suffrage. Because of this failure, Anthony and Stanton left the AERA to form the National Woman Suffrage Association in 1869.

—*Judith E. Harper*

See also
Women and the Antislavery Movement

For Further Reading
Anthony, Katharine. 1954. *Susan B. Anthony: Her Personal History and Her Era.* Garden City, NY: Doubleday; Barry, Kathleen. 1988. *Susan B. Anthony: Biography of a Singular Feminist.* New York: New York University Press; Harper, Ida Husted. 1899. *The Life and Work of Susan B. Anthony.* Indianapolis, IN: Bowen-Merrill; Venet, Wendy Hamand. 1991. *Neither Ballots nor Bullets: Women Abolitionists and the Civil War.* Charlottesville: University Press of Virginia.

ANTILITERACY LAWS

Slaveowners in the U.S. South thought they had ample reason to curtail the spread of literacy among slaves. Literate slaves might forge passes, read newspapers, or communicate conspiratorial plans. Thus, in 1740, after the Stono Rebellion of 1739, South Carolina enacted a ban on educating slaves, and other colonies and states followed suit. Later, several states enacted antiliteracy laws between 1829 and 1834 after abolitionist publications began mounting. In South Carolina, the nullifiers—radical proslavery men—led the way in imposing new restrictions.

Antiliteracy laws, however, never became universal across the slave South. Some states, like Tennessee and Kentucky, never enacted antiliteracy laws. Of the four states that did maintain such laws from the 1830s through the Civil War, three—North Carolina, South Carolina, and Georgia—banned anyone from teaching any African American, whether slave or free, to read or write; Virginia banned schools for blacks but not private tutoring.

The best example of enforcement of such laws was in Norfolk, Virginia. There, Margaret Douglass, a white seamstress who ran a school for free black children, spent a month in jail in 1854 for violating the state's antiliteracy law. Teaching slaves or free blacks to read or write took place in the private sphere fairly widely, whatever the law, but so did the punishment of anyone's efforts to teach slaves and of slaves' efforts to learn.

In Jacksonian America (1824–1845), literacy seemed a badge of liberty, citizenship, and a tool for achievement. When various states, Northern and Southern alike, were launching new efforts to establish common schools, some Southern states enacted new restrictions to restrict the access of blacks to literacy. The fact that those restrictions targeted free blacks and slaves displayed an effort to narrow the meaning of black freedom. In the antebellum North, the pattern was ragged, yet most communities permitted black schools, many jurisdictions invested public funds in black schools, and by the 1850s Boston's public schools had been racially integrated.

The South's antiliteracy laws died when slavery did. In summer 1865—after the surrender at Appomattox but before ratification of the Thirteenth Amendment—Freedmen's Bureau and American Missionary Association schools sprouted across the Southern landscape. No legislature had yet repealed an antiliteracy law, but every such law had become a dead letter. When the black codes of 1865–1866 mentioned literacy, they specified that the masters of apprentices should see that their charges learned to read and write.

In the 1870s, every Southern state created a system of public schools that, on a segregated basis, might give all children access to literacy. Moreover, new institutions of higher education for African Americans—like Hampton Institute, Howard University, Fisk University, and Atlanta University—emerged soon after emancipation. Not only were such institutions now legal, but some received public funds, either state or federal, and each trained black teachers for the new black elementary schools. Especially among young people, black illiteracy began to decline.

—*Peter Wallenstein*

See also
Stono Rebellion
For Further Reading
Cornelius, Janet Duitsman. 1991. *"When I Can Read My Title Clear": Literacy, Slavery, and Religion in the Antebellum South.* Columbia: University of South Carolina Press; Foner, Philip S., and Josephine F. Pacheco. 1984. *Three Who Dared: Prudence Crandall, Margaret Douglass, Myrtilla Miner—Champions of Antebellum Black Education.* Westport, CT: Greenwood Press; Woodson, Carter Godwin. 1968. *The Education of the Negro Prior to 1861.* New York: Arno Press.

ANTONIO
See *Johnson, Anthony*

APARTHEID

A term derived from Afrikaans meaning "separation," apartheid refers to systematic political, social, and economic organization along racial lines. The South African government's official policy from 1948 to 1994, apartheid became a byword for racial discrimination in the modern world. Many opponents depicted it as a system of effective slavery, and the Anti-Slavery Society for the Protection of Human Rights condemned it.

Some analysts view apartheid as a means of securing white political supremacy by methods that were economically irrational and unproductive. Others stress that it was primarily an economic strategy aiding the growth of South Africa's capitalist economy by ensuring the availability of cheap black labor. Recent scholarship challenges the view that apartheid was a single cohesive policy and emphasizes variation in its application at different times and its more flexible, pragmatic character.

Apartheid became the policy of the predominantly Afrikaner National Party in the 1948 election campaign, but it was based on earlier segregationist measures passed by previous colonial and local English-speaking governments. Since the late-nineteenth and early-twentieth centuries, black landholding had been restricted to small and overcrowded reserves while pass laws (which required blacks to carry special documentation) prevented Africans from living and working freely in the towns. The 1910 Act of Union, which created the modern South African state, excluded blacks from voting.

Apartheid went further than earlier segregationist measures. In the first decade of National Party government, the focus of a legislative barrage was the extension of racial separation and discrimination. The Population Registration Act (1950) classified all South Africans by race; the Immorality Act (1950) prohibited sexual contact between whites and other South Africans, in an attempt to maintain white "purity"; and the Group Areas Act (1950) enforced separate residential areas in towns; segregation in education and all public amenities followed. Pass laws were extended to African women. These laws generated sustained opposition by organizations like the multiracial African National Congress (ANC) and the Pan-Africanist Congress, but the state banned and silenced opponents. In 1960, the police shooting of unarmed demonstrators against the pass laws at Sharpeville highlighted the brutality of the apartheid state, although Western powers continued providing investment and support to South Africa, which they saw as a bastion against communism's spread in Africa.

In the 1960s apartheid was extended still further with the implementation of "separate development." Eight (later ten) Bantustan homelands were created, defined along imposed ethnic lines, and African political rights were confined to them. In 1970, homeland citizenship was imposed on all Africans, thus depriving them of South African nationality and any claim to representation in its government. The main impact of "separate development" involved the forced removal of over 3.5 million black South Africans from farms and settlements in the rest of the country to the homelands on grounds that they were foreign aliens in "white" South Africa, where they were entitled to work only as migrants.

During the 1970s and 1980s, "separate development" began to collapse. The homelands failed to attract investment and were not economically viable, and manufacturing industries needed a permanent labor force rather than migrant workers. The number of urban Africans living in illegal "squatter camps" around South African cities grew rapidly despite state attempts to force them back to the homelands. Most important, internal resistance in the form of strikes in Durban and Natal in the early 1970s and the Soweto Township uprising in 1976 demonstrated unified black opposition to the state and alarmed foreign investors. Accordingly, some reforms were made such as easing the pass laws, removing segregation in public facilities, and limiting parliamentary representation in 1983 to Indian and mixed-race voters (some of whom were descendants of slaves in the former Cape Colony), but not to Africans. These reforms only rallied further opposition, and by the mid-1980s, most black townships were in open revolt.

The government responded with a heavy hand, killing many people and detaining others without trial. International condemnation of apartheid grew, but it was not until the Cold War ended in 1989 that the West indicated that it was no longer prepared to tolerate apartheid to bolster its position against the Soviet bloc. This indication, together with continued mass internal resistance, persuaded Premier F. W. de Klerk to try to dismantle apartheid while still retaining some power for his National Party. In 1990, ANC leader Nelson Mandela was released from jail as key segregationist legislation was repealed, and in 1994, a new constitution finally abolished apartheid and established a Government of National Unity elected by universal franchise. Yet the enormous social and economic inequalities in modern South Africa and the trauma of so many years of repression are legacies that are less easy to remove.

—*Nigel Worden*

For Further Reading
Lipton, Merle. 1985. *Capitalism and Apartheid*. London: Gower Publishing House; O'Meara, Dan. 1996. *Forty Lost Years: The Apartheid State and the Politics of the National Party, 1948–1994*. Athens: Ohio University Press, and Johannesburg: Ravan Press; Posel, Deborah. 1991. *The Making of Apartheid, 1948–61: Conflict and Compromise*. Oxford: Clarendon Press; Worden, Nigel. 1995. *The Making of Modern South Africa: Conquest, Segregation, and Apartheid*. New York: Blackwell.

APOLLINARIS SIDONIUS, GAIUS
(C. 431–489)

Gaius Apollinaris Sidonius was an important figure in the ecclesiastical hierarchy of late-Roman Gaul. His views on the moral and ethical aspects of slavery appear in several letters among his surviving writings. Born into the aristocratic landowning elite of Gallo-Roman society, Sidonius retained his wealth and upper-class ideals throughout a successful clerical career. Nevertheless, as a prominent bishop, he often confronted moral questions that arose from Christianity's contact with contemporary society's realities. Slavery was one of the issues Sidonius addressed on several occasions, sometimes as a result of his personal involvement in the matter.

Like many of his peers and contemporaries, Sidonius owned large tracts of land, which were organized into a self-supporting working estate that provided him with a source of wealth. Many of the estate workers were slaves, who either tilled the land as unfree cultivators or who were employed in Sidonius's household as clerks, readers, and personal servants.

Sidonius's letters reveal his attitudes toward the status and treatment of the unfree. That he regarded slaves as persons of low type appears most clearly in a letter to St. Ambrose, in which Sidonius rejoiced that an acquaintance had finally ended a relationship with a slave girl and married a woman of high birth. Sidonius leveled little approbation at the aristocratic seducer. Instead, the "shameless" slave girl was censured as a "domestic Charybdis" from whose clutches the man had thankfully escaped. Sidonius seemed equally scornful when mocking a servile "reader" in his service who, through incompetence, lost in transit some letters his master eagerly awaited. Sidonius described the slave as a "blockhead"—but did not punish him when he groveled in shame.

The slaves of Sidonius's household and estate do not seem to have been treated unfairly. Indeed, Sidonius displayed a certain compassion in the case of a freedwoman of his who eloped with a slave belonging to his friend Pudens. Since unions between slaves and free persons were unlawful, Sidonius suggested that Pudens should promptly give the "ravisher" his liberty, thereby removing criminality from the elopement and conferring legality on the couple's marriage. It is clear that the incident was considered a serious matter, for Sidonius remarked that his friendship with Pudens would have ended had the latter not professed ignorance of the slave's "shameful" abduction of the freedwoman.

Although he made no apologies for regarding slaves as base individuals, Sidonius did not condone their abuse by cruel masters. Thus, when the landowner Lampridius was brutally murdered by his own slaves, Sidonius remarked that the deceased had perhaps invited such a fate by treating his slaves badly.

In another letter, Sidonius complained to the Breton warlord Riothamus that soldiers under his command roamed the countryside enticing slaves from the estates upon which they toiled. It is this type of writing, with its insight into the anxieties and personal concerns of the still-Roman, slaveowning upper classes, that makes Apollinaris Sidonius such a useful source for contemporary attitudes toward slavery in late antiquity.

—*Tim Clarkson*

See also
Bacaudae Insurrection
For Further Reading
Dalton, O. M., ed. 1915. *The Letters of Sidonius.* Oxford: Clarendon; Stevens, C. E. 1933. *Sidonius Apollinaris and His Age.* Oxford: Clarendon.

AN APPEAL TO THE CHRISTIAN WOMEN OF THE SOUTH
(1836)

Angelina Grimké wrote the abolitionist pamphlet *An Appeal to the Christian Women of the South,* and it was published by the American Anti-Slavery Society of New York in 1836. The work aroused such intense disfavor in the South that Southern postmasters intercepted and destroyed copies of it to prevent its distribution. In the North, the pamphlet sparked interest in abolitionism and quickly increased Grimké's standing in the abolitionist movement.

In the pamphlet, Grimké addressed Southern women as a woman born and raised in the South herself. As such, she thought she could reach and influence the thinking of other Southern women. The women, in turn, could persuade their brothers, fathers, and husbands to change the laws. She called upon women as sisters, wives, and mothers and urged them to try to understand that slavery violated natural law, Christianity, and human law. God, she argued, created all human beings in his image; therefore, no one could be treated as a "thing" the way Southerners treated slaves. Using the Bible, she showed that slavery in the South was not at all like biblical slavery, for Southern slaves lost all of their rights as human beings. Pointing to the Declaration of Independence, she appealed to Southern women to recognize the equality of slaves as human beings with a natural right to freedom.

As Grimké saw it, Southern women could do more than just understand the injustice of slavery; they

A master spies on his two apprentices, waiting to use his stick if one appears idle in this William Hogarth plate entitled The Fellow 'Prentices at their Looms.

could pray over it, speak about it, and act against it by freeing any slaves they owned, educating them, and paying them wages. She also asked women to send petitions to their state legislatures demanding an end to slavery. She argued: "Speak to your relatives, friends, acquaintances, be not afraid . . . to let your sentiments be known. . . . Try to persuade your husband, father, brothers and sons that slavery is a crime against God and man." She even advised Southern women to stand firm against "wicked laws" that dehumanized people. She wrote, "Slavery must be abolished . . . there are only two ways in which it can be effected, by moral power or physical force, and it is for you to choose which of these you prefer."

Grimké's *Appeal* was not unique in its content; many abolitionists used similar arguments when writing against slavery. Her *Appeal* was unique, however, because it was the first and only abolitionist tract written by a former Southern woman to Southern women. Grimké's family name was well known in Charleston, South Carolina, where she was born and raised, and that fact made her *Appeal* even more controversial among Southern women. When copies of her pamphlet reached Charleston as part of a mass mailing of abolitionist literature ("the great postal campaign" of 1835–1837), the postmaster publicly burned them. Charleston police even advised Grimké that she would not be permitted to visit the city ever again, and she never did.

—*Mary Jo Miles*

See also
Abolition, United States; Grimké, Angelina; Grimké, Sarah Moore
For Further Reading
Ceplair, Larry. 1989. *The Public Years of Sarah and Angelina Grimké: Selected Writings, 1835–1839.* New York: Columbia University Press; Lerner, Gerda. 1964. *The Grimké Sisters from South Carolina.* Boston: Houghton Mifflin.

APPRENTICESHIP

Apprenticeship was an established form of European bound labor in which a person, usually an adolescent child, was contracted to serve an employer for several years in order to learn and be allowed to practice a trade. Apprenticeship helped create paternalistic ideas about labor relations that heavily influenced thinking about slavery. The practice developed in early-medieval European towns as tradesmen gathered in guilds and attempted both to ensure quality of goods and to restrict competition. In a standard apprenticeship contract or indenture, a tradesman promised to house an adolescent and teach him a trade; in return, the tradesman exercised parental authority over his charge for a specified number of years (seven in English practice). Apprentices were unmarried and usually lived and worked in the master's household. A master's authority included corporal punishment and possibly even selling the apprentice's contract without his consent. Since many trades were mastered a few years before the apprenticeship ended, the masters then had the benefit of a skilled, inexpensive, and pliant workforce.

Reports of abused and runaway apprentices indicate possible systematic exploitation, but apprenticeship did serve a vital social function in which kinship and business connections were strengthened through governing other people's children, and apprenticeship was also a way of providing for destitute children. Masters provided gifts and patronage when an apprenticeship ended, and former apprentices, now town freemen, could practice their trade and hope to become masters in their turn. It was a typical medieval social institution since it relied on hierarchical ties of obligation and patronage between those involved and because it established strict lines of demarcation between the free and the unfree.

As Europe's economy increasingly diversified in and after the sixteenth century, apprenticeship gradually shifted from household paternalism to a more stratified use of labor in which social mobility was less likely. Developing mercantilist ideas meant that apprenticeship came to be considered as a useful tool for state control of labor. For example, the 1563 Statute of Artificers in England attempted to reduce unemployment by extending apprenticeship to the entire country, thus forcing masters to accept apprentices and putting the idle to work. Europeans accepted this regulated and forced labor, and when they faced labor shortages in the New World, they adapted easily to utilizing slavery and indentured servitude.

Traditional apprenticeship became part of the variety of bound labor found in colonial America, especially in urban areas, and was also often a transitional stage in the emancipation of slaves. Laissez-faire ideas meant that apprenticeship came under increasing attack in Britain and its colonies, where the strongest defenders of apprenticeship were small-scale artisans who were dependent on the cheap labor of a few apprentices to survive. The coming of the factory system in the nineteenth century caused the death of household industries and with them, apprenticeship in its traditional form.

—Gwilym Games

See also
Indentured Servants; Paternalism; Serfdom in Medieval Europe; Transition from Slave Labor to Free Labor (Africa, Caribbean, Latin America, North America, South Africa)
For Further Reading
Dunlop, O., and R. C. Denman. 1912. *English Apprenticeship and Child Labor*. New York: Macmillan; Morris, Richard B. 1946. *Government and Labor in Early America*. New York: Columbia University Press; Thompson, E. P. 1968. *The Making of the English Working Class*. London: Pelican.

APTHEKER, HERBERT (1915–)

Herbert Aptheker, the author of the definitive work *American Negro Slave Revolts* (1943), was born in Brooklyn, New York, on July 31, 1915. After receiving his Ph.D. from Columbia University in 1943, Aptheker began a scholar-activist sojourn that helped shape and change how the field of African American history is understood. Aptheker's career achievements include the editing and writing of over 80 books, of which over 40 volumes consist of the personal letters and scholarly works of the American educator and writer W. E. B. DuBois. Aptheker's wife, Fay, whom he married in 1942, ably assisted him in these scholarly efforts.

Although Aptheker was born the son of affluent Russian immigrants, he said that a black woman and nursemaid, Angelina Corbin, helped elevate his racial horizons as a young man. Aptheker reflected that "Annie raised me as much as mother. I loved her and mother loved her" (this and subsequent quotations are from the author's interview with Aptheker in 1995). His intellectual curiosity was challenged by Ulysses S. Grant's biography, which asserted that slaves in the United States were accurately portrayed by the stereotyped Sambo image. Reflecting on the strength of Annie's character, Aptheker said of this historical interpretation: "It can't be true. It was impossible that her people were like that." His social consciousness was further pricked in 1932 when he traveled in the Depression-era South and saw how the "barbarism" of peonage and Jim Crow degraded the black populace. After returning, he wrote a regular column, "The Dark Side of the South," in his high school newsletter exposing this racial injustice.

Aptheker believes that these early experiences led to his interest in the African American resistance to oppression. Searching for historical truth, Aptheker's master's thesis analyzed Nat Turner's rebellion and was published in 1966. His dissertation was the comprehensive interpretation of American Negro slave revolts. He also published two essays with the same title as his dissertation in successive issues of *Science and Society* in 1937. Two years later, he published "Maroons within the Present Limits of the United States" in the *Journal of Negro History,* and International Publishers published his work on slave resistance with *The Negro in the Civil War* in 1938 and *Negro Slave Revolts in the United States, 1526–1860* in 1939. When his dissertation was published in 1943, it became a watershed in slavery historiography.

In that work, Aptheker tried to address and refute the racist assumptions of U. B. Phillips and others, who stated that "slave revolts and plots very seldom occurred in the United States . . ." and that the slaves themselves were mentally defective, docile, and submissive. *American Negro Slave Revolts* challenged, in Aptheker's words, "the racism of the dominant historical profession and of the society it mirrored and served . . . [but also] further substantiated its thesis, that the African-American people, in slavery, forged a record of discontent and of resistance comparable to that marking the history of any other oppressed people." Aptheker defined a revolt as "a minimum of ten slaves involved; freedom as the apparent aim of the disaffected slaves; contemporary references labeling the event as an uprising, plot, insurrection."

The impact of the book on the historical profession was polar, with generally, white historians rejecting its thesis and black historians praising the author and his scholarship. A favorable review in 1944 noted that the book was scholarly, penetrating, and scientific while a negative one in 1951 argued that the research was so subjective that it did not deserve to be defined as history. The polarity of these two reviews reflected Aptheker's leftist politics and the effects of the Cold War, which further divided the historical profession on clear ideological grounds. One historian in favor of civil rights recalled that the work "was the single most effective antidote to the poisonous ideas that Blacks had not a history of struggle" (Bracey, 1993). By the 1970s, most historians accepted Aptheker's thesis either by incorporating or modifying its assumptions in their own work. George Rawick would agree that slaves "fought back in constant struggle"; Eugene Genovese accepted the "slaves' rebellious spirit"; John Blassingame and Mary Berry argued that "slaves engaged almost continuously . . . in . . . conspiracies, rebellions"; Leslie H. Owen thinks that "again and again bondsmen attacked slavery"; Peter Wood's and Gerald Mullin's work affirmed Aptheker's premise; and Vincent Harding's book presented a wide pattern of multilayered resistance within slave culture (all

cited in Shapiro, 1984). Aptheker's book forced historians to see rebellion as an essential characteristic of people held in bondage and illuminated a tradition of which all Americans can be proud.

—*Malik Simba*

For Further Reading
Aptheker, Herbert. 1993. *American Negro Slave Revolts.* 6th ed. New York: International Publishers; Bracey, John. 1993. "Foreword." In Herbert Aptheker, *American Negro Slave Revolts.* New York: International Publishers; Shapiro, Herbert. 1984. "The Impact of the Aptheker Thesis: A Retrospective View of American Negro Slave Revolts." *Science and Society* 48: 52–73.

ARCHAEOLOGICAL RECORD OF THE SLAVE TRADE

The African slave trade existed for four centuries and was one of the largest forced migrations in history. Slavery itself has existed throughout history and prehistory all over the world, but the African slave trade is best known because it is the most historically documented. But using historical records alone to understand the slave trade offers an incomplete picture regarding the slaves' everyday life. Often the documents were written by people who were directly involved in the slave trade or by apologists who were trying to justify it, and because it was illegal for slaves to become literate, there is little documentation regarding their perspective of slavery or details of their everyday life. Because archaeological research provides details about slavery that are often overlooked in the written record but present in the archaeological record, archaeology offers a good way to better understand the slave trade and the lives of those involved in it.

Archaeology is a subdiscipline of anthropology, and archaeologists study the living conditions, behavior, and way of life of humans in the past by examining the material remains that humans have left behind—the archaeological record. Through analysis of remains pertaining to slavery, archaeology can give insight into the context of everyday plantation life, the African American response to enslavement, and the processes of interaction between slaves and masters.

Archaeology is interpretive in nature, and interpretations are often based on remains that are selective and incomplete because of decay, corrosion, and disturbance, and to compound the problem, many traditional African artifacts were made from more perishable materials than contemporary European artifacts. Additionally, the material that archaeologists deal with often consists of what individuals discarded or lost rather than items that were kept and passed on from generation to generation. Interpreting an archaeological site is similar to completing a puzzle: an attempt is made to determine the larger picture by placing together small pieces of data. Although some pieces may be missing, it is still generally possible to get a good idea of the larger picture.

Slavery is somewhat difficult to identify through archaeological efforts alone because slavery pertains to status and it is difficult to determine when material remains point to the presence of a social status. The use of historical documents in conjunction with archaeology has been the most successful approach in the study of slavery. Documenting the process of the slave trade archaeologically is also difficult because any traces left are ephemeral. It is necessary to look at slave sites that are a consequence of the slave trade to find implicit evidence of it and to determine how the trade impacted the lives of those victimized by it. The archaeology of the slave trade encompasses the archaeology of slavery and plantation life, some slave cemeteries and burials, and former slave quarters, and this type of archaeology in the United States began in 1968 with the work of Charles Fairbanks.

The archaeological record of slavery reveals a material culture unique to the African presence in the New World. African American ethnic patterns and information on living conditions of the enslaved are visible, and the material remains that reflect ethnicity offer implicit evidence as to the African origins of those who were sold into slavery. Archaeological evidence of African and African American ethnicity stems from several sources: objects presumably brought over from Africa, re-creations of African-style or African-influenced objects, cultural practices that are detectable from physical remains, mortuary patterns, and European-American materials that were modified or reinterpreted by slaves so they had an African American meaning.

It is generally assumed that enslaved Africans took very few personal goods on the transatlantic voyage, but excavation has revealed that some goods did survive the journey. The remains of carnelian beads, Indo–Pacific Ocean cowry shells, an ebony ring, and a Ghanaian smoking pipe are artifacts found in slave contexts that indicate an African source. Besides objects from Africa, the archaeological record also contains re-creations of African-style objects. A large ceramic complex found in Jamaica is a form of African material culture that was re-created in the New World, and there are also remnants of African-style architecture at plantation sites. Colonoware, an unglazed, low-fired earthenware, has often been cited as the most widespread material indicator of slave presence in the New World. However, colonoware has been found in various African American slave/Native

American contexts and apparently was made by both cultures, so the presence of colonoware in the archaeological record does not necessarily presuppose the presence of enslaved African Americans.

Some cultural practices leave physiological evidence that reveals information about ethnicity. In New York City's African Burial Ground, skeletal evidence has been found of a dental mutilation that is consistent with a rite of passage performed in West Africa, and mortuary patterns on the Newton Plantation in Barbados indicate the use of burial mounds that have strong connections to African burial customs. Evidence that African Americans were reworking European-American materials to produce an African American meaning has also been found at various sites. Spoons incised with African-style motifs, bottoms of cast-iron kettles, parts of dolls, and pierced coins that may have been used for ritual or decorative purposes are some examples of reworked European-American materials found in the archaeological record in a slave context.

There is currently not much direct evidence about the actual process of the slave trade, but the archaeological record does offer indirect evidence of this process, and it also offers a way to understand what life was like for the enslaved African Americans who were victims of the African slave trade. The material remains reveal that despite attempts by European and Anglo masters to suppress African cultural influences, they continued to persist throughout the New World and to influence the culture of African Americans during the period of slavery and into freedom.

—*Lori Lee*

See also
African Burial Ground; Domestic Slave Trade in the United States; Plantation Archaeology
For Further Reading
Ferguson, Leland. 1992. *Uncommon Ground: Archaeology and Early African America, 1650–1800.* Washington, DC: Smithsonian Institution Press; Singleton, Theresa. 1991. "The Archaeology of Slave Life." In *Before Freedom Came: African-American Life in the AnteBellum South.* Ed. Edward Campbell, Jr., and Kym Rice. Charlottesville: University Press of Virginia; Singleton, Theresa, ed. 1985. *The Archaeology of Slavery and Plantation Life.* San Diego: Academic Press.

ARISTOMENES (*FL. SEVENTH CENTURY B.C.*)

The seventh-century-B.C. Greek hero Aristomenes led his people, the Messenians, in a revolt against Sparta, which had defeated and annexed Messenia in the First Messenian War (735

B.C.). As was their custom, the victors had reduced the vanquished population to the state of Helots, serfs bound to the land, and exacted a yearly tribute of half their produce. Hence, Messenians had been slaves for almost a century when they rebelled under the leadership of Aristomenes, a member of the Aepytid family.

Aristomenes inspired and organized his countrymen to fight against the oppressors and also secured help from Sparta's enemies, Argos and Arcadia. He was at first successful in freeing his people from bondage, but unfortunately, this freedom lasted only a few years. After a series of victories, such as those at Derai and at Stenyclarus, Aristomenes was betrayed by his Arcadian ally, King Aristocrates, and was routed by Sparta in the Battle of the Great Trench (631 B.C.) during the Second Messenian War.

Despite this serious setback, Aristomenes did not yield. He retreated with faithful followers to Mount Eira (Ira) in northern Messenia, and from there he led sorties against the Spartans for 11 years. He was twice taken prisoner and managed to escape, but when the Spartans conquered his stronghold and captured him for a third time, they took Aristomenes to Sparta and threw him to his death in a deep pit. One legend says that his fall was broken by an eagle and that he managed to escape from the pit by holding onto the tail of a fox. According to this legend, he died in exile on the island of Rhodes.

There are many ancient legends about Aristomenes, and much of what we know about him derives from the *Description of Greece* written in the second century A.D. by the Greek geographer Pausanias, who in turn based his work mainly on a now-lost epic *Messianica* written by the Cretan poet Rhianus in about 230 B.C. It is likely that the story's romantic embellishments come from Rhianus. Pausanias himself testified that in the second century, Aristomenes was still a celebrated hero in Messene because of his unrelenting fight against his people's enslavement. Pausanias's work also reports that after Messene's resurgence in the fourth century B.C., its inhabitants erected a statue to Aristomenes in their stadium and returned from Rhodes what they believed to be his bones to bury with great honors.

Whatever the exact historical details of Aristomenes' life, the multiplicity of references to him in ancient Greek texts, and the fact that the basic heroic actions attributed to him are consistently the same, leave little doubt that Aristomenes did indeed exist and that he fought to emancipate the Messenians.

—*L. Natalie Sandomirsky*

See also
Helots
For Further Reading
Grote, George. 1951–1957. *History of Greece*. 12 vols.

Boston: J. P. Jewett; Huxley, George Leonard. 1962. *Early Sparta*. London: Faber and Faber; Pausanias. *Description of Greece*.

ARISTOTLE'S POLITICS

According to Aristotle (384–321 B.C.), slavery is a necessary and natural part of a state, for the state consists of households and households consist of masters and slaves. Masters and slaves cannot exist without each other. The master rules with foresight, an intellectual power that enables him to develop plans and supervise those who put those plans into effect; slaves provide the physical force that brings the master's foresight to fruition. As the intellect or soul is superior to the body, so too is the master superior to the slave, and it is in the inferior's best interests to be ruled by a superior. In the *Politics*, Aristotle argues that this form of slavery, the subjection of an inferior by a superior, is natural and ethical.

Aristotle calls the slavery enforced on captives of war "conventional" as opposed to the natural slavery of the inferior. He advises against waging war for the primary purpose of taking slaves, implying that it cannot be assumed that those conquered in battle have been proved to be inferior. Taking captive slaves disrupts the natural relationship between master and slave, a relationship that is symbiotic and therefore mutually beneficial. Although admitting that slaves, as property, have no right to exercise choice and no share in the happiness that is the goal of the state, Aristotle insists that slaves and masters have a common interest and that slavery is in the best interest of those judged to be naturally inferior. Nevertheless, he notes that masters rule primarily out of self-interest and cautions that this self-interest should not threaten the slave's life, for a man cannot be a master without slaves to follow his rule.

In classifying slavery in a Platonic sense, Aristotle limits the study of the slave to what he describes as servile branches of knowledge—including cooking and farming. Regarding the slaves' character, he warns masters to raise their children with as little exposure to slaves as possible lest their offspring acquire servile attitudes and habits. He admits that slaves may exhibit excellent character attributes, such as temperance, courage, and justice, but he credits the master's influence as the source of slave virtue.

Aristotle cautions that because of their foundational role in the households that constitute the state, unvirtuous slaves can harm the household and the state. In a tyranny, slaves can be used as informers to undermine the master's position, or be emancipated and added to the tyrant's forces. Slaves can also be used by a state's enemies to weaken the state from within and make it susceptible to attack. Therefore, Aristotle urges masters to instill self-control in their slaves so they will not be tempted to disloyalty.

—*Mary-Ellen Cummings*

See also

Augustine (Saint); Greece; Homer's Theory; Plato's *Laws*

For Further Reading

Jowett, Benjamin, trans. 1885. *The Politics of Aristotle Translated into English with Introduction, Marginal Analysis, Essays, Notes, and Indices.* 3 vols. Oxford: Clarendon Press; Newman, W. L. 1887–1902. *The Politics of Aristotle.* 4 vols. Oxford: Clarendon Press.

ART, ANCIENT

Slavery in ancient Greece, Rome, the Near East, and Egypt was a fact of life during the earliest period of recorded history. Generally, no single race or group was enslaved by another society. Rather, people became slaves after being captured in war, because they had violated the law, or to satisfy unpaid debts.

Slaves' lives in these cultures, and how each society viewed slaves and slavery, influenced the ways in which slaves were depicted in the various forms of media. In societies not heavily dependent upon slave labor, few depictions of slaves survive. Ancient Near Eastern cultures were unable to absorb many captives because of their weak economies, so slaves in those cultures were mostly domestic slaves, performing tasks that did not require close supervision and were not seasonal. In first-millennium Babylonia, slaves engaged in trade, ran taverns and workshops, taught other people various trades, and pawned and mortgaged their property. In biblical cultures there were no temple slaves, and it was most likely freeborn people, not slaves, who constructed Jerusalem's temple and royal palace.

Slavery was vital to Greek and Roman economies, and slaves held many responsible positions, including being doctors, teachers, writers, accountants, and overseers. Slaves were depicted fairly frequently in art, sometimes openly, as slaves in relation to masters, and at other times "hidden," depicted but not recognized as slaves, at least not by the modern viewer.

Several political monuments in the ancient world showed slaves in their most demeaning and vulnerable state, as war captives. One such monument is the Column of Trajan in Rome, constructed around A.D. 110–113 to commemorate victories over the Dacians. Textiles and paintings showing similar battle-

Roman slaves working in a kitchen.

related scenes also depict slaves or people about to become enslaved.

Representations of household slaves are rather common. A first-century-B.C. funeral stele from western Asia Minor depicts male and female servants in smaller scale than a deceased couple, and servants of senators are depicted smaller than the senators themselves on the Arch of Constantine (c. 130 A.D.) in Rome. A first-century wall painting in Pompeii portrays a banquet at which one slave removes a guest's shoes while another offers a cup of wine to the guest. Several centuries earlier, a Bulgarian vaulted burial chamber boasted a frieze showing a seated couple dining amid a retinue of servants. A gem carved by the fifth-century-B.C. artist Dexamenos of Chios shows a seated woman facing a maid who holds a mirror and a wreath.

Examples of "hidden" slaves occur frequently in religious art, since many popular cults attracted slaves to their membership. A Herculaneum wall painting represents a sacrifice to Isis and a double choir singing hymns, and some of the worshipers portrayed are undoubtedly slaves. Similarly, scenes depicting initiation and fertility rites in the cults of Dionysus, Demeter, Artemis, and other gods and goddesses probably include slaves, who may have accompanied their owners as they worshiped or were adherents themselves.

Because slaves could hold high-ranking positions in Greco-Roman society, the portrayal of a school scene on a grave relief from 185 A.D., now in Trier, Germany, could be showing another "hidden" slave—the teacher. Similarly, scenes related to the healing god Asclepius may include a slave physician.

Slaves or servants in antiquity were not necessarily looked down upon or enslaved because of color, and dark-skinned men were often depicted in mosaics in Greco-Roman bath and domestic settings. Baths, though an integral and positive aspect of daily life, were thought to pose certain dangers, such as falling, drowning, demons, or the fear of grudging envy of one person toward another because of the other's beauty or good fortune, all too visible in the baths. To battle these demons and the so-called evil eye, various *apotropeia,* images to repel evil, were employed. Among these images were dark-skinned persons and the phallus, since both evoked laughter, which protected against evil. Therefore, the dark-skinned, hyperphallic male bath attendant, usually a slave, depicted in numerous mosaics functioned as a popular image to ward off the evil lurking in the baths.

—*Valerie Abrahamsen*

For Further Reading
Bartchy, S. Scott. 1992. "Slavery." In *Anchor Bible Dictionary.* New York: Doubleday; Clarke, John. 1996. "Hypersexual Men in Augustan Baths." In *Sexuality in Ancient Art.* Ed. Natalie Boymel Kampen. Cambridge: Cambridge University Press; Grant, Michael, and Rachel Kitzinger, eds. 1988. *Civilization of the Ancient Mediterranean: Greece and Rome.* New York: Charles Scribner's Sons; Wiedemann, Thomas. 1981. *Greek and Roman Slavery.* London: Croom Helm.

ART, MODERN

Modern art, which begins with the Renaissance in the sixteenth century and extends into the twentieth, is intimately connected with slavery, for the rise of modern art and modernity coincided with the rise of the Atlantic slave trade and New World slavery. The fall of Constantinople to the Ottoman Turks in 1453 produced two important events that led to the emergence of both the Atlantic slave trade and modern art. First, the Ottoman Turks diverted the flow of Caucasian slaves and servants from the Black Sea and the Balkans to Islamic markets, thereby depriving Mediterranean Europe of its major source of slaves and opening up sub-Saharan Africa as an alternative slave source. Second, the Turks took a flood of scholarly refugees to Italy, and they introduced Italians to the Greek language, literature, and culture, which led to a cultural Renaissance and the rise of modernity.

Given the centrality of the slave trade to the settlement and development of the New World, the single most striking feature of the relationship between slavery and modern art is the relative paucity of images that are concerned with slavery. Until the rise of antislavery thought in the 1760s and 1770s, artists virtually ignored the West African trade. They sometimes alluded to the trade by including images of blacks, but the formal beauty with which these blacks are depicted points to the common humanity between blacks and whites rather than to an emphasis on blacks as "natural slaves" or subservient beings.

For example, Albrecht Dürer's and Hieronymus Bosch's scenes of *The Adoration of the Magi* (1504 and c. 1490–1510, respectively) both include black kings as a possible link between the African trade and Europe, and the mid-sixteenth-century image of the *Miracle of the Black Leg* (artist unknown) shows two saints replacing the leg of a white man with that of a dead black man. But these images refer only indirectly to the Atlantic slave trade, and they neither defend nor condemn slavery; there was essentially no need to do so. Most artists were preeminently occupied with aesthetic issues rather than social concerns, and the first two and a half centuries of the Atlantic trade coincided with profoundly dignified images of blacks by such canonical artists as Albrecht Dürer,

Drawing of the slave Katharina by Albrecht Dürer.

Hieronymus Bosch, Diego Velázquez, Peter Paul Rubens, and Rembrandt.

With the rise of antislavery thought, two different types of slavery images emerged: "high art" paintings and sculpture by established "masters" and propaganda pieces, often in the form of prints or engravings that originally appeared as book illustrations whose purpose was to defend or condemn slavery. "High art" depictions of slavery continued to emphasize aesthetic considerations over social commentary, but they now began to reinforce racial stereotypes that were linked to the proliferation of the Atlantic trade. Anne-Louis Girodet's famous painting of the French military captain Jean-Baptiste Belley (1797), for example, portrays the former Saint Domingue slave in elegant grandeur: in a richly ornamented officer's uniform, he stoically leans against a marble bust and gazes, after the fashion of eminent men of the time, up and into the distance. But at the same time, Belley is depicted with an enormous sexual organ that is clearly discernible beneath his elegant pants, reinforcing the stereotype of virility and sexual prowess in black men.

Propaganda pieces constituted the vast majority of slave imagery until the mid- to late-nineteenth century.

The first antislavery images appeared as visual counterparts to the writings of the French philosophes in the 1770s. The Quakers, who led the antislavery movement in both Great Britain and the United States, tended to associate visual arts with luxury and extravagance, and they rarely embellished their writings with images. Two of the best-known antislavery images—Josiah Wedgwood's medallion of a supplicating slave underneath the inscription, "Am I Not a Man and a Brother?" and the cross section of the *Brookes* slave ship (artist unknown)—were thought of as symbols of Christian humanitarianism and the evils of slavery, never as art.

Images defending slavery generally focused on the positive effects of the system—happy, contented slaves within an orderly and organic social system, for instance—and drawings associated with pseudo-scientific treatises that defended innate racial differences, such as an illustration for Joseph Virey's treatise on polygenesis (1824), showed blacks as being more similar to apes than to whites. The Haitian Revolution became an important source of images, both for abolitionists, who viewed barbarism and bloodshed as the inevitable result of a slave system, and for proslavery advocates, who linked barbarism with emancipation.

The major differences between European and American depictions of slavery involved perceptions of the color line, slave sexuality, and America's self-conscious status as a democracy. The tensions in the United States caused by a slave society that embraced freedom and democracy resulted in a virtual absence of slave imagery in the arts until the rise of abolitionism in the 1830s. Additionally, unlike images that portrayed slavery in the West Indies, the moral and sexual codes in the United States prevented artists from portraying black sexuality or the sexual component of the slave system. The rigid color line was enforced in virtually all images of slavery in the United States, by both proslavery and antislavery artists; blacks were typically portrayed as different from whites, and few images by U.S. artists depict blacks or slaves as objects of sexual desire.

The French painter Jean-Auguste-Dominique Ingres's portrayal of the seductions of slavery, *Odalisque with a Slave* (1842), would have been excoriated if it had been painted in the United States because it violated the strict moral codes that kept sexuality out of the public sphere. Similarly, book illustrations such as Thomas Stothard's *The Voyage of the Sable Venus* (1801), which shows the goddess Venus as a nude black woman, and William Blake's engraving, *Europe Supported by Africa and America* (1790), an image of three nude women holding each other upright by use of their hands and a large rope, would have been unacceptable to an American public, both because of the nudity and sexual suggestiveness and because of the linking of dark-skinned and seductive women to national identity and the meaning of the United States.

The first efforts to depict slavery from the point of view of the slave occurred in the mid-nineteenth century, and the radical uncertainty and alienation of slave subjectivity corresponded to the rise of abstraction in art and ultimately coincided with the emergence of modernist abstraction. J. M. W. Turner's *The Slave Ship* (1840) attempts to convey the chaos, death, and destruction associated with slaves being thrown overboard during a storm. Théodore Chassériau's *Study of a Nude Black* (c. 1836–1838) evokes, through the portrayal of an athletic black man floating amid a blue background and distended body parts, the void of disorientation and alienation associated with slave subjectivity. It is no coincidence that abstraction and modernism in the twentieth century coincided with an increasing interest in African art and subjectivity by white Europeans and Americans. As Henry Louis Gates, Jr., has suggested, "It is not too much to argue that European modernity manifested itself as a mirrored reflection of the mask of blackness" (Gates, 1996).

—*John Stauffer*

See also
Art, Ancient; Caste; The Enlightenment; Literature; Racism
For Further Reading
Davis, David Brion. 1986. *From Homicide to Slavery: Studies in American Culture*. New York: Oxford University Press; Devisse, Jean, and Michael Moliat. 1979. *The Image of the Black in Western Art. Vol. 2*. New York: William Morrow; Gates, Henry Louis Jr. 1996. "Europe, African Art, and the Uncanny." In *Africa: The Art of a Continent*. Ed. Tom Phillips. New York: Guggenheim Museum; Honour, Hugh. 1989. *The Image of the Black in Western Art. Vol. 4*. Cambridge, MA: Harvard University Press.

THE ASHANTI

The rise of the Ashanti (or Asante) people in western Africa virtually ended slave exporting from areas under their control, but they actively bought and captured slaves from other areas. The net result was an increase in the number of slaves exported from the Gold Coast. Ashanti rulers had a large number of domestic slaves, but this practice did not expand much beyond royal households. The main reason for its limitation was the tremendous demands of transatlantic slave trading.

The Ashanti's rise characterized the movement of African state power from the Sudan toward the west coast as a consequence of the slave trade. These new states threatened both the more established coastal states and European powers. During the seventeenth and eighteenth centuries, European powers maintained rather isolated garrisons at the pleasure of local coastal powers. Thus, a somewhat natural alliance formed between coastal states and the new inland powers.

The Ashanti rose to power in the early-eighteenth century, learning much from the failure of the Akwamu, who had never established an administration that was capable of tying all of its subjects into a cohesive unit, which would have made it possible to control trade between the interior and the coast. The Ashanti, however, first secured the northern areas of Bono, Banda, Gonja, and Dagomba, and only then did they move to confront European traders.

Slavery among the Ashanti was not a simple matter. There were at least five forms of slavery (or slavelike status) within the area. *Akoa* was a term used to identify subject-to-client relationships, an important concept as the principle of seniority was well-established in most African societies. *Awowa* referred to people who had pawned themselves for a debt owed. *Odonko* identified a person purchased as a slave, *domum* was someone captured and enslaved as a result of war, and *akyere* indicated someone living in a village designated for slaves to be used in human sacrifice. Additionally, *panyarrins* described the forcible seizure of persons for debt and was often included as a type of slavery. As one scholar notes, "A man became the standard of price" (Reynolds, 1974).

Although the Ashanti were mainly concerned with consolidating trade and not with warfare, they found themselves in a position where war with Britain was inevitable. The Ashanti reached the coast at a time when Britain was firmly entrenched there, and the interests of the two were inevitably at cross-purposes. The First Ashanti War (1824) forced the British to change their policy and follow a more conciliatory path under the leadership of the merchant-administrator George Maclean. He used a system of informal jurisdiction over the coast, coupled with a peaceful yet resolute policy toward the Ashanti. Unfortunately, when Britain resumed more direct rule over Gold Coast states in 1843–1844, it neglected Maclean's lessons.

Britain found itself in constant conflict with the Ashanti, and the conflicts tended to involve slave trading, which the Ashanti wished to continue practicing despite British opposition. In 1772, a judicial decision had abolished slavery in England itself. Great Britain later abolished the slave trade (1807) for British subjects and in 1811, imposed heavy penalties on any subjects engaged in it. By 1840, Britain had virtually eliminated the Atlantic slave trade with the aid of the United States and other European powers. Other powers had left the Gold Coast by 1872, and any Ashanti hopes of establishing a European-style government

A European trader negotiates with an Ashanti slave trader in this anonymous early-nineteenth-century illustration.

along the coast vanished. In 1874, the British convincingly drove that point home with a punitive expedition against the Ashanti capital at Kumasi.

—Frank A. Salamone

For Further Reading
Klein, A. Norman. 1994. "Slavery and Akan Origins." *Ethnohistory* 41: 627–656; McSheffrey, Gerald M. 1983. "Slavery, Indentured Servitude, Legitimate Trade, and the Impact of Abolition in the Gold Coast, 1874–1901: A Reappraisal." *Journal of African History* 24: 349–368; Reynolds, Edward. 1974. *Trade and Economic Change on the Gold Coast: 1807–1874.* New York: Longman; Wilks, Ivor. 1993. *Forests of Gold: Essays on the Akan and the Kingdom of Asante.* Athens: Ohio University Press.

ASIAN/BUDDHIST MONASTIC SLAVERY

Buddhist monasteries have always been a major economic force throughout Asia, with large land domains, stores of wealth, and in earlier times, slaves. Early Chinese Buddhist communities inherited from India scriptures that described a slavery system in which all property was collectively owned by the *sangha* (the community of monks and nuns). Property was supplied largely through donations from local elites and some factions of the central state. According to these Indian scriptures, the Buddha had allowed donations of slaves—along with land, buildings, robes, and other property—to the *sangha* (as a corporate body; slaves were not the private property of specific monks). Large Buddhist monastic communities began developing in China during the fourth and fifth centuries, and these institutions were still a major economic force, although seriously weakened, in the ninth and tenth centuries.

Chinese monastic slavery related to the expansion of cultivated landholdings into peripheral areas. Throughout the medieval period, the state tried moving people from densely populated, good land to cultivate tougher land. Generally, slaves (*nupei*) worked the uncleared hilly land, and peasants and serfs tilled the lowland, which had a longer history of cultivation. Various means were used to induce people to break new ground, including tax incentives and forced deportation to agricultural and military colonies. These colonists were often placed under the supervision of

Buddhist monks, and some became, in effect, monastic slaves.

Beginning in the fifth century, during a period of military action by the northern Wei, certain dislocated and relocated families were designated "sangha households" (sengqihu) and had the duty of maintaining the monasteries. Of the grain they produced, a certain portion was called "sangha millet" (sengqisu) and was placed in the monastic granaries. If these households met their quotas, they sometimes enjoyed the influence of the monastery as a tax shelter. There was also a class of slaves called "Buddha households" (fotuhu), which consisted mainly of state slaves and convicts whose sentences of death or hard labor had been commuted to a life of supervised ownership by monasteries.

Another class of monastic serfs were called "households held in perpetuity." Lay servants were also called "garden folk" (yuanmin or shouyuanmin, perhaps derived from the Sanskrit ārāmika). Households made up of these monastic serfs were subject to a prohibition against marrying externally, and the monasteries claimed any children they had. The households' dependence on their monastic owners was thus hereditary, but unlike slaves, they had some economic freedom to cultivate and engage in trade.

In modern times, with the demise of the legal institution of slavery, monasteries rely upon hired labor, and movements stressing social welfare have led to increased numbers of monks and nuns involved in construction, education, and preventive medicine. Slavery is no longer a part of Asian monasticism.

—Eric Reinders

See also
Buddhism; China (Ancient, Late Imperial, Medieval); East Asia

For Further Reading
Gernet, Jacques. 1995. *Buddhism in Chinese Society: An Economic History from the Fifth to the Tenth Centuries*. New York: Columbia University Press; Twitchett, Denis C. 1955–1956. "Monastic Estates in T'ang China." *Asia Major* 5 (1): 123–146.

THE ASIENTO

The *asiento* was an agreement between a private contractor and the Spanish government in which the entrepreneur or company purchased a monopoly over the importation of a certain number of slaves, at a set price and in a specified time, to Spanish America. The origin of this type of agreement lay in the introduction of plantation agriculture to Spain's Caribbean possessions in the 1500s. That type of agricultural economy demanded the large-scale importation of African slaves, but in the Treaty of Alcaçovas (1479), Castile had surrendered all claims to sub-Saharan Africa to Portugal. Thus, for much of the sixteenth century, slaves were imported into Spanish America under a rather erratic system of special licenses, mainly granted to Portuguese businessmen, but Spanish agriculturalists in the New World found this system a generally unsatisfactory means of supplying their labor needs.

The union of the Spanish and Portuguese crowns in 1580 stimulated a more regularized slave import system, the *asiento*. In 1595, the crown concluded the first such contract with a Spaniard with Portuguese connections, but the Portuguese rapidly dominated the system. From factories along Africa's western coast, Portuguese vessels carried slaves to designated ports in Spanish America. The standard of importation was a *pieza de Indias*—a young adult male in good physical condition. Women, children, and older males counted as fractions of a *pieza de Indias*. Spanish officials, their salaries often paid from the original *asiento* contract, received the slaves at Havana, Cartagena, Veracruz, and other ports. Occasionally the *asentistas* (the individuals who "worked" the *asiento*) were even permitted to transport the slaves to the interior.

The successful Portugal rebellion for independence from the Spanish crown in 1640 occasioned a brief hiatus in the *asiento* system, but the coincident sugar revolution in Spain's Caribbean economy increased demands for slave labor. By 1662 the *asiento* had been revived, but now with an added international participant—the Dutch. Technically, the latter were barred from such trade as they were heretics, but Dutch capital and maritime power allowed them to dominate the *asiento* through dummies and subcontractors until the late-seventeenth century. As these newcomers supplanted the Portuguese in the Gulf of Guinea, if not along the entire coast of West Africa, they were in an excellent position to supply slaves to Spanish America.

The Dutch participation in this slave trade revealed that the *asiento* had become an international prize. After a French Bourbon assumed the Spanish crown in 1700, French merchants were awarded the *asiento* in the early-eighteenth century. Not only were there profits to be gained from the slave trade, but with the cooperation of corrupt New World officials, the *asiento* also provided a cover for importing contraband finished goods into Spanish America. Although such contraband was imported during the era of the Portuguese *asiento*, it grew to massive amounts during the Dutch participation and was a continual source of concern to the Spanish crown.

So great a prize was the *asiento* that in the Treaty of Utrecht (1713), which ended the War of the Spanish Succession, British subjects were awarded the monopoly for 30 years, and from African trading posts, the Royal African Company supplied to the South

Seas Company slaves bound to Spain's New World possessions. Although profits to the British were erratic and they often faced Spanish obstructionism and harassment, the accompanying contraband traffic compensated the South Seas Company for its trouble. Sometimes, war between Spain and Britain in the early-eighteenth century signified a temporary interruption of the *asiento*, but when Britain was victorious, it then demanded and received the return of the monopoly until the full period of British rights, not counting the war years, was fulfilled.

By the 1750s, reformist Bourbon officials had started attacking the institution, but contracts were awarded to Spanish businessmen until 1789. In that year, the *asiento* was abolished, and other means were employed during the brief remaining period of Spain's participation in the transatlantic slave trade.

During the *asiento* era, approximately 900,000 African slaves entered the New World by this system. Not only was it a significant part of the transatlantic commerce in slaves, it also had a tremendous impact upon the economic and human history of Spanish America, particularly the Caribbean.

—*Jerry W. Cooney*

See also
Alcaçovas, Treaty of; Dutch Slave Trade; *Piezas de Indias;* Portuguese Slave Trade; Royal African Company; Sugar Cultivation and Trade; Utrecht, Treaty of
For Further Reading
Palmer, Colin. 1981. *Human Cargoes: The British Slave Trade to Spanish America, 1700–1739.* Urbana: University of Illinois Press; Rawley, James A. 1981. *The Transatlantic Slave Trade.* New York: Norton.

ATLANTIC ABOLITIONIST MOVEMENT

By the 1770s, Western cultural developments had converged with transatlantic imperial crises to provide society with the language and opportunity for collective opposition to slavery and the slave trade. Natural rights philosophy, the Enlightenment critique of traditional authority, British Protestantism's emerging faith in the individual's capacity for virtue, and new economic theories suggesting that free labor and free trade best promoted economic progress all undermined the older justifications for slavery. American Quakers revitalized their moral opposition to warfare during the Seven Years War (1756–1763), extended their critique of violence to include slavery itself, and dedicated themselves to eliminating slaveholding within their own ranks. The American and French Revolutions, fought for liberty and equality, encouraged others to join the abolitionist movement.

Fearing that radical experimentation might undermine the social order, early Anglo-American and French abolitionists supported modest measures for eliminating slavery. They generally favored ending the slave trade, emancipating slaves gradually, and compensating slaveholders for their losses. In the newly independent United States, Quakers, evangelicals, and several revolutionary leaders established the first state abolition societies to promote these aims. Between 1780 and 1808, abolitionists secured legislation preventing slavery's expansion into the Northwest Territory, freeing the children of slaves in the Northern states after apprenticeships of approximately 20 years, and prohibiting U.S. participation in the transatlantic slave trade.

Inspired by antislavery advocates in the United States, Quaker and evangelical abolitionists in England campaigned against British participation in the transatlantic slave trade, hoping that a diminished slave supply would encourage West Indian planters to treat their slaves more humanely and ease the transition to free labor. Operating through the Society for Effecting the Abolition of the Slave Trade (1787), the British abolitionists won the patronage of influential figures in Parliament, but despite a massive public campaign far surpassing that of their U.S. counterparts, they failed to overcome the powerful slave trading interests until 1807. That year marked the beginning of their efforts against foreign participation in the transatlantic slave trade as well, but justifiable international suspicion of British motives limited their success.

In 1788, following the example of Anglo-American abolitionists, the French reformer Jacques-Pierre Brissot de Warville organized a group of enlightened nobles and philosophes into the Société des Amis des Noirs. During the 1789 meeting of the Estates General in Paris, the society condemned slavery but limited its immediate goals to supporting colonial mulatto representation and abolishing the slave trade. Planter and merchant representatives easily suppressed the initiatives of the sanguine and poorly organized group.

Insurrectionary slaves, rising in rebellion when Spanish and English troops invaded the French colony of Saint Domingue (modern Haiti), eclipsed the group's moderate efforts. Desperate to secure the loyalty of the insurrectionists, French commissioners issued a decree in 1793 freeing loyal slaves, and the National Convention in Paris abolished slavery in 1794. Napoleon forcibly reinstituted slavery in the colonies but failed to subdue the revolutionaries in Saint Domingue, who represented 80 percent of France's former colonial slave population. The resulting relative marginality of French colonial slavery opened the way for its eventual abolition in 1848.

Anticolonial nationalism, not abolitionism, led to the emancipation of most Latin American slaves. Revolutionaries like Simón Bolívar granted freedom to slaves willing to join the military campaigns for independence, but most nationalist leaders, many of whom owned large landholdings and numerous slaves, supported such measures only reluctantly. Although willing to endorse freedom for slaves who would assist them in a war effort, they balked at full-scale, immediate emancipation. The newly independent mainland Latin American republics along the Atlantic seaboard eventually passed gradual emancipation acts, beginning with Argentina in 1813 and ending with Venezuela in 1854. Spanish Cuba and independent Brazil, however, resisted this trend toward emancipation.

Following legislative prohibition of both British and U.S. participation in the transatlantic slave trade, antislavery advocates explored new, moderate measures to promote emancipation. British abolitionists proposed registering all West Indian slaves to protect them from flagrantly exploitative abuses and to set a legal precedent for more substantial parliamentary intervention. In the United States, the American Colonization Society (1816) popularized the idea of emancipating Southern slaves and transporting them to colonies in Africa, thereby eliminating the potential threat of a much reviled free African American population. But planter intransigence and the expansion of slavery into new U.S. territories led Anglo-American abolitionists in the 1820s to reject gradualism and demand more radical, immediate action. Religious developments reinforced this tactical shift, as evangelicals seeking to hasten the millennium became less willing to tolerate compromise with slaveholding sinners. This later generation of abolitionists also benefited from the more active participation of middle-class white women who increasingly viewed slavery as an affront to new domestic ideals.

British abolitionists, armed with new conviction and organizational strength, and pointing to the recent slave revolts in Barbados, Demerara (British Guiana), and Jamaica, convinced Parliament to pass the Emancipation Act in 1833. Not entirely pleased with the statutory provisions to compensate slaveholders and the apprenticeships required of slave children, abolitionists successfully supported legislation to eliminate lengthy work requirements in 1838. Having promoted the emancipation of 750,000 British West Indian slaves, abolitionists turned their attention toward slavery and the slave trade elsewhere. They organized the World Anti-Slavery Conventions of 1840 and 1843 to encourage emancipation in the Southern United States, they scored significant successes in curtailing the slave trade by advocating the searching of European vessels, and they later helped secure British diplomatic support for the Union during the U.S. Civil War.

Parliamentary supremacy over Great Britain's distant colonies simplified the task of British abolitionists, but a decentralized federalist political system granting great autonomy to slaveholding states hampered the U.S. antislavery advocates. In 1833, William Lloyd Garrison established the American Anti-Slavery Society, and that group condemned the racial prejudice implicit in the colonization movement and called for immediate, uncompensated emancipation. Members of the society even came to consider the U.S. Constitution a proslavery document and preferred dissolution of the Union over compromise with slaveholders.

Garrison's strict stance, and his support for other controversial issues like women's suffrage, alienated some of his followers, and in 1840, these critics formed the Foreign and American Anti-Slavery Society. Most of these abolitionists viewed the Constitution as an antislavery blueprint that gave the federal government the right to dismantle slavery. Black abolitionists—particularly fugitives from the slave South like Frederick Douglass and William Wells Brown—played an important role in healing some of the rifts, eloquently reminding contending factions in both Britain and the United States to combat dogmatism and tackle the immediate problem of slavery. Despite the conflicts between the various abolitionist groups, they managed to convey to Southerners that their abolition ideas were widely accepted by the Northern public. In this sense, they helped fuel the sectional animosity that resulted in both the Civil War and the eventual emancipation of 4 million Southern slaves.

Independent Brazil and Spanish Cuba remained the last major bastions of slavery in the Americas. In both countries, the example of U.S. abolition, British success in ending the transatlantic slave trade, the efforts to attract European immigrants, and the rebellious activities of slaves facilitated emancipation. Only in Brazil did there exist an organized abolitionist movement. The lawyer and parliamentarian Joaquim Nabuco led a small group of secular-minded abolitionists from northeastern Brazil where slave-based sugar production was in serious decline. In 1871, despite the opposition of coffee planters in southwestern Brazil, the government passed a gradual abolition law requiring lengthy indentures for former slaves. An emancipation law offering current slaves immediate freedom passed in 1888, but by that time, slaves had already begun to take matters into their own hands by fleeing their masters in large numbers. In Cuba a gradual abolition law was passed in 1880, and full emancipation came in 1886.

After slavery was abolished in the West Indies, British antislavery advocates directed their attention toward emancipation in Africa. To reinforce that goal, they supported a naval squadron along the African coast to enforce abolition of the transatlantic slave trade, promoted the "legitimate trade" in tropical staples, and encouraged missionary activity to spread Christianity. But this campaign also served to legitimize Britain's growing imperial ambitions in the region.

While British naval power effectively prohibited the transatlantic trade in the late-nineteenth century, it also challenged the sovereignty of African nations. Even though new world markets for tropical staples offered Africans an alternative to the international traffic in slaves, the growing labor employed in the production of such commodities was often indistinguishable from domestic slavery, and missionary explorers, discovering the great extent to which Africans utilized slaves, became key proponents of greater colonial authority. International antislavery agreements, like the Brussels Act (1890), authorized direct intervention to end domestic slavery and the slave trade, but the fine line distinguishing domestic slavery from other profitable forms of labor exploitation was drawn with an eye toward promoting economic benefits. While greatly expanding European colonial power in Africa, the success of such ventures in eliminating slavery was minimal.

Various forms of human bondage—though often difficult to classify definitively as slavery—continue to this day. The United Nations, the Working Group of Experts on Slavery, the London-based Anti-Slavery Society, and other organizations have challenged exploitative labor contracts, forced relocation, the pawning of individuals for debt, the betrothal of children, convict labor, and prostitution.

—Anthony A. Iaccarino

See also
Abolition (Africa, British Empire, Latin America, Scandinavia, United States); Abolitionist Confederation; Brazilian Anti-Slavery Society; Closing of the African Slave Trade; Compensated Emancipation; Emancipation Proclamation; Immediatism; Quakers; Société des Amis des Noirs; Somersett Case

For Further Reading
Azevedo, Celia M. 1995. *Abolitionism in the United States and Brazil: A Comparative Perspective.* New York: Garland; Davis, David Brion. 1975. *The Problem of Slavery in the Age of Revolution, 1770–1823.* Ithaca, NY: Cornell University Press; Davis, David Brion. 1984. *Slavery and Human Progress.* New York: Oxford University Press; Fladeland, Betty. 1972. *Men and Brothers: Anglo-American Antislavery Cooperation.* Urbana: University of Illinois Press.

ATTUCKS, CRISPUS
(C. 1723–1770)

Crispus Attucks, a mulatto and former slave of African and Native American descent, is noted as the first person killed in the Boston Massacre, but little else about him is certain. Apparently Attucks was the slave of Deacon William Browne of Framingham, Massachusetts, until November 1750, when he escaped at the age of 27. As a free black in colonial America, Attucks worked on a whaling ship, and there he met other American colonists who disapproved of Britain's colonial policies. He died on March 5, 1770, the first person to fall at the hands of the British soldiers stationed in Boston.

Although his background remains obscure, Attucks played an important role in the event that caused his death. Court records and the testimony of other participants in the melee indicate that Attucks led a mob of 50–60 men to the Boston Custom House on King Street. The jeering crowd pressed forward and began to throw snow and ice at the British soldiers stationed at the Custom House, and according to one eyewitness, Andrew, a slave of Oliver Wendell, Attucks struck at a soldier. Colonial essayist Samuel Adams later told the court a different story, claiming that Attucks was not the person who started the riot.

Whatever Attucks did that night, a violent episode ensued between the mob and the British soldiers under Capt. Thomas Preston's command. Several shots were fired, and five civilians were killed, including Attucks, and his conduct during the event played a prominent role in the trial that followed. The documents used to indict the British soldiers for the massacre identified Attucks as the first individual the soldiers fired on. The same documents accused the soldiers of participating in an unprovoked altercation with uncontrollable force and malice. Responding to the plaintiffs' tactics, John Adams, the British soldiers' defense attorney, focused on Attucks's actions and argued that Attucks was the person who formed the mob and led the attack on the soldiers. Eventually, the court found two British soldiers guilty of manslaughter, and they were branded and given clemency.

After his death and the end of the War of Independence, the name of Attucks continued to receive much attention. Throughout the antebellum period, several African American military regiments named themselves the Attucks Guard; between 1858 and 1870, many of Boston's African Americans held annual Crispus Attucks Day celebrations; and in 1888, an Attucks memorial was constructed on the Boston Common. His name became a symbol of courage for all Americans, particularly African Americans.

—Eric R. Jackson

For Further Reading
Fisher, Ruth Anna. 1942. "Manuscript Materials Bearing on the Negro in British America." *Journal of Negro History* 27 (1): 83–93; Livermore, George. 1970. *An Historical Research Respecting the Opinions of the Founders of the Republic on Negroes as Slaves, as Citizens, and as Soldiers.* New York: Augustus M. Kelley; Quarles, Benjamin. 1961. *The Negro in the American Revolution.* New York: Norton; Simmons, William, J. 1968. *Men of Mark: Eminent, Progressive, and Rising.* New York: Arno.

AUGUSTINE (SAINT)

Saint Augustine

Aurelius Augustinus (A.D. 354–430) was the greatest Western Christian theologian between the close of the apostolic age and the high Middle Ages. In his extensive writings he codified previous theological reflections and added his own creative insights, thereby decisively shaping succeeding Western Christian theology. He made significant contributions to the Christian doctrines of the Trinity and original sin and to the Christian interpretation of society and history.

Born in North Africa, the son of a pagan father and a Christian mother, Augustine trained as a young man in classical rhetoric. Though his mother was steadfast in her efforts to bring him to accept Christianity for himself, Augustine resisted, believing it inferior to classical philosophy. At 29 he went to Italy and came under the influence of Ambrose, the Christian bishop of Milan, and Augustine began to look upon Christianity with greater favor.

Increasing doubts about other alternatives, the appeals of Ambrose's teachings, and a mystical experience all led Augustine to embrace Christianity wholeheartedly in 387. He returned to North Africa intent upon founding a monastery. His longing to live a quiet contemplative life was thwarted, and against his desires, he was ordained a priest and then in 395, bishop of Hippo. Although he led a most active life in this office, he still found time to write many profound, complex, and powerful treatises in which he stated his convictions concerning the most fundamental problems of Christian thought and action. He remained in Hippo the rest of his life and died there when the Vandals attacked the city.

Augustine's views concerning slavery are best understood in the context of his beliefs concerning human nature and original sin. He believed that all humans are bound by original sin. Adam, though created sinless, was also endowed with free will. He could have chosen not to sin, but instead he disobeyed God and sinned. Since then, he and his descendants have been in a state of original sin from which no one can escape by his or her own efforts. Indeed, in the state of original sin one cannot choose not to sin, and to be redeemed from a sinful state requires an act of God.

This view of human nature and original sin underlies Augustine's interpretation of society and history as well as his attitude toward slavery. Believing slavery to be a consequence of human sin, he wrote in *The City of God*, "The prime cause, then of slavery is sin, which brings man under the dominion of his fellow— that which does not happen save by the judgment of God, with whom is no unrighteousness, and who knows how to award fit punishments to every variety of offence" (xix, 15). In the same work, Augustine notes that we do not read of biblical slavery until the time of Noah: "For it is understood, of course, that the condition of slavery is justly imposed on the sinner. That is why we do not hear of a slave anywhere in the Scriptures until Noah, the just man, punished his son's sin with this word; and so that son deserved this name because of his misdeed, not because of his nature" (xix, 19). Furthermore, although slavery was not a part of God's original intention nor of humanity's uncorrupted state, it became a part of the "natural order of things." Consequently, Augustine apparently believed slaves should accept their condition and make the best of it.

> But by nature, as God first created us, no one is the slave either of man or of sin. This servitude is, however, penal, and is appointed by that law which enjoins the preservation of the natural order and forbids its disturbance; for if nothing had been done in violation of that law, there would have been nothing to restrain by penal servitude. And therefore the apostle [Paul] admonishes slaves to be subject to their masters, and to serve them heartily and with goodwill, so that, if they cannot be freed by their masters, they may themselves make their slavery in some sort free, by serving not in crafty fear, but in faithful love, until all unrighteousness pass away, and all principality and every human power be brought to nothing, and God be all in all. (xix, 15)

Nevertheless, Augustine acknowledged that slavery is contrary to the basic equality of all men as human beings, and on one occasion he proclaimed that a deacon who had purchased several slaves must free them before entering a monastery. He also refused to accept the concept of slaves as mere chattel. Instead, he drew upon Mosaic law, which ordained humane treatment of slaves, an attitude refined by Christian teachings on charity and universal brotherhood (see *City of God*, xix, 15–16; *Expositions on the Psalms*, 124, 7; *Sermons*, 21, 6–7). Although Augustine never dared to ask slaveowners to beg a slave's pardon after inflicting an unjust punishment or losing one's temper with a slave, he advised them quietly to humble themselves before God and to show the man concerned, by means of a friendly word, that the injustice of which he had been made a victim was at least recognized (*Sermons*, 211, 5, 4).

Augustine did not hesitate to say that a slave must not be handled in the lighthearted manner that a man might deal with his own money or his own horse, and that this was no less true when a slave's market value happened to be lower than that of a horse (*Commentary on the Sermon on the Mount*, 1, 19, 59). Yet the fact remains, St. Augustine believed human sinfulness to be the root problem. Therefore, slavery and coercion could be accepted, and he was more concerned to ennoble the existing relation between master and slave than to abolish it.

—*Jerry D. McCoy*

For Further Reading

Brown, Peter. 1967. *Augustine of Hippo*. Berkeley: University of California Press; Meer, Frederick van der. 1961. *Augustine the Bishop*. London: Sheed and Ward; Oates, Whitney J., ed. c. 1948. *Basic Writings of St. Augustine*. 2 vols. New York: Random House.

AUTOBIOGRAPHIES

Autobiographies by slaves in the United States served as a principal means by which the victims of the peculiar institution and abolitionists could offer an alternative perspective on slavery. For abolitionist groups like the Massachusetts Anti-Slavery Society, they provided eyewitness accounts that contradicted owners' claims of a paternalistic and even beneficent institution. They offered a vision of a nightmare society, filled with violence, torture, and promiscuity, in which all members, both black and white, were degraded by an uncontrolled exercise of power. Because of the potential effect of these autobiographies, abolitionist societies published dozens of them between 1760 and 1865. They were one of the most popular early-nineteenth-century literary forms, especially among Northern white female readers.

For the writers, these autobiographies presented an opportunity to tell their experiences in their own words. In doing so, they were able to claim an identity and selfhood that slavery had denied them. But this privilege came at a price. The authors could not assume that the readers would accept the story's veracity or even the narrator's humanity, so various devices were used to validate both the writers and their experiences. One such device was the authentication letter, a statement from one or more prominent whites that said they knew the author, that he or she was a trustworthy person, and that they had good reason to believe the story was true. The author was thus put in a position of dependence on whites, much as he or she had been in slavery; the writer's word alone counted for little.

Another technique for engaging the reader was to indicate the inhumanity and even sadism of the treatment experienced under slavery, and the slave narratives went into great detail about the cruelties inflicted on innocent victims. Whippings were shown to be, not merely straightforward punishment, but arbitrary acts resulting from the immoral character of masters. Such people enjoyed drawing blood and eliciting screams. Drawings were often included of torture devices, with explicit directions on how they were used. Such detail substantiated the writers' claims.

Another convention was to show the lengths to which slaves would go to gain their freedom. Henry "Box" Brown nailed himself in a shipping crate and was sent to the North as goods. Much of his narrative relates to the suffering he endured during the transportation. William and Ellen Craft were able to escape because she was light enough to pass for white. They dressed her as a master, with William as her servant. They managed to travel overland to freedom by making her appear to have a broken arm (because she could not write and one had to sign hotel registers and other papers) and a toothache (because her speech would give them away). Despite a number of close calls, they reached the North. Interestingly, the narratives that are now considered the most important pay relatively little attention to this aspect of the slaves' stories.

The most important means by which narrators made themselves and their stories convincing was through their self-presentation as people very similar to their readers. In one of the earliest and more important narratives, Olaudah Equiano presented himself as an English gentleman. The engraved image of him in the 1789 edition of his narrative shows a figure indistinguishable in dress and manner from his intended audience; the difference comes in skin color and hair texture. This identification is reinforced in the text as he depicts the culture and people of his African childhood. His Africans display close parallels in family structure, moral probity, diligence in work, and spirituality to the British. Equiano himself is the model of the hard-working entrepreneur who deals honestly with everyone. The flawed characters in his autobiography are those whites whose association with slavery and the slave trade have made them greedy, cruel, and generally uncivilized. He directed his narrative specifically to members of the British Parliament and clearly sought to present himself as a worthy subject. He called on them, out of common humanity, to end slavery.

Equiano's work is international in its frame of reference, but two major U.S. texts focus on national and local issues. Frederick Douglass became famous as a result of his 1845 *Narrative of the Life of Frederick Douglass*. He had managed to escape seven years earlier and by 1841 had become a successful lecturer on the abolitionist circuit. His book was written to counter charges that one so articulate could not have been a slave. In his story, Douglass gave particular attention to what Robert Stepto (1979) has asserted is the principal theme of the narratives: the link between literacy and freedom. Douglass's story of how he came

to be able to read and write, though it was against the law and against his master's explicit orders, is connected to his sense of self and desire for freedom. The escape from a slave mentality was for him more important than the physical escape, about which he said nothing in this first version of his autobiography.

Harriet Jacobs, in *Incidents in the Life of a Slave Girl* (1861), provides a distinct perspective as she describes what it meant to be a young woman in a social order in which white men had no limits on the exercise of their power. Her master constantly tried to seduce her, and, because of this, Jacobs was subject to his wife's jealous rage. Her appeal is to the understanding of virtuous white women who have not had to face the kinds of pressures imposed upon slave women. Both Jacobs and Douglass, more than other narrators, demanded recognition of their equality with their audience.

The slave narrative tradition did not end with the Civil War. Some 65 narratives were published by ex-slaves from 1870 to 1930, and during the Depression, the collection of oral histories was one aspect of the Federal Writers Project (over 2,500 narratives were collected in 17 states). About 6,000 narratives exist in one form or another, offering the voices of one group of victims of history. The tradition has been continued in literature with fictional versions, such as Ernest Gaines's *The Autobiography of Miss Jane Pittman* (1971) and Toni Morrison's *Beloved* (1987).

—*Keith Byerman*

For Further Reading
Andrews, William L. 1986. *To Tell a Free Story: The First Century of Afro-American Autobiography, 1760–1865*. Urbana: University of Illinois Press; Davis, Charles T., and Henry Louis Gates, Jr., eds. 1985. *The Slave's Narrative*. New York: Oxford University Press; Sekora, John, and Darwin Turner, eds. 1982. *The Art of Slave Narrative: Original Essays in Criticism and Theory*. Macomb: Western Illinois University Press; Stepto, Robert B. 1979. *From Behind the Veil: A Study of Afro-American Narrative*. Urbana: University of Illinois Press.

BABYLONIAN MUSHKENUM

There have been many attempts to make a clear determination of *mushkēnum* (an ancient Near Eastern social category), but none of them has been considered satisfactory by all scholars. *Muskēnum*, a loanword from the Sumerian existing as early as the middle of the third millennium B.C., is an Akkadian participle of *shukēnum*, a term having the root meaning of "rendering oneself prostrate." *Mushkēnum* has often been translated as commoner, and as a collective plural of poor or destitute. The term had a wide linguistic, chronological, and geographic range of usage, and is also found in Ugaritic, Aramaic, biblical Hebrew, and Arabic. In the Old Babylonian period (c. 2000–600 B.C.), the term was used in the Code of Hammurabi, the laws of Eshnunna, texts from Mari, and later at Alalakh and Ugarit.

It is in the Code of Hammurabi that the terminology has caused confusion. The code divided male society into three categories: *awīlum*, so-called nobles; *wardum*, slaves; and the ambiguous *mushkēnum*. The Babylonians did not always adhere to this division, and many people did not fit into any category. Some scholars have argued that all subjects of the king were considered *mushkēnum*. Although apparently of a lesser status, *mushkēnum* could own slaves. In fact, the slave of a *mushkēnum* who married a freewoman enjoyed more privileges than the slave of an *awīlum*. Moreover, there was a lesser penalty for those who assisted a fugitive slave of an *awīlum* as opposed to a *mushkēnum*. As in Hammurabi's code, the *mushkēnum* in the laws of Eshnunna also had a similar dependency on the state. It has even been argued that all who owned a house in Eshnunna were considered *mushkēnum* (i.e., state dependents). The Mari archives used *mushkēnum* as a collective term, and they were occasionally mentioned in opposition to skilled laborers.

Many of a *mushkēnum*'s obligations and privileges were personal and did not relate to status. The term may have been generic, referring to all people whose economic resources were dependent on the crown. The *mushkēnum* may have received a conditional land grant by the crown as a remuneration for a type of service. Robert Adams has suggested that *mushkēnum* might refer to the rural population or to former nomads. Giorgio Buccellati posits that in the northern Euphrates Valley, *mushkēnum*, when associated with *awīlum*, may have referred to land tenure.

In the Late Assyrian period (c. 900–600 B.C.), *mushkēnum* were contrasted with the wealthy and were associated in lists of syllables with the poor or weak. The Hebrew Bible also exhibits this latter usage, as there the term signified forced labor (Exod. 1:11), misery (Deut. 8:9), or underprivileged (Eccles. 4:13).

—*Mark W. Chavalas*

For Further Reading
Adams, Robert Mc. 1982. "Property Rights and Functional Tenure in Mesopotamian Rural Communities." In *Societies and Languages of the Ancient Near East: Studies in Honour of I. M. Diakonoff*. Ed. J. N. Postgate. Warminster, Eng.: Aris and Phillips; Buccellati, G. 1991. "A Note on the Muskēnum as Homesteader." *Maarav* 7: 91–100; Soden, W. von. 1964. "Muskēnum und de Mawālī des frühen Islam." *Zeitschrift für Assyriologie* 56: 133–141; Speiser, E. A. 1958. "The Muskēnum." *Orientalia*, n.s., 27: 19–28.

BACAUDAE INSURRECTION

In the late-third century A.D., several uprisings by peasants, agricultural slaves, and other lower-class elements occurred in the Roman Empire's western provinces. Contemporary writers called these insurgents Bacaudae, a name of uncertain origin. The social conditions that fomented the Bacaudae insurrections probably originated in the second century when plague and war created economic and social upheaval in many rural areas of Gaul and Spain, prompting repression by landowners and subsequent discontent among the rural poor.

The first recorded Bacaudae insurrection occurred in about 283 or 284, when numerous insurgents rampaged in Gaul. Imperial authorities, in the person of co-emperor Maximian, eventually succeeded in crushing the uprising within a few years. Bacaudae are not mentioned again until more than a century later when in 407, a large uprising of northwestern Gaul's agricultural poor wreaked havoc for 10 years until suppressed by imperial forces. Bacaudae were also active in other parts of Gaul and in Spain throughout the first half of the fifth century. Among their alleged aims was the desire to establish their own state, a state that owed no allegiance to Rome. This aim, and the objective of securing personal freedom from imperial authorities, have invited contemporary and modern observers to draw parallels between the fifth-century Bacaudae and the Germanic barbarians of a generation later who finally overthrew Roman rule in Gaul and Spain.

The Bacaudae differed from common bandits and brigands as their objectives seemingly included some measure of social change. Typical among their targets were upper-class rural magnates, whose estates were attacked and confiscated by Bacaudae and whose workers and slaves were liberated. Sometimes, the Bacaudae reduced landowners themselves to servile status, forcing them to toil on lands formerly their own. Slaves from the confiscated estates and elsewhere joined the Bacaudae ranks and played a prominent role in the uprisings. The proportion of slaves to other groups within the Bacaudae is unknown, since contemporary writers used common terms that denoted slaves and agricultural peasants alike.

Sources that mention Bacaudae were written by literate men from Roman society's upper classes. Their accounts of peasant uprisings and social upheaval in the countryside are, therefore, biased and disparaging toward the lower-class elements who formed most of the revolts' participants. An early fifth-century comic work has survived in which a wealthy Gallo-Roman named Querolus receives insight into the social structure and laws of a Bacaudae community. If the situation depicted in this work is authentic and historical rather than satirical and rhetorical, it would appear that the Bacaudae organized themselves along egalitarian lines and dispensed a primitive system of natural justice. The latter included punishments administered to captured landowners and forcible enslavement so that, as Querolus learned, "a man became the slave of his own slaves" (Thompson, 1952). Whatever the rhetorical or anecdotal nature of the work, it perhaps reflects contemporary perceptions of the Bacaudae, at least among the wealthy upper classes whose livelihoods were most threatened by the marauding bands.

—Tim Clarkson

See also
Apollinaris Sidonius, Gaius
For Further Reading
Drinkwater, J. F. 1984. "Peasants and Bagaudae in Roman Gaul." *Classical Views* 3: 349–371; Thompson, E. P. 1952. "Peasant Revolts in Late-Roman Gaul and Spain." *Past and Present* 2: 11–23; Van Dam, Raymond. 1985. *Leadership and Community in Late Antique Gaul*. Berkeley: University of California Press.

BAKER, MOSES
(1731?–1828)

Moses Baker was one of several African American black loyalists credited with laying the basis for the Jamaican practice of Afro-Christianity or native baptism. Baker was born into New York City's free black community and learned to read and write in an Anglican-sponsored Society for the Propagation of the Gospel school. He became a barber; married Susannah Ashton (a free black woman); and because of his Tory sympathies, was transported, along with his wife and children (Polly, Charles, and John), by the British to Kingston, Jamaica, in the spring of 1783.

In Kingston, Baker encountered George Liele, underwent a spiritual conversion, and, encouraged by Liele and fellow African Americans like George Vinyard and George Lewis, established a network of Afro-Christian or Ethiopian Anabaptist chapel/congregations that crisscrossed the island. In an 1803 narrative, Baker recounted how he fell on hard times, took to drinking alcohol, and became blinded. Using evangelistic language, Baker described his conversion from doom to redemption. Liele baptized him, and Baker then experienced a conversion that restored his spiritual and physical well-being. He moved to St. James Parish where, with assistance of planters Isaac Lascelles Winn and Samuel Vaughan, he constructed a chapel known as Crooked Spring and purchased a house plot in a community called Martha Brae.

Like Liele, Baker embarked on a mission to emancipate blacks. He traveled from estate to estate and amassed a following of several thousand. He encountered Moravian missionaries in Jamaica and was arrested during the Second Maroon War (1795–1796) on charges of sedition. Baker would have been transported to British Honduras had sympathetic planters not intervened on his behalf. In addition to achieving freedom for blacks, Baker was directly responsible for George Vinyard's formation of a chapel/congregation in Westmoreland Parish. Nineteenth-century Baptist missionaries later absorbed this congregation and chapel, eclipsing Baker, Liele, and the others.

—John W. Pulis

See also
Black Loyalists; Jamaica; Narratives; Slave Preachers
For Further Reading
Baker, Moses. 1803. "An Account of Moses Baker, a Mulatto Baptist Preacher near Martha Brae." In *Evangelical Magazine and Missionary Intelligencer* 11: 365–371; Brathwaite, Edward. 1971. *The Development of Creole Society in Jamaica*. Oxford: Oxford University Press; Pulis, John W., ed. 1997. *Moving On: Black Loyalists in the Afro-Atlantic World*. New York: Gar-

land; Rippon, John, ed. 1801. *The Baptist Annual Register*. London: Brown and James.

BALAIADA MOVEMENT
(1838–1841)

The Balaiada Movement in the northern Brazilian province of Maranhão was part of a wave of social unrest that marked the regency years (1831–1840) during the minority of Pedro II, the second emperor of Brazil. The occupation of one of the movement's leaders, that of basket maker (*balaio* means "hamper," a type of basket), gave the movement its name. The rebellion started as a confrontation between local elites, but it eventually spread to the rural poor and to slaves who fled in great numbers to join the rebellion.

Nineteenth-century Maranhão was characterized by small producers of cotton and cattle, and there was a substantial slave population in the cotton areas. In 1823, the estimated slave population in Maranhão was 97,132 out of a total population of 164,836; in 1867, the estimate for the province was about 50,000 slaves out of a total population of about 500,000 (IBGE, 1990).

The revolt began in 1838 in the southern part of Maranhão when Raimundo Gomes and a few friends attacked the prison in Vila da Manga to free Gomes's brother. From there, the group began marching through the region, gaining followers and support wherever they went. The situation created great apprehension in São Luís, the provincial capital. The leaders of the movement, Raimundo Gomes, Manoel Francisco dos Anjos Ferreira (the basket maker), and Cosme, a fugitive slave from the prison in São Luís, were all members of the lower class. Cosme became the leader of an army of 3,000 runaway slaves, which gave the movement the characteristics of a slave rebellion. In August 1839, the rebels conquered Caxias, the second-largest city in the province. There they settled down, created a provisional administration, and sent a commission to São Luís to negotiate an armistice.

The Balaiada rebels were not literary people. The written sources documenting the movement and its ideology are very restricted, but they do stress the rebels' belief in basic social values like the Catholic faith, the emperor, and the constitution. The rebels did not demand social or economic changes, but their frequent invocations of "sacred liberty" can be seen as an expression of the dream of personal emancipation for slaves, who were the driving force of the movement.

The rebels were unable to maintain the unity of the movement, which in the end was defenseless against government troops. The government's attack on Caxias was commanded by Luís Alves de Lima y Silva, later to become a famous general and the duke of Caxias. An amnesty was decreed for all rebels except the slaves, who were sent back to captivity, and Cosme, who was hanged in São Luís in 1842.

The Balaiada Movement is remarkable because it was one of the few comprehensive and prolonged slave rebellions in Brazil. Mostly, Brazilian slaves expressed their resistance in a passive or an individual way—some committed suicide while others ran away. Militant rebellion, as seen in the Balaiada Movement, was out of the ordinary as a solution.

—*Birgitte Holten*

See also
Palmares; *Quilombos*
For Further Reading
Fausto, Boris. 1995. *História do Brasil*. São Paulo: Editora da Universidade de São Paulo; IBGE, ed. 1990. *Estatísticas históricas do Brasil*. Rio de Janeiro: Fundação Instituto Brasileiro de Geografia e Estatística.

BALL, CHARLES
(1780–?)

Charles Ball was the author of *Slavery in the United States: A Narrative of the Life and Adventures of Charles Ball* (1837), which was first released anonymously as *The Life and Adventures of a Fugitive Slave* (1836). This antebellum slave narrative, viewed by some literary scholars as an archetype of African American literature, was used by abolitionists to dramatize the immorality of Southern slavery because of its sometimes symbolic presentation of the plight of individual slaves. Like Charles Ball, most successful slave runaways were adult males; thus, slave men wrote most of the slave narratives. For abolitionists, the critical component of all slave narratives was their firsthand recitation of the evils of slavery per se. However, the narratives universally point to the importance of "literacy, identity, and freedom" for antebellum slaves; indeed, the inclusion of these three points in most narratives is a convention of the slave narrative form.

For slaves, attaining literacy was linked to both personal identity and freedom, and obviously, without it, no narrative would have been possible. Various criticisms were directed at the slave narratives: abolitionists were accused of appropriating slaves' lives in ways similar to those used by slaveowners themselves, and skeptical readers found some of the narrative prose too polished or sophisticated to have been written by slaves. Nevertheless, most were proved to be authentic. Ball's own narrative has been compared with other contemporary accounts of events, agriculture, landmarks, and local types in South Carolina.

Ball's narrative addressed several questions concerning the slave's life, including how black slaves felt about white owners. He distinguished among his several owners as a slave in South Carolina, Georgia, and Maryland, criticizing one for being arbitrary in dispensing punishment although he also conceded that he had loved that particular master very much. Thus, the "intimacy" and ambivalence produced by slavery were both shown. Ball also recalled that he noticed a clear difference between African-born and native-born American slaves—Africans resisted slavery more.

Apparently Ball was familiar with African ideas because his own grandfather was a pure African who taught him certain African religious perspectives and especially cautioned him about the hypocrisy of white Christians, whose version of Christianity, he said, was "false" and really "no religion at all." Ball's relationship with his grandfather may have prepared him for the environment in which he found himself when he was sold to an owner from South Carolina: there, he had the experience of living among Africans who practiced both African folk religions and Islam. Historians have noted that the retention of African mores was facilitated when many Africans found themselves together in close proximity; and Ball recounted the practice of African rituals and mores in the slave quarters, such as burial practices based on certain West African beliefs that the deceased returned to the African homeland after death, or, at the very least, to a Christian heaven that would allow for retribution by slaves. Slave Christians, according to Ball, believed fervently in the idea that they would change places with whites in the world to come; that the last would become first.

—*Dale Edwyna Smith*

For Further Reading
Davis, Charles T., and Henry Louis Gates, Jr., eds. 1985. *The Slave's Narrative.* New York: Oxford University Press; Kolchin, Peter. 1993. *American Slavery, 1619–1877.* New York: Hill and Wang; Nichols, Charles H. 1963. *Many Thousand Gone: The Ex-Slaves' Account of Their Bondage and Freedom.* Bloomington: Indiana University Press; Raboteau, Albert J. 1978. *Slave Religion: The "Invisible Institution" in the Antebellum South.* New York: Oxford University Press.

BANDEIRAS

Bandeiras were movements of territorial expansion in colonial Brazil ranging from small cohesive groups of 15–20 men to larger expeditions of several hundred. *Bandeirantes* (participants in *bandeiras*) took the Portuguese flag to new territories and in so doing, encroached upon the boundaries of Indian habitation. They also brought back Indian slaves in slave-raiding expeditions that sometimes lasted two years or longer.

The *bandeirantes* used Amerindians, bond or free, as scouts, guides, porters, and food gatherers for their expeditions. Horses, which gave them the supreme advantage of mobility, were one of their few expenses. Some *bandeirantes* used firearms, but others did not because they were expensive and rusted in the tropical forests. Instead, they used bows and arrows or steel swords. The *bandeirantes* also used mastiffs to hunt Indians.

They were recognized for their skill as woodsmen and trackers, and they traveled light, often raiding Indian villages for food. Sometimes they dressed in high boots, wore suits of animal skins, and used padded cotton armor, but on other occasions they marched barefooted through the jungle. They consistently wore wide-brimmed hats and grew beards to protect themselves against the rain, sun, and jungle insects.

Antônio Raposo Tavares, perhaps the most famous of the *bandeirantes*, organized a 1628 expedition that traveled south and west from São Paulo with 60 whites, 900 *mamelucos* (mixed Amerindian-white Brazilians), and over 2,000 Indians. His expedition also included several city officials and chaplains.

The *bandeira* movement, conducted initially by residents of the São Vincente captaincy known as Paulistas, began with a cycle of Indian hunting during the late-sixteenth century. Any Indian tribe could be captured in a just war, and the *bandeirantes* could legally wage war on any tribe that threatened Portuguese rule. Until 1639, the *bandeirantes* were able to capture Indians with relative ease because of their superior weapons and military tactics. They advanced southward until they reached the Jesuit villages among the Guaranis where they found thousands of Indians already trained in useful occupations.

The *bandeirantes* pursued runaway Indians who had fled from settlers because the settlers forced them to perform backbreaking labor. Plantation owners needed workers and were willing to purchase Indian slaves from Paulistas, who transported them great distances from their original homes. The distance from home generally corresponded with the difficulty involved in the slaves' escaping.

Bandeirantes also searched for stones and precious metals. Their exploration made colonization in remote areas feasible, and they settled on the most efficient routes for travel and transportation across the hinterlands. They were active in the late-seventeenth and early-eighteenth centuries with the great gold rush in present-day Minas Gerais in Brazil. The *bandeira* movement ended in the eighteenth-century cycle of settlement in territories away from coastal areas.

—*Sharon Landers*

See also
Sugar Cultivation and Trade
For Further Reading
Boxer, C. R. 1962. *The Golden Age of Brazil, 1695–1750: Growing Pains of a Colonial Society.* Berkeley: University of California Press; Hemming, John. 1984. "Indians and the Frontier in Colonial Brazil." In *The Cambridge History of Latin America.* Ed. Leslie Bethell. Cambridge: Cambridge University Press; Schwartz, Stuart B. 1978. "Indian Labor and New World Plantations: European Demands and Indian Responses in Northeastern Brazil." *American Historical Review* 83 (1): 43–79; Vianna, Hélio. 1970. *História do Brasil.* São Paulo: Edições Melhoramentos.

BANNEKER, BENJAMIN (1731–1806)

Benjamin Banneker was an eighteenth-century rationalist who was also a self-taught mathematician, astronomer, author, surveyor, humanitarian, and inventor. Born the free son of a mulatto mother and a black father, Banneker learned some skills from his grandmother Molly Welsh, a Quaker schoolteacher who taught him the rudiments of an elementary education, and another Quaker, George Ellicott, loaned him astronomy books. Banneker combined his limited education with an unusual mathematical ability and earned a reputation for remarkable innovation.

Because clocks and clock makers were rare, Banneker as a young man had seen only two timepieces— a sundial and a pocket watch—but at the age of 22 he constructed a wooden clock, using the pocket watch as a model. First he drew a diagram of the watch's internal mechanism, and then he converted the diagram into three-dimensional parts. Built almost entirely of hand-carved, hard-grained wood wherever possible, the clock not only kept the time but also struck the hour.

In the late 1750s, Banneker began studying astronomy. After mastering astronomical concepts through books loaned by Ellicott, Banneker predicted eclipses and calculated the cycle of the 17-year locust. Later dubbed "the black Poor Richard," Banneker published more than 10 annual farmers' almanacs for the Mid-Atlantic states beginning in 1792. Finding that no publisher would take on an unknown black man's almanac, he wrote a 12-page letter on August 19, 1791, and sent a copy of his 1792 almanac to Thomas Jefferson, then secretary of state under President George Washington, refuting the pervasive belief that "blacks are inferior to whites." Jefferson responded by sending a copy of the almanac to the French Royal Academy of Sciences in Paris and Britain's House of Commons, and Banneker's 1792 almanac became the first scientific book published by a black American.

Banneker later participated in a historical survey of the future District of Columbia. He brought to the project a knowledge of astronomy and related instruments as well as a familiarity with surveying. As the first black presidential appointee in U.S. history, he assisted Major Andrew Ellicott during the preliminary survey from February to April 1791 and helped establish lines for some of the major points in the city. Accounts of Banneker's contributions include the legend that he played a pivotal role in saving the city, but Silvio A. Bedini's exhaustive search of surviving documents challenged the legend that Ellicott was able to reconstruct master city planner L'Enfant's proposals for the city from Banneker's memory.

Banneker was dedicated to exploring and applying natural law for the betterment of the human race. He proposed a federal government office entitled "Secretary of the Peace" and wrote *Plea of Peace* (1793). He supported public education, the prohibition of capital punishment, and the abolition of the militia. Antislavery organizations highlighted his achievements to science as an example of what African Americans can achieve.

—*Yolandea Wood*

For Further Reading
Allen, Will W. 1971. *Banneker: The Afro-American Astronomer.* Freeport, NY: Libraries Press; Bedini, Silvio A. 1972. *The Life of Benjamin Banneker.* New York: Charles Scribner's Sons; Green, Richard L., ed. 1985. *A Salute to Black Scientists and Inventors.* New York: Empak.

BANTU CULTURE

The word Bantu is derogatory when referring to a people or to their culture and is, in fact, a linguistic designation. Bantu languages are spoken by peoples from southeastern Nigeria across the African continent to Kenya and south to the Cape of Good Hope. Bantu-speaking peoples share a common grammar and logic, like people of European ancestry who speak Romance languages. "Proto-Bantu" is an early language and culture shared by Africans living in this enormous area.

There are approximately 3,000 ethnic groups in sub-Saharan Africa. Those speaking Bantu languages are one of the largest, and their culture includes diverse and various traditions. Many attempts have been made to classify culture based on the concept that a cultural area consists of several societies with certain common features, but with regard to Africa, the areas are too large to be meaningful, as each includes widely different forms of social and political characteristics. G. P. Murdock (1931) studied small clusters of peoples and grouped them according to linguistic and ethnohistorical characteristics. Although not completely accurate, this appears to be the best approach to understanding what is often called "Bantu culture."

There are more than 20 major groups of Bantu-speaking peoples. They include the Bemba of Zambia; Chagga, Gisu, Konjo, and Kikuyu of Kenya; Ganda of southern Uganda; Herero of Namibia; Kongo of northern Angola and southwestern Zaire; Lozi of Zimbabwe; Luba of southern Zaire; Mambwe of Zambia; Ngoni of South Africa; Nyakyusa of Tanzania; Shona of South Africa; Songe of Zaire; Swazi of South Africa and Swaziland, Tonga of Zambia; Tswana and Kgalagadi of Botswana; Yao of northern Zimbabwe; and Zulu and Xhosa of South Africa.

What all these various African peoples share with regard to their culture is the linguistic structure of their languages and the oral traditions they follow in singing, dancing, reciting, performing, sculpting, and painting their history and culture. The social, economic, and political organizations of the various Bantu-speaking peoples reflect the wide range of areas they occupy. The economy can be pastoral; sedentary agriculture; a combination of hunting, gathering, and agriculture; or fishing and river trade. Their kinship systems, religious practices, and political organizations are similarly diverse.

In southern Africa, the characteristic social unit seems to have been an extended patrilineal family headed by an elder male and including his wives, their unmarried children, married sons, and their families. Although social and labor organization was not uniform throughout the area, it is safe to say that women usually cared for the children, prepared the food, and cultivated and gathered the food crops while the men were responsible for keeping the cattle, hunting, tool-making, and engaging in various crafts.

As for political organizations, the area of south-central Mozambique may serve as one example. Near the end of the first century A.D., groups of households known as *nyika* became established as social units under the authority of a chief. By the tenth century, settlements known as *mapungubwe*, which included many *nyika*, had developed on the upper Limpopo River in southeastern Africa. This type of settlement was the first to feature stone enclosures called *zimbabwes*, and by the early-tenth century, such settlements exhibited marked social differentiation.

The arts and crafts of the Bantu-speaking peoples can be discussed as a whole because while the art of various peoples differs in form, the traditional roles of art and the artist in the cultural life of the society are similar. The artist is valued and supported by his or her community, and the objects of art are valued both for their aesthetic value and for their functionality.

The poetic and narrative forms of the oral tradition of Bantu-speaking peoples are rich and diverse but generally consist of myths; poetry, of which the praise poem is the most popular; and folktales, the best known being the animal trickster tale. In the Bantu tales, the trickster is a hare, as is the case in African American folktales. Proverbs and riddles make up the final category of the oral traditions. The cultural traditions of Bantu-speaking peoples today reflect the political issues of modern times and make use of new technology. Zulu drama is quite successful as serialized radio plays, and protest theater in South Africa makes use of the ancient traditions of praise poetry, proverbs, riddles, and folktales.

The idea that the drum is the only musical instrument in Africa is most inaccurate. There is an enormous variety of musical instruments on the continent, and they vary from region to region. The instruments of Bantu-speaking peoples consists of percussion instruments, strings, and winds. They range from simple to complex, and the instruments serve various purposes from social to religious.

Among some groups there can be restrictions as to the age, gender, or social status of the player. Among the Xhosa, only girls play the Jew's harp, which is a modern replacement for the ancient mouth bow. In Zimbabwe, lamellaphones, or thumb pianos, are used for keeping cattle content while they are grazing. All Bantu languages are tonal, that is, the tone or pitch of the word determines its meaning, so most of the musical instruments can be referred to as talking, with the talking drums being the best known. Zulu solo songs traditionally were accompanied by the ugubhu, a gourd bow. The instrumental melody was influenced by the tone requirements of the song's lyrics, but the tuning of the bow was determined by the vocal scale of the singer's voice. Today, the Zulu use Western guitars in the same antiphonal way and an interdependence between voice and instrument is maintained.

Some of the principal instruments of the Bantu-speaking peoples include rattles, clappers, and bells. Lamellaphones—the name varies from region to region—are unique to Africa and are used to accompany songs. In Tanzania and Malawi, gourds are used to simulate military band music. Lutes, fiddles, harp lutes, lyres, and harps abound throughout the Bantu-speaking areas. The Zulu ugubhu, Swazi makhweyane, Sotho lesiba, and Tsonga xizambi are string instruments that are still in use today.

The structure of the music is similar throughout the

continent as well as being characteristic of African American music. Basically, it is polyrhythmic and polymetric, complex, and cannot easily be equated with Western metrical systems. Four fundamental concepts govern the African system of timing: metronome sense, recurring patterns or themes (call and response), strophes and cycles that can be divided in more than one way, and patterns that can be shifted out of order, resulting in cross rhythms. Examples of interlocking techniques are prominent features in the drumming of the Gogo Bantu-speaking women of Tanzania and Mozambique and the drumming and dance of the Ngwayi of northeastern Zambia.

Like music, dance is highly developed and complex and is used for a variety of purposes ranging from social to religious, recreation to ritual. It is also divided by age, gender, and social status. There are four principal dance formations used by Bantu-speaking peoples: a group using a formal floor pattern, a group using a free-flow floor pattern, a group using formation with a leader emerging as solo dancer, and a solo dancer.

The architecture of the Bantu-speaking peoples varies by region. Franco Frescura's *Rural Shelter in Southern Africa: A Survey of the Architecture, House Forms, and Constructional Methods of Black Rural Peoples of Southern Africa* (1981) is informative.

The traditional religions of the Bantu-speaking peoples vary in ritual but consist, nevertheless, of some basic beliefs. Those beliefs are the idea of a supreme being who is the creator of everything, communication with the spirits of ancestors, and interaction between the living and the dead or the seen and the unseen. Although often described as pagan by outside observers, the traditional religions are and were pantheistic. In other words, the early Bantu did not see God as a personality; instead, they saw all laws, forces, and manifestations of the universe as God, and they worshiped and tolerated the worship of all gods of various groups. Thus, it was relatively easy for Christian missionaries to convert the Bantu-speaking peoples. For an insightful study of this topic see John S. Mbiti's *African Religions and Philosophy* (1990).

—*Nagueyalti Warren*

See also
Drums
For Further Reading
Bottignole, Silvana. 1984. *Kikuyu Traditional Culture and Christianity: Self-Examination of an African Church*. Nairobi: Heineman; Maxwell, Kevin B. 1983. *Bemba Myth and Ritual: The Impact of Literacy on an Oral Culture*. New York: Peter Lang; Murdock, George Peter, ed. 1931. *The Evolution of Culture*. New York: Macmillan; Sempebwa, Joshua Wantate. 1978. *The Ontological and Normative Structures in the Social Reality of a Bantu Society: A Systematic Study of Ganda Ontology and Ethics*. London: Macmillan.

BANTU MIGRATION

Many of the African peoples who became victims of or participants in the slave trade shared a common cultural bond in their linguistic origins. The word Bantu mainly refers to the linguistic classification of more than 200 different African languages. The Bantu migration, however, refers to the movement across the African continent of the various speakers of Bantu languages. Bantu speakers, although diverse in culture and lifestyle, seem to share a common origin. Extending over most of subequatorial Africa, the Bantu-speaking peoples probably are descendants of the original peoples of Guinea, Nigeria, and present-day Cameroon. Linguistic evidence points to these regions as the origin of Bantu people.

Represented in Nigeria are virtually all the indigenous races of Africa. Over several millennia, the Bantu have migrated in all directions, carrying the Iron Age into many areas of Africa. Anthropologists speculate that Bantu and semi-Bantu peoples migrated east and intermingled with Sudanese blacks. They had reached as far as Madagascar by 700 A.D., and the area the Bantu currently occupy includes approximately one-third of the African continent. Prior to their migration, approximately 2,000 years ago, the areas of central and southern Africa were dominated by the Pygmies and the San (Bushmen).

Anthropologist George P. Murdock postulates that the Bantu migration began as a result of their acquiring certain foods crops from Malaysia. These crops, which included banana, taro, and yam, enabled them to penetrate the tropical rain forest and spread across the southern part of Africa. Other scholars believe that the route of migration lay eastward, suggesting that the Bantu crossed the southern Sudan and then moved south. This movement began in at least the third century A.D.

The reason for the Bantu migration is presently unknown, but the initial migration took place at the Neolithic stage of development. The Bantu people made pottery and cultivated palm oil and yam crops before their southward expansion, but there is confusion regarding their use of metallurgy. Evidence of ironworking dates to the sixth century B.C. in the upper Nile and to the fifth century B.C. in Nigeria. By the third century B.C., iron smelting had spread as far as Gabon and the Congo, which would seem to indicate that the Bantu took a knowledge of metallurgy with them when they migrated south and east. At least one source suggests that once the techniques of metallurgy were known, they spread quickly through sub-Saharan Africa and had reached as far south as the present-day Transvaal region and KwaZulu/Natal by the third or fourth century A.D.

The Bantu are thought to have first reached Zimbabwe around the fifth century A.D. The San, who were probably the original inhabitants, were driven into the desert by the Bantu-speaking peoples. In a slow but steady progression, another group of Bantu moved east toward the Indian Ocean and then south along the coast. Still another group moved south onto the Zimbabwe plateau and spread into the highlands of western Mozambique. When Bantu farmers spread as far as the Cape of South Africa they encountered the Khoi, pastoral nomads who had inhabited the area since the first century A.D.

The Khoi probably provided sheep and cattle for the newly arriving Bantu, and evidence of ceramic remains and those of domestic animals indicate that there was a long and stable history between the Khoi and the Bantu in the South African region. Additional evidence of their long-term interaction is the presence of click sounds in many Bantu languages, a characteristic of the Khoisan language. The Bantu of South Africa—the Zulu, Xhosa, Sotho, and Tswana—all incorporate click sounds and also use Khoisan-derived words for domestic animals, words that are not used north and east of the Kalahari Desert.

Some scholars believe the division of the Bantu into two major branches, eastern and western, took place at the very beginning of the Bantu migration. Others claim it occurred much later and in the area centered on the lower Congo River. The western Bantu migration proceeded directly south from Cameroon through an area where cattle, sheep, and their agriculture were not well adapted. As a result, the Bantu spread westward below the tropical forest, arriving west of the Okavango River in southern Angola around the middle of the first century A.D. When they acquired cereal crops and domesticated cattle and sheep, these Bantu expanded even further into the savannas of southern Angola and western Zambia. Eventually, the languages of this western group split into Umbundu and Bantu, the Bantu being farther south. Today they include the languages of southern Angola, northern Namibia, and northwestern Botswana: Ambo, Herero, Kwangari, Nyaneka, Ndombe, Ngonyelu, and Ngumbi.

—*Nagueyalti Warren*

For Further Reading

Bohannan, Paul, and Philip Curtin. 1971. *Africa and the Africans.* Prospect Heights, IL: Waveland Press; Murdock, George P. 1981. *Atlas of World Cultures.* Pittsburgh: University of Pittsburgh Press; Murdock, George P. 1983. *Outline of World Cultures.* New Haven, CT: Human Relations Area Files; Nurse, Derek. 1980. *Bantu Migration into East Africa.* Nairobi: University of Nairobi Institute of African Studies.

BARBADOS

First settled by Europeans in 1627, Barbados quickly became the first true English colonial slave society in the Americas. Initially its settlers struggled to find a niche in the emerging Atlantic economy, despite their advantageous position east of the main Lesser Antilles arc. If Barbadians could find a suitable staple crop, they could exploit the island's proximity to the winds and currents and gain privileged access to transatlantic markets. Although they failed in their initial efforts to discover such a crop, planters soon laid the groundwork for dramatic changes that made Barbados England's most prized colony. Land distribution policies in the 1630s promoted large-scale holdings, and serious attempts to produce labor-intensive staples—particularly tobacco, cotton, and indigo—led planters to recruit large numbers of English indentured servants. Thus, Barbadians were poised to take advantage of an acute shortfall in Brazilian sugar production during the early 1640s and put their abundant labor supply to work on the new crop. Sugar shaped Barbadian society from that point on.

Once the sugar boom began, a declining availability of English indentured servants, coupled with shifts in imperial policy that stimulated the slave trade, made it more expensive for planters to import English servants than African slaves. Blacks soon outnumbered whites, and thanks to slave labor, Barbados exported about two-thirds of all sugar shipped from the English Caribbean during the mid-seventeenth century. The sugar trade was so profitable that by 1670, 70,000 people, three-quarters of them slaves, packed into the island's 166 square miles. The population of Barbados exceeded that of Virginia and Massachusetts, and at over 400 people per square mile, Barbados had a population density four times that of England. By 1800, Barbados supported 600 people per square mile, compared to about 75 on the larger island of Jamaica.

Barbados differed from other American slave societies in several important respects. First, its early commitment to black slavery, coupled with its small size, meant that the process of creolization (a process of social and cultural synthesis roughly corresponding to the proportion of native-born people in a plantation society) began and finished earlier than in most Caribbean societies. Creoles began to outnumber Africans sometime in the early-eighteenth century, and by 1807, the island's 5,496 Africans made up only 7 percent of the slave population. Second, female slaves outnumbered males by 1715, with significant consequences for family and cultural life. Finally, slaves outnumbered free persons by "only" four or five to one throughout the eighteenth and early-nineteenth

Slave labor enabled Barbados to become a major exporter of sugar by the mid-seventeenth century.

centuries, in distinct contrast to rival sugar colonies like those on Jamaica and in British and Dutch Guiana.

The early creolization of Barbadian society, the island's small size, its lack of refuges where autonomous communities of runaway slaves could develop, and its comparatively high proportion of whites made it more difficult to sustain African ways there than in other sugar-based slave colonies. Nevertheless, Barbadian slaves maintained a synthetic but distinctly West African cosmological vision. Music forms and post-emancipation social and political philosophies reflect a similar rootedness in African cultures, albeit much synthesized from diverse African origins and constantly modified to fit Barbadian conditions.

Plantation managers typically organized Barbadian slaves into three or four gangs, grouping them by age rather than gender. Thus, women often composed the majority even on the heavily burdened "first gang" while the very young and very old of both sexes performed lighter tasks on the fourth gang. As the supply of white indentured servants declined in the late-seventeenth century, many male slaves were trained as artisans, and slave women replaced whites in domestic service. A disproportionate number of these artisans and domestic servants lived in the port city of Bridgetown. Most slaves, however, remained on the plantations, where they worked 12-hour days and 6-day weeks at the demanding and sometimes dangerous tasks required by sugar cultivation. Additionally, many slaves worked for themselves. Black women dominated the ranks of Bridgetown's hucksters and street vendors, selling among other things produce and livestock from small plots cultivated during the interstices of their work weeks. Thus, they created their own economic life; here, as in the cultural sphere, men and women partially overcame the notoriously severe Barbadian slave regime to create some self-autonomy.

—*James D. Rice*

See also
Comparative Slavery in the Americas; English Caribbean; Indentured Servants; Sugar Cultivation and Trade; West Indies

For Further Reading
Beckles, Hilary McD. 1990. *A History of Barbados: From Amerindian Settlement to Nation-State.* Cambridge: Cambridge University Press; Beckles, Hilary McD. 1989. *Natural Rebels: A Social History of Enslaved Black Women in Barbados.* New Brunswick, NJ: Rutgers University Press; Dunn, Richard S. 1973. *Sugar and Slaves: The Rise of the Planter Class in the*

English West Indies, 1624–1713. New York: Norton; Handler, Jerome S., and Frederick W. Lange. 1978. *Plantation Slavery in Barbados: An Archaeological and Historical Investigation.* Cambridge, MA: Harvard University Press.

BARNBURNERS

One faction of the New York State Democratic Party, the Barnburners, opposed slavery's extension into new territories and, in 1848, broke with the other faction, the Hunkers, over this issue. The two groups had long coexisted uneasily because of disagreements on fiscal and social policies. Congressional introduction of the Wilmot Proviso (1846), an amendment against extending slavery into territory acquired in the Mexican War, provided a focus for the split. When the state convention in Syracuse, New York, elected Hunker delegates to the national convention and refused to consider the proviso, Barnburners walked out. At a mass meeting they resolved not to support any pro-extension candidate for president and elected their own national convention delegates. The convention refused to recognize the Barnburners' delegation or to endorse the proviso and nominated Lewis Cass, who was unacceptable to Barnburners. These delegates then proceeded to call their own convention, reaffirmed their anti-extension stand, and nominated Martin Van Buren as their presidential candidate. It was then that they were named Barnburners, for they were accused of being like the Dutch farmer who burned his barn in order to rid it of rats.

Meanwhile, Liberty Party members and Conscience Whigs were searching for an anti-extension presidential candidate who would be attractive to voters. The three anti-extension forces coalesced to form the Free Soil Party, which endorsed Van Buren's nomination and affirmed uncompromising support for the proviso.

Barnburners joining the Free Soil Party were motivated by various interests. While on the surface the main issue was support for the proviso, some Barnburners were most concerned with party control in New York State, others with wresting control of the national party from Southerners, still others with getting their share of patronage. Historians usually divide them into two groups, one exemplified by the politically minded Senator John Adams Dix, whose support for the Wilmot Proviso was restrained and who overlooked slavery's moral issues. The other was represented by Preston King, a congressman from upper New York State and an early proponent of the proviso who saw moral evil in slavery.

Most anti-extensionists were not abolitionists. A majority of the Barnburners were essentially racist and received support from a racist constituency. They repeatedly stated that they wanted slavery excluded from the new territories in order to preserve the rich new land for free white labor.

The 1848 election, which brought mostly Whig victories and elected Zachary Taylor president, prompted Barnburners and Hunkers to reunite. The Barnburners rejoined the state Democratic Party without obtaining any commitment to the proviso, rationalizing that slavery was instituted by local law, that the Fifth Amendment to the Constitution already prevented the federal government from creating conditions of bondage anywhere on U.S. soil, and that the Wilmot Proviso was redundant.

When Congress, aware that growing tensions between North and South threatened the Union, passed the Compromise of 1850, most former Barnburners supported it, but party unity remained shaky in both major parties. Although the more politically inclined former Barnburners remained Democrats, many of the more liberal ones, like King, joined the Whig Party in 1854 when that party reorganized to become the Republican Party.

—*L. Natalie Sandomirsky*

See also
Conscience Whigs; Free Soil Party; Wilmot Proviso
For Further Reading
Blues, Frederick J. 1973. *The Free Soilers: Third Party Politics 1848–1854.* Urbana: University of Illinois Press; Donovan, Herbert. 1925. *The Barnburners: A Study of the Internal Movements in the Political History of New York and of the Resulting Changes in Political Affiliations, 1830–1852.* New York: New York University Press; Foner, Eric. 1995. *Free Soil, Free Labor, Free Men.* New York: Oxford University Press.

BARRACOONS

Generally located some miles upriver, at the convergence of rivers, or where a river meets the sea, barracoons—enclosures or barracks (sometimes called factories) used for temporary confinement of slaves—formed one link in the African-European transatlantic slave trade. Secure from capture, slavers could signal when the coast was clear to come down the river with their shipments of captives. African traders retained sovereignty over the forts and factories that linked internal and external trade on that continent; few whites remained at these posts because of malaria and other diseases. Europeans paid for permission to build permanent or semi-permanent structures, which ranged from permanent forts like the castle at Elmina in Ghana to huts. The entire factory might consist of a barracoon, store, warehouse, living quarters, and a wharf. Europeans paid custom duties and business fees to conduct business. The entire factory, including the barracoon, could change owners frequently.

From the trader's perspective, barracoons prevented slaves from forming kinship ties, escaping, or dying, and slavers could use the barracoon as a holding pen until a shipload of slaves was collected. Black traders exhibited much sophistication by retaining sovereignty over forts and factories and deciding which commodities they would accept. African landlords guarded white slave traders' lives and property and stood responsible for their debts. In return, traders were expected to adhere to accepted standards of conduct. In this way, a partnership was formed to facilitate the sale of human captives.

Europeans paid an annual rent and a head tax on slaves exported. They might also have had to supply guns in the event of war, but they received reciprocal agreements to build forts, to move among specified villages, and to protect them from competitors. Barracoons allowed Europeans to haggle over prices and negotiate at leisure. The protracted trading process included festivals and entertainment and could take several days. Prices were determined by a highly volatile and fluctuating market, and payment could be in iron, silver, or copper bars; cowry shells; guns; or liquor. Slave prices were based on the ideal slave—a healthy adult male of five feet or more in height. The rate of sale was only three or four slaves per day, so completing the loading of a large ship might consume six months.

Caravans brought slaves and other commodities to the factories over miles of hostile territory that were often plagued by warring factions, so slaves normally arrived at a barracoon depressed, starved, abused, and exhausted. Most slaves entering the Atlantic trade originated in western and central Africa, but some came from eastern Africa. All were combined so people from different parts of Africa with various cultures and languages were housed together. Sold through African brokers, the new slaves faced harsh, psychological terror from leaving their villages to arriving on the coast to enduring a sea voyage that could last several months and cover vast distances.

—*Yolandea Wood*

See also
Elmina

For Further Reading
Law, Robin. 1991. *The Slave Coast of West Africa 1550–1750: The Impact of the Atlantic Slave Trade on an African Society*. Oxford: Clarendon Press; Rawley, James A. 1981. *The Transatlantic Slave Trade: A History*. New York: Norton; Tibbles, Anthony, ed. 1994. *Transatlantic Slavery: Against Human Dignity*. London: HMSO.

BASIL THE GREAT
(329–379)

Basil the Great, bishop of Caesarea; Gregory of Nazianzus; and Basil's brother Gregory of Nyssa, one of the Cappadocian fathers of Eastern Christianity, were known especially for their work on the doctrine of the Trinity. Basil's writings also advocated social justice for the poor and oppressed, and he urged masters to treat their slaves with kindness. Basil, a classical scholar and a social and ecclesiastical reformer, was too valuable to the church to engage in a life of monastic solitude. In 364, his friend Gregory of Nazianzus persuaded Basil, against his will, to accept ordination as a presbyter; Basil eventually became archbishop of Caesarea, supervising 50 bishops.

Basil fought politicians, monks, heretics, and even his own family and friends for the sake of church unity and social justice. He served as a social, theological, and political conscience in a time of turmoil for the Eastern Church, when Arianism threatened orthodoxy. In 368, his friend Eusebius, bishop of Samosata, invited Basil to visit him, but Basil turned him down, explaining that he had to care for those impoverished by hail, floods, and earthquakes. The letters to Eusebius speak of the spiritual union of all people under one master. During this time, Basil preached his homily of consolation. He lived a simple life, dressed in sackcloth, worked for the poor and the widowed, and even distributed his inheritance among Caesarea's poor. He built a church, a clergy house, and a hospital, none of which remains today.

Basil's letters demonstrate an awareness of social inequality, but he speaks of a spiritual unity that transcends secular divisions. Only people who labored in holiness had hope. Every Christian should work at that which has been assigned him and work within his ability. The letters show Basil in the midst of the turmoil when the emperor Valens threatened to divide Cappadocia. In Epistle 74, Basil hears the struggle for life in the marketplace, where creditors demand their money and men are beaten with whips. There is no direct mention of slavery in the correspondence, but there is a clear attitude of disgust with social injustice. The old institutions were gone, the government was gone, the rulers were gone, and despair was everywhere.

Basil wrote letters to support the old and the young who suffered and against the taxation of the Cappadocian farmers. In Epistle 90, Basil lamented that the church was plagued by heretics and the desert was filled with destitute people. How the older men grieve, he wrote, as they compared the older state to the present, but the young were to be pitied most because they were unaware of their depravity. To the bishop Valerian, Basil wrote there was a famine of love in both church and state. When Valens tortured the Eastern Catholics from 369 to the end of his reign, Basil wrote to the Alexandrians in 373 as their spiritual leader, urging them to keep the faith amid the tortured and dishonored bodies, the exiled, and the plundered property.

Two works specifically mention slavery and affirm the fact that Basil sought, not to overthrow the social structure, but to reform from within one's boundaries. Question 11, "Concerning Slaves," of *The Long Rules* refers to the example of St. Paul's epistle to Philemon, in which Paul urged the master to forgive his runaway slave Onesimus and treat him with kindness. By returning to his master, wrote Basil, the slave was obeying God, not the master. However, if the master should treat his slave harshly or force him to disobey God, then the church should intervene. In Chapter 55 of his work on monastic rules, Basil tells the poor never to do evil because of their social condition or to bemoan it. Again, this idea reflects the thought of St. Paul who, because of his faith, was content in whichever situation, including imprisonment, he found himself (Phil 4:11).

—*Judith T. Wozniak*

See also
Gregory of Nazianzus
For Further Reading
Deferrari, Roy Joseph, et al., eds. 1951–1987. *The Fathers of the Church.* 70 vols. Washington, DC: Catholic University of America Press; Farrar, F. W. 1907. *Lives of the Fathers: Sketches of Church History in Biography.* London: Adam and Charles Black.

BEECROFT, JOHN (1790–1854)

John Beecroft was a trader and British government official in West Africa who spent the last 25 years of his life engaged directly or indirectly in the fight against the slave trade. Until arriving in West Africa in 1829, Beecroft had been at sea and had also spent 9 years as a prisoner of war in France. In West Africa, he was in charge of the department of works on Fernando Po in the Bight of Biafra from 1829 to 1834 and remained after the evacuation of the settlement as a partner in a trading firm. He combined his maritime experience and his local knowledge when he led several expeditions inland by river for Robert Jamieson, a Liverpool palm oil merchant. Jamieson wanted to establish trading links away from the coast, not only as good business, but also as a way of encouraging African chiefs to give up their trade in slaves.

In 1835, Beecroft ascended the Niger to Lokoja in the steamer *Quorra* and the following year explored the Cross River. In Jamieson's specially built steamer *Ethiope*, he went further up the Niger in 1840 and up the Cross and Old Calabar Rivers in 1842. His findings were reported to the Royal Geographical Society, but he concluded that "there appears too formidable an array of difficulties to render [commerce on the Niger] likely to be of any practical benefit to Africa or Europe" (Dike, 1956).

During these years of trading and exploration, Beecroft established an unrivaled network of connections with African chiefs, gaining their friendship and respect. As the British government's antislavery policy became more interventionist, Beecroft's services were sought by the local naval authorities, and on nine occasions between 1844 and 1849, he accompanied naval officers on missions to secure antislaving treaties. When Foreign Secretary Henry Palmerston decided to appoint British consuls in West Africa in 1849, Beecroft was the obvious choice as consul for the Bights of Benin and Biafra.

Beecroft was active in supporting British economic and political interests in West Africa, including a further attempt in 1850 to secure a treaty with Dahomey, one of the most notorious slaving states. He was also responsible for ousting Jack Anna Pepple, another supplier to the illegal traders. But it was also at this time that the extension of British rule began. Beecroft was closely involved with the capture of Lagos in 1851, officially intended to turn it from "a nest for slave traders . . . to become a port of lawful trade" (Dike, 1956), but within 10 years it had become a British colony.

Beecroft died in office in 1854. His principal contribution to the abolition of the slave trade was in using his influence with African chiefs to cut off the supply of slaves to illegal slavers and to help provide the more stable conditions required by legitimate traders. Much of his work also laid the groundwork for later colonialism.

—*Anthony Tibbles*

See also
Jaja (Jack Anna Pepple), King of Opobo; Lagos
For Further Reading
Dike, K. O. 1956. "John Beecroft, 1790–1854." *Journal of the Historical Society of Nigeria* 1 (1): 5–14.

BELIZE

Belize was an unusual colony in the Caribbean because it lacked a sugar plantation economy and a different form of slavery developed there to extract economically important tropical woods. Slavery in Belize reflected the vagaries of the Anglo-Spanish imperial struggle to assert dominion in Central America's Caribbean coastal zone. Specifically, Yucatán and the Bay of Honduras composed a major hemispheric source for mahogany and logwood, the latter an important dye fixative for European textile manufacturers. England's capture of Jamaica from Spain in 1655 provided a secure base for exploiting Yucatán logwood and harassing Spanish shipping from there. Jamaica's capture fostered English cutting operations in Yucatán and to the south in Belize, where the British later introduced slavery.

Although seventeenth-century reports note a Spanish slave trade associated with logwood extraction, and even though English Puritans had established plantation slavery on Providence Island to the southeast by the mid-1630s, pinpointing slavery's advent in Belize remains difficult. Settlement was spontaneous and at first only sporadic, and the loose alliance of mostly uneducated buccaneers and adventurers created no formal political organization and left no written records. But by 1723, the British had introduced slavery into Belize in response to a growing market demand for the region's forest resources.

If slavery was integral to the forest industry, it also was the most potentially destabilizing aspect of the settlement's economy, and slaves mounted resistance from the first. This posed a serious threat because the ability to control the slave population would determine the settlement's very survival, especially in the face of Spanish attacks and the offer of freedom to escaped slaves.

Spanish officials in Yucatán, Guatemala, and Honduras mounted episodic attacks and granted freedom to escapees to undermine a growing English foothold in Caribbean Central America. Yet slavery was well established in Belize by 1737, when the first manumission was reported, and by 1745 slaves outnumbered whites for the first time.

Major slave revolts occurred in 1765, 1768, 1773, and 1820. The 1773 insurrection along the Belize River paralyzed the logwood industry and led proprietors to contemplate the possible end of their settlement owing to a rumored slave alliance with Spanish forces. Slave escapes persisted and were sufficient to sustain Maroon communities (settlements composed of runaway slaves) in the colony's interior for some time. Slave knowledge of these settlements apparently encouraged what would be the last major insurrection in 1820.

In defending their way of life, and what they claimed was an especially "benign" form of slavery, Belize proprietors argued that work conditions in the forest demanded that far more leeway be granted slaves than was allowed in the disciplined regimes of Caribbean and U.S. plantations. Slaves worked in the

bush for much of the year in small teams with considerable autonomy, scouting the forest and extracting logwood and mahogany under conditions that required them to be armed for hunting and protection against wild animals or Spanish and Mayan attacks. Indeed, in 1798 the proprietors were obliged to call on slaves to help defend against an all-out Spanish attempt to destroy the settlement. This event is enshrined in national ideology, in a discourse of racial democracy whose ideals remain both a challenge and an inspiration today.

Slavery endured in Belize until the declaration of abolition throughout the British Caribbean in 1838, preceded by several years of slave "apprenticeship." By that time, escaped English slaves had established communities in Yucatán, Guatemala, and Honduras, where descendants of those escaped slaves, and the populations with whom they mixed, reside today.

—*Michael C. Stone*

For Further Reading
Bolland, O. Nigel. 1988. *Colonialism and Resistance in Belize: Essays in Historical Sociology*. Belize: Cubola Productions; Bolland, O. Nigel. 1977. *The Formation of a Colonial Society: Belize from Conquest to Crown Colony*. Baltimore: Johns Hopkins University Press; Burdon, John, ed. 1931–1935. *Archives of British Honduras*. 3 vols. London: Sifton Praed; Stone, Michael C. 1994. "Caribbean Nation, Central American State: Ethnicity, Race, and National Formation in Belize, 1798–1990." Ph.D. dissertation, Department of Anthropology, University of Texas at Austin.

BENIN

Benin is the name of three separate polities in the history of slavery in Africa: the Benin Kingdom, Benin City, and the modern nation of Benin. The earliest, the Benin Kingdom, was an important destination for European traders interested in obtaining slaves and other commodities. The kingdom, internationally known for the high quality of its artistic bronzes, was founded in the fourteenth century and entered the historic realm in 1485 when Portuguese navigators exploring Africa's western coast first made contact. Centered in western Nigeria, at times the kingdom expanded as far west as Lagos, north to the Oyo Kingdom, and east to the Niger River. Ethnically, the Benin Kingdom was primarily Edo, although the state's boundaries did not include all of the Edo population. Other ethnic groups encompassed within the kingdom included Yoruba and Igbo.

In contrast to most of the major ports of call in the Atlantic trade, the Benin Kingdom and its capital, Benin City, were not on the coast but were located

A Benin king and his attendants are shown in this seventeenth-century brass bas-relief.

over 50 miles inland. Benin traded with Europeans, obtaining metal, guns, powder, salt, and cloth in exchange for palm oil, ivory, cloth, and slaves. Benin also maintained extensive African trade networks, obtaining leather, stone beads, livestock, and slaves from the interior in exchange for objects of local and European origin.

Benin City was located in low-lying country, originally covered with primary rain forest, which had been significantly altered owing to extensive cultivation around the city. A ditch-and-wall system six miles in circumference encircled the city, which was divided into two unequal parts. The larger contained the bulk of the town's settlement, and the smaller was made up of the elite district and palaces. European visitors to Benin City were struck by the spaciousness of the settlement, which contrasted with the cramped conditions prevalent in European cities.

Initial Portuguese contact was motivated by a desire to obtain slaves who could be exchanged for gold in the Fanti villages of the Gold Coast. By the sixteenth century, the Portuguese had established a Catholic mission at Benin. In the seventeenth century, other European nations began competing with the Portuguese as Dutch, French, and English traders began calling at Benin. By the mid-1600s, a significant market in Benin cloth had developed, and Europeans

purchased it for trade elsewhere in West Africa. When the number of slaves who were easily available on the Slave Coast to the west increased, European trade at Benin diminished throughout the eighteenth century. Benin's inland location and the difficulty of entering its rivers with larger vessels led most Europeans to bypass Benin, but some slave trading did continue there through the 1830s. The ivory and cloth trade did little to compensate for the diminished slave trade, and the palm oil trade, which had begun at the time of the first European contact, was unable to develop on the same scale as in regions closer to the coast or along navigable stretches of the Niger Delta.

The decreasing ability to attract European trade and the growth of Fulani power to the north led to a weakening of Benin's influence. Finally, in 1897, the British conquered Benin City after a massacre of members of a British trading party and incorporated it into the British zone of the lower Niger River. It was then that the richness of the Benin artistic tradition became known, as the British removed vast numbers of art objects from Benin City for sale to the European public. Analysis of the bronze artwork has demonstrated the existence of a highly developed metalworking tradition in Benin dating from well before European arrival.

Benin is also the current name of the country formerly known as Dahomey. It lies to the west of the old Benin Kingdom, which is in modern Nigeria, and constitutes the central region of Africa's Slave Coast. Several important slave-trading states existed on the Slave Coast, including the Hueda, Allada, and Dahomey states, but Benin certainly ranks as one of western Africa's most highly organized trading centers.

—*Kenneth G. Kelly*

See also
Slave Coast; Trade Goods
For Further Reading
Bradbury, R. E. 1964. *The Benin Kingdom and the Edo-Speaking Peoples of South-Western Nigeria.* London: International African Institute; Bradbury, R. E. 1973. *Benin Studies.* London: International African Institute and Oxford University Press; Connah, Graham. 1975. *The Archaeology of Benin: Excavations and Other Researches in and around Benin City, Nigeria.* Oxford: Clarendon Press; Ryder, A. F. C. 1969. *Benin and the Europeans, 1485–1897.* New York: Humanities Press.

BERBICE SLAVE REVOLT (1763–1764)

The Berbice slave revolt was an uprising in the Dutch colony of Berbice (later part of British Guiana and today part of Guyana) that lasted from February 1763 to April 1764. The insurgents almost achieved their initial objective, which was to drive all whites from the colony. Planned long in advance by two leaders named Coffy and Accara, a group of domestic slaves started the rebellion after a deadly epidemic, probably yellow fever, had begun among the white population. Carrying the revolt from the banks of the Canje River to plantation after plantation, the slaves killed many whites and set their houses on fire.

Completely demoralized, the whites who could escape flocked to St. Andries Fort at the junction of the Berbice and Canje Rivers. Except for the fort and a few plantations, the whole colony was in rebel hands by late March 1763. The few white men bearing arms would not have been a match for the insurgents, but relief troops from the Dutch colonies of Suriname and St. Eustatius eventually arrived. Two vessels from the latter appeared just in time to repel a massive slave attack on May 13, 1763, in which an estimated 2,000 slaves participated. Troops sent from the United Provinces (later known as the Netherlands) arrived later to defend the colony.

The attack's failure sowed discord among the slaves and turned tactics into a bone of contention, with Coffy opting for peaceful coexistence. He may have pursued a treaty such as the one concluded in Suriname between Maroons (fugitive black slaves) and the colonial government. For a little while, new danger arose for colonial authorities when a group of white soldiers from Suriname joined the Berbice rebels, leaving the Corantine region on the border on Guyana and Suriname exposed to a possible linkup of the rebellion with the Suriname Maroons. Not trusting these whites, the insurgents killed many of the turncoats. These events might have been successful, but at this point the sting had already been taken out of the revolt and the swift early successes gave way to a war of attrition. However skilled the slaves were in guerrilla warfare, their lack of provisions, arms, and ammunition became important in the long run. By the time the rebels eventually started surrendering, Coffy had already committed suicide after tasting defeat in a dispute with a fellow rebel leader. The black prisoners of war met a harsh fate with 128 being sentenced to death; they were broken on the wheel, hanged, or burned alive.

Maltreatment, including bad or insufficient food and cruel punishment, was the reason given by the predominantly Creole slaves to account for their uprising. They even identified some planters as the main culprits. Slaves outnumbered whites on the plantations by a wide margin, which probably helped the rebellion to spread rapidly. Harsh treatment may have been common, but it did not extend to the plantations of the Society of Berbice, a joint-stock company that governed the colony largely independent of the West India Company. The few slaves working on that company's plantations showed little inclination to join the rebellion.

The uprising destroyed most of the plantations in Berbice. Besides material damage, there were serious demographic consequences. The number of whites fell from 286 in 1762 to 116 in 1765 (not counting the relief forces), victims of the epidemic or murder. Many black lives were lost as well. Out of 1,451 Society of Berbice slaves and 2,700–2,800 private slaves in 1762, only 1,072 and 1,392, respectively, were still alive in June 1764. They died from disease, lack of food, or battle wounds, or they were executed after having been found guilty. Berbice's slave regime is not known to have undergone significant changes as a result of the rebellion, nor did events have any influence on Dutch metropolitan ideas about slavery and abolition.

—*Wim Klooster*

See also
Dutch Caribbean
For Further Reading
Goslinga, Cornelis Ch. 1985. *The Dutch in the Caribbean and in the Guianas 1680–1791*. Dover, NH: Van Gorcum; Hartsinck, Jan Jacob. 1770. *Beschryving van Guiana, of de Wilde Kust, in Zuid-America*. Amsterdam: G. Tielenburg; Netscher, P. M. 1888. *Geschiedenis van de koloniën Essequebo, Demerary en Berbice, van de vestiging der Nederlanders aldaar tot op onzen* tijd. The Hague: Martinus Nijhoff.

BERLIN WEST AFRICAN CONFERENCE (1884–1885)

The Berlin West African Conference, which established rules allowing for the partitioning of Africa, began November 15, 1884, and concluded February 26, 1885, after passing the Berlin Act. Except for Switzerland, all major European powers, the United States, and the International Association of the Congo attended; no African representatives were invited. German Chancellor Otto von Bismarck presided over the conference.

European powers began searching for colonies globally because of a combination of economic and social factors, including a need for new markets and cheap raw materials, a desire to invest surplus capital, and the status that colonial possessions gave one in the international community. Europe was not technologically equipped to colonize the African interior fully until the late-nineteenth century. Britain and Portugal became alarmed in 1879 when French and Belgian interest in the Congo basin threatened their territorial claims there, and as Germany attained world power status in the early 1880s, it also began claiming African territories. The scramble for Africa had begun, and it was under these conditions that the first major colonial conference of modern times occurred.

Initially, the conference's purpose was to resolve the Congo basin issue, but it quickly expanded. On February 26, 1885, the conference ratified the Berlin Act, which established several guidelines. First, European nations agreed to consult with other powers before making African territorial claims; second, conference participants agreed that territorial claims would not be considered valid until the territory was annexed and effectively occupied; third, delegates agreed that legitimate title to a territory could be acquired through treaties with African rulers. Fourth, conference participants agreed to recognize spheres of influence, extending into the hinterland, as an integral part of coastal claims, and fifth, navigation on the Congo and Niger Rivers would be accessible to all conference participants.

The abolition of slavery within Africa was necessary as Africa became more integrated into the world economy because the political structures required to maintain the slave trade were incompatible with cash-cropping. Africa had been incorporated into the world economy before the Berlin Conference, but the conference marked Africa's political incorporation. Conference participants condemned the slave trade but agreed upon no common action because the issue was not seriously discussed. Each participant would end the slave trade in its own territories.

The conference established many of Africa's modern geopolitical boundaries, reflecting that although the conference's subject matter was Africa, proposals were designed to solve European problems. European conflict was postponed, but Africa was left with a legacy of geopolitical boundaries adhering to no clear ethnocultural, geographical, or ecological rationale. Upon independence, many of these artificial states found internal multiethnic cooperation limited, interstate boundary disputes abundant, and development troublesome. Accordingly, the process of building African nation-states has been difficult.

—*Eric Martin*

See also
Abolition (Africa, British Empire); Africa; Capitalism; Marxism

For Further Reading
Boahen, R. Adu. 1987. *African Perspectives on Colonialism*. Baltimore, MD: Johns Hopkins University Press; Crowe, S. E. 1942. *The Berlin West Africa Conference, 1884–1885*. Westport, CT: Negro Universities Press; Wallerstein, Immanuel. 1986. *Africa and the Modern World*. Trenton, NJ: Africa World Press.

THE BIBLE

The Bible mentions slavery as a social institution and as a theological metaphor. The institution described is of different periods and kinds, depending on which book of the Bible one reads. Composed between c. 1200 and 125 B.C., the books of the Old Testament refer to kinds of slavery and dependent labor in the context of Bronze and Iron Age Near Eastern civilizations. The books of the New Testament, written between c. A.D. 70 and 120, concern themselves with the Greco-Roman era. Vocabulary poses further difficulties. The Hebrew word for slave, *'ebed*, means various things besides an actual chattel slave; indeed, the word often refers to military subordinates, royal courtiers, or a speaker's self-abasement before a deity. The Greek word *doulos* in the New Testament presents a similar ambiguity. Yet even when the original phraseology clearly designates a chattel slave, biblical translators since Luther and the King James Version have employed the euphemism "servant" to mollify the harshness of the slavery described.

Many key figures in the Old Testament are slaveholders. Their slaves are chattel; slave ownership appears as an unquestioned part of daily life, as normal as possessing oxen, sheep, camels, or donkeys. When Abram went to Egypt to reside there as an alien, he found favor from the pharaoh who gave him "male and female slaves" (Gen. 12:16, New Revised Standard Version), and after his covenant with Yahweh, Abram circumcised "all the slaves born in his house or bought with money" (Gen. 17:23). The patriarch was polygamous and had the slave Hagar as his secondary wife (Gen. 21:8–21). His son Isaac grew to own slaves and used them for manual labor (Gen. 26:25). Isaac's son and heir, Jacob, became "exceedingly rich, and had large flocks, and male and female slaves, and camels and donkeys" (Gen. 30:43). Another slaveholder was the suffering Job, whose challenge to God included Job's fair dealing with his slaves' complaints (Job 31:13–15).

At the height of its political hegemony, the Kingdom of Israel and Judah under the United Monarchy employed public slaves of state (1 Sam. 8:10–22), a practice that biblical writers claim dated back to the time of Joshua's conquest (Josh. 9:22–27) and continued into their own time. Those descendants of the Canaanites "whom the Israelites were unable to destroy completely—these Solomon conscripted for slave labor, and so they are to this day. But of the Israelites Solomon made no slaves" (1 Kings 9:20–22; parallel in 2 Chron. 8:7–10). Foreign slave labor built Solomon's Jerusalem temple, and the number and attendance of Solomon's court and temple slaves left even the opulent queen of Sheba breathless (1 Kings 10:2–5; parallel in 2 Chron. 9:3–4).

Some ancient Hebrews experienced enslavement. Joseph was sold into slavery by his brothers (Gen. 39–41), which some saw as a divine test of his character (Ps. 105:17–19), and from the wife of his Egyptian master Potiphar, the teenaged Joseph discovered firsthand the sexual vulnerability of a slave (Gen. 39:1–23). The Moses and the Exodus story provides a later narrative of enslavement in which Hebrews were forced into manual labor, refused basic supplies such as straw for brick making, and beaten by rod-wielding taskmasters (Exod. 5:1–23).

This kind of dependent labor, which allowed the Hebrews to continue to live in their own family communities, was not exactly chattel slavery. It was more analogous to the form of serfdom endured by ancient Sparta's Helots. Helotry is the subjugation of a neighboring, conquered population, not as "property" that can be bought, sold, or removed from family communities, but as an unfree workforce of the state. Interestingly, the fifth and tenth plagues (diseased livestock and death of the firstborn) that affected the people of the Exodus killed not only Egyptians but also some of their non-Hebrew slaves, apparently chattels (Exod. 9:20–21 and 11:5). Although liberated from Egyptian bondage, the ancient Hebrews after the Exodus continued using slavery as a theological metaphor to understand their covenantal relationship with their God, Yahweh, who had freed them, by calling themselves Yahweh's "possession" (Exod. 19:4–6 and 20:1–3).

Admonishments to serve Yahweh by remembering the Exodus "out of Egypt, out of the house of slavery [lit. 'slave-quarters']" recur throughout the Old Testament (Exod. 13:3 and 20:2; Lev. 25:42; Deut. 6:20–25; Josh. 24:17; Judg. 6:7–10; 1 Kings 9:9), and in biblical accounts of the Babylonian Captivity, when King Nebuchadnezzar II conquered Jerusalem and made its inhabitants "slaves to him and his sons" in Babylon (2 Chron. 36:20), the Exodus theme is echoed (Ezra 6:19–22 and 9:8–9). But in no place is the admonishment to remember the Exodus more prominent than in the Old Testament slave laws.

Found in Exodus 21, Leviticus 25, and Deuteronomy 15, the principal slave laws concern debt-bondage and manumission. The slaves discussed are of different kinds: foreigners and fellow Hebrews, apparently of low social rank. According to some biblical scholars, the three sets of laws functioned together in a single, comprehensive system of social welfare legislation to offset the debt-slavery that was rising in ancient Israelite society.

The material specific to destitute Hebrews enslaved by wealthy Hebrews does appear more humanitarian than the Laws of Hammurabi and other extant Mesopotamian legal collections that attempted to initiate periodic releases of debt-slaves. In the seventh year of bondage, one's Hebrew slave "shall go out free, for nothing" (Exod. 21:2). At this manumission, "you shall not let him go empty-handed" but provide livestock, grain, and wine (Deut. 15:13–14). The freedman then may "return to the possession of his fathers" (Lev. 25:41). Kidnapping to procure Hebrew slaves was considered a capital offense, a violation of the commandment, "You shall not steal" (Exod. 20:15; Deut. 5:19): "If a man is found stealing one of his brethren, the people of Israel, and if he treats him as a slave or sells him, then that thief shall die" (Deut. 24:7). Another law prohibited returning an escaped slave to his master (Deut. 23:15–16). Although designed to curtail and perhaps even to end debt-slavery, these laws apparently went unheeded, as debt-slavery of fellow Hebrews continued to be common throughout the biblical period (2 Kings 4:1; Amos 2:6 and 8:6). Judah's King Zedekiah tried to end it with his own large-scale manumission legislation (Jer. 34:8–22).

Foreign slaves did not enjoy the same benevolence in manumission or treatment. Israelites "may buy male and female slaves from among the nations around them," and "they may be your property" (Lev. 25:44–45). If a man strikes his slave "with a rod and the slave dies," the master is to be punished, unless the slave survives "a day or two," because "the slave is his money" (Exod. 21:20–21). Such religious concern for proper treatment of slaves is evident in the later wisdom literature of the Old Testament known as the Apocrypha: "Do not abuse slaves who work faithfully" (Sirach [Ecclus.] 7:20). Yet this concern exhibits no problem with regular disciplining of those disobedient: "For a wicked slave there are racks and tortures" (Sirach [Ecclus.] 33:27).

In the New Testament there are many references to slaves and slavery. There are individuals like the Roman centurion's slave (Luke 7:1–10; Matt. 8:5–13), the slave of the Jewish high priest (Mark 14:47; Matt. 26:52; Luke 22:50–51), the Ethiopian eunuch (Acts 8:27-40), the maid Rhoda (Acts 12:13-15), and the slave-girl fortune-teller of Philippi (Acts 16:16–24). Slaves also appear in Jesus' parables. One parable even praises the shrewdness of a trickster slave for dishonest business management in preparation for his fate (Luke 16:1–13). The goal of the parables is not so much to describe the behavior of actual slaves and masters as to communicate early Christian ethics through the slavery allegory. Dealing ostensibly with problem of debt among domestic slave stewards in Palestine, the parable of the unforgiving slave (Matt. 18:23–35) is not about slaves as a social order at all but about early Christians in Matthew's church (who may or may not have been actual slaves).

Warning of beatings "light" to "severe" and dismembering for unfaithful and lazy slaves, the gospel admonitions about watchfulness are not to inform readers about the ancient treatment of slaves but about the eschatological judgment of God (Luke 12:35– parallel in Matt. 24:45–. This allegorical use of slavery to express, not social description, but religious beliefs reveals that slavery was taken for granted in the time of the gospel writers. No extant saying of Jesus condemns the institution as intrinsically evil.

The apostle Paul, self-identified as "a slave of Jesus Christ" (Rom. 1:1) and even "a slave to all" (1 Cor. 9:19), also employs rhetorical use of slavery as metaphor. His language of "redemption" originates from the economic transaction that effects the legal manumission of a Roman slave (Rom. 8:23; 1 Cor. 6:20 and 7:23). Paul wrote that among baptized Christians, "there is no longer slave or free" (Gal. 3:28; parallel in Col. 3:11), yet he also addressed actual slaves in early Pauline congregations, which demonstrates that his theological statements about slavery did not translate into social activism. In 1 Corinthians 7:21–24, Paul advises believers in Corinth baptized as slaves "not to be concerned about it" unless they have manumission opportunities. In his letter to Philemon, the apostle described his prison encounter with Onesimus, an unbaptized slave and perhaps (but not necessarily) a runaway. Paul asked the Christian master's permission to use Onesimus in the service of Pauline missionary activities, probably a roundabout manumission request, which was legal under the Roman law of slavery (Philem. 11; see also Col. 4:9).

The New Testament letters include early Christian adaptations of Greco-Roman domestic codes of household management, which commanded slaves "to obey your earthly masters with fear and trembling, in singleness of heart, as you obey Christ" (Eph. 6:5; parallel in Col. 3:22). "Those who have believing [i.e., Christian] masters must not," exhorts the author of 1 Timothy, "be disrespectful to them on the ground that they are members of the church" (1 Tim. 6:2). Slaves must "accept the authority of your masters with all deference, not only those who are kind and gentle, but also those who are harsh" and endure even unjust "beatings" (1 Pet. 2:18–21). Masters, too, have directions to "stop threatening" their slaves (Eph. 6:9) and to treat them "justly and fairly" (Col. 4:1), and slave dealers belong in the same class as "fornicators," "liars," and "perjurers" (1 Tim. 1:10; see also Rev. 18:13).

This evidence shows that early Christians such as Paul and his followers had attitudes about chattel slavery that resembled those in the wider Greco-Roman world, and historically, the Bible has been used in debates over the moral legitimacy of slavery. Indeed, scriptural justification was the central pillar in the eighteenth-century proslavery argument while at the same time, abolitionist clergy found evidence in the Bible to justify the opposite and thus support their antislavery theology. In evaluating the merits of either position for scholarly biblical exegesis, we must appreciate the difference between ancient and modern slavery. We must also consider the tension between our time and the biblical periods and not absolve slavery or downplay its significance in ancient life.

—*J. Albert Harrill*

See also
Augustine (Saint); Babylonian *Mushkēnum*; Christianity, U.S. Antebellum South; Egypt, Ancient; Greece; Ham, Curse of; Hammurabi, Code of; Helots; Judaism and the Antebellum South; Mesopotamia; Paul (Saint); Proslavery Argument, General; Roman Empire; Slave Preachers; The Torah; Weld, Theodore Dwight

For Further Reading
Beavis, Mary Ann. 1992. "Ancient Slavery as an Interpretive Context for the New Testament Servant Parables with Special Reference to the Unjust Steward (Luke 16:1–8)." *Journal of Biblical Literature* 111 (1): 37–54; Chirichigno, Gregory C. 1993. *Debt-Slavery in Israel and the Ancient Near East*. Sheffield, Eng.: Sheffield Academic Press; Harrill, J. Albert. 1995. *The Manumission of Slaves in Early Christianity*. Tübingen, Germany: J. C. B. Mohr; Swartley, Willard M. 1983. *Slavery, Sabbath, War, and Women: Case Issues in Biblical Interpretation*. Scottdale, PA: Herald Press.

BILBAO, FRANCISCO BARQUÍN (1823–1865)

Francisco Bilbao was a Chilean author and political polemicist who criticized the Catholic Church for its enslaving effect upon individuals and society. A major nineteenth-century Chilean thinker and intellectual progenitor of Chile's Radical Party, Bilbao spent much of his life in exile because of his strongly voiced opinions. He studied at the Instituto Nacional under Andrés Bello and José Victorino Lastarria and produced his most famous article, "La sociabilidad chilena" (The nature of Chilean society), while still a student. This article condemned both Catholicism and the state as modern versions of slavery; Bilbao believed that Chile's colonial heritage was the main obstacle to the country's social equality and political democracy. The debilitating effects of tradition and dogma prevented Chileans from attaining full personal freedom and respect for individual rights; reason, fraternity, and love were the basis for future Chilean democracy. These ideas, voiced early in Bilbao's life, dominated his career.

Francisco Bilbao paid dearly for his determined attacks upon his country's traditional power structures. He was arrested and put on trial for publishing "La sociabilidad chilena" and was convicted of blasphemy, sedition, and immorality. Threatened with imprisonment, Bilbao left for France in 1844 and spent six years traveling in Europe, where he felt content with like-minded authors such as Jules Michelet, Edgar Quinet, and Felicité Robert de Lamennais.

Bilbao returned to Chile in 1850 and continued his attacks. With friends Santiago Arcos and Eusebio Lillo Robles, he established the underground Sociedad de Igualdad (Society of Equality), which took for its motto the French Revolution's cry, "Liberty, Equality, Fraternity." Bilbao continued criticizing church and state; in "Las boletines del espiritu" (Spiritual bulletins) and "Mensajes del proscripto" (Messages from an outlaw) he railed against Chile's historical development and blamed its archaic power structure, oligarchic dominance, public servility, and useless traditions for enslaving Chileans' minds and hindering societal development. These new attacks were even more threatening than previous ones because many of the younger clergy began siding with Bilbao. He narrowly escaped prison again by fleeing to Peru, dressed as a priest.

From Peru, Bilbao headed for Europe a second time, but he was shocked and disillusioned to find that the liberal France he remembered had been replaced by the empire of Napoleon III. Bilbao began doubting the future of European liberty and, instead, turned to America as humanity's best hope for freedom. "América en peligro" (America in danger) stressed America's responsibility to proceed where Europe had faltered and continue developing a free republican society based on reason, tolerance, and amity. Bilbao argued that Catholicism and republicanism were exclusive because the former required blind obedience and faith in the unexplained while the latter was inherently rational and conscious. In "El Evangelio Americano" (The American evangelist) Bilbao made this point forcefully when he wrote, "We hand over our conscience to the priest and to the Church and then we think we can keep our autonomy for our political affairs!"

Francisco Bilbao was a major intellectual force in nineteenth-century Chilean politics and letters. His exposé of Chile as a society enslaved by Catholicism and as an outmoded oligarchic authority fell within the "black legend" school of thought, which condemned Spain's colonial heritage in Latin America. His ideas constituted the founding platform for the Chilean Radical Party and greatly influenced future generations.

—*Karen Racine*

For Further Reading
Crawford, W. Rex. 1961. *A Century of Latin American Thought*. Cambridge, MA: Harvard University Press; Donoso, Armando. 1913. *Bilbao y su tiempo*. Santiago: Zig Zag; Lipp, Solomon. 1975. *Three Chilean Thinkers*. Waterloo, Ont.: Wilfred Laurier University Press; Varona, Alberto J. 1973. *Francisco Bilbao*, revolucionario de América. Panama City: Ediciones Excelsior.

BIRNEY, JAMES G. (1792–1857)

An abolitionist and third-party presidential candidate in 1840 and 1844, James G. Birney won pivotal votes that had the unintended effect of helping to elect the proslavery candidate James K. Polk in the latter election. Born into a Kentucky slaveholding family, Birney became a slaveholder when he was six, yet he never advocated the institution, both because of his family and because of his education. He studied at Transylvania University and later at Princeton, and after studying law in Philadelphia, he returned to Danville, Kentucky, to practice law. His father favored emancipation despite being a slaveholder himself, and in Philadelphia, Birney was further introduced to antislavery sentiment. Despite these factors, Birney gained ownership of even more slaves through his marriage in 1816.

In 1818, he moved to northern Alabama's Madison County, where he entered state politics, ignored his plantation, and increased his visibility as an attorney. As a member of the Alabama Constitutional Convention (1819), Birney was largely responsible for a constitutional provision prohibiting the introduction of slaves into the state for sale. Compensated emancipation was also provided upon an owner's consent. Elected to the state legislature in 1819, Birney was a founder of the University of Alabama. Birney was noted for his antislavery views, and after he opposed the state's support of Andrew Jackson's presidential candidacy, he was not reelected. By 1823, he had a lucrative law practice in Huntsville, Alabama. One of his more prominent clients was the Cherokee Nation, and he increasingly became an advocate for the Cherokee and an opponent of slavery. Raised an Episcopalian, he converted to Presbyterianism in 1826 and started supporting gradual emancipation.

During the next decade, Birney gained notoriety as an opponent of slavery, but he was not yet an abolitionist. In August 1832, he became an American Colonization Society agent, traveling across the South lecturing on the society's objective—to encourage black Americans to emigrate. Birney believed that Kentucky was an ideal state in which to advocate his antislavery sentiments, and he promoted his views in lectures and letters to newspapers and friends. Gradually recognizing that colonization was not the answer to slavery, in 1834, he wrote his "Letter on Colonization," first published in the Lexington, Kentucky, *Western Luminary* and reprinted in other newspapers and as a pamphlet. In this letter, he attempted to justify his resignation from the Kentucky Colonization Society and thus added to his standing among antislavery forces.

Living in Danville, Kentucky, Birney helped found a state antislavery society and planned to publish a newspaper advocating his views. After being personally threatened and having his mail interrupted, Birney moved across the Ohio River to New Richmond, Ohio (near Cincinnati), and published his paper there. Birney had become an abolitionist, and his pamphlet "The American Churches, the Bulwarks of American Slavery," published in 1835, was an established abolitionist tract. In 1839, he emancipated his 21 slaves at an estimated cost to him of $20,000.

In January 1836, Birney's inaugural issue of the *Philanthropist* attacked slavery, Democrats, and Whigs and advocated political action for abolitionists. The publication added to the distrust of and opposition to Birney's ideas, and his public appearances were frequently threatened with violence. He remained in Ohio until September 1837, when he moved to New York to become executive director of the American Anti-Slavery Society. Birney's belief in abolishing slavery by constitutional or legal means differed from the views of followers of William Lloyd Garrison, the best-known abolitionist. Birney's philosophy, using political action to end the institution of slavery, increased his national visibility.

In 1840, an Albany, New York, antislavery convention nominated Birney as the newly formed Liberty Party's candidate for president; he garnered 7,100 popular votes. Four years later, Birney had a determining impact on the presidential election. Running once again as the Liberty Party's nominee, he won 62,300 votes nationally, but more significant were his 15,812 votes in New York. Without Birney's role, these votes would probably have gone to the Whig candidate Henry Clay; instead, Democrat Polk won New York's electoral votes and the election. Polk and his party defended slavery and, if anything was learned politically from the election of 1844, it was the power of the vote in the attempt to end slavery.

In 1845, Birney suffered a crippling fall from a horse and remained partially paralyzed for the rest of his life. He continued writing in opposition to slavery—pamphlets, letters, and other antislavery tracts—but late in life, he became a bitter recluse. Birney died in New Jersey on November 25, 1857, a unique figure in the antislavery movement who proved difficult to label or characterize—a slaveowner who opposed slavery. As strident as other abolitionists in his antislavery views, Birney advocated a constitutional end to bondage. Through his writing, public speaking, and presidential candidacy, Birney became an important figure in the American antislavery movement.

—*Boyd Childress*

For Further Reading
Birney, William. 1969. *James G. Birney and His Times; The Genesis of the Republican Party.* New York: Bergman; Fladeland, Betty. 1955. *James G. Birney: Slaveholder to Abolitionist.* Ithaca, NY: Cornell University Press.

BLACK BELT

A geographical region spreading across much of the cotton-growing area of the southern United States, the Black Belt was a stronghold of the South's agricultural heartland and slavery. At first glance, the region seems to defy an accurate description. Two lines of thought define the Black Belt: one defines it as a distinct southern geographic region, and the other, used by sociologists, describes the same region's demographic characteristics.

Geographically, the Black Belt is the crescent-shaped 300-mile area stretching from central Alabama to northeastern Mississippi and even into Tennessee, although one noted sociologist believed the region extends into Georgia, both Carolinas, and even western Mississippi (Odum, 1936). It is an unusually flat region about 20–25 miles wide and is situated between 200 and 300 feet below the upland areas lying north and south. The region includes 5,000 square miles, 75 percent of which is in Alabama. The region drains primarily into the Alabama and Tombigbee River systems. Long considered one of the most desirable southern agricultural regions, the Black Belt takes its name from the rich black soil—calcareous soil formed from large deposits of Selma chalk. With its fertile soils, the region was ideal for cultivating cotton.

The presence of a large slave population to tend cotton planting and production led sociologists and historians to use the term Black Belt to describe the plantation society that emerged. This social science definition stems from the large black population that tilled the rich soil, as at the zenith of "king cotton" in the South, blacks constituted over two-thirds of the region's population. Some historians have concluded many white planters and farmers even avoided the region.

Throughout history, the Black Belt has been generally identified with Alabama. A Creek cession of land in 1816 opened Alabama's Black Belt for settlement, and by the 1820s, cotton and corn were the major crops farmed in the region. Only the Mississippi River valley produced more cotton than the Black Belt. More extensive settlements had developed by the 1830s, and the region remained a dominant cotton area until the end of the century when the boll weevil invaded the South and caused agricultural diversification and an emphasis on livestock production. Between 1830 and 1860, Alabama's Black Belt was easily the state's most productive region—it was home to the greatest number of slaves and was the stronghold of the state's Whigs. The region claimed three of the state's five capitals, including the current capital of Montgomery, and a significant number of plantations. With water travel available on a number of rivers, including the Alabama and Tombigbee, there was not much rail development. That fact helped preserve the region during the Civil War, as Union armies made few invasions into the area. Even in 1880 cotton production was still the major occupation of Black Belt residents.

Tenancy became a way of life in the region after cotton declined, and the area became nearly synonymous with poverty. In *Let Us Now Praise Famous Men* (1936), James Agee and Walker Evans depicted this poverty through text and vivid photography. Although little attention is paid to the Black Belt today, in history the region is still as distinct and as recognizable as the Carolina Piedmont and the Virginia Tidewater.

—*Boyd Childress*

For Further Reading
Odum, Howard W. 1936. *Southern Regions of the United States*. Chapel Hill: North Carolina University Press.

BLACK CARIBS (GARIFUNA)

At European contact the Arawakan-speaking island Caribs of the Lesser Antilles had close cultural, political, and military ties with mainland South American Carib groups. This affinity conditioned the cultural heterogeneity that evolved under a developing system of Caribbean slavery and marronage, cross-cultural marriage, and opportunistic trade and military alliances between Amerindian groups, escaped African slaves, and European colonial forces.

Island Carib settlements fiercely resisted European occupation and forged contingent alliances that adroitly played colonial forces against one another. In 1605, the *Caraibe* (their French appellation) allied under French command against Spanish and English forces, but at mid-century they would also combat French permanent settlement. Native insurgency precipitated a 1659 English-French treaty designating St. Vincent as Carib territory. Later pacts enabled French West Indian merchants to exploit extensive island-mainland Carib cultural links and trade networks. But Dutch, English, and Spanish forces nurtured their own alliances, and the individualistic spirit of local indigenous political leadership undermined Pan-Amerindian resistance prospects, favoring instead the emergence of "colonial tribes" whose heterogeneous ethnic formations reflected the historical exigencies of massive European colonial displacement.

The supposed cohesion of a distinct Carib ethnicity is belied by a readiness to cultivate strategic kinship, trade, and military links with neighboring indigenous groups, African Maroons (fugitive slaves and their descendants), and European merchants. To muster Caribs as "ethnic soldiers," Europeans fostered complex relations with native leaders and enlisted the Caribs to hunt renegade African slaves. This employment brought the Caribs firearms and manufactures, precluded their own enslavement, and mediated the worst effects of European militarization and settlement while furthering Carib cultural, linguistic, and biological hybridization. But colonial conflict also moved Carib groups to assimilate African Maroons, and the European effort to distinguish the sociocultural product of this process on the basis of race fomented ethnic conflict based on culturally specious but politically productive discrimination between black (phenotypically African), red (phenotypically Indian), and yellow (light-skinned) Caribs.

Early-eighteenth-century French and English settlement of St. Vincent introduced slavery, which in turn produced a marked African admixture and Carib multilingual propensities by the 1720s. English encroachment upon Carib lands for sugar plantations fueled unrest in the 1770s, and war in 1779 returned the island to France, with Carib assistance. Britain regained control in 1783, but long-standing indigenous-removal plans followed the English victory in the Carib War (1795–1796).

Black Carib internment and decimation by malnutrition and epidemic disease preceded their 1797 deportation to Roatán (an island off the coast of Honduras), where the English hoped they would harass coastal Spanish Honduras. A Black Carib–Spanish alliance resulted instead, but factions of that alliance broke away and fled to coastal Guatemala and British Honduras (Belize). Their descendants are known today as the Garifuna (from their Carib-warrior honorific, *Kalinago*), and over 70,000 Garifuna inhabit northwest Central American Atlantic coastal settlements, demographically depleted but economically sustained by migrant remittances from urban North America.

Garifuna assertions that they (unlike Afrocreoles) were never enslaved are evidence of the renewed significance of ethnic identity and heritage, and the same is true of linguistic revival efforts, the continued *Jonkonnu* tradition, and a renaissance of Garifuna ancestor rites, sacred drumming, dance, and song in Central and North American communities alike.

—*Michael C. Stone*

See also
Jonkonnu (John Canoe)
For Further Reading
Gonzalez, Nancie L. 1988. *Sojourners of the Caribbean: Ethnogenesis and Ethnohistory of the Garifuna.* Urbana: University of Illinois Press; Helms, Mary W. 1969. "The Cultural Ecology of a Colonial Tribe." *Ethnology* 8: 76–84; Kerns, Virginia. 1983. *Women and the Ancestors: Black Carib Kinship and Ritual.* Urbana: University of Illinois Press; Whitehead, Neil Lancelot. 1990. "Carib Ethnic Soldiering in Venezuela, the Guianas, and the Antilles, 1492–1820." *Ethnohistory* 37 (4): 357–385.

BLACK LEGEND

Julián Juderías coined the term Black Legend in *La Leyenda negra y la verdad histórica* (1914) in interpreting the attitude with which Spain's enemies referred to the bloody, cruel conquest of the New World by Spaniards. Conceptually, the term came to encompass the entire Spanish colonial era as one of stagnation and superstition. Images of tyrannical, greedy Spaniards are much older as they appear to have started when Aragon seized Sicily, Sardinia, and Naples during the thirteenth century. Bartolomé de Las Casas published his *Short Account of the Destruction of the Indies* in 1542 in an effort to convince the Spanish monarch to stop exploiting the Indians and to concentrate on their peaceful conversion to Catholicism, and the book was used as propaganda to fuel prejudice against Spain. Envy and fierce competition between Catholicism and Protestantism, which began with the beginning of the Reformation in 1517, fanned the flames.

Las Casas's work was published in Dutch in 1578 (there were 16 reprints in the Low Countries within 40 years); French in 1579; English in 1583 (under the title *The tears of the Indians, being an historical and true account of the cruel massacres and slaughters of above twenty millions of innocent people, committed by the Spaniards in the islands of Hispaniola, Cuba, Jamaica, &c.: as also in the continent of Mexico, Peru, & other places of the West-Indies, to the total destruction of those countries and Popery truly display'd in its bloody contours, or, A faithful narrative of the horrid and unexampled massacres, butcheries, and all manner of cruelties, that hell and malice could invent, committed by the popish Spanish part on the inhabitants of West-India together with the devastations of several kingdoms in America by fire and sword, for the space of forty and two years, from the time of its first discovery),* German in 1597; Latin in 1598; and Italian in 1626. Theodore de Bry, whose woodcuts remain popular today, gruesomely illustrated the Latin version.

An Amsterdam version of Las Casas, circa 1620.

Spain created a White Legend in order to try to counter the Black Legend's negative effects. The *leyenda blanca* painted Spaniards as stoic bearers of religion and civilization to the New World's ignorant, savage inhabitants. General Francisco Franco later added a new hue to the palette when he tried to reconstruct Spain's imperial past. He dropped the "ignorant savage" portion and emphasized the heroic attempts of Spaniards to protect the Indians and bring them the rewards of Catholicism and civilization—his version was dubbed *la leyenda rosa* ("the rose-colored legend").

Today, as Miguel Molina Martínez suggests, increased knowledge of the effects of "virgin soil" disease epidemics has caused a major revision of the Black Legend. As revealed by the violent emotions raised during the five hundredth anniversary of Columbus's 1492 landing in the Americas, however, the Black Legend is clearly not just a remnant of the past, despite our scientific enlightenment. It continues to engender negative stereotypes of Spaniards, Spanish culture, and, by reflection, all Hispanic peoples.

—*Lynne Guitar*

For Further Reading
Gibson, Charles. 1971. *The Black Legend: Anti-Spanish Attitudes in the Old World and the New.* New York: Knopf; Molina Martínez, Miguel. 1991. *La Leyenda Negra.* Madrid: NEREA; Quarta, Pietro Luigi. 1993. "Reflexiones acerca de la leyenda negra en la historia de España." *Rivista di studi politici internazionali* 60 (1): 92–100; Sánchez, Joseph P. 1990. *The Spanish Black Legend: Origins of Anti-Hispanic Stereotypes.* Albuquerque: Spanish Colonial Research Center.

BLACK LOYALISTS

Black loyalists were African Americans who served the British forces in various capacities during the American Revolution. Lured by proclamations promising manumission in return for service to the Crown (and by the republican ideology of liberty, equality, and fraternity), many blacks (some free, some indentured, most enslaved) declared their independence from slavery, joined the British, and toiled as victualers, laborers, and aides-de-camp. They served as auxiliaries to British, Hessian, and Loyalist militias and organized into formal military units like the Black Pioneers and the Ethiopian Regiment. Although the number of these loyalists is uncertain, scholars estimate that perhaps 100,000 black loyalists (and perhaps an equally large number of enslaved blacks) were evacuated, along with white loyalists, when peace was declared.

Loyalist communities began forming soon after the Revolution began. The British shifted and moved these loyalists from one location to another as military activities unfolded in Massachusetts, Pennsylvania, and New York and later in Georgia, South Carolina, and the West Indies. Populations in Savannah, Georgia; Charles-Town, South Carolina; and New York swelled as refugees, both black and white, migrated to British-controlled areas. The single largest black community formed in and around New York City. That city's population began increasing soon after the British occupation, and it had expanded to over 25,000 by 1783. Blacks lived in "Negro quarters," barrack-like domiciles converted from housing seized, confiscated, and leased from Americans.

Some indication of the black community's size and viability can be obtained by looking at evacuation returns and firsthand accounts of black festivities. *The Book of Negroes*, a listing by name, age, gender, place of origin, etc., of black people transported on British ships in the 1780s, shows an aggregate total of just over 3,000. Besides providing services to the Crown, blacks formed free communities. Eyewitness accounts of "Ethiopian balls," festivities attended by whites, at-test to such the importance of such events in both the black and the white communities.

Despite proclamations assuring their liberty, the black loyalists' plight was insecure, and negotiations concerning their disposition assumed top priority as the Revolution ended. Sir Guy Carleton, hoping to honor the British proclamations, interpreted Article 7 of the Treaty of Versailles (1783) to mean that blacks within British-controlled areas as of a given date were free. Despite this effort, military correspondence is replete with accounts of former slaveowners entering British-controlled areas to reclaim what they considered their property—slaves. Both sides confiscated slaves, and British or British-affiliated agents engaged in illicit trade to the West Indies throughout the Revolution.

The transport and relocation of black loyalists constituted one of the largest diasporas in the Atlantic region. Between July 1782 and November 1783, the British evacuated Wilmington, Delaware; Savannah, Georgia; Charles-Town, South Carolina; and New York City. Britain estimated that 50,000 tons of shipping would be necessary to remove the military, the loyalists, and their baggage, so with less than 30,000 available at any one time, Carleton opted for a series of mini-evacuations. Four separate convoys left Savannah in July 1782: the largest went to New York, the second to Charles-Town, the third to St. Augustine, and the fourth to Jamaica. Three convoys sailed in December 1782 from Charles-Town: the first and largest went to New York, the second to Jamaica, and the third went to England. New York was the last and largest port evacuated. A small number of blacks left there in June 1783 for Jamaica, a larger convoy departed for the Bahamas in August and October, and another group went to Canada in November 1783.

Organizing convoys resolved transportation issues but not relocation. It was one thing to offer a home away from home for white loyalists, quite another for blacks. Most blacks were transported to the Canadian Maritimes where they established communities in Nova Scotia and New Brunswick. Dissatisfied with Canada, substantial numbers opted for transport to England, and finding life in England little better, they later left for Sierra Leone in West Africa. A small, but influential, number of blacks opted for transport to Jamaica. Among the more notable of these were Moses Baker and George Liele, folk or itinerant preachers who laid the basis for the island's practice of Afro-Christianity. The history of black loyalists remains one of the untold stories. Although investigations into their diaspora have been undertaken, we know little concerning their plight and future in the Old World or the New.

—*John W. Pulis*

See also
Baker, Moses; Jamaica; Sierra Leone
For Further Reading
Hodges, Graham, ed. 1996. *The Black Loyalist Directory: African Americans in Exile after the American Revolution.* New York: Garland Publishing; Pulis, John W. 1997. "Bridging Troubled Waters: Moses Baker, George Liele, and the African-American Diaspora to Jamaica." In John Pulis, *Moving On: Black Loyalists in the Afro-Atlantic World.* New York: Garland Publishing; Quarles, Benjamin, 1960. *The Negro in the American Revolution.* Chapel Hill: University of North Carolina Press; Wilson, Ellen. 1976. *The Loyal Blacks.* New York: Capricorn Books.

BLACK NATIONALISM

Black nationalism is based on the conviction that blacks share a common ethnic background, cultural identity, worldview, and historical experience. Nationalist consciousness has inspired great movements throughout human history, and although the objectives may vary, nationalist movements generally espouse certain universal ideals, the most prevalent being freedom and equality. Historical circumstances often shape these ideals. Occasionally nationalism aims at institutional reforms within an existing polity that are designed to create a conducive environment for realizing defined and articulated objectives.

Racial/ethnic solidarity is perhaps the leitmotiv of black nationalism. The forging of this solidarity is often geographically exclusive, confined to a particular location—the United States, Africa, or the Caribbean. Sometimes it is geographically unifying, embracing several regions where peoples of African descent are found. This transatlantic thrust is both a reaction to and a reflection of the historical practice of justifying the dehumanization of all blacks because of the alleged barbaric and heathenish condition of Africa. The practice of mobilizing black consciousness of domination, oppression, and exploitation in pursuit of justice gives black nationalism the character of a resistant phenomenon, but black nationalism vigorously affirms the unique cultural and historical identity of blacks and insists upon the intrinsic essence and validation of their heritage.

Black nationalism has assumed varied forms throughout its history. "Integrationism" affirms black identity with, and subscription to, a particular state's values, and integrationists evince a determination to belong, to become accepted as an integral element of a state or nation. "Emigrationism," or separatism, entails the search for a new national identity external to the state or nation. At times emigrationism has been aimed at effecting relative isolation—either spatial or cultural—from an oppressor state's material and cultural influences, albeit within the same geographical confines. Spatial isolation is often described as "internal statism"; in cultural isolation, blacks construct race and ethnically based institutions and values to defend against the destructive influences of the hegemonic group they share territory with.

The history of black nationalism in the United States exhibits all of the aforementioned dimensions. Black nationalism originated with slavery and oppression, and the earliest expressions of black nationalism were the slave revolts/plots and the antislavery organizational efforts of free blacks in the North. Slavery induced a consciousness of shared experience and group solidarity. By the mid-nineteenth century, this consciousness, particularly the underlying experience of deprivation and dehumanization, had led to a determined struggle to define and assert an identity.

Blacks mobilized their resources in demanding an end to bondage and the granting of full citizenship, and nationalists such as Lott Cary and Paul Cuffe proposed solutions that were meant to enhance the cause of racial and social elevation, both within the United States and in Africa. Cooperative efforts of free blacks in New York, Philadelphia, Boston, and all of Ohio from the late-eighteenth century to the first half of the nineteenth represented the greatest expression of national consciousness to that time. These blacks clearly manifested a desire to end slavery and discrimination and to become fully integrated as Americans. Their failure to achieve integration unleashed an emigrationist consciousness and movements that mobilized black solidarity toward the assumption of an external national identity in Africa or the Caribbean.

The passage of the Fugitive Slave Act in 1850 heightened emigrationist consciousness. Led by Martin R. Delany, emigrationists proposed creating an independent black nationality abroad, and they urged blacks to build their own nation where they could develop their potential unburdened by slavery and racism. The outbreak of the U.S. Civil War in 1861 temporarily halted this trend as blacks, including emigrationists, were optimistic that the war would ultimately destroy slavery. For blacks, the Civil War was a war for freedom and the realization of the elusive American national identity. This expectation was only temporarily realized during the war itself and the Reconstruction period that followed, 1861–1877, and the end of Reconstruction meant a revival of black nationalism. With aspirations betrayed and threatened by a renewed Southern offensive, blacks embraced emigration in both its external and its internal dimensions. Some blacks sought a new beginning in Africa, others looked toward Haiti, and still others turned to the lands of the West and Southwest, in the direction of Oklahoma and Kansas.

By the early-twentieth century, black nationalism had coalesced into a strong Pan-African movement. Knowledge and consciousness of shared historical experiences of slavery, colonial exploitation and domination, and racism's pervasive and ubiquitous character, compelled blacks in the United States, the Caribbean, and Africa to engage in a common struggle. The ethos of shared experience, identity, and cultural and historical heritage created and sustained the solidarity that Pan-Africanism represented, and Marcus Garvey was most forceful in projecting this consciousness in the first two decades of the twentieth century.

The civil rights movement of the 1960s in the United States witnessed the flowering of black nationalism and consisted of a curious mixture of integrative and separatist values—from the moderate approaches of the National Association for the Advancement of Colored People to the militant traditions of Black Power, the Black Muslims, and the Black Panthers. Attempts by blacks to exercise control over their communities and such vital sectors and resources as education, religion, economics, and culture, and to wrest these vital aspects of their lives from the control and influence of forces and agents deemed hostile, represent enduring expressions of nationalism. Black cultural nationalism was most pronounced and productive during the Harlem Renaissance of the 1920s, when black artists, musicians, and writers used their talent and vocations to express, define, and project a consciousness of identity and nationalism.

Within the United States today there are loud echoes of past traditions of black nationalism. Integrationism shapes the consciousness of many black conservatives who harbor faith in "the American dream" and the notion of progress through industry and self-help. Cultural nationalist and separatist aspirations and values inform the vision of a black America that the Black Muslims and proponents of Afrocentrism project. But historically, the role of black nationalism cannot be forgotten as it served to challenge the prevailing image of black slavery in American society in the nineteenth century.

—*Tunde Adeleke*

For Further Reading
Essien-Udom, Essien Udosen. 1969. *Black Nationalism: A Search for Identity in America.* New York: Dell; McAdoo, Bill. 1983. *Pre-Civil War Black Nationalism.* New York: David Walker Press; Pinkney, Alphonso. 1976. *Red, Black, and Green: Black Nationalism in the United States.* Cambridge: Cambridge University Press.

BLACK SLAVEOWNERS

Slavery in the United States has traditionally been portrayed as an institution based on race. Generally speaking, this conviction is correct, but its propagation has led to the almost universal belief that all slaveowners were white and that all slaves were of African descent. In reality, while there were no white slaves, there were many black slaveowners from the colonial period to the Civil War. Census records, deeds of sale, wills of free blacks providing for the disposition of slaves, and records of freedom suits brought by slaves against free blacks attest that there were numerous black masters in the United States.

Records identify Anthony Johnson as perhaps the earliest black slaveowner, for Johnson, a former slave himself, acquired John Casor, a slave, in the 1650s. This early in the development of slavery in the American colonies, before custom had fully crystallized into law, no one questioned the propriety of a black man owning a slave. In fact, a local court sanctioned the right of free blacks to own slaves when it ruled not to give Casor his freedom when he sued Johnson for it. Another noteworthy case involving a freedom suit, was initiated by Sarah, a slave, against Mary Quickly in the 1660s. Again, no claim was made that Quickly, being a black woman, had no right to own a slave, and the grounds for the suit were unrelated to the color of the defendant. Although some states initiated legislation forbidding blacks to own slaves, none became law. A 1670 Virginia law specifically stated that blacks were not barred from buying any of "their own nation."

In 1830, approximately 3,700 free African Americans, mostly in the lower South, owned nearly 12,000 slaves. Some black masters held many slaves. Antoine Decuir and Martin Donatto owned 75 and 70 slaves, respectively. A Louisiana colony of free Creoles, descended from an eighteenth-century French settler and an African slave, contained 411 free persons who owned 276 slaves by 1860. One free black Virginian held 71 slaves, and two free blacks in South Carolina each owned 84 slaves. Two African-born mulatto brothers owned rice plantations in South Carolina worked by 100 slaves, and William Ellison, also of South Carolina, owned over 60 slaves prior to the Civil War. William Johnson, son of a white father and a mulatto woman, operated three barber shops in Natchez, Mississippi, owned 1,500 acres of land, and had at least 15 slaves.

There were two kinds of black masters and black slaveowning. Most black slaveowners had some personal interest in their property. State policy toward manumission was responsible for this type of slaveholding, as most black slaveowners had purchased

A slave is flogged by his black owner while another bound slave, perhaps awaiting a similar fate, looks on.

husbands, wives, or children and were not able to emancipate them under existing state laws. Phil Cooper, a slave in Virginia, became the chattel property of his wife in 1828 when she purchased him from his master, and Ermana, a slave woman, was the property of her husband—neither could legally be freed by the spouse. There were, moreover, some affluent free blacks who purchased relatives or friends, thus rescuing them from the worst features of slavery if not bondage. This was a benevolent form of slaveholding in which the slaves were not seen as, or treated as, slaves per se by their black masters but were merely technically enslaved.

The second type of black master was of a much different nature. There were some black masters who most assuredly did not practice a benevolent form of slaveownership. These masters considered their blacks as chattel property; bought, sold, mortgaged, willed, traded, and transferred fellow blacks; demanded long hours in the workshops and fields; severely disciplined recalcitrant blacks; and hunted down escaped slaves. These black masters had few pangs of conscience about selling children away from their parents or separating loved ones. For these free black planters, slaveholding was neither a philanthropic gesture nor a strategy for uniting family members. In these instances, free black masters had a real economic interest in the institution of slavery and owned slaves to improve their own economic status.

Two general characteristics of black masters were their racial heritage and their economic standing. The largest slaveholding free black planters were mulattoes, as slaveownership was a mark of membership in the free mulatto aristocracy. It would seem that, despite their own slave heritage, many black masters entertained few misgivings about the institution of slavery.

Although slaveowning was spread across the economic spectrum of the free black community, it was concentrated near the top. In 1860, almost half of the free blacks with real estate worth $2,000 or more owned slaves, and owning more than two or three slaves was confined to the economic elite since, whatever their desires, few free blacks could afford to own any slaves at all. Two of the wealthiest free blacks, Justus Angel and Mistress L. Horry, each owned 84 slaves. Cyuprian Ricard, who purchased an estate with 91 slaves in Louisiana, and Charles Rogues and Marie Metoyer, who had 47 and 58 slaves, respectively, were all members of the elite black class. Their need for labor, skilled and unskilled, drew them to the institution as it was the only viable source of labor in the South. Furthermore, one of the best capital investments in the South, besides land, was slaves.

Wealthy free blacks drew distinctions between themselves and poorer free blacks and slaves. The fact that free blacks in the South owned slaves underscores the distance that freedom placed between the free and the enslaved. Black masters were often trying to fit in with white society, and because they lived in a society in which more than 90 percent of the black population was slaves, their principal goal was to preserve their freedom. To avoid slipping backward into bondage, they had to give their freedom substance, and one way to do that was to become a slaveholder. The Civil War and emancipation removed from these free blacks their labor force, a significant capital investment, a means of belonging to white society, and often, their economic status.

—*Sharon Roger Hepburn*

See also
Ellison, William
For Further Reading
Koger, Larry. 1985. *Black Slaveowners: Free Black Slave Masters in South Carolina, 1790–1860.* Jefferson, NC: McFarland; Russell, John H. 1916. "Colored Freeman as Slave Owners in Virginia." *Journal of Negro History* 1 (July): 233–242; Schweninger, Loren. 1990. "John Carruthers Stanly and the Anomaly of Black Slaveholding." *North Carolina Historical Review* 67 (April): 159–192; Woodson, Carter G. 1925. *Free Negro Owners of Slaves in the United States in 1830.* Washington, DC: Association for the Study of Negro Life and History.

BLAIR EDUCATION BILL

In the United States, the legacy of slavery endured long after emancipation as former slaves struggled for political, social, and economic opportunity. According to an 1880 survey of the United States, 7 out of 12 children and one voter out of seven could not read or write, with the Southern states having disproportionate numbers of illiterates. To ameliorate this national crisis, the chairman of the Senate Education and Labor Committee, Henry W. Blair, a Republican from New Hampshire, introduced the Blair education bill in 1881, and it proposed equal distribution of federal funds for the instruction of black and white children. Although the bill did not deal with segregation, minimum standards of fairness toward newly freed blacks were required and "separate but equal" public educational systems were to be instituted.

The bill suggested a 10-year commitment of federal money, beginning with $15 million in the first year and decreasing by $1 million each successive year. Approximately 75 percent of the money would have gone to the South because the aid was to be allotted in proportion to state illiteracy rates. In various incarnations, the bill was passed by the Senate in 1884, 1886, and 1888, but it never reached the floor of the House of Representatives. By 1890, interest in the Blair bill had died completely. Had it been passed, this legislation would have allowed the Southern states to improve and expand their school systems to make education more readily available to impoverished whites and particularly newly freed blacks, 47.7 percent of whom were illiterate in 1883 compared to the 6.96 percent national average for whites.

The Blair bill was controversial and hotly debated, especially in the South. Worried that too many children were "growing up in absolute ignorance of the English alphabet" and arguing that "ignorance is slavery," Blair sought equal access to education for all, and especially blacks, in the hope of eradicating one of the legacies of slavery that continued to keep freedmen in bondage despite legal emancipation (Crofts, 1971). Blair's supporters viewed universal education as a prerequisite for solving problems of moral degeneration, economic lethargy, and uninformed voting that had existed in the post–Civil War era since an intelligent and industrious citizenry could better promote financial and political stability. Northern and Southern educators, Southern independents and Republicans, and blacks, among others, strongly endorsed the bill.

Ultimately, party politics, long-held racial beliefs, and suspicions of federal intervention in education defeated the bill. Many Democrats suspected that the legislation was politically motivated, designed to alleviate a tax surplus that had resulted from the high protective tariffs the Republican Party favored. Although proponents of the bill argued that it was the nation's responsibility to help the overburdened South, its opponents believed that federal intervention was unconstitutional and would result in the usurpation of states' rights since education was a power reserved for local governments.

Furthermore, many people perceived the Blair bill to be a costly and futile ploy to improve the lot of black Southerners, most of whom were deemed to be incapable of learning. Others worried that too much education would "spoil a good plow-hand" and enable educated blacks to compete economically and politically with Northern and Southern whites. Northern Republicans, who supported the bill but then sought reconciliation with the South, did not aggressively promote the legislation and abandoned the freedmen. In the end, the failure of the Blair bill reflected the divisive racial and political climates that continued to plague the nation in the era after Reconstruction, which ended in 1877.

—*Constance J. S. Chen*

For Further Reading
Crofts, Daniel W. 1971. "The Black Response to the Blair Education Bill." *Journal of Southern History* 37 (1): 41–65; Going, Allen J. 1957. "The South and the Blair Education Bill." *Mississippi Valley Historical Review* 44 (2): 267–290; Woodward, C. Vann. 1971. *Origins of the New South, 1877–1913*. Baton Rouge: Louisiana State University Press.

BLANCHARD, JONATHAN (1811–1892)

Influenced by nineteenth-century evangelical Protestantism, Jonathan Blanchard strove to correct the ills of society in the United States as an abolitionist, pastor, and educator. Following preparatory studies at Chester Academy in Vermont, Blanchard entered Middlebury College, also in Vermont, where he learned debate and parliamentary procedure. While there, he founded the *Undergraduate*, the first of several newspapers he would eventually establish.

Upon graduation from Middlebury, Blanchard assumed duties as preceptor of Plattsburg Academy in New York State. He often found his duties frustrating but proposed measures for improving the educational system. Here, also, he advocated the immediate abolition of slavery, a campaign he soon undertook with characteristic vigor.

While engaged in theological studies at Andover Seminary in Massachusetts, Blanchard met Theodore Weld, and Blanchard left school in September 1836 to become a lecturer for the American Anti-Slavery Society as one of Weld's 70 "disciples." He was sent to Harrisburg, Pennsylvania, where he met his future wife, Mary Avery Bent. Blanchard traveled throughout the region attempting to solicit support for the abolitionist cause.

Blanchard returned to his theological training in 1837 at Lane Seminary near Cincinnati, Ohio. He preached in black churches and continued working for abolition. Called to preach in the Sixth Presbyterian Church, he eventually accepted the position of full-time minister there, a church that had been formed as the result of a schism over proslavery attitudes at Cincinnati's First Presbyterian Church. When Blanchard was ordained a Presbyterian minister on October 31, 1838, two of the people at his ordination were Lyman Beecher and Calvin Stowe. While in Cincinnati, Blanchard had become acquainted with the influential Beecher family, and his wife had developed a strong friendship with Harriet Beecher Stowe.

Besides continuing his local antislavery work, Blanchard traveled to London as a delegate to the World Anti-Slavery Convention in 1843. In 1844, he journeyed to Quincy, Illinois, to deliver the commencement address to the Adelphi Theopolis Mission Institute, a school known for its abolitionist work. While in the region he took the opportunity to visit Knox College in Galesburg, Illinois, which had offered him its presidency. In November 1845, the Blanchard family moved to Galesburg, and Blanchard was installed as president of the college—a position he held until 1858.

Before he left for Knox College, Blanchard held a four-day debate with Nathan Lewis Rice over the question of whether slaveholding was a sin. This debate was eventually transcribed and published. Although removed from the fray of abolitionist work in rural Illinois, Blanchard made a strong attempt to maintain his former level of work. In 1850, Blanchard wrote a open letter, spanning seven newspaper columns, to Stephen A. Douglas concerning the Fugitive Slave Act. On October 13, 1854, Blanchard debated Douglas in Knoxville, Illinois, and in the debate Douglas sought to show that Blanchard was an extremist.

Blanchard's fervor would eventually cause problems at Knox College and with George W. Gale, founder of Galesburg, with the result that in 1858, Blanchard was in need of employment. He held a pastorate and lectured regionally until he was called to assume the presidency of the Illinois Institute (a Wesleyan Methodist school in Wheaton, Illinois, that stood for abolition, opposition to secret societies, and temperance). Blanchard restructured the board of trustees of the institute and named to it Owen Lovejoy, younger brother of the famed abolitionist martyr Elijah P. Lovejoy. It was the younger Lovejoy who, as a congressman, would sponsor the bill that abolished slavery in the United States.

Blanchard has been called a "minority of one." His self-recognized vehemence and sublimated tendency for vengeance seemingly kept him from rising into the inner circle of American abolitionism. His work was devoted, his spirit was strong, and his acquaintances were numerous, but his personality kept him from moving beyond regional to national importance.

—*David B. Malone*

For Further Reading
Detzler, Wayne A. 1961. "The Outreach and Origin of Jonathan Blanchard's Social Theory." M.A. thesis, Department of History, Wheaton College, Wheaton, Illinois; Kilby, Clyde S. 1959. *Minority of One*. Grand Rapids, MI: Berdinans; Taylor, Richard S. 1977. "Seeking the Kingdom: A Study in the Career of Jonathan Blanchard, 1811–1892." Ph.D. dissertation, Department of History, Northern Illinois University, De Kalb, Illinois.

BLEEDING KANSAS

Bleeding Kansas refers to the violent confrontation between proslavery and antislavery forces in Kansas Territory following the passage of the Kansas-Nebraska Act in May 1854. The Kansas-Nebraska Act repealed the Missouri Compromise (1820) by allowing popular sovereignty to determine whether or not slavery would be allowed into the territory west of Iowa and Missouri, which was a part of the Louisiana Purchase territory. Passage of the Kansas-Nebraska Act rekindled the sectional controversy over slavery, which had been held at bay by the 1820 Compromise, and initiated a chain of events in the mid-1850s that contributed to violent skirmishes on the plains. These skirmishes, in Bleeding Kansas, were the first informal battles of the U.S. Civil War.

A single question lay at the heart of the matter: should slavery be extended to the Kansas Territory? Prior to the Kansas-Nebraska Act, the Missouri Compromise (1820) had abolished slavery north of 36° 30' north latitude (Missouri's southern border). But once the Kansas-Nebraska Act passed the U.S. Congress, undoing the clearly defined boundary and allowing popular sovereignty to determine slave status in the territories, debate began as to whether the territory was to be settled slave or free.

Everyone understood that Nebraska would enter the Union as a free state; Nebraska lay to the north of the newly created Kansas Territory, and plantation agriculture seemed unlikely to thrive on the windswept, barren plains. But Kansas, south of Nebraska and just west of proslavery Missouri, was another matter. Northern abolitionists staunchly opposed the spread of slavery into any western territory, including Kansas. Southerners interpreted Northern antislavery rhetoric as a threat to their economic survival and way of life, and not surprisingly, Southern proslavery forces fought hard to ensure that Kansas would join the Union as a slave state, thereby preserving the balance of power in the U.S. Congress.

In June 1854, only a month after the controversial act passed Congress, President Franklin Pierce opened the territory for settlement. Settlers poured into Kansas from Missouri and other neighboring states, most of them seeking pristine farmland. In this regard, the land rush in Kansas was no different from that experienced in other territories, but the question of slavery hung thickly in the air. Whether or not the slave question motivated the settlers who moved to the region, all who staked a claim in Kansas soon took one side of the issue or the other. New Englanders organized the New England Emigrant Aid Society, and antislavery New Englanders began migrating to Kansas under the company banner. Meanwhile, proslavery Missourians had the same idea. If the matter were to be solved by popular sovereignty, as stipulated in the Kansas-Nebraska Act, each side was determined to form a majority in the region.

Part of the problem arose from the vague language of the Kansas-Nebraska Act, which stated that Kansans could "form and regulate their domestic institutions in their own way," subject only to the Constitution. Such broad language left the spirit of the law open to interpretation in a politically unorganized territory at a moment in history when settlers with opposing viewpoints were pouring into the region with the expressed purpose of "forming and regulating" domestic institutions after either the Northern or Southern pattern, which further intensified sectional grievances. Confrontation erupted almost immediately.

Most of the settlers who lived in Kansas in 1855 had migrated from neighboring Missouri, which meant that initially, the majority of the people living in Kansas favored slavery. When it came time to elect a territorial legislature in 1855, therefore, it seemed as though a proslavery legislature would be elected. However, mistrusting popular sovereignty and leaving nothing to chance, "border ruffians" from Missouri crossed into Kansas and stuffed the ballot box with 5,000 bogus proslavery votes. The election was thus illegal, but the territorial governor, Andrew Reeder, failed to dispute the fraudulent election even though he personally denounced it. It proved difficult to dispute the illegal election in a politically unorganized territory, and President Pierce, ever mindful of Southern Democratic votes, offered no support to Reeder if the latter were to challenge the election results. The illegally elected Kansas legislature passed several laws, including a strict slave code and a law punishing anyone who espoused antislavery beliefs.

Antislavery settlers and Northern abolitionists were outraged by the turn of events and set out to form their own antislavery legislature. By autumn 1855, the steady migration of New Englanders had resulted in an antislavery majority in Kansas. The new majority demanded another election for a constitutional convention to be held in Topeka, Kansas, in October 1855. Delegates to the Topeka Convention applied for statehood and also passed a law outlawing both slaves and free blacks from Kansas Territory, perfectly expressing both antislavery and racist views in one stroke. Furthermore, the delegates decided to hold a general election in January 1856 so Kansans could elect a legal—and an antislavery—legislature and governor. Kansas then had two governments, each claiming legitimacy.

Settlers continued to stream into Kansas, and tensions rose with each passing day. Events began to happen very quickly. On May 21, 1856, border ruffians attacked Lawrence, Kansas, an antislavery town. They set buildings on fire, destroyed businesses, and intimidated residents. Abolitionist John Brown reacted murderously to the Lawrence incident, hacking to death several of the border ruffians during a night raid he staged on May 24 with seven other antislavery supporters. The violence escalated from there and led to open warfare between the two sides. It took swift action by federal troops to quiet the quarreling Kansans, but approximately 200 people had died before they were able to do so.

Meanwhile, other national events served to divide proslavery and antislavery forces in Kansas. Both the caning of Senator Charles Sumner by Representative Preston Brooks in 1856 and the Dred Scott decision of the Supreme Court in 1857 added fuel to the fire. Further, a chain of ill-advised and shortsighted political decisions by President James Buchanan underscored tensions rather than dissipating them.

The fraudulently elected proslavery legislature in Kansas organized its own election of delegates for a constitutional convention to meet at Lecompton, Kansas, in October 1857. The purpose of the convention was to draft a document requesting admission to the United States as a legal state. The move was similar to the one that had been made by delegates at the Topeka Convention, which meant there were now two applications for admission to the United States, one as a free state, the other as a slave state—with the supporters of each claiming to legitimately represent popular sovereignty in Kansas.

At this critical juncture, Buchanan appointed Robert J. Walker as territorial governor of Kansas in 1857. Walker had been elected to the U.S. Senate from Mississippi, and he placed the Union above sectional conflicts. He saw in the Kansas conflict an opportunity for popular sovereignty to succeed, even as the success of popular sovereignty might help his Democratic Party. Walker, with Buchanan's blessing, pledged to the free-state voters that the new constitution would be submitted to a fair vote.

But Walker only increased the polarity between the two sides. Essentially, the Lecompton constitution made Kansas a slave state, but to assuage the antislavery voters, Walker persuaded the proslavery convention delegates to allow voters to vote on only one clause in the constitution, "with slavery" or "with no slavery," rather than on the whole constitution. Voters could vote one way or the other, but the "with no slavery" clause excluded even those slaves already residing in Kansas, even though they could not be "interfered" with under other terms of the constitution. The election was set for December 21, 1857.

Antislavery voters boycotted the election, claiming that the entire process and the Lecompton Convention were rigged to favor the minority proslavery forces. At this crucial moment, President Buchanan reneged on his promise to Walker regarding a fair vote and chose instead to support the Lecompton Convention, knowing full well that the convention would vote to become a slave state in spite of the antislavery majority then living in Kansas. Buchanan depended heavily on Southern congressmen for political support, which explains this capitulation to Southern interests.

Walker resigned, and the result of Buchanan's political bargain was increased sectionalization and a step closer to civil war. Northern abolitionists, antislavery Northern Democrats, Republicans, and the antislavery majority in Kansas were incensed by the turn of events. On December 21, 1857, when the proslavery clause of the Lecompton constitution passed at the convention, the acting governor in Kansas, Frederick Stanton, called for another election to vote on the Lecompton constitution. On January 4, 1858, Kansans voted overwhelmingly to reject the constitution. Stubborn and concerned more about his own political career than about popular sovereignty, Buchanan stuck to his position and continued to back the Lecompton constitution. He forced the bill through Congress, even though he splintered the Democratic Party into sectionalized, warring factions. The U.S. Congress accepted the proslavery Lecompton constitution in March 1858.

Southerners felt certain that Kansans would now accept the slavery clause because to reject the slavery clause, they would have to reject the constitution itself, which would delay Kansas statehood until the population reached a population of 90,000. But Kansans held firm to their convictions. When the matter came to a vote on August 2, 1858, Kansas voters rejected the Lecompton constitution by a vote of 11,300 to 1,788. The events inspired by Bleeding Kansas now came to an end; the antislavery forces had won. Kansas was admitted as a free state on January 29, 1861, only three months before the firing on Fort Sumter began the U.S. Civil War.

—*Julie R. Nelson*

See also
Brooks-Sumner Affair; Brown, John; Fugitive Slave Act of 1850; Lecompton Constitution; Pottawatomie Massacre

BODIN, JEAN (1530–1596)

The Renaissance French jurist, political theorist, and administrator Jean Bodin attacked slavery's natural law foundation in his *Six Books of the Commonwealth* published in 1576. Bodin was trained in Roman law and in the cus-

tomary law of northern France, but his writings display the formal clarity of a scholastic argumentation seeking to uncover and explain the universal laws of political systems. French Renaissance literary criticism also influenced his *Commonwealth*, as did the tension between inalienable individual freedom and the need for absolute monarchy. French religious wars (Catholic versus Calvinist Huguenot) forced Bodin into a fairly neutral corner, one that required a rethinking of established orthodoxy on many issues, including slavery. Bodin developed conclusions about slavery in Chapter 5 of Book 1 in the *Six Books of the Commonwealth,* which he wrote while a household member of the Duke of Alençon, who led a political party that stressed the absolute monarch's application of tolerant rationalism in dealing with the era's religious struggles.

Bodin posited that slavery was either natural and profitable to the commonwealth or unnatural and unprofitable. References to Aristotle's ideas about natural law traditionally upheld slavery as nature (and among Christians, God) had created some people to be servile and some to be leaders. History, of which Bodin was well informed, showed that all civilizations had used slaves, from the Flood to the present and that even the "holiest of men" used slave labor. Slavery began as a charitable act that saved the lives of captives and criminals who would otherwise have been slain. He countered the natural capacity notion by arguing that better or wiser men often became slaves of meaner or stupider men and that even men of seemingly servile nature should not be deprived of natural liberties. "We must not measure the laws of nature by men's actions, be they ever so old and inveterate" (Tooley, 1955). He attacked custom and usage by demonstrating that like slavery, human sacrifice, of which none of his readers would presumably approve, was also used by many peoples—indeed, often by pious ones. Just as free will often undoes God's plan for humans, even turning the vile into the pious, so it was with human sacrifice and slavery. Regarding the "charity" behind slavery, of what use is a corpse to a captor when he can command labor from the living slave? Charity is not self-serving; slavery is.

Whatever profitability slaves provide a commonwealth is offset by the fears that are induced in the general populace and by the cruel culture that naturally attends the institution. Bodin drew heavily on classical history for examples of slave treachery and the resultant vengeance exacted by masters or the state. Since slaves were untrustworthy, they were traditionally deprived of arms and a role in warfare. Bodin traced the historical relationship of Christianity to slavery, noting numerous examples of late-classical manumission and manumission following the early

Muslim example of freeing converts. He claimed that slavery caused political unrest wherever it existed in Christian Europe until it vanished by the time of the High Middle Ages.

Bodin treated contemporary slavery as a perversion of divine will, arguing that the Portuguese and the Spanish had revived large-scale slavery by converting Africans from Islam and illicitly retaining them as slaves. Bodin also witnessed a revival of slavery among the Tatars, Turks, and people of the Barbary Coast. France, conversely, freed slaves who entered the country, according to anecdotal evidence that he presents. Ultimately, though, natural law is subsumed by divine law, which states clearly that servitude as a penalty or restitution should last no more than seven years, as was Jewish (and Tatar) custom. After that period of time, it is up to the slave to choose freedom or continued service.

Yet Bodin was no simple idealist. He recognized that the newly enfranchised could easily become unemployed beggars or brigands, so he urged incremental manumission and providing persons with a trade when slavery was involved. Bodin's combination of moral, practical, and historical arguments to end slavery is intriguing, but his detachment from the terribly important colonial experience and the waning interest in argument by historical example lessened the potential effect of his ideas.

—*Joseph P. Byrne*

For Further Reading
Bodin, Jean. 1962. *The Six Bookes of the Commonweale.* Ed. K. D. McRae. Cambridge, MA: Harvard University Press; Bodin, Jean. 1986. *Les six livres de la république.* Paris: Librairie Arthème Fayard; Tooley, M. J., ed. and trans. 1955. *Six Books of the Commonwealth by Jean Bodin.* Oxford: Basil Blackwell.

BOERS

Boers (literally meaning "farmers") were descendants of Dutch, German, and French Huguenot settlers who arrived in what is now South Africa in the seventeenth and eighteenth centuries. A fiercely independent people who fell under British control, the Boers used a strict, Calvinist biblical interpretation to justify their continuation of slavery long after the institution had been officially abolished in the rest of the British Empire. In fact, British attempts to end the Boer practice of enslaving southern Africa's native peoples was one cause of a massive Boer migration away from British control and into Africa's interior.

While still under seventeenth-century Dutch control, Cape Colony Boers imported slaves—mainly from territories controlled by the Dutch East India Company such as Borneo, Burma, Madagascar, and Bengal. Lesser numbers of West African slaves were also imported. Between 1652 and 1808, when the slave trade had officially ended, the Boers imported at least 63,000 slaves into southern Africa, and by the early 1700s, they had also begun enslaving large numbers of native peoples. Although the Boers were supposed to register their slaves, by the 1720s it was common practice for individual Boer families simply to capture and enslave indigenous people as they saw fit, and by the 1730s, Boers were conducting large-scale, well-organized slave raids on neighboring tribes. They usually attempted to capture children instead of adults on these raids because children were easier to train and less likely to escape than adults. Britain's abolition of the slave trade in that country in 1807 and subsequent efforts to suppress the international trade led to more frequent Boer slave raids as imported slave prices rapidly rose to about $2,000 in the 1820s.

During the Napoleonic Wars, Britain took control of Cape Colony and was officially ceded the territory in 1814. Boers immediately clashed with the British government over the treatment of slaves, the former contending that what occurred between master and slave was a domestic matter outside of the scope of colonial government. British attempts to prevent any mistreatment of slaves and servants were met with hostility and later, open rebellion. A series of circuit courts had been established by the British in 1813 to hear complaints about mistreatment. These courts were dubbed "black courts" by Boers, who often refused to recognize their verdicts and ignored their summonses. When a British party attempted in 1815 to arrest a Boer who had ignored three summonses, open rebellion began. The British easily put down the rebellion, but the hanging of six rebels at Slagter's Nek created martyrs for Boer independence and symbols of British repression and injustice toward Boers.

Hostility between the two sides further deteriorated in 1828 when the British attempted to limit the Boers' authority over their slaves. For many Boers, the final break came in 1833 when the British formally abolished slavery in the British Empire and freed southern Africa's 35,000 slaves. Although Britain promised compensation for the loss of slaves, the Boers soon learned that this reimbursement was payable only in London. For the agrarian Boer economy, which was almost entirely slave-based, Britain's action spelled ruin. In 1834, the average Boer farm had between four and seven slaves, and the number on larger farms rivaled the slave populations of plantations in the southern portion of the United States. Consequently, many Boer families decided to migrate beyond British control by moving into Africa's interior and taking their slaves with them. These Boers became known as Voortrekkers, or pioneers, and their mass migration became known as "the great trek." Eventually, thousands undertook this journey to escape British control.

The Voortrekkers established a number of small, independent republics. With the notable exceptions of Transvaal and the Orange Republic, by the mid-1850s most of the territory settled by the Voortrekkers had been absorbed into expanding British colonies in southern Africa. Within Transvaal and the Orange Republic, slavery remained common, and Boers continued to organize slave raids against neighboring tribes well into the 1870s. The Second or Great Boer War (1899–1901) eventually brought these two republics under British rule. The Boers continued to use certain means, such as the apprentice system and pass laws (which did not allow freedom of movement without documentation), to perpetuate virtual slavery among southern Africa's native peoples, and it was these practices that eventually evolved into the modern system of apartheid.

—*Tom Lansford*

See also
Apartheid
For Further Reading
Le May, G. H. 1995. *The Afrikaners*. Oxford: Oxford University; Macmillan, William. 1963. *Bantu, Boer, and Briton*. Oxford: Clarendon; Ransford, Oliver. 1972. *The Great Trek*. London: Murray.

BOLIVAR, SIMON

Designated El Libertador (the Liberator) of northern South America by his contemporaries, Simón Bolívar was of instrumental importance in achieving that region's independence from Spain in the early-nineteenth century. His struggle with that metropolis resulted, eventually, in the abolition of African slavery in a good portion of the continent.

The scion of a wealthy family, Bolívar was born on July 24, 1783, in Caracas, Venezuela. During the course of his life, he defeated the Spaniards in New Granada (Colombia, Ecuador, and Venezuela), Peru, and upper Peru (Bolivia) at the battles of Boyacá (1819), Carabobo (1821), and Ayacucho (1824); was president or dictator of Gran Colombia (formerly New Granada) and Peru from 1819 to 1830; and contributed to the emancipation of numerous slaves in South America.

Bolívar, who sought arms and refuge from Haitian president Alexandre Pétion, promised him, after arriving in Port-au-Prince in 1815, to free "his brothers [as] a condition for his aid" (Madariaga, 1952). The Liberator had freed his own bondsmen prior to this meeting, years before Abraham Lincoln raised his voice in the Anglo-Saxon world by issuing the Emancipation Proclamation in 1863 (Masur, 1948).

Bolívar kept his promise to Pétion in the years ahead. In Angostura (now Ciudad Bolívar), Venezuela, at the inauguration of the congress that established Gran Colombia after the victory at Boyacá, Bolívar lobbied for the "confirmation of the absolute freedom of the slaves [which he had decreed in 1816], as I would plead for my very life and for the life of the Republic" (Lecuna, 1951). In addition, slavery was outlawed in the post-Ayacucho Bolivian constitution, which Bolívar submitted to the national legislature in 1826. He described bondage as the "negation of all law" and a "crime" in the letter that transmitted the document to the legislators (Lecuna, 1951).

Bolívar argued, according to one scholar, that the "desire for independence and nationality would assert itself" over racial differences among the revolutionaries during the war against Spain (Belaunde, 1938). This unifying force (i.e., the quest for freedom), so the argument went, would motivate the insurgents to defeat the enemy and forge new nations in Latin America. Although events since the independence era have contradicted Bolívar's prediction of ethnic harmony, and given that military and political considerations influenced his antislavery sentiments, the historical record nevertheless substantiates the Liberator's sincerity (and partial success) regarding the ending of slavery in the Americas.

Bolívar died of tuberculosis in relative poverty on his way to voluntary exile in Europe on December 17, 1830, near Santa Marta, Colombia. Ironically, Bolívar passed away in the house of a sympathetic Spaniard who provided a clean shirt for his corpse.

—*Fidel Iglesias*

See also
Latin America
For Further Reading
Belaunde, Victor Andrés. 1938. *Bolívar and the Political Thought of the Spanish American Revolution*. Baltimore: Johns Hopkins University Press; Lecuna, Vicente, comp. 1951. *Selected Writings of Bolívar*. Ed. Harold A. Bierck, Jr. New York: Colonial Press; Madariaga, Salvador de. 1952. *Bolívar*. Coral Gables, FL: University of Miami Press; Masur, Gerhard. 1948. *Simon Bolívar*. Albuquerque: University of New Mexico Press.

BONAPARTE, NAPOLEON
See *Napoleon Bonaparte*

BONIFACIO DE ANDRADA E SILVA, JOSE (1763–1838)

Known to most Brazilian schoolchildren as "the patriarch of Brazilian independence," José Bonifácio was a bold and often cantankerous statesman at the center of Brazilian politics in the tumultuous years of 1819 through 1835. His most controversial positions included his stand favoring emancipation. Writings condemning slavery as a backward, immoral institution cost him dearly toward the end of his political life but made him a hero to later abolitionists.

Bonifácio was hardly a constant champion of the poor and oppressed. He was of impeccably elite heritage, feared popular participation in government affairs, and remained committed to principles of monarchy despite eventual entanglements with Brazil's Emperor Pedro I. But he despised Brazil's entrenched aristocrats even more than he distrusted republicans, and he railed against the aristocrats' oversized, unproductive estates and lampooned their pretension to noble titles.

Decades of study, travel, and work in Europe exposed Bonifácio to both Enlightenment ideals and the chaotic aftermath of revolution, and each profoundly marked his political thought. Although born in Brazil, like many sons of Brazilian elite he studied at the Portuguese university at Coimbra and afterward, remained in Europe attending diplomatic posts within the Portuguese royal bureaucracy. In 1819, he returned to a Brazil that was embroiled in a slow struggle toward independence of an uncertain character. He soon became Dom Pedro's closest adviser and counseled him on his decision to break with the mother country and establish an independent Brazilian empire in 1822. Advocating a constitutional monarchy guided by the highly educated and dedicated to domestic economic development, Bonifácio linked conservative political ideas to a progressive social and economic program, a combination that defined the character of his career (Viotti da Costa, 1985).

Even before the empire's birth, Bonifácio called for emancipation and promotion of immigration to increase free labor. He employed immigrant labor on his own estate in Santos, São Paulo, a practice that set him apart dramatically from fellow landowners. In 1825, he wrote a treatise against slavery. Suffused with Enlightenment influences, the treatise argued that slavery violated civil society's founding principles and that men could not be property (Falcão, 1963). Bonifácio's economic arguments against slavery were not original. He advocated adoption of advanced, mechanized production and demonstrated the practical advantages of a free workforce. Although ignored at the time, 50 years later the prominent abolitionist Joaquim Nabuco incorporated these arguments into his own persuasive attacks on slavery.

After an influential but tumultuous stint as tutor to the prince regent (later to rule for decades as Pedro II), José Bonifácio was forced from power. He died in a Brazil that was still dependent on slave labor and many years away from experimenting with his social and economic programs.

—*Bryan McCann*

For Further Reading
Falcão, Edgard Cerqueira, ed. 1963. *Obras científicas, políticas a sociais de José Bonifácio de Andrada e Silva.* São Paulo: E. C. Falcão; Freyre, Gilberto. 1972. *A Propósito de José Bonifácio.* Recife, Brazil: Ministério de Educação e Cultura; Viotti da Costa, Emilia. 1985. *The Brazilian Empire: Myths and Histories.* Chicago: University of Chicago Press.

BOSTON FEMALE ANTI-SLAVERY SOCIETY (1833–1840)

In its brief seven-year history, the Boston Female Anti-Slavery Society conducted three national women's conventions, organized a multistate petition campaign, brought suit against Southerners bringing slaves into Boston, organized elaborate and profitable fund-raisers to keep male antislavery organizations financially solvent, and sponsored the Grimké sisters' lecture series throughout New England.

The society organized annual antislavery fairs at which handmade items and luxury items donated from European antislavery societies were sold, and these fairs quickly became the social event of the Christmas season for Boston residents. Additionally, the society published 15 volumes of *The Liberty Bell,* a literary annual first published in 1839. Maria Weston Chapman served as editor, and each volume included poetry, reflective essays, biographical sketches, and short stories written by distinguished political and literary figures. The sale of these books also provided both fund-raising and moral suasion opportunities for the society.

The Boston Female Anti-Slavery Society associated itself with both the American Anti-Slavery Society and the New England Anti-Slavery Society and supported both organizations with financial contributions. The Boston Female Anti-Slavery Society, much like the Philadelphia Female Anti-Slavery Society, included both white and black women in its membership. More important, the Boston organization consisted of two diverse religious groups: evangelicals—those belonging to Baptist, Presbyterian, and Congregational denominations—and liberals—including primarily the Quaker and Unitarian members. Initially, a coalition of these two divergent groups constituted the Boston organization. Both evangelicals and liberals were drawn to antislavery by their religious commitment to emancipation, and despite their differences, the women worked well together and made great strides toward their goals.

Religious differences finally split the society in 1840 after several years of bitter fighting between the factions began in 1837. Although it officially disbanded in April 1840, Maria Weston Chapman led the liberal faction in declaring the dissolution illegal based upon the society's original constitution, and she continued to operate the organization under the same name. In addition to its religiously liberal membership, the Chapman-run faction closely allied itself to William Lloyd Garrison and his antislavery beliefs. This society existed on paper into the 1850s, and its primary activity was the annual antislavery fair. The evangelical women formed a new society in 1840, the Massachusetts Female Emancipation Society, but this group had disappeared by the mid-1840s.

Prominent members of the Boston Female Anti-Slavery Society included liberal members Maria Weston Chapman, Lydia Maria Child, Anne Warren Weston, Henrietta Sargent, Caroline Weston, and Thankful Southwick and evangelical members Mary Parker, Martha Ball, Lucy Ball, and Catherine Sullivan. Despite appearances, the evangelical women held a majority in the society, but the liberal members' names appeared in the antislavery literature more frequently as they were more outspoken than their evangelical sisters.

—Sydney J. Caddel

See also
Child, Lydia Maria; Grimké, Angelina; Grimké, Sarah Moore; Women and the Antislavery Movement

For Further Reading
Boylan, Ann M. 1994. "Benevolence and Antislavery Activity among African American Women in New York and Boston, 1820–1840." In The Abolitionist Sisterhood: Women's Political Culture in Antebellum America. Ed. Jean Fagan Yellin and John C. Van Horne. Ithaca, NY: Cornell University Press; Chambers-Schiller, Lee. 1994. "'A Good Work among the People': The Political Culture of the Boston Antislavery Fair." In The Abolitionist Sisterhood: Women's Political Culture in Antebellum America. Ed. Jean Fagan Yellin and John C. Van Horne. Ithaca, NY: Cornell University Press; Hansen, Debra Gold. 1993. Strained Sisterhood: Gender and Class in the Boston Female Anti-Slavery Society. Amherst: University of Massachusetts Press.

BOZAL

The word *bozal* is of Spanish origin and was commonly used in Spain and in Spain's American colonies from the thirteenth through the eighteenth centuries to identify black people born in Africa, black people of African origin recently removed from their country, persons not expressing themselves properly in Spanish, beginners in an exercise, and those who were simple, idiot, or inane. When one speaks in terms of livestock, *bozal* means savage or wild, and slaves introduced to the Americas or Spain directly from Africa were listed as *bozales*. The sixteenth-century Portuguese used *bozal* in the same fashion the Spaniards did; today its use is limited to referring to livestock and commonly suggests the wild nature of the animals.

In the early years of the slave trade, African slaves recently introduced to the Americas were thought to be prone to run away and rebel. In those same years, enslavers thought that the Africans' stubbornness resulted from their geographical origin and their way of life. Time and practice demonstrated that this characteristic was not an innate one—some *bozales* had a well-developed culture, including knowledge of the Islamic religion and handwriting—and later the less well-developed *bozales* were called *bozales torpes* (dull *bozales*) or more commonly, *bozalones*.

After an incident on San Juan Island (now Puerto Rico), Emperor Charles V advised against introducing any more *gelofes* (who were clearly obstinate to slavery) or any other Negro raised with the Moors, as it was thought that *gelofes* were *soberbios, e inovedientes, revolvedores e incorregibles* ("arrogant and disobedient, turbulent and incorrigible"). Consequently, the search for and capture of blacks to be slaves was then limited to specific regions to ensure submission and to make enslavement easier.

A slave's origin was also identified by using a geographic reference (rather than ethnic) applied to the probable place of origin: *nacilav* ("nation"), *tierra* ("land"), *lugar* ("place"), or *natural de* ("born in"). So a *bozal nación São Tomé* or a *bozal nacilón Angola* (*bozal* of São Tomé nation or *bozal* of Angola nation) did not indicate ethnic origin but was arbitrarily employed identification pointing toward a geographical origin and some probable cultural characteristic. Slaves born out of Africa (i.e., in Spain or New Spain) were called *criollos* ("creoles"). Slaves acculturated to Spanish life, customs, and language were characterized as *ladinos* ("cultured"). The description, *Joseph negro esclavo entre ladino y bozal* (Joseph, Negro slave between *ladino* and *bozal*) meant that the slave was in the process of being acculturated.

—Juan M. de la Serna

See also
Africa
For Further Reading
Aguirre Beltrán, Gonzalo. 1972. *La población negra en México. Estudio ethnohistórica.* Mexico City: Fondo de Cultura Económica; Bastide, Roger. 1972. *African Civilization in the New World.* New York: Harper and Row; Palmer, Colin. 1976. *Slaves of the White God: Blacks in Mexico 1570–1650.* Cambridge, MA: Harvard University Press.

BRANDING OF SLAVES

A brand is a mark made by burning the skin with a hot iron. The branding of domestic animals to indicate ownership is an ancient and universal practice, and the practice was also used until modern times on human beings for the same reason—to indicate ownership and therefore to signify slave status. Furthermore, branding was one of many methods used to punish delinquent slaves.

The Babylonian law code of Hammurabi mentions the branding of slaves, there are similar references from the New Babylonian Empire, and comparable evidence is found in both Pharaonic and Ptolemaic Egypt. The Persians may have branded slaves as well, although the evidence is ambiguous and may refer to tattooing instead. The custom was almost unknown to the Greeks and was relatively rare among the Romans, both of whom seem to have preferred tattooing. Again, problems in terminology (i.e., words that can mean either "brand" or "tattoo") make certainty elusive, and much of what was once assumed to be evidence of branding has been shown recently to refer to the much more prevalent practice of tattooing. Such misapprehension is perpetuated by mistranslation of the sources and by misleading lexicographical entries.

Branding slaves as a penalty was fairly common in the Middle Ages in Europe. In the later Middle Ages, when methods of cruelty and torture grew more refined and the penal system became increasingly harsh, the procedure grew yet more common. People convicted of certain crimes would have their social status reduced to that of a slave, and then they could be branded to make their degradation manifest. In England, runaway slaves were branded on various parts of the body, though most often on the cheek or forehead. Galley slavery was well known in France after

A man brands a newly purchased slave in this undated engraving from an antislavery book published in Ohio.

the beginning of the fifteenth century, and anyone condemned to the oars was branded on the forehead with the letters GAL. Similarly treated were people who were condemned to work in the French navy-yard prisons. Penal slaves condemned to forced labor in Russia also were customarily branded on the forehead, with an abbreviation of the name of their accompanying punishment. In the nineteenth century, all of these types of branding were formally discontinued.

Slave traders and trading companies often branded slaves to indicate ownership, but as the slave changed hands among agents and shippers, others might add additional brands for various reasons. A brand could indicate that a contractor had paid the appropriate export duties, a royal design denoted the slave's state of permanent servitude to the crown, and a cross signified that the provision requiring baptism of slaves had been fulfilled. Thus, when slaves came to the New World directly from Africa and the West Indies, they were likely to be branded already. If not, they might be so marked by their new owners. Branding was used by slaveowners in the United States to punish runaways, and such branding was often done on the face and usually with the owner's initials or with R for "runaway." This was just one of many brutalities inflicted on slaves; others included whipping, beating, shackling, dismemberment, and mutilation before abolition put an official stop to such practices.

—*Mark T. Gustafson*

See also
Tattooing
For Further Reading
Blassingame, John W., ed. 1977. *Slave Testimony: Two Centuries of Letters, Speeches, Interviews, and Autobiographies.* Baton Rouge: Louisiana State University Press; Jones, C. P. 1987. "Stigma: Tattooing and Branding in Graeco-Roman Antiquity." *Journal of Roman Studies* 77: 139–155; Miller, J. C. 1988. *Way of Death: Merchant Capitalism and the Angolan Slave Trade, 1730–1830.* Madison: University of Wisconsin Press; Sellin, J. T. 1976. *Slavery and the Penal System.* New York: Elsevier.

BRAZILIAN ANTI-SLAVERY SOCIETY

The Brazilian Anti-Slavery Society was founded in Rio de Janeiro on September 7, 1880—the fifty-eighth anniversary of Brazil's independence. The organization's founders met in the home of Joaquim Nabuco, a member of Parliament and Brazil's chief abolitionist. A few days before, Nabuco had presented a bill to eliminate slav-

ery in Brazil before 1890. The Brazilian Anti-Slavery Society existed primarily to agitate against slavery, and its members arranged public meetings in Rio de Janeiro and other major cities, supervised the establishment of abolitionist clubs, and raised money for emancipating slaves.

The first issue of the society's journal, *0 Abolicionista,* appeared in November 1880. The first campaign in the abolitionist press denounced slavery's legality, at least for a large number of Brazil's slaves, and abolitionists maintained that slaves imported from Africa after passage of a bill on November 7, 1831—in which Brazil banned the slave trade but failed to enforce the law—and their descendants, were illegally enslaved. The journal thus prepared the ground for numerous lawsuits filed by descendants of illegally imported slaves. The journal blamed slavery for the economic and industrial backwardness of Brazil and called for the abolition of slavery to stimulate immigration, further industry and agriculture, and improve the moral character of the nation by creating a new working class of freedmen and immigrants.

After a heartening beginning in 1880 and 1881, the society then had a long period of inactivity. Abolitionist clubs and societies declined in number and activities when abolitionist leaders were not reelected to Parliament in 1881. Nabuco left for London, where he wrote *0 abolicionismo* (1883), Brazil's most widely distributed abolitionist manifesto.

The northern province of Ceará, where there were only a few slaves, did not experience the general feeling of defeat. Hearing rumors that a steamer in the harbor of the capital was carrying slaves to be sold illegally elsewhere in Brazil, the boatmen of Fortaleza (the capital of Ceará and also known by that name) blockaded the port and demanded that the slaves be put ashore. After this victory, antislavery agitation predominated in Ceará. In a generally festive mood, abolitionists visited street after street, parish after parish, convincing slaveowners to emancipate their slaves. On March 25, 1884, slavery was abolished in Ceará. From then until 1888, when slavery was abolished in all of Brazil, Ceará became a haven for runaway slaves. In the neighboring province of Amazonas, where there were also very few slaves, a similar movement appeared, and slavery ended there on May 24, 1884.

But even though the antislavery movement enjoyed remarkable success in the remoter regions, the advancement of the idea throughout the country was quite slow. Only a small fraction of the population, mainly in the large cities, was influenced at all by the initial campaign, and it was commonly accepted that abolition would require a long and difficult struggle. Nobody could predict that the abolition of slavery would be accomplished in less than 10 years.

The Brazilian Anti-Slavery Society itself experienced only a fleeting existence. As early as 1882, the English-language newspaper *Rio News* noticed and reported its disappearance, but its ideas continued and were eventually successful—even long before expected.

—*Birgitte Holten*

See also
Abolitionist Confederation; Lei Aurea
For Further Reading
Conrad, Robert. 1972. *The Destruction of Brazilian Slavery*. Berkeley: University of California Press; Nabuco, Joaquim de Araújo. 1977. *Abolitionism: The Brazilian Anti-Slavery Struggle*. Chicago: University of Illinois Press; Nabuco, Joaquim de Araújo. 1880–1881. *0 Abolicionista: Orgão da Sociedade Brazileira Contra a Escravidão*. Rio de Janeiro: Brazilian Anti-Slavery Society; Toplin, Robert Brent. 1992. *The Abolition of Slavery in Brazil*. New York: Athenaeum.

BREEDING OF SLAVES

Because the slave population in the United States was unique in that it reproduced itself, the question of whether slaveowners there utilized a deliberate breeding strategy has long been debated. A combination of historical circumstances no doubt contributed to a gradual but consistent increase in the native-born black slave population of the United States after the American Revolution, including the acquisition of the Louisiana Territory in 1803 and then the lands gained in the war with Mexico, both of which resulted not only in the westward expansion of the United States but also in the westward expansion of slavery. In 1808, the constitutional ban on African importations went into effect, and though importations had been deliberately increased in anticipation of the ban in the decades immediately preceding it, the market demand for slaves after the ban went into effect had to be met solely by the natural increase of native-born slaves. At the same time, technological innovations in agriculture resulted in an antebellum cotton boom, which added to the increased demand for black slaves.

Initially, so-called surplus slaves from the older settled areas of the South were moved westward, both with their owners and alone after being sold. From 1810 through 1860, approximately 500,000 black slaves made the involuntary migration from Virginia and the Carolinas to Kentucky, Tennessee, Alabama, Mississippi, and other Deep South states. Of particular interest for people who are inclined to conclude that slave breeding was at least a consideration of slaveowners is the fact that unlike the strategy utilized during the colonial period, slave women and men were equally in demand in the old Southwest and sales of women and men were roughly equal. At least one historian has suggested that the odds of a slave couple being separated by sale were one in three, and slave women in their childbearing years were rarely allowed to remain without a mate, whether it was one of her own choosing or one selected by her master. Slave women almost invariably recalled being forced into sexual relationships, both with other slaves and with whites, including the owner. "Encouragement" to reproduce often included rewards of leisure time, colorful cloth for dresses, and even cash. Occasionally, an owner might promise a particularly fertile slave woman her freedom after she had produced a certain number of healthy children. Despite continual interference, slave marriages tended to be long-lived, and families tended to be stable.

The flourishing internal trade in slaves suggests that the so-called surplus was constant over a period of five decades. In addition, larger commercial brokerages operating in Southern coastal cities were responsible for acquiring, auctioning, and transporting hundreds of slaves annually. Additional slaves were also purchased and sold along the southwestern internal slave trade route, either overland or by sea via New Orleans. Some historians have insisted that slave traders were despised in a society that, nevertheless, used the acquisition and possession of slaves as an indicator of wealth and status.

The birthrate of Africans in the United States steadily increased and the death rate decreased after the American Revolution, and indeed, native-born slaves had begun to outnumber Africans even before that. It is possible that tropical diseases in the West Indies and in South America contributed to the continued low birthrate of Africans in those countries, but in their own words, former slaves recounted to interviewers hired by the federal government during the 1930s the deliberate, artificial, and forced creation of slave "marriages" or even more temporary sexual liaisons for the clear purpose of producing offspring.

Women singled out for their fertility were referred to by the slaves themselves as "breed women," and women who failed to reproduce recalled being sold. When slaveowners had many more female than male slaves, "breeding males" or "stockmen" were sometimes hired specifically to impregnate slave women. In other situations, a favored male hand might be allowed to take more than one wife at a time as a kind of reward. Thus, former slaves recalled pairings of slaves by the white owner, the exertion of "influence" of one kind or another in order to pair a particular slave couple, rewards offered and given for producing offspring, the sale of women who did not reproduce after a period of time (although one historian has suggested that slave women might have used abortion techniques since documentary evidence has been found to show that some slave women who were considered infertile did in fact reproduce after emancipation), the "renting" of stud males, or the male owner himself impregnating female slaves. It seems clear that both promiscuity among the slaves and at least a version of polygamy for slaves was strongly supported by slaveowners.

Slavery was meant to be a profit-making venture. Because slaves were sold as a hedge against inflation or bankruptcy, to mortgage property, or as collateral for loans; bequeathed in wills; and used as an indicator of social status as well as laborers, slaveholders strongly encouraged the "production" of slave infants either by wedded couples or by slaves placed together arbitrarily for that purpose.

—*Dale Edwyna Smith*

See also
Domestic Slave Trade in the United States
For Further Reading
Escott, Paul D. 1979. *Slavery Remembered: A Record of Twentieth-Century Slave Narratives.* Chapel Hill: University of North Carolina Press; Sutch, Richard. 1975. "The Breeding of Slaves for Sale and the Westward Expansion of Slavery." In *Race and Slavery in the Western Hemisphere.* Ed. Stanley L. Engerman and Eugene D. Genovese. Princeton, NJ: Princeton University Press.

BRITISH ANTI-SLAVERY SOCIETY
See The African Institution

BRITISH EMPIRE
See Abolition, British Empire

BRITISH PROSLAVERY ARGUMENT
See Proslavery Arguments, British

BROOKS-SUMNER AFFAIR

The Brooks-Sumner Affair was a brutal attack that occurred on May 22, 1856, on the U.S. Senate floor against Massachusetts senator Charles Sumner by South Carolina representative Preston Brooks. The assault was one inci-

dent in a series of events in the 1850s connected with the debate on slavery, and it represented the growing hostility between anti- and proslavery forces and an increasing sectional and political rivalry that eventually led to the U.S. Civil War.

On January 23, 1854, Democratic senator Stephen A. Douglas of Illinois, an advocate of westward expansion and a potential candidate for the presidency, introduced the Kansas-Nebraska bill in the U.S. Senate. The bill called for creating two territories from part of the Nebraska Territory. Territory to the west of Iowa would become Nebraska Territory, and land west of Missouri would become Kansas Territory. Both territories would have the right of popular sovereignty to decide whether they would be free or slave states.

Douglas, hoping to gain support from Southern legislators for his bill, supported the principle of popular sovereignty that had been established by the Compromise of 1850, which effectively voided the line between free and slave territory established by the Missouri Compromise (1820). After lengthy debate, Congress finally passed the Kansas-Nebraska bill. Antislavery forces in Congress, Massachusetts senator Charles Sumner included, argued that passage of the measure represented a conspiracy of proslavery forces to expand slavery. Sumner, an avid abolitionist and one of the most vocal congressional opponents of slavery, believed that if slavery could be prevented from expanding to new territories, it would eventually fade away.

The passage of the Kansas-Nebraska Act placed the focus of the slavery question in the new territories, especially Kansas, where political and moral questions would be addressed violently in the upcoming months. In March 1855, fraudulent voting in Kansas helped elect a proslavery territorial legislature there. This proslavery legislature, based in the town of Lecompton, dismissed the few antislavery delegates and enacted slave codes. Later that summer, antislavery forces called their own meeting in Topeka and established an extralegal, antislavery legislature that passed laws prohibiting slavery and made formal application that Congress admit Kansas Territory as a free state. President Franklin Pierce condemned the antislavery Topeka legislature, recognized the proslavery Lecompton legislature, and showed his support for the territorial administration by sending troops and appointing proslavery judges in Kansas.

Antislavery forces, especially the New England Emigrant Company, which organized to promote the movement of antislavery settlers to Kansas, appealed to Sumner to champion the cause of preventing Kansas from becoming a slave state. Sumner realized that Kansas's request for statehood would be a topic on the Senate floor over which antislavery and proslavery forces would clash. In March 1856, Douglas condemned Kansas's antislavery forces, and Sumner defended antislavery attempts to make Kansas a free state.

On May 19, 1856, Sumner began a two-day speech, "The Crime against Kansas." In the speech, which was meant to arouse Northern sentiment against violence in Kansas between pro- and antislavery proponents and the growing influence of proslavery forces in Congress, Sumner first recognized that the main congressional proponents of slavery were Senators Stephen A. Douglas of Illinois and Andrew Butler of South Carolina. Sumner then detailed the crime committed against Kansas, which was allowing slavery forces to invade the once-secure free territory. Only restoring the Missouri Compromise line, continued Sumner, could ameliorate the crime committed by Congress and proslavery advocates.

Sumner also condemned President Pierce for supporting the illegally elected Kansas proslavery government, reprimanded U.S. senators who supported slavery, and then, in a series of personal attacks, focused his anger on South Carolina senator Andrew Butler. Sumner informed the crowded Senate chamber that Butler had taken up with "the harlot, slavery," ridiculed his inability to control his drooling, and accused him of being an incompetent fool. Sumner also maligned South Carolina by belittling the importance of that state's contribution to society. Southern congressmen reacted vehemently with threats and insults, but Sumner refused any special protection from his supporters.

Preston Brooks, determined to protect the honor of Butler (his relative) and the state of South Carolina as well as to strike a blow against the antislavery forces in Congress, planned his response. Since Brooks considered Sumner to be a social inferior, the Southern code of honor prevented him from challenging Sumner to a duel. Instead, Brooks decided to teach Sumner a lesson. On May 22, just two days after the conclusion of "The Crime against Kansas" speech, Brooks and a cohort, South Carolina representative Lawrence M. Keitt, who stood nearby to prevent anyone from interfering, entered the Senate chamber soon after the day's session had ended and approached Sumner, who was seated at his desk. Brooks informed Sumner that his "Crime against Kansas" speech was both libelous against the state of South Carolina and demeaned the honor of Senator Butler who happened to be a close relation. Without waiting for Sumner to respond, Brooks began beating Sumner with his walking cane.

The attack was so vicious that Brooks's hollow cane broke into pieces from the impact of the blows. Sumner, unable to avoid the blows because he was trapped at his desk, which was bolted to the floor, finally tore the desk from its fastenings and collapsed bloody and unconscious on the Senate floor. Keitt, who had kept onlookers from interfering with the attack, ended the blows by warning Brooks that if he continued the beating, Sumner might die.

After the attack, Brooks received hundreds of canes from Southern proslavery sympathizers. The injuries Sumner sustained in the attack prevented him from returning to the Senate for three years, but Massachusetts reserved his Senate seat until he was well enough to do so. In the House of Representatives, legislators failed to pass a recommendation expelling Brooks. Soon after the vote, Brooks defended his attack on Sumner and tendered his resignation; South Carolina voters immediately returned Brooks to Congress by an overwhelming vote. Brooks's beating of Sumner helped sway many conservatives to the Republican Party and persuade them to take up a strong antislavery stance.

—*Craig S. Pascoe*

See also
Bleeding Kansas
For Further Reading
Blue, Frederick J. 1994. *Charles Sumner and the Conscience of the North*. Arlington Heights, IL: Harlan Davidson; Donald, David Herbert. 1960. *Charles Sumner and the Coming of the Civil War*. New York: Knopf; Potter, David M. 1976. *The Impending Crisis, 1848–1861*. New York: Harper and Row; Sewell, Richard H. 1988. *The House Divided: Sectionalism and Civil War, 1848–1865*. Baltimore, MD: Johns Hopkins University Press.

BROWN, HENRY "BOX" (C. 1816–?)

Henry Brown gained fame through an extraordinary escape to freedom. Born a slave in Virginia's Louisa County, Brown was sent to work in Richmond, Virginia, at age 13 when his master died. At about the age of 20 he met and married another Richmond slave, Nancy, and they lived as happily as possible under slavery for about 12 years. In August 1848, she and their three children were suddenly sold to a Methodist preacher from North Carolina.

No longer deterred from seeking to escape slavery—as Brown later noted, now "my family were gone" (Stearns, 1969)—he concocted an approach that, though dangerous, might work. He had a carpenter make a wooden box, two feet by two and a half feet by three feet, and took it to a white friend, Samuel A. Smith, a shoe dealer, and Smith's free black employee, James Caesar Anthony Smith. Asked what the box was for, Brown exclaimed, to "put Henry Brown

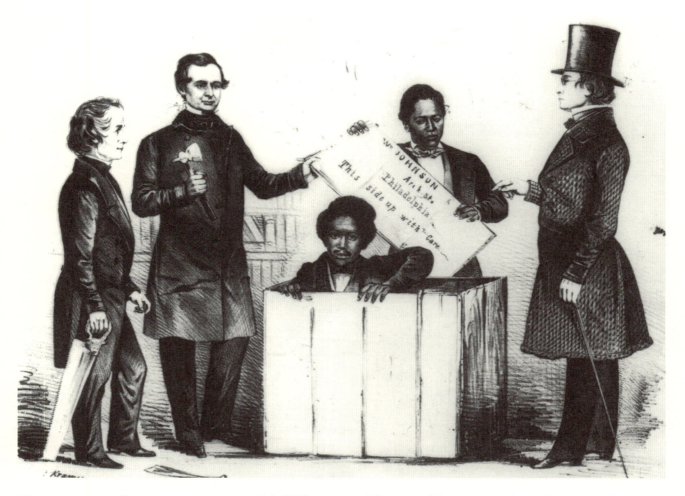

The resurrection of Henry "Box" Brown in Philadelphia, to which he escaped from Virginia by packing himself in a small box.

in!" The two Smiths marked the box "right side up with care"; addressed it to William A. Johnson, Arch Street, Philadelphia; and on March 29, 1849, shipped it by Adams Express.

Brown took with him a container of water and had three small holes for air, yet he thought he would die when, for parts of the journey, he traveled in the crate upside down. But the trip ended at last—after 27 hours—and like Lazarus from the dead, Brown rose from the box when four men (including William Still, a black abolitionist, and James Miller McKim, a white one) from the Philadelphia Vigilance Committee, associated with the Underground Railroad and the Pennsylvania Anti-Slavery Society, collected the box and opened it. As for Samuel Smith, he went to the Virginia penitentiary for attempting in May 1849 to ship two more boxes, each containing a slave man, north to freedom.

Henry Brown took the name Henry "Box" Brown and, after moving to Boston, became active in the abolition movement as a witness to the horrors of slavery even at its best. He told crowds his tale, and abolitionist Charles Stearns published Brown's narrative, "written from a statement of facts made by himself" (Stearns, 1969). In January 1850, Brown attended a giant antislavery convention in Syracuse, New York. Also at the Syracuse meeting was James Caesar Anthony Smith, who, having made his way north after Samuel Smith's conviction in Richmond, now assumed the moniker "Boxer" for his role in boxing up Brown. Some people in Boston painted a panorama, "Mirror of Slavery," that depicted scenes from slavery and Brown's flight, and "Box" Brown and "Boxer" Smith toured the Northeast with the panorama and the famous crate.

On August 30, 1850, slave catchers nearly kidnapped Brown, and in order to put himself beyond their reach and that of the new Fugitive Slave Act, Brown left for England. He spent the next four years telling his story in Great Britain, but there is no record of what happened to him after the mid-1850s.

—*Peter Wallenstein*

See also
Abolition, United States; Fugitive Slave Act of 1850; Underground Railroad

For Further Reading
Ripley, C. Peter, ed. 1985. *The Black Abolitionist Papers: The British Isles, 1830–1865.* Chapel Hill: University of North Carolina Press; Stearns, Charles. 1969. *Narrative of Henry Box Brown.* Philadelphia: Rhetoric Publications; Still, William. 1968. *The Underground Railroad.* New York: Arno Press.

BROWN, JOHN
(1800–1859)

John Brown was a radical abolitionist whose die-hard commitment to the destruction of slavery in a raid on Harpers Ferry in 1859 prefaced the U.S. Civil War. Brown was born at Torrington in northwestern Connecticut in 1800 and was one of six children reared under the strict supervision of Calvinist parents Ruth and Owen Brown. In 1805, the family moved to the village of Hudson in Ohio. Owen Brown, a tanner and shoemaker by trade, was an abolitionist who supported the creation of antislavery educational establishments, including Western Reserve College and Oberlin College in Ohio. Reared in this reformist environment, the young Brown imbibed strict discipline, antislavery tenets, and religious conversion.

Brown's professional life was plagued by debt, insistent creditors, and failed business schemes—the failures coincided with his burgeoning public commitment to antislavery. During the 1840s, Brown was in touch with antislavery leaders like Gerrit Smith and Frederick Douglass. On January 15, 1851, Brown helped found the League of Gileadites, which attracted 44 members including progressive whites, free blacks, and runaway slaves. The primary aims of this radical group were to promote physical resistance toward the Fugitive Slave Act of 1850 and to protect runaway slaves from pursuing slaveowners. Despite these antislavery rumblings, it was not until the mid-1850s that the true extent of Brown's commitment against slavery materialized.

In 1855, Brown and his sons moved to Kansas where they settled along the Osawatomie River. The future statehood status of this territory, whether it would enter the Union as a slave or free state, was in fierce dispute. After one failed attempt to destroy Lawrence, a free-state town, proslavery forces attacked again on May 21, 1856, and destroyed it. Three days later, Brown and his group sought out five Southern settlers along Pottawatomie Creek and killed them all. Throughout the rest of the year, Brown and his sons fought for antislavery principles against the proslavery forces in Kansas and Missouri.

During this period, Brown became known as "Osawatomie Brown" or "Old Osawatomie." For some abolitionists, he came to symbolize a holy crusade against slavery; for many proslavery and Southern sympathizers, he was a hated figure. This sectional divide around the exploits of a heroic/antiheroic personality helped to clarify the complex nature of the growing sectional divisions in the United States prior to the Civil War.

By the mid-1850s, Brown had planned a raid on the federal armory at Harpers Ferry in northern Virginia. It was well stocked with arms and strategically well placed for easy access to the slave South down the Appalachian Mountain range. By summer 1859, Brown had secured financial backing from a "secret six" group (Gerrit Smith, Samuel G. Howe, Franklin Sanborn, Theodore Parker, George L. Stearns, and Thomas W. Higginson) and a band of loyal followers. His 21 followers included 2 former slaves, Shields Green and Dangerfield Newby; 3 free blacks, Osborne P. Anderson, John A. Copeland, and Lewis Leary; and 16 radical whites. The youngest follower, 20-year-old William H. Leeman, explained clearly the nature of their plan in a letter to his mother: "We are now all privately gathered in a slave state, where we are determined to strike for freedom, incite the slaves to rebellion, and establish a free government" (Oates, 1970).

The raid began on the evening of October 16, 1859. Thirty-six hours later, and after 15 deaths, the raid was over, and Brown had failed to accomplish his stated objective of slave armed insurrection. Brown was taken to Charles Town a few miles away, tried by state law for treason, and hanged. His corpse was later transferred to his family's farm near Lake Placid in upstate New York.

The historical significance of John Brown has been debated ever since his death. Whence arose his passionate antislavery beliefs? The source was probably less an epiphany than it was environmental, which can be traced directly to his family upbringing, work in abolitionist circles, and acquaintance with the slave-free conflict during the 1850s. Was Brown mad, vainglorious, or heroic? Psychological portraits are invariably sketchy precisely because they are so indeterminate, and it is undeniable that Brown's actions were either praised or condemned according to sectional division. It is also ironic that the military actions of Brown are still questioned, yet those of subsequent Union and Confederate soldiers are acclaimed. Was he a bumbler, a deliberate martyr, or politically sagacious? Clearly, the raid was well planned if poorly executed. Faced with the inevitability of his execution, it is probable that Brown chose martyrdom as a fitting climax to his actions.

The historical jury is still out on several of these issues, but there are some irrefutable points. Brown has often assumed heroic proportions among African Americans because of his commitment to the cause of freedom. Furthermore, Brown's raid and its consequences revealed the underlying reality of the antebellum sectional crisis—namely, slavery.

Northerners praised Brown's principles even if many of them disagreed with his methods. Southerners condemned the event even as they used it to galvanize popular support for their cause. On October 25, 1859, the *Richmond Enquirer* wrote: "The Harper's Ferry invasion advanced the cause of Disunion more than any other event." Most concretely of all, the raid was the opening shot of the Civil War. As Brown's parting words noted: "The crimes of this guilty land will never be purged away but with blood"(Oates, 1970). This was less a prophecy than a direct recognition that it would take a major war to abolish slavery.

—*Jeffrey R. Kerr-Ritchie*

See also
Harpers Ferry Raid
For Further Reading
DuBois, William E. B. 1909. *John Brown.* Philadelphia: G. W. Jacobs; Finkelman, Paul, ed., 1995. *His Soul Goes Marching On: Responses to John Brown and the Harpers Ferry Raid.* Charlottesville: University of Virginia Press; Oates, Stephen B. 1970. *To Purge This Land with Blood: A Biography of John Brown.* New York: Harper and Row; Quarles, Benjamin. 1974. *Allies for Freedom: Blacks and John Brown.* New York: Oxford University Press.

BROWN, WILLIAM WELLS (C. 1814–1884)

An abolitionist and writer, William Wells Brown was born a slave even though his father was a white slaveholder. As a youth he was taken to St. Louis where he lived and worked for three different owners. He was hired out for various jobs: farmhand, servant in a tavern, for a brief time handyman in Elijah Lovejoy's printing office, worker on Mississippi River steamboats, assistant in his owner's medical office, and handyman for James Walker, a slave trader who took him along on three trips to New Orleans. Brown's work in the doctor's office inspired him later to study and practice medicine, and his work in a tavern led to his later activism in the temperance movement. His various work experiences provided a wealth of information for him to draw on when he became an antislavery activist.

Since childhood, Brown had thought of escaping from slavery, and when his last owner, a St. Louis commission merchant and steamboat owner, took him to Cincinnati as a servant, Brown seized his chance. Traveling on his own and falling ill, he chanced upon Wells Brown, an Ohio Quaker who housed and fed him for about a week until he was able to continue his journey. Assuming the status of a free person, Brown took his benefactor's name and was thereafter known as William Wells Brown. Later he dedicated the first edition of his narrative to Wells Brown.

Brown lived for several years in Cleveland, then in Buffalo for nine years before moving close to Rochester, New York. During much of that period he worked on Lake Erie steamers, taking advantage of the opportunity to help other fugitives reach Canada. Largely self-educated, he lectured on temperance and in 1843 became a lecturer for the Western New York Anti-Slavery Society. In 1847 he moved to Boston where he lectured for both the Massachusetts and the American Anti-Slavery Societies. William Lloyd Garrison recognized Brown's talents as a speaker, and Garrison and other New England abolitionists sponsored Brown's tours. For his part, Brown was loyal to Garrison and his cohorts and continued to work with them after many other antislavery advocates had shifted their support to electoral politics or free soil tactics.

In 1848, Brown represented the American Peace Society at a peace congress in Paris, and there he met Victor Hugo and other European reformers. While he was abroad, Congress enacted the new Fugitive Slave Act, which made it much more dangerous for him to return to the United States. He traveled and lectured extensively in England, joining former slaves William and Ellen Craft at some public meetings and at others exhibiting a panorama to add a visual dimension to his lectures on slavery. The panorama was not well received, but Brown's lectures were always impressive. He and other slaves and former slaves had the stamp of authenticity when speaking of the institution, and many people who would not listen to a white abolitionist were moved by Brown's forceful presentation. Yet he wished to return to his native country and finally agreed, reluctantly, to permit English abolitionists to purchase his freedom.

After returning to the United States, Brown devoted himself to antislavery work with another series of lecture tours. As the North became more free soil in sentiment, Brown met a much warmer reception from audiences. He also wrote more than a dozen books, pamphlets, and plays, beginning with the *Narrative of William W. Brown, a Fugitive Slave, Written by Himself* (1847), which quickly became a best-seller. The 3,000-copy first edition sold out within six months, and three more editions followed; a total of 10,000 copies was sold in two years. It was one of only a few slave narratives that were written by the subject rather than dictated to abolitionists.

In 1856, Brown supplemented his lectures by reading one of his works, a three-act antislavery drama entitled "Experience; or How to Give a Northern Man a Backbone." Although he never published this first play, it met with enthusiastic response. At the end of 1856, he planned a second drama, *The Escape; or, A Leap for Freedom*, the first known play to be published by an African American. Brown often read it, too, during his extensive travels in the antislavery cause.

His lectures and dramatic readings were based primarily on his personal experiences as a slave, and it was his novel *Clotel; or, The President's Daughter* (1853) that became his most controversial work. Published in London, *Clotel* was based on the rumor that Thomas Jefferson had fathered a slave daughter by his personal servant Sally Hemmings. As a novel it was flawed, parts of it virtually lifted from Lydia Maria Child's story "The Quadroons." Yet as one of the earliest novels published by an African American, it adds to Brown's significance as a pioneer writer for his race. *Clotel* was not published in the United States during Brown's lifetime, though he wrote three variations on its theme for domestic readers.

Another of Brown's innovations was a travel book, *Three Years in Europe; or, Places I Have Seen and People I Have Met* (1852), written from the perspective of a former American slave. It included articles and letters Brown had contributed to the London press and American antislavery papers during his European sojourn. In contrast to other travel accounts, Brown's book compared the freedom he found in England with the slavery he had suffered in his native land. In a letter to his last owner, Brown wrote of his affection for the United States but also of his hatred for "her institution of slavery."

Brown pioneered in yet another area by writing a history of African Americans. Although he was not a trained historian, he called attention in four books to the contributions of African Americans in the American Revolution and in the country's Civil War. Later editions of *The Black Man; His Antecedents, His Genius, and His Achievements* (1863) and *Rising Son; or, The Antecedents and Advancement of the Colored Race* (1874) included biographical sketches of the more than 100 African American men and women Brown believed represented the best of their race.

Brown recruited for the Union Army during the Civil War and continued his efforts for civil rights. He also undertook the practice of medicine, combining it with lecturing and writing. Temperance remained one of his major concerns. Late in life, Brown traveled through the South and wrote of that experience in his last book, *My Southern Home; or, The South and Its People* (1880). Brown, who rose out of slavery by his own efforts, produced more than a dozen publica-

tions, broke ground for later African American writers in several fields, and was himself a significant American writer.

—*Larry Gara*

See also
Craft, William and Ellen; Fugitive Slave Act of 1850; Garrison, William Lloyd; Underground Railroad
For Further Reading
Brown, Josephine. 1856. *Biography of an American Bondman by His Daughter*. Boston: R. F. Walcutt; Brown, William Wells. 1847. *Narrative of William W. Brown, a Fugitive Slave, Written by Himself*. Boston: Anti-Slavery Office; Farrison, William Edward. 1969. *William Wells Brown: Author and Reformer*. Chicago: University of Chicago Press; Yellin, Jean Fagan. 1972. *The Intricate Knot: Black Figures in American Literature, 1776–1863*. New York: New York University Press.

BRUSSELS ACT (1890)

The General Act for the Repression of the African Slave Trade, known as the Brussels Act, was a treaty negotiated by the Brussels Conference of 1889–1890. It was signed in Brussels on July 2, 1890, by all the European powers that had colonies in Africa—Britain, France, Germany, Italy, Portugal, and Spain; by the other signatories of the Berlin Act of 1885—Austria, Belgium, Denmark, Holland, Russia, Sweden, and the United States; and by the Congo Independent State, the Ottoman Empire, Persia, and the Sultanate of Zanzibar. As the first comprehensive treaty against the African slave trade, it was thus a landmark in the antislavery campaign and set a precedent for the human rights movement. Although regarded as a humanitarian instrument, it also served the purposes of the European colonial powers, as it presented the conquest and exploitation of Africa as being antislavery "actions," and thus good.

Chapters 1 and 2 of the act covered actions to be taken against the slave trade at its source in Africa. They declared that the colonial powers could best attack the slave trade by establishing administrations; building fortified posts; eliminating porterage by constructing road, rail, water, and telegraphic communications; by protecting missionaries and trading companies; and by initiating Africans into agricultural labor and the "industrial arts."

Having thus established that the occupation and exploitation of Africa were antislavery measures, the signatories bound themselves to outlaw the slave trade, capture and transport of slaves, and the castration of males. They undertook to prevent raids, arbitrate in local wars, control caravan routes and ports of embarkation, repatriate or resettle freed and fugitive slaves, and educate liberated children. To disarm resistance and enable governments to control the lucrative trade in munitions, the traffic in arms and ammunition, particularly in precision weapons, was to be limited in a zone stretching right across the continent and a 100 nautical miles offshore between latitudes 20° north and 22° south.

Chapter 3 provided for the suppression of the slave trade by sea. The British, to secure the agreement of other powers to mutual rights to visit, search, and arrest slavers, agreed to restrict those rights to a "slave trade zone," which included the coasts of the Indian Ocean from Baluchistan in the north to the Quelimane River in Mozambique to the south and covered Madagascar, the Red Sea, and the Gulf. The rights were also limited to vessels of less than 500 tons (except for very small fishing craft, which were exempt). Strict rules were laid down to control the granting of flags to native vessels.

All crews and legitimate passengers were also to be issued with identity papers, and passengers were to board and land only in controlled ports. Slaves found were to be freed, as were fugitive slaves, other than criminals, who reached ships of war. To minimize disputes between signatories, the procedure for stopping, searching, and arresting suspects was carefully described.

Chapter 4 bound all signatories, in Africa and elsewhere, in whose territories slavery was legal to pass laws against the import, export, transport of, and trade in slaves and the mutilation of males. Illegally imported slaves were to be freed and repatriated or assisted in earning a living. Liberation offices were to be established to care for them. The Ottoman Empire, Persia, and Zanzibar all pledged active cooperation.

Chapter 5 established two bureaus. One, in Zanzibar, was to centralize information that might lead to the arrest of slavers and keep a record of all captures. The other, in Brussels, was to collect and publish information received from signatories on the measures they were taking to carry out the Brussels Act, statistical information on the number of slaves liberated, and information on the traffic in slaves, arms, and liquor. British attempts to have this latter bureau perform a supervisory role were resisted so it became little more than an information office.

Chapter 6 provided for the restriction of the spirits traffic within the same zone as the restriction of the arms traffic. In areas not yet "contaminated" by the trade, spirits were to be banned. In areas of the zone where there was already an established trade, the spirits were to be subjected to customs duties or, if manufactured locally, to rising excise duties.

Chapter 7 effectively left in force all of Britain's existing treaties against the slave trade except for any clauses that contradicted the provisions of the Brussels Act. Provision was also made for powers that did not sign the act to adhere to it.

Attached to the Brussels Act was a separate declaration allowing import duties to be imposed in the basin of the Congo—a modification of the Berlin Act insisted on by King Leopold II of Belgium. Since the United States had not ratified the Berlin Act, this provision could not be included in the Brussels Act and had to be incorporated in a separate declaration, which all powers but the United States had to sign. The Dutch, whose traders in the Congo were competing with the Belgians, were persuaded to accept this declaration only with great difficulty.

The Brussels Act came into force in 1892. It was ratified in full by all powers except France, whose parliament refused to accept the provisions for the detention of suspected slavers and the verification of the flag. However, the French introduced regulations that virtually implemented these articles, and they ratified the rest of the treaty.

The impact of the act is hard to estimate. It was flawed in that it contained no mechanism either for enforcement or for monitoring results. However, no colonial power could tolerate the disorders of slave raiding, and that problem was soon ended in all but the remoter areas and large-scale slave trading was gradually suppressed as the sources of slaves dried up, although small-scale dealing continued until the end of colonial rule. It was also in the interests of the colonial rulers to end the export of slaves from their territories as they sought to exploit all available manpower themselves.

In 1919, the Brussels and Berlin Acts were both abrogated by the victorious allies—Britain, France, Belgium, Portugal, Italy, the United States, and Japan—as part of the general peace settlement after World War I. For the colonial powers, the acts had served their purpose. They had rallied popular support to the conquest of Africa and given the colonial powers an excuse to make war on those peoples who resisted, who were often also active slave raiders and traders. In 1919, the colonial powers claimed that treaties against the slave trade were no longer needed. In the event, this claim proved overoptimistic, but the powers no longer wished to be tied by the commercial clauses of the Berlin Act and wanted separate agreements concerning the traffic in spirits and arms.

The acts were replaced by three treaties signed at St. Germain, France, in 1919, and the slave trade figured in only a single article in only one of the treaties. That article bound the signatories to watch over the preservation of and supervise the improvement of the moral and material well-being of native peoples and to secure the complete suppression of slavery in all its forms and of the slave trade by land and sea.

The Brussels Act was only one factor in reducing the slave traffic, and it did not protect Africans against the exploitation of their colonial rulers. However, it brought the evils of the slave trade forcefully to public attention and bound signatories to cooperate to suppress it. Humanitarians regarded the act as a triumph, and the principles embodied in it were passed on to the League of Nations and, ultimately, to the United Nations.

—*Suzanne Miers*

See also
Abolition (Africa, British Empire); Brussels Conference; League of Nations
For Further Reading:
Miers, Suzanne. 1975. *Britain and the Ending of the Slave Trade*. London: Longman Group and Africana Publishing.

BRUSSELS CONFERENCE (1889–1890)

The Brussels Conference was the first international conference convened for the express purpose of negotiating a treaty against the African slave trade. It met from November 1889 to July 1890 and resulted in the signature of the General Act for the Repression of the African Slave Trade of 1890, known as the Brussels Act.

The British had tried to secure such a treaty at the Congress of Vienna (1814–1815), and when that effort failed, they had built up a unique network of treaties with other maritime powers and with African and Asian rulers and peoples. These agreements granted them the right to search the shipping of the other countries and laid down procedures for the arrest and trial of suspected slavers. Although these rights were often reciprocal, in practice only the British consistently exercised them, and rival powers became convinced that Britain was using the suppression of the slave trade to interfere with their commerce. In 1855, France refused to grant the British more than the right to verify that suspected vessels were entitled to fly the French flag. Those whose papers were in order could not be searched or arrested, even if they were seen to be carrying slaves.

By the early 1880s, the Atlantic slave trade had ended, but the traffic was still rife in Africa and slaves were still being exported to the Muslim world. Some traveled under guise of the pilgrimage, but many sailed in small vessels (dhows) from the eastern coast of Africa. By this time, the European colonial powers and Leopold II, the king of the Belgians who was building a personal empire in the Congo basin, were dividing up Africa and the islands of the Indian Ocean. The danger was that as they took over the coasts they would attract trade and avoid the expense of policing the seas by allowing slavers to sail under their flags. This possibility was particularly serious in the case of France because the British had no treaty with that country.

Similarly, the powers in the interior of Africa that tolerated the slave trade, and a lucrative arms traffic that supported it, might draw away commerce from more scrupulous neighbors. Neither the slave trade nor the arms trade on land or sea could be ended without international cooperation, and Britain's existing hodgepodge of treaties, which were aimed primarily at the maritime slave traffic, were no longer adequate. Another loophole in the treaty network was that slaves could still be exported on European ships under the guise of contract labor.

At the Berlin West African Conference of 1884–1885, the British tried to get the export slave trade, and the overland traffic that fed it, declared a crime against the law of nations that all powers were bound to suppress. All they could get agreement to, however, was a declaration in the Berlin Act that the maritime trade was forbidden by international law and that the operations that furnished the slaves "ought likewise to be forbidden"; also, the powers that territories in the basin of the Congo merely bound themselves to "help in suppressing slavery and especially the slave trade" and to improve the well-being of "native tribes." No practical measures or common action were agreed upon, and there was no time limit for enforcement.

In the next few years, the European advance into Africa, spearheaded by missionaries, traders, prospectors, and adventurers, was resisted by peoples anxious to preserve their independence, protect their trade, or carve out conquests of their own. The resulting conflicts increased the slave raiding and slave trading that were endemic in much of the continent. By the late 1880s, British settlers on the shores of Lake Malawi, French missionaries around Lake Tanganyika, and King Leopold's posts in the far interior were all threatened by a widespread resistance movement of Arabs and Swahili traders and their African allies who were importing quantities of arms and ravaging large areas. To impose their rule, the imperial powers needed to disarm their enemies and end all wars and raids.

As the "scramble" for Africa gained momentum, it was clear that the antislavery movement could be used to rally previously lukewarm domestic support for colonial ventures. The interest of the British public had already been galvanized by the appeals of David Livingstone to end the scourge by bringing Christianity, commerce, and civilization to the heart of Africa. In 1888, Cardinal Lavigerie, the French founder of the missionary order the Society of Our Lady of Africa, or the White Fathers, whose missionaries in eastern Africa had to abandon some of their stations, launched a "crusade" against the slave trade. To rally support, he toured European capitals with a papal blessing calling for volunteers to fight the slavers and founding antislavery societies as he went.

The idea of a conference in Brussels was first mooted in the British Foreign Office in response to Lavigerie's crusade, which had made a deep impression in Britain. The British government, which was anxious to retain leadership of the antislavery movement and fearful of the havoc that might be created by the cardinal's crusaders, suggested to King Leopold II that he might convene a conference of the European powers that were colonizing the African coast to get their cooperation against the exporting of slaves. The aim was to get other powers, particularly France, to share in the odium and expense of policing the seas, and the British thought an invitation from the king would arouse less suspicion than one emanating from London.

The proposal met with skepticism in Brussels and opposition in Germany, but the British, prodded by a resolution introduced in the House of Commons by supporters of the British and Foreign Anti-Slavery Society, renewed it in the spring of 1889. Both King Leopold and the Germans had now come to realize that such a conference could be tailored to serve their interests. The Germans, who had to quell a rebellion when they first took over their East African territory, wanted to prevent arms from reaching their enemies. Leopold also wanted to control the arms traffic, but for commercial as well as military reasons; he wanted public approval for his conquests in the interior; and he was determined to levy import duties, which had been forbidden in the Congo basin by the Berlin Act.

The act had also stipulated that there should be free trade on the Niger River, as well as on the Congo, and the British, who were now extending their control on the Niger, decided to use the conference to prohibit the liquor traffic in areas of Africa "uncontaminated" by it and to impose duties on it elsewhere. This aim pleased the very vocal temperance societies in Britain; the British Charter Company, which was seeking to gain a monopoly of trade on the Niger; and the governors of the West African colonies, who were anxious to raise revenue by taxing liquor but fearful of driving trade away to rival territories.

To achieve these diverse aims, all the African colonial powers—Britain, France, Germany, Portugal, the Congo, Italy, and Spain—had to be included in the conference as well as the other signatories of the Berlin Act—Holland, Belgium, Russia, Austria, Sweden, Denmark, and the United States. The Ottoman Empire, which had territories in Africa and was a major importer of slaves, was invited for the further reason that its presence would avoid the impression that the conference was launching a Christian crusade. Zanzibar was asked as a sop to the sultan, whose territories were then being divided between Britain and Germany, and Persia was included because it was a Muslim state and believed to be cooperating against the slave trade.

The conference was attended by many leading diplomats, by experts on Africa, by representatives of trading companies, and by observers from humanitarian bodies. Over many months the delegates hammered out the Brussels Act—a treaty designed to end the slave trade while serving the imperialist cause. The act that finally emerged, although flawed, was comprehensive and detailed and thus a great advance over the Berlin Act and a landmark in the antislavery movement.

—Suzanne Miers

See also
Abolition (Africa, British Empire); Africa; Berlin West African Conference; Brussels Act; Vienna, Congress of
For Further Reading
Miers, Suzanne. 1975. *Britain and the Ending of the Slave Trade*. London: Longman Group and Africana Publishing.

BUDDHISM

Slavery appears in Buddhist tradition as an existential metaphor and as one kind of economic capital of monastic institutions. Historically, to the extent that slavery was practiced in the cultures that embraced it, Buddhism condoned slaveowning. Slavery was partly justified by the Buddhist doctrines of karma and rebirth: those who do bad deeds will suffer the results of those deeds, whether in this or in future lifetimes. Conversely, any suffering or low status experienced now results from previous bad deeds. Therefore, if you suffer as a slave, it must be because of moral transgression in an earlier life, and bearing the burden without anger or violence may lead to a better rebirth. The Buddha exhorts masters to treat slaves well but also tells slaves to bear their lot in life patiently. Yet beyond a pleasant rebirth, the ultimate goal of Buddhist beliefs is manumission from enslavement to desire, which binds us to the painful birth and death cycle (samsara).

Thus, slavery appears in Buddhist scriptures as a metaphor for the human condition: we are enslaved to the cycle of rebirth, to our egotistical delusions, and to our passions. In the Lotus Sutra (Saddharma-pundarika-sutra), Buddha tells a parable of a dung

The Wheel of Transmigration depicts the different realms into which one may be reborn in order to learn necessary lessons. This logic can be used to argue that slaves are working off "bad karma" from a previous life.

sweeper who is unaware that the friendly master he serves is really his rich father and that he is the rightful heir to a great fortune. Menial servitude (although in this case not really slavery) is a metaphor for the dire condition of the people who live in ignorance of their true Buddha nature. Another rhetorical use of the slavery motif is to express devotion, as in the name of the famous Thai monk, Buddhadāsa ("slave of Buddha").

Buddhism's historical founder, Gautama Sākyamuni, was born a prince of a small state at the foot of the Himalayas. He left home to become an ascetic, experienced a spiritual awakening, and became known as the Buddha ("one who has awakened"). During a long teaching career, the Buddha gained numerous disciples. Consistent with the rhetoric of withdrawal from the world, the Buddha and his disciples did not cultivate their own food but lived on donations. Initially, they wandered, living in marginal areas or donated dwellings. Although they were allowed to build only rudimentary shelters by themselves, they could accept grander accommodations from wealthy laity. Initially, the monastic life was determined directly by Buddha's judgments, but after his death, monastic codes (vinaya) were recorded and transmitted in various versions according to sectarian and local differences. Until the reign of King Asoka (274–236 B.C.), the Buddhist community (sangha) was relatively small and only one of many monastic communities. Asoka sponsored Buddhists and several other sects, precipitating their increased institutionalization. By dispatching missionaries and expelling dissident Buddhists, Asoka stimulated Buddhism's spread into central and eastern Asia.

Buddhism, from the beginning, was a movement that thrived on the laity's sponsorship. Land, buildings, animals, precious metals, cloth, and food were donated. Doctrinally and ritually, Buddhist clerics claimed a status beyond the secular world, but inevitably monastic institutions conformed to many aspects of their surrounding social world, which included slavery. In Buddhist scriptures, slavery is an assumed background to the narratives, and slaves were among the donations to the sangha. Various terms were used: kalpikāra ("bondsmen"), kapyāri ("proper slave"), kalpiyakāra ("proper bondman"), parivāra, dāsa, and ārāmika (there are problems of precise translation for these last three). To the extent that people could be "donated," they were, in any case, chattel.

Although people could be given to monks and monasteries, slaves could not be ordained as monks or nuns unless they were legally freed. If they were freed, they received new names since Buddha specifically ruled against using the old name. In the rules on admission to the order is the story of a runaway slave who was ordained as a monk. When the owners came and wanted to take him back some people objected, and the case was reported to Buddha, who decided that no slave should receive ordination. In their exclusion from ordination, slaves were not alone: similar rules applied to robbers, convicts, debtors, underage boys, runaways without parental permission, the diseased, and anyone in royal service. Women were admitted to the sangha only after some lobbying, and even then with significant reservations.

In several of the vinayas, Buddha allows the donation and use of domestic servants and slaves, along with land, mats, livestock, utensils, and medicine. One tradition preserves a story of King Bimbisāra (a major donor who lived the same time as Buddha) asking the Buddhist monk Pilindavaccha if he needed an "attendant for a monastery" or "park keeper" (ārāmika). Pilindavaccha first sought the permission of the Buddha, who replied, "I allow monks a monastery attendant." Bimbisāra gave Pilindavaccha 500 such attendants, and they lived in a separate compound. Here, the gift was to a specific monk. The influx of these workers (and others) necessitated the monastic office of "superintendent of monastery attendants" to oversee their labors.

A somewhat later vinaya, of another tradition, has a parallel version of the story. In it, the donated servants are initially forced to work in the king's house as well. The slaves objected, saying, "We belong to the noble ones"—the plural is important here as it indicates a shift from gifts to individual monks to the collective sangha. To clarify whose slaves were whose, the Buddha allowed the monastic slaves to have a separate dwelling: "Henceforth having quarters for the proper bondmen constructed is approved." The location was determined to be outside the king's city and outside the monastery.

Occasionally, slaves were employed to perform acts specifically forbidden of monks (e.g., handling silver and gold), and the retinue of important people often included slaves who delivered invitations to monks and carried food offerings. Perhaps by the beginning of the first century there were a few large monasteries with vast servant populations attached, but numerous smaller establishments had no such endowment. As monasteries declined in economic power and as antislavery movements grew, slavery in the service of Buddhism became obsolete.

—Eric Reinders

See also
Asian/Buddhist Monastic Slavery; China (Ancient, Late Imperial, Medieval); East Asia
For Further Reading
Gernet, Jacques. 1995. *Buddhism in Chinese Society: An Economic History from the Fifth to the Tenth Centuries.*

New York: Columbia University Press; Schopen, Gregory. 1994. "The Monastic Ownership of Servants or Slaves: Local and Legal Factors in the Redactional History of Two Vinayas." *Journal of the International Association of Buddhist Studies* 17: 145–173.

BULKING CENTERS

Bulking centers were the principal places for international commerce, including commerce in slaves, along Africa's coast and generally were linked to the presence of many Europeans, Americans, and/or Arabs or to major African state-enterprises with strong commercial ties to outside interests. In these centers, the outsiders bulked large quantities of trade goods for both the African market and exterior markets. When African state-enterprises were involved, state monopolies served similar purposes, with Africans regulating trade and acting as principal merchants. Such centers were advantageous for outsiders as they permitted a rapid turnaround of goods brought to Africa in exchange for slaves and commodities. Quick transactions inevitably improved profits and lessened exposure of ships' crews to tropical diseases and fevers.

From the earliest non-African contact with Africa's coast, outsiders attempted to establish linkages with existing African commercial networks and to identify coastal locations where their commerce could enjoy security and protection. Along the east coast, the Arabs generally sought islands that were secure from mainland attack and where, through special arrangements with landlords, they practiced unique cultural patterns. Over time, Pate, Lamu, Malindi, Pemba, Zanzibar, Kilwa Kisiwani, and Mozambique acquired importance as ports of call for most merchants trading along the east coast. In West Africa, the Portuguese and their successors initially obtained possession of islands well beyond the coast (Cape Verde Islands, São Tomé, Príncipe, Fernando Po) where they established elaborate commercial enterprises. They later extended their networks to islands closer to the coast, which they obtained through contracts with indigenous landlords (Gorée, Bolama, Îles de Loos or Los Islands, and Bance). Africans also utilized the islands as bulking centers, especially during the transition period from commerce in slaves to commodities.

The advantages of the islands off the west coast as bulking centers were significant during the slave-trading period. On the Îles de Loos, for example, an absence of mangrove swamps and the presence of steady sea breezes significantly reduced the incidence of fever, the bane of Europeans visiting the coast. Friendly landlords profiting directly either as merchants themselves or as recipients of rents, taxes, and customs gave stability to commercial ventures requiring significant capital investment.

During the height of slaving on this coast (1750–1790), Liverpool's Barber and Bolland Company maintained a major bulking center on Factory Island, one of the Îles de Loos. Barber (or his agents) constructed buildings that served as housing for merchandise, residences for himself and his workers, a shop for making and storing rope/rigging, a place for ship repair and storing shipwright supplies, blacksmith shop, and wine warehouse. Barber also maintained two barracoons (corrals for salable slaves), a wharf for loading and unloading ships, a slip for ship repairs, a large trading vessel permanently anchored at the wharf, and a large number of longboats for trading in neighboring rivers. Barber's enterprise extended onto the mainland where he operated numerous agencies and employed more than 450 subagents or employees. From his Factory Island bulking center, Barber sold directly to buyers (both African and European) and indirectly to agents marketing his products along the coast.

A second type of bulking center was represented by clusters of factories operating within a small area. Such was the case in the Rio Pongo, located approximately 50 miles north of the Îles de Loos. Here more than 20 European, Euroafrican, African American, and African merchants (and their descendants) operated factories at the beginning of the nineteenth century, often within walking distance of each other. Although none of these was as elaborate as the one on Factory Island, each generally consisted of a shop, warehouse, house, and barracoon.

Factors established relationships with landlords for mutual advantage and often specialized in products or markets. Merchants competed for market shares but often cooperated openly by bunching commodities when captains arrived searching for cargoes of commodities or slaves. Such clusters also served as magnets for traders from the interior seeking adequate supplies of firearms or other manufactured goods and expecting to conduct business in the African fashion. The merchants of such clusters operated, then, in two ways: rapid turnarounds for Europeans in European languages and slow bargaining for Africans in indigenous languages. Collectively, the clusters provided significant markets (entrepôts) for both African and outside merchants.

A third type of bulking center associated with slave trading consisted of mainland forts/towns. These centers (Elmina, Cape Coast, Lagos, Benin, Warri, Luanda, Benguela) were controlled by official European monopoly enterprises or African state commerce. In both cases, slave trading became regulated and taxed, generating significant income to local political elites.

—*Bruce L. Mouser*

See also
Barracoons; Benin; Factors; Gorée Island; Middle Passage; Slave Villages
For Further Reading
Brooks, George E. 1993. *Landlords & Strangers*. Boulder, CO: Westview Press; Curtin, Philip. 1969. *The Atlantic Slave Trade*. Madison: University of Wisconsin Press; Debbasch, Yvan. 1988. "L'Espace du Sierra-Leone et la politique francaise de traite a la fin de l'Ancien Regime." In *De la traite a l'esclavage*. Ed. Serge Daget. Paris: Harmattan; Mouser, Bruce L. 1973. "Trade, Coasters, and Conflict in the Rio Pongo from 1790 to 1808." *Journal of African History*, 14 (1): 45–64.

BURGOS, LAWS OF (1513)

The Laws of Burgos, promulgated on December 27, 1512, were passed in an attempt to regulate the relationship between Spaniards and Indians in the New World. As the sixteenth century began, there was a rivalry over the Taino, the native people of Hispaniola. The opposing sides were Spanish *encomenderos*—conquistadors to whom groups of Taino had been "commended" for labor tribute, theoretically in exchange for Christian training and induction into "civilized" ways of life—and Dominican friars—who believed that the exploitative *encomienda* system was not the best way to convert the natives. "Are these not men?" asked the Dominican friar Antonio de Montesinos in a famous 1511 sermon in which he demand that natives be treated like proper vassals of the crown.

The Spanish crown appointed a royal council of theologians and legal specialists to meet at Burgos to study conflicting requests and recommendations and to decide whether the Indians were, as suggested by Aristotle, "natural slaves" or whether they had the capacity to become fully functioning crown subjects. "While recognizing the freedom of the Indians and their right to humane treatment," the council "concluded that they must be subject to coercion and kept close to the Spaniards in order that their conversion be effected" (Hanke, 1949). In other words, the council decided that the *encomienda* system was just and that it would, if properly regulated, provide the medium by which Spain could fulfill its obligation to Christianize the natives, as per the Papal Donation of 1492. The regulations the council developed were known as the original Laws of Burgos.

These laws decreed that the Indians were to be relocated into new villages where they could see and emulate their Spanish *encomenderos* and thus be kept from backsliding into habits of "idleness and vice" as they had done when they lived far from their *encomenderos* (Preamble and Article 1, Laws of Burgos). Eleven of the 35 articles deal specifically with religious matters. For example, the *encomendero* was "obliged to erect a structure to be used for a church" in each new village, "and in this said church he shall place an image of Our Lady and a bell with which to call the Indians to prayer, and the person who has them in *encomienda* shall be obliged to have them called by the bell at nightfall and go with them to the said church, and have them cross themselves and bless themselves, and together recite" the basic Catholic prayers (Article 3).

Many of the articles detail the proper treatment of the Indians, including restrictions against using Indians as beasts of burden (Article 11); division of the work year into periods for gold mining and periods when the Indians were to be allowed to tend their own fields (Article 13); allowing the Indians to celebrate on Sundays and feast days (Article 14); provision for minimum meat rations to be fed to the Indians (Article 15); restrictions against women more than four months pregnant being sent to the mines and provision that they be given only light household tasks (Article 17); provision that the Indians should be given and restrictions against allowing them to sleep on the ground (Article 19); provision for a gold peso per year as salary to each Indian laborer (Article 20); restrictions against beating or whipping any Indian and establishing fines for anyone who "should call an Indian dog, or address him by any name other than his own" (Article 24).

Encomenderos argued that the Laws of Burgos were too restrictive, and Dominicans argued that the laws did not provide adequate protection for the Indians. King Ferdinand agreed with the friars, and amendments to the Laws of Burgos were promulgated on July 28, 1513. These included protection for Indian women, who "shall not be forced to go and come and serve with their husbands, at the mines or elsewhere, unless it is by their own free will" (Amendment 1); for Indian children under age 14, who were not to be assigned adult tasks but only "tasks proper to children, such as weeding the fields and the like," and for Indian children without parents, who were to be provided with guardians "of good conscience" (Amendment 2); for unmarried Indian women, who were to be assigned to tasks in the village and not sent to work with the men (Amendment 3); and for any and all Indians who learned to wear clothes and to lead Christian lives, thus showing their competency "to live by themselves and govern themselves," that they be allowed to do so (Amendment 4).

In addition to trying to regulate relationships between Spaniards and Indians, the Laws of Burgos also attempted to bring the Indians to Christianity and to integrate them into the new colonial society in a "just" manner. Unfortunately, the laws were not very effective.

—Lynne Guitar

For Further Reading
Hanke, Lewis. 1935. *The First Social Experiments in America: A Study in the Development of Spanish Indian Policy in the Sixteenth Century.* Cambridge: Cambridge University Press; Hanke, Lewis. 1949. *The Spanish Struggle for Justice in the Conquest of America.* Philadelphia: University of Pennsylvania Press; Parry, John H., and Robert G. Keith, eds. 1984. *New Iberian Worlds: A Documentary History of the Discovery and Settlement of Latin America to the Early Seventeenth Century.* New York: Times Books; Simpson, Lesley Byrd. 1966. *The Encomienda in New Spain: The Beginning of Spanish Mexico.* Berkeley: University of California Press.

BURKE, EDMUND
(1729–1797)

Edmund Burke's name is connected with conservatism, and he is widely known for his famous counterrevolutionary essay *Reflections on the Revolution in France* (1790), but Burke hated slavery. Born in Ireland, Burke was raised as a Protestant in a Catholic milieu. He went to London in 1750 and entered English political life as a Whig politician in the British Parliament in 1765. An eloquent writer and orator, Burke engaged in political issues that included the Irish case, the American Revolution, India and the role of Governor Warren Hastings, and the French Revolution. It was the outbreak of the French Revolution that led him to break with the Whigs in 1791.

To call Burke a conservative is too simplistic. He had an organic vision of society that did not allow for sudden or revolutionary changes, but throughout his life, Burke took stands that can be labeled liberal or enlightened. His ideas on political and civil liberty, and slavery, fit his organic and enlightened worldview. Liberty meant, according to Burke, social freedom. Liberty was embedded in society and was "another name for Justice, ascertained by wise Laws and secured by well constructed institutions," as he wrote in 1789 (O'Brien, 1992). Burke gave political support to American independence but felt uneasy about the freedom the American revolutionaries claimed and the slave system in which many of them were engaged.

As early as 1757 he uttered strong feelings of discontent about the slave trade and slavery in the West Indies and North America, and he thought the West Indian slaves were worse off than their counterparts in the American colonies. The natural increase in the slave population in Virginia was, according to Burke, a "blessing derived from a more moderate labor, better food, and a more healthy climate" (Burke and Burke, 1835). In the West Indies, the death rate among the slaves was very high owing to bad treatment and harsh working conditions. Burke proposed better treatment, including religious instruction, not only for the sake of humanity, but also to prevent unrest and insurrection.

In 1765, Burke spoke against the seating of Americans in the House of Commons, because in his opinion that would mean the seating of slaveowners. Burke, like most of his contemporaries, did not want a revolutionary solution to the problem of slavery; he proposed gradual reform, for he believed that slaves were not prepared for immediate abolition. As early as 1780, Burke developed a plan for ameliorating the slave trade and slavery entitled, "Sketch of a Negro Code."

In 1789 and 1791, Burke supported motions by William Wilberforce in the House of Commons for abolition of the slave trade; in both cases the majority of the House voted against. In April 1792, a compromise was presented to the House by Henry Dundas: before the slave imports from Africa could be stopped, it was necessary to improve the conditions of the West Indian slaves. Now a majority was in favor of a gradual abolition of the slave trade, but the proposition did not have the status of a bill and the House of Lords was not willing to cooperate, so matters were postponed to a later date.

Also in April 1792, Burke retrieved his "Sketch" of 1780 from his papers and sent it to Dundas. Besides a more humane treatment of the slaves and rules for the slave trade, Burke proposed to introduce "civilization and gradual manumission" in preparation for future abolition. By civilization he meant education, religious and moral instruction, and the encouragement of family life among slaves (Cone, 1964). Burke's ongoing support for abolition had a considerable influence on the political campaign against the slave trade.

—Angelie Sens

For Further Reading
Burke, Edmund, and William Burke. 1835. *An Account of the European Settlements in America.* Boston: J. H. Wilkins; Cone, Carl B. 1964. *Burke and the Nature of Politics: The Age of the French Revolution.* Lexington: University of Kentucky Press; Freeman, Michael. 1980. *Edmund Burke and the Critique of Political Radicalism.* Oxford: Basil Blackwell; O'Brien, Connor. 1992. *The Great Melody: A Thematic Biography and Commented Anthology of Edmund Burke.* Chicago: University of Chicago Press.

BURNS, ANTHONY
(C. 1830–1862)

Anthony Burns ranks with Frederick Douglass and Harriet Tubman as being among the more famous fugitive slaves in U.S. history. Born in Stafford County, Virginia, he was hired out at the age of seven and subsequently worked for several masters. He had a hand mangled in a sawmill accident, but he learned how to read and write, and in his teens he became a Baptist preacher. Employment in Richmond, Virginia, in 1853 finally offered him a realistic opportunity to escape, and in February 1854 he stowed away on a ship bound for Boston by way of Norfolk.

On May 24, about 11 weeks after arriving in Massachusetts, Burns was on his way home from his job at a clothing store when he was arrested on a false charge of robbery, taken to the federal courthouse, and confronted by his owner, Charles F. Suttle. The next morning Burns was taken before the fugitive slave commissioner, Judge Edward G. Loring, for what was intended as a quick hearing under the Fugitive Slave Act and a quiet return to slavery in Virginia. But a failed rescue effort on May 26 led to the death of a jailer, and continued intervention by Bostonians like Burns's black pastor, Leonard A. Grimes, and a white lawyer, Richard Henry Dana, extended the procedure until June 2. Judge Loring then determined that Burns was indeed the fugitive slave being sought. Hundreds of state militia and more hundreds of federal soldiers ushered Burns to the docks for his return to Virginia. At enormous cost, the federal act had been enforced.

In despair after his capture, Burns had regarded quiet cooperation with the slave catchers as his safest method of behavior. He was correct that he otherwise faced cruel treatment on his return, but the fracas associated with his being rendered back to slavery also led to his eventual freedom. For many weeks following his return to Richmond on June 12, 1854, he was kept manacled in a filthy jail cell. Then Suttle sold him to David McDaniel, a slave trader and planter from Rocky Mount, North Carolina. Within a few months people in Boston's black community discovered Burns's new whereabouts, and McDaniel agreed on a purchase price that would permit Burns to return North, this time as a freeman. Burns arrived back in Boston one year after he had stepped off the steamer that carried him out of slavery the first time.

Burns's wish to study to become a trained preacher took him to Oberlin College in Ohio in summer 1855 and later to Fairmont Theological Seminary in Cincinnati. Sales of his biography helped finance his education. By 1860 he was the minister of a black church in Indianapolis, and he became the pastor of a congregation of fugitive slaves, Zion Baptist Church, in St. Catharines on the Canadian side of Lake Ontario. Still weak from his 1854 ordeal, Burns died of tuberculosis soon after moving to his new home.

—Peter Wallenstein

See also
Canada; Fugitive Slave Act of 1850
For Further Reading
Boston Slave Riot and Trial of Anthony Burns. 1854. Boston: Fetridge and Company; Finkelman, Paul. 1996. "Legal Ethics and Fugitive Slaves: The Anthony Burns Case, Judge Loring, and Abolitionist Attorneys." *Cardozo Law Review* 17 (May): 1793–1858; Pease, Jane H., and William H. Pease. 1975. *The Fugitive Slave Law and Anthony Burns: A Problem in Law Enforcement*. Philadelphia: J. B. Lippincott; Stevens, Charles Emery. 1973. *Anthony Burns: A History*. Williamstown, MA: Corner House Publishers.

BUXTON, SIR THOMAS FOWELL
(1786–1845)

Thomas Fowell Buxton succeeded William Wilberforce as the leader of the British parliamentary campaign against slavery in 1824. He led the abolitionist party in the House of Commons, which finally achieved an emancipation act in 1833 and thereafter advocated proposals for bringing all forms of slaving by illegal traders to an end.

Buxton's early life had a significant influence on him. His mother was a member of the Society of Friends and encouraged his interest in social issues, such as reform of the criminal law and prison systems. He became a member of Parliament in 1818 and soon developed an interest in the slavery question. With Wilberforce and others he was a founding member of the Society for the Mitigation and Gradual Abolition of Slavery throughout the British Dominions in 1823. Formation of the society was the start of the renewed campaign against slavery, but it moved slowly and with limited demands lived up to the "Gradual" in its title.

Buxton did not marshal his forces well, either in mobilizing public opinion or behind the scenes. The number of slave revolts, economic factors, and a change of government were probably more effective than the humanitarian antislavery campaign. However, Buxton's evidence of the decline of the slave population in the Caribbean over the 20 years before 1830 was a factor in the case for abolition.

Buxton was not returned to Parliament in 1837, and he turned his attention to the illegal slave trade, which was still very active on the West African coast. His treatise *The African Slave Trade and Its Remedy*

(1840) proposed various measures including improvements in the antislavery patrols of the Royal Navy, the "civilization" of Africa by the introduction of Christianity, and the increased encouragement of legitimate trade to push out slaving. To this end he inaugurated the African Civilization Society at an enthusiastic meeting in London in June 1840. More important, he persuaded the British government to mount an expedition to the Niger River to establish a European-style farm in the lower Niger Valley.

The expedition was vigorously opposed by people who had direct experience of Africa, including MacGregor Laird, who had explored the Niger in the early 1830s, and Robert Jamieson, a Liverpool palm oil merchant. Jamieson's *An Appeal to the Government and People of Great Britain against the Proposed Niger Expedition* (1840) argued in favor of free trade and against government intervention, which, he said, would lead to a monopoly, force prices down, and prevent further development.

The expedition was a total disaster. Within two months, 48 of the 145 settlers had died of disease, and the remainder had to be rescued, many by Jamieson's steamer *Ethiope*. The failure of the expedition resulted in the dissolution of the African Civilization Society and effectively brought Buxton's career to an end. He had been created a baronet in 1840, and a statue, which now stands in Westminster Abbey, was erected by public subscription.

—Anthony Tibbles

See also
Wilberforce, William
For Further Reading
Temperley, Howard. 1991. *White Dreams, Black Africa.* New Haven, CT: Yale University Press.

BYRD, WILLIAM
(1674–1744)

The second William Byrd of Virginia was one of that colony's most prominent slaveholding planter aristocrats, and he distinguished himself as a lawyer, colonial official, and writer. He inherited a large James River plantation, its slaves and the family home, Westover, from his father, William Byrd (1652–1704), who had obtained part of his fortune through land speculation and the traffic in African slaves. The son William Byrd later accumulated more land and slaves, which enabled him to enjoy an elegant and cultivated lifestyle.

The number of Byrd's African slaves exceeded 200. On occasion he imported them directly—in June 1710 he paid £23 each for 26 who arrived at Westover; others he acquired when he took over the estate at Mount Folly of his deceased father-in-law, Daniel Parke. Besides African slaves, Byrd also owned several Native Americans, mentioning three by name in his diary. Byrd, like many Virginia planters, occasionally sold slaves to pay his creditors.

Although Byrd tried to be a kindly master, referring to his slaves and servants as "my family," his paternalism also had a harsh side. As detailed in his *Secret Diary,* Byrd often talked with his slaves, listened to their troubles, prescribed cures for their illnesses, and advised them on personal matters. He made sure that they were adequately clothed, and as a strict observer of the Sabbath, he tried to keep their Sunday work to a minimum. However, he personally whipped slaves whose behavior displeased him, or he might induce an unruly slave to vomit, which he found to be an effective punishment. He ordered others to be tied by the leg or fastened with a bit in their mouth, but he never branded them, and usually he maintained discipline with threats, not punishment. Occasionally a slave escaped, but this occurred less frequently at Westover than at other Virginia plantations.

Byrd was well aware that it was because his vast estates were worked by slaves that he was able to "live in a kind of independence of everyone but Providence" (Wright and Tinling, 1941), yet he gradually came to disapprove of slavery as not being Christian and of the people who trafficked in human cargo. He strongly advised the prohibition of slavery in the new colony of Georgia. He felt uncomfortable with the inhumanity of slavery and regretted the cruelty it engendered. But severity was necessary, he conceded, because the vast numbers of slaves made them insolent. He claimed that slavery led to laziness among whites who detested work "for fear it should make them look like slaves."

His greatest concern, however, was the possibility of a servile uprising. He feared that a leader, perhaps a white leader, might arise to lead the slaves in a rebellion that "would tinge our rivers . . . with blood" (Wright and Tinling, 1941). Although Byrd himself engaged in the transatlantic slave trade, he had great contempt for the self-righteous New Englanders who carried rum and slaves up Virginia rivers, once characterizing them as "felons." Despite Byrd's reservations about slavery, as a Virginia planter he recognized the reality of its economic value.

—Charles H. McArver, Jr.

For Further Reading
Hatch, Alden. 1969. *The Byrds of Virginia.* New York: Holt, Rinehart and Winston; Marambaud, Pierre. 1971. *William Byrd of Westover.* Charlottesville: University of Virginia Press; Wright, Louis B. 1940. *The First Gentle-*

A slave market in the Byzantine Empire.

men of Virginia. San Marino, CA: Huntington Library; Wright, Louis B., and Marion Tinling, eds. 1941. *The Secret Diary of William Byrd of Westover, 1709–1712.* Richmond, VA: Dietz Press.

BYZANTINE ECLOGA

Around the year 726, Byzantine emperors Leo III and Constantine V issued a collection of laws to supplement the great legal corpus formulated by their predecessor Justinian two centuries earlier. These supplementary laws, or *Ecloga,* added numerous details to Justinian's slavery legislation. Besides expanding on numerous aspects of the Justinian Code, the *Ecloga* also provided simplified interpretations of how laws worked in practice. For example, the legal position related to emancipating slaves was both extended and clarified, and the Orthodox Church was given a greater role. The means by which a slave could gain freedom were presented in clear, unambiguous terms and became subject to direct clerical influence.

A slave became free if his master emancipated him publicly in a church or in the presence of three or five witnesses. If there were no public enfranchisement, then a letter from the master, signed by witnesses, was sufficient, as was a will. Other methods of manumission included some in which the church's influence is clearly visible. For instance, with his master's consent, a slave could become a priest or monk, or the master, or his heir, might act as sponsor to a slave's receiving "holy and salvation-bringing baptism." Any slave wishing to become a Christian, but whose master was non-Orthodox, could do so and was promptly freed, the basis of this law being that no non-Orthodox person should be permitted to possess a Christian slave, the fine for such possession being 30 pounds of gold paid directly to the state coffers. "Non-Othodox" at that time usually implied affiliation to Judaism, paganism, or a Christian heresy. Jewish masters who kept Christian slaves and had them circumcised were themselves executed by the state, as were any non-Orthodox masters who tried to coerce Christian slaves into renunciating their faith.

Religious elements are visible, too, in the *Ecloga*'s refinement of the laws of reenslavement. A freedman who fell back into slavery could not revert to the service of a non-Orthodox former master, even if the latter subsequently converted to Christianity. Likewise, a freedman who found himself reenslaved could appeal to the church and make a case for regaining his liberty.

Any unjust return of a freedman to bondage was viewed as a serious crime: anyone who abducted a freedman and sold him as a slave was punished by amputation of a hand. One of the harsher laws in the *Ecloga* condemned a maidservant, whether freed or freeborn, to slavery if she was found to be consorting with her mistress's husband.

The slavery laws contained in the *Ecloga* differ from those codified by Justinian in detail rather than in substance. The incorporation of Christian and clerical influence testifies to the growing importance of the Orthodox Church in Byzantium, but it seems rather to overlay rather than to underpin the text. Of equal interest and importance is that the main corpus of classical Roman slavery law was still functioning largely unchanged into the eighth century.

—*Tim Clarkson*

For Further Reading
Freshfield, Edwin, ed. 1926. *A Manual of Roman Law: The Ecloga.* Cambridge: Cambridge University Press.

CADIZ

The city of Cádiz is located in southwestern Spain's Andalusian region. Its harbor is both a link between the Atlantic Ocean and the Mediterranean Sea and a central reference point in the international trade routes between America, Europe, and Africa, and its geographical placement gave Cádiz a significant role in the history of Spanish slavery between the sixteenth and eighteenth centuries. There were few slaves in northern Spain during the early modern period, and through the fifteenth and sixteenth centuries, the majority of Spain's slaves were concentrated in a geographical triangle whose three corners were all in southern Andalusia: Ayamonte, Seville, and Cádiz.

Fifteenth-century Portuguese expansion in the Atlantic Ocean was the major reason for the presence of the first slaves in Cádiz. Known as "blacks," most of them came from Jalof and Saõ Tomé (islands off the coast of West Africa) to work as domestic servants for members of the upper strata of local society. As the fifteenth century ended, documents show a change: most slaves appearing in municipal or parish registers started being called "Moros," and they came from North Africa's Maghreb area. The predominance of Moors among the slave population of Cádiz diminished in the sixteenth century after the organization of the trade monopoly with America and the *asiento* (monopoly right to carry slaves to Spanish lands). As a result of this monopoly, numerous ships arrived in Cádiz harbor with hundreds of black slaves, and these slowly replaced the Moors as the major type of local slave.

Cádiz marriage books of the first half of the seventeenth century show that slaves named *Negros* and *Morenos* constituted almost 80 percent of all of the city's slaves who married; another 11 percent of the slaves registered in Cádiz marriage books were named *Berberiscos,* 5 percent had the name *Mulatos,* and all the others were named *Pardos* or *Membrillos cochos.* The geographical origins of these slaves were diverse during the first half of the seventeenth century, but most of them came from Angola and others from Portugal and the Portuguese and Spanish-American territories. The predominance of black Angolan slaves diminished after the 1640 Portuguese rebellion against Spain, as commercial relations between Spanish and Portuguese merchants suffered because of the political troubles. In 1663, the British traders John Mathews and Robert Broque sold more than 125 African slaves in Cádiz, and the price of slaves from 1663 to 1675 varied between 180 and 220 pesos of 8 silver reals for each man or woman. As the seventeenth century ended, commercial relations with the Portuguese slave traders improved, and Cádiz again became a marketplace to which hundreds of African slaves (called Moros, Berberiscos, Turcos, and blacks) were brought to be sold.

In Cádiz, African blacks organized their own religious association, the Cofradia de Nuestra Senora de la Salud, San Bello y Santa Ifigenia. Many of these slaves worked as domestic servants in the wealthier sectors of Cádiz society whereas Moros were employed in the worst jobs, like building city walls or street cleaning.

Available data suggest that in the first half of the seventeenth century, there were at least 3,000 slaves in Cádiz. This figure increased so that by the end of the century, there might have been at least 6,000 slaves (about 10 percent of the population) living in the city. This slave population included children of slaves born in Spain but consisted mostly of slaves who had been brought to the city in slave ships. During the eighteenth century, the Cádiz slave trade diminished considerably, and the number of slaves freed by their owners slowly increased.

—*Paloma Fernández-Pérez*

See also
Spain
For Further Reading
Fernández-Pérez, Paloma. 1997. *El nuestro familiar de la metrópoli. Redes de parentesco y consolidación de lazos mercantiles en Cádiz, 1700–1812.* Madrid: Siglo XXI de España; Franco Silva, A. 1992. *Esclavitud en Andulaucia 1450–1550.* Granada: Servicio de Publicaciones de la Universidad de Granada; Lobo Cabrera, M. 1990. "La esclavitude en la España moderna: su investigación en los últimos cincuenta años." *Hispania* 176; Phillips, W. D., Jr. 1990. *Historia de la esclavitude in España.* Madrid: Siglo XXI de España.

CALHOUN, JOHN C.
(1782–1850)

Although he served as vice-president and as a cabinet officer in two presidential administrations, John C. Calhoun is most remembered as being a staunch supporter of slavery and states' rights. No Southern politician of the antebellum period was more widely experienced than South Carolina's Calhoun, and as congressman, senator, cabinet member, and vice-president he was as powerful and influential as any American before his death in 1850. Yet, despite Calhoun's national stature, history recognizes him more as the strategist who engineered the antebellum defense of slavery.

Calhoun was a significant slaveholder himself and, not surprisingly, viewed slavery as an economic good. He was interested in agriculture and scientific farming and had mining interests in northern Georgia. His largest landholdings were near Pendleton, South Carolina, where he owned a 1,000-acre cotton plantation named Fort Hill, and he owned another cotton plantation in Alabama's Black Belt in Marengo County. Calhoun owned over 150 slaves at the two operations, and he also utilized slave labor at his gold mine located near Dahlonega, Georgia. Calhoun added several large land grants to his already considerable interests, and in later years, he went into serious debt because of land investments and several poor harvests.

Calhoun had grown up with slaves and was considered a good and fair master. The historical record shows his slaves were rather fond of their master. He was convinced of the inferiority of blacks and believed them incapable of freedom. He defended slavery on moral and economic grounds and rejected the "necessary evil" defense, convinced the institution was the foundation of a Southern society based on agriculture. Over the last two pivotal decades of his life, Calhoun did not waver in his belief that slavery was a "positive good," one that was benevolent to the inferior race.

Calhoun saved his most vitriolic attacks for Northerners who were critical of slavery, especially abolitionists. Calhoun charged that Northern contentions that slavery was a sin and immoral were baseless, and he did not mince words when provided a public audience. Unlike several of his more enlightened Southern colleagues, Calhoun opposed emancipation, and, to the satisfaction of many of his fellow slaveowners, his was a major voice defending the existence of slavery.

Calhoun was born on March 18, 1782, near Abbeville in South Carolina. In 1802 he left South Carolina for Yale and returned two years later a graduate and a Unitarian. Calhoun began the study of law in Charleston and graduated from Connecticut's Litchfield Law School in 1806. His early years practicing law proved unfulfilling, and he entered politics in 1808. His early experience led to his election to Congress in 1811, where he served until 1817 when he was appointed President James Monroe's secretary of war. A war hawk in Congress, Calhoun served eight years in the cabinet, reorganizing the War Department and overseeing its significant growth. Aspiring to the presidency, Calhoun settled for the vice-presidential post under John Quincy Adams in 1825. As the Democratic Party emerged with the meteoric rise of Andrew Jackson, Calhoun found that party's states' rights platform compatible with his doctrine of nullification, and when Jackson easily carried the presidency in 1828, Calhoun was again elected vice-president.

The year 1828 was pivotal for Calhoun. He anonymously penned the so-called South Carolina Exposition, which continued the states' rights stand, and introduced his interpretation of the doctrine of interposition, which argued that a state had the right to veto any federal legislation that it found to be unconstitutional. The entire argument centered on opposition to the protective tariff of 1828, and Calhoun and South Carolina led the charge. As a split developed between Jackson and Calhoun, South Carolina nullified the tariffs of 1828 and 1832 and threatened secession. The volatile Calhoun was elected to the Senate in December 1832 and resigned as vice-president. In time, a lower tariff measure was passed as a compromise and the secession crisis was averted.

From the Senate, Calhoun further developed his defense of slavery as a positive good and opposed the growing national antislavery movement, moving away from defending the institution as a necessary evil for Southern economic development. Confronting abolitionists at every turn, Calhoun's defense of the South's right to protect its constitutional guarantee to own slaves further increased his position as a national political figure. He briefly considered a run for the presidency in 1840 and was appointed secretary of state under President John Tyler in April 1844. Slavery again became an issue, and Calhoun pushed for allowing slavery in the annexed Texas territory. He left the State Department when James K. Polk was elected and returned to the Senate in late 1845. One final time Calhoun rose to defend states' rights, this time over the Compromise of 1850 and California statehood. Seeing the South being pushed into a minority position on slavery, Calhoun argued against the compromise. Too weak to read his own speech, Calhoun heard his words read for him on the Senate floor. He appeared in the Senate for the final time on March 13, 1850, and died on March 31. Like so many Southerners who fought to defend states' rights and, thus, slavery, Calhoun never strayed from his views.

—Boyd Childress

For Further Reading
Bartlett, Irving. 1993. *John C. Calhoun: A Biography.* New York: Norton; Calhoun, John C. 1957–. *The Papers of John C. Calhoun.* Ed. Clyde N. Wilson. Columbia: South Carolina University Press; Coit, Margaret L. 1950. *John C. Calhoun, American Portrait.* Boston: Houghton Mifflin.

CALHOUN'S DISQUISITION ON GOVERNMENT

The bitter sectional debate over slavery in the United States led some to question the merit of that country's constitutional system and to seek a philosophical alternative. John C. Calhoun began writing his *Disquisition on Government* in spring 1845. It was the first of two major philosophical inquires into the nature and character of representative government in general and of the U.S. government in particular and was to have been a preliminary "inquiry into the elements of political science, preliminary to a treatise on the Constitution of the U. States" (Spain, 1951). The second work was *A Discourse on the Constitution and Government of the United States* published in 1852. Calhoun did not live to see either book in print.

The underlying theme of both works is how best to secure and safeguard the interests and the way of life of a minority against the will of democratic majorities. It was in his *Disquisition* that Calhoun redefined and developed his doctrine of the "concurrent majority," which he had first described during the nullification discussions of the late 1820s. It was Calhoun's hope that his political works would be considered among the great philosophical books of his century.

In the *Disquisition,* he argued that the nature of man is such that he is a social being. Mankind is physical and moral, and Calhoun assumed that man is inherently self-centered. This self-centeredness leads to self-preservation and, therefore, "implies an unusual excess of the individual over the social feelings" (Post, 1953). Calhoun further concluded that man cannot exist without government of some sort and that representative government is the best government.

He argued that true representative government would be sympathetic to all points of view and thus must provide adequate protection for every minority: region, district, class, and economic. It is the ideal of the protection of the minority that underscores the philosophy of his first work, and it is in that work that Calhoun's ideas are fully developed. He believed that the framers of the Constitution so worried about the tyranny of the majority that they insisted on the Bill of Rights; he was trying to carry that concept to a higher level.

The actual impact of the *Disquisition on Government* is difficult to measure. The book itself was largely ignored by a country on the brink of civil war, and while Calhoun's views on Southern politics and particularly his views on economics and slavery were well known and documented, some of the views expressed in this book were less known. The most important result seems to have been its use in a conference on reforming Maryland's constitution held during the winter of 1850–1851, at which delegates from the Eastern Shore (which was the strongest slaveholding district in the state) claimed that the state's constitution was a compact and used Calhoun's views as expressed in the *Disquisition* to show that the compact was designed to protect the minority from the "ruthless actions of the majority" (Green, 1930). Calhoun would have agreed with those delegates that the compact idea made more sense than the fundamental law theory, which was then being hotly debated.

The principal value of Calhoun's *Disquisition on Government* lies in its defense of the minority, an argument that goes well beyond the beliefs of any of his contemporaries and one that has recently become increasingly important in a democratic society.

—*Henry H. Goldman*

For Further Reading
Bancroft, Frederic. 1928. *Calhoun and the South Carolina Nullification Movement.* Baltimore: Johns Hopkins University Press; Green, Fletcher M. 1930. *Constitutional Development in the South Atlantic States, 1776–1860: A Study in the Evolution of Democracy.* Chapel Hill: University of North Carolina Press; Post, C. Gordon, ed. 1953. *A Disquisition on Government and Selections from the Discourse.* New York: Liberal Arts Press; Spain, August O. 1951. *The Political Theory of John C. Calhoun.* New York: Bookman Associates.

CANADA

Slavery within the geographical region that is now Canada may be separated into three distinct categories: the pre- and postcontact Amerindian slavery practices, the enslavement of Amerindians and Africans in the New France colony, and the expansion of slavery in British Canada from the conquest of Quebec in 1759 until the final abolition of slavery in British North America took effect in 1834.

Slavery as a term applied to Amerindians in the eastern and Great Lakes regions must be used with caution because the extreme subordination of individuals there was often linked to the adoption of war captives or was a prelude to ritual execution according to mourning/war practices. Recent scholarship has, through linguistic and other means, more closely linked fictive kinship adoption with permanent subordination status. In the Pacific coastal regions of what is now British Columbia, the slave status of captive peoples was unambiguous. Slavery among Native Americans in those areas was highly developed and persisted into the nineteenth century. Amerindian societies of the far north also frequently featured slavery as a social component.

Slavery among French colonists in the St. Lawrence Valley and Acadia assumed a dual character. Amerindian slaves came to be utilized in the colony as a result of intra-Amerindian warfare, which secured a small but steady supply of enslaved captives of French-allied tribes. Slaves of African origin, fewer in number than their Amerindian counterparts until after the British conquest, were mainly an occasional byproduct of a system designed to supply agricultural labor to the French-held islands in the Caribbean. New France had a chronic undersupply of labor. Indentured servants were generally hard to attract to the colony; furthermore, they only served for a few years before settling as free citizens or returning to France. The need for labor was such that Canadians sometimes resorted to ransoming English captives of local Amerindians for use as bonded domestic servants until the English could manage to repay the French who had ransomed them.

Slaves in French Canada between 1640 and 1760 were mostly concentrated in the towns of Montreal, Quebec, and Three Rivers where both male and female slaves were mainly employed as domestic servants. Agricultural slavery was only occasionally practiced on the small-scale family farms of the St. Lawrence Valley. As a result of the domestic nature of slavery in New France, it has often been characterized as a more "paternal" or "personal" system than was seen elsewhere in North America at the time. Although many of the depredations of large-scale, plantation-based exploitation were absent in New France, enough evidence of resistance among the slaves exists to raise questions concerning the nature of this paternalism.

The British acquisition of Canada following the Seven Years War (1756–1763) and the influx of Loyalists from all colonies following the American Revolution brought fundamental changes to the practice of slavery in Canada. In lower Canada (Quebec), the enslavement of people of African origin increased under the British while the enslavement of Amerindians began a permanent decline. Nevertheless, most slaves in lower Canada remained in the hands of the French-speaking populace, a phenomenon sustained by the British Parliament's Quebec Act (1774), which allowed for the continuance of French customary law in matters related to slavery.

The immigration of Loyalists from the 13 new United States meant the arrival of significant numbers of slaves in upper Canada (Ontario) and the Maritime regions, and the new environment transformed the practices of slavery that Loyalists had developed in the American colonies. Adapting to new environmental realities, slaves were mostly employed in domestic service and in a variety of small-scale commercial and agricultural activities. Occasional emancipation also added to the substantial free black population of the Canadas.

The abolition of slavery in British Canada was a gradual and irregular process. Before the formal act of abolishment was passed by the British Parliament in 1833 (to take effect the following year), slavery had been steadily abridged by local judicial rulings and legislative efforts. After slavery within its boundaries formally ended in 1834, Canada's role in North American slavery changed: Canada then served as a place of refuge and resettlement for thousands of escaped U.S. slaves until that country's civil war.

—*William H. Foster III*

See also
American-Canadian Relations
For Further Reading
Trudel, Marcel. 1990. *Dictionnaire des esclaves et de Leurs Propriétaires au Canada Français*. Ville LaSalle, Quebec: Éditions Hurtubise; Trudel, Marcel. 1960. *L'esclavage au Canada Français*. Quebec: Les Presses Universitaires Laval; Winks, Robin W. 1971. *The Blacks in Canada, a History*. New Haven, CT: Yale University Press.

CANNON, PATTY HANLEY (1764?–1829)

Patty Cannon led the nineteenth century's most successful kidnapping ring in the abduction of free blacks. Cannon's gang, which included over 30 white thugs and a black confederate, terrorized blacks from Philadelphia, Pennsylvania, to Accomac, Virginia. Responsible for sending a number of free blacks into slavery, Cannon's operation illuminates the dangers that freed slaves and free-born people living within a slave nation faced.

Much of Cannon's life remains a mystery. Born about 1764, she spent most of her life in Delaware. She married Jesse Cannon and produced several children, one of whom she later confessed to strangling three days after its birth. Jesse, killed by poison, also figured among Cannon's 11 acknowledged murder victims. One of her daughters married a Joe Johnson, and he did much of the gang's kidnapping work. Cannon supervised blacks imprisoned in the two Cannon-Johnson homes, each located in heavily wooded sections along Delaware's southern border with Maryland near the Nanticoke River, while her son-in-law captained ships and bands taking captives to the South. With easy access to Chesapeake Bay, the gang operated by both land and water.

In the United States, free blacks risked being kidnapped and sold into slavery. Although kidnapping occurred throughout the nation, residents of states bordering the Mason-Dixon line were in greatest jeopardy, and Delaware was a good site for the Cannon-Johnson gang. On the Chesapeake's eastern-shore peninsula, whites viewed freeborn and emancipated blacks, who by 1819 already outnumbered slaves, as a threat. Antikidnapping laws could not be enforced in such a hostile situation, and newly opened cotton country in the old Southwest created a huge demand for slaves just after the African slave trade had been abolished. Kidnapping could be a highly lucrative and relatively safe occupation. In abducting slaves, kidnappers risked death at the hands of angry slaveholders, but by abducting freeborn or emancipated blacks, kidnappers faced only a slight risk since the victims and their families had little legal recourse and few powerful supporters.

The exact number of Cannon's kidnapping victims is unknown, but is estimated to be over two dozen. Slave testimony collected in Delaware's Federal Writer's Project shows that while Quakers sent runaway slaves north to freedom, Cannon shipped free blacks south into slavery. Arrested in 1829 for killing a slave trader, Cannon confessed to murdering 11 people and admitted to playing a role in 12 other deaths. She committed suicide in jail on May 11, 1829, by taking poison, but at a posthumous trial in October 1829, the Delaware court convicted Cannon of the murder of 3 children and sentenced her to hang.

In subsequent years, Cannon acquired immortality in print. Featured in both George Alfred Towsend's 1884 collection, *The Entailed Hat*, and R. W. Messenger's 1926 novel, *Patty Cannon Administers Justice*, Cannon's nightmarish legend has become part of American folklore.

—*Caryn E. Neumann*

For Further Reading
Miller, M. Sammy. 1975. "Legend of a Kidnapper." *Crisis* 82 (April): 118–120; Wilson, Carol. 1994. *Freedom at Risk: The Kidnapping of Free Blacks in America, 1780–1865.* Lexington: University of Kentucky Press.

CAPE COAST CASTLE
See Fort Carolusburg

CAPE COLONY

The Dutch East India Company established a colonial settlement around what is now Cape Town on Africa's southernmost tip in 1652. The colony rapidly expanded as settler pastoral farming grew, and by the time of the British takeover in 1795, Cape Colony extended from the Orange River in the north to the Fish River in the east. The Dutch East India Company traded slaves in South Asia and the East Indies and extended its use of slave labor to the colony. The first slaves arrived with the earliest settlers in 1652, and more followed after settler farming was established in 1658. Subsequently, slaving expeditions went from Cape Town to Mozambique and Madagascar, but most slaves came from South and Southeast Asia aboard vessels carrying other trading goods between Batavia (now Djakarta) and Europe. This European colony in Africa used primarily Asian slaves.

By 1838, when slavery legally ended, there were 36,000 slaves in the Cape Colony. The Dutch East India Company used slaves on its cattle and defense posts and on public works in Cape Town and sold slaves to colonists for employment on grain and wine farms in the southwestern part of the colony. Pastoralist farmers owned some slaves, although indigenous Khoi and San inhabitants commonly worked on frontier farms, and most residents had slaves as domestic servants and artisans.

Profits obtained from slave labor in the colony could be as high as those made by owners of eighteenth-century slave plantations in the Caribbean and North America, and contrary to contemporary opinion and that of more recent apologists, some Cape slaves were treated just as brutally as in other colonial slave societies. Although the East India Company offered slaves nominal protection from their owners' worst abuses, it was the late 1820s before the British government was able to obtain effective control over physical punishment. Slaves were restricted from traveling without a pass, could be sold at public auction, and until the 1820s, were unable to marry. Some acquired small amounts of money or livestock from earnings permitted by their owners, but the majority lacked any personal resources.

Although most Cape settlers associated slaves and indigenous people with manual labor, class and wealth differences were not as absolutely associated with race as was the case in many transatlantic slave colonies. In the seventeenth and early-eighteenth centuries, a number of freed slave women became wives and mothers to European settlers, but eighteenth-century manumission levels declined. Only in Cape Town did a significant "free black" (ex-slave) community emerge. Some free blacks owned slaves themselves, but generally they lacked the resources to challenge the settlers' monopoly of wealth and status.

The Cape Colony slaves came from various places, spoke many languages, and practiced many belief systems. They also often worked alongside indigenous Khoi laborers, particularly on frontier farms, so a strongly distinctive slave culture like the one in the colonial Americas did not develop. Rather, slaves contributed to a broader popular culture, infusing both settler and indigenous elements. Slave languages, especially those from the East Indies, played an important part in the emerging language that later became Afrikaans. Together with political exiles brought by the Dutch from Asia, slaves formed the basis of Cape Town's thriving Muslim community; indeed, Cape Muslims wrote the earliest Afrikaans texts in Arabic script.

Until the nineteenth century, the Cape Colony depended on imported slaves to maintain its labor force. Most of these slaves were male, and there was thus a sexual imbalance. Even where family ties formed, couples could be separated and children sold. But after the slave trade was abolished in 1807, a higher proportion of slaves were Cape-born (children of slave women), and more extended slave kinship networks emerged. Families were still often separated from each other among different owners.

Slaves resisted their condition in numerous ways. Rebellion was difficult because slaves were physically separated in relatively small units on remote farms. Many slaves ran away, some escaping from the colony altogether and becoming part of the mixed Oorlam and Griqua societies of the Orange River region and beyond. A runaway slave community also existed for almost a century in subterranean caves on Cape Hangklip near Cape Town, frustrating attempts by the authorities to capture them. Not all slaves tried to rebel or run away. Historian Robert Shell (1994) argues that paternalism and deference, particularly among female household domestic slaves, inhibited open resistance, although other scholars contest this argument.

Important changes occurred in Cape Colony slave society in the early-nineteenth century. Abolishing the slave trade eliminated external supplies, and high infant mortality levels made it difficult to maintain slave numbers from local births. Wine farms, where many slaves worked, suffered a slump in the late 1820s, and wool production, the colonial economy's boom sector, was less dependent on slaves. As colonial settlement expanded in the eastern Cape a more mobile labor force was needed. Hence, merchants and new commercial pastoral farmers began opposing slavery and opting for cheap wage labor. Slaves themselves became more assertive and laid complaints against their owners to the authorities. There were two rebellions: an uprising of over 300 slaves in Cape Town's hinterland (1808) and a smaller revolt in the northern Cape's remoter Bokkeveld region (1825). Neither was very widespread, and both were swiftly crushed, but colonists were alarmed. When the British Parliament abolished slavery (1833), allowing a four-year period until final emancipation, slaveowners offered only muted opposition.

Slave emancipation did not alter colonial social structure. As elsewhere in the British colonies, no land or capital was provided as compensation for the freed slaves. Although some moved to towns and villages, and particularly to mission stations, many others remained on farms as permanent or seasonal workers. Families were united, and many women withdrew from farmwork, but most freed slaves lacked the resources to obtain a truly equal position in Cape society.

Slavery had a major impact on the Cape Colony's economy and society. Additionally, slavery's coercive nature influenced other types of labor use. Khoi and San children captured in raids were indentured as forced workers, and in the eastern Cape during the early-nineteenth century, settler farmers captured and enslaved some indigenous Africans. These labor methods were extended to the southern African interior after the 1830s. Slave raiding occurred in the Delagoa Bay region, and indentured labor was widely used in the states established in the Transvaal by colonial migrant farmers.

—*Nigel Worden*

See also
Great Trek
For Further Reading
Armstrong, James, and Nigel Worden. 1989. "The Slaves, 1652–1834." In *The Shaping of South African Society, 1652–1840*. Ed. Richard Elphick and Hermann Giliomee. Cape Town: Maskew Miller Longman; Shell, Robert. 1994. *Children of Bondage: A Social History of the Slave Society at the Cape of Good Hope, 1652–1838*. Hanover, NH: Wesleyan University Press; Worden, Nigel. 1985. *Slavery in Dutch South Africa*. Cambridge: Cambridge University Press; Worden, Nigel, and Clifton Crais, eds. 1994. *Breaking the Chains: Slavery and Its Legacy in the Nineteenth-Century Cape Colony*. Johannesburg: Witwatersrand University Press.

CAPITAES DO MATO

Capitães do mato or *Capitães do campo* ("bush captains") were persons dedicated to capturing black runaway slaves in Brazil. In 1612, each parish of the captaincy of Pernambuco had designated bush captains, and by 1625 in Bahia, the town council of Salvador had set a schedule of rewards for those recovering runaway slaves. The *capitães do mato* worked on a commission basis with rewards based upon the distance involved in the capture. Often the *capitães do mato* were free blacks or mulattoes who assembled their own troops consisting of free mulattoes, Negroes, Amerindians, and half-breeds. These men could not carry weapons legally unless they were on expeditions.

Recaptured slaves were jailed until their masters paid the stipulated reward. Sometimes the bush captains captured old or sick slaves who were no longer useful, and on one occasion the city of Salvador publicly auctioned prisoners to pay for expenses. Occasionally innocent slaves, who were on legitimate business, were seized and held until the captain received a payment. Sometimes bush captains used recaptured slaves for extended periods before informing the rightful owners and claiming their rewards.

Inventories of property almost always listed slaves who had escaped, and planters often hired *capitães do mato* to recapture them. Although the bush captains succeeded in recapturing many slaves because of their superior weapons, *mocambos* or *quilombos* (settlements of runaway slaves) continued to be a strong attraction. As the slave population in Brazil increased with the expansion of sugar production, the number of runaways also increased, and planters feared that the survival of the *quilombos* would encourage further escapes. The most important contributing factor in the incidence of successful slave escapes, however, was probably the frontier nature of the region and its unstable military condition.

One the chief duties of the *capitães do mato* was to find and destroy *quilombos*. After the early-seventeenth century runaway slaves were a problem, not only for their masters, but also for all residents because of the example they set for the remaining slaves. The slave hunters faced a difficult task since the slaves would flee when the *capitães do mato* approached and hide nearby until the armed slave hunters had left. Then they would return to their respective villages.

Most *quilombos* were in inaccessible areas and had fewer than 100 residents. At times, new runaway villages were established by slaves who had fled from another *quilombo* to escape recapture. The bush captains often destroyed the smaller *quilombos*, but they were unable to stop the formation of new runaway colonies.

In the early-eighteenth century, many slaves in the mining areas worked under lax supervision, and geographic isolation and inadequate policing contributed to a fair number of runaways. Dragoon patrols in the mining areas employed *capitães do mato* to help control the movement of contraband gold and diamonds because the bush captains knew the backlands and

could guide soldiers into the remotest areas. These bush captains received rewards proportionate to the seizures they made.

—*Sharon Landers*

See also
Palmares; *Quilombos*; Slave Catchers
For Further Reading
Boxer, C. R. 1962. *The Golden Age of Brazil, 1695–1750: Growing Pains of a Colonial Society*. Berkeley: University of California Press; Fagan, Brian. 1993. "Brazil's Little Angola." *Archaeology* 46 (July): 14–19; Schwartz, Stuart. 1992. *Slaves, Peasants, Rebels: Reconsidering Brazilian Slavery*. Urbana: University of Illinois Press; Wood, Russell A. 1984. "Colonial Brazil: The Gold Cycle c. 1690–1750." In *The Cambridge History of Latin America*. Ed. Leslie Bethell. Cambridge: Cambridge University Press.

CAPITALISM

Capitalism is form of socioeconomic organization that favors the accumulation of capital through the production of commodities for market sale to achieve maximum profit. The capitalist mode of production is characterized by private ownership of the means of production and separation of the producers from those means. An economy is considered capitalist when the capitalist mode of production dominates. In many capitalist countries, some productive capital is owned by the state but most of it is privately owned. Conversely, communist countries may allow a degree of private capitalist enterprise, but state ownership predominates.

The form of labor power employed for the production of goods can vary. Capitalism historically has had two major variant modes of production: one employed free labor sold on the labor market; the other was based on slave labor. Historians recognize three general areas in which the slave variant of capitalism occurred: the Americas up to the end of the nineteenth century, the Banda Islands in the Dutch East Indies (Indonesia) between the late-seventeenth and mid-eighteenth centuries, and the Indian Ocean slave colonies of the eighteenth and nineteenth centuries.

The terms "free" and "slave" apply to differences in relationships of production. Slavery is the most dramatic means of controlling labor by the capitalist class while free labor is the most advanced. In Marxist terms, an argument can be made that, in reality, there is no difference between slavery and the sale of labor in a free market. Everything produced in a capitalist economy is produced through labor, and all labor, both free and slave, is a commodity. Capitalism, Marx wrote, can therefore be regarded as wage slavery.

Elements of capitalism, such as private enterprise, capital accumulation, commodity production, and wage labor, existed in late-medieval Europe, but it was not until the sixteenth and seventeenth centuries that a combination of economic and social factors combined to enable Europe to experience a "commercial revolution." New sea routes in the fifteenth century opened up West Africa and the New World, and banking and merchant classes amassed significant capital and established systems of banking and financial networks for investment. Population increase and the growth of urban centers stimulated commerce, and a new entrepreneurial class demanded luxury items and New World products such as sugar and tobacco. New attitudes and ways of thinking about profits, competition, and the formation of capital evolved.

New nation-states supported and regulated trade through protective tariffs, colonial domination, and naval power, and they waged economic warfare with rival states. This new mercantile capitalism was based on trade, finance, the extraction of precious metals from newly conquered land, and the production of goods through plantation agriculture based on slave labor.

Slave labor and the slave trade played crucial roles in the growth of commerce and establishment of an Atlantic commercial empire in the seventeenth and eighteenth centuries. Merchants and investors gained large profits from overseas ventures in a new trading system that linked Europe, the New World, and Africa. The slave trade was highly valued and affected national economic policies aimed at protecting private enterprise.

Slavery emerged in this capitalist system as a form of high-intensity labor to work the profitable colonial plantations—large tracts of land devoted to monocultural production. Free European laborers were not attracted to the plantations, which offered very arduous work with little reward. Furthermore, such laborers were not readily available, for the European population boom of the sixteenth century leveled off in the seventeenth.

The eighteenth century was a period of expansion in trade, especially world trade, and increases in market, agricultural, and manufacturing production. The Industrial Revolution, which began in England in the second half of the eighteenth century, led to the development of a new capitalism based on mechanized industry. Industrial capitalism continued to expand in the nineteenth century and spread from Great Britain to other European countries and the United States. New technologies and production methods, such as the spinning jenny, the steam engine, and the factory system, were adopted to maximize profit. Urban manufacture and mining production increased tremendously, fueled by capital accumulated by commercial and agricultural activities and by an influx of surplus rural labor.

Especially important for both industrial capitalism and slavery were technological advances in cotton manufacturing and the growth of the British textile industry. A series of inventions in the eighteenth century led to the mass production of textiles. Cotton became extremely popular, and the demand for raw cotton combined with the invention of the cotton gin heightened the profitability of the Southern plantation economy in the United States, which, in turn, increased the attractiveness of slave labor.

The profits made through slave labor in the New World stimulated banking and investment in industrial entrepreneurial activities in Britain. However, the degree to which the profits of the slave trade were directly invested in capital formation in Britain has been debated. It is now thought that the level of capital transfer was not as significant as previously claimed. Rather, it is believed that most of the profits remained in the pockets of planters and merchants.

Regardless of the degree of capital investment in industry, the development of modern capitalism was significantly affected by the wealth generated through slavery and the slave trade and monopolized by an entrepreneurial class that was able, in the nineteenth century, to effect political and economic change. Nineteenth-century entrepreneurs embraced the notion of laissez-faire, a policy of nonintervention in the economy by the government that had developed from the ideas of the Enlightenment of the eighteenth century.

Economic liberals promoted freedom in trade, freedom of production, and the free expression of consumer demand. Free trade, they contended, would provide for the well-being of both the individual and society. However, by the end of the nineteenth century, many people felt that the state had to fill the necessary role of providing those things that the marketplace could not, such as education, road systems, regulating monopolies, and improving the condition of the working class.

The role of free trade in the abolition of slavery has been debated. Current scholars are generally of the opinion that the slave trade was not destroyed by developing industrial capitalism, nor did the maintenance of the slave trade conflict with the emergence of a free trade economy. The slave trade continued to be important for capitalist production in the Atlantic basin in the nineteenth century as long as slavery lasted.

—*Jeanne Schock*

See also
Abolition, British Empire; Marxism
For Further Reading
Beaud, Michel. 1983. *A History of Capitalism 1500–1980.* Trans. Tom Dickman and Anny Lefebvre.

New York: Monthly Review Press; Beckles, Hilary. 1984. "Capitalism and Slavery: The Debate over Eric Williams." *Social and Economic Studies* 33: 171–185; Patterson, Orlando. 1979. "On Slavery and Slave Formations." *New Left Review* 117: 31–67.

CAPOEIRA

Capoeira is a dance, martial art, ritual, and game developed by colonial Brazil's African slaves. Many of its elements are clearly of African origin, and have analogs in other parts of Africa's diaspora, but nowhere else did a similar game grow into such a rich, complex, immediately recognizable cultural phenomenon. Capoeira is uniquely Brazilian.

The game's central element is stylized combat between two players surrounded by a ring of singers and musicians. After an elaborate, competitive, improvisational dance that can last anywhere from a few seconds to a few hours (although a few minutes is most common), players leave the ring and join the musicians. Two new participants then enter the ring, setting the pattern for a potentially endless succession of dance/combat accompanied by music.

Capoeira certainly existed in some form by the mid-eighteenth century, and probably before. It was part of those slave practices prohibited by owners, and thus its origins remain shrouded in mystery. With little distinction between capoeira and street fighting, adepts of the game earned reputations as local toughs and were employed as bodyguards. By the nineteenth century, police in Rio de Janeiro and Bahia characterized capoeira as an urban scourge, a dangerous weapon of slaves and free blacks, and vigorously repressed its practice.

Capoeira was not legalized until well into the twentieth century, and only since the 1940s has it become somewhat codified and standardized. Today, as capoeira spreads throughout the world, it is marked by tremendous flexibility and variation in all of its aspects. One constant is that slave resistance and African heritage remain central to the game's popular memory. Many accompanying songs recall slavery, and some almost certainly date from the nineteenth century. Capoeira masters frequently teach the game's demanding physical maneuvers with reference to a slave's movements when inhibited by shackles and in teaching its subtle musical variations, recall the slaves' need to communicate secretly. Although often historically questionable, these maneuvers purposefully invoke the game's origins and traditions.

Capoeira melds central and western African characteristics. Bantu influence appears most prominent, particularly in capoeira music and lyrics. The game's principle musical instrument is the *berimbau*, a single-string percussion instrument and a resonating gourd with clear central African antecedents. The word *capoeiraangola* designates a slow, crafty style of play performed close to the ground. It is widely considered to be older and closer to an African cultural heritage, but the word is imprecise as a geographical reference. (This style of play is often contrasted with *capoeira-regional*, a faster, more acrobatic variant.) In general, African influences on the game await further study.

—*Bryan McCann*

For Further Reading
Holloway, Thomas H. 1989. "'A Healthy Terror':Police Repression of *Capoeiras* in Nineteenth-Century Rio de Janeiro." *Hispanic American Historical Review* 69: 637–676; Lewis, J. Lowell. 1992. *Ring of Liberation: Deception Discourse in Brazilian Capoeira*. Chicago: University of Chicago Press; Rego, Waldelior. 1968. *Capoeira Angola, ensaio sócio-etnográfico*. Salvador: Editora Itapuã; Thompson, Robert Farris. 1983. *Flash of the Spirit: African and Afro-American Art and Philosophy*. New York: Random House.

CAPTAINS OF SLAVE SHIPS

Captains of slave ships played a crucial role in conducting the transatlantic slave trade. Not only did a voyage's profitability depend upon their abilities, but the treatment of the enslaved and of the crew was under their control.

The captain's duties were numerous and demanding. He had to navigate and sail the ship, and he had to be able to control and discipline the crew and the enslaved Africans. For trading, he needed a knowledge of Africa's coast and had to possess sufficient business acumen to negotiate with both sellers and buyers and often to find a return cargo to take home.

Owners recognized the value of previous experience in the slave trade when employing captains, and it became an essential requirement. In England after the Dolben Act (1788), all captains had to have served on two voyages as a chief mate or surgeon or on three voyages as a mate to qualify for appointment.

The captains were generally well-seasoned and experienced men. Stephen Behrendt (1991) examined the records of captains of 2,876 voyages, mainly from Liverpool and Bristol, between 1785 and 1807. About 80 percent came from a commercial family background—mercantile, shipping, or other trading activity. Many had had previous experience in the West Indies trade and slaving. Their average age on appointment was 30; few were less than 25 years old. However, most captains made fewer than four voyages, partly because of the high mortality rate among them. Twenty-seven percent of Behrendt's sample died on a slave voyage (nearly two-thirds of them on the African coast). Examination of another group of Dutch captains showed a lower death rate—about 15 percent—but, again, most made fewer than four voyages and over half made only one.

The rewards for captains could be substantial. Most were paid bonuses for successful voyages in addition to their wages, and they were often allowed slaves for their own benefit and undertook naval commissions. There is evidence that many Dutch captains smuggled extra slaves for their own benefit and sometimes cargo, like ivory. Some also kept young Africans on board for sexual gratification.

The risks encountered were significant. There was the continuous threat of an onboard revolt, lack of discipline and desertion among the crew, disease, and—in the last analysis—death. The captains who survived often made sufficient money to invest in other activities, and many left a considerable fortune when they died. One of the most successful French captains, Pierre van Alstein, made enough money on eight voyages to buy a country estate and become a member of the nobility. After retirement, several captains from Lancaster, England, invested their profits in later slave voyages.

Several contemporary accounts by slave captains survive. John Newton (1725–1807) is probably the best known of the captains, not only because his published journals contain one of the most detailed descriptions of everyday life in the trade, but also because he later fought vigorously for abolition. His hymn "Amazing Grace" has been a particular favorite of black congregations for generations. Newton served in the Mediterranean trade, was press-ganged into the Royal Navy, worked as a trader on the African coast, spent almost a year in virtual slavery in Sierra Leone, and served as first mate on a slave ship. In 1750, he took command of the *Duke of Argyle* for the first of three slaving voyages. In 1755, he left the sea and worked as a customs officer for nine years before becoming a clergyman. After his ordination, he was influential in opposing the slave trade through preaching, writing, and giving evidence to parliamentary inquiries.

Hugh Crow (1765–1829), who captained the last British slaver, the *Kitty's Amelia,* began his career as a boatbuilder, served on board ship, and worked for three years as a mate in the West Indies trade. He made six voyages as a mate on a slaver before gaining his own command in 1798. Crow also wrote about his experiences and was unrepentant about them.

A less well-known figure, the Scotsman James Irving (1759–1791), had a different experience, which is recounted in his letters and journal. He was employed as a surgeon in the West Indies and slave trade before undertaking his first voyage in charge of a slaver in 1789. He had the misfortune to be shipwrecked and kept in slavery on the Barbary coast for 18 months. He returned to the trade almost immediately and died in the mid-Atlantic in December 1791. With him perished 47 of the 253 Africans on board.

—Anthony Tibbles

For Further Reading
Behrendt, Stephen D. 1991. "The Captains in the British Slave Trade from 1785 to 1809." *Transactions of the Historic Society for Lancashire and Cheshire* 140: 79–140; Crow, Hugh. 1970. *Memoirs of the late Captain Hugh Crow of Liverpool.* London: F. Cass; Martin, Berbard, and Mark Spurrell. 1962. *The Journal of a Slave Trader, John Newton, 1750–1754.* London: Epworth Press; Schwarz, Suzanne. 1995. *Slave Captain: The Career of James Irving in the Liverpool Slave Trade.* Wrexham, Eng.: Bridge Books.

CARIBBEAN

See **Danish West Indies; Dutch Caribbean; English Caribbean; French Caribbean; Spanish Caribbean; Transition from Slave Labor to Free Labor, Caribbean;** *individual islands*

CARTOGRAPHY

The act of mapping Africa during the era of the Atlantic slave trade can be equated to the creation of a controlled fiction in which the myths used to justify slavery and the exploitation of African resources were reinforced through a framework that appeared to be both rational and scientific. However, it was partly through the translation of real knowledge about the continent's interior into cartography in the late-eighteenth century that the image of Africa as the wild, uncivilized, "dark" continent was stripped away, which furnished the incipient antislavery movement with an image of Africa that better coincided with European notions of civilization.

Under the direction of Prince Henry the Navigator, Portuguese ships rounded Cape Bojador in 1434, and other voyages eventually had reached almost as far as Sierra Leone by the time of Henry's death in 1460; by 1488 and Bartholomeu Dias's rounding of the Cape of Good Hope, the whole of the West African coast was known. Following closely behind these voyages of exploration were the slave traders. The Portuguese crown,

This map, dated approximately 1547, from the Vallard Atlas, *shows West Africa from the European perspective—upside down. The cartographer's imagination was called into play to fill in the enormous gaps in European knowledge of the interior of the continent.*

determined to maximize returns from its monopoly on trade with Africa, tried to use its monopoly of geographical knowledge to regularize trade for its own citizens and to exclude the trade of other nations.

Although the idea that Henry the Navigator established a school of cartography at Sagres in Portugal has largely been discredited, he did hire Jafuda Cresques, a leading Majorcan cartographer, to help consolidate the ever-growing knowledge of the African coastline. Being able to offer Portuguese navigators the most recent charts minimized their risks and thus maximized the crown's percentage of the profit. Under King John II, this monopoly on commercial knowledge was extended; Portuguese pilots who gave or sold charts to foreigners were to be executed.

This tendency to treat cartographic knowledge as a commercial secret was further reinforced by the establishment of the Armazém da Guiné e Índias (Store-

house of Guinea and the Indies) in the early-sixteenth century. This organization regulated both the content and the use of charts of Africa: pilots were given a copy of the most-up-to-date chart available and had to hand it back immediately upon returning along with a full report of any new discoveries. Such details were then added to the king's standard chart. This method of control came to be copied by the Spanish and, later, by the Dutch.

Such state-sponsored attempts to monopolize geographical knowledge and the trade that went with it were destined to fail. The Cantino map of 1502, for instance, obtained through bribery for the duke of Ferrara, was a copy of the Portuguese standard chart. Although the map presents an accurate delineation of the African coast, it highlights another trend that came to dominate the cartography of the slave-trade period. Starved for accurate information about the interior of

Africa, the cartographer inserted captions describing the goods available along the coast. Slaves were listed simply as one of this array of commodities, thereby equating the trade in grain with the trade in people in the mind of the map user.

But the Cantino map goes further than that, for it defines the African continent only in terms of its relationship to Portugal. Possession is defined by representations of the Portuguese flag in the interior and by the right to name places. Thus, even at this very early stage in the slave trade, Africans were stripped of the semblance of agency on their own continent. This depiction of mercantile relations within a framework of power, control, and authority became the established policy until the late-eighteenth century.

It was in the representation of the interior of Africa that the pattern of domination and condescension came to be expressed most fully. Rather than confess their ignorance of Africa beyond the coast, cartographers preferred to fill the continent with exaggerated and embellished depictions of what they thought they knew. For example, the second-century cosmographer, Ptolemy of Alexandria, had used the accounts of a Greek merchant in describing the Nile as originating below the equator in two great lakes, which were filled by waters coming down from the snowcapped Mountains of the Moon. After the middle of the sixteenth century, this crude sketch of the interior was supplemented by the account of the travels of the Italianate Moor, Leo Africanus, in North Africa, the Sahara, and the Sudan. Both Ptolemy and Leo Africanus remained the fundamental sources for the cartography of Africa until the late-eighteenth century.

Together, Ptolemy and Leo did not provide enough information to fill a map, so the later cartographers embellished the empty spaces with images of wild animals. By filling the interior with animals and not towns or other structures associated by the Europeans with civilization, and doing so within a framework that claimed to be authoritative by virtue of being scientific, cartographers stressed the notion of Africa as a wild, uncivilized place in need of domination.

The state of knowledge is clearly portrayed in the 1665 map "Africae novae descriptio" by the Dutch cartographer, Jan Blaeu. Although Blaeu showed the kingdoms named by Leo, he drew their vague boundaries with a confident hand. After adding Ptolemy's rivers and lakes, Blaeu filled in the gaps with chains of mountains, for which he had no evidence, and wild animals. Thus, he crafted a representation of Africa and its inhabitants that emphasized the wild and untamed. Ideology, not knowledge, had been allowed to fill the gaps in European knowledge.

But, in the mid-eighteenth century, this situation was redressed by the French cartographer, J. B. Bourguignon d'Anville. By stripping his maps of all superfluous imagery, he exposed the limits of European knowledge about Africa, prompting his audience to fill in the huge gaps.

The challenge was taken up by the Royal African Association in the late-eighteenth century. Founded in 1788, the association helped organize missions into the African interior, and the resulting geographical information helped to "rehumanize" Africans in European cartography. Instead of lists of commodities and pictures of wild animals, the names of towns and states could be inserted onto maps. Europeans, therefore, could identify structures that they equated with civilization and begin to see the inhabitants of the interior of Africa as a market rather than as a commodity.

—*Richard Raiswell*

See also
Mortality of the Slave Trade; Portuguese Slave Trade
For Further Reading
Barker, A. 1978. *The African Link: British Attitudes to the Negro in the Era of the Atlantic Slave Trade, 1550– 1807.* London: Frank Cass; Hallett, R. 1965. *The Penetration of Africa: European Enterprise and Exploration Principally in Northern and Western Africa up to 1830.* London: Routledge; Marshall, P. J., and G. Williams. 1982. *The Great Map of Mankind: British Perceptions of the World in the Age of Enlightenment.* London: J. M. Dent and Sons; Wallis, H. 1986. "'Things Hidden from Other Men,' The Portuguese Voyages of Discovery." *History Today* 36 (June): 27–33.

CARTWRIGHT, SAMUEL (1793–1862)

New Orleans physician Samuel A. Cartwright was one of the principal architects of the medical facet of the antebellum South's proslavery argument, writing essays on supposed physiological differences between blacks and whites in defense of African slavery. Specifically, he sought to prove that certain anatomical characteristics suited blacks to slavery rather than to freedom.

In one essay, Cartwright described supposed differences between the respiratory systems of blacks and whites. He argued that the blacks' smaller lung size precluded their inhaling a sufficient amount of fresh air, thus limiting the amount of oxygen drawn into the blood. Accordingly, Cartwright insisted, their minds became clouded by ignorance. The "cure" he advanced was physical labor as slaves as that would improve the lungs' capacity to oxygenate the blood and clear their minds of ignorance. For this reason, Cartwright wrote, blacks preferred slavery over freedom, and whites' enslavement of them represented a benevolent act. If given their freedom, Cartwright maintained, blacks would indulge in the idleness to which they were naturally prone, and the lack of physical labor would cause their minds to once more be enveloped in a shroud of ignorance.

Cartwright endeavored to show that his claims with respect to racial differences were in perfect conformity with the Scriptures. Although many of his contemporaries feared that scientific research undermined the scriptural version of a single creation, Cartwright insisted that physiological and biblical justifications for slavery did not contradict one another and were actually interdependent. He claimed, for instance, that physiological findings concerning blacks' knees sustained the veracity of the biblical Curse of Canaan (Ham). According to this belief, God cursed Canaan's descendants in Africa and declared that they be slaves. The Hebrew verb *canah*, Cartwright argued, meant the submission of oneself and the bending of the knee. Anatomical investigation of the knee structure of Canaan's descendants enslaved in the U.S. South, Cartwright argued, showed that slaves' knees bent in a manner similar to that described in Scripture. Both physiology and the Bible, Cartwright concluded, sustained the notion that Africans were meant to be enslaved.

Ultimately, Cartwright blamed Northern and Southern sectional discord in the United States on abolitionists who, ignorant of physiological findings that supposedly proved the suitability of blacks for slavery, continued to insist that slaves should be freed. Once the Northern medical establishment accepted his claims, Cartwright contended, the abolitionists would recognize the blacks' incapacity for freedom, and once the abolitionists ceased their clamoring, Cartwright concluded, sectional animosity over slavery would dissipate and the prospect of disunion would diminish.

—*John J. Zaborney*

See also
Ham, Curse of; Proslavery Argument, United States
For Further Reading
Genovese, Eugene D. 1974. *Roll, Jordan, Roll: The World the Slaves Made.* New York: Vintage Books; Guillory, James Denny. 1968. "The Pro-Slavery Arguments of Dr. Samuel A. Cartwright." *Louisiana History* 9 (4): 209–227; Kolchin, Peter. 1993. *American Slavery: 1619–1877.* New York: Hill and Wang.

THE CASE OF OUR FELLOW CREATURES

Published in 1783 by English Quakers, *The Case of Our Fellow Creatures* called upon the British Parliament to prohibit the slave trade and extend "relief" to slaves in the West Indian colonies. Together with a June 1783 abolition petition to the House of Commons, the pamphlet signaled the beginning of British Quaker abolitionism and prepared the way for the immensely popular abolition campaigns of the late 1780s and early 1790s.

The Quaker initiatives of 1783 departed from established practice. Although the discipline imposed by the religious society barred members from the slave trade, British Quakers chose to lobby for abolition in the early 1780s only after receiving repeated appeals for active canvassing from Philadelphia Quakers. The London Yearly Meeting, the governing body for the Society of Friends, resolved on June 16, 1783, that slavery demanded the "humane interposition of the legislature" and the following day petitioned the House of Commons for abolition. Praise from politicians for their principled stand moved the Friends to further activity, even though the House of Commons tabled their petition.

Meeting for Sufferings, the executive committee of the London Yearly Meeting, appointed a subcommittee to "embrace all opportunities" to promote abolition of the slave trade. At its first meeting in September 1793, William Dillwyn and John Lloyd were assigned to draft "an Address to the publick," which was published less than two months later as *The Case of Our Fellow Creatures, the Oppressed Africans, Recommended to the Serious Consideration of the Legislature of Great Britain, by the People Called Quakers.*

The work denounced slaving almost exclusively on moral grounds: the slave trade caused war and destroyed families in Africa; it abrogated the biblical injunction to "do unto them as we would they should do unto us"; it conflicted with the values of a free people; and it inverted government's obligation to protect the innocent and punish the criminal. If readers imagined themselves as slaves, the pamphlet suggested, Britons would no longer ignore the injustice. And as national sins brought national punishments, government had a duty to act expeditiously. The Quakers were confident that many members of Parliament held the slave trade "in the utmost abhorrence," and *The Case of Our Fellow Creatures* assured them that abolition would serve commercial policy, since the richness of African soil offered the prospect of a profitable, humane commerce in staple crops to replace the commerce in slaves.

The Society of Friends expended substantial energy and resources on the pamphlet. In May 1784, Friends presented copies to King George III and each member of Parliament. Meeting for Sufferings printed 10,000 copies in August 1784 for dozens of Quaker correspondents across England and instructed them to direct the booklets to town corporations, justices of the peace, clergy, commissioned officers, merchants, school headmasters, and others "in situations which may afford them an opportunity of discouraging the traffic." Philadelphia Friends published 5,000 copies for distribution in North America. Before the 1787 founding of the Society for Effecting the Abolition of the Slave Trade, no British antislavery tract was more widely circulated.

—*Christopher L. Brown*

See also
Atlantic Abolitionist Movement; Quakers
For Further Reading
Clarkson, Thomas. 1808. *The History of the Rise, Progress, and Accomplishment of the Abolition of the African Slave Trade by the British Parliament. Vol. 1.* London: Longman, Hurst, Rees, and Orme; Davis, David Brion. 1975. *The Problem of Slavery in the Age of Revolution.* Ithaca, NY: Cornell University Press.

CASTAS

The word *casta* is of medieval Iberian origin and was originally used by the Portuguese to describe Hindu society. In India, *casta* meant a group of persons sharing the same social rank defined by different grades of racial purity, and belonging to a particular *casta* carried certain privileges and prohibitions like wearing specified clothing, using special dishes forbidden to others, carrying arms, and engaging in handiwork as a mere dilettante. Because the *castas* were highly endogamic, there was no opportunity to move from one to another.

Spanish concepts of *casta* were closely related to the ideas of cleanliness of blood and of religion—i.e., Catholicism without suspicion of being Jewish or Moorish. These were the determining factors defining the abilities necessary to occupy positions of moral and political authority. Nevertheless, in Spanish society possibilities of vertical social mobility did exist based upon personal capabilities without paying attention to birth origin and class.

Magnus Mörner believes that the Spanish American regime of *castas* was characterized by the transfer of late medieval, hierarchical, and corporative Castilian society into a multiethnic reality. Initially, a dichotomy of conqueror/defeated or master/slave governed this society, and a strong feeling of "pureness of blood" was no less important among the Indian population. This sixteenth-century society was relatively open to receiving offspring of opposite racial groups, like Indians and Spaniards, but as time progressed, the society gradually became stratified and closed. Those members of the community who were products of miscegenation were segregated because they could be absorbed neither by the conquerors, since there were not enough privileged positions for all, nor by the Indians, because they did not share the same physical characteristics.

This policy created a floating society that was chaotic and scattered. Offspring of racially mixed groups were called *castas* in New Spain, and accordingly, the system included descendants of Spanish-Indian, Spanish-black, and Indian-black ancestry. As a result, colored, scientific, and euphemistic classifications appeared. Nicolás León's *Las castas del México colonial* (1924) listed 50 distinct *castas* and included the proportion of African, Indian, and Spanish blood in each of them. Nevertheless, only a few appeared widely in parish archives and colonial institutions. The following list suggests some of the possible *castas* that appeared in colonial Mexico.

FATHER	MOTHER	OFFSPRING
Spaniard	Indian	Mestizo
Spaniard	Mestiza	Castizo
Castizo	Española (Spanish woman)	Spaniard
Spaniard	Negra	Mulato
Spaniard	Mulata	Morisco
Indian	Negra	Zambo/Loco (Wolf)
Indian	Mulata	Pardo
Zambo	Negra	Chino

There were no religious sanctions against exogamic marriage among *casta* members in New Spain because there was no heritage to protect. Skin color was the primary determinant of an individual's social status, although some people could escape from this policy if they had wealth or power. Additionally, *casta* members were obliged to pay tribute as Indians did, and regulations prohibited them from carrying firearms or occupying positions in state and church bureaucracy, professions, and prestigious guilds. They were relegated to being semiskilled workers like sellers, petty traders, domestic laborers, or vaqueros (cowboys). The *casta* system was abolished in Mexico in 1812, but nevertheless, it was used as a means of discrimination in Mexican society until the Mexican Revolution began in 1911.

—*Nora Reyes Costilla*

For Further Reading
Mörner, Magnus, ed. 1970. *Race and Class in Latin America.* New York: Columbia University Press; Mörner, Magnus. 1967. *Race Mixture in the History of Latin America.* Boston: Little, Brown.

CASTE

There is a strenuous argument among social scientists over whether the word "caste" can be used anywhere other than in referring to India. The major characteristics of India's caste system are that castes are hereditary, ranked hierarchically, religiously based, theoretically rigid, endogamous, tied to occupations, and politically supported. Additionally, there are rules of ritual purity to prevent or cleanse contamination.

As the slave trade and transatlantic slavery ended, the number of slaves in African societies increased, especially in those areas where plantations flourished. These slaves began forming a common identity and often acted in concert to achieve certain goals. Control over their daily life was limited, however, because of the power of African monarchs to enforce effective jurisdiction over their activities. Thus, numerous slave revolts marked late-nineteenth-century Africa.

Reforms that slaveowners developed had the effect of making slavery more like a caste status. For example, in Zanzibar, slave families were specifically encouraged, and plots of land were given to nuclear families. This marriage within a group that is tied to a particular occupation is the definition of caste. Moreover, effective legislation granted specific rights to slaves, as in Calabar where slaves received immunity from execution. In general, codified rights and duties were attached to slave status, and the position was inherited by a married couple's offspring (Manning, 1990).

In South Africa and the United States, it can be and has been argued that the relationship between the races had caste-like characteristics. Certainly, both apartheid and segregation had hereditary, rank, religious, endogamous, occupational, and hierarchical aspects. There was, moreover, a stunning lack of social mobility in both systems and clear aspects of ritual purity tied to contamination beliefs.

—*Frank A. Salamone*

For Further Reading
McSheffrey, Gerald M. 1983. "Slavery, Indentured Servitude, Legitimate Trade, and the Impact of Abolition in the Gold Coast, 1874–1901: A Reappraisal." *Journal of African History* 24: 349–368; Manning, Patrick. 1990. *Slavery and African Life: Occidental, Oriental, and African Slave Trades.* Cambridge: Cambridge University Press.

CATILINARIAN CONSPIRACY

The attempted coup d'état by Lucius Sergius Catilina in Rome in 63 B.C. was the most serious domestic challenge to the Roman government in Italy between the civil wars of the Roman generals Marius and Sulla (91–88 B.C.) and the conflict between Pompey the Great and Julius Caesar (49–48 B.C.). According to the primary sources, Cicero's *Speeches against Catiline* and Sallust's *Conspiracy of Catiline,* Catilina attempted his revolutionary takeover of Rome in the name of disaffected citizens and the lower classes. His subordinates most likely arranged slave uprisings in Apulia, in south-central Italy, as a diversionary tactic and also may have enlisted rural slaves, including gladiators, into the army.

Catilina himself was apparently ambivalent about using slaves, and there is no evidence that he offered slaves any prospects for alleviating the conditions of their slavery if they joined his movement. The major plans proposed by Catilina centered on economic reform, including debt cancellation and land redistribution, and those would have benefited the lower classes only marginally and slaves not at all. The only possible benefit to slaves would have been freedom gained by fighting in the army and a share of any land distribution, but there is no evidence that these benefits were offered. Most likely, the conspirators intended to capitalize on slave discontent and use slaves to further their own plans for personal gain and social reform, which did not include changes in the system of slavery.

The importance of slave participation in the Catilinarian conspiracy is that it foreshadowed the ways slaves were employed by great gang leaders in the 50s B.C., the most violent decade of the republic. Slaves were used increasingly to supply the manpower for individuals who chose to gain power and office through force rather than through traditional, competitive means. Some of those ambitious men spoke about helping the poor, but none offered help to the slaves.

The Catilinarian conspiracy made clear which types of slavers were best suited for rebellion: farmworkers, gladiators, former gladiators, and slaves recently freed to provide protection for their former masters. These slaves and freedmen were more easily incited to revolt and were accustomed to bearing weapons. In this regard, the Catilinarian conspirators may have learned something from the Spartacus uprising (73–71 B.C.), in which rural slaves and gladiators formed the bulk of the army. Similarities between the Spartacus rebellion and the Catilinarian conspiracy are often noted in later sources.

As a result of the increasing use of slaves and freedmen to help form personal armies and to incite rebellion against the government, measures were introduced to keep the number of rural slaves, gladiators, and freed slaves under control. Julius Caesar enacted a law requiring that one-third of the shepherds be freemen. Limits were placed on the number of gladiators that could be exhibited and how many slaves could be liberated. Thus, the increasing use of slaves to force through social programs for free persons in the 60s and 50s resulted in stricter regulations regarding the slaves themselves.

—*Robert W. Cape, Jr.*

See also
Spartacus
For Further Reading
Annequin, Jacques. 1972. "Esclaves et affranchis dans la conjuration de Catilina." *Actes du colloque sur l'esclavage.* Paris: Les Belles Lettres; Bradley, K. R. 1978. "Slaves and the Conspiracy of Catiline." *Classical Philology* 73: 329–336; Dumont, J. C. 1987. *Servus: Rome et l'esclavage sous la républic.* Rome: École française de Rome.

CATO
(234–149 B.C.)

Marcus Porcius Cato, called "the Censor" and also known as Cato the Elder, was one of the most influential politicians and intellectuals of the Roman Republic. He was often characterized by his fiercely conservative beliefs, suspicion of things Greek, and harsh attitudes toward slaves.

Cato the Censor was not born into the Roman nobility—he came from more humble origins outside the city—yet through persistent effort and the patronage of one of Rome's patrician families, he rose to the highest offices in the state and became the leading proponent of the conservative policies linked with the noble class. He fought with distinction in the Second Punic War (218–202 B.C.), was elected consul in 195, and became censor in 184. Cato was known for his harsh strictures against immorality, but it was his actions during his tenure as censor, when it was his job to inquire into public morals, that earned him notoriety in the ancient world.

Cato is considered to be the founder of Latin prose literature, and his many works—including speeches, history, general advice, and a treatise *On Agriculture*—provide some of the earliest evidence for Roman slave practices, especially agricultural slavery. In Chapter 2 of *On Agriculture,* Cato outlines what a master can expect to hear when he inspects his property and finds the work is not done: the slaves are lazy; they could not work because of sickness, rain, or holidays; or they have run away. He offers remedies for almost every excuse: if they are sick, they should not be fed so much (because they need less sustenance and reducing the amount given reduces costs); if it rains, there are things they can do inside; on holidays they

can find other sorts of labor, such as working on a public road or clearing bushes.

If the master finds he has equipment or animals—or sick or old slaves—in bad shape or in abundance, he should sell them to save or earn money: "Sell worn-out oxen, blemished cattle, blemished sheep, wool, hides, an old wagon, old tools, an old slave, a sickly slave, and whatever else is superfluous. The master should have the selling habit, not the buying habit" (Cato and Varro, 1934).

Chapter 5 of the same work provides a wealth of information about the duties of the farm overseer *(vilicus),* who was either a slave or a freedman. The overseer was responsible for monitoring the slaves at all times. Cato advises him to settle disputes between slaves fairly; to provide adequate food, drink, and clothes; and to be a model for them so they will work hard, be loyal, and stay sober.

By the time of Plutarch (c. A.D. 48–120), Cato had become the exemplar of the inhumane slaveowner because of other statements of Cato's that do not survive and because of Cato's general dislike of Greeks (Plutarch was Greek). Plutarch recorded in his *Life of Cato* that Cato boasted he had never paid more than 1,500 drachmas for a slave and claimed that old or sick slaves should be sold or not fed because they were no longer useful.

Plutarch also related that in order to keep male slaves content, Cato encouraged them to visit female slaves for sex—but set a fixed price for each visit. It is not known whether this money went to the women (as part of their *peculium*—a portion of the master's wealth set aside for a slave's use) or to Cato. His slaves were not allowed to enter another person's house without an explicit order to do so, and when they were asked anything about Cato or his wife, they were to say they did not know. Finally, Plutarch stated, Cato became harsher toward his slaves as he got older, often beating them if they prepared a meal incorrectly. He also used to foment dissent among his slaves so they would not trust one another and form an alliance against him.

Plutarch's picture of Cato as the harsh slave driver, which seems to be confirmed by information in Cato's own writings, has remained virtually intact until the present. Alan Astin (1987) presented strong arguments against the validity of this view, arguing that the passages Plutarch cited probably came from a lost speech in which the points were made strongly for rhetorical effect. Astin's thesis has had an impact on the scholarly consensus, but it has not yet affected the popular image of Cato as the archetypal conservative Roman who acted inhumanely toward his slaves.

—*Robert W. Cape, Jr.*

See also
Roman Republic

For Further Reading
Astin, Alan E. 1978. *Cato the Censor*. Oxford: Clarendon Press; Cato, Marcus Porcius, and Marcus Terentius Varro. 1934. *On Agriculture*. Trans. William Davis Hooper and Harrison Boyd Ash. Cambridge, MA: Harvard University Press; Dumont, J. C. 1987. *Servus: Rome et l'esclavage sous la republic*. Rome: École française de Rome.

CEDDO

The *ceddo* were slave warriors among the Wolof, Serer, and Fulbe peoples of Senegambia (basin of the Senegal and Gambia Rivers in West Africa). They lived by a code that placed great emphasis on courage, generosity, and loyalty. They provided many members of the fighting forces of all Senegambian kingdoms, served as messengers, and became some of the most important chiefs. They dominated the court, protected the king, and were the most dependable part of the army. In Wolof kingdoms, authority was often divided between chiefs of freemen, Muslims, and *ceddo,* but the *ceddo* chiefs tended to receive those offices closest to the king. In conferences with Europeans, the person seated next to the king was usually the farba, the most important slave chief.

The institution of slave warrior was common in much of Africa. It is not clear how far back it goes, but when the first Portuguese navigators visited Senegambia, the kings already had large entourages, which probably included many slave dependents. Expansion of the use of slave warriors came after the mid-seventeenth century, when the development of West Indies sugar cultivation increased the demand for slaves from Africa and contributed to the creation of more centralized and more warlike states.

Slave warriors were important in most of the kingdoms that developed at this time, and in kingdoms where they already existed, their use increased. The kingdom of Segou was dominated by the *tonjon,* essentially slaves of the state. The Alafins of Oyo, the most powerful Yoruba kingdom, used slaves as bodyguards, administrators, messengers, and soldiers. Slave warriors were found in most Muslim states of the savanna and in central and eastern Africa.

The value of slaves lay in the fact that they had no family and therefore no allegiance except to the king. They served at his pleasure and had no rights to any office or any land. They could accumulate wealth and often received slave wives as booty from their wars, but both could just as easily be taken from them.

They were known for their colorful clothes, their long hair, and their hard-drinking, hedonistic lifestyle.

They usually had privileged access to guns and horses. In the West African state of Ashanti, for example, when repeating rifles were acquired, they were entrusted to soldiers purchased in the slave markets of northern Ghana. The *ceddo* disdained sustained labor. Although they sometimes worked their own fields, most of their food came from the labor of their wives. Boys taken prisoner in slave raids were often used as grooms and porters, and those who served well, often became *ceddo.*

The *ceddo* tended to live either at the court or in their own distinct villages. In the Wolof kingdom of Kajoor, there were 16 *ceddo* villages. Because of their loyalty to the king, they were not only his bodyguards but also in charge of the administration of the court. In theory, their privileges depended on loyal service. In fact, slave warriors could sometimes act independently in their own collective interest. In Segou, *tonjon* sometimes chose the rulers, and in the 1880s, the powerful farba of Kajoor dealt independently with the French and thus betrayed his king, Lat Dior Diop.

—*Martin A. Klein*

CELTS

The position of slaves in Celtic society is difficult to assess since surviving documentary evidence for that society's structure is meager and often controversial. Nevertheless, ancient texts like the Welsh and Irish law codes suggest that in the early medieval period at least, slavery played an important role. As a social institution within the tribal system it served two useful purposes: it provided a grouping within which the very lowest members of a tribe or clan could be included, and it acted as punishment for serious crimes in a society that had no jails.

Warfare provided the main source for slaves among Celtic nations, as it did originally in the classical world. Just as Roman law defined slavery as a product of war, so too does the Welsh word for slave, *caeth,* derive from the Latin word *captus* ("captive"). Poor conduct in war could also reduce a freeman to slavery: the Irish laws show that warriors who fled the field of battle or received a wound in the back were in danger of losing their liberty.

For Ireland, the surviving legal texts exist mainly in manuscripts of the twelfth to fourteenth centuries, although the society portrayed in them is purportedly that of a period some 700 years earlier. The ultimate origin of the texts lies with the professional lawyers, or *brehons,* who formed one of the higher-status social groupings in the tribal hierarchy. Collectively, the legal texts are often referred to as the Brehon Laws.

Early Irish society revolved around a tribal system in which all inhabitants of tribal territory were graded according to a hierarchy of status. The Brehon Laws show that beneath the lowest grade of freemen were three grades of the unfree: *bothach, sen-cleithe,* and *fuidhir.* The first two may have originated as prisoners of war, or more probably as descendants of such captives, and although usually born within tribal territory, they were denied almost every basic right afforded to free tribesmen. Forbidden to bear arms, to appear as witnesses in judicial cases, or to leave tribal territory, both the *bothach* and the *sen-cleithe* should nevertheless be properly regarded as living "without rights" rather than in slavery.

The *fuidhir* seems to have been so low in the social hierarchy that members of this group can be defined as true slaves. By origin a war captive, a criminal, a bankrupted debtor, an outcast, or a fugitive from another tribe, a *fuidhir* possessed no rights whatsoever, not even the right—so fundamental to Celtic societies—to sue for compensation if a relative was murdered. Nor could a *fuidhir* inherit property of any kind. Instead, he was bound forever in service to his master—usually a *flaith* ("nobleman")—who would generally set the *fuidhir* to work on the poorest parts of his land.

In Wales, the most comprehensive legal code is known today as the Law of Hywel Dda, a text that, although much amended throughout the Middle Ages, originated during the tenth-century reign of King Hywel and seems to have preserved archaic laws from still earlier times. Like contemporary Ireland, early medieval Wales was essentially a tribal society, and its legal systems were founded on centuries of custom and tradition. Close similarities therefore exist between the law codes of the two areas. Just as the Irish grouped the unfree members of their society into various grades, so a similar grading process probably operated in Wales, at least for female slaves, who were graded according to the nature of their work. A higher-grade slave woman was described as *gweinyddol* ("servant") and was defined as "one who goes neither to quern nor spade" (one who does not go to take part in agricultural labor).

In Wales, slaves seem to have been afforded certain basic rights, rights that were denied to Ireland's *fuidhir.* Thus, a Welsh slave suffering insult or injury could claim *sarhaed* ("compensation") in the same manner as a freeborn person, although, of course, the *sarhaed* for a slave was less than that for a free individual. Another important right was that the slave was protected by law from being killed after a first offense of theft, although subsequent offenses were in some instances punishable by amputation of a limb. Even in cases where execution was permitted, monetary compensation could be paid by the slave's lord to the victim of the crime so that the slave would be saved from death. Any freeman who made a slave pregnant was obliged by law to provide her lord with a woman to perform the slave's duties until the child's birth, and should the slave die during the birth, her lord was to be compensated with her monetary value.

Celtic slaves were overwhelmingly illiterate and insignificant in the activities of tribal elites, and they were consequently largely ignored by contemporary writers. The Irish and Welsh law codes seemingly imply that slaves in early-medieval Celtic society had little freedom but few hardships and, being rather akin to serfs of a later period, were unlikely to suffer the severe and punitive conditions that were the norm for slaves in many other cultures.

—*Tim Clarkson*

See also
Ireland, Scotland, and Wales, Raids on
For Further Reading
Ginnell, Laurence. 1917. *The Brehon Laws.* Dublin: West; Jenkins, Dafydd. 1986. *The Law of Hywel Dda.* Llandysul, Wales: Gomer; Wade-Evans, A. W. 1909. *Welsh Medieval Law.* Oxford: Clarendon.

CENTRAL AFRICA

The background to slavery in central Africa lies in the sixteenth-century expansion of people like the Luba-Lunda, the Nyamwezi, the Swahili, and the Yao who established long-distance trade routes both to the east and to the west. This trade initially involved transactions with the coastal Portuguese and the Omani Arabs in African commodities of gold and ivory for cotton products and European weaponry.

The excessive demand for slaves was prompted by the imperial developments of the Omani Arabs, commercial demands for slaves in other parts of the East Indian area, and by the labor needs of Portuguese plantations in Brazil and French plantations on Mauritius. By the nineteenth century, Kilwa and Muscat were cities of embarkation for tens of thousands of slaves per year.

There are striking similarities in central African slavery between that which gravitated toward the east coast and that to the west coast. Toward the west coastal area of the Kingdom of Kongo and the Mbundu, the slave trade with the Portuguese had profound effects. With the baptisms of the king of the Kongo, Mani Nzinga Nkuwu, in 1491 and his successor, Nzinga Mbemba in 1622, a type of covenant was established between those rulers and the king of Portugal. A part of this covenant

Slave caravans wended their way across Central Africa to the east coast, where Arab slave traders awaited them well into the nineteenth century.

was the understanding that slaves would be provided for the Portuguese island and overseas colonies. The covenant was soon broken, and the Kongo lost monopoly control of the trans-African trade to lesser chiefs who were engaging in their own profit sharing with Portuguese adventurers.

Kongo rulers in the sixteenth and seventeenth centuries tried to stop the slave trade because of the many "evils" visited on their kingdoms, which prompted a Portuguese invasion of Kongo and the neighboring Angola-Ndongo of the Mbundu people. The mid-seventeenth-century resistance to the Portuguese was led by Queen Nzinga, who migrated to Matamba in Angola once the Portuguese had destroyed Ndongo. After her death in 1663, the entire region, including the eastern lands of the Ovimbundu and Imbangala (also in Angola), became settled by Portuguese planters who used slave labor. These regions also were a major source for slaves bound for Brazil until the late-nineteenth century.

Paralleling the development of slavery was the disruption of royal succession in central Africa with the intrusion of the Ngoni from southern Africa, the Cokwe traders from the west, and Arab traders from the coast. Slaving became a thread that connected each intrusion. The Bemba of present-day Zambia were able, with the help of Arab traders, to stop the Ngoni, but in doing so, they solidified their own in-

fluence in raiding central Africa for slaves with the assistance of Nyamwezi and Swahili traders. The royal leader of the Bemba, Chileshe, eventually became a wealthy trade merchant with a centralized government in Lubemba (in present-day Zambia).

The Cokwe were late arrivals to the slave trade, and their expansion led to dominance in the Zimbabwean areas of Katanga, Kasai, and Kwango. The Cokwe moved from being prominent traders in wax and ivory to being traders in slaves. Arab traders aligned themselves with various royal leaders. One such individual was Msiri, who ruled the Nyamwezi-Yeke and who, by 1870, had become the dominate power in the area of Kazembe west of the Luapula River. Msiri's power base revolved around his acquisition of European weaponry in exchange for slaves, copper, and ivory. His assassination on December 20, 1891, led to popular revolts and the disintegration of law and order in the region.

Arab and Swahili merchants also forged an alliance with the Nyamwezi leader, Mirambo, whose capital was at Urambo in present-day Tanzania. His growth in power collided with the interests of coastal merchants who tried to coerce compliance through a boycott of Mirambo's merchandise. Mirambo was able to negotiate a truce because of a well-armed mercenary army and an alliance with the Arab trader Tippu Tip.

Tippu Tip arrived in the area of the Luba in the late 1850s, and by the 1860s, his slavers were in the Bemba and Lungu areas (all in present-day Zambia). Warfare and slaving ensued, with Tip defeating the local chieftains. Relying on a large army and kinfolk connections, Tip traded slaves, ivory, and copper.

By the 1870s, central Africa was a slaving center, and Nyangwe (on the Lualaba River leading into the Congo River) was its largest market. This area eventually came under Tip's control as well, and with this added territory, Tip commenced to solidify his bureaucratic state. He made Kasongo his capitol in 1875 and consolidated his control over the areas north of the Luba Kingdom of Kasongo Kalombo (in present-day Zimbabwe).

Slavery and slave raiding became a way of death for millions of lost souls in central Africa as a result of starvation, famine, and attrition through ceaseless labor. Slavery as a reality did not cease until equally coercive, if not less deadly, labor practices, like the corvée, were implemented when direct colonialism was established in the area in the late-nineteenth century.

—*Malik Simba*

For Further Reading
Davidson, Basil. 1969. *A History of East and Central Africa*. London: Longman; Miers, Suzanne, and Igor Kopytoff. 1977. *Slavery in Africa*. Madison: University of Wisconsin Press; Miller, Joseph C. 1988. *Way of Death*. Madison: University of Wisconsin Press; Vansina, Jan. 1966. *Kingdoms of the Savanna*. Madison: University of Wisconsin Press.

CENTRAL AMERICA

The transition from colonialism to independence in Central America was nonviolent: it was declared by an assembly of notables on September 15, 1821, and the Central American Federation (Costa Rica, El Salvador, Guatemala, Honduras, and Nicaragua) detached itself from Mexico on June 29, 1823. Unfortunately, the years that followed were characterized by conservative-liberal clashes over common issues (e.g., church-state relations) debated in other Latin American states in the early national period. The federation dissolved in 1838 because "stagnation, class antagonism, political tyranny and anarchy replaced the relative tranquillity and stability of the Hispanic era" (Woodward, 1985).

The abolition of African slavery was enacted by the National Constituent Assembly of the federation on April 24, 1824. Liberals engineered this law in the face of weak opposition since "involuntary servitude was never so critical [there were at least 100 slaves in Costa Rica and 800 in Guatemala in 1824] to the Central American economic system. . . . The ex-slave simply became one of the mass of persons living more or less at a subsistence level" (Rout, 1976). Of course, the abolition decree was ignored by many owners. Several hundred bondsmen in Guatemala, for example, complained in 1826 to the Federal Congress of the Central American Federation about their continued enslavement (Rout, 1976). Nonetheless, Central American slavery was abolished in the 1820s as a result of demographic, economic, and political considerations, including the availability of Indian labor and scarcity of slaves, the agriculture of the isthmus, and constitutional compromises.

The harvest of indigo, a major crop in colonial Central America, was confined to about two months of the year. Consequently, the "seasonal labor needs made the use of negro slaves difficult and costly. Slaves were expensive and in short supply. . . . So the obraje owners were thrown back upon vanishing Indians for their labor needs" (MacLeod, 1973). The indigenous peoples of the region were exploited after independence according to "colonial patterns [that] contributed to the permanence of compulsory forms of labor recruitment [such as debt-peonage] that, in turn, were more likely to occur where the prosperity of commercial agriculture created demands," which resulted in burgeoning settlements (Lindo-Fuentes, 1995). El Salvador and Guatemala, the centers of indigo production, were home to 248,000 inhabitants (33 per square mile) and 595,000 people (15.25 per square mile), respectively, in 1820 (Lindo-Fuentes, 1995). Increased coffee cultivation later in the century increased these statistics because it was more labor intensive than indigo production.

Article 13 of the 1824 constitution outlawed slavery in the federation as part of a conservative-liberal compromise on church-state relations, federalism, and individual liberties in Central America. "Leaders in both parties recognized the need for modernization and a rational approach to economic problems, as the utilitarian influence of Jeremy Bentham on both sides illustrates" (Woodward, 1985). By the early-nineteenth century, many Latin American intellectuals viewed slavery as an outdated institution and an impediment to development along Western lines. However, it was easier to emancipate the slaves than to empower them in a population (about 65 percent Indian, 31 percent *ladino* or of mixed ancestry, and 4 percent white) of more than 1 million persons (Woodward, 1985). The freedmen were effectively disenfranchised, economically and politically, during the federation years.

The Central American Federation lasted less than two decades because of the five states' competing interests. African slavery was terminated in the second year of the union as a result of slavery's relative insignificance, the existence of Indian laborers, the seasonality of indigo production, and the tenets of nineteenth-century liberalism. The modern-day African experience in the region is, to some extent, a legacy of the federation years; in other words, the exclusion of blacks from mainstream society was one outcome of the period. That is why, "Culturally and racially, the Central American insists on depicting himself as Spanish, according to Salvador Mendieta" (Rout, 1976).

—*Fidel Iglesias*

For Further Reading
Lindo-Fuentes, Héctor. 1995. "The Economy of Central America: From Bourbon Reforms to Liberal Reforms." In *Central America, 1821–1871: Liberalism before Liberal Reform.* Ed. Lowell Gudmundson and Héctor Lindo-Fuentes. Tuscaloosa: University of Alabama Press; MacLeod, Murdo J. 1973. *Spanish Central America: A Socioeconomic History, 1520–1720.* Berkeley: University of California Press; Rout, Leslie B., Jr. 1976. *The African Experience in Spanish America: 1502 to the Present Day.* Cambridge: Cambridge University Press; Woodward, Ralph L., Jr. 1985. *Central America: A Nation Divided.* New York: Oxford University Press.

CERVANTES, MIGUEL DE (1547–1616)

The best-known writer in the Spanish language, and author of *Don Quijote de la Mancha*, Miguel de Cervantes spent five years of his life in Algiers as a slave. After participating in the Battle of Lepanto (1571) and serving as a soldier in Italy, Algerian pirates apprehended Cervantes's ship in 1575 as it was returning to Spain. The letters of recommendation he carried with him convinced his captors that he was an important individual. More or less autobiographic details of his slavery experience appear frequently in his work. "The Tale of the Captive" (*Don Quijote*, Part 1, Chapters 37–42), notwithstanding its fantastic development and ending, recounts some important details of the lives of many Christian Europeans who saw themselves reduced to slavery in North Africa.

The lives of Christian slaves in Algeria were markedly different from those of Muslim slaves in Spain or Italy. They received periodic visits from the Christian friars who acted as mediators to rescue the wealthiest among them through the payment of ransom money, and religious observance was tolerated. Still, the harshness of their lives in captivity is vividly portrayed in most testimonies. Algiers was a multilingual and multinational society in which an important group of renegades (Christians converted to Islam)

had managed to gain sufficient ascendancy to place themselves between the Turkish conquerors and the Arab and Berber Islamic population. Cervantes's own master was one of these Muslim converts. Originally from Venice, his name was Hasan Baja, and he had been the male lover of a former governor of Algiers. Later portrayed in Cervantes's writing as the archetypal "Muslim sodomite," he had protected Cervantes from certain death after one of his escape attempts was discovered. Cervantes was about to be shipped to Istanbul when rescue finally arrived after his family in Spain put together 500 escudos for his ransom.

Cervantes's portrayal of slavery in Spain is somewhat sparse. He was already in Italy during the campaign of Don Juan de Austria against the Moriscos (people of Muslim descent) of Granada (1568–1570), which ended in the destruction of their society and the enslavement of thousands. On the issue of black slaves, Cervantes presented the most complex picture of any Christian European author of his time. In Chapter 29 of *Don Quijote*, Part 1, Sancho Panza dreams of becoming a lord of black vassals in a mythic African kingdom. He plans to sell them in Spain, buy a title of nobility, and retire to his village.

In one of the *Exemplary Novels*, "The Jealous Extremaduran," a black slave man called Luis presents an ironic twist to the already popular stereotype that associated blacks with music, since music was one of the few ways for black slaves to earn money. Luis wants to learn how to play the guitar, yet he is tone deaf. He has also been castrated and is a heavy drinker. Cervantes attacked the slave masters principally, for instance, having Don Quijote attack those who released old slaves when they could no longer be of use: "Throwing them into the street with the title of free men, they turn them slaves to starvation, from which their only escape is death itself" (*Don Quijote*, Part 2, Chapter 24).

—*Baltasar Fra-Molinero*

For Further Reading
Camamis, George. 1977. *Estudios sobre el cautiverio en el Siglo de Oro.* Madrid: Gredos; Canavaggio, J. F. 1990. *Cervantes.* New York: Norton; Friedman, Ellen G. 1983. *Spanish Captives in North Africa.* Madison: University of Wisconsin Press.

CEUTA, CONQUEST OF (1415)

The conquest of Ceuta occurred on June 23, 1415, as Prince Henry's Portuguese forces attacked Morocco's rich northeastern coastline at what had been Moorish North Africa's most flourishing port along the Strait of Gibraltar's southern shore. In the region there were abundant lemon and orange groves, sugarcane fields, teeming fisheries, and bazaars with extensive amounts of worked coral. Ceuta was left undefended by a rebel leader who withdrew his fleet to Granada, preoccupied by hostilities between himself and another warring domestic Moorish faction, and Prince Henry capitalized on this serious "oversight." The Portuguese believed that by possessing Ceuta they would control the Strait of Gibraltar and thus end the earlier harassment of their Mediterranean trade by Moorish vessels. Ceuta would be Portugal's first step toward penetration of the African continent.

With a fleet of 240 vessels, including 27 galleys, and a papal bull bestowing upon the Christian invaders all rights and privileges of a crusade, Henry's forces sacked Ceuta. Contemporary chroniclers described the Portuguese sailors' boorish manners in the lavish bazaars. In their search for gold they ripped open sacks of expensive spices and pepper and wantonly destroyed jars of oil and honey. They also proceeded to remove thousands of alabaster and marble columns from the Moorish palaces, and they carried these back with them to Portugal when the campaign ended. Appointed governor of Ceuta, Henry was to supervise any future trade in Africa. In 1443, Portuguese incursions into West Africa became profitable when they discovered the island of Arguin, which was to become the first focus of Portuguese trade with Arabs, Tuaregs (a West African tribe in the region of modern Mali, Niger, and Nigeria), and the slave-raiding kings of Africa's Guinea coast.

When gold and slaves began appearing in Portugal the population was ecstatic, and the people forgot their earlier accusations that Henry and his legions had wasted public funds on exploratory voyages. By then, Henry had acquired absolute suzerainty over Madeira and the nearer Azores, and he held a West African trade monopoly. Portuguese trading companies and merchants applied for licenses to trade at Arguin and the islands beyond, and furnishing each vessel with a Knights of Christ banner, traders set out to return with an abundant bounty of slaves, which during the initial stages of discovery reached over 300. Prince Henry usually claimed one-fifth (*quinto real*) of the slaves as payment and reflected pleasurably upon the "salvation" of what he considered to be otherwise lost souls. Historically, Europeans initiated the slave trade, and its associated ravaging and pillaging of Africa's interior, after the conquest of Ceuta.

—*Talaat Shehata*

For Further Reading
Livermore, H. V. 1947. *A History of Portugal*. Cambridge: Cambridge University Press; Livermore, H. V. 1971. *The Origins of Spain and Portugal*. London: Allen and Unwin; Watt, William Montgomery. 1967. *A History of Islamic Spain*. Edinburgh: Edinburgh University Press.

CHAVANNE, JEAN-BAPTISTE (D. 1791)

As a landowner and a veteran of the French forces that fought in the American Revolution, Jean-Baptiste Chavanne exemplified the important role free *gens de couleur* ("people of color") played in Saint Domingue (modern-day Haiti) before the French Revolution. Despite their wealth and military service, people like Chavanne were excluded from political participation in the exclusively white local colonial assembly formed in Saint Domingue in 1789.

In Paris, leaders who were free people of color, like Vincent Ogé and members of the Société des Amis des Noirs, failed to convince the National Assembly to redress this injustice. Consequently, the colonial law enacted on March 8, 1790, declared that, as in France, all property-owning and tax-paying men in the colonies who were over 25 would be active citizens and therefore could vote. The law did not explicitly mention the free people of color as citizens, however, and it delegated to the all-white colonial assemblies the right to create their own local legislation regarding citizenship. By not specifically addressing the concerns of the free people of color, the law perpetuated racial discrimination in Saint Domingue.

Disgusted with this decision, Ogé left France, purchased arms in Great Britain and the United States, and arrived in Saint Domingue on October 21, 1790, planning to use force to push the colonial assemblies into acknowledging the rights of the free people of color. Ogé's friend Chavanne joined him, and together they gathered a force of 200 and captured the town of Grande-Rivière in the northern province. They disarmed the white population and issued letters to the colonial assembly demanding political rights. The assembly's response was to send troops to disband the insurgents.

Defeated, Chavanne and Ogé escaped to Spanish territory, but they were extradited to French territory and put on trial in February 1791. Sentenced to death, both were broken on the wheel in Le Cap (Cap Haitien), and their heads were placed on spikes along roads leaving the town—Chavanne's was placed on the road to Grande-Rivière. Thirty-five other participants in the revolt were also executed.

The martyrdom of Ogé and Chavanne shocked many people in France and turned them against the white leadership in Saint Domingue, and in May 1791, the French National Assembly granted political rights to the few people of color born of two free parents. The revolt led by Ogé and Chavanne prefigured the massive slave insurrection of August 1791, which forever altered Saint Domingue's political landscape, and in April 1792, after that insurrection, the National Assembly vindicated Ogé and Chavanne by declaring free people of color full citizens with equal rights. This law stated that the only relevant separation in the colonies was that between the free and the enslaved—a separation that itself was eliminated in late 1793 when slavery was abolished in Saint Domingue.

—*Laurent Dubois*

See also
Haitian Revolution; Ogé, Jacques Vincent
For Further Reading
Benot, Yves. 1989. *La révolution française et la fin des colonies.* Pa. s: Editions de la Découverte; Davis, David Brion. 1975. *The Problem of Slavery in the Age of Revolution.* Ithaca, NY: Cornell University Press; Fick, Carolyn. 1990. *The Making of Haiti: The Saint Domingue Revolution from Below.* Knoxville: University of Tennessee Press.

CHAVIS, JOHN
(1763–1838)

As a free black conservative teacher and preacher, the Reverend John Chavis announced that the abolition of slavery would add to the problems of his enslaved brethren, and in 1831 he referred to Nat Turner's revolt as an "abominable insurrection" (Hudson, 1976). Concern for his personal welfare overrode his concern for and identification with enslaved blacks, as the Turner rebellion had made it impossible for Chavis to continue his life's work when North Carolina's frightened whites nearly expelled all free blacks from the state.

Chavis was born in the West Indies, according to some sources, although an exact location is not identified and he could also have been born near Oxford in Granville County, North Carolina, at a place known locally as the Reavis Cross Roads. In 1832, Chavis described himself as "a free born American [who] saw service in the Revolutionary War" (Hudson, 1976). Chavis somehow managed to receive an extraordinary education by attending Washington Academy (now Washington and Lee University) and, according to some sources, attending but not graduating from the College of New Jersey (now Princeton University). Chavis had been sent to school as an experiment to see if black people could learn the same as

whites, and the experiment obviously succeeded—Chavis excelled in both classics and rhetoric.

In 1801, the Presbyterian Church licensed Chavis to preach. Chavis also began teaching in Fayetteville, North Carolina, and later moved to Franklin, Wake, and Chatham Counties where he continued teaching and preaching to blacks and to whites. By 1808 he had married a woman named Frances and settled in Raleigh where he opened a private integrated school, but was forced to separate his black and white students. He taught the white children in day school, charging them $2.50 for tuition, and the blacks in night school from sundown until 10 P.M. He charged black families $1.75 tuition (probably per year).

Vigorously involved in the politics of the 1800s, Chavis identified himself a Federalist. He opposed Andrew Jackson's election, stating that Jackson was a backwoods countryman without benefit of "blood or training." Clearly, Chavis favored the aristocracy, and perhaps even thought himself part of it, until he was stripped of the vote in summer 1835 when the North Carolina General Assembly decided blacks, including freemen, could not cast ballots.

On June 13, 1838, Gales and Son published a pamphlet written by Chavis entitled *Letter upon the Atonement of Christ,* the sale of which provided income for Chavis and his wife; in addition, the Presbyterian Church voted to support them for the remainder of their lives. For years after his death, Chavis's work as a minister and educator seemed forgotten, but after 50 years of obscurity, Charles Lee Smith, an educator, resurrected the name and had a large park and housing project in Raleigh, North Carolina, named in Chavis's honor.

—*Nagueyalti Warren*

For Further Reading
Cooper, Richard. 1985. *John Chavis: To Teach a Generation.* Raleigh, NC: Creative Productions; Franklin, John Hope. 1943. *The Free Negro in North Carolina 1790–1863.* Chapel Hill: University of North Carolina Press; Hudson, Harold Gossie. 1976. "John Chavis." In *Dictionary of Negro Biography.* Ed. Rayford W. Logan and Michael R. Winston. New York: Norton; Knight, Edgar W. 1930. "Notes on John Chavis." *North Carolina Historical Review* 7: 326–345.

CHEROKEE SLAVEOWNERS

The Cherokee, one of the Five Civilized Tribes whose territory once extended from North Carolina to Alabama, became slaveowners in their attempt to assimilate into white society. The Cherokee often intermarried with whites, and by the 1830s several Cherokee leaders had white blood. Most Cherokee adopted their slaveowning white neighbors' plantation culture in the hope of avoiding removal or extermination, but Cherokee slaveowners tended to be less harsh and cruel than the Southern planters they imitated. Originally, the Cherokee made slaves of their prisoners of war, but this enslavement was not always a permanent situation since some prisoners were later adopted into the tribe. Before Europeans settled the southeastern part of what is now the United States, chattel slavery did not exist in Cherokee society because making a profit was unimportant to them. Only after accepting aspects of white culture, like a central government, commerce, and increased productivity, did Cherokee society support numerous slaves.

In 1828, the Cherokee organized a republic with its capital at New Echota in Georgia and organized the government according to a constitution similar to that of the United States. They had a slave code that predated the constitution, a series of laws concerning black slaves within Cherokee lands. Few of these laws involved slave rebellion or insubordination, and most punishments were reserved for the master rather than the slave. Indians marrying slaves, buying merchandise from slaves, or selling them liquor were punished. Cherokee tradition probably influenced these laws since masters were both responsible for and had absolute power over their slaves.

Slaveholding Cherokee organized and ran the Cherokee republic. Their prosperity and status brought them respect both within the tribe and in Southern white society, and most Cherokee slaveholders spoke English and were part white. They farmed more acres and owned more businesses—mainly mills, ferries, and taverns—than nonslaveholders, and as a group, the Georgia Cherokee had considerably more wealth than the North Carolina Cherokee, who resisted adopting white culture and had relatively few slaves.

Although editorials in the *Cherokee Phoenix* in the 1839s favored abolition with compensated emancipation, most Cherokee probably accepted their white neighbors' views and regarded blacks as inferior. Cherokee laws excluded blacks and mulattoes from voting or holding office in the Cherokee republic, and free blacks who moved onto Cherokee land were regarded as unwelcome intruders and were required to obtain a residence permit. The Cherokee could not marry slaves, but they could marry free blacks, and the 1835 census listed a small number of Cherokees with African blood.

Slaves owned by the Cherokee were allowed to establish chapters of the African Benevolent Society, an outgrowth of the American Colonization Society, within the republic. Missionaries who proselytized among the Cherokee converted more blacks than Native Americans. The Moravians, the first missionaries to the Cherokee, established a mission school at Spring Place, the home of James Vann, a wealthy Cherokee slaveowner. Their church services were integrated as were those of the American Mission Board, which followed the Moravians and established several schools and churches for the Cherokee. Slaves were allowed to attend church services and mission schools along with the missionaries' children, which became a problem in Georgia as that state's code prohibited the instruction of blacks. Although most Cherokee probably treated their slaves better than the whites did, they also considered slaves to be their property, and Cherokee law protected property. Thus, slaves were sold in payment of debt and to settle estates.

Despite their having accepted Southern plantation culture and slavery, when gold was discovered in Georgia the state government demanded that the Cherokee be removed to Indian Territory in Oklahoma. Even though they won their case before the Supreme Court, the Cherokee were forced to leave Georgia, and many took their slaves with them during their removal to Oklahoma. Most Cherokee slaves left no records of their treatment, but Henry Bibb, one slave who belonged to a Cherokee after removal to Oklahoma said, "If I must be a slave, I had by far, rather be a slave to an Indian, than to a white man" (Mails, 1992).

—Elsa A. Nystrom

See also
Seminole Indians
For Further Reading
Mails, Thomas E. 1992. *The Cherokee People: The Story of the Cherokees from Earliest Origins to Contemporary Times*. Tulsa, OK: Council Oaks Books; Perdue, Theda. 1979. "The Development of Plantation Slavery before Removal." In *The Cherokee Indian Nation: A Troubled History*. Ed. Duane H. King. Knoxville: University of Tennessee Press; Wilkins, Thurman. 1988. *Cherokee Tragedy*. Norman: University of Oklahoma Press.

CHILD, LYDIA MARIA (1802–1880)

Coupling an eighteenth-century sensibility with a nineteenth-century radical's passion to free the slaves, Lydia Maria Child was one of the antislavery movement's most brilliant essayists. From her *Appeal in Favor of That Class of Americans Called Africans* (1833) to *Romance of the Republic* (1867), Child was a tireless and accomplished advocate of the human rights of black Americans. Clear-sighted in her analyses of Southern slavery, Child discerned its links to the social lot of white women and also found time to investigate comparative religions.

Child's first book, *Hobomok* (1824), treated the shocking subject of miscegenation (marriage or cohabitation between a white person and a member of another race), yet literary Boston welcomed the novel and its author with open arms. Soon, Child was writing essays and short stories to popular acclaim and editing *The Juvenile Miscellany,* an enormously popular children's magazine. Finding belles lettres insufficiently lucrative, Child turned her energy and talent to domestic guides like *The Frugal Housewife* (1829) and *The Mother's Book* (1831).

Both of the latter books sold extremely well until Child published her exhortatory *Appeal;* after that, she was labeled a radical and ostentatiously shunned. Undeterred, Child joined the Boston Female Anti-Slavery Society, accompanied George Thompson on his U.S. tour, and published *Authentic Accounts of American Slavery* (1835), *The Evils of Slavery and the Cure of Slavery* (1836), and an *Anti-Slavery Catechism* (1836).

Although dismayed by the antislavery movement's dissent over the role of women in abolition, Child continued to oppose the institution. In the early 1840s, she edited the *National Anti-Slavery Standard* and published short stories and essays opposing slavery. Yet in 1843, after separating her finances from her husband's, Child stepped out of the antislavery limelight, exhausted by the internecine quarrels that plagued the movement at the time.

In the 1850s and 1860s, her energy renewed, Child attended antislavery gatherings and asked permission to nurse John Brown in prison. She also helped to raise funds for the families whose sons and fathers had died in the raid on Harpers Ferry, engaged in a letter-writing campaign with Virginians who were outraged at Brown's supposed treachery, and composed antislavery treatises like *The Patriarchal Institution* and *The Duty of Disobedience to the Fugitive Slave Law* (1860). In addition, Child penned proemancipation articles that were printed anonymously and edited Harriet Ann Jacobs's *Incidents in the Life of a Slave Girl* (1861), a slave narrative that focuses on the sexual exploitation of women born as slaves. A section of the last book reappeared in Child's *Freedmen's Book* (1865), a compendium intended to instill racial pride in people long subjugated to the lash. When that work appeared, Child was lobbying for the redistribution of confiscated plantation lands.

In 1870, she attended the closing meeting of the Massachusetts Anti-Slavery Society and the last antislavery festival. Nine years later, she wrote her last article, a tribute to William Lloyd Garrison.

—*Barbara Ryan*

See also
Jacobs, Harriet Ann; Women and the Antislavery Movement
For Further Reading
Karcher, Carolyn L. 1994. *The First Woman in the Republic: A Cultural Biography of Lydia Maria Child.* Durham, NC: Duke University Press; Meltzer, Milton, and Patricia G. Holland, eds. 1982. *Lydia Maria Child: Selected Letters, 1817–1880.* Amherst: University of Massachusetts Press.

CHILDREN

African societies introduced children to work and discipline early, partly because polygamy, which was almost universal, meant large families. In rural areas small boys were taught to herd goats and sheep while their toddler sisters often carried the most recent baby strapped to their backs. Children of both sexes were sent into fields to chase birds away from plantings (which was later also the case for slave children in the Americas). Urban children, especially girls, were given age-appropriate tasks from carrying small pots of water to the house to helping prepare meals. Boys ran errands for their fathers, and some were apprenticed by the time they were six or seven in order to develop skills as artisans.

Although child labor was not associated solely with slavery, there were major differences between the two labor practices. Slave children lacked the extended kinship network of older family members and relatives, which provided much security, and it was their parents who chose the tasks they performed, not their owners. Still, when enslaved by Africans, children had the benefit of a culture that believed in indoctrination and informal education. Slave children usually stayed with their mothers until they were old enough to perform tasks beyond the household, and if a slave woman gave birth to a child by a royal man, that child could eventually achieve power in his own right. Conversely, slave children born into slave families rarely escaped from bondage except by running away.

Children were enslaved under various circumstances. Some were sold away from drought and famine or when their parents were unable to pay a debt. Some were captured in the warfare that characterized political upheaval over time in African societies. Few of these children were transported in the Atlantic slave trade, although some were born aboard slave ships.

Slavery was mostly benign in African societies, but there were occasions when slave children suffered in-

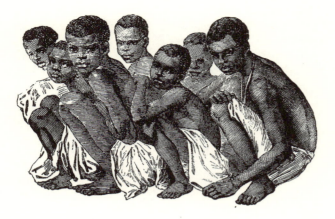

Young boys such as these were prized by slave traders.

forming light tasks to avoid mischief and to instill the slavery work ethic.

In Brazil, some masters treated slave children like pets—throwing them bits of food from the table and generally allowing them to play with their own children until they until they were old enough to work. In Brazil and the West Indies, fathers rarely had any involvement with their children even if they lived in the same house, and most of the children resided in quarters where they were surrounded and reared by females. The same was true in North America. Without male input, either financial or emotional, young boys grew up without knowing how to act as fathers, and as a result, there emerged in the New World a matriarchal system that was in contradistinction to the patriarchal system that characterized African societies.

North American slave children usually remained with their mothers until they reached 10 or 12. Some enlightened owners preferred keeping families intact, but as the frontier opened and labor needs increased, boys and girls were increasingly sold away from their mothers, and brothers and sisters often went in different directions. Parents, when they were together, attempted to provide affection for their children, especially when they were small. In female-centered households, older women provided the love and comfort that would have been forthcoming from extended kin in Africa.

In slave societies, children played as time and opportunity allowed, and their attire depended upon climate and age. In Africa, youths of both sexes frequently went naked until they were 8 or 10, and the same was true in the tropical and temperate climates in the New World. Otherwise, they wore homespun muslin fabrics and had a limited wardrobe. Many went barefoot through adulthood.

Education was generally limited, with some masters allowing their slave children to obtain rudimentary reading skills, but through time, education was prohibited for all but the most favored children of house slaves. Home discipline was strict in the Americas, partly to instill self-discipline to ward off harsh punishments from owners. By the time the boys neared puberty, they were often placed in the fields in rural areas, and children of both sexes were put to work picking cotton and cutting tobacco. Girls were taught to work in the house at tasks like setting and clearing tables or carrying water to the fields when they were large enough to carry the pots. Young girls were subject to rape in these New World societies, and half-castes were often sold as prostitutes—as in Africa, where lithe pubescent girls were frequently sold as concubines.

Whether in Africa, where slavery's burden was generally less harsh, or in the Americas, slavery deprived children of the loving comfort of an extended family

humane treatment. One such instance occurred when a young girl, Swema, was sold with her mother to Arab slave traders in central Africa. The long march, combined with her frailty, caused Swema to faint. Her captors believed her dead and placed her in a shallow grave before continuing to the Zanzibar slave market. Fortunately, Swema recovered consciousness and was able to alert passersby before she actually suffocated.

Although examples of treatment regarding slave children are limited and we lack evidence for earlier periods in history, we have John Haggard's report on how the Muslim Swahili punished disobedient slave children in East Africa in the nineteenth century. Haggard observed little children dragging long wooden poles that had been attached to their necks by heavy metal collars. The poles varied in length from "a foot long to twelve or fourteen feet . . . I noticed a boy in the water . . . with one at least twelve feet long and as big round as a clothes post. He could hardly drag it after him" (King, 1995).

Europeans varied in their attitudes and behavior toward African slave children. The first examples we have come from the Dutch in southern Africa's Cape Colony. In the mid-seventeenth century, they captured a slaver containing 174 Angolan children off the Brazilian coast. These children proved easier to assimilate than adults, and thus the Dutch came to prefer children as slaves and transported considerable numbers of them from Madagascar to the slave lodge in the Cape Colony. There the children were provided with a daily dose of brandy and "two inches of tobacco" while they were taught the Dutch language and Christian prayers. The French also favored children in some of their possessions because children were more easily trained and suffered less from the depression of separation from their lineage systems. Both the French and Dutch put children to work per-

that was the birthright of those who were born and raised in freedom.

—*Patricia Romero*

For Further Reading
King, Wilma. 1995. *Stolen Childhood: Slave Youth in Nineteenth Century America*. Bloomington: Indiana University Press; Robertson, Claire, and Martin L. Klein, eds. 1983. *Women and Slavery in Africa*. Bloomington: Indiana University Press; Romero, Patricia. 1997. *Lamu: History, Society, and Family in an East African Port City*. Princeton, NJ: Markus Wiener Publishers; Shell, Robert. 1994. *Children of Bondage*. Johannesburg: University of Witwatersrand Press.

CHINA, ANCIENT

The ancient civilization that formed along the great bend of the Huang Ho (Yellow River) in northern China ranks as one of the earliest cradles of civilization in human history, as archaeologists have unearthed pottery shards in the region that date back as much as 10,000 years. Historical and anthropological evidence suggest that the Chinese farmed, cultivated silk, and domesticated animals during the prehistoric period and that this East Asian development occurred completely independent of any Western Eurasian influences. Accordingly, the social structures that developed in the region were not based upon Western models, and institutions like slavery that evolved in China were distinctly dissimilar from any counterparts to the west.

Chattel slavery, as it was known in the west, did not exist in ancient China. Although slaves may indeed have been owned by others, the slaves were seldom in a situation where they faced abject powerlessness. Rather, what existed in China was a complex society in which the nature of one's societal membership was based upon various dependency relationships.

In general terms, Chinese society was divided into two broad categories: *liangmin* ("good people") and *jianmin* ("inferior people"). Within the category of the *jianmin* there existed a hierarchy of status that included all individuals who were viewed as "base" or "mean." This group did include slaves, but it also included other people who were at levels of servitude that made them less than free. Law codes generally reflected the varying status of individuals by exacting different punishments for those who committed similar offenses based upon the social level of the perpetrator.

Some Marxist scholars have maintained that slavery existed in China from the time of the Hsia (Xia) dynasty (2205–1766 B.C.), but that claim is based upon theoretical assumptions rather than substantive evidence. The Marxist notion that a slave economy necessarily precedes a feudal structure presupposes that slavery had to exist before the end of the Chou (Zhou) dynasty (1122–221 B.C.), a time of great cultural achievement in ancient China.

That argument is rather specious. Historical documentation for the Hsia dynasty is lacking as the period is noted more by myth and legend than by historical evidence. The Shang or Yin dynasty (1766–1122 B.C.), which was the successor to the Hsia, is historically well documented, and there is no evidence to support widespread use of slavery in China at that time. Although there is ample evidence to support the notion that Shang society maintained class-based dependency relationships, confirmation of any large-scale trading of slaves does not exist in the historical record.

Some evidence from the study of royal tombs of the Shang period supports the belief that practices such as self-immolation and burying people alive were used during that era. It is believed that those who were marked for such deaths were non-Shang "barbarians," probably war captives who had been reduced to slavery. This custom also seems to have been used by the Shang in dedicating new buildings.

During the more than six centuries of Shang rule, wars of conquest extended the boundaries of China to the south and east. These conflicts, which were primarily to collect tribute and to loot and plunder, also provided an opportunity for the taking of war captives, who might then have become slaves of the state. Although this hypotheses is speculative, Shang familiarity with "barbarians" increased throughout the period of the dynasty, and after it ended, the practice of slaveholding in China seems to have been more common, if not yet institutionalized, during the Chou and subsequent dynasties.

During the time of the Chou, a regimented class system remained in effect in China. Peasants were not considered slaves, but they lived in a state of near serfdom as they were bound to the land, unable either to flee from it or to own it. By this time in Chinese society, slaves were considered to be beyond the traditional class structure, and they generally consisted of outsiders—war captives or criminals—who could be purchased and used as laborers.

Even though some form of slavery existed in ancient China, it is apparent that it was used on a small scale. It can be said that ancient China was a society that owned slaves, but it cannot be said that it was a slave society on a par with subsequent civilizations such as classical Greece and Rome.

—*Junius P. Rodriguez*

See also
Marxism

For Further Reading
Li, Zeming. 1990. "On China's Ancient Slaves in Agricultural Production." *Che hsueh she hui ko.* 2: 95; Wang, Guimin. 1990. "*Zhong-ren* (Commoners) in Shang Supposed To Be Slaves." *Zhongguoshi yanjiu* 1.

CHINA, LATE IMPERIAL

Although certain types of slavery did exist in ancient and medieval China, contact with the West would alter the institution. The first contact between Europeans and the Chinese dates back to the time of the Han dynasty (206 B.C.–A.D. 220) when merchants from the Roman Republic (and later the Roman Empire) traversed the Silk Road to trade for exotic oriental goods. Subsequent interaction between Eastern and Western civilizations tended to be sporadic, as vast distances and the many difficulties associated with long-distance commerce made contact between the two regions less and less frequent. For the people who did conduct a successful east-west trade, the potential for profits was tremendous, and occasionally the lure of riches prompted someone to seek a practical route for safe sustained trade between Europe and China.

As a result of the Crusades (1095–1272) and the travels of Marco Polo (1271–1295), European interest in goods from the Orient was piqued once more, and increased overland trade developed again along the ancient Silk Road. During the fifteenth century, European navigators progressively strove to circumnavigate Africa while others like Christopher Columbus sailed west to reach the east. By 1514, Portuguese sailors had reached the coast of southeastern China, and the fate of imperial China would thereafter be inextricably tied to the ever-expanding interests of Europeans.

War captives were a potential source of slaves, and the Chinese discovered this fact in reverse during the imperial period. When the Mongols invaded and conquered China during the thirteenth century, many Chinese were enslaved in the process. Later, when the Manchu established the Ching (Qing) dynasty (1644–1912), more Chinese were enslaved. Many of these newly enslaved bondsmen became personal retainers (*bugu*) of their new imperial lords. Since both the Mongols and the Manchu were outsiders, each tried to rely upon the cooperation of the indigenous Chinese to bolster the image of its new dynasty. As a result, many Chinese slaves found themselves in positions of power and influence in both the Mongol and Manchu administrations. Many of the Manchu bondservants performed high-level tasks for the Manchu emperors that in previous dynasties would have been performed by eunuchs.

Occasionally, the owners of large numbers of slaves were absentee owners who placed the responsibility of their bondsmen in the hands of a trusted slave overseer. These "master slaves" often owned their own property, which sometimes included their own slaves. This anomaly of Chinese owning other Chinese was unsavory to many, and when slave revolts or peasant uprisings occurred, it was often the property of the "master slaves" that was targeted first.

Although some elements of slavery continued to exist in the late imperial period, another common practice, the removal of Chinese for labor in other world areas, also became a labor concern during this era. In the nineteenth century, when Great Britain and other European nations made a concerted effort to end the African slave trade, Chinese coolies began to be exported in large numbers, partly as a replacement labor force. By the late 1840s, substantial numbers of Chinese male laborers were being shipped under contract, mainly from Amoy (Xiamen) but also from Macao and other ports, to satisfy the pressing demand for cheap labor in newly developing areas like Cuba, Peru, Hawaii, Sumatra, and Malaya.

The process was certainly prompted by the worldwide effort to abolish the African slave trade, but it was also encouraged by the introduction of foreign shipping, which made this practice more cost-effective. In this new labor trade under foreign flags, Chinese "crimps" (procurers of laborers) often committed excesses in the process of recruiting and keeping the human cargoes in depots (barracoons) for transfer, and some foreign vessels nearly duplicated the conditions and practices of the earlier African slave trade.

Occasionally, reformers within China sought to end the practice of slavery. During the Taiping Rebellion (1850–1864), the rebel leader Hung Xiuquan (Hung Hsiu-ch'üan) implemented a far-reaching plan of social reforms that included the abolition of slavery, prostitution, and the trading of wives. The defeat of the rebel movement and the suicide of its leader brought an end to those reforms.

In 1909, in the final years of imperial rule, the Ching leaders decreed that slavery was abolished in China, but the practice persisted until 1949 when the People's Republic of China was founded. Although the practice of slavery did exist at various times in China's long history, the extent of its use does not justify the classification of China as being a slave society. It appears that the presence of an ample peasantry largely mitigated the need for large-scale slave labor in China.

—*Junius P. Rodriguez*

For Further Reading
Pulleyblank, E. G. 1958. "The Origin and Nature of Chattel Slavery in China." *Journal of the Economic and*

Social History of the Orient 1: 185–220; Tsai, Shih-shan Henry. 1996. *The Eunuchs in the Ming Dynasty.* Albany: State University of New York Press.

CHINA, MEDIEVAL

As used here, "medieval" refers to the period in China during which a feudal economy and society emerged as the primary characteristics of civilization and life. In terms of dynastic chronology, this period would correspond with the Ch'in (Qin) through the T'ang dynasties (roughly second century B.C. through the tenth century A.D.). It was during this time that slavery became common and more institutionalized in China. Although war captives and foreigners (or "barbarians") remained a common source of slaves, many individuals often signed themselves into a form of voluntary slavery to avoid the excessive burdens of imperial taxation. During the medieval era, two Chinese rulers made an effort to abolish the practice of slavery, but neither met with success. Rather than supporting abolition on any moral or ethical grounds, these rulers sought to enhance the power of the state by eliminating the feudal holdings in land and slaves of the wealthy.

Sometime around 100 B.C., Tung Chung-shu, a famous follower of Confucius, advised Emperor Wu that reforms were necessary if an agricultural crisis that threatened China's well-being were to be averted. His reforms included the limitation of ownership of both land and slaves. His suggestions were never implemented because the wealthy families, who would have been threatened by such changes, opposed them and pressured the government against such drastic innovations.

In A.D. 9, the reformer Wang Mang attempted to destroy the power of the great private estates by ordering that their lands be nationalized and distributed among tax-paying peasants. He also decreed that the current practice of private slavery should be changed, but not destroyed. He proposed this drastic policy because so many peasants lived on the tax-free estates that there were not enough taxpayers to support the central government. In particular, many small farmers sought protection from the "counting tax" by becoming tenant farmers or personal retainers of some great man who had ample power to shield them from the imperial tax collectors. Some impoverished farmers even sold themselves or their children into slavery.

During the Ch'in dynasty, large numbers of slaves belonging to the state were used as laborers on large-scale projects. Ambitious public works programs, which included land reclamation, road building, and canal construction, were completed during this era

with a workforce that consisted largely of slave laborers. It appears that holdings in slaves during this era were quite extensive. In the third-century-A.D. Han dynasty, the Chinese jurist Ma Tuan-lin promulgated the following policy:

> In accordance with the suggestion made by responsible officials, the limitation of slave ownership should be as follows: For kings and dukes the maximum number of male and female slaves each of them is allowed to own is 200; for counts and imperial princesses, 100; and for counts who reside in the capital and its environs and for all officials and commoners, 30. Slaves over the age of sixty or below that of ten are not included in this limitation. (Fitzgerald, 1969)

There were four common ways people acquired private slaves: slaves could be given to individuals by the government, they might submit to self-sale, they might become slaves by commendation, or they might be inherited. Of these four processes, commendation was the most vague, because the individuals who submitted themselves to this process were given a status somewhere between that of a slave and that of a commoner. Through commendation, one became a personal retainer *(bugu)* of another. Slaves with this status could not be sold, but they could be given away to another. Many of the privately owned slaves were employed as household servants while the slaves who belonged to the state generally worked as agricultural laborers, on state public works projects, in convoys, or as army attendants.

—*Junius P. Rodriguez*

For Further Reading
Fitzgerald, Charles P. 1969. *The Horizon History of China.* New York: American Heritage; Hsu, Cho-yun. 1965. *Ancient China in Transition: An Analysis of Social Mobility, 722–222* B.C. Stanford, CA: Stanford University Press; Wilbur, Clarence M. 1943. *Slavery in China during the Former Han Dynasty, 206* B.C.–A.D. *25.* Chicago: Field Museum of Natural History.

CHRISTIANA RIOT

The most violent incident of African American resistance to the Fugitive Slave Act of 1850 occurred on September 11, 1851, near Christiana, Pennsylvania. That morning, Maryland slaveowner Edward Gorsuch, six of his relatives, and three U.S. marshals bearing federal warrants ar-

This 1851 illustration shows slave hunters being attacked by free African Americans during the Christiana Riots, the most violent instance of resistance to the Fugitive Slave Act of 1850.

rived at the tiny Quaker village of Christiana and surrounded the house of William Parker, a local black farmer.

The posse demanded the surrender of Nelson Ford and Joshua Hammond, two slaves who had run away from the Gorsuch farm in 1849 and were hiding inside the Parker home. Parker's wife sounded a horn, and dozens of neighbors—both black and white—responded. Two Quakers advised the posse to retreat, but Gorsuch refused, declaring, "My property I will have, or I'll breakfast in hell" (Slaughter, 1991). After a heated verbal exchange, shots were fired, and when the confusion subsided, Gorsuch lay dead and three members of his party were nursing serious wounds.

The affair quickly assumed national importance. Southern proslavery newspapers and the abolitionist press waged a fierce propaganda battle, each attempting to use the incident to sway public opinion. The former viewed the riot as a breach of Southern property rights under the U.S. Constitution and saw abolitionist provocation as the cause. The latter blamed slaveholding interests and cast the rioters in the liberty-loving tradition of the heroes of the American Revolution.

Fearing political repercussions, President Millard Fillmore dispatched a company of U.S. Marines and some 40 Philadelphia policemen to Christiana to apprehend those involved. Nearly 40 blacks and 6 whites, some with tenuous links to the incident, were arrested. But the 5 blacks who were most responsible for Gorsuch's death—including Parker, Ford, and Hammond—escaped to Canada West (now Ontario), where requests for their extradition went unheeded.

Federal prosecutors sought to make examples of the rioters and charged them with treason. A grand jury indicted and imprisoned 36 blacks and 2 whites until they could be tried before the U.S. circuit court in Philadelphia. The trial of Castner Hanway, a white miller alleged to have directed the rioters in their attack on the posse, became the test case upon which the fate of the other 37 rested. But his trial, which ironically convened on the second floor of Independence Hall, only served to show the weakness of the government's case. The available evidence proved insufficient to substantiate the charges, and after Hanway was acquitted in early December, the prosecution waived all remaining indictments and the rioters were released.

The incident at Christiana, and its aftermath, demonstrated the difficulty of enforcing the Fugitive Slave Act. The incident also polarized public opinion regarding the law. Southerners were outraged that none of the rioters was convicted. At the same time, federal efforts to punish the rioters increased sympathy for the abolitionists in the North. As a result of the riot, therefore, sectional tensions increased, and the nation moved closer to civil war.

—Roy E. Finkenbine

See also
Fugitive Slave Act of 1850; Slave Catchers
For Further Reading
Slaughter, Thomas P. 1991. *Bloody Dawn: The Christiana Riot and Racial Violence in the Antebellum North.* New York: Oxford University Press.

CHRISTIANITY, U.S. ANTEBELLUM SOUTH

Christianity's spread among African American slaves during the nineteenth century coincided with the moral battle between the North and South over slavery during the antebellum era, and the basis of the mission to convert slaves was formed within the context of the North-South clash. Southerners accepted the challenge of instituting plantation missions largely because doing so was perceived as being in their best interest. Two proponents of plantation missions, Charles C. Jones and William Capers, proposed the direction the program should take. Basically, these leaders advocated modifying slaves' belief and behavior to make them compatible with the white evangelical worldview. Jones and Capers believed that Christian slaves would be better slaves in that their duties and responsibilities would be clearly defined during religious instruction. Part of "the gospel of Christ," this dogma was also functional for a social order based on master-slave relations. Hence, "the conversion of slaves became the means of saving the South" (Mathews, 1977).

Mission theorists Jones and Capers were both ministers and slaveholders. Similarly, Bishop Leonidas Polk, who owned a large Louisiana plantation, and a Bishop Mead of Virginia urged planters to teach their slaves the Christian religion. In fact, the major Southern denominations encouraged planters to bring the gospel to blacks. There had long been an alliance between ministers and planters. Prior to America's permanent settlement there was an alliance in England between businessmen and ministers to promote American colonization, and as during the antebellum years, divines initiated that alliance. Regarding the plantation missions, "Southern planters recognized that control of their slaves' religious lives was a means of social control" (Reimers, 1965).

Some missionary theorists owned slaves partly because they desired "properly" trained servants, yet a larger motive was to assure an orderly Southern society—that is, one that kept blacks in a subservient position. Planters and preachers held Sunday school classes for the slaves, and Southerners sought to demonstrate that slavery was a "positive good" through the antebellum plantation mission. Still, Northern abolitionists labeled Southerners "sinful and wicked." In 1858, Abram Pryne described slavery as having begun in "robbery, piracy, and murder; and having this indescribably wicked beginning, it ought to die" (Mathews, 1977). In response, Southerners felt compelled to defend slavery against the Northern attack. Christianization of blacks had been a rationale for slavery for centuries, and it was this belief that assuaged the conscience of Southerners more than anything else. There had been occasional efforts to convert blacks to Christianity but never a wholehearted and systematic attempt. Greater efforts to do so occurred during the antebellum era during the moral battle between the North and the South over slavery.

Mission theorists Jones and Capers believed that Christian slaves would be better slaves. Self-interest was the basic motive for this view since the anticipated result would be an orderly, hierarchical Southern society consisting of Christian masters and slaves. Allied with self-interest was a peripheral motive of compassion and concern by some Southerners for their slaves' spiritual growth and development. Perhaps converting slaves was the right thing to do. Historian Donald G. Mathews suggests that if slavery was a "positive good" as argued, then conversion of slaves "would be living proof of God's favor, and conscience might be satisfied" (Raboteau, 1980).

Slaveholders' "sins" were identified with other vices upon which all Christians agreed: fornication, adultery, theft, kidnapping, procuring, and murder. This fact embarrassed some Southern clergymen, and one evangelical slaveholder was compelled to damn "the curse of slavery" (Mathews, 1977). Although such expressions of guilt and concern were not universally felt in the South, they indicate that a moral crisis did exist in the minds of some Southern clergymen and laymen. Albert Raboteau (1980) notes in his analysis that there had always been sporadic and occasional "eruptions of Christian conscience," suggesting that slavery was wrong and that converting blacks to Christianity was the proper thing to do.

Regardless of the motives responsible for bringing the plantation missions into being, an evaluation of their triumphs and shortcomings shows that the idea was a failure. Since the objective was the slaves' "proper" socialization, leaders anticipated that the final product would be an obedient and submissive Christian slave, but from the missions' beginnings there were inherent misgivings. Blacks and whites were taught the same religion, although certain biblical verses were emphasized for the slaves' consumption. Despite contrary arguments, past and present, the spirit of equality is the essence of biblical doctrine, and criticism levied against the mission plan recognized this fact. Samuel Seabrook, who observed the plantation mission, expressed apprehension in his *Management of Slaves* (1834) regarding an emergence of egalitarian ideals. Seabrook feared the latent function of mission teachings—transmitting egalitarian ideals inherent in Christian doctrine.

Raboteau's (1980) argument that some slaves found the "message of docility" obnoxious and rejected it as the "white man's religion" is supported by slave testimony. Although some slaves accepted the teaching and did their best to "incorporate it in their lives," there was greater resentment and rejection of the "message of docility" than social scientists have recognized or acknowledged.

John W. Blassingame's *Slave Testimony* (1977) presents a massive systematic compilation of "black response to bondage." Reproducing various primary sources such as letters, speeches, autobiographies, and interviews, this work reflects slaves' attitudes and perceptions of Southern society. In a letter from Canada, one Henry Bibb castigated his former master in caustic and accusing words: "Vain is your religion—base is your hypocrisy." He continued his condemnation adding: "And whilst you continue in such an unhallowed course of conduct, your prayers, your solemn fasts and ordinances are an abomination to the Lord, from which he will turn his face away, in disgust, and will not hear or look upon." Just sampling expressions of slaves' attitudes and perceptions of Southern society, especially how that society related to and affected them, supports the conclusion that the missions failed and that many slaves rejected the "special" brand of Christianity designed for them. Considering data on Southern culture that includes the slaves' perspective results in a more complete and more comprehensive account of the sociology of master-slave relations.

Members of various Protestant denominations sought to establish a solid or integrated South by advocating different forms of Christianity for blacks and whites, forms that were designed to inculcate separate and distinct value and behavioral systems. This "rule of gospel order" was hierarchical in nature and placed a greater emphasis upon slaves' submission to earthly masters than to a heavenly master. Inherent in this type of biblical exegesis were the seeds of failure.

Despite the missions' failure, a slaveholding ethic matured that was explicit and systematically expressed. Variations of its expression existed, but it included two basic tenets: a belief in the inherent inferiority of black people and the belief that Christianity and slavery were compatible. This Southern Christian slaveholding ethic was accompanied by proslavery ideology that envisioned a structured slaveholding social order. Within the context of plantation missionary work designed to benefit the slaves, these two ideas led to a merger of white racism and Christianity and the result was what has been called "Christian racism" (Smith, 1972).

Origins of the associations among slavery, white racism, and Christianity in Western culture have become uncertain to today's scientific and technological minds, but it has been argued that "modern racism" in the West is connected to and grounded historically in cultural ideas and religious beliefs. The Ham doctrine, for example, which legitimized belief in black inferiority, was a central part of Christian theology from the sixteenth to the nineteenth centuries. Indeed, it is ironic that the faith which many believe holds a common message of liberation was for many centuries an active agent in the perpetuation of slavery.

—*James H. Rasheed*

See also
Ham, Curse of; Proslavery Argument, United States; Racism

For Further Reading
Mathews, Donald G. 1977. *Religion in the Old South.* Chicago: University of Chicago Press; Raboteau, Albert J. 1980. *Slave Religion.* New York: Oxford University Press; Reimers, David M. 1965. *White Protestantism and the Negro.* New York: Oxford University Press; Smith, Hilrie Shelton. 1972. *In His Image, but . . . Racism in Southern Religion, 1780–1910.* Durham, NC: Duke University Press.

CHRISTOPHE, HENRI (1767–1820)

Henri Christophe was a military leader and statesman who fought against slavery during the French occupation of Saint Domingue, the western portion of Hispaniola. After independence, he ruled the northern province of the new country. Born on the island of Grenada, a former French colony ceded to Britain shortly before his birth, Christophe grew up fluent in both French and English but illiterate. Supposedly sent to sea as a cabin boy at age nine, he thus landed on Saint Domingue. Two years later, he reportedly served under Comte d'Estaing, side by side with American insurgents, during the siege of Savannah. Later, he worked at an inn, La Couronne, in Saint Domingue where he rose from scullion to manager. He must have become a free black at some point, for it would have been almost impossible for a slave to occupy the latter position.

Henri Christophe, portrait by Richard Evans.

In the early 1790s, Christophe was a member of the French armed forces and was assigned as an aide to Toussaint Louverture. The commander appreciated his reliability, organizational talents, and loyalty and promoted him rapidly to brigadier. During the rest of that decade, as Toussaint continued leading the war of liberation, Christophe fought valiantly at his side to safeguard his people's freedom from slavery.

By 1801, Christophe was leading troops against General Leclerc and the army sent by Napoleon to reinstate French control, restore white supremacy, and reinstitute slavery for blacks and limited rights for mulattoes. Christophe was second in command when, having repulsed the French, the chief of the army of liberation, Jean-Jacques Dessalines, proclaimed the independence of the territory under its old Arawak name, *Haiti,* and declared himself emperor. When Christophe realized that the new emperor's bloody tyranny was destroying Haiti, he allied himself with the mulatto general Alexandre Pétion and others to arrange the assassination of Dessalines in 1806.

Cooperation between blacks and mulattoes did not last long. Christophe soon found himself warring with Pétion, in whose mind the revolt against Dessalines was but a first step toward a mulatto takeover of Haiti. In 1807, Christophe controlled the north, Pétion the south. Christophe had the northern assembly elect him president of the State of Haiti and commanding general of the armed forces. Meanwhile, the southern senate elected Pétion president of the Republic of Haiti. Each man aspired to unify the country under his own rule. To defeat Pétion, Christophe built a navy and negotiated with the British. He sought international recognition and needed British naval noninterference with any blockade he might mount in the south. Pétion also sought British guarantees, but Britain steered a neutral course, doing what best suited its own interests in Grenada. The civil war lasted for years, with neither Haitian leader being powerful enough to oust the other. An uneasy truce existed after 1811, when Pétion was reelected president and Christophe declared himself king.

Although this change of title no doubt satisfied his vanity, Christophe was also motivated by a desire to enhance his country's prestige abroad, in a world still dominated by monarchies, and on the island itself. He took the change seriously, charging the assembly with drafting a new constitution. He appointed a nobility, built elegant palaces—principal among them, Sans Souci—and held court in the style of European monarchs. But all was not pomp and circumstance. Christophe also built formidable fortifications, particularly the Citadel high on the Pic de la Ferrière. Inaccessible, impregnable, this fortress was meant to resist any invader. He continued his efforts to improve

living conditions, and his main concerns were reviving the economy and restoring agricultural production. For this purpose he instituted the *fermage,* which meant that the government could seize abandoned plantations and lease them. Tenants had to share one-fourth of their gross revenue with workers, house them, and provide medical assistance. In exchange, the field hands worked long hours and could not leave the plantation at will. Government overseers strictly enforced regulations on both tenants and workers.

As the economy suffered from a manpower shortage, owing to the needed maintenance of a large army to deter a greatly feared new French invasion or an assault by Pétion, Christophe also tried to involve the military in agriculture by granting plots of land proportionate to rank. Thanks to all these measures, sugar production increased tenfold, but the population resented the harsh work discipline.

Although jealously safeguarding his black nation's prerogatives, Christophe did not indulge in vindictiveness against whites. Like Louverture before him, he preached tolerance, believing that white knowledge and skills were needed to develop Haiti. He issued proclamations welcoming trade with neutral powers, sent envoys to capitals of seafaring nations, and invited foreign merchants to establish commercial relations with Haiti.

He requested help from the British abolitionist William Wilberforce to institute a Haitian educational system, for Christophe was persuaded that education was the key to the future. The establishment of elementary schools in the main cities was followed by the creation of the Royal Academy for secondary education, from which students would proceed to royal colleges. Christophe strove to impose a work ethic and to strengthen society's moral fiber by outlawing concubinage, severely punishing theft, and forcing participation in Christian church rites.

Thanks to Christophe's strict measures, conditions in the country improved rapidly. Yet the population was dissatisfied: imposed Catholicism conflicted with the native voodoo, working conditions were too much like the days of slavery, the military found itself forced into working on what it felt were undignified projects, and Christophe was becoming more self-important and tyrannical. When Pétion's successor, Jean-Pierre Boyer, attacked the north, Christophe's officers wavered. At this moment Christophe suffered a paralytic stroke and could not resist the general unrest. Realizing that his rule was at an end, Christophe shot himself on October 8, 1820. At that time disrespect for him was so great that his body was thrown into a lime pit, where it remained until 1847 when he finally received proper burial in the Citadel.

—*L. Natalie Sandomirsky*

See also
Dessalines, Jean-Jacques; Louverture, Toussaint; Pétion, Alexandre Sabès; Wilberforce, William
For Further Reading
Cole, Hubert. 1967. *Christophe King of Haiti*. New York: Viking Press; Ott, Thomas. 1973. *The Haitian Revolution*. Knoxville: University of Tennessee Press; Ros, Martin. 1994. *Night of Fire*. New York: Sarpedon; Vandercook, John W. 1928. *Black Majesty: The Life of Christophe, King of Haiti*. London: Harper.

CHURCH AND SLAVERY IN LATIN AMERICA

The Roman Catholic Church, as an institution, sustained a legal opposition toward slavery. Beginning in the fifteenth century, popes expressed their position in different papal bulls and letters to monarchs. In 1537, Pope Paul III ordered that Indians should not be reduced to slavery *(Veritas ipsa)*; Pius II, in a 1462 document addressed to the local ruler of the Canaries, condemned the slave trade as a crime and criticized the Christians that dared to enslave Negroes; and Urban VII, in a 1639 document addressed to the Cámara Apostólica de Portugal (Apostolic Chamber of Portugal), supported his predecessors' position on slavery and defended the freedom of Indians from Brazil, Paraguay, and Rio de la Plata.

In 1741, Pope Benedict XIV, in letters addressed to the bishop of Brazil and to the king of Portugal, advocated freedom for the Indians of those kingdoms. Pius VII in 1814, in a letter addressed to the king of France, condemned any declaration by a member of the church, or by any Christian, that recognized the slave trade as being legal. Gregory XVI, in a bull of 1837 *(Supremo apostolatus fastigio)*, forbade trade in Africans and Indians. Clearly, the Vatican sustained a continued position condemning the slave trade.

The converting of slaves to Christianity and liberation movements fall into four distinct periods: 1492–1550, 1550–1600, 1600–1683, and 1683 to the end of slavery. In the first, from 1492 to 1550, laws and dispositions to evangelize and regulate slavery activities came from royal *cédulas* ("decrees"). Bartolomé de Las Casas in 1560 rectified a previous statement declaring that captivity of the Negroes was as unjust as that of the Indians. Mexico's Bishop Fray Alonso de Montúfar, in a letter addressed to the Spanish king, declared that as long as the Negroes received the holy gospel and did not make war on Christians, there was no reason to enslave them.

From 1550 to 1600, the church celebrated the *sinodos diocesanos* ("diocesan synods") in which the idea of converting Negroes and slaves to Christianity was conceived. In the first attempt, which occurred on Hispaniola (c. 1539), it was decreed that all Negro slaves imported from Guinea should be baptized before they were delivered to their buyers. The next synod met in 1576, and all dispositions taken in the preceding meeting were sustained. Members of the third synod, in 1610, were worried about maintaining the process of Christianizing the slaves so they also ordered all masters to honor the right of their slaves to be buried in a cemetery in the vicinity of a church. A synod of the Mexican clergy gathered in 1565 and recommended that all masters protect the slave family unit.

From 1600 to 1683, there was a critical movement against slavery in Lima and Cartagena, identified by the writings of the Jesuit Alonso de Sandoval who wrote *Naturaleza, policia sagrada y profana, costumbres y ritos, discipline y catecismo evangelico de todos los etiopes* [Nature, sacred police and profane, uses and rites, discipline and evangelical gospel of the etiopes]. These four books were mainly an ethnological and pastoral compendium.

In 1603, in the Dominican convent of Lima, Fray Martin de Porres, a Peruvian Negro, was ordained a priest and promised to live in poverty and help the poor without distinction. Later he was canonized by Pope John XXIII. Also in the seventeenth century, Peter Claver, "slave of the Negroes for ever" as he called himself at the moment of his ordination, committed his life to protect the slaves in today's Colombian cities of Cartagena and Tunja. He died in Cartagena in 1654 and was made a saint by Leo XIII in 1888, the same year slavery was finally abolished in Brazil.

The Cuban synod of 1681 regulated such events as the days and occasions when slaves might dance or go out to sell their products and even signaled where the slaves could cry over their dead. In 1680–1681, while the Cuban synod was meeting, Capuchin friars Francisco José de Jaca and Epifanio de Morains (of French origin) preached in Cuban churches against illegal slavery. They were arrested in 1682; judged in Spain, they won their case in 1683 but could not return to Cuba. Finally, in 1686, the Holy Office in Havana expressed its favorable opinion of the 11 propositions of the friars, which might be summarized in four ideas: African slavery is unjust, slaves are free, it is just to free slaves, and masters that do not free their slaves cannot receive a Christian pardon.

Finally, from 1683 to the end of slavery, the Holy Office and the Colegio de Propaganda Fide observed those recommendations approved in the Jaca and Morains case. In Brazil, arguments by Monseigneur Paula Rodrigues in São Paulo and Father Antonio Ferreira Visoso in Rio de Janeiro resulted in a national polemic to abolish slavery, and this polemic became the best known effort of the Catholic Church to free the slaves from their sufferings.

The Africans were subject to the jurisdiction of the Inquisition although their slavery status reduced the Holy Office policies to establish the slaves' responsibilities and to promulgate their sentences. Abjuring the Christian deities and beliefs and practicing sorcery were the most common causes of the slaves being judged by the Inquisition.

Members of secular church and religious orders owned most of the church's slaves in Hispanic America. Not only friars but even cloistered nuns used to own slaves. In almost every province of Hispanic America, Jesuits reaped an economic benefit from slave labor on their plantations and in other commercial enterprises.

—*Juan Manuel de la Serna*

For Further Reading
Alberro, Solange. 1988. *Inquisición sociedad en México.* Mexico City: Fondo de Cultura Económica; Gutierrez, A. Ildefonso. 1992. "La Iglesia y los Negros." In *La historia de la Iglesia en Hispanoamérica y las Filipinas. Fifteenth to nineteenth centuries.* Ed. Pedro Borges. Madrid: Biblioteca de Autores Cristianos; Laviña, Javier. "Iglesia y Esclavitud en Cuba." *América negra* 1 (June): 11–29; Saez, J. Luis. 1994. *La Iglesia y el negro esclavo en Santo Domingo: Una historia de tres siglos.* Santo Domingo: Patronato de la Ciudad Colonial.

CHURCH MISSIONARY SOCIETY

The Church Missionary Society (CMS) was the Church of England's principal mission arm and was founded as the Society for Missions in Africa and the East in 1799. The name was changed to the Church Missionary Society in 1813. The CMS established missions in India and Africa, sending its first missionaries to Sierra Leone in 1804 and continuing its activities in other British territories thereafter. Early support centered among anti–slave trade (and later antislavery) advocates in the British Parliament and among evangelicals known as the Clapham Sect. Many of the society's directors supported a London-based school for Africans and prepared, from that experience, to deliver Christian British civilization to Africa through missions and schools.

From the beginning, the society taught that education, industry, conversion, and self-improvement would end African slave trading. Accordingly, it established schools near Sierra Leone (the Rio Pongo Mission, 1806–1816) to educate children of African headmen and local merchants (many of whom were slave traders) and of Freetown's settlers. The CMS believed its students would become the vanguard of African social and economic change. The Rio Pongo Mission failed to end either slave trading or slavery, but it did bring new technologies to Africa and improved linkages to world commodities economies.

After 1814, the society began concentrating operations in the Freetown region, where Royal Squadron vessels landed large numbers of slaves (recaptives) taken from captured slave vessels. The society established schools and maintained missions to transform these liberated Africans into Christians, into industrious British subjects, and perhaps into teachers and missionaries. In many cases, the society obtained student converts by purchasing their freedom and assigning them European names. These redeemed and Anglicized Africans helped produce Freetown's Christianized Krio (Creole) society.

From Sierra Leone, the CMS expanded its activities to the slave coast (Ibo and Yoruba Missions in southern Nigeria established in 1841), where indigenous states (Abomey, Oyo, Abeokuta, Benin) had enthusiastically supported the slave trade, and to eastern and southern Africa. Generally, the CMS interpreted its aims as serving coastal Anglican communities, initiating a civilizing mission on the African continent, and spreading Christianity (and the Anglican doctrine) among Africans.

—*Bruce L. Mouser*

See also
African Squadron; Benin; The Ibo; Names and Naming; Recaptives; Sierra Leone; Wilberforce, William

For Further Reading
Grove, C. P. 1948. *The Planting of Christianity in Africa.* London: Lutterworth; Hole, Charles. 1896. *The Early History of the Church Missionary Society for Africa and the East.* London: Church Missionary Society; Jakobsson, Stiv. 1972. *Am I Not a Man and a Brother?* Uppsala, Sweden: Almqvist and Wiksells; Stock, Eugene. 1899. *The History of the Church Missionary Society.* London: Church Missionary Society.

CICERO
(106–143 B.C.)

Marcus Tullius Cicero was a leading politician and intellectual of the late Roman Republic, and his vast corpus of personal letters, public speeches, and philosophical essays is the most extensive single body of literary evidence for social practices in the period prior to the Roman Empire. It is likely that Cicero owned only a small number of slaves compared to the hundreds owned by other leading men in Rome, yet the wealth of detailed information and, more often, incidental remarks about slavery in his writings allow us to know more about common practices and social customs than is possible from the writings of a large slaveowner. From Cicero, we know that it was customary for Romans to free slaves after seven years; that runaway slaves could be the concern of high-ranking officials in the provinces; that slaves could be recommended to the circles of important politicians; and that the attachment between master and slave could be very close.

Cicero's attitude toward slavery was probably typical of the mid-sized slaveowner in the Roman Republic. Unfortunately, there is little or no direct evidence for the attitudes of large-scale and small-scale slaveowners. Yet the importance of Cicero's writings goes beyond their unique status as sources, for they provide the first Roman evidence of a distinction between real and philosophical views of slavery. Slavery was a given condition in the ancient Greek and Roman worlds and among early Christians as well. It was considered a natural power relationship between two people, one of whom owed his life to the other. The Latin term for slave, *servus*, derives from *servare*, meaning "to save," so it refers to the slave's status as a person "saved," a prisoner of war who could have been killed.

Slavery was the lowest state a human being could be in, but the Romans generally thought that slaves deserved respect as human beings. Cicero and most Romans rejected Aristotle's view that there are peoples who are slaves by nature. One of Cicero's most influential works, *On Duties,* includes his well-known statement: "Let us also remember that justice ought to be preserved even toward the lowest level of persons. The lowest level is the condition and fortune of slaves. Those who advise us to use them as we would hired workers don't give bad advice: work must be done; but justice must be shown" (*On Duties,* 1.41). There is some evidence in Cicero's writings of an ongoing debate about whether slavery was just or not, but the basic Roman opinion that slavery was necessary and that slaves should be treated humanely probably mitigated the extreme positions enough to diffuse the debate.

Cicero's relationship with a slave whom he later freed, Marcus Tullius Tiro, was one of the most celebrated relationships between slave and master (later former master) in antiquity. Tiro served Cicero as his secretary and, later, as his literary executor. He published some of Cicero's writings after his death and wrote an influential biography about his former master. Earlier, in the 40s B.C., Tiro became acutely ill, and Cicero's letters attest to his great concern for his former slave. Cicero may have had fairly close relationships with some of his other slaves. When a young slave named Sositheus died, Cicero lamented that "it has moved me more than, it seems, the death of a slave should" (*Letters to Atticus,* 2.12.4).

Despite the close attachment Cicero expressed for his slaves in his personal letters and the idealistic view he took of them in his philosophical essays, he was not above making disparaging comments and insinuations about slaves in his speeches. That practice must represent, to a large degree, popular attitudes about slaves, which were largely negative: slaves lie, cheat, steal, etc. Since his audience was composed largely of slaveholders, Cicero would capitalize on their prejudice and fears to prove his point at the moment. That tendency demonstrates the danger of using all of Cicero's writings equally to reconstruct his personal views.

Cicero's rhetorical and philosophical works have had an enormous impact on Western thinking for the past 2,000 years. Several directly influenced the early church fathers, and Cicero's views on slavery were generally in keeping with early Christian beliefs. His treatise *On Duties* exercised an especially formative influence on European ideas during the Renaissance and the Enlightenment. The work was widely read in the eighteenth and early-nineteenth centuries, and it is likely that Cicero's comments on slavery helped reinforce the notion that slavery was natural (though the Romans did not consider any race to be "naturally" servile) while his encouragement of justice toward slaves was ignored.

—*Robert W. Cape, Jr.*

See also
Roman Republic
For Further Reading
Dumont, J. C. 1987. *Servus: Rome et l'esclavage sous la républic.* Rome: École française de Rome; Etienne, R. 1972. "Cicéron et l'esclavage." *Actes du colloque d'histoiré sociale.* Paris: Les Belles Lettres; Garland, A. 1992. "Cicero's familia urbana." *Greece and Rome* 39: 163–172; Wood, N. 1988. *Cicero's Social and Political Thought.* Berkeley: University of California Press.

CINQUE, JOSEPH (1811?–1852?)

The man who came to be known as Joseph Cinqué was the leader of a successful revolt in which 38 slaves under his command seized the slave ship *Amistad* and attempted to return to Africa. When U.S. authorities thwarted that plan, Northern abolitionists pursued legal appeals on behalf of Cinqué and his colleagues, appeals that eventually led to their release and repatriation to Africa.

Cinqué was born Sing-gbe in a region of West Africa now known as Sierra Leone. The year of his birth is generally accepted as 1811, although some sources claim he was born in 1817. Sing-gbe, a member of the Mende tribe, was captured by slave traders in 1837 or 1838 and forcibly removed to the infamous Portuguese slave factory on the island of Lomboko off the coast of West Africa. He left behind a wife and three small children. On Lomboko, Portuguese slavers called him "Cinqué," a phonetic approximation of Sing-gbe, and prepared him for transportation to the slave market in Cuba. The voyage aboard the Portuguese slaver, *Tecora,* was exceptionally harsh even by the grim standards of the usual transatlantic voyage in a slave ship. More than half of the men, women, and children who left Lomboko did not live to see Havana. Since the importation of slaves into Cuba was illegal, slavers gave the Africans Christian names and falsely listed them as Cuban-born. Sing-gbe was thereafter known as Joseph Cinqué.

Two Spanish planters, José Ruiz and Pedro Montes, bought Cinqué and 38 other slaves in Havana and loaded them and some other slaves aboard a 120-ton schooner, the *Amistad,* for the short run up the Cuban coast to Puerto Principé. The slaves were connected by a long chain threaded through their neck rings and fastened to the inside of the wooden hull of the *Amistad* in the cramped, dark hold of the ship. For two days and nights they pitched and rolled in terror as the *Amistad*'s crew fought an unexpected storm that drove them far off course.

Using a rusted nail pried from the floor planks of the hold, Cinqué methodically worked at the bracket that anchored the slaves' chain to the hull. Once free, the slaves broke into the cargo hold where they armed themselves with cane knives. Then, under cover of darkness on the first night of calm, Cinqué led the slaves out of the hold. On deck they found an exhausted captain and crew asleep, with only one man awake at the helm. Within minutes the deck of the *Amistad* was awash with the blood of the captain, Ramón Ferrer, and his crew. Two of the crew members were killed; four survived. Two of the survivors evaded the slaves and slipped off the ship in a lifeboat. They eventually reached the port of Havana and told the story of the *Amistad* mutiny. The other two survivors, Ruiz and Montes, were spared because Cinqué needed their navigational skills to pilot the *Amistad* to its new destination—Africa.

For 63 days Ruiz and Montes, who were expert seamen, deceived Cinqué by setting a northeasterly course by day and turning hard north by night. Ruiz and Montes intended the zigzag path to lead them, not to Africa, but to the United States, where slavery was legal and the rights of slaveholders recognized and protected. The land they eventually spotted, which Cinqué assumed to be an island off the African coast, was Long Island off the coast of New York City. The *Amistad* was intercepted by a U.S. Coast Guard cutter and escorted under arms to the port of Montauk, New York, where Cinqué and his compatriots were arrested and imprisoned.

When the news of the *Amistad's* capture reached Havana, Spanish and Cuban authorities demanded the return of the ship and its slave cargo. The penalty for slave insurrection in Cuba was burning at the stake, the fate that awaited Cinqué and his band if they were returned to Havana. U.S. president Martin Van Buren, eager not to offend the powerful slavery interest in Congress, ordered their return to Spanish authorities. Northern abolitionists, however, filed a lawsuit in federal court to block Van Buren's action.

For almost two years, a protracted legal battle played out in the federal court system. At stake were both the lives of Cinqué and his fellow Africans and the important legal principle of a human being's right to resist enslavement forcibly. While the highly publicized case proceeded through the appellate process, with the abolitionists winning at each level and the appeal carried to the next level by the government, Cinqué, free on bond posted by wealthy New England abolitionists, lived comfortably in Farmington, Connecticut. A powerful speaker with a charismatic physical presence, Cinqué took to the lecture circuit, and the fees he earned helped pay the mounting legal bills. Although he spoke only Mende, Cinqué's speeches were translated into English and widely distributed throughout the North.

The cause won the support of former president John Quincy Adams, an ardent abolitionist and respected elder statesman. Adams, who was also a skilled litigator, personally pleaded the case for the *Amistad* insurgents before the U.S. Supreme Court in 1841. The Court ruled in Cinqué's favor, declaring that he and his fellow mutineers were free to return to Africa. Joseph Cinqué returned home in 1842.

His subsequent life is not clearly documented. Some accounts claim he died barely a decade after his return to Africa; others contend he lived until 1879 and was buried on the grounds of the American Missionary Association compound in Sierra Leone.

Regardless of his ultimate fate, Joseph Cinqué remained an important symbolic presence for slaves in the United States and, after the abolition of slavery there, for African Americans. In 1939, on the centennial anniversary of the *Amistad* mutiny, a major artwork was unveiled. *The Amistad Murals* by the noted African American artist Hale Woodruff commemorated Joseph Cinqué's seizure of freedom.

—*Frederick J. Simonelli*

See also
Amistad Case

For Further Reading
Barber, John W. 1840. *A History of the Amistad Captives*. New Haven, CT: E. L. and J. W. Barber; Cable, Mary. 1971. *Black Odyssey: The Case of the Slave Ship Amistad*. New York: Viking Press; Hoyt, Edwin. 1970. *The Amistad Affair*. New York: Abelard-Schuman.

CIRCUMCELLIONS

Circumcellions were fanatical members of the Donatist branch of the Christian religion in North Africa. They served as shock troops in defending Donatism and attacking both official Catholicism and rich landholders from about A.D. 317 until the seventh-century Arab invasions. Ancient sources agree that circumcellions were peasants, primarily from Numidia and Mauretania in northern Africa, who revolted in part against Roman economic repression and corrupt taxation policies. Their name derived from their tendency to live around the sites *(cellae)* of Christian martyrs' tombs, where they could receive food. Their Christianity was puritanical and unforgiving of past official Roman persecution and of Catholic Christians who had acquiesced to pagan demands to renounce their religion and/or surrender copies of the Scriptures to authorities.

As Donatists, circumcellions believed that their profession was Christianity's one true form. Led by their bishops and priests they acted on this belief by torturing, plundering, and burning the property of their rivals and by actively seeking martyrdom, even as victims at pagan sacrifices. St. Augustine, contemporary bishop of the African city of Hippo Regius, wrote of them, "They lived as robbers, died as circumcellions and were honored [by fellow Donatists] as martyrs" (Epistle 88). At a conference of Orthodox and Donatist bishops at Carthage in 411, Donatism was formally outlawed, but it apparently remained a majority religion in Numidia until the Muslim conquests. Circumcellion violence reached its height in the 390s, and the undisciplined movement had become unpopular by the 430s.

Although early Christians accepted slavery as being divinely ordained, the natural result of man's fallen nature, they generally insisted upon the recognition of mutual rights and obligations between owners and slaves. Although slaves could be cruelly handled and abused, they were not to seek to change their lot. Perhaps influenced by circumcellion activity, the Council of Gangra (c. 341) condemned both overly ascetic practices and anyone who, under the pretext of religion, taught slaves to resist their masters, fail to obey fully, or flee service. Circumcellions, driven by their re-vilement of both the Roman state (a foreign occupying force) and state-sanctioned Catholic authorities, often targeted rich estates and sought to overturn the social order: "Slaves and masters found their positions reversed. Rich men driving comfortable vehicles would be pitched out and made to run behind their carriages, now occupied by their slaves" (Frend, 1971).

An implacable enemy of Donatism, St. Augustine both recorded and attacked the outrages of the circumcellion armed bands: "What master was there who was not compelled to live in dread of his own slave, if the slave had put himself under the protection of the Donatists? Under the threat of beating, and burning, and immediate death, all documents compromising [even] the worst of slaves were destroyed, that they might depart in freedom" (Epistle 185). Economic hardship, Berber self-assertion, and religious conviction led to the localized violence that apparently liberated any number of slaves, yet the circumcellions developed no theoretical or theological stance to challenge Catholic orthodoxy regarding the natural disposition of the slave.

—*Joseph P. Byrne*

See also
Augustine (Saint)
For Further Reading
Frend, W. H. C. 1969. "Circumcellions and Monks." *Journal of Theological Studies,* n.s., 20: 542–549; Frend, W. H. C. 1971. *The Donatist Church.* New York: Oxford University Press; Jones, A. H. M. 1959. "Were Ancient Heresies National or Social Movements in Disguise?" *Journal of Theological Studies,* n.s., 10: 280–298; Saumagne, C. 1934. "Ouvriers agricoles ou rôdeurs de celliers? Les Circoncellions d'Afrique." *Annals d'histoire économique et sociale* 6: 351–364.

CIVIL WAR, UNITED STATES

The Civil War in the United States began after decades of discord between Northern and Southern states. Various economic, political, and social issues led to the disagreement, yet slavery seemed to be at the heart of each problem. Since slavery predominated in the South, Southerners felt increasingly isolated and threatened by attempts to hinder or ban slavery. Whereas slaveholders had earlier seen slavery as a necessary evil that was inconsistent with the ideals of the American Revolution, by the 1830s, Southerners believed slavery to be a positive good.

This change in attitude was partially a result of slavery's benefits. Unlike in the more industrialized North, slaves were the principal form of wealth in the agricultural South; in 1860, 4 million slaves had a

A series of illustrations from Harpers' Weekly History of the Civil War *shows various African American soldiers' experiences during the Civil War.*

market value of $3 billion. Slavery, however, was not only a means of providing a large labor force, it also served as a means by which white supremacy could be preserved. This aspect was especially important for some people whose sole claim of superiority came from the color of their skin.

Slaveholders also became much more defensive of slavery as the antislavery movement intensified and produced more abolitionists, like William Lloyd Garrison, who called for an immediate end to slavery without compensation to slaveowners. As a result, the South became a dangerous place to express antislavery sentiments.

During the 1840s, the national debate dealt more with slavery's expansion into the western territories than with the actual abolition of slavery. Southerners believed that it was their constitutional right to take their slaves into the territories with them and that Congress lacked the power to prevent them from doing so. Northerners opposed the expansion of slavery, some on moral grounds and others for economic reasons. Despite opposing the expansion of slavery into the new territories, many Northerners did not oppose the institution of slavery in areas where it already existed, as they feared that if slavery ended, emancipated slaves would flock to the territories and take land that could be used by whites.

After several heated debates in Congress, Senator Henry Clay of Kentucky proposed a compromise bill in 1850. The bill included five measures: (1) the admission of California as a free state; (2) the creation of New Mexico and Utah territories, in which residents would be allowed to choose whether or not to permit slavery; (3) the paying of Texas's debts in return for that state's promise not to seek to widen its western border; (4) the end of the slave trade in Washington, D.C.; and (5) the creation of a new fugitive slave law, which would require that runaway slaves be returned to their masters and authorize the use of federal power to enforce the law.

Congress ultimately approved Clay's bill, which became known as the Compromise of 1850. Despite widespread acceptance of the compromise, it soon became obvious that it offered only a temporary solution to the problem, as its vague language left much open to debate. However, the greatest problem with the Compromise of 1850 was its failure to confront the issue of the expansion of slavery directly. Instead, Congress placed a seal of approval on the theory of popular sovereignty, that is, allowing settlers to choose whether or not they wanted slavery. Consequently, Congress sent out mixed signals to people on both sides of the debate.

In 1854, Congress passed the Kansas-Nebraska Act, which established Kansas and Nebraska as territories and ruled that popular sovereignty should settle the issue of slavery in the two areas. Conflict erupted almost as soon as President Franklin Pierce signed the bill into law in May 1854. When Missouri slaveowners moved into Kansas Territory, they immediately clashed with antislavery settlers. Soon the conflict, known as Bleeding Kansas, turned deadly, and fighting continued for four years until the antislavery forces emerged as the victors.

The slavery issue split both the Whig and Democratic parties down sectional lines, with Northern Whigs and Democrats taking sides against their Southern counterparts. At the same time, several political groups joined to form the Free Soil Party and oppose slavery's expansion. However, the major disintegration of the political parties came with the passage of the Kansas-Nebraska Act. Many Northern Democrats left their party, as did Northern Whigs, and most of these men, along with members of the Free Soil Party, created the new Republican Party, which took a firm stance against the expansion of slavery.

As tensions grew between North and South, the antislavery movement increased as well. Southerners were outraged at the publication of the novel *Uncle Tom's Cabin* (1852), which sold 500,000 copies and strengthened the antislavery movement in the North. Written by the Northern abolitionist Harriet Beecher Stowe, *Uncle Tom's Cabin* told of the horrors of slavery; it was banned in the South.

Yet some Southerners criticized slavery. Although slavery was immensely profitable for some, others argued that slavery would ultimately ruin the prospects of all. In his book *The Impending Crisis of the South and How to Meet It* (1857), North Carolinian Hinton Rowan Helper argued that slavery was an inefficient system that stunted the South's economic growth and hurt the nonslaveowning majority. He believed that by focusing on agriculture and ignoring natural resources and industry, the South was becoming "a cesspool of ignorance and degradation." Most of all, Helper expressed his hatred of the wealthy planter class, whose arrogance and greed prevented poor whites from prospering.

The book was banned by Southern states, and people who were caught owning a copy were fired from their job, arrested, and some even executed. However, Helper's ideas did receive support. Not only did his book appeal to poor whites in the South, it was also used as a propaganda tool by Republicans, who distributed 100,000 edited copies in 1858.

Despite attacks from antislavery supporters, Southerners still had a powerful voice in national politics, a power that was reflected in the Supreme Court decision in the Dred Scott case. In this case a slave, Dred Scott, argued that since his master had moved him from Missouri to free territory, he was a freeman. In 1857, the U.S. Supreme Court ruled that since slaves were not U.S. citizens, they could not sue in federal courts. Chief Justice Roger B. Taney wrote that slaves could be moved anywhere as they were the property of their owner, and he found the Missouri Compromise, or any other attempt by Congress to limit slavery's expansion, to be unconstitutional.

Although Southerners were jubilant following that court decision, their excitement turned to fear following John Brown's raid on Harpers Ferry, Virginia, in 1859. Brown, a lifelong abolitionist and participant in the struggles of Bleeding Kansas, planned to end slavery through force. With a small band of men, including runaway slaves, Brown took control of the U.S. arsenal at Harpers Ferry. Ultimately, Brown was hanged for his actions, thus becoming a martyr for the abolitionist movement and proving to Southerners the importance of political power.

Relations between North and South deteriorated rapidly after 1859. At the 1860 Democratic National Convention, Southerners pushed for a platform that included a federal slave code for the territories. When Northern Democrats refused to accept the idea, Southern Democrats left the convention, which split the Democratic Party and allowed the Republican candidate for president, Abraham Lincoln, to win the election of 1860.

In December 1860, South Carolina and seven other slave states seceded from the Union and formed the Confederate States of America. In an attempt to appease the eight slave states that remained in the Union, Kentucky senator John J. Crittenden offered a compromise that stressed the protection of slavery below the Missouri Compromise line of 36° 30' and promised compensation to owners of runaway slaves. Lincoln opposed the Crittenden Compromise, and the measure was defeated. Although Lincoln still hoped to appease the remaining eight slave states, his promises not to interfere with slavery or with the Confederacy could not stop the war. Soon after the Confederate attack on Fort Sumter in April 1861, four more slave states seceded, and only the border states of Missouri, Kentucky, Maryland, and Delaware remained, precariously, in the Union.

Although the South's reason for the war was the protection of slavery and Southern sovereignty, Lincoln's initial desire was to protect the Union. He did not wish to interfere with the institution of slavery, and he even ordered his generals to return any slaves who escaped behind Union lines and to help prevent slave rebellions.

However, organized slave rebellions were not common during the war. Instead, many slaves simply refused to cooperate with their masters, especially when the slaveowners went to war and left their wives in control of the plantations. Slaves often took this opportunity to work at a slower pace or leave their work altogether. Home guards were established to maintain order and to prevent slaves from running away. Since the presence of the Union army led many slaves to cross Union lines to freedom, slaveowners told their slaves stories about the cruelty of Union soldiers in an attempt to frighten the slaves into staying on the plantations.

Many slaves did remain on the plantations out of loyalty or fear of the unknown. Others ignored the warnings of their masters and fled across Union lines and provided the Union army with information about Confederate activities. Although slaves were at first returned to their masters, the confiscation acts of 1861–1862 ruled that slaves who crossed Union lines should be considered contraband of war and freed from slavery. Behind Union lines, the escaped slaves found life to be almost as harsh as plantation life. Those who remained with the Union troops labored with little or no compensation and lived in crowded camps with inadequate shelter, food, and clothing. Others moved into urban areas where they faced poverty, overcrowding, and disease. Fortunately, the former slaves received some help from sources such as the Freedmen's aid societies and missionary societies, which provided them with supplies and educational opportunities. At the same time, the escaped slaves formed tightly knit communities and began to demand equal rights.

The slaves that remained behind played an important role in the Confederate war effort. In the absence of white workers, some slaves were put to work in factories and mines and on the railroads; others served in home guard units, replacing white men who went off to war. The use of slaves in the home guard was especially prominent in Louisiana, where slaves formed almost half the state's population. Slaves also often accompanied the Confederate army to help carry supplies and build forts. This work was unpopular among slaves and slaveowners alike, for slaves found it to be particularly difficult work and slaveowners disliked sending their best slaves to the front—they thus reserved this work for their most uncooperative slaves.

As the war continued, Lincoln realized the need to redefine the Union's war goals. Although Lincoln's original goal was simply to preserve the Union, he faced criticism from abolitionists who wished to make the war one to end slavery. He also faced problems abroad as European nations seemed increasingly sympathetic to the South's claims that the Confederacy was fighting for its independence. Fearing that Europe would intervene economically or militarily on the South's behalf, Lincoln realized that freeing the slaves must become a priority. This was a difficult decision for Lincoln, for while he personally opposed slavery, he was not convinced that blacks and whites could ever live together peacefully. However, he believed that emancipation might be the only way to quiet his critics and preserve the Union.

Lincoln began to draft a document that would order an end to slavery but did so secretly since he was concerned that outside observers might interpret his decision as a sign that the Union was wearing down after a series of Confederate victories. Although not a Union victory per se, the Battle of Antietam (or Sharpsburg) repelled a Confederate invasion of the North and provided Lincoln with the opportunity to issue a draft of the emancipation proclamation on September 22, 1862. In the final Emancipation Proclamation, which became law on January 1, 1863, Lincoln ordered that all slaves in areas under rebellion were free as of that date. The proclamation did not apply, however, to slaves in the four border states or to slaves in areas occupied by Union troops.

Technically, the Emancipation Proclamation did not legally free any slaves, for such an action required a constitutional amendment. Symbolically though, the proclamation had a significant impact on the Northern war effort. It appeased abolitionists, and it also prevented foreign intervention by making the war a war for slavery's abolition rather than one of Northern aggression against the Confederacy. Moreover, the Emancipation Proclamation encouraged the thousands of slaves who remained in the South, giving them hope that freedom was just around the corner.

Following the announcement of the Emancipation Proclamation, Lincoln approved the use of black troops in the Union army. Many Union soldiers disagreed with Lincoln's decision, but the need for more men was greater than the prejudice of individuals. Sadly, black soldiers were not treated as equals. At first denied the opportunity to fight, when necessity did demand that black soldiers enter battle, they often went in without adequate training or supplies. Until 1864, black soldiers received less pay than their white counterparts and had few opportunities for advancement.

In spite of this discrimination, black soldiers played a vital role in the Union victory. The Fifty-fourth Massachusetts Regiment, formed primarily of Northern free blacks, gained fame for their courageous but ill-fated attack on Fort Wagner, South Carolina, on July 18, 1863. Despite losing over 250 men during the attack, the Fifty-fourth went on to participate in other battles in South Carolina, Georgia, and Florida. The First South Carolina Volunteers, which consisted entirely of fugitive slaves, had a reputation not only for bravery and skill in battle but also for recruiting large numbers of slaves into the regiment. In all, 200,000 blacks served in the Union armed forces, making up 10 percent of the total Union enlistment. Of these 200,000 black men, approximately one-third gave their lives for the cause of freedom.

When the war ended, Lincoln had met his goal of preserving the Union, but he would not live to see the painful process of reconstruction. Lincoln also achieved a second goal, one he had not intended: the end of slavery. In 1865, the Thirteenth Amendment to the Constitution abolished slavery throughout the United States. This would be but the first step on the road to equality for black Americans.

—*Jason H. Silverman*

See also
Confiscation Acts; Emancipation Proclamation
For Further Reading
Gerteis, Louis S. 1973. *From Contraband to Freedom: Federal Policy toward Southern Blacks, 1861–1865.* Westport, CT: Greenwood Press; Glatthaar, Joseph. 1990. *Forged in Battle: The Civil War Alliance of Black Soldiers and White Officers.* New York: Free Press; Potter, David M. 1976. *The Impending Crisis, 1848–1861.* New York: Harper and Row; Quarles, Benjamin. 1953. *The Negro in the Civil War.* Boston: Little, Brown.

CLARKSON, THOMAS (1760–1846)

Called by Samuel Taylor Coleridge "the moral Steam-Engine, or the Giant with one Idea" (letter from Coleridge to Daniel Stuart, February 1809), Thomas Clarkson was a leader in Britain's abolitionist movement from 1786 until his death. A virtual professional reformer who organized petition drives throughout the country and lobbied members of Parliament, he was also the movement's first historian.

Born in Wisbech in Cambridgeshire on March 28, 1760, Clarkson entered Cambridge University in 1779 with the intention of becoming a clergyman. But his life's direction changed when he entered and won a 1785 Latin essay contest on the question of whether it was right to enslave others against their will. Research done for his essay convinced Clarkson of slavery's evil, and determined to see the transatlantic slave trade abolished, he published an expanded translation of his work, *An Essay on the Slavery and Commerce of the Human Species, Particularly the African.* A Quaker bookseller, James Phillips, published the book in June 1786 and introduced Clarkson to others, including Granville Sharp and James Ramsay, who shared his views.

Clarkson soon began lobbying members of Parliament to legislate the abolition of the slave trade. When he met William Wilberforce, who became leader of the parliamentary drives to abolish the slave trade in 1807 and slavery itself in 1838, the two men discussed Clarkson's *Essay*, and Wilberforce encouraged him to collect further evidence and sources. On May 22, 1787, Clarkson, Sharp, Philip Sansom, and nine Quakers (John Barton, William Dillwyn, George Harrison, Samuel Hoare, Joseph Hooper, John Lloyd, James Phillips, Richard Phillips, and Joseph Woods) formed the Society for Effecting the Abolition of the Slave Trade. The society was organized to collect money and information to be used to pressure Parliament into taking action.

Clarkson, the London Committee's principal agent, began his first tour of the provinces in June 1787, promoting the cause and gathering evidence in Manchester and the major slave ports of Bristol and Liverpool. In 1788, he covered England's southern coast; in 1790, Scotland and northern England; in 1791, he returned to northern England. He traveled about 35,000 miles in all and organized local committees wherever he went. For much of Britain, Clarkson embodied the abolitionist movement. His travels enabled him to gauge public sentiment toward the slave trade, and his exhaustive research quickly established him as the subject's leading authority. From slave ships' muster books, Clarkson collected statistical evidence proving the high mortality rate for English seamen engaged in the trade. His records of slave ships' dimensions demonstrated the cruelty of the transatlantic voyage, and he gathered evidence proving that Africa would be more profitable as a trading partner than as a source of slaves. He also identified witnesses and arranged their transportation to London to testify against the trade.

Clarkson continued writing against the trade as well. In 1787 he published *A Summary View of the Slave-Trade, and of the Probable Consequences of Its Abolition*, an abridged version of his *Essay*; in 1788, *An Essay on the Impolicy of the African Slave Trade*; and in 1789, he produced a diagram of a slave ship. Clarkson's publications and provincial work were co-ordinated with Parliament's legislative campaign.

On February 11, 1788, George III ordered the Privy Council Committee for Trade and Plantations to begin investigating British commercial relations with Africa and the nature of the slave trade, which transported to Europe's American colonies approximately 80,000 Africans a year, more than half of them in British ships. On May 9, 1888, Prime Minister William Pitt, substituting for Wilberforce who was ill, introduced the subject of the trade in the House of Commons. That session passed a bill sponsored by William Dolben that regulated the dimensions of slave ships.

Wilberforce began Parliament's investigation of the trade on May 12, 1789, after the Privy Council report was presented, and from 1789 to 1792 the House of Commons heard evidence and witnesses produced mainly by Clarkson against the trade and evidence and witnesses brought forward by proslavery interests. In 1792 a bill abolishing the trade passed in the House of Commons only to be defeated in the House of Lords, partly because excesses of the French Revolution and the subsequent Reign of Terror made Britain reluctant to undertake substantial economic or political reforms.

Until physical exhaustion forced his retirement in 1794, Clarkson relentlessly continued his activities, risking his life gathering evidence that threatened the profits of some of Britain's wealthiest citizens. Throughout the parliamentary campaign of 1788–1794, Clarkson organized petitions around the country and beyond. In August 1789 he went to France to try to convince the new government to abolish the French slave trade. He failed.

Clarkson came out of retirement in 1805 to make a highly successful organizing tour throughout the country that helped to sustain revived efforts to abolish the trade, a goal achieved in 1807. In 1808, Clarkson published his indispensable two-volume *History of the Rise, Progress, and Accomplishment of the Abolition of the Slave Trade*, which later led to false charges by Wilberforce's sons, after Wilberforce's death in 1833, that Clarkson had exaggerated his own contributions and diminished those of their father.

After 1807, Clarkson turned his efforts to the problem of slavery beyond Britain, working with the African Institution to see that provisions of the 1807 law were enforced and making several European trips to persuade rulers to outlaw the trade in their dominions. He also worked to abolish slavery in the British West Indies, becoming with Wilberforce a vice-president of the British and Foreign Anti-Slavery Society, which was formed in 1823, though age and health made his position largely honorary. Hoping that Haiti would prove that freed slaves could be self-governing, Clarkson maintained correspondence with that country's despotic ruler, Henri Christophe, until the latter's suicide in 1820. Clarkson also corresponded with the U.S. abolitionist William Lloyd Garrison. Clarkson made his last public address in June 1840 to the Anti-Slavery Convention in London. He died on September 26, 1846.

—*Vincent Carretta*

See also
Abolition, British Empire; The African Institution; Garrison, William Lloyd; Ramsay, James; Sharp, Granville; Ships; Wilberforce, William

For Further Reading
Wilson, Ellen Gibson. 1990. *Thomas Clarkson: A Biography*. New York: St. Martin's.

CLAVER, PETER
(1580–1654)

The Jesuit Pedro Claver was the son of landed peasants in Verdú in the Spanish region of Catalonia. After studying in Barcelona and Majorca, he requested an assignment to Spanish America, where he arrived in 1610 and where he became a priest in 1616. Initially, he was assigned pastoral work with the Indian population but then he was sent to Cartagena. Before 1615, Cartagena was the only port in Spanish America authorized to import slaves. Its population consisted of 2,000 Spaniards and between 3,000 and 4,000 blacks. Claver was entrusted with the religious instruction of newly arrived Africans.

His mentor was Alonso de Sandoval, the Spanish author of *De instauranda aethiopum salute* (1627, 1647), which makes an extensive classification of the different black peoples of Africa and includes a thorough method for evangelizing Africans in Spanish colonies. The presence of Muslims among West African peoples, especially the Wolofs, Bambaras, Mandingas, and Fulas of West Africa, is mentioned in relation to futile attempts at conversion. Sandoval was opposed to the slave trade rather than to the entire institution of slavery, and he considered evangelization of Africans in the New World a pressing issue.

Jesuits were among the most important slaveowners in Spanish America, and converting blacks was not considered a priority for the church authorities of the day in Cartagena. Sandoval and Claver were the only two priests given the task of ministering to African slaves, and they were helped by 18 interpreters, who were also slaves. When slave ships arrived, Peter Claver appeared with his assistants to offer the sick and the old water, oranges, lemons, brandy, perfumed water, and tobacco. He baptized those who were dying and started a program of religious education with the rest. His ministry included care of the sick, the old, and the abandoned. Sandoval and Claver saw the need to buy slaves themselves, slaves who would remain attached to the Jesuit house in Cartagena.

Claver had admirers among the urban aristocracy, but he was also accused of encouraging "insolence and laziness" among the slaves, whose religious activities were viewed as a loss of productivity. He confronted slaveowners when they impeded slave marriages, and he became a regulator of public morality. Being adamantly opposed to African dances and music, he removed drums and other musical instruments used in public gatherings, considering them idolatrous since they were used to honor the dead, and at times he was seen whipping the participants. Besides ministering to black slaves, Claver was entrusted with the spiritual care of prisoners who had been condemned to death, including British subjects persecuted by the Inquisition for their Anglican faith.

Claver's superiors in the Jesuit order had an ambivalent attitude toward his well-known zeal and methods. Once he was forbidden to own money and foodstuffs, which he kept in his cell and used to gain ascendancy among Cartagena's enslaved population. His request to be sent to Africa as a missionary after the Portuguese revolt against Spain (1640) interrupted the slave traffic was denied. He was also unsuccessful in his wish to extend his work with blacks in other Caribbean cities. In their yearly reports to Rome, his Jesuit superiors tended to register a poor opinion of his intellectual capabilities. Unlike Sandoval, Claver did not leave any writings about his work.

By the time he died, Claver had become a celebrity in Cartagena and throughout the Viceroyalty of Peru. The Catholic Church proclaimed him a saint on January 15, 1888, in a somewhat belated effort to join the antislavery movement in Europe and the Americas. A Catholic sodality, the Knights of Peter Claver, was founded to promote more harmonious race relations.

—*Baltasar Fra-Molinero*

For Further Reading
Sandoval, Alonso de. 1987. *Un tratado sobre la esclavitud (De instauranda aethiopum salute)*. Madrid: Alianza Editorial; Valtierra, Ángel, SJ. 1980. *Pedro Claver: El Santo Redentor de los negros. Cuarto Centenario de su nacimiento 1580–24 de junio–1980*. Bogotá: Banco de la República.

CLIENTELA *SYSTEM*

The word *clientela* was used throughout Roman history to designate the unequal social relationship of a client or sponsored free male (*cliens, salutator, togatus, parasitus*), and any of his dependent family members, to a patron or a sponsoring citizen, whether male or female (*patronus/patrona, advocatus*). *Clientela* differed from *tutela* ("tutelage") and from slavery in that the client was not bodily in the patron's power under the law. The client was generally a Roman citizen and the head of his own family (*paterfamilias*). He received food, money, and/or legal representation and had legal obligations (e.g., avoiding giving testimony against the patron) as well as social ones (e.g., greeting the patron each morning—*salutatio*).

In the early republic (c. 500–300 B.C.), *clientela* existed primarily between noble "patrician" patrons and non-noble citizen "plebeian" clients, who were poorer and had fewer rights under the law. The Twelve Tables

(450 B.C.) included a severe law protecting clients from economic abuse by their patrons: "If a patron shall have defrauded a client, he shall be sacer," i.e., might legally be slain (8.21). It was not legal to pay a patron money for his services after 204 B.C., but that restriction was frequently circumvented in the late republic (150–44 B.C.). Freedmen became clients of their former owner (Dionysius of Halicarnassus, in *Antiquitates Romanae* [4.22.4], claimed that the legendary king Servius Tullius started the practice in the sixth century B.C.). The Twelve Tables assigned inheritance of any intestate Roman citizen-freedman to his patron freedmen's obligations, and this extended beyond other clients' obligations.

After development of a plebeian aristocracy, which itself had a large share in patronage, different social/political relationships were designated as "patronage" although they did not always involve legal sanctions. Roman generals were considered patrons of those they conquered (e.g., C. Fabricius of the Samnites in 278 B.C.) and of soldiers to whom they dispersed booty or land. Such patronage was handed down through generations in the male line and bestowed honor on the family of the general; for example, a hereditary network of clients was exploited politically by Pompey the Great (106–48 B.C.). Such patronage, combined with gifts of citizenship, enabled direct political support in Rome: Julius Caesar extended citizenship to the residents of the Po Valley for this purpose.

Literary patronage, common from the middle republic (300–150 B.C.) on, involved the sponsorship of impecunious poets, playwrights, historians, and other artists by wealthier members of society; it became almost institutionalized under the emperors. In the late republic and empire (44 B.C.–A.D. 476), provinces and municipalities within and outside Italy would rely for representation of their interests on Roman patrons; social/business groups such as the collegia had their own patrons to represent them before the emperor.

Acts of patronage by wealthy municipals in the late empire extended even to the informal protection of neighbors against imperial tax collectors and political help in having public obligations remitted; in exchange, clients gave money, services, or the ownership of their lands. This sort of patronage is closely linked to the practice of using *coloni* (free poor) in the Roman Empire, itself a forerunner of medieval serfdom.

—*Jerise Fogel*

See also
Coloni; Roman Empire; Roman Republic
For Further Reading
Badian, Ernst. 1958. *Foreign Clientelae*. Oxford: Clarendon Press; Carcopino, Jerome. 1941. *Daily Life in Ancient Rome*. London: Routledge.

CLOSING OF THE AFRICAN SLAVE TRADE

Efforts to end the African slave trade began in the late-eighteenth century, but the trade continued well into the late-nineteenth century. The African slave trade's closing occurred in two phases. The first concerned suppression of West Africa's slave trade, which generally involved transporting slaves to the major Western Hemisphere slave nations such as the United States and Brazil. The second phase centered around attempts to end exportation of eastern African slaves to Arabian states.

Denmark became the first major European state to abolish the slave trade in 1792. Nonetheless, Britain was the primary force behind suppressing Africa's slave trade from 1807, upon abolition of the trade within the British Empire, to the essential end of international trade in African slaves at the close of the nineteenth century. Prior to 1807, Britain was the largest participant involved in the trade. British slave traders shipped Africans to Britain's West Indian colonies, various states of South and Central America, and the Southern part of the United States. Although parliamentary efforts to abolish the trade began in the 1780s, British slave traders and West Indian plantation owners who depended on slave labor presented a powerful, economic bloc that repeatedly defeated abolitionist legislation. Not until 1807 could Thomas Clarkson and William Wilberforce convince Parliament to abolish the slave trade within the empire. In 1811, Parliament followed its abolition act with another law making involvement in the slave trade a felony for British citizens.

Within the legislation, the British government offered to pay bounties for captured slave ships and for each slave captured in transport. Captured slaves were freed and relocated to a colony in Sierra Leone. That colony became the center of Britain's efforts to end West Africa's trade, and the capital of Sierra Leone, Freetown, became the major base for British naval units involved in suppressing the trade and the home of the courts that tried slavers.

In 1808, two British naval ships went to Africa with orders to intercept slave vessels. The conclusion of the Napoleonic Wars in 1815 freed more naval resources, and Britain steadily increased the antislavery squadron's size. Britain also conducted diplomatic offensives aimed at ending the trade by negotiating with other nations to cease involvement and, more important, allow the British navy to stop, search, and if necessary arrest non-British citizens engaged in the trade. For instance, in 1815, Portugal agreed to end its involvement in the trade north of the equator and to allow Britain to stop suspected slave ships.

In this undated illustration, Arab traders throw slaves overboard to avoid being caught with slaves by British naval vessels engaged in suppressing the slave trade.

By the 1820s, most nations, with the notable exception of the United States, had granted the British rights to search and capture vessels involved in the trade. Additionally, Britain was able to insert "equipment clauses" in most of these treaties, which allowed them to seize empty slave ships if they were rigged to transport slaves. Other nations, including France and eventually the United States, also stationed antislavery squadrons along the coast of West Africa, and by the 1830s, these squadrons were capturing, on average, approximately 30 slave ships per year and freeing nearly 5,000 slaves per year. Nonetheless, the 80,000–90,000 slaves that continued to be transported to the Americas dwarfed these numbers.

The United States was the major impediment to the European powers' attempts to suppress the trade. The United States refused to grant rights to other nations to stop and search U.S. ships, and the net result was that other nations' slavers sailed under the U.S. flag to escape the antislavery squadrons. Additionally, Americans provided the bulk of the slave ships, and by the 1850s, two of every three slave ships captured had

been outfitted in U.S. ports. Nonetheless, substantial progress in curtailing the trade was accomplished. By the 1830s, all major European powers were backing British efforts to end the trade, and eventually they included the "equipment clause" in the Quintuple Treaty (1841).

In the 1840s, Britain also began efforts to eliminate the supply of slaves either by offering subsidies to native rulers to end involvement in the trade or by taking direct military action against those who refused to cooperate. For instance, the British military acquired the Lagos territory when its ruler refused to end that kingdom's prolific slave trade, and Britain instituted a tight naval blockade of Dahomey for the same reason. The British also purchased Denmark's former slave colonies in 1850.

Diplomatic efforts to involve the United States in suppressing the trade proved successful when a portion of the Webster-Ashburton Treaty (1842) pledged that the United States would dispatch a small naval squadron to patrol with the British so that suspected slave ships flying the U.S. flag could be stopped without incident. Known as joint cruising, this effort proved to be more symbolic than effective. U.S. officials refused to act upon British intelligence about suspected slave ships, and even as late as 1860, some 20 slave ships were outfitted in the port of New York alone without interference from U.S. customs officials.

The U.S. Civil War and the subsequent Union blockade of Southern ports effectively ended the large-scale transport of West African slaves. From 1860 to 1864, the number of slaves transported to the Western Hemisphere dropped from approximately 25,000 to 7,000. The Washington Treaty (1862) further strengthened abolition efforts between the United States and Britain by finally allowing the British to seize suspected slave ships sailing under the U.S. flag. Hence, despite slavery's continuation in Cuba until 1886 and in Brazil until 1888, the British antislavery squadron's ability to stop and search suspected slave ships had largely ended the West African trade by the 1870s.

Britain also played a leading role in efforts to suppress East Africa's slave trade. Major slave trade routes in eastern Africa extended from the southern states, like Zanzibar—the prime supplier of eastern African slaves—to the Muslim states of the Middle East and some Near Eastern and Asian areas like Mauritius and India. Additionally, South America imported a small number of these slaves.

As with the West African trade, Britain was able to negotiate a series of treaties with various nations involved in the eastern trade. In 1841, the sultan of Zanzibar formally outlawed the slave trade outside of Zanzibar, and by 1856, all major slave-importing areas, including Persian Gulf sheikdoms, Somali chiefdoms, and Persia, had officially banned the slave trade. The British once again attempted to use naval force to suppress the trade, but some 20,000 slaves per year continued to be exported to areas that had formally banned the trade. British squadrons were only able to free on average some 1,000 of these slaves per year. Slavers continued to export slaves because an internal slave trade within Zanzibar and surrounding areas persisted. Consequently, slaves imported into Zanzibar were usually secretly transported from that sultanate to other markets.

Public outrage against the slave trade's continuation, encouraged by reports from explorers like David Livingstone, compelled the British government to attempt to negotiate a complete end to slave exporting from Zanzibar. Under threat of a naval blockade, the sultan acquiesced and closed Zanzibar's slave markets in 1873. In 1877, the sultan appointed a British naval officer to oversee compliance among the various chiefdoms that composed Zanzibar.

With the major source of slaves gone, the eastern slave trade dramatically declined, but still it continued. Many slavers shifted operations to Mozambique, where Portuguese authorities were less inclined to enforce anti–slave trade measures, until the Portuguese bowed to international pressure in 1880 and established a joint-patrol system with the British. By the mid-1880s, Mozambique's slave trade was mostly suppressed. Eventually, 17 nations, including all major European powers, the United States, the Ottoman Empire, Persia, and Zanzibar, signed the Brussels Act (1892), which formally charged each of the nations to take steps to suppress what remained of the trade.

Imposing European prohibitions on the slave trade as European powers carved Africa into colonies during the period known as "the scramble for Africa" meant the external trade had more or less ended by the early 1900s, although a slave ship was discovered in the Persian Gulf as late as 1920. Africa's internal slave trade continued well into the twentieth century, and in the end, only the formal abolition of slavery as an accepted institution throughout Africa effectively ended the slave trade.

—*Tom Lansford*

See also
French Slave Trade; General Abolition Bill; Palmerston Act; Sierra Leone; Wilberforce, William
For Further Reading
Alpers, Edward. 1975. *Ivory and Slaves*. Berkeley: University of California Press; Mannix, Daniel, and Malcolm Cowley. 1962. *Black Cargoes: A History of the Atlantic Slave Trade*. New York: Viking; Miers, Suzanne. 1975. *Britain and the Ending of the Slave Trade*. New York: Longman; Ward, William. 1969. *The Royal Navy and the Slavers*. New York: Pantheon.

COARTACION

*T*he term *coartación* is historically related to the Spanish Empire, but it is also related to an economic system that used slave labor in production activities. The term was first used in sixteenth-century Spain when it was mentioned in the ninth version of the *Laws of the Indies* (Ortíz, 1986), but the best way to characterize it is through its use in nineteenth-century Spanish colonies.

Except for macrolevel studies of slavery and the scarce documentation of the processes involved under *coartación*, there is very little written on the topic. Despite the paucity of sources, however, an inductive analysis of the available documents provides a reconstruction of the term's main elements. *Coartación* must be studied as a dynamic phenomenon operating within certain parameters in the context of power relationships.

Coartación was a legal mechanism that allowed a

slave to move toward freedom. Slaves paid an appraised amount in order to participate in a long process that had as its main objective, self-emancipation. With this initial payment, slaves entered into a self-staged program of action within the system, which meant that in all formal documents they would be considered *coartados* and not slaves. From this moment on, they began ascending the social scale that had attempted to maintain them in the most inferior levels. They not only achieved a different nominal position than slaves not entering the process but also were assigned fixed appraisal prices that could not be changed even if their owners changed. The latter provision certainly was beneficial for slaves, but for owners interested in selling them, it posed a problem. Since slaves were merchandise, a prospective buyer's need was insufficient justification to purchase them. Slaves had to be considered a good long-term investment, but their involvement in an emancipatory process made them a risky purchase. The few studies on this topic suggest that slaves who had not entered the emancipatory process were sold at higher prices than those who had begun the procedure.

It is important to understand that *coartación,* characterized as the payment of an appraised and fixed price, was not the only mechanism available to slaves seeking to free themselves in pre-abolition times. Nor did it represent a clear-cut way of achieving freedom. The mechanism was only a small step in a long process that generated its own contradictions and tensions, and it certainly merits more scholarly attention.

—*Víctor Torres-Vélez and Carlos BuitragoOrtíz*

For Further Reading

Bergad, Laird W.; Fe Iglesias Garcia; and Maria del Carmen Barcia. 1995. *The Cuban Slave Market, 1790–1880*. New York: Cambridge University Press; Ortíz, F. 1986. "Los negros esclavos." In *Revista bimestre cubana 1916* (annual yearbook); Scott, Rebecca. 1993. "Explaining Abolition: Contradiction, Adaptation, and Challenge in Cuban Slave Society 1860–1886." In *Caribbean Slave Society and Economy: A Student Reader*. Ed. Hillary Beckles and Verene Shepherd. New York: New Press.

COBB, HOWELL
(1815–1868)

A proponent of Southern unionism, Howell Cobb was elected Speaker of the U.S. House of Representatives in 1849 and held that position during the hotly debated Compromise of 1850, playing a key role in its passage. Born in Jefferson County, Georgia, Cobb was reared in Athens, Georgia. Attending Franklin College (now the University of Georgia), he graduated with a bachelor's degree in 1834. He studied law for two years and gained admittance to the Georgia bar in 1836. Using the family's political influence, he secured a position as solicitor general of Georgia in 1837. Always attracted to politics, he ran successfully for a congressional seat in 1842, representing a pro-Union district in northeastern Georgia.

While serving in Congress from 1843 to 1851 and 1855 to 1857, Cobb supported Texas annexation, the Mexican War, and slavery's expansion into the territories. Despite his position on these issues, he was regarded as a moderate among national Democrats. Although a slaveowner, the states' rights doctrine and secessionist views of John C. Calhoun were anathema to Cobb. During his tenure as Speaker of the House, the debate over California's admission as a free state threatened the Union. Cobb, much to the chagrin of many Southerners, supported the Compromise of 1850. Under its provisions, California became a free state, and the South received a stronger federal fugitive slave law.

Passage of the Compromise of 1850 preserved the Union but created a major upheaval in Southern politics that did not spare Cobb's home state. The weakening of the national Whig Party created chaos in Georgia politics as did a split among Georgia Democrats. Georgia Whigs and Democrats realigned themselves into two factions—the States' Rights Party representing secessionist sentiments and the pro-Union, Constitutional Union Party. Resigning from Congress, Cobb returned to Georgia to lead the forces of the Constitutional Union Party as its gubernatorial candidate in 1851.

Cobb served a successful two-year term as governor, but he had national political ambitions and campaigned vigorously for the 1856 Democratic presidential nominee, James Buchanan. When Buchanan became president, Cobb won a cabinet appointment as secretary of the Treasury. Exerting great influence in the administration, one political pundit described Cobb as "the president as much as if he were sworn in" (Simpson, 1973).

As 1860 approached, Cobb desired the Democratic presidential nomination but failed to win it and instead witnessed the disintegration of the national Democratic Party. He resigned from the cabinet after the election of Republican candidate Abraham Lincoln. Returning to Georgia he supported the immediate secession of his state from the Union—joining his antebellum political foes and reversing his previous position on several issues. In February 1861, he presided over a convention of seceded states in Montgomery, Alabama, which created the Confederate States of America. Disappointed at not securing the Confederate presidency, he organized a regiment and fought in several major Civil War engagements in the eastern theater. Following the war he practiced law in Macon, Georgia, until his death in 1868.

—*Mary Ellen Wilson*

For Further Reading
Cook, James F. 1995. *The Governors of Georgia, 1754–1995*. Macon, GA: Mercer University Press; Greene, Helen Ione. 1946. "Politics in Georgia, 1853–1854: The Ordeal of Howell Cobb." *Georgia Historical Quarterly* 30 (2): 185–211; Simpson, John Eddins. 1973. *Howell Cobb: The Politics of Ambition*. Chicago: Adams Press.

CODE NAPOLEON
See Napoleon Bonaparte

CODE NOIR

The Code Noir was the centerpiece of French legislation regulating the status of slaves and freedmen in the French Antilles during the eighteenth century. Signed by Louis XIV in March 1685, it also was a blueprint for the Louisiana code, where it created similar conditions. Louis made his intentions clear in the Preamble: the code was to "maintain the discipline of the . . . Roman Church and to regulate the state and quality of slaves in our said Islands." It established the religious and legal framework of master-slave relations in the French colonies until the end of the ancien régime in 1789.

Slaves were defined as movable property and treated accordingly. As valuable assets necessary for the plantation economy, they were often a part of trials over financial disputes, so the code outlined legal procedures to be followed. Although the main purpose of these regulations was to safeguard the colonial economy (e.g., by preventing the separation of slaves from their plantation during debt litigation), they also provided a modicum of protection for slaves. Legally seized slave couples and children, for example, could not be separated. Slaves enjoyed no civil rights and could own no property. Precluded from public office, they could neither appear as a party nor be admitted as witnesses in court; slave depositions could only be used to help judges seek evidence elsewhere.

Discipline for a potentially rebellious slave population was harsh and designed to protect the socioeconomic status quo, though codification probably tended to prevent the most flagrant abuses. The code targeted slave violence. Slaves were forbidden to carry arms or to congregate, and violence against free persons was punished severely, if necessary by death. Even minor theft was typically punished by beating and branding with the fleur-de-lis. Fugitive slaves could have their ears cut and shoulder branded; repeat offenders were hamstrung—or executed. Still, in previous regulations, runaways could be shot on sight. Slaves were also forbidden to trade valuable commodities. The sale of sugarcane was expressly forbidden, on pain of whipping for the slave and a fine for both the master and the buyer.

Numerous articles were aimed at providing minimal standards of care. Slaves were to be given weekly rations of 2.5 pots of manioc flour and 2 pounds of salt beef, or similar provisions, and provided with two outfits of clothes per year. Masters were required to care for physically incapacitated slaves. Torture was outlawed, though chaining or beating was accepted. Masters and overseers who killed a slave would be brought to court. Finally, abused slaves could appeal to the royal procureur, the representative of crown interests in the Parlements.

The code contained liberal provisions for manumission. Masters aged 20 and above were granted complete powers of enfranchisement, and freedmen could not be forced to work for former masters. In theory, at least, freedmen were considered citizens with full civil rights.

The Roman Catholic Church was firmly established as an expression of Louis XIV's aggressive Catholic absolutism, exemplified in the watchwords "one king, one law, one faith." Slaves were to be baptized and instructed in Catholicism, and all subjects were ordered to observe Sundays and church holidays. Interracial sexual relations, impossible to eradicate in a rude colonial society in which there was a paucity of white women, were highly regulated. Free (married) subjects who had children with slave concubines were condemned, but an unmarried freeman might marry his slave concubine in church and thus legitimize and enfranchise his wife and children in one stroke. Slave marriages required the consent of the master, but masters were prohibited from forcing slaves to marry. Masters were responsible for burying deceased baptized slaves in designated cemeteries; unbaptized slaves were buried at night in a convenient field.

Scholars are divided on the extent of the code's humanitarianism, as well as on its implementation, and gauging real conditions of slave life has been difficult. George Breathett called it "one of the most significant humanitarian developments in the history of colonial Haiti" (Breathett, 1988), yet Joan Brace argued that "it did almost nothing to improve the slaves' human and civil status" (Brace, 1983). Still, the evidence indicates somewhat improved conditions after the code was implemented, at least in theory. Judging from later legislation, enforcement was difficult, and by

1789, French planters were known as the most efficient slaveowners in the region.

Briefly abolished with slavery in 1794, the code was reintroduced with the restoration of the French monarchy in 1814. Louis-Philippe finally dismantled it and guaranteed the civil rights of free people of color, though slavery itself lasted until 1848 in the French empire.

—*William L. Chew III*

See also
French Caribbean; Société des Amis des Noirs
For Further Reading
"Edit du Roi, Touchant la Polices des Isles de l'Amérique Françoise. Du mois de Mars 1685." 1980. In *Le Code Noir, ou Recueil des reglemens rendus jusquà présent. Concernant le Gouvernement, l'Administration de la Justice, la Police, la Discipline & le commerce des Negres dans les Colonies Françoises.* Basse-Terre: Société d'histoire de la Guadeloupe; Brace, Joan. 1983. "From Chattel to Person: Martinique, 1635–1848." *Plantation Society* 2 (1): 63–80; Breathett, George. 1988. "Catholicism and the Code Noir in Haiti." *Journal of Negro History* 73 (1): 1–11; Stein, Robert Louis. 1988. *The French Sugar Business in the Eighteenth Century.* Baton Rouge: Louisiana State University Press.

CODES

Slave codes, sometimes called "black codes," were separate sets of legislation created by white leaders and lawmakers to control black slaves in the interest of peace and order in a slave society. After formally institutionalizing slavery, whites felt that each action by a slave that threatened the property or safety of others also had the potential to weaken or even destroy slavery. Therefore, slave codes were intended to perpetuate slavery as much as to protect life and property. Slave codes were only marginally intended to protect the slaves themselves.

In the United States, slave codes consolidated numerous existing laws that whites had enacted over the years while attempting to determine the social order of the new colonies. Virginia lawmakers passed that colony's first complete slave code in 1705, and it defined who would be slaves and who could own slaves, detailed punishments for slaves who owned guns or ran away, and even created punishments for whites who aided or married slaves. But laws existed before 1705 that addressed all of these same issues. As early as 1630, Hugh Davis was punished for having sexual relations with a Negro, and by 1639, no Negro could own arms. As early as 1640, blacks who escaped were treated more severely than white indentured servants who did the same. By 1682, the legislature clearly stated that "all Negroes" would be slaves. Slowly but surely, white leaders and lawmakers were removing the slave's legal personality. In comparison to penalties imposed on white offenders, the treatment of blacks grew increasingly worse, mirroring the relative decline of their condition socially as well.

Enslavement was a gradual process—one that progressed from a vague, fluid form in the seventeenth century to a hardened yet flexible form in the nineteenth. In the British mainland colonies, several decades lapsed between settlement and the creation of separate codes for slaves by white leaders and lawmakers. These first decades, and indeed, the first several generations in the colonies, witnessed a conflict over the place of Africans and African Americans in colonial society. As the population grew and spread out, colonial life became more complex, and race relations became more tense. As the black population in the colonies increased, white leaders intensified efforts to repress blacks and to define the precise social, economic, and even physical place of the black slave. Steadily, slavery emerged as a formal institution, bolstered by new sets of laws specifically aimed at protecting white interests and the slave system while also limiting black rights and protection under the law.

Colonial codes went through continual revision as new concerns and problems emerged. Virginia legislators significantly revised their code in 1748 and again in 1848–1850 in response to new threats from the slave community: poisoning in the eighteenth century and arson in the nineteenth. The revisions reflected value and belief changes in the society as a whole, and the democratic fervor and humanitarian spirit of the American Revolution shaped Virginia lawmakers' view of the codes. Newly enlightened lawmakers disallowed dismemberment, reduced many previous felony charges to misdemeanors, granted the benefit of clergy to slaves, made it more difficult to execute slaves, and realized that the extenuating circumstances slaves faced often led to poor behavior. While helping to balance the scales of justice, these reforms also perpetuated the system of slavery by stemming the revolt that was brewing in the slave community.

Slave codes placed slaves in a precarious position: the slave was both a person and a nonperson before the law. As a person, lawmakers defined the slave's position in society and controlled his or her behavior just as they defined and controlled other groups of people. Laws specified which unlawful acts applied to slaves and prescribed appropriate punishments for violators. Lawmakers also described the few rights slaves had before the law, which included being tithable individuals in colonial revenue arrangements. The lawmakers defined slaves as nonpersons, as property before the law. Slaves could be bought and sold,

Slave codes made it legal to burn slaves who attacked their masters. Slaves could be executed even for killings undertaken in self-defense.

inherited as real or personal property, accounted as part of an owner's estate, taken for payment of debt, and disputed in court cases on ownership. The theft of a slave, because slaves were property of great value, was a felony.

Slaves recognized that the social and legal order in which they lived did not include them as members but instead defined them as enemies. Slaves therefore had to act for themselves and in accordance with their own notions of what was right, what was wrong, and what was just if they wished to have any power over their own lives. If a slave killed an overseer who was whipping him to death, a slave court classified the act as a capital crime even though the slave might have called the killing self-defense. Whereas a planter called slaves who stole food from the plantation stores "thieves," the slaves themselves felt they were due a "take" of the plantation's produce since their labor had created it. Although threat of force kept most slaves outwardly obedient, individually and communally, slaves developed their own code of ethics, rules, and values.

—*Laura Croghan Kamoie*

See also
Code Noir; The Enlightenment; Indentured Servants; Latin American Law; Manumission Laws
For Further Reading
Finkelman, Paul, ed. 1988. *Statutes on Slavery: The Pamphlet Literature.* New York: Garland; Higginbotham, A. Leon. 1978. *In the Matter of Color: Race and the American Legal Process.* New York: Oxford University Press; Schwarz, Philip J. 1988. *Twice Condemned: Slaves and the Criminal Laws of Virginia, 1705–1865.* Baton Rouge: Louisiana State University Press; Watson, Alan. 1989. *Slave Law in the Americas.* Athens: University of Georgia Press.

COFFIN, LEVI
(1789–1877)

Abolitionist and Underground Railroad operator Levi Coffin was born and spent his youth in North Carolina where his Quaker family's antislavery views influenced his attitude toward the institution. His views deepened at the age of 7 when he saw a coffle of shackled slaves being transported. Later he saw a slave physically attacked without provocation, and at age 15 he helped liberate a free African American who had been kidnapped into slavery.

In 1821, Levi and his cousin Vestal Coffin organized a school for African Americans, but local slaveholders forced its closure. Coffin also helped organize a local manumission society that favored gradual emancipation. When the moderate organization voted to support the forced removal or colonization of freed slaves, Coffin resigned. Like many North Carolina Quakers, he found it difficult to espouse antislavery in a slave state.

In 1826, Coffin and his wife Catherine moved to Newport (now Fountain City) in Wayne County, Indiana. Learning that fugitive slaves occasionally traveled through Newport, where assistance was improvised and sometimes ineffective, Coffin made it known that his home was open to fugitive slaves. Soon he was providing temporary shelter, food, and clothing to fugitives and transportation to antislavery workers farther north. He established a network of Underground Railroad workers that served about 100 refugees per year. None was ever captured. Coffin's position as a prosperous businessman provided a degree of protection since he was open about his antislavery activity, and while he was in Indiana he became known as "president of the Underground Railroad."

Coffin also helped African Americans living in the Newport area. He served on a Quaker committee that provided schools for black children, visited their homes, and provided aid as needed. He was also active in the temperance movement, but his abolitionist views were the most controversial, even among Quakers. Although they had distanced themselves from slavery, many Friends objected to William Lloyd Garrison's call for immediate emancipation, favoring instead a program of gradual emancipation and colonization. In 1843, Coffin helped establish a separate Indiana Yearly Meeting of Anti-Slavery Friends, and there were two separate yearly meetings for 13 years until a growing Northern free soil sentiment made abolitionism more acceptable to conservative Quakers.

In 1844, Coffin and another Quaker abolitionist visited Canadian settlements of former slaves who had found a haven within the British Empire. In Canada he contacted many he had helped on the journey north, and the two also visited schools for black children and encouraged refugees to acquire as much education as possible. Although many of the former slaves were in better condition than had been reported, some new arrivals were in desperate need of clothing and other essentials, and after returning home, Coffin raised money and collected clothing for the refugees. The 1844 trip was the first of several he made to visit black settlements in Canada.

Coffin also played a major role in the free labor movement. As a merchant he became increasingly uncomfortable about dealing in cotton and other merchandise that depended on slave labor for its production and distribution, and influenced by John Woolman's example of refusing to wear fabrics dyed by slaves, and a growing free labor movement among abolitionists, Coffin reluctantly agreed to move to Cincinnati in 1847 to manage a wholesale depository of free labor goods. As part of his new position, Coffin traveled to eastern cities to observe free labor stores and factories that bought cotton and other supplies from mostly small-scale Southern farmers who did not own slaves. Abolitionists purchased a cotton gin and moved it to Mississippi to be operated with free labor. Coffin traveled south to locate cotton planters using only free labor, and there he spoke freely of his antislavery views, his nonconfrontational approach and Southern background enabling him to do so without serious consequences. His free labor business was highly successful, and the move to Cincinnati proved to be permanent.

When the Coffins arrived in Cincinnati, they feared their Underground Railroad work was over, but they soon learned that it was needed more than ever, for fugitive slaves passing through the Ohio city found little aid upon which they could count. Coffin quickly organized a network similar to the one he had established in Newport, and once again his home became the center of such activity. The Coffin home was also the meeting place of the Anti-Slavery Sewing Society, which provided essential clothing for fugitives traveling through Cincinnati. Demands on Coffin's time were especially heavy after passage of the Fugitive Slave Act in 1850, as increasing numbers of slaves left Kentucky and other Southern states and many of Cincinnati's African Americans fled to Canada to avoid kidnapping.

It was in Cincinnati that Coffin received national attention for his work with fugitives. The character Simeon Halliday, a Quaker abolitionist in Harriet Beecher Stowe's *Uncle Tom's Cabin,* was a composite of Coffin and Thomas Garrett of Wilmington, Delaware. Eliza Harris, another of Stowe's characters, was modeled after a fugitive Coffin had assisted. Some years after the Civil War, Charles T. Webber depicted Coffin and his wife in a famous painting of the Underground Railroad.

Coffin considered the Civil War divine punishment for slavery. As a Quaker nonresistant he did not openly support the Union military cause, but he nursed the wounded and provided supplies for those preparing to defend Cincinnati against threatened Confederate raids. He traveled extensively to work with former slaves, called contrabands, within the Union lines. He helped organize the Western Freedman's Aid Commission and traveled to England to raise money for its work. In 1867 he attended an International Anti-Slavery Conference in Paris. Coffin's autobiography, published in 1876, remains one of the more reliable accounts of the Underground Railroad by a participating abolitionist.

—*Larry Gara*

See also
Garrett, Thomas; Stowe, Harriet Beecher; Underground Railroad
For Further Reading
Coffin, Levi. 1876. *Reminiscences of Levi Coffin, Reputed President of the Underground Railroad.* Cincinnati: Western Tract Society; Haviland, Laura S. 1881. *A Woman's Life-Work: Labors and Experiences of Laura S. Haviland.* Chicago: Publishing Association of Friends; Mabee, Carlton. 1970. *Black Freedom: The Nonviolent Abolitionists from 1830 through the Civil War.* New York: Macmillan; Siebert, Wilbur H. 1898. *The Underground Railroad from Slavery to Freedom.* New York: Macmillan.

COLES, EDWARD (1786–1868)

Edward Coles's role in slavery is intriguing. Born into an Albemarle County, Virginia, slaveowning family, he is best known for his opposition to slavery, and he represented Thomas Jefferson's hope that slavery would be removed in a generation after the American Revolution.

Coles decided slavery was immoral during his education at the College of William and Mary in Virginia (1805–1806). He agonized for over a decade about how to put his belief into effect, and during that time, he conducted a correspondence with Jefferson trying to convince him to lead a campaign against slavery. Coles's conviction that slavery was immoral stemmed from his understanding of natural rights and laws, and his perception that Jefferson shared these beliefs, and Jefferson's status, made him the obvious leader in Coles's mind.

Disillusioned by Jefferson's refusal, Coles decided to leave Virginia and free his own slaves. In 1819, he finally went to Illinois, emancipating his slaves along the way. Coles's delay illustrates the practical problems connected with manumission in the United States. He worried about maintaining his own livelihood without a slave labor force, the well-being of his slaves after emancipation, and the economic burden of posting a bond for the manumitted slaves. His move to Illinois solved each of these problems.

In Illinois, he took a leading role in the opposition to a movement to allow slavery. In 1824, while governor, he worked to prevent the calling of a constitutional convention that would have written a constitution allowing the introduction of slavery. As part of the Northwest Territory, slavery had been forbidden, but after statehood, Illinois, Indiana, and Ohio all debated the legality of introducing slavery. Coles's role in Illinois was important because he threw into the opposition his status as governor and his past relationships with fellow Virginians Jefferson and James Madison. Coles's opposition played a significant part in the defeat of the convention party, and his actions helped maintain the integrity of the nonslave Midwest.

Coles's beliefs reveal the paradoxes of early-nineteenth-century antislavery efforts. Although he opposed slavery for moral reasons, he believed that emigration was the best option for African Americans. He was an early member of the American Colonization Society, which established Liberia as a removal destination, and as late as the mid-1850s, he was offering to pay the expenses of his former foreman to scout in the Caribbean for a suitable removal site. Coles was shocked when the former slave declined the offer, arguing that he was an American and had no wish to leave. That incident reveals the extent to which antislavery and an acceptance of diversity could be separated. Although professing a belief in the equality of African Americans, Coles was unable to imagine the United States as a multiracial nation.

In 1833, Coles moved from Illinois to Philadelphia, and his visible role in the antislavery movement ended. His family split during the Civil War, with one son fighting for the Union and the other for the Confederacy. Coles died in 1868 having lived to see slavery finally ended.

Coles's life is important for its symbolism. His antislavery beliefs were idealistic, based on a sincere acceptance of the humanity of African Americans and thus the immorality of slavery. Yet, he often seemed unable to carry those beliefs to their logical ends and could not accept the idea of a multiracial nation. Coles's life illustrates the essential dilemmas posed by slavery for many white Americans in the nineteenth century.

—*Kurt E. Leichtle*

COLONI

*C*oloni were tenant farmers of the Roman Empire and Europe in the Middle Ages, and occasionally, some among this group were slaveowners. The word *colonus* derives from the Latin verb *colo* ("to cultivate" or "to live in"). In Latin literature *colonus* is sometimes used to denote an inhabitant of a Roman or Latin colony, partly in the original sense of a peasant. Beginning in the first century B.C., it was used more specifically to designate a rent-paying tenant farmer. Tenancy first became a significant phenomenon in Italian agriculture in the late-second century B.C., when public land and private landowners' estates were rented to *coloni*. It became still more important during the Principate (27

B.C.–A.D. 180) when tenants also farmed imperial estates, but slave-run estates did not disappear. The two forms of exploitation were complementary.

A mixed form of management, whereby a slave bailiff ran one part of a property with slaves while *coloni* took leases on the other part, existed in several cases. Roman legal writers also attest to slave tenants, or quasi-*coloni*, who obtained leases from their masters. The control of *coloni* on estates owned by absentee landlords was mainly exercised by entrusted slaves or freedmen. The tenants' contracts were short term (normally five years). Rents seem initially to have been paid solely in cash, but there is evidence for a sharecropping system on senatorial and imperial estates in Italy and North Africa beginning in the second century A.D. On African estates, the tenants' obligations also included a fixed number of labor services, perhaps in accordance with local pre-Roman agrarian customs. The social and economic conditions of the provincial tenants are difficult to determine, given the paucity of contemporary sources, but uniform legal practices progressively extended to all parts of the Roman Empire. In principle, the *coloni* were independent in running their own farms and bore the full risk of crop failure.

There was a wide range of categories of tenants. *Coloni* often employed their own slaves and thus were not *kleinpächter* ("small farmers") but must be regarded as "middlemen." Other more humble tenants regarded the landowner as their patron, and debt pushed them toward a de facto state of dependence on the landowner. The law was very harsh to tenants who did not fulfill their obligations, but that fact does not suggest that there was a continuity between the free tenants of the early Roman Empire and the bound *coloni* of late antiquity. The inclusion of *coloni* for tax purposes started apparently on the imperial estates at the end of third century and first became universal with fiscal legislation in A.D. 366.

—*Jesper Carlsen*

See also
Bacaudae Insurrection; Circumcellions; Latifundia; Roman Empire
For Further Reading
Johne, Klaus-Peter; Jens Köhn; and Volker Weber. 1983. *Die Kolonen in Italien und den westlichen Provinzen des römischen Reiches*. Berlin: Akademie-Verlag; Kehoe, Dennis P. 1988. *The Economics of Agriculture on Roman Imperial Estates in North Africa*. Göttingen: Vandenhoeck and Ruprecht; Neeve, Pieter Willem de. 1984. *Colonus: Private Farm Tenancy in Roman Italy during the Republic and the Early Principate*. Amsterdam: J. C. Gieben; Scheidel, Walter. 1994. *Grundpacht und Lohnarbeit in der Landwirtschaft des römischen Italien*. Frankfurt am Main: Peter Lang.

COLUMBUS, CHRISTOPHER
(1451–1506)

Christopher Columbus went ashore on San Salvador (Watlings Island) in the Bahamas on October 12, 1492, on the first of four voyages to the Americas, all of which departed from Spanish ports. By 1502, when his final expedition sailed across the Atlantic, it was increasingly evident that the "two worlds [old and new], which God had cast asunder, were reunited, and the two worlds, which were so very different, began on that day [when Columbus stepped on American soil] to become alike" because of the trend toward "biological homogeneity" that resulted from the Columbian voyages (Crosby, 1972). Indian and African slaves were to be the victims of this transoceanic connection.

Columbus realized the value of native labor once he arrived in the Greater Antilles. According to a passage in his journal (dated December 16, 1492), the Taino of Hispaniola were "fitted to be ruled and to be set to work, to cultivate the land and to do all else that may be necessary" pursuant to the Spaniards' wishes (Columbus, 1960). An uprising in 1495 against Isabela—the first European colony in the Americas—resulted in the transporting of hundreds of Indian captives to Spain and their sale at the slave market in Seville (Granzotto, 1985).

The Black Legend of Iberian cruelty toward the pre-Columbian Americans—exemplified by that incident—was accurate to some extent, and unfortunately, the New Laws (1542), which outlawed their enslavement, did not end the mistreatment. The Dominican friar Bartolomé de Las Casas, who was instrumental in the enactment of these statutes, tried to liberate the natives by acknowledging their souls—in other words, their bondage was illegal since they were human beings.

Church and state were unable to improve the living conditions of the indigenous peoples because of stiff resistance from the conquistadors (conquerors) who followed Hernán Cortés into Mexico and Francisco Pizarro into Peru in 1519 and 1531, respectively. European-introduced diseases (e.g., measles, smallpox, and typhus) coupled with the exploitation unleashed by these Spanish adventurers decimated the Indian populations.

African slaves stepped into this demographic vacuum in the centuries that followed, and the numbers involved in the Atlantic slave trade were significant. Since the "shortage of labor was most pressing in the islands and littoral of tropical America, where the swords and maladies of the Old World had made the cleanest sweep of the aborigines and where the profits to be made from the mass production of tobacco, rice, indigo, coffee, and especially sugar were potentially the greatest" (Crosby, 1972), about 90 percent of the 8–10 million Africans brought, by 1850, to the Americas, settled in the circum-Caribbean. In this way, the result of Columbus's voyages involved the multifaceted transformation of three worlds: Africa, America, and Europe.

It is unlikely that Columbus comprehended the full implications of his landing on October 12, 1492. Moreover, his complicity in the Black Legend was tempered by positive assessments of the man, including a description of him as a "learned man of great experience . . . he was very moderate and modest . . . [and] so strict in matters of religion that for fasting and saying prayers he might have been taken for a member of a religious order" (Columbus, 1959). Columbus was a product of his time. He "never once considered that the relationship between Spaniards and Indians could be anything but a master-slave relationship" (Granzotto, 1985), and his actions and words made him partly responsible for what happened after the Old and New Worlds collided in the late-fifteenth century.

—*Fidel Iglesias*

See also
Central America; Latin America; New Spain
For Further Reading
Columbus, Christopher. 1960. *The Journal of Christopher Columbus.* Ed. L. A. Vigneras. New York: Bramhall House; Columbus, Ferdinand. 1959. *The Life of the Admiral Christopher Columbus.* Ed. Benjamin Keen. New Brunswick, NJ: Rutgers University Press; Crosby, Alfred W., Jr. 1972. *The Columbian Exchange: Biological and Cultural Consequences of 1492.* Westport, CT: Greenwood; Granzotto, Gianni. 1985. *Christopher Columbus, the Dream and the Obsession: A Biography.* Garden City, NJ: Doubleday.

COLUMELLA'S DE RE RUSTICA

Lucius Junius Columella, a Spanish compatriot and contemporary of the Stoic philosopher Seneca, composed agricultural treatises in the time of the emperor Nero (A.D. 54–68). He possessed a detailed knowledge of earlier Roman agricultural writers, and his writings reveal the conceits and pretensions of an upper-class first-century Roman polymath. Columella frequently quoted Vergil's *Georgics,* he cast Book 10 in the poetic meter of epic, and he composed a work on astrology, which is now lost. His extant work consists of *De re rustica* (On farming) in 12 books and a substantial fragment of a shorter work, *De arboribus* (On trees).

De re rustica provides valuable evidence on slavery in the High Roman Empire and on Roman masters' attitudes toward their slaves. Columella exhibited a seemingly humanitarian concern for slaves: he recommended friendliness of masters to their slaves, suggested that masters take account of slave opinion and expertise, and advised that masters regularly inspect slave living quarters (1.8.15–18; cf. 11.1.18–19). He also had a high regard for the authority of the agricultural writer Julius Hyginus, who was a freedman (1.1.13).

When read in context, these passages show that Columella's concern for chattel property was purely utilitarian. He recommended exemption from work or even freedom for slave women who produced children (1.8.19), and he provided notes on slave children in farming (8.2.7; 11.2.44). Columella identified the advantages of keeping slave overseers *(vilici)* illiterate (1.8.4–5), stated that slaves should be well-clothed so that they could work in any weather (1.8.9–10; cf. 11.1.21), and paired acquiring slaves with acquiring cattle (4.3.1–2).

Columella's work betrays aristocratic class biases and Roman group stereotypes of the servile classes. He stated that entrusting important matters to slaves led to a decline in husbandry (1. Preface.2; cf. 1.7.3–4), and he spoke of the corruption of slaves in the master's absence (1.1.20). Columella also wrote of the superiority of free to slave labor when the master could not supervise (1.7.6–7), slaves' negligence and greed (1.7.5), and the worthless, spoiled urban slave (1.8.1–2; cf. 1.8.6–7).

Grim realities of Roman slavery emerge from Columella's work: masters must avoid slave absences from the farm (11.1.23); they may employ chained slave gangs (1.6.3; 1.9.4), who live in underground prisons (1.6.3); tenant farmers *(coloni)* and slaves *(servi)* may be fettered (1.7.1); and fear is a means of controlling slaves (1.2.1), although excessive cruelty should be avoided (11.1.25). This information on Roman slavery is incidental, and like most classical authors, Columella took the institution of slavery for granted.

—*Craige Champion*

See also
Cato; *Coloni;* Latifundia; Seneca; Varro; *Vernae*
For Further Reading
Bradley, Keith R. 1987. *Slaves and Masters in the Roman Empire: A Study in Social Control.* New York: Oxford University Press; Columella, Lucius Junius. 1941. *On Agriculture.* Trans. Harrison Boyd Ash. London: Heinemann; White, K. D. 1970. *Roman Farming.* Ithaca, NY: Cornell University Press.

COMFORT WOMEN

"Comfort women" is a euphemism for a system of sexual enslavement conducted by the Japanese military during World War II. The English term comes from the Japanese *jugun ianfu.* The women involved were neither volunteers nor prostitutes but slaves. There is no certainty as to the number of women involved; estimates range from around 70,000 to 200,000. Korean women are thought to have composed perhaps 80 percent of the total.

Korean women were generally recruited for service through deception or even outright abduction. Their recruiters were not all Japanese; Koreans also knowingly were agents for the Japanese military in recruiting women for sexual service. Occasionally, fathers were paid to send their daughters into service, though it is unclear just how precisely they knew the kind of work their daughters would be doing. "Comfort stations" for Japanese soldiers were established in all areas where there were concentrations of Japanese troops: China (including Manchuria), Burma, Indonesia, the Philippines, Korea, and other locations in East and Southeast Asia.

The gathering of Korean women to serve as sexual slaves must be seen against the backdrop of several other aspects of Japan's expansion in Asia. Japan's annexation of Korea in 1910 began a period of colonial rule that ended only with Japan's defeat by the United States in 1945. Although Japanese rule in Korea was never benign, it became increasingly harsh as Japan prepared for, and then conducted, a full-scale invasion of China in 1937. Two developments in particular paved the way for the widespread use of sexual slaves, and for the high degree of institutionalized bureaucratization exemplified by the comfort women system.

First, as Japan's need for labor increased, the government began a system of mandatory labor service for Koreans, many of whom were sent abroad. They were required not only to work in mines and factories in Japan but also to serve the Japanese economy by developing such relatively undeveloped places as Sakhalin Island. The second development was the most notorious assault in the Japanese invasion of the mainland, the "rape of Nanking." The Japanese attack on this important Chinese city in December 1937 was accompanied by a horrifying display of murder and rape of civilians, with victims numbering in the tens of thousands. Stung by international criticism, the Japanese military leadership sought ways to avoid such incidents in the future, and the decision to establish comfort stations as a sexual outlet for Japanese soldiers became an integral part of Japanese war planning. In some records, the women being transported to the front lines were simply referred to as "military supplies."

The Korean women who became sexual slaves came from various backgrounds, though it appears that most of them were from rural areas characterized by poverty and minimal education. To some of the women, the lure of a job seemed an attractive alternative to a life of rural poverty. Others—those who were abducted rather than deceived—had no choice. The conditions in which they lived during their enslavement were uncomfortable at best, appallingly inhumane at worst. Women attempting to escape were punished severely, sometimes by physical mutilation or even execution. Their captivity ranged from weeks to years. They were raped repeatedly, in many cases being forced to serve as many as 30 or 40 soldiers a day, every day. Besides the humiliating sexual service, many of the women were also required to render various other duties. There were provisions made for medical examinations of the comfort women, though it is clear that the concern of the Japanese leadership was for the health of the soldiers, not for the women.

Since comfort women were sent to all parts of the Japanese empire, at Japan's surrender in 1945 many of them were left with no way to get home and no money. In some parts of the empire, Japanese soldiers indiscriminately murdered many comfort women at war's end. Some did eventually make their way back to Korea, but many continued to live in exile. Whether in Korea or abroad, however, their prospects after the war were bleak. Few were able to establish any kind of family life, either because they were viewed as tainted or because their harrowing experience had created a psychological barrier to marriage. The combination of unsanitary conditions, repeated rape, and forced abortions left many women physically incapable of bearing children, and they frequently had no family to turn to for support.

The issues of responsibility and compensation for the plight of the women, though raised with increasing frequency in recent years, have yet to be resolved. Reluctant to admit to any official involvement in the comfort stations, the Japanese government finally acknowledged the official nature of wartime sexual enslavement. It has denied compensation claims and refused to issue an apology, accepting only the establishment of a private fund to which individuals may contribute money for survivors. The comfort women issue has caused strains in Korean-Japanese relations and has also become part of a broader women's movement in Asia.

—J. Michael Allen

See also
Kim Hak-sun; Korean Council; Sexual Slavery, Japanese military; Yun Chông-ok
For Further Reading
Dolgopol, Ustinia, and Snehal Paranjape. *Comfort Women, an Unfinished Ordeal: Report of a Mission.* Geneva: International Commission of Jurists; Hicks, George. 1995. *The Comfort Women: Japan's Brutal Regime of Enforced Prostitution in the Second World War.* New York: Norton; Howard, Keith, ed. 1995. *True Stories of the Korean Comfort Women.* London: Cassell; Watanabe, Kazuko. 1994. "Militarism, Colonialism, and the Trafficking of Women: 'Comfort Women' Forced into Sexual Labor." *Bulletin of Concerned Asian Scholars* 26 (4): 3–15.

COMMONWEALTH V. JENNISON (1783)

For many scholars, *Commonwealth v. Jennison* (1783) represents the proverbial "last nail in the coffin" that buried, and thus abolished, slavery in Massachusetts. A few years earlier, several Massachusetts towns had complained that the state's constitution did not have an antislavery clause; subsequently, the state constitution of 1780, in a Declaration of Right, declared that "all men are born free and equal, and have certain natural, essential, and unalienable rights." The age of revolutionary fervor had created an atmosphere that favored freedom over slavery throughout Massachusetts and in some of the other colonies. Also, because of the early proliferation of white labor in Massachusetts and a numerically small slave population, merchants and farmers had turned to immigrant white labor to meet their labor needs; thus, slavery had never solidified its economic stranglehold on this state. It was in this historical context that *Commonwealth v. Jennison* arose and was decided.

Quaco (also known as Quo and Quock) Walker's pursuit of his freedom began when he escaped from Nathaniel Jennison, who claimed to be Walker's master. Walker's flight took him to the nearby farm of Seth and John Caldwell, whose brother had been, at one time, Walker's legal master. The brother had passed away, and when his widow married Jennison, her property (including Walker) became his.

Seeking to reclaim his property by marriage, Jennison, along with several cohorts, accosted Walker, beat him severely, and returned him to slavery. The Caldwells, in turn, hired the noted lawyer, Levi Lincoln, to be Walker's lawyer when Walker sued Jennison for assault and battery. This first case, *Quock Walker v. Jennison*, was heard in June 1781, and a jury decided in favor of Walker, awarded him £50, and declared that he was a "freeman." When Jennison sued the Caldwell brothers on the grounds that they had "seduced Quock Walker for plaintiff's service," another jury contradicted the first and in *Jennison v. Caldwell*, found in favor of Jennison and awarded him £25 for the loss of his slave's service.

The third and last case involving these litigants took place in April 1783 when state authorities indicted and charged Jennison with assault and battery on Walker. In *Commonwealth v. Jennison*, the state attorney general, Robert Paine, claimed that a free citizen of Massachusetts had been unlawfully attacked. According to Paine, Walker was a free citizen because of a verbal contract of manumission made to him by his deceased master and renewed by his widow.

Refuting proslavery arguments by Jennison, Chief Justice William Cushing, referring to the Declaration of Right and the American Revolution, which favored freedom, declared that the accused was guilty of assault and battering a freeman with "rights and privileges wholly incompatible and repugnant to its [slavery] existence." What initially had begun as a slave case between the Caldwell brothers and Jennison over who would have the rights to the labor of Quock Walker ended up establishing the philosophical basis for antislavery as the policy of the state of Massachusetts.

—*Malik Simba*

For Further Reading
Cushing, J. D. 1961. "The Cushing Court and the Abolition of Slavery in Massachusetts: More Notes on the Quock Walker Case." *American Journal of Legal History* 5: 118–119; Higginbotham, A. Leon, Jr. 1978. *In the Matter of Color.* New York: Oxford University Press; Zilversmit, Arthur. 1967. *The First Emancipation.* Chicago: University of Chicago Press.

COMPARATIVE SLAVERY, RECENT DEVELOPMENTS

Since the 1980s, scholars have looked increasingly at slavery in the United States as a phenomenon comparable to other forms of unfree and semifree labor outside the New World. The appearance of Peter Kolchin's *Unfree Labor* (1987) and Shearer Davis Bowman's *Masters and Lords* (1993) marks the beginning of a new subfield in comparative slave studies. Both books compare the antebellum U.S. South with roughly contemporaneous European societies, offering new interpretations of the nature of slavery in the United States and questioning previous assumptions. Indeed, debate has started on the relationship between slavery, serfdom, and capitalism and on the definitions of free and unfree labor in the context of Old World and New World history.

Although Kolchin and Bowman support strikingly different views of U.S. slavery, they both refer to Immanuel Wallerstein's "modern world system" approach, and his studies have been enormously influential in redefining the concepts of free and unfree labor. According to Wallerstein, during the sixteenth century a complex interrelation of different factors, most importantly demographic and geographic expansion and price increase, created a European world economy that from the beginning was characterized by a capitalist mode of production.

The single most important consequence of this process was the "discontinuity between economic and political institutions" (Wallerstein, 1979). Within the global economy of the capitalist world system, there grew a distinction between stronger states in the "core" and weaker states on the "semiperiphery" and "periphery." Within the capitalist mode of production, characterized by a single division of labor spread on a global scale, core states and peripheral states differed in the way labor was "recruited and recompensed in the labor market" (Wallerstein, 1979). In core states, wage labor was the norm while in semiperipheries and peripheries, sharecropping and various forms of coerced labor, ranging from serfdom to slavery, were widespread. Therefore, wage labor became associated with diversified agricultural and industrial activities within core areas, where workers were employed in the production and trade of finished products. Conversely, unfree labor became synonymous with monocultural agriculture within peripheral areas, where workers were forced to participate in the process of production and exportation of raw materials to core countries.

This model links the emergence of slavery and serfdom to the spread of a global capitalistic mode of production, thereby questioning the orthodox Marxist assumption which holds that capitalism is based exclusively on wage labor. Historians of slavery are recognizing an important implication of this model: the range of societies with which to compare slave systems increases enormously if we follow Wallerstein's suggestions. Conceptualizing these suggestions has been a necessary step in moving away from the idea of strict comparative slavery, and some historians have started looking at New World slavery as one of the many forms coerced labor took in peripheral economies. Not all historians agree with Wallerstein's view, of course, but they have incorporated it in looking for new directions of comparison.

Kolchin's and Bowman's monographs give precise ideas of two different reactions to Wallerstein's model and of two different ways of using it. Since both comparisons involve the U.S. South and eastern Europe, they explore potentially similar kinds of issues: the rise and demise of unfree labor systems, the ideology of landed elites, and the defense of conservatism from external threats. However, Kolchin's comparison of slavery in the United States and serfdom in Russia focuses upon labor relations, control, and management while Bowman's comparison of the U.S. South and Prussia considers almost exclusively the worldview of elites. Inevitably, both works compare elements considered common to each case with different results in the end. Still, their points of departure are similar: the rise of unfree labor systems in Old World and New World peripheries is clearly linked in both studies with expansion of the European world economy.

Bowman's *Masters and Lords* acknowledges its debt to Wallerstein's model by treating the "consolidation of Junkerdom and then planterdom as peripheral landed elites" (Bowman, 1993) actively involved in producing and exporting raw material to core states. He considers the U.S. South and East Elbia (in Prussia) as "relatively *backward* peripheries" playing an important role in transforming the United States and Germany from semiperipheries to core areas in the nineteenth century.

That view is essential to his central argument, according to which Junkers (members of the Prussian landed aristocracy) and planters functioned as capitalistic entrepreneurs engaged in production for the world market. By the mid-nineteenth century, serfdom no longer existed in East Elbia, making comparison with the South's slave system difficult to support if Bowman did not share Wallerstein's view on the relation between types of labor and capitalism. In fact, Bowman elaborates this idea, stating that "although capitalist development since the fifteenth century has certainly furthered proletarianization in core areas by promoting greater reliance on free wage labor in conjunction with technological advances, this does not mean that only a free-labor economy qualifies as capitalist" (Bowman, 1993). In other words, the conservative, reactionary, and antimodern ideology of planters and Junkers rested upon different, but related, systems of labor control, which were part of the same capitalist mode of production.

In stark contrast with Bowman's work, Kolchin's *Unfree Labor* is heavily influenced by Eugene Genovese's approach to slavery in the United States. It is possible to see Kolchin's monograph as a way of reinforcing the strength of Genovese's approach by transferring it to a comparative context. Kolchin sees American planters and Russian landowners essentially behaving in a "paternalistic" way toward their subjects. Like Genovese, he sees paternalism as being incompatible with capitalistic production so that in the end, both the antebellum South and pre-1860s Russia share a status as "prebourgeois" societies. Interestingly enough, this general rejection of the link between capitalism and slavery/serfdom does not prevent Kolchin from acknowledging his intellectual debt to Wallerstein.

Although in a milder form than Bowman, Kolchin recognizes that "the concept of a European core versus periphery to the east and west" (Kolchin, 1987) is important in his comparative analysis of the rise of unfree labor systems at the two extreme ends of the European world economy. He sees U.S. slavery as a particular labor system born in a process similar and related to the rebirth of serfdom at the periphery of the European economy in the sixteenth century. Without a hint of the role of the two peripheries in the world market, or of the link between this role and the form coerced labor took in the South and in Russia, there is enough to make one wonder how far one can argue (as Kolchin does) that slavery and serfdom are related and similar phenomena without acknowledging a general similarity in origins and structure between the various types of labor employed in the peripheries of the world system.

The next step in studying comparative slavery seems to be engaging in a more comprehensive comparison between slavery and other forms of labor control and management that developed outside Wallerstein's core areas of the world system. In an article published in 1996, Stanley Engerman attempts to compare systematically differences and similarities between serfdom and slavery within the general context of ancient and modern coerced labor systems. Even if this article is but a start of sustained research and analysis, it hints at very important issues that must be considered in future studies of comparative slavery. Among them, certainly the most important is the relativity in defining "free labor." Even though the article is titled "Slavery, Serfdom, and Other Forms of Coerced Labor," Engerman goes beyond the limits imposed by the analysis of classical forms of unfree labor to consider diverse topics like indentured servitude, convict labor, debt bondage, and "related systems which involve a loss of worker control over his (or her) options for a limited period of time" (Engerman, 1996). In explaining the ambiguity of the word "voluntary" when used in reference to indentured labor, Engerman states that "if it is argued that giving up control in the workplace is coercive, this would mean that almost all labor contracts, even with otherwise free labor, were restrictive" (Engerman, 1996).

This last point makes the work of historians of comparative slavery far more complicated than it used to be since they can no longer assume the meaning of freedom as an absolute category opposed to slavery and related to certain working conditions. Slavery and freedom are categories that will be subject to continuous scrutiny and redefinition as comparative studies of societies based on free and unfree labor proceed in future years.

—*Enrico Dal Lago*

See also
Comparative Slavery in the Americas
For Further Reading
Bowman, Shearer Davis. 1993. *Masters and Lords: Mid-19th Century U.S. Planters and Prussian Junkers.* New York: Oxford University Press; Engerman, Stanley. 1996. "Slavery, Serfdom, and Other Forms of Coerced Labor: Similarities and Differences." In *Serfdom and Slavery: Studies in Legal Bondage.* Ed. M. L. Bush. New York: Longman; Kolchin, Peter. 1987. *Unfree Labor: American Slavery and Russian Serfdom.* Cambridge, MA: Belknap Press; Wallerstein, Immanuel. 1979. *The Capitalist World-Economy.* Cambridge: Cambridge University Press.

COMPARATIVE SLAVERY IN THE AMERICAS

Modern slavery evolved in various Western Hemisphere colonies at different rates and with different results. European colonial leaders eventually turned to the African slave trade to fulfill colonial labor needs, and the nature of slavery in each colony varied. The plantation complex—an economic and political order centering on forced slave labor—characterized Brazil, most of the Caribbean islands, French Louisiana, and the British American South. Shared economic and labor organization created similarities between these colonies, like hierarchical social structures, agriculture often based on one cash crop, and a lack of self-sufficiency for staple goods. Additionally, disparate environments, cultures, and social and political organization resulted in different circumstances and opportunities for slaves and very distinct racial relations.

Two variables were most critical in influencing the African American experience in the Americas under slavery. The first was the type of work slaves did and the nature of the work environment. The primary daily activity of slaves was working—in the fields or mills, in "the big house," or on the docks and when they finally had time, for themselves and their families. Slave experiences varied greatly according to whether one worked in a mine, on a ranch, in an urban area, or on a plantation. For those slaves who found themselves in the fields of the Americas, experiences differed between those working with sugar, tobacco, coffee, cotton, or rice.

The second determinant of the African American experience under slavery was the slave community's demographic composition. The ethnicity, gender, and sheer number of the African American population dictated the slaves' ability to establish families and communities, to produce offspring and thus reproduce the population naturally (as opposed to continued forced importation), to maintain a cultural heritage, and to attempt to control the degree to which the master's culture was assimilated.

Most plantation slaves worked in one of two labor systems. Under the task labor system, slaves were assigned several specific tasks to complete within a day. When those tasks were finished, slaves could have time to themselves to spend however they wished. Slaves who worked on rice and long-staple-cotton plantations, in the naval stores industry, or in skilled labor positions worked under the task system. The benefits of this system for slaves included less supervision, more autonomy, and more free time. Many slaves who worked in this system were less acculturated and more able to maintain various elements of their African culture because of their infrequent contact with white society. South Carolina used the task system on its plantations, and that state's densest slave populations were in the coastal areas where rice, indigo, and long-staple cotton thrived and in Charleston where the service sector provided plentiful job opportunities. Plantation owners often lived in Charleston, away from the malarial environment of the swampy coast, so those plantation slaves had little contact with white society and maintained enough of their African culture to develop a new language, Gullah, which was virtually unintelligible to local whites.

The gang system was the most characteristic labor organization system of the plantation complex in the Americas. Wherever tobacco, sugar, or short-staple cotton grew, slaves worked in large groups or gangs under the strict supervision of white overseers from sunup to sundown. Close supervision by and frequent contact with whites meant that slaves working in gangs had less autonomy and less free time.

Sugar plantations in Brazil, the Caribbean, and Louisiana provide the most typical picture of the gang system in action. Sugar was a grueling crop to tend. The work was hot and physically taxing, and workers were expected to labor up to 24 hours straight during harvest. Heat exhaustion, accidents, and equipment failure in the sugar mills took their toll on slaves' lives. High mortality rates and low birthrates forced planters to rely on the continuing African slave trade to maintain slave populations, which meant that slaves throughout the plantation complex were largely African in culture and custom. Populations on these plantations were generally not self-sustaining because the sex ratio was male dominated. Consequently, marriages were infrequent, reproduction rates low, family and community formation more difficult, and miscegenation rates high.

An exception to this description of slavery under the gang labor system was in Virginia. Within two generations of being brought to this Chesapeake Bay area, Africans were establishing families and communities through natural increase, and by the mid-eighteenth century, Virginia planters no longer relied on the African slave trade. A more even sex ratio, a less demanding crop (tobacco), and a different planter-class mentality all contributed to the reproductive success of slaves in Virginia. Planter paternalism in the U.S. South, based on racist notions of slave inferiority, encouraged family development among slaves partly because planters believed families to be more stable and less likely to rebel. Virginia planters called their slaves their "black families" and felt that as leader of the plantation family, they had a right to intrude into slave life and attempt to shape it. Consequently, this close interaction in Virginia created the most acculturated plantation slave society in the Americas. Slaves were able to develop families and communities, but they were less able to maintain any direct African influences.

In Brazil and the Caribbean, planters were less concerned with shaping slave life and more concerned with maintaining social order and making profits. The greater the slave population within a society, the more paranoid the planter class became about slave insurrection and resistance. To maintain the status quo, Brazilian and Caribbean white leaders and planters resorted to urgent and openly repressive means of maintaining order and stability. Savage punishments, slave-hunting militias, bounties on fugitives, legal incentives to surrender fugitives, and strict slave codes characterized life in the plantation complex. Fewer family ties, a harsh work and living environment, and certain African cultural elements like voodoo and marronage (establishing communities of runaway slaves) coalesced to create a more volatile, openly resistant, and defiant slave population. Consequently, slaves in Brazil and the Caribbean were more likely than slaves elsewhere in the Americas to escape, establish independent guerrilla villages, individually attack owners through poison or arson, and organize armed rebellion.

Slaves also worked under other arrangements and in other environments. In mainland Spanish America, Brazil's backcountry, and northern British America, slavery was but one of many labor systems employed. African slaves were used for various tasks, but these societies were not slave societies. In mainland Spanish America, a black majority never existed, and Indian labor systems were far more important and influential in shaping Spanish-American economic development. African slaves were incorporated into these labor arrangements as miners, farmers, and carriers. In small areas where plantations existed, like coastal Venezuela, demographic patterns were similar to the rest of the plantation complex.

In southern and western Brazil, slaves worked on ranches and in mines—areas where the social structure was more fluid and flexible. In Brazil and Spanish America, miscegenation rates were high, and peo-

ple of mixed ancestry were common. The social system was therefore a complicated caste system in which status depended on race, lineage, and economic position, not solely a racist system with white on top and all shades of brown and black below, as in the North and South of the United States. In northern British America, slaves became jacks-of-all-trades, worked in factories or on the docks, or helped around the farm. The typical slaveowner owned only a few slaves, making family life and community development for slaves more difficult. The close nature of racial relations meant that slaves in the Northern part of the United States were highly acculturated, and manumission rates and social acceptance of freed blacks in these regions were high.

As much as life differed for slaves throughout the Americas, many commonalties also existed in their experiences. All slaves were slaves for life and inherited slave status from their mother. Throughout the Americas, slavery was imposed only on people of color. All slaves were defined by law as both human beings and pieces of property, and all societies passed laws to protect the slaves' humanity against the master's power to exploit—and in all societies a gap existed between these laws and actual practice. Everywhere, planters and leaders used religion as a means of supporting slavery, not weakening it, and officially, the church showed little interest in interfering with the institution of slavery. Wherever slavery existed, slaves struggled against their status as unfree and inferior. Organized armed rebellion occurred infrequently throughout the Americas, but escaping and other forms of passive resistance were common, everyday means of survival.

—*Laura Croghan Kamoie*

For Further Reading
Berlin, Ira, and Philip D. Morgan, eds. 1993. *Cultivation and Culture: Labor and the Shaping of Slave Life in the Americas*. Charlottesville: University Press of Virginia; Curtin, Philip D. 1990. *The Rise and Fall of the Plantation Complex: Essays in Atlantic History*. Cambridge: Cambridge University Press; Degler, Carl N. 1971. *Neither Black nor White: Slavery and Race Relations in Brazil and the United States*. New York: Macmillan; Klein, Herbert S. 1967. *Slavery in the Americas: A Comparative Study of Virginia and Cuba*. Chicago: University of Chicago Press.

COMPENSATED EMANCIPATION

Compensated-emancipation programs compelled slaveholders to free their slaves but offered them restitution through the labor of the ex-slaves (euphemistically called apprenticeship), monetary payment, or both. Depending on the compensation terms, freedom for the slave could be immediate and unconditional, or gradual with full freedom for the slave delayed long enough for the owner to recoup as much of his or her investment as possible.

Debates over compensated emancipation focused foremost on whether to free the slaves. After examining the religious, economic, and ideological grounds for emancipation, the debate shifted to the question of compensation. At issue was the protection of slaveowners' property rights, specifically whether the state had the right to deprive owners of their property without compensation. For the people who considered slavery evil, the critical question remained whether slaveowners deserved restitution for participating in an immoral institution.

The total cost and the compensation terms varied from place to place. Some compensated-emancipation plans spread the expense between taxpayers, slaveholders, and the slaves, but other programs, seeking to free nonslaveholders and the state from any financial burden, placed the full cost on the owners and the slaves. Slaveowners bore part of the burden of compensation, for they lost the legal right to owning the slave's lifelong labor. When governments used state funds to recompense owners, the expense fell on taxpayers, both slaveowners and nonslaveowners. The slaves, who were typically required to serve years of apprenticeship before receiving complete freedom, paid for a portion of their emancipation with their labor.

Compensated-emancipation plans ranged from those that freed only the unborn, leaving all living slaves still enslaved, to those programs that freed and compensated owners for the youngest and oldest slaves while deferring freedom for slaves in their prime years. Typically, compensated-emancipation programs offered freeborn status to all children born on or after a specified date, with the manumission being either unconditional or delayed until satisfaction of an apprenticeship.

Usually, few of the principal characters involved in compensated-emancipation programs—the state, the slaveholders, and the slaves—expressed full satisfaction with the policy. Frequently, slaveowners bemoaned the compensation level, and many did not receive the promised restitution. Slaves facing gradual emancipation often found the terms unacceptable, and many chose to escape from their apprenticeship. The high cost of financial compensation proved too burdensome for many nations, leading, in some instances, to revised legislation that ended slavery without the benefit of compensation.

The northern part of the United States inaugurated the trend toward compensated emancipation during the late-eighteenth century. During the early-nineteenth century, European nations instituted compensated-emancipation programs in their colonies: Great Britain enacted its policy in 1833, France and Denmark issued compensated-emancipation decrees in 1848, and the Dutch followed in 1863. With the exception of Cuba and Brazil, Latin American and Caribbean nations ended slavery and compensated owners during the 1850s and 1860s. In 1870, Cuba issued a free-birth decree, and in 1880, that country passed a law freeing the remaining slaves after an eight-year apprenticeship. By 1886, two years ahead of schedule, slavery had ended in Cuba. In 1871, Brazil enacted a free-birth law that provided both gradual emancipation and compensation for owners.

The cases of the United States and Great Britain in its colonies illustrate the varieties of compensated-emancipation programs. During the time of the American Revolution, the states in the northern portion of the United States enacted laws repealing the legal basis of slavery within their respective state boundaries. Acknowledging the legal rights of owners to their slave property, gradual-abolition laws freed no living slave, only conferred partial freedom on the future issue of slave mothers and deferred full freedom for these semifree children until they had served apprenticeships that typically lasted till their mid- or late-twenties. The plans confirmed the owners' property rights to living slaves, relieved the state and nonslaveholding citizens of the financial burden of compensation, and split the fiscal responsibility between the owners (who lost the right to the lifelong labor of the freeborn children) and the free children (who paid for their emancipation with years of unpaid labor).

Amid the chaos of the U.S. Civil War, an attempt was made by President Abraham Lincoln to introduce a plan for compensated emancipation. Hoping to remove the cause of dissension and war between North and South and thereby restore the divided nation, in 1862, Lincoln proposed to free the slaves in the remaining slave states in the Union, pay partial compensation to the owners for their property losses, and remove the freed slaves through colonization. Unlike the gradual-abolition laws in the North, Lincoln's proposal, which never became law, would have used national funds to compensate slaveholders and to colonize the freed slaves.

In the British colonies, taxpayers, slaveowners, and slaves bore the cost of compensating slaveowners. Britain's 1833 Emancipation Act abolished slavery throughout the colonies, freeing all slaves—immediately and unconditionally for children under age six, gradually for the others—and indemnified slaveowners for their losses. The state allocated a fund of £20 million to pay direct monetary compensation to slaveowners. Slaveholders assumed partial costs, for they lost their rights to the lifelong labor of their slaves and, as some complained, received less than the full market value for them. Slaves over age six paid a portion of the cost of their emancipation with apprenticeships of up to six years. In 1838, following loud complaints about abuses suffered under the emancipation act, Britain enacted a new law freeing all remaining slaves unconditionally.

—*Patience Essah*

See also
Free Birth, Law of
For Further Reading
Blackburn, Robin. 1988. *The Overthrow of Colonial Slavery, 1776–1848.* London: Verso; Davis, David Brion. 1975. *The Problem of Slavery in the Age of Revolution, 1770–1823.* Ithaca, NY: Cornell University Press; Fogel, Robert William. 1989. *Without Consent or Contract: The Rise and Fall of American Slavery.* New York: Norton.

CONCUBINAGE

Concubinage is the act of entering into a lasting sexual relationship with a person of a different social status, usually free. The word stems from a Latin word meaning "to lie with" and denotes an alternative to marriage when social circumstances prohibit legal marriage between unequals. Throughout the history of concubinage, one finds laws and decrees from secular and religious groups warning against the mistreatment of slaves as human beings, but this mistreatment did not include their sexual exploitation.

The Old Testament recognizes the acceptability of concubinage as a moral relationship necessary for the Hebrew race's procreation. Concubines were acquired by purchase from poor Hebrew families captured in time of war or taken in payment of a debt. All slaves were treated as commodities, but a female slave was also subject to sexual exploitation for the pleasure of the male members of the household and for breeding slave children. The highest position a female slave could achieve in Hebrew society was to become a childbearing concubine to her master; the lowest position was that of professional prostitute.

In ancient Greece, concubinage was a moral relationship and was often made by contract. Some wealthy men lived with concubines who were considered the man's sexual property just as the legal wives were, and the rape or seduction of a concubine drew the same penalties as offenses committed against a wife. Married Athenian men were permitted by law to copulate with prostitutes, and female slaves were always available to their masters and to their masters'

friends for sexual purposes. Rarely did a slave rise to concubine status. Prostitutes bought young slave girls or collected abandoned female infants, trained them in prostitution, and kept them in brothels to ensure an income. In the Hellenistic period, abandoned infants automatically were given slave status unless someone proved them freeborn. When older, the female infants worked as prostitutes and were banned by law from entering into a legal marriage.

When Rome captured the Greek city-states, enslaved Greeks were especially mistreated because they were newcomers or foreigners. Since cross marriage between slaves and nobles was seen as a disruption of the social order, Roman men took concubines. Although Roman women were not allowed to refuse sex with their partners, if the woman initiated concubinage, she was blamed for aiding in the destruction of the empire. But when the Roman emperors tried to make it attractive by law for men to marry, they still refused. Concubinage became a social problem because of the illegitimate children such a relationship produced. When slave women became freewomen in the first century, many became concubines for economic reasons.

In A.D. 52, Emperor Claudius proclaimed that if a woman chose to be the concubine of a slave, then she was reduced to slavery. Slaves could amass money and buy freedom, and freeborn women often married slaves to improve their social status in a complex slave society, but there was much prejudice against a freewoman cohabiting with a slave. There was little incentive for men to marry female slaves, and only a few of the imperial household attained positions of influence as the freedwomen concubines of the emperors, as Helena, the mother of Constantine did. Since a concubine could not become empress, Constantine's father dismissed Helena to take a legitimate wife. Constantine fought hard to change marriage laws between unequals, and Helena used her imperial wealth to build churches and promote the monastic movement in the East. Vespasian, Marcus Aurelius, and Antoninus lived with concubines, and Justinian granted concubines a status almost equal to that of legal wives and made their children legitimate.

The barbarian tribes did not seem to view concubinage as a permanent relationship and tended to uphold the importance of marital fidelity. Germanic tribal laws considered concubinage, usually with slave girls, an accepted, but not sexually exclusive, relationship involving no property rights. What distinguished concubinage from marriage under Germanic law was the intention to form a permanent union. Under Visigoth law, a master could have sex with a slave, but he was fined if he prostituted her. Visigoth law also provided that slaves who could provide evidence about an adulterous relationship should be tortured to get information. Under Lombard law, sexual relations with a betrothed woman were treated as adultery, even if the woman was a slave. There are many instances recorded of people of the lower classes escaping to live with the barbaric tribes rather than continue to live oppressed under the rule of Rome.

The rise of concubinage forced the church to tolerate the practice, although it did so reluctantly. During the early Middle Ages, the Christian church tended to look the other way when it came to concubinage. Many priests were "married" to concubines, and although the hierarchy and the public protested against clerical concubinage, the practice continued until the Reformation. Many parents encouraged their daughters to become concubines until in the twelfth century, the church emphasized chastity, celibacy, and virginity as the perfect states. In the ninth century, Pope Nicholas I cited John Chrysostom, the fourth-century church father and patriarch of Constantinople, who taught that it was not intercourse that made the marriage but the intention, suggesting that concubinage was marriage between consenting adults. The church fought against the prohibition of legal marriage between people of unequal social classes.

The word "concubine" faded from popular use in the fifteenth century when the word "mistress" in French and English was used to mean both a woman that a man wanted to marry and a kept woman. Sexual relations between masters and slaves or servants were not universally approved, but they were not exceptional. Where slavery existed, as in Spain, Italy, and the New World, women were left unprotected and available for sex with little opportunity to resist. For the wealthy, there was something that resembled concubinage, or the keeping of an auxiliary "wife" without legal standing but with a degree of permanence. Eventually, the word "mistress" came to mean someone who specialized in love and sex apart from marriage; the meaning of concubinage as a legitimate relationship between social unequals was thus transformed into an illicit love affair.

—*Judith T. Wozniak*

For Further Reading
Brundage, James R. 1987. *Law, Sex, and Christian Society in Medieval Europe.* Chicago: University of Chicago Press; Gottlieb, Beatrice. 1993. *The Family in the Western World.* Oxford: Oxford University Press; McNeill, John T., and Helena M. Gamer. 1990. *Medieval Handbooks of Penance.* New York: Columbia University Press; Pomeroy, Sarah B. 1995. *Goddesses, Whores, Wives, and Slaves.* New York: Schocken Books.

CONDORCET, MARIE-JEAN-ANTOINE-NICOLAS CARITAT, MARQUIS DE (1743–1794)

Marie-Jean-Antoine-Nicolas Caritat, marquis de Condorcet, was an outstanding, internationally known French intellectual, *philosophe*, mathematician, secretary of the French Academy, member of the Academy of Sciences, political theorist, and politician during the early part of the French Revolution. During his life, Condorcet never stopped protesting against injustice and defending the rights of the oppressed and victimized, especially slaves and women. Condorcet was a leading member of the French abolitionists who organized the Société des Amis des Noirs in 1788. Condorcet, like many of his fellow abolitionists and political friends, fell victim to the Reign of Terror and died in prison in March 1794, seven weeks after the National Convention had abolished slavery in all French territories (February 4, 1794).

In several writings, Condorcet showed his profound disgust of the slave trade and slavery. In one of his works, *Remarques sur les pensées de Pascal* (Remarks on the thought of Pascal), written in 1776, he wrote that natural rights, bestowed on every human being, came first and that no other rights or laws could surpass the right of freedom—certainly not the argument that abolishing slavery would violate the property rights of the colonists.

Four years later, using the pseudonym Joachim Schwartz, Condorcet wrote *Réflexions sur l'esclavage des nègres* (Reflections on the enslavement of Negroes), a pamphlet against slavery and a program to abolish slavery gradually. Condorcet held that slavery was not human and could not be tolerated under any circumstances. In fact, slavery was nothing less than a capital crime. Condorcet wrote at the beginning of the pamphlet: "Friends. Although I do not have the same color as you, I have always considered you as my brothers. Nature has bestowed you with the same mind, the same reason, the same virtues as whites. With whites I mean only the ones in Europe, because I would insult you if I would compare you to the whites in the colonies" (Schwartz, 1788).

In 1788, the same year the Société des Amis des Noirs was founded by Brissot de Warville, the *Réflexions* was reissued and served as a guiding principle for the society. In the *Réflexions,* Condorcet reiterated that freedom was an inalienable human right and slavery a crime against humanity. He showed that the arguments the defenders of the slave trade and slavery used were wrong. If these defenders say, Condorcet wrote, that most slaves are convicted criminals or prisoners of war and that enslaving them is nothing more than a deed of humanity because these slaves are saved from a certain death, then they are twisting the truth. And even if the slave trader were to go free, the plantation owner would have committed a crime because he would be a receiver, even though he might think he was smart in letting others commit the actual theft.

Another argument the defenders of the trade and slavery often used was that only blacks were physically fit to do the work on the land in a hot climate and that without Negro slaves, the plantations would be ruined. Even if this argument were true, slavery would still be a crime; the loss of colonial riches can never be an argument to legalize slavery. Furthermore, it would be wrong to think that sugar, indigo, coffee, and spices could only be cultivated on plantations worked by slaves. Economically the cultivation of these crops would be better on small plots of land worked by free citizens—whether laborers, tenants, or owners of the land—no matter what color they might have. Condorcet even went so far as to assume that free blacks working the land would not only enlarge the yield but also improve the quality of the crops. With this argument, Condorcet silenced the people who said that blacks are lazy and stupid by nature. Only slavery kept them in such a state, and only freedom could change the situation.

The role of society and the state is to protect the citizens and their natural and civil rights, Condorcet continued. Laws that violate these rights are therefore crimes. Since the state has the obligation to protect every citizen and to maintain law and order to do so, it would be wise, Condorcet argued, to give slaves their freedom step by step. That would be in the best interest of free citizens and the slaves to be freed.

First of all, the slave trade had to be abolished immediately and every violation of the abolition law punished severely as a crime of theft. As a consequence, slaveowners would ameliorate their slaves' condition, because not to do so would harm themselves financially. Second, all slaves born on plantations should be manumitted immediately. The danger here would be that slaveowners might treat pregnant black women badly and perhaps cause miscarriages. Condorcet offered two solutions to this problem. According to one, pregnant slaves should be registered by an independent inspector who would visit the plantations every two months. If a miscarriage was reported, the woman had to be set free. The other solution was that children born of a slave mother would remain enslaved until they reached the age of 35. Other slaves should be offered the possibility of buying their freedom or they should be manumitted after a certain number of years, depending on their age and the date on which the new law would be issued. Condorcet calculated that 70 years after that date, all slaves would be free.

Life after slavery would be totally different. Blacks and whites would live together in the overseas territories, and these territories could also function as settlements where Jews and, in this case, French Protestants could be free citizens and enjoy all the civil rights they did not have in Europe. Condorcet not only possessed an enlightened view of a future in which the world would be a better one for all humankind, he also firmly believed that progress toward this better world was not just something to hope for but would be determined by historical laws. The first years of the French Revolution offered favorable conditions for progress in the right direction, and especially during the years 1789–1791, Condorcet tried to convince the new politicians and pressure groups to share his and the Amis des Noirs' political stand against slavery.

—Angelie Sens

See also
Société des Amis des Noirs
For Further Reading
Badinter, Elisabeth, and Robert Badinter. 1990. *Condorcet (1743–1794): Un intellectuel en politique.* Paris: Librairie Fayard; Baker, Keith Michael. 1975. *Condorcet: From Natural Philosophy to Social Mathematics.* Chicago: University of Chicago Press; Condorcet. 1996. *Politique de Condorcet: Textes choisies et présentés par Charles Coutel.* Paris: Editions Payot et Rivages; Schwartz, Joachim [Condorcet]. 1788. *Réflexions sur l'esclavage des nègres.* Paris: Froullé.

CONFISCATION ACTS (1861–1862)

Two confiscation acts were passed by Congress during the U.S. Civil War, and this legislation authorized military authorities to appropriate permanently any property, including slaves, owned by Confederate citizens. The two acts were thus the first small steps taken to erode the legal foundations of slavery in the United States.

Union forces advancing south immediately confronted the problem of what they could legally do with captured Confederate property. Since Lincoln's administration insisted that Confederates were rebellious insurgents rather than foreign belligerents, the laws of war giving nations the right to seize the property of enemy aliens might not apply. Some specific legislative act was necessary that would allow the North legally to seize and retain the South's war-making matériel. On August 6, 1861, therefore, Congress passed with little debate the first Confiscation Act to allow military forces to keep any rebel war-making property.

Did this "property" include slaves? If so, the first Confiscation Act might easily have been a de facto emancipation proclamation. Southerners certainly understood it as such. They angrily referred to the Northern law as an emancipation act and passed their own harsh confiscatory legislation to exact revenge against what they believed to be the Union's poorly concealed declaration of war against their slave "property."

Slaves performed essential military service throughout the Confederacy, and some Northerners, like General Benjamin Butler, believed that slaves should be considered "contraband of war" and thus seized and kept with the same justification the Union army might use to keep a captured Confederate musket or cannon. The authors of the first Confiscation Act specifically provided that slaves directly employed in aiding the Confederate military effort could be confiscated, but the act contained no provisions for deciding whether these individuals might subsequently be emancipated. As a result, the army was flooded with thousands of runaway slaves whose legal status remained in limbo.

The ambiguity of this and other provisions caused Congress to pass a second Confiscation Act in July 1862. This act authorized the government to seize any property owned by rebellious Southerners. Sponsored by more radical antislavery congressmen, many Northerners understood this act to be a first step toward total emancipation, treating the slaves of rebel owners as "captives of war" and unequivocally declaring them "forever free."

The second Confiscation Act did not resolve the basic legal confusion over whether the Confederates were rebels or foreign enemies. It referred to rebels as "traitors," implying they were simply wayward U.S. citizens who might nevertheless possess certain basic rights in a court of law, such as a hearing to determine whether their property might be taken from them. But using the phrase "captives of war" to describe confiscated slaves suggested that Confederate slaveowners were waging war as foreign belligerents, which afforded indirect legal recognition of the Confederacy as a foreign nation, something Lincoln's administration very much wished to avoid.

Lincoln had his doubts about these and other matters, so much so that he took the unprecedented step of sending a message to Congress stating his objections to the bill and indicating he would veto it if certain changes were not made. He believed the law incorrectly implied that Congress could end slavery in a state, and he suggested that the wording should be altered to give the national government ownership of confiscated slave "property" prior to freeing those slaves. Lincoln took pains to indicate that he had no objections to liberating slaves, as such—indeed, even as he wrote this message, he was working on a preliminary draft of the Emancipation Proclamation.

Congress took Lincoln's suggestions for changing the bill's wording, and it became law in the fall of 1862. In the final analysis, both of the confiscation acts were relatively ineffective where slavery was concerned, for just six months after passage of the second one, Lincoln freed the slaves using his powers as commander in chief. Yet the acts did set certain precedents. They marked the first congressional attempt to address the issues of emancipation and slavery's legal status during the Civil War, and they implied that such issues were national rather than local in scope. The confiscation acts are best remembered for their symbolic value, as milestones on the difficult road Northerners took from fighting a war to save the Union to fighting a war to end slavery.

—*Brian Dirck*

See also
Abolition, United States; Civil War, United States; Contraband; Emancipation Proclamation; Lincoln, Abraham
For Further Reading
Frederick, Duke. 1966. "The Second Confiscation Act: A Chapter of Civil War Politics." M.A. thesis, Department of History, University of Chicago; Syrett, John. 1971. "The Confiscation Acts: Efforts at Reconstruction during the Civil War." M.A. thesis, Department of History, University of Wisconsin, Madison.

CONFRATERNITIES

Confraternities are voluntary organizations directed by laypeople that add social and religious stability in times of political turmoil. These societies use symbols and rituals to give members a feeling of *communitas* in a heterogeneous group, encouraging unstructured human relations to develop. The popularity of confraternities ranged from medieval Florence to nineteenth-century Brazil, and documents identify slaves enjoying the full privileges of confraternity membership, including the rise to leadership positions over white elites.

The characteristics and history of the confraternities of the Italian Renaissance came to the Americas via the Portuguese slave trade. While Italian confraternities declined in the sixteenth century as parish clergy gained control once held by the laity, the Brazilian confraternities were weakened by parallel forces of the late-eighteenth century. Entire families joined the Italian confraternities, but evidence that slaves participated in membership activities is not clearly documented until colonial Brazil. In both cultures confraternities thrived where social bonds were dense and multifaceted, where social roles overlapped, where personal relationships granted security and stability in a fragmented world. In Renaissance Italy, the fragmentation tended to be distinguished by social role: customer, partner, competitor, kinsman, neighbor, friend. In Brazil, the fragmentation also was based on race and ethnicity. In both cultures confraternities were closely connected to the church: the mendicant orders in Florence and the local parishes in Brazil. By focusing on symbols like the cross, the Eucharist, and the lives of Jesus, Mary, and the saints, confraternities provided a common, interrelated set of symbols around which a diverse people could unite through organized devotion in a divided community.

In eighteenth-century Brazil, confraternities provided social welfare for their members and their families, including ministry to prisoners and burying the dead. After the mid-sixteenth century the confraternities increasingly fell under the clergy's control, and social heterogeneity was structured into a social hierarchy that was exclusive rather than inclusive. Local processions gave way to an emphasis on private adoration and meditation, and flagellation was rejected for an appreciation of interior discipline.

In the Brazilian gold-mining capital of Vila Rica, early-eighteenth-century confraternities consisted of whites, blacks, and mulattoes. The bylaws of some confraternities prohibited membership of people born in Africa, and the confraternity Irmandade da Senhora das Merces e Redencao might have played a role in ransoming the freedom of slaves. Also, the membership rolls of Santo Antonio and Nossa Senhora do Terco reveal the admission of men and women—free, freed, and slave. Families joined as units with their slaves. The bulk of the nonwhite membership of Merces e Perdoes consisted of slaves and, especially, ex-slaves.

At a time when slaves and outcasts often were buried in faraway places, confraternities provided space inside the church for burial. Donald Ramos's research suggests that the Brazilian confraternities assisted in the Portuguese acculturation of the Africans, including slaves. Slaves thus were provided a shelter under which they could maintain African traditions and develop a leadership structure. In the black confraternity of Nossa Neshora do Rosario of Antonio Dias Parish in the eighteenth century, 80.9 percent of the male leaders and 65.4 percent of the female leaders were or had been slaves. Some confraternities in Brazil owned slaves and used them to maintain the church and to generate funds.

During the late-nineteenth century, Brazilian confraternities suffered economic weakness and, as in sixteenth-century Italy, they were unable to resist clergy control. With the shift in wealth, many confraternities could not maintain their independence from local parish authorities. Ronald Weissman's description of the Italian confraternities could be applied to those that moved several years later from Portugal into the

Americas: autonomous lay institutions, corporate character with ties to the community, social heterogeneity, synthesis of interior spirituality and collective action, festive character, cultural fluidity, and ambiguous boundaries.

—*Judith T. Wozniak*

For Further Reading
Eisenbichler, Konrad, ed. 1991. *Crossing the Boundaries: Christian Piety and the Arts in Italian Medieval and Renaissance Confraternities.* Kalamazoo, MI: Medieval Institute Publications; Ramos, Donald. 1986. "Community, Control, and Acculturation: A Case Study of Slavery in Eighteenth Century Brazil." *The Americas* (4): 419–451; Weissman, Ronald F. E. 1982. *Ritual Brotherhood in Renaissance Florence.* New York: Academic Press.

CONFUCIANISM AND SLAVERY

Although Confucianism's canonical texts contain numerous references to slaves of various kinds, apparently there was no specific Confucian position or treatment of the topic. It is difficult to distinguish between specific Confucian attitudes to slavery and state policies, because throughout most of Chinese history, Confucianism was the official ideology of rulership and Confucians determined and administered much of the legal structure.

Generally, traditional Chinese law restricted slaves' conduct in various ways: the punishment for crimes committed by slaves was harsher than for the same crimes committed by a free person, and the punishment for crimes committed against slaves was correspondingly lighter. Owners could determine female slaves' marriages, and male slaves who had sexual relations with freewomen in the owner's household were severely punished, but men could use their unmarried female slaves as sexual partners. If such intercourse produced the birth of a child (especially a son), the slave might become a concubine and gain somewhat higher status. Otherwise, the children of slaves were generally considered chattel, and the owner determined their fate.

In legal terms, slaves were considered children: they had a lesser status as witnesses or instigators of lawsuits. Masters had a legal right to beat slaves provided there was no demonstrable intent to kill, but even killing disobedient slaves had slight legal consequences for masters. Sometimes, the master was not allowed to kill the slave but could petition the government to execute the slave instead. In the Qing dynasty (1644–1912), if a slave accused his master and the accusation was true, the slave still received a beating and imprisonment because of the unfiliality of the act. If the accusation was proved false, the slave was strangled to death.

Yet some Confucians spoke for the humane treatment of slaves. Dong Zhongshu (c. 179–104 B.C.) and others argued against the unequivocal right of masters to kill their slaves, and the law codes were modified to prevent wanton cruelty. As a Confucian saying goes, "Of all things brought forth by Heaven, man is the most precious" (*Hou Hanshu*). As a humanistic philosophy, Confucianism encouraged the humane treatment of slaves, stressing the obligations of both the superior and the subordinate. Some Confucians challenged the notion that wise ancient sage-kings (or philosopher kings) had tolerated slavery. Yet Confucianism does not posit equality as a social virtue: differences in power are inherent in nature. The central Confucian term *li* ("rites" or "propriety") refers to behavior which recognizes hierarchy that is consistent with the reality of natural difference and is conducive to social and cosmic harmony.

As a discourse contending that hierarchy is natural, Confucian attitudes included a resistance to slaves wearing fine clothing or any other outward sign of a higher status. Contemporary and later commentators condemned the conferral of a ceremonial cap by one Liu He on a male slave: "A male slave was capped; and the world was [thrown into] anarchy" (Wilbur, 1943). Much of Confucian literature concerns the correct signs and rituals appropriate for persons of specified ranks, and the principle of rank varied according to context: generally, older over younger, male over female, parent over child, and ruler over ruled. The relationship of slave to owner was subsumed under the last.

Maintaining rank had significance beyond social control: power differences were seen as inherent in the order of the universe. Heaven and earth, *yin* and *yang*—the conceptual building blocks of Confucian and other Chinese thought—bespoke the justification of power differences. If slaves wore the garments of their owners, the harmony of the cosmos was at stake. A strong antislavery movement, led by Confucians but also under some western influence, developed during the Qing dynasty, and gradually the power to buy and sell slaves was restricted, certain forms of slavery and banishment were abolished, and the inequitable punishment of slaves who broke the law was lightened. Most forms of slavery were legally abolished in 1910 shortly before the dynasty ended.

The attitudes of Confucius toward slavery and the proper fashion to periodize ancient society were debated in mainland China during the 1950s and early 1960s. The debate was largely ideologically driven and based on arbitrary philology. Zhao Jibin interpreted Confucius's well-known injunction to love "men" *(ren)* to mean "love the class of slaveowners."

According to Marxist historiography, societies move from primitive communism to slaveowning to feudalism to capitalism and finally to socialism. The division between the slaveowning and feudal periods was variously assigned to the later years of the Zhou dynasty (1122–221 B.C.), the Warring States period (403–222 B.C.), or the Qin dynasty (221–206 B.C.). From the May Fourth movement (1919 into the early 1920s) onward, Confucius was attacked as a reactionary and associated with all the past evils, like slave burial and foot binding. His nostalgia for the ancient enlightened rulers certainly seemed to support this view.

Views of Confucius have varied in the People's Republic. Scholars such as Yang Rongguo, Ren Jiyu, and Zhao Jibin and other writers said Confucius was of the slaveowning class and tried to preserve the status quo—a widespread view during the Cultural Revolution (1967–1976). But Guo Moruo argued throughout the 1950s that Confucius was a progressive, even a revolutionary, who helped in the transition from a slave society to a feudal society. Indeed, burial of live slaves (to accompany owners into the afterlife) declined during the Zhou dynasty, and Confucianism was associated with the rejection of live burial. The influential historian of philosophy Feng Youlan said that Confucius represented the reactionary slaveowning class, but also that he reformed himself and became a representative of the new emerging landlord class (which was victorious). The term *ren,* he argued, was an inclusive term for all humanity.

—*Eric Reinders*

See also
China (Ancient, Late Imperial, Medieval)
For Further Reading
Louie, Kam. 1980. *Critiques of Confucius in Contemporary China.* New York: St. Martin's; Meijer, Marinus J. 1980. "Slavery at the End of the Ch'ing Dynasty." In *Essays on China's Legal Tradition.* Ed. Jerome Alan Cohen, R. Randle Edwards, and Fu-mei Chang Chen. Princeton, NJ: Princeton University Press; Wilbur, C. Martin. 1943. *Slavery in China during the Former Han Dynasty, 206 B.C.–A.D. 25.* New York: Russell and Russell.

CONJURE

As slavery developed in seventeenth-century America, there emerged a distinct slave culture born of African and European-American heritage. Contemporary African American culture has been greatly influenced by this earlier slave culture, which flourished during the period before the U.S. Civil War. An integral aspect of the slave culture was a well-established belief system known as "conjure." To some people, conjure is nothing more than witchcraft, a version of voodoo; to others, it is a component of slave religion as practiced in the slave quarters—namely, an alternative religious system that ran counter to Christian doctrine.

The African American folk meaning of conjure leans toward conjure as the use of natural and artificial materials for medicinal and quasi-medicinal purposes, or in short, folk pharmacy. Conjure involved rituals whereby conjurers, men of power who enjoyed a measure of authority in the slave community, used herbal concoctions, roots, and powders and called upon the spirits to perform "magic."

Conjure served numerous functions within the slave community. It was a means of social control in the slave quarters where white control often inhibited free outward expressions and actions. Whereas the power of the master limited fighting, divorce and other marital issues, and family disputes, conjure served as a vehicle for expressing and alleviating feelings of anger and jealousy and was often used to settle disputes of varying nature.

Slaves often employed conjurers to aid in romance, and conjure was also used in the form of good-luck charms to ward off sickness, misfortune, or another's animosity. Moreover, conjure allowed slaves, to some extent, to exercise power over their masters, and it was often invoked to make masters kind and forgiving or to prevent slaves from being whipped. Of course, there was danger in too heavy a reliance on conjure. A slave exercising conjuration who escaped an offense without chastisement, for whatever reason, may have had his belief in conjuration strengthened only to receive a harsh punishment the next time he tested his master's power.

Conjure could be used for both good and evil, and conjure spells could be undone with the proper counter ritual or potion. With so many spells, incantations, and curses being placed on the plantation, the conjure doctor gained equal business removing the work of other conjurers. Only a conjure doctor could remove the work of another; white man's medicine was useless in treating conjure spells.

Slaves perceived the world and their place in it with conjure at the center of the supernatural world. For slaves, conjure made sense of the mysterious and was a way to try to direct forces that were otherwise beyond their control. It gave slaves the power, or at least the perception of the power, to govern their lives, which were severely restricted by the chains of bondage. Conjure represented the slaves' psychological defense against total dependence on, and submission to, their masters.

The strength of conjure within the slave community illustrates clearly the African element in their culture as conjure combined African and European-American magical lore and fused together various African religious rites. Conjure, a powerful link to the slaves' African past, seems to have been most pronounced in areas where slaves were concentrated in large numbers. In some respects, conjure can be seen as a process of cultural interaction between acquired Christianity and inherited African religious traditions. Although heavily Christianized, blacks in slavery molded their own distinctive religious forms from a mixture of Christian and African elements so that slave religion coexisted alongside conjure, which filled needs unmet by Christianity.

Not all slaves believed in conjure. Many viewed it as irreligious or unchristian, a form of witchcraft or devil worship. Others had, at one time, unsuccessfully tried its powers and had their confidence turn into disbelief. But there were whites who believed in the power of conjuration and occasionally even sought the power of conjurers for certain things. Regardless of its success rate, conjure served a real function in the slave community.

With considerable variation, conjure was practiced throughout the New World slave societies. Since conjuration was often practiced underground or in secret, and is encompassed in a shroud of mystery, documentation is scanty. Discussion of conjuration is, therefore, relatively tentative and speculative. Nevertheless, there is sufficient evidence to show that it did exist and had an important role in the slave community.

—*Sharon Roger Hepburn*

See also
Conjurers
For Further Reading
Brown, David H. 1990. "Conjure/Doctors: An Exploration of a Black Discourse in America, Antebellum to 1940." *Folklore Forum* 23 (1–2): 3–46; Levine, Lawrence W. 1977. *Black Culture and Black Consciousness: Afro-American Folk Thought from Slavery to Freedom*. New York: Oxford University Press; Raboteau, Albert J. 1978. *Slave Religion: The "Invisible Institution" in the Antebellum South*. New York: Oxford University Press; Smith, Theophus. 1994. *Conjuring Culture*. New York: Oxford University Press.

CONJURERS

During the 1930s, an African American representative of the Federal Writers Project interviewed Marrinda Jane Singleton, a Virginia ex-slave born in 1840. "The practice of conjuration," she recalled, "was carried on by quite a few. The Negroes who were from the Indies and other Islands were greatly responsible for these teachings. Although much of it was handed down from the wilds of

Africa. A brewin' of certain concoctions . . . was believed to wuk charms or spells on the persons desired."

In those few words, Singleton touched upon most of the features of "conjuring." Although conjurers did not form an autonomous, institutionalized religion, they drew upon common notions about the interdependence of the spiritual and material worlds to manipulate the former into affecting the latter. The faith in the ability of conjurers to influence supernatural forces was rooted in West African beliefs about the thin, indistinct, and porous boundary between the material and supernatural worlds. These beliefs suggested it was possible to maintain continuing relationships with ancestors, spirits, and gods—and even enlist their aid in temporal affairs. African-born slaves were considered especially qualified to serve as conjurers, and they found the warmest reception in places where the black majority was largest and where memories of Africa were closest, like the Sea Islands of South Carolina and Georgia.

Despite their contacts with the spiritual world, conjurers served very concrete purposes. Consolidating functions that in West Africa would be divided between numerous specialists, in the New World they used charms assembled from herbs, roots, feathers, dirt, and other items to cure the sick; attracted potential mates to their clients; identified thieves and other evildoers; and protected clients from encountering harm at the hands of masters, ghosts, witches, and neighbors. Conjurers could also do harm. As one former slave recalled, "I was conjured once an' don' wan' to be conjured no mo' . . . de spell brung big bumps under both my arms."

The immediate purposes also served greater ends. The widespread belief that conjurers could identify thieves, witches, and other culprits served to check antisocial behavior among slaves, and community harmony would be more likely to prevail if disputants appealed to conjurers rather than coming to blows. Conjurers also reminded believers that masters were not the only powerful force in their world; thus, their existence provided a defense against psychological dependence upon whites. This independent source of power was especially evident when whites consulted conjurers, and equally so when planters betrayed their fears by attempting to suppress conjurers' activities. Conjuring often complemented Christianity as both forms of belief allowed slaves to exercise some control over the mysterious and harsh forces of nature and of human society. While conjurers addressed immediate problems—a mysterious illness or an impending whipping—Christianity provided a framework for understanding long-term developments. Although some Christian slaves believed conjurers to be in the devil's service, more often the two belief systems coexisted.

—*James D. Rice*

See also
Christianity; Obeah; Voodoo
For Further Reading
Genovese, Eugene. 1974. *Roll, Jordan, Roll: The World the Slaves Made*. New York: Pantheon Books; Levine, Lawrence. 1977. *Black Culture and Black Consciousness: Afro-American Folk Thought from Slavery to Freedom*. Oxford: Oxford University Press; Raboteau, Albert J. 1978. *Slave Religion: The "Invisible Institution" in the Antebellum South*. Oxford: Oxford University Press; Roberts, John W. 1989. *From Trickster to Badman: The Black Folk Hero in Slavery and Freedom*. Philadelphia: University of Pennsylvania Press.

CONSCIENCE WHIGS

Conscience Whigs was the name given to the abolitionist wing of the Massachusetts Whig Party of the 1840s whose adamant opposition to the territorial expansion of slavery led to the formation of the Free Soil Party in 1848. During the early 1840s, debate over the annexation of Texas spurred the antislavery sentiments of Northern Whigs, and Massachusetts Whigs adopted a resolution opposing annexation. However, once Congress passed a resolution favoring annexation in February 1845, the Massachusetts Whig leadership, led by Daniel Webster, called for a halt to further opposition. Continued opposition might harm national party unity, and Webster, who aspired to the Whig presidential nomination in 1848, was anxious to downplay sectional issues within the party.

Despite this directive, several youthful party members refused to end their public agitation. These young Whigs, including Charles Sumner, Charles Francis Adams, and John Palfrey, decried the decision to put party interests before individual conscience in this matter. Soon labeled Conscience Whigs, they organized an anti-Texas rally in Boston in November 1845. While Adams chaired the event, Sumner shared the podium with the radical abolitionist William Lloyd Garrison and emerged from the rally as a forceful new voice against slavery. The Conscience Whigs now drew closer to the Garrisonian abolitionists, and the party split into factions, with the more moderate leaders being called Cotton Whigs because of their conciliatory position on Texas and their tendency to underscore the important economic ties between the South and the cotton-manufacturing interests of Massachusetts.

The onset of war with Mexico in spring 1846 was highly unpopular throughout New England and helped swell the ranks of the Conscience Whigs. In an effort to gain control of the state party, that faction's leaders acquired a newspaper, the Boston *Whig*, and with Adams as editor, vigorously criticized the war and the Whig Party for its muted stance on slavery. Introduction of the Wilmot Proviso into Congress in August 1846 augmented the factional infighting. The proviso, which would have banned slavery from territory acquired from Mexico, became the focal point of the Conscience-Cotton conflict. At the state convention of the Massachusetts Whig Party in September, Webster successfully led a platform fight to exclude the antislavery agenda proposed by the Conscience Whigs, including a resolution endorsing the proviso.

Speculation that Zachary Taylor, a Louisiana slaveholder and military hero of the Mexican War, was under consideration for the 1848 Whig presidential nomination led to the final rupture between Conscience and Cotton Whigs. At a convention in September 1847, the Conscience Whigs pressed for a resolution stating that Massachusetts Whigs would support for president only a candidate who was on record as opposing the extension of slavery. The Cotton Whigs, certain that Taylor could win the White House, defeated this resolution.

Now ready to leave the party, the Conscience Whigs waited until Taylor's nomination at the Whig national convention in June 1848 before calling a meeting of all state members opposed to his candidacy. At this breakaway meeting, the Conscience Whigs rallied around the slogan, Free Soil—Free Labor—Free Speech, and sent delegates to a convention in Buffalo, New York, where they joined forces with other disaffected Whigs, antislavery Democrats, and members of the Liberty Party. From this Buffalo convention arose the new antislavery Free Soil Party, pledged to the Wilmot Proviso and with Martin Van Buren as its standard bearer and Charles Francis Adams as its vice-presidential nominee.

—David L. Ferch

See also
Free Soil Party; Garrison, William Lloyd; Wilmot Proviso

For Further Reading
Brauer, Kinley. 1967. *Cotton versus Conscience: Massachusetts Whig Politics and Southwestern Expansion, 1843–1848.* Lexington: University of Kentucky Press; Brock, William. 1979. *Parties and Political American Dilemmas, 1840–1850.* Millwood, NY: KTO Press; Donald, David. 1960. *Charles Sumner and the Coming of the Civil War.* New York: Knopf; Holt, Michael. 1992. *Political Parties and American Political Development from the Age of Jackson to the Age of Lincoln.* Baton Rouge: Louisiana State University Press.

CONSIDERATIONS ON THE KEEPING OF NEGROES

The Quaker abolitionist John Woolman published two antislavery tracts: *Some Considerations on the Keeping of Negroes* (Philadelphia, 1754) and *Considerations on the Keeping of Negroes, Part Second* (Philadelphia, 1762). The first presented Woolman's moral objections to slavery; the second contested rationalizations for slaveholding and implicated slaveowners in the transatlantic commerce in "fellow creatures." Both essays helped launch Quaker abolitionism in the United States and contributed to changing attitudes toward slavery that culminated in the antislavery movements of the late-eighteenth and early-nineteenth centuries.

Woolman first drafted *Some Considerations on the Keeping of Negroes* after witnessing plantation slavery in 1746 during visits to Quakers in Virginia and North Carolina, but he withheld the manuscript until encouraged in 1750 by his ailing father to prepare it for publication. The Quaker Overseers of the Press approved and printed the essay in 1754, the first antislavery pamphlet endorsed and published by the Society of Friends.

Starting from a belief in human equality—"all nations are of one blood," he wrote—Woolman pleaded for charity to the oppressed and restraint in the acquisition of wealth. The Lord had provided for Quaker settlers in America, and society and family benefited more from the example of moral practice than riches. Therefore, Christians were obliged to sympathize with slaves and "make their case ours," even if at the cost of material gain. Unlike his Quaker predecessors Benjamin Lay and Ralph Sandiford, Woolman spared slaveholders from invective. Because he understood the power of habit and interest, Woolman sought merely to disquiet slaveholders by questioning custom, exposing error and inconsistency, and arousing conscience.

Woolman published the second pamphlet at his own expense, preferring not to draw from the Quaker funds because they included contributions from Quaker slaveholders. He believed, too, that the book would receive more careful study if available only through purchase. This second pamphlet exhibited the insight gleaned from several years of entreating slaveholders to free their slaves. Working from similar principles and aims but with less caution than before, Woolman confronted prevailing apologies for slavery. He spoke for the capacities of Africans and their right to equality. Drawing from travel narratives to Africa, he illustrated the "barbarous proceedings" that led to the enslavement and transportation of Africans to the Americas. It was possible in theory, said Woolman, for slaveholders to treat slaves humanely, but few, if any, acquired slaves with charitable intentions or with beneficial effects.

Both pamphlets assisted early attempts by the Philadelphia Yearly Meeting to dissuade Quakers from the sale, purchase, and possession of slaves. In 1754, the Overseers of the Press delivered part one of *Considerations* to the yearly meeting in both England and North America, and passages from the pamphlet were included in a landmark 1754 epistle to the Friends from Philadelphia Yearly Meeting declaring slavery a sin.

Although the essays most influenced the Society of Friends, they circulated widely. The Quaker propagandist Anthony Benezet cited lines from the 1754 tract in the preface to his *Observations on Inslaving, Importing, and Purchasing of Negroes* (1759) and sent both essays with the antislavery pamphlets he distributed in North America and shipped to England. The essays were reprinted and bound with the first American edition of *The Journal of John Woolman* (1774) and with various editions of *The Works of John Woolman* published on both sides of the Atlantic in succeeding decades.

—*Christopher L. Brown*

See also
Quakers; Woolman, John
For Further Reading
Cady, Edwin H. 1966. *John Woolman: The Mind of the Quaker Saint.* New York: Washington Square Press; Drake, Thomas. 1950. *Quakers and Slavery in America.* New Haven, CT: Yale University Press; Gummere, Amelia Mott. 1922. *The Journal and Essays of John Woolman.* New York: Macmillan; Moulton, Phillips P. "The Influence of the Writings of John Woolman." *Quaker History: The Bulletin of the Friends Historical Association* 61 (2): 3–13.

CONTEMPORARY SLAVERY

As the twentieth century ends, slavery still exists in several areas of the world, and the United Nations Working Group on Contemporary Forms of Slavery meets regularly in Geneva to discuss this abhorrent situation. Most shocking, chattel slavery—the sale and ownership of one person by another—exists in the Sudan and Mauritania, and reports from human rights organizations and journalistic accounts document the activities of Arab slave traders selling African children. In addition to chattel slavery, the United Nations Supplementary Convention on the Abolition of Slavery, the Slave Trade, and Institutions and Practices Similar to Slavery (1956) mentions four other forms of slavery: child slavery, bonded labor, enforced prostitution, and the servitude of indigenous peoples.

Anti-Slavery International (ASI), originally the British and Foreign Anti-Slavery Society founded in 1839, is the oldest international human rights group, and it regularly publicizes modern forms of slavery and seeks to eliminate all forms of servitude. Based in Great Britain, this organization issues a quarterly newsletter and special reports on topics ranging from slavery in Brazil to child labor in Nepal. Working with other nongovernment organizations, ASI provides extensive, documented research to various governments and international bodies, including the United Nations.

In several parts of Asia, human rights organizations have reported on both bonded labor and child slavery. In India, Pakistan, and Nepal, children are forcibly employed in the handmade woolen carpet industry. According to an article in the *Atlantic Monthly,* the number of children involved ranges from 500,000 to almost 1 million in Pakistan alone. Iqbal Masih, a Pakistani boy freed from bonded labor became an internationally known activist against child labor. After he was murdered in 1995, the Bonded Labor Liberation Front charged that the 12-year-old was killed by the "carpet mafia." Although this accusation was never proved, the boy's death sparked worldwide outrage and focused attention on the plight of enslaved child laborers.

The children weave on looms in substandard, unsanitary carpet factories, and often they work from sunrise to late at night with virtually no relief. Their wages are barely a pittance, and they are often entrapped in a debt-bondage system that forces them to use their meager earnings to repay loans incurred by their families. Some children are kidnapped off the streets and are then forced to pay off their own ransom.

In U.S. congressional hearings in March 1996, a special UN human rights monitor, Gaspar Biro, reported on the existence of chattel slavery and modern-day slave markets in the Sudan. The victims are mainly indigenous African women and children from the southern Sudan who have been abducted by Arab tribal militias. Biro testified: "I have talked to people, mainly women, children and elderly who were in the worst shape I have ever seen human beings in my life. Inhuman and degrading treatment of the victims by their captors is widespread. Many victims of these violations and abuses are forcibly converted to Islam and are given Arabic names" (U.S. Congress, 1996).

Biro's testimony was corroborated by Kevin Vigilante, a physician who led a fact-finding investigation to Khartoum in 1995 for the Puebla Program on Religious Freedom at Freedom House. Vigilante reported that human beings were sold for $15. "Slavery not only exists in Sudan, but it is increasing and becoming institutionalized," declared the Brown University medical faculty member (U.S. Congress, 1996).

In early 1995, Vigilante and his delegation were the first human rights group to enter northern Sudan in more than a year, and they documented widespread "government-sponsored abductions of children, and a campaign of 'cultural cleansing' targeted at African Christians and animists" (U.S. Congress, 1996). The group charged the Arab government of Sudan with the enslavement of African Christians and asked the U.S. government to speak out against chattel slavery in Sudan. The Sudanese bishop Macram Mas Gassis reported that almost 30,000 children in the Nuba Mountains—the location of his diocese—had been sold into slavery with the approval of the government in Khartoum.

Although the Islamic Republic of Mauritania outlawed slavery on July 5, 1980, human rights organizations and journalists have charged that slavery still exists there. In early 1996, the journalist Samuel Cotton interviewed black Mauritanians in various refugee camps who charged that slavery is still a way of life in their country. Garba Diallo, a Mauritanian scholar in Denmark, conducted an investigation which indicated that slaves were being taken across the Senegal River from Mauritania to Senegal. According to a 1994 study by the organization Human Rights Watch/Africa: "Black Africans in Mauritania are subjected to de facto discriminatory government policies, such as forced Arabization, with serious consequences for their civil and political rights. Slavery continues to exist in Mauritania, especially in the countryside. Its persistence is due to inadequate efforts by the government to educate slaves about their rights and to prosecute slaveholders for continuing to own slaves. Those slaves who attempt to escape are sometimes subjected to severe punishment and torture" (U.S. Congress, 1996).

Despite the publication of numerous human rights reports and the testimony of eyewitnesses, the issue of slavery still fails to ignite major world protests such as those against apartheid. Some commentators attribute the silence to the pressure of Arab and other Third World governments to stifle discussion of these human rights abuses. Another possible factor may be the lack of searing visual images. Michael Dottridge, director of Anti-Slavery International, has complained, "There's always the 'show-me-the-picture' problem." Slavery in the twentieth century does not involve whips, chains, and public auctions. Rather, it is sustained through complex relationships such as forced labor, debt-bondage, and the rarely observed activities of modern-day Arab slave traders. These forms of slavery, unfortunately, cannot easily be captured by a camera.

—*Donald Altschiller*

See also
American Anti-Slavery Group
For Further Reading
Miers, Suzanne. 1996. "Contemporary Forms of Slavery." *Slavery and Abolition* 17: 238–246; Rone, Jemera. 1995. *Children in Sudan: Slaves, Street Children, and Child Soldiers.* New York: Human Rights Watch; Silvers, Jonathan. 1996. "Child Labor in Pakistan." *Atlantic Monthly* (February): 79–92; U.S. Congress, House of Representatives. Committee on International Relations. 1996. *Slavery in Mauritania and Sudan.* Joint Hearings. March 13, 1996. Washington, DC: Government Printing Office.

CONTRABAND

If one applies the broadest definition of the word "contraband" to the trade in slaves, much of the slave trade after 1807 would fall into this category since the governments of Great Britain and the United States outlawed the trade early in the nineteenth century. Still, even though the illegal import and export of slaves into the United States and other nations continued for much of that century, despite the attempts to suppress it by those nation's navies, that trade is not generally considered "contraband." In practical application, contraband slavery refers to the period of the U.S. Civil War and the slaves that escaped to or were delivered to Union territory. Those slaves were considered legitimate contraband of war; labor was deemed a valuable commodity that was subject to confiscation by either belligerent faction.

Federal policy about contraband slavery did not come about by purposeful mandate; instead, it was a response to the actions of the Union general Benjamin Butler in the opening phases of the war. Butler, who originally commanded the Eighth Massachusetts Volunteers, was commissioned for political reasons rather than military experience. The opinionated and willful man had shown his contempt for the Confederacy and for the chain of command by occupying Baltimore, Maryland, on May 13–14, 1861, without the authorization of his commanding general, Winfield Scott. On May 22, Butler was given the command of Fort Monroe near Newport News, Virginia, which he occupied with no opposition. Scott then expressly forbade him to take any further action without formal authorization.

Butler was soon presented with another opportunity to assert his personality when three slaves belonging to a colonel of the Confederate army escaped behind Butler's lines. When the colonel asked for their return, Butler indignantly refused on the grounds that they would be put to work against the Union building fortifications. Butler held the slaves as contraband of

An undated drawing by Edwin Forbes depicts fugitive slaves entering Union lines in a farm wagon called a "schooner." A few laggards appear on a distant hill, one waving his hat for joy at the sight of the Union soldiers.

war, claiming that they were valuable workmen, and as word of his actions circulated, Fort Monroe became a destination for scores of escaping slaves who soon renamed it "Fort Freedom." By May 27, 67 slaves had sought refuge; by July, that number had increased to about 900 men, women, and children.

Responsibility for establishing refugee camps and employment for escaped slaves fell largely upon the army. At the time of Butler's decision, the Fugitive Slave Act of 1850, which dictated that the failure to return an escaped slave to a master was a criminal offense, remained in effect. Federal marshals bore the burden of restoring fugitive slaves to their former owners, and in the border states, many owners offered exorbitant "apprehension fees" to any civilian or military personnel who could return a contraband fugitive.

As the war progressed and more and more slaves fled to Union lines, it became a matter of course to consider all masters as disloyal. Refugee slaves came to be considered the captured property of the Union army and were put to work at various tasks. At Fort Mon-

roe, the general's quartermaster doled out heavy labor to the contraband slaves, like loading and unloading supply vessels or constructing earthworks and fortifications. Some became servants of ranking officers, and a few others acted as scouts through the swamps and forests of the area. These men were paid modest sums for their efforts, with certain deductions for the upkeep of their families. The army also issued "certificates of liberation" to the former slaves that it employed. Butler established a school for the fugitives, with day classes for children and night classes for adults.

Campaigning armies and established forts attracted refugee slaves, at times by the thousands. Contraband slaves were not always as welcomed as they were at Fort Monroe—many Yankees were bitterly prejudiced and thought that the refugees would contribute to the demoralization of the entire army. Certain commanders, like Ulysses S. Grant, employed slave men in making entrenchments and bearing equipment and assigned slave women to work in the kitchens and hospitals during his western campaigns in Mississippi.

Other refugee slaves could be put to work for pay on confiscated or abandoned plantations that were leased to white tenants. Far more were not as fortunate: following the siege of Vicksburg, 30,000 contraband slaves died on the ravaged streets from disease and starvation. Eastern philanthropists were basically unable to improve the squalor of the refugee camps, which were almost always short of housing and food.

In 1863, enlistment in the army became another option for the employment of contraband slaves. There had been great support for this idea since the outset of the war by abolitionists, but opposition remained strong and feelings over black troops were quite divided. Before the establishment of black regiments and the Emancipation Proclamation, black troops were enrolled in Union militias as early as 1861 in the taking of New Orleans. One even finds precedent for contraband slavery and the employment of black troops in the American Revolution, when Lord Dunmore offered freedom to any slave who would take up arms against the American rebels. It is estimated that as many as 25,000 slaves were persuaded to side with the British.

President Lincoln decided that the secession of the Southern states had made the Fugitive Slave Act of 1850 null and void and endorsed the contraband ruling at Fort Freedom, referring to it as "Butler's fugitive slave law." In July 1862, the second Confiscation Act declared that it was an offense for any member of the Union forces to relinquish an escaped slave to an owner and also established that escaped slaves of disloyal masters were "forever free." In a way, General Butler's decision can be considered as the first step toward actual emancipation.

—*David A. Johnson*

See also
Confiscation Acts

CONVICT TRANSPORTATION

onvict transportation to distant colonies has been practiced by several major powers, but the most well-known is that from Great Britain to Australia in the eighteenth and nineteenth centuries. Convicts were not slaves in a legal sense as they were not bought and sold and their descendants were free. Yet they were used in occupations that would not otherwise have attracted labor, like building roads, clearing land, and maintaining public works.

The British system, which dated back to the seventeenth century and was legitimated by the Transportation Act of 1718, used convicts to develop plantations in the Caribbean and the southern American colonies. After the American Revolution, Britain sought other locations for transportation, and the most important of the new areas was on the southeast coast of Australia, claimed for Britain by Capt. James Cook in 1770. The colony of New South Wales was established in 1787, and the first fleet of convicts arrived on January 26, 1788, which is still commemorated as Australia Day. The initial landing was at Botany Bay, but settlement was quickly moved to the current site of Sydney, which had a better water supply. The name "Botany Bay" remained popular in Britain to describe all convict settlements in Australia.

Convict settlements were extended to Van Diemen's Land (Tasmania) in 1803, and it became a distinct colony in 1825, notorious for the rigor of its systems of punishment and imprisonment. Smaller colonies were created at Newcastle in New South Wales and at Moreton Bay near the modern city of Brisbane. Remote Norfolk Island was dreaded as a place of secondary punishment from 1788 to 1806 and 1826 to 1855. Transportation was extended to Western Australia between 1850 and 1868, by which time it had been abandoned in the eastern colonies. Convicts were not transported to the colonies of South Australia or Victoria though many former convicts went from Van Diemen's Land to Victoria in the early 1850s to search for gold. Most Australian colonies had convicts, but they were numerically most important in New South Wales and Van Diemen's Land.

The original purposes of transportation to Australia have been debated by historians. One was to clear the overcrowded prison hulks anchored in the Thames and Medway Rivers and Portsmouth Harbor because the prison system was unable to cope with the pressures created by industrialization and the end of the Napoleonic Wars. The number transported reached a peak between 1828 and 1843. Although estimates vary slightly, the total transported between 1788 and 1868 was 160,000—divided between 78,000 to New South Wales, 66,000 to Van Diemen's Land, 10,000 to Western Australia, and smaller numbers to Norfolk Island and elsewhere.

Transportation lasted from 1788 until 1851 in New South Wales and until 1853 in Van Diemen's Land. Most of the convicts were English and included women in eastern Australia but not in the western part. One-quarter were Irish; Scottish law inhibited overseas transportation. The abolition of slavery in Mauritius and the Caribbean in 1834 led to a small number of ex-slaves being transported from those areas for various offenses, but most convicts were of British or Irish origin, with Londoners being strongly represented in the early transports.

The brutality of the convict system has been a subject of debate, with the strongest condemnation being found in Robert Hughes's popular book *The Fatal Shore* (1987). Penal centers like Port Arthur, Norfolk Island, or the Newcastle coal mines were especially feared, and much attention is given in popular accounts to flogging and other severe punishments. Many convicts were assigned to employers, especially as shepherds, and some were able to reunite with their families.

A ticket-of-leave system allowed many convicts to enter civilian life, and some became very prosperous—some even formed the first police force in New South Wales. These freed "emancipists" were an important element in Sydney and were assimilated into society between 1810 and 1821; many families in New South Wales and Tasmania were anxious to obscure the "convict stain" of their ancestry. Convict labor was essential to public works, the early mining and wool industries, and some rural settlements. By the 1840s, the policy was being attacked as a form of slavery and was replaced by paid assistance for free settlers from the British Isles.

—*James Jupp*

COROMANTEE

Coromantee (Cromantyn, Kormantan, Kormantin) refers to the town of Kormantin located along the Gold Coast (now the Republic of Ghana) and was also the name given to Gold Coast slaves in many parts of the New World. Founded by members of a black ethnic group, the Fanti, Kormantin became a major port for British and Dutch merchants in the seventeenth century. The first European traders arriving on the Gold Coast, the Portuguese, showed no interest in Kormantin, and initially, neither did the Dutch, even after receiving permission from the king of Kormantin to trade in 1624. But after 1631, when the British received local authorization to build a trade fort in Kormantin, the town became a leading commercial center in the Atlantic trade in gold and slaves. The British first built a lodge on the Gold Coast and expanded it later into a full-fledged fort complete with barracoons (cells or barracks) for holding slaves bound for the Americas.

From 1631 to 1665, Kormantin remained the headquarters of the British trade on the Gold Coast. Following Britain's conquest of Jamaica in 1655, there was a rise in the demand for slave labor on the island, and Kormantin served as the primary port for meeting that demand. Consequently, Gold Coast slaves in Jamaica and elsewhere in the Americas were called Coromantees, and the name persisted long after the British had lost control of their fort at Kormantin. New World slaveholders claimed that Coromantee slaves were strong, warlike, and prone to instigating and leading slave plots and revolts.

The lucrative trade in gold and slaves at Kormantin soon attracted the attention of the Dutch. In 1665, during the Second Anglo-Dutch War, the Dutch and their African allies captured the fort and renamed it Fort Amsterdam. The trade in gold and slaves at Kormantin remained profitable during the Dutch tenure (1665–1868), and the many reconstructions of Fort Amsterdam during this period provide eloquent testimony of the importance of the slave and gold trade at Kormantin.

Gold Coast rulers were keenly aware of the favorable trade opportunities at Kormantin. During the Dutch capture of the Kormantin fort, the king of Kormantin used the occasion to advance his economic prospects by agreeing to help the Dutch in exchange for monetary payment and an agreement on the part of the Dutch to pay duties on each trade ship calling at Kormantin. Similarly, in 1807, partly because of the need to obtain and protect access to coastal trading, members of the Ashanti people invaded and looted the fort.

Following the abolition of slavery, declining profits coupled with the rising cost of maintaining the forts compelled the Dutch and the British to agree to an exchange of their forts on the Gold Coast. This 1867 agreement placed the fort at Kormantin in the hands of the British once again, and they controlled it until Ghana achieved independence in 1957.

—*Patience Essah*

For Further Reading
Boahen, Adu. 1975. *Ghana: Evolution and Change in the Nineteenth and Twentieth Centuries*. London: Longman; Daaku, Kwame Yeboa. 1970. *Trade and Politics on the Gold Coast, 1600–1720: A Study of the African Reaction to European Trade*. Oxford: Oxford University Press; van Dantzig, Albert. 1980. *A Short History of the Forts and Castles of Ghana*. Accra: Sedco Publishing; Dickson, Kwamina B. 1969. *A Historical Geography of Ghana*. Cambridge: Cambridge University Press.

COURTS OF MIXED COMMISSION

Courts of mixed commission were international courts operating throughout the Atlantic region between 1819 and 1871 to adjudicate cases of slave vessels suspected of violating treaties ending the slave trade between Great Britain and various states of Europe and the Americas. The treaties generally stipulated that a court be located in territory belonging to each of the signing countries.

Two commissioners, one from the country that had

arrested the slaver and one from the slaver's country, would hear a case. If acquitted, the vessel was immediately returned to the owners, who could appeal for compensation for losses. If condemned, the slaves on board were immediately landed and emancipated and the vessel was taken as a prize and auctioned, with the proceeds being divided between the two countries. The court could not prosecute the crew, who were turned over to their country's authorities. British commissioners were paid generously as an inducement to brave the oftentimes dangerous climate (in Sierra Leone, for example, commissary judges received a staggering £3,000 per year), but despite that inducement, many of the commissions, and the proctors representing the accused, were not legally qualified.

Before 1845, most of the cases were tried in the first courts established in 1819: the Anglo-Portuguese commission in Rio de Janeiro (after Brazilian independence in 1822, it became an Anglo-Brazilian commission), the Anglo-Spanish in Havana, the Anglo-Dutch in Suriname, and three commissions in the British colony of Sierra Leone. An Anglo-Brazilian commission was added to Sierra Leone in 1826, and other courts were established, after 1842, in Luanda (Angola), Boa Vista (Cape Verde Islands), Spanish Town (Jamaica), Cape Town (South Africa), and, in 1862, New York (United States).

In 1831, France agreed to mutual search of vessels, but that country never agreed to a mixed commission; insisting, instead, that the vessels be taken to its national court. Many countries followed the French model. Only Chile, the Argentine confederation, Uruguay, Bolivia, and Ecuador agreed to the mixed courts (all between 1839 and 1841) after the original four were established, and these countries waived their right to establish a court on their territory and the right to send a commissioner to Sierra Leone.

In theory, the bilateral treaties signed with Britain called for reciprocity at all levels of the antislavery enforcement process, but, as with the naval patrols, the administration of justice was largely done by the British. Of 623 cases heard between 1819 and 1845, 528 were adjudicated in Sierra Leone, which consequently received an estimated 65,000 liberated Africans. Oftentimes, British commissioners heard the cases alone because the other countries involved had not bothered to replace their commissioners.

The process became even more exclusively British after the Palmerston Act (1839), which, among other aggressive measures, sanctioned the prosecution of Portuguese, and later Brazilian, slavers at British vice-admiralty courts. In fact, British officers of the African Squadron were largely turning to the vice-admiralty courts by 1845, which severely curtailed the use of the courts of mixed commission.

—*Jeff Pardue*

See also
African Squadron; Palmerston Act; Sierra Leone
For Further Reading
Bethell, Leslie. 1966. "The Mixed Commissions for the Suppression of the Transatlantic Slave Trade in the Nineteenth Century." *Journal of African History* 7 (1): 79–93; Eltis, David. 1987. *Economic Growth and the Ending of the Transatlantic Slave Trade*. Oxford: Oxford University Press; Fyfe, Christopher. 1962. *A History of Sierra Leone*. Oxford: Oxford University Press.

CRAFT, WILLIAM (1827–1900) AND ELLEN (C. 1826–1890)

William and Ellen Craft gained national attention in the United States because of the circumstances of their escape from slavery in 1848. The two married in Macon, Georgia, while both were slaves, and later they decided to flee the South in search of freedom. William, a cabinetmaker whose master allowed him to work independently, used his earnings to buy disguises and pay for travel costs, and the two obtained passes to leave Macon during the Christmas season.

Ellen, the daughter of a former master, wore dark glasses and a muffler to hide her face while posing as an elderly and ailing master, with William playing the part of a faithful servant. With her right arm in a sling, the illiterate Ellen was able to avoid signing hotel registers or other documents. They traveled by train and steamer without incident until they reached Baltimore, the last slave city on their journey. Maryland law required masters to sign and post bond for any slaves accompanying them to the North, but William's plea for his master's urgent need of medical care persuaded the railroad agent to waive the requirement. On the train they met a free African American who directed them to a Philadelphia abolitionist.

After resting briefly in Philadelphia the Crafts continued to Boston accompanied by the former slave and abolitionist William Wells Brown. They had a second wedding in Boston, where they remained for two years. There, William worked as a cabinetmaker and Ellen trained as a seamstress, and they were both active in the antislavery movement. In October 1850, when agents of their masters appeared in Boston with warrants for their arrest under the new Fugitive Slave Act, the Crafts fled the United States. Assisted by other abolitionists they went first to Nova Scotia and then to England.

The Crafts attended British antislavery meetings and attracted attention when they visited the Crystal Palace Exhibition of 1851. Their five children were born in England, where they lived until after the U.S. Civil War. In 1868 they returned briefly to Boston, then moved to Georgia to manage an industrial school financed by English and American abolitionists. After the Ku Klux Klan burned the school, the Crafts supervised a similar project located on a Bryan County, Georgia, plantation. That site later became the Craft family plantation.

The Crafts frequently spoke publicly about their dramatic escape, which relied solely on their ingenious plan. While in England they told their story in the book, *Running a Thousand Miles for Freedom; or The Escape of William and Ellen Craft from Slavery* (1860). Their association with the Underground Railroad was typical of many other escapes from slavery. Although they eventually received valuable assistance, it was only after reaching the North that they received any help beyond their own resources.

—*Larry Gara*

See also
Brown, William Wells; Fugitive Slave Act of 1850; Underground Railroad
For Further Reading
Blackett, R. J. M. 1978. "Fugitive Slaves in Britain: The Odyssey of William and Ellen Craft." *Journal of American Studies* 12: 41–62; Craft, William and Ellen. 1860. *Running a Thousand Miles for Freedom; or The Escape of William and Ellen Craft from Slavery.* London: William Tweedie; Still, William. 1883. *The Underground Railroad.* Philadelphia: William Still; Woodson, Carter G., ed. 1926. *The Mind of the Negro as Reflected in Letters Written during the Crisis, 1800–1860.* Washington, DC: Association for the Study of Negro Life and History.

CRANDALL, PRUDENCE (1803–1889)

Prudence Crandall became famous in 1833 when she defied Northern racial prejudice by accepting black students into her Canterbury, Connecticut, female boarding school. Abolitionist leaders seized on Crandall's action and Connecticut's violent reaction as a means to promote antislavery and to demonstrate to white Northerners the danger slavery and prejudice posed to their own civil liberties. When Sarah Harris, the daughter of a local black farmer and abolitionist, asked to attend the all-white school so that she could learn enough to teach black children, Crandall could not say no. The school's board of visitors demanded that Crandall remove Harris; if she did not, they would remove the white pupils. Crandall refused, then took her stand against racism further: she dismissed the white students and announced she would take only black students. The school for black girls opened on April 1, 1833.

The town's attack proceeded on two fronts, in the courts and the state legislature and through intimidation. Urged by a prominent member of the board of visitors, the Connecticut state legislature passed a "black law" in 1833 requiring local approval for schools to admit out-of-state black students and instituting onerous fines for those who violated the new policy. The authorities arrested Crandall, but she would not post bond so the town was forced to jail her, an action abolitionist leaders eagerly publicized. Her trial in August 1833 ended in a hung jury, but she was found guilty in October by the state supreme court. That decision was overturned on appeal because of a technicality.

All this time Crandall continued her school, which endured boycotts by the town's storekeepers, churches, and doctors. Townspeople smashed windows and dumped manure in the well; they insulted Crandall and the black students on the street and threw manure and dead animals at them. One student was arrested for vagrancy and threatened with public whipping. The terrorism continued after the court decisions—including an arson attempt while Crandall, her husband, and the students were sleeping, and a midnight attack on September 9, 1834, by a mob that smashed windows and downstairs rooms with clubs and iron bars. The mob attack convinced Crandall that the danger was extreme, and she reluctantly closed the school.

After Crandall gave up her school she dropped from the public eye. In the mid-1870s a regiment of black soldiers raised money to assist her, and several of her black students did become teachers. Although her antislavery stand occurred during only a small portion of her life, Crandall's principles and her sufferings on behalf of those principles placed her in the community of martyrs who were admired and publicized by abolitionist speakers and newspapers throughout the antebellum period.

—*Andrea M. Atkin*

For Further Reading
Foner, Philip. 1984. "Prudence Crandall." In *Three Who Dared: Prudence Crandall, Margaret Douglass, and Myrtilla Miner—Champions of Antebellum Black Education.* Ed. Philip S. Foner and Josephine F. Pacheco. Westport, CT: Greenwood Press; Fuller, Edmond. 1971. *Prudence Crandall: An Incident of Racism in Nineteenth-Century Connecticut.* Middletown, CT: Wesleyan University Press.

CRASSUS, MARCUS LICINIUS
(C. 115–53 B.C.)

Marcus Licinius Crassus, known for his primary role in suppressing the Spartacus servile rebellion, was a Roman soldier and an aristocratic politician. In his youth he served with his father in Spain, where he later fled during the bloody purges of Gaius Marius and Lucius Cornelius Cinna. He joined Lucius Cornelius Sulla during the civil war against the Marians (83–82 B.C.) and distinguished himself in the Battle of Colline Gate in 82 B.C. During the proscriptions of Sulla, he amassed a fortune (his surname was Dives, meaning "the rich") by money-lending, educating his slaves and selling them at high prices, and speculating in real estate.

Crassus owned numerous slaves, including some who were scribes, readers, silversmiths, stewards, and table servants. He trained or taught many of them himself, considering it his duty to treat slaves as "the living tools of household management" (Adcock, 1966). He purchased hundreds of slaves who were skilled as builders and architects. Then he bought houses that were on fire and those adjoining as well at very low prices. Using his slaves to rebuild the residences, Crassus became the city's biggest landlord.

Meanwhile, he pursued a political career, rising to the position of praetor in 73 B.C. When Spartacus led an uprising of gladiators and slaves in 73 B.C. (the Servile War) and defeated several Roman armies, the terrified Senate bestowed a proconsular command on Crassus. He conducted a vigorous six-month campaign, even resorting to the old practice of decimation when some of his troops displayed cowardice. He pursued the rebels into southern Italy. In an effort to pen up Spartacus, probably on the promontory of Scyllaeum, Crassus ordered his soldiers to dig a ditch 15 feet wide and deep, which was backed by a rampart. After two unsuccessful breakout attempts Spartacus managed to escape, but the Roman troops slaughtered thousands of his followers.

Crassus then twice defeated breakaway rebel contingents commanded by Cannicus and Castus. Subsequently, Crassus hunted down Spartacus and the remnants of his band and routed them. Spartacus supposedly died in the fighting, but his body was never identified. Crassus closed his campaign by having 6,000 prisoners crucified along the Appian Way between Capua and Rome.

Gnaeus Pompeius Magnus (Pompey) intercepted and killed several thousand of the fugitives and then claimed partial credit for suppressing the Spartacus insurrection, thus alienating Crassus. The Senate decided that Crassus's victory did not merit a triumph and granted him a mere ovation, although with the special honor of a laurel wreath instead of the traditional myrtle.

Despite their differences, Pompey and Crassus served together as consuls in 70 B.C. After his consulship Crassus remained in the Senate and gave his support to promising young politicians, including Gaius Julius Caesar. Crassus served as censor in 65–64 B.C., and in 59 he joined Pompey and Caesar in the First Triumvirate. In 55, he and Pompey again served as consuls. After receiving a special command in Syria, Crassus crossed the Euphrates River and attacked Parthia. He suffered a disastrous defeat in 53 B.C. at Carrhae in Mesopotamia, where he died.

—*Charles H. McArver, Jr.*

See also
Spartacus
For Further Reading
Adcock, F. E. 1966. *Marcus Crassus Millionaire.* Cambridge: Cambridge University Press; Crook, J. A.; Andrew Lintott; and Elizabeth Rawson, eds. 1994. *The Cambridge Ancient History. Vol. 9.* New York: Cambridge University Press; Marshall, B. A. 1976. *Crassus: A Political Biography.* Amsterdam: A. M. Hakkert; Ward, A. M. 1977. *Marcus Crassus and the Late Roman Republic.* Columbia: University of Missouri Press.

CREOLE LANGUAGES

Creole languages, spoken natively by millions of people around the globe, have their origin in settings of extended cultural contact. Because they are first languages, they meet the full range of their speakers' communicative needs. Because they are human languages, they are characterized by stylistic repertoires and socially conditioned variations and are subject to linguistic change. Creole languages are describable by systematic grammatical rules and, as such, are amenable to standardization.

Creolization, as it is generally understood, can result from the nativization of a pidgin as occurred with Sango in the Central African Republic and with Tok Pisin in Papua New Guinea. Alternatively, as in the Caribbean, creolization can result when the setting in which adults attempting to learn a second language is characterized by extreme cultural, psychological, and/or social distance from native speakers of that language. In settings where the politically subordinate, or substrate, population greatly outnumbers the politically dominant, or superstrate, population, there is inadequate access to the superstrate language for true learning to occur. For example, in Haiti, where speakers of the substrate languages greatly outnumbered speakers of French, the second generation (i.e., the African American population) did not learn French but created Creole. In such settings, although second-language acquisition is initiated, it does not proceed very far, and the varieties the learners develop become the language of children born into the community.

Alternatively, when there is adequate access to the superstrate language for acquisition to occur but the relationship between the two groups is characterized by extreme cultural and psychological distance, the superstrate population's language and culture will be rejected in favor of the Creole culture and language emerging in the substrate community. A third possibility, which is only beginning to receive attention, involves modification of the superstrate language by a white Creole population because of intense contact with a substrate population.

The word *Creole* has its origin in the Spanish/Portuguese terms for persons, either European American or African American, born in the New World. Thus, a Creole language was originally a language spoken by a Creole population. In 1770, the first published study of a Creole language appeared in a grammar that was intended to regularize and develop Hoch Kreol, a variety of Dutch spoken by the Danish West Indies' white population. Seven years later, Moravian missionary Christian Oldendorp, in remarking on Negerhollands, the variety of Dutch used by the black population in that same colony, used the word *Creole* when referring to "every European language which is spoken in a corrupted manner [by Negroes] in the West Indies" (Oldendorp, 1987). It is this second meaning (i.e., the languages of the African American population in the Caribbean) that linguists in the twentieth century usually have in mind when they speak of Creole language. The rapid expansion of Creole studies since the mid-1970s had included a broadening in focus from the study of Caribbean Creole languages to the study of creolization as a process of contact-induced language creation around the globe.

There is now general agreement that the Creole languages are genetic hybrids. In settings where political power is unevenly distributed among groups (e.g., colonies), vocabulary tends to be drawn primarily from the superstrate population while phonology is initially sharply constrained by the native languages of the substrate population. Sources of Creole syntax remain a hotly debated issue, with some researchers arguing that like phonology, Creole syntax has its source primarily in the substrate languages; others argue that Creole syntax reflects linguistic universals. There is additional substantial disagreement about theories of Creole genesis and about the centrality of definitional criteria, for example, whether structural criteria and/or historical circumstances are either necessary or sufficient to identify a language as a Creole language.

—Robin Sabino

See also
Gullah

For Further Reading
The Encyclopedia of Language and Linguistics, s.v. "Pidgins and Creoles" and "Pidgins, Creoles, and Change." 1994. Ed. R. E. Asher. New York: Pergamon Press; Holm, John. 1988–1989. *Pidgins and Creoles*. 2 vols. Cambridge: Cambridge University Press; *International Encyclopedia of Linguistics*, s.v. "Pidgins and Creoles." 1994. Ed. William Bright. New York: Oxford University Press; Oldendorp, C. G. A. [1777] 1987. *A Caribbean Mission*. Ed. and trans. Arnold R. Highfield and Vladimir Barac. Ann Arbor, MI: Karoma Publishers.

CRITTENDEN COMPROMISE

On December 18, 1860, in an effort to avoid destroying the United States over the unresolved issues of slavery and states' rights, Kentucky senator John Jordan Crittenden presented several proposals to the U.S. Senate, including six possible amendments to the Constitution and four resolutions.

Crittenden's proposals included these stipulations. One, in lands already in possession of the United States (or yet to be acquired north of 36° 30'), slavery would be prohibited; south of the line, slavery would be protected as property. Two, Congress could not abolish slavery in areas under federal control in the slave states. Three, Congress could not abolish slavery in the District of Columbia without compensation to the owners and the consent of the states of Maryland and Virginia. Four, Congress could not interfere with the interstate transportation of slaves. Five, Congress would have to compensate owners of fugitive slaves. And six, Congress should not have the power to interfere with slavery where it already existed by the passage of constitutional amendments that would alter the fugitive slave law or interfere with slavery in the states.

Crittenden's compromise also included the following four resolutions. First, the fugitive slave law was constitutional, and therefore it should be enforced. Second, any state laws (personal liberty acts) that conflicted with the fugitive slave law were to be null and void and should be repealed by the states. Third, Congress should amend the fugitive slave law to remove certain passages that were offensive to Northern citizens. Fourth, Congress should enforce and further strengthen laws forbidding the foreign slave trade.

The Senate appointed a committee of 13 and the

House a committee of 33 to review Crittenden's plan. On December 22, 1860, the Senate committee rejected the plan because President-elect Lincoln and the Republicans refused to compromise on the extension of slavery into the territories. In February and March 1860, Congress passed a resolution to prohibit interference with slavery in the states by the federal government, but it was not ratified by the states.

The rejection of these proposals was a terrible blow to those hoping for a peaceful solution to the nation's problems. Crittenden received approbations from many Americans for his efforts to reach an agreement between North and South, and moderates from both sections of the nation earnestly hoped for an acceptable alternative to the specter of disunion. A convention of the states of the upper South held in Washington, D.C., February 4–27, 1861, endeavored to modify the Crittenden Compromise, but it failed to satisfy either section of the country and eventually only added to the confusion and distrust between the two regions. The Crittenden Compromise was a desperate effort to salvage a disintegrating Union, and by rejecting that effort, the U.S. government faced the grim reality of not only the breakup of the Union but, ultimately, civil war.

—Ron D. Bryant

See also
Peace Convention
For Further Reading
Coleman, Mrs. Chapman. 1871. *The Life of John J. Crittenden.* Philadelphia: J. B. Lippincott; Kirwan, Albert D. 1962. *John J. Crittenden: The Struggle for the Union.* Lexington: University of Kentucky Press.

CROWTHER, SAMUEL AJAYI (C. 1806–1891)

An ex-slave, educator, missionary, linguist, translator, statesman, and pioneer Africanist, Samuel Ajayi Crowther also was the first African bishop of the Anglican Church. Born in Osogun, an Oyo-Yoruba town in present-day Nigeria, Crowther was captured in 1821 when his town was destroyed during a war fought in lands controlled by the Yoruba people. En route to the Americas after being sold by his captors to slave traders, British African Squadron vessels captured the Portuguese slave ship Crowther was being carried on near Lagos. The British took the *Esperanza Felix* to Sierra Leone, Britain's experimental colony for ex-slaves, where its crew was imprisoned and its slaves were freed.

In Sierra Leone, Ajayi distinguished himself as an industrious, intelligent, humble, and highly capable young man. These qualities endeared him to Church Missionary Society (CMS) agents who witnessed his conversion and baptism in December 1825, when he took the name Samuel Crowther after a prominent British CMS supporter. Crowther became fluent in English within six months, and in 1826 he followed a missionary to England, where he studied briefly at the parish school in Islington. Returning to Freetown, he became the first student to enroll at Fourah Bay College, West Africa's first institution of higher learning. Crowther later taught in various mission and government schools, including Fourah Bay College.

As part of a philanthropic movement to eliminate the West African slave trade at its source, three expeditions were sent into regions adjoining the Niger River to open them to the gospel, and Crowther accompanied all three. These trips allowed him to demonstrate his qualities of leadership and endurance, qualities that made a lasting impression on his superiors in Sierra Leone and England. Ordained a priest in 1844, he worked with a Reverend Townsend to establish a strong CMS church in Abeokuta in present-day Nigeria between 1845 and 1846. He worked assiduously for years as superintendent of the Niger Mission, opening several mission stations from Bonny and Brass in the Niger Delta, to Onitsha in central Igboland, and Lokoja and Jebba in the Sudan's Islamic Nupe country.

Through time, with astuteness and patience, Crowther witnessed the conversion of kings and commoners, the extirpation of repugnant customs like human sacrifice and the gradual abolition of other customs such as polygamy, slavery, and the slave trade. He persistently advocated progressive measures regarding Africa's agricultural and industrial development and consistently supported using Africans to evangelize the "dark continent" in continuing partnership with Europe.

A versatile linguist, he compiled and wrote the first major dictionary and grammar of the Yoruba language and also translated the English Bible and the baptismal service into the same language. By any standard, these were significant achievements, and they brought him considerable recognition. He visited England several times, interviewed and corresponded with the famous British foreign secretary, Lord Palmerston, and was received at Windsor Castle by Queen Victoria and Prince Albert. Based upon his literary works, Oxford University conferred on him the honorary degree of Doctor of Divinity in 1862. Despite opposition from white clergymen, who resented being led by Africans on racial grounds and especially by this upstart ex-slave, the archbishop of Canterbury made Crowther the first Anglican bishop of West Africa in 1864. Crowther's experience became a powerful propaganda weapon for the CMS: his story an epic of the antislavery movement, and his long and eventful life an illustration of the redeeming grace of the gospel.

—*Funso Afolayan*

See also
Abolition, British Empire; Church Missionary Society; Sierra Leone; Slave Coast; The Yoruba

For Further Reading
Ajayi, Joseph Ade. 1965. *Christian Missions in Nigeria, 1841–1891: The Making of a New Elite*. London: Longman; Ayandele, Emmanuel. 1966. *The Missionary Impact on Modern Nigeria*. London: Longman; Crowther, Samuel. 1970. *Journal of an Expedition up the Niger and Tshadda Rivers*. London: Frank Cass.

CUBAN SLAVE MARKET

Nineteenth-century colonial Cuba was characterized by the great scale of its sugarcane cultivation and export. Slavery was the basis of this production, but it was not until the late-eighteenth century that slavery became very visible. Between 1790 and 1800, as a partial consequence of the Saint Domingue revolt and the Napoleonic period, Cuba's market experienced the beginning of its commercial hegemony in producing and exporting the island's tropical products.

After that time, with its resulting growth of haciendas, or plantations, Cuba's slave market experienced a stable period of regular imports, totaling about 325,000 imported slaves. The greatest magnitude of imports occurred between 1815 and 1820 when 140,000 slaves entered Cuba. It is not by chance that the first Anglo-Spanish treaty against the African slave *trata* ("traffic") was proposed in 1817 or that as a consequence, a radical increase of slave imports followed. Although these years saw the largest number of slaves entering Cuba of any period, very little fluctuation was registered in price, with the average sale price going from 341 pesos to 470 pesos per slave. A second period of notable slave importing occurred from 1821 to 1835, but it was characterized by short fluctuations in both the magnitude of the number of imports and the slave prices. During a third period, from 1836 to 1850, price stability returned with the average slave selling at 400 pesos or less, though imports declined slightly. Not until after 1850 did Cuba's market experience a drastic change.

In 1857, world sugar prices rose incredibly from 4 to 14 cents per pound, and slave prices in Cuba also rose, from an average of 393 pesos per slave in 1850 to an average of 809 pesos in 1859. The incredible aspect of the price increase was that these values remained

A trader from the country barters poultry for a slave in a mid-nineteenth-century Cuban market.

the same until the movement to abolish slavery began in 1868, which demonstrates that the emancipatory process was unrelated to sugar plantation productivity. The continued dependence of sugar planters on slavery demonstrates the market's profitability (Bergad, Iglesias, and Barcia, 1995).

During this period, slaveowners maintained their sugar plantations' efficiency, which required a secure and continuous slave supply, but such a supply was not always available because occasionally it was threatened, mainly by the anti-trade politics of several governments. At such times, owners were forced to seek other means of satisfying their needs. For example, owners would then prefer acquiring female slaves over the equally subordinate males, because uncertainty about the future availability of slaves meant owners wished to ensure a local supply based upon the reproductive potential of female slaves. As a result, although long-term fluctuations aimed toward gender equity in slave acquisition, short-term fluctuations were very different because owners sometimes preferred purchasing female slaves. When political or economic factors were stable, prices and rates of slave acquisition tended to favor males.

These trends and fluctuations all demonstrate a very solid slave market in Cuba. In the long run, both imports and prices remained stable, but the market reacted with periods of high fluctuation that were influenced by any change against its well-being. This slave market was totally geared to a highly productive sugar industry. Despite all the political obstacles, the Cuban slave market maintained consistent imports and evidently monetary profitability from the enterprise until the time Cuba began to emancipate the slaves in 1880.

—*Víctor Torres-Vélez and Carlos BuitragoOrtíz*

For Further Reading

Bergad, Laird W.; Fe Iglesias Garcia; and Maria del Carmen Barcia. 1995. *The Cuban Slave Market, 1790–1880*. New York: Cambridge University Press; Higman, Barry W. 1993. "The Slave Population of the British Caribbean: Some Nineteenth-Century Variations." In *Caribbean Slave Society and Economy: A Student Reader*. Ed. Hillary Beckles and Verene Shepherd. New York: New Press; White, Deborah Gray. 1983. "Female Slave: Sex Roles and Status in the Antebellum Plantation South." *Journal of Family History* 8 (Fall): 248–261.

CUCUTA, CONGRESS OF (1821)

A small town located in the northeastern corner of present-day Colombia, Cúcuta was the site, from May until October 1821, of a constitutional and legislative assembly whose delegates promulgated the Constitution of 1821, which gave legal form to the Republic of Gran Colombia, which included Venezuela, New Granada (Colombia), and Ecuador. This republic had been provisionally established in 1819 by the patriot forces fighting for independence against Spain in northern South America. Elected as president and vice-president of the republic were Simón Bolívar and Francisco de Paula Santander, respectively.

Initial debates at Cúcuta involved the institution of slavery. The delegates quickly ratified two earlier decrees, namely, those ending the slave trade within the former colonies and guaranteeing the liberty of any slaves who gained their freedom, under the various patriot governments, in the military campaigns against Spain. However, with respect to the remaining slave population and its status within Gran Colombia, disagreement prevailed. Within the coastal complexes of Venezuela and Colombia and the western Colombian mining enclaves, the economic fortune of the Creole elite was heavily dependent upon slave labor, and they blocked any attempt by the delegates to abolish slavery outright. The more strident opponents of slavery, led by the president of the congress, Colombian José Félix de Restrepo, reached a compromise, and it was embodied in the 1821 Cúcuta Slave Law.

Restrepo's solution was a manumission system designed to compensate slaveowners for the loss of slaves. The law stipulated that slave children would be free, but only after attaining the age of 18. Until reaching this age, the children of slaves were required to pay for their maintenance by serving their mother's owner, who in turn would educate the child and prepare him to lead the life of a free citizen. Yet even at 18, the child, legally a free adult, was not entirely liberated, as he was to be presented to a local commission with a record of his conduct, and the commission was authorized to decide his future occupation. This same principle of compensation, and of devolving authority upon local interests to implement it, was applied to adult slaves. Under the law, the freedom of deserving slaves would be paid for through imposing a series of inheritance taxes. Few slaves were manumitted on this basis because the committees appointed to administer the policy lacked any power to compel the payment of taxes. Indeed, in Gran Colombia, more slaves were manumitted voluntarily than through observance of the 1821 law.

In 1827, made aware of how easily the system was being evaded, Bolívar issued a decree designed to reorganize it and to strengthen the law. Unfortunately, the collapse and dissolution of Gran Colombia in 1830 nullified his effort and led to a further weakening of the program within the successor republics. Not until the mid-nineteenth century would all slaves be freed and the institution of slavery completely dismantled in this part of Spanish America.

—*Russ Davidson*

See also
Abolition, Latin America; Angostura, Congress of; Bolívar, Simón
For Further Reading
Bushnell, David. 1970. *The Santander Regime in Gran Colombia*. Westport, CT: Greenwood Press; Lombardi, John V. 1971. *The Decline and Abolition of Negro Slavery in Venezuela; 1820–1854*. Westport, CT: Greenwood Press; Masur, Gerhard. 1969. *Simón Bolívar*. Albuquerque: University of New Mexico Press.

CUDJO
(C. 1680–1744)

Cudjo (or Cudjoe or Kwadwo) was the leader of Jamaica's Maroons (fugitive black slaves) during the First Maroon War (1730–1739) between the British colonial government and the communities of runaway slaves in the island's mountainous interior. With his sister, Nanny, and his brothers Accompong, Johnny, and Quacu, Cudjo led 5,000 rebel slaves in a successful armed resistance to reenslavement, forcing the British government to grant them a degree of semiautonomy that continues in force today under Jamaica's independent government. This achievement places Cudjo among the ranks of the most successful opponents of slavery in the history of the Americas.

According to Maroon oral tradition, Cudjo was the son of Naquan, a prince or chief of the Akan, a Kormantine people of West Africa's Gold Coast region in what is modern-day Ghana. Captured with 600 of his tribespeople by Spaniards, Naquan was sold into slavery in Spanish Jamaica in the 1640s. Shortly after his arrival he instigated a revolt against his new masters and led them into the island's rugged interior, establishing the first community of Maroons (from the Spanish *cimarron,* "wild"). Runaways continued to increase the Maroon population, especially during the English conquest of Jamaica in 1655 when many former Spanish slaves took advantage of the chaos to flee enslavement. Cudjo was born into this free community in the late-seventeenth century and succeeded to the chiefdom upon his father's death at the advanced age of 90.

To protect the Maroon community from frequent British raids against them, Cudjo divided them into five towns, three in the eastern Blue Mountains and two in the nearly impenetrable Cockpit Country in the west, and placed his sister and brothers in charge of different communities. Once open hostilities of the First Maroon War erupted in 1730, command of the Maroons divided between Cudjo in the west and Nanny in the east. Under their leadership, the Maroons practiced a highly skilled form of guerrilla warfare, complete with a form of camouflage known as "ambush" and an elaborate communications system using native horns and drums. After a series of Maroon successes, which proved the futility of attempting to subdue the rebels, a new British governor, Edward Trelawny, sent Colonel John Guthrie to sue for peace. After an extended negotiation in which Guthrie attempted to cajole Cudjo and Nanny into yielding as many points as possible, an agreement was reached on March 1, 1739.

Although Cudjo failed to gain his foremost wish—to be repatriated to West Africa—the treaty terms provided unprecedented liberty to the former slaves: the Maroons were ceded the lands they held at the armistice; the British and the Maroons observed a three-mile "no man's land" between their respective territories; Cudjo and his successors had full sovereignty over their people, except the power to execute malefactors; and the Maroons agreed not to harbor future runaway slaves, returning any they found to the British authorities in exchange for a bounty. This last provision has complicated the Maroons' relationship with descendants of other Africans in Jamaica. Known for many years by the enslaved and free black communities as "the king's Negroes," the fiercely independent Maroons stand as symbols of both collaboration and successful resistance to slavery.

Cudjo died suddenly at Nanny Town in the Blue Mountains five years after peace was concluded and was succeeded by his brother, Accompong. The epitaph on his now-lost grave marker, written by Stephen Gregory Harris, a Briton who had settled among the Maroons many years earlier, read: "Cudjoe, a Maroon Forever Free." The impact of Cudjo's military victory is suggested by Milton McFarlane, one of Cudjo's descendants, who remarked that "it probably would have taken them [the British abolitionists] twice as long [to abolish slavery] had it not been for the Maroon victory that gave the British cause to think" (McFarlane, 1977).

—*Thomas W. Krise*

See also
Drums; English Caribbean; Jamaica; Trelawny Town Maroons
For Further Reading
Agorsah, E. Kofi, ed. 1994. *Maroon Heritage: Archaeological, Ethnographic, and Historical Perspectives*. Barbados, Jamaica, and Trinidad and Tobago: Canoe Press of the University of the West Indies; Edwards, Bryan. 1793. *The History, Civil and Commercial, of the British Colonies in the West Indies*. London: John Stockdale; Long, Edward. 1774. *The History of Jamaica*. London: T. Lowndes; McFarlane, Milton C. 1977. *Cudjoe of Jamaica: Pioneer for Black Freedom in the New World*. Short Hills, NJ: Ridley Enslow.

CUGOANO, QUOBNA OTTOBAH
(B. 1757?)

The most radical participant in Britain's abolitionist movement during the eighteenth century, Cugoano was the first person of African descent to write a jeremiad attacking the transatlantic slave trade and the institution of slavery itself and to advocate the slave's moral duty to resist. Cugoano was born in the coastal village of Agimaque or Ajumakoon of present-day Ghana around 1757. When he was about 13, fellow Africans kidnapped him, sold him into slavery, and transported him to Grenada where he worked in a slave gang for almost a year. Owned by one Alexander Campbell, Cugoano spent another year "at different places in the West-Indies" until Campbell took him to England in late 1772. Advised by friends to become baptized so he might not be returned to slavery, Cugoano was baptized as John Stuart (or Stewart) at St James's Church, Piccadilly, in London on August, 20, 1773. We do not know how he gained his freedom, but the painter Richard Cosway soon employed him. Cugoano joined William Green, another Afro-Briton, in 1786 in appealing to Granville Sharp to save another black, Henry Demane, from being sent to the West Indies after having been kidnapped in England. With a writ of habeas corpus, Sharp rescued Demane as the ship was setting sail.

Cugoano published *Thoughts and Sentiments on the Evil and Wicked Traffic of the Slavery and Commerce of the Human Species, Humbly Submitted to the Inhabitants of Great-Britain, by Ottobah Cugoano, a Native of Africa* (1787), probably written in collaboration with Olaudah Equiano. Cugoano refuted proslavery arguments that slavery was divinely sanctioned, that Africans gladly sold members of their own families into slavery, that Africans were especially well suited for slavery, and that West Indian slaves led better lives than Europe's poor. He argued that the enslaved had not only the moral right but also the duty to resist and that every Briton shared the blame for the evil of slavery, which threatened Great Britain with divine retribution. He also condemned European imperialism throughout the world, especially in the Americas. Defending his friend Equiano, Cugoano criticized the implementation of the Sierra Leone settlement, but he supported the principle behind it, believing that trade with Africa should replace trade in Africans.

With Equiano and other "sons of Africa," Cugoano continued the struggle against slavery with letters to newspapers and leading abolitionists like Sharp. Cugoano also wrote privately to George III, the prince of Wales, Sharp, and Edmund Burke, though no responses from any of them are extant. Cugoano published a shorter version of his 1787 book entitled *Thoughts and Sentiments on the Evil of Slavery; or The Nature of Servitude as Admitted by the Law of God, Compared to the Modern Slavery of the Africans in the West-Indies; in an Answer to the Advocates for Slavery and Oppression Addressed to the Sons of Africa, by a Native* (1791), in which he thanked Sharp and William Wilberforce for their efforts against slavery and announced his intent to open a school for Afro-Britons. Henri Grégoire reported that Cugoano married an Englishwoman, but there is no other record of that fact, nor do we know when or where Cugoano died.

—*Vincent Carretta*

See also
Abolition, British Empire; Equiano, Olaudah; Grégoire, Abbé Henri; Sharp, Granville; Sierra Leone; Wilberforce, William

CURACAO SLAVE REVOLT
(1795)

On August 17, 1795, a slave revolt erupted on the island of Curaçao in the Dutch Antilles. After about a month the colonial government succeeded in suppressing the revolt by a combined policy of military force, isolation and starvation, and betrayal. The use of a Catholic priest, one Father Schinck, as an intermediary proved not to be successful, but his account of the events is one of the most important sources, since he wrote down the slaves' reasons to revolt.

Curaçao was predominantly a trading colony, but there were also plantations worked by slaves. The revolt started on one of the plantations in the western part of the island when some 40 or 50 slaves, led by Tula, surnamed Rigaud, refused to go to work and marched to other plantations nearby to pick up other slaves. On one of those plantations Tula met with Bastiaan Carpata, the other leader of the revolt. The slaves were armed and had prepared their actions thoroughly. Some free people of color, free blacks, and a handful of Maroons (escaped slaves) reportedly joined the revolting slaves. Soon it became clear that the slaves demanded their freedom.

By 1795, Curaçao had been the stage of conflicts and disorders for some years. In the 1780s, warfare in the Caribbean and problems resulting from the Dutch Patriot movement had aroused political tension among several groups of whites on the island. In the 1790s, the problematic situation became even worse as financial problems increased and support from the motherland became more difficult to obtain. The precarious situation left its traces on the treatment of slaves. Abuses were reported, such as the farming out of slaves, forcing them to work on Sundays, and punishing the whole slave force of a plantation for an offense one of them had committed.

But what seems to have triggered the slave revolt of 1795 were two main events: the slave revolt on Saint Domingue (1791) and the French defeat of the Dutch and the formation of the Batavian Republic (1795). These were the events to which the revolting slaves referred. The slave revolt on Saint Domingue had a clear impact on the inhabitants of Curaçao, whether free or enslaved, whether black or white, and in the years following 1791, the colonial government issued several regulations stating that it was forbidden for non-white Haitian refugees to enter or to stay on the island. The Batavian Revolution, partly inspired by the Patriot movement and uprising of the 1780s and partly by the French Revolution, complicated colonial relations. Since the Batavian Republic was believed to have copied the French constitution and laws—and since the French Convention had abolished slavery in February 1794—it seemed only logical that slaves under Dutch rule should enjoy the same rights as the former French slaves did.

The revolt lasted about a month, and during that time, several rebellious slaves (men, women, and children) were taken prisoner or killed. The military force employed to suppress the revolt consisted for the most part of the Corps of Free Coloreds and Blacks. The colonial government tried to sabotage the revolt by promising the rebellious slaves, except their leaders, a "general pardon" (amnesty). The government also promised manumission for slaves who would capture the leaders of the revolt alive; any free coloreds or blacks who did so would get a sum of money instead.

After the revolt was suppressed, the government stated that the slaves had intended to kill all the whites and form a black government. Neither Tula nor Carpata had ever spoken of such a plan, but Tula confessed to the plan after he had been severely tortured on the rack (reinstated for this occasion). The damage to the property of the plantation owners seems to have been considerable. Most rebellious slaves returned to the plantations. Of the rest, the leaders were hanged after heavy torture, others were flogged or sold, and free persons were banned from the island.

In order to prevent future uprisings, not only were the leaders of the revolt severely punished, but the colonial government also issued a new slave rule in which the rights, the duties, and the treatment of the slaves were written down. Sunday was the slaves' day off; working hours were limited from 5 to 11 in the morning and from 1 until dusk; masters had to supply their slaves with food; slaves had to be clothed by their masters in order to cover their nakedness; punishment was allowed only for someone who had committed an offense; runaway slaves had to be reported to the police; and slaveowners were not allowed to give their slaves firearms. Several reiterations of these rules in the following years indicate that they were not followed.

—Angelie Sens

For Further Reading
Goslinga, Cornelis Ch. 1990. *The Dutch in the Caribbean and in Surinam, 1791/95–1942*. Maastricht, Neth.: Van Gorcum; Hoog, Levina de. 1983. *Van rebellie tot revolutie. Oorzaken en achtergronden van de Curaçaose slavenopstanden in 1750 en 1795*. Leiden: Universiteit van de Nederlandse Antillen; Paula, Alejandro F., ed. 1974. *De slavenopstand op Curaçao. Een bronnenuitgave van de originele overheidsdocumenten*. Curaçao: Centraal-Historisch Archief.

CURRY, JABEZ LAMAR MONROE (1825–1903)

Scholar, diplomat, and educational reformer, Jabez Lamar Monroe Curry was best known during his lifetime as the general agent of the Peabody Education Fund, which promoted public education in the South after the U.S. Civil War. He was born in Georgia and grew up in Alabama, the son of a slaveowning planter. While a law student at Harvard (1843–1845), Curry was exposed to Horace Mann's public school advocacy. Although the Northern states adopted free public education, it was generally reviled in the South; in his later years, Curry was to become the foremost advocate of public schools in his native region.

Curry was elected to the Alabama legislature and to both the U.S. and Confederate congresses. He also served briefly as an aide in the Confederate army. After the war, he taught English for 13 years at Richmond College, now the University of Richmond.

In 1881, Curry was appointed general agent of the Peabody Education Fund, and under his leadership, the endowment funded the creation of state normal schools for teachers of both races throughout the South. The first of these schools was the Peabody Normal School in Nashville, Tennessee. Curry dispensed funds from the Peabody endowment as seed money to cover the start-up costs of free school systems and tirelessly toured the South addressing legislatures and promoting the concept.

Curry was appointed minister to Spain in 1885, but three years later he returned to the Peabody Fund, where he served for another decade. In 1890, he was appointed agent for the Slater Fund, which supported black public education in the South. He returned to Spain in 1902 as Theodore Roosevelt's ceremonial ambassador extraordinary.

National reconciliation was Curry's passion throughout his postwar career. When the United Confederate Veterans held their sixth reunion at Richmond, Virginia, in 1896, Curry sought to reconcile Southern pride with patriotism, declaring that "recognition of the glorious deeds of our comrades is perfectly consistent with loyalty to the flag and devotion to the Constitution and the resulting union" (Curry, 1969).

—*Edward F. Heite*

For Further Reading
Curry, J. L. M. 1969. *A Brief Sketch of George Peabody, and a History of the Peabody Education Fund through Thirty Years*. New York: Negro Universities Press.

DAHOMEY

Located in West Africa's Bight of Benin region, Dahomey (now Republic of Benin) lies between modern-day Togo and Nigeria and is bordered to the north by Niger and Burkina Faso. Founded on the Abomey Plateau by the Aja people in the early-seventeenth century, Dahomey and its capital, Abomey, remained landlocked until a series of early-eighteenth-century expansions enabled it to gain access to the Atlantic.

Domestic slavery was a common feature in Dahomey society, and the state was also a leading participant in the Atlantic slave trade. An estimated one-fifth of all the slaves sold into slavery in the Americas came from the Bight of Benin region, an area that includes Dahomey. Most of these slaves were exported to Brazil, especially to the Bahia region, where they worked in the mines and on the sugar, tobacco, and coffee plantations.

Dahomey obtained its slaves through purchase, raids, and wars. From its seventeenth-century founding, Dahomey was involved in wars for territorial expansion and defensive wars against enemy states, and it battled its way south toward the coast in order to be able to trade with European merchants. Dahomey's wars for expansion began under Wegbaja (c. 1650–1685) who is credited with creating the state's strong military. Agaja Trudo (1708–1740) took Dahomey's tradition of expansion and defense to new heights in the eighteenth century, conquering neighboring states, particularly to the south toward the slave markets and ports along the Atlantic. Agaja conquered and incorporated the states of Allada in 1724 and Whydah in 1727, thereby giving Dahomey direct coastal access to trade with the Europeans. Dahomey's wars, though not fought primarily to obtain slaves, produced war captives who were usually sold into slavery in the New World or enslaved locally.

Noted for having an efficient administrative structure, Dahomey instituted policies to control and regulate the Atlantic trade. Although the kings of Dahomey sold a significant portion of the slaves, they did not monopolize the trade. State policy restricted local traders who were not subjects of Dahomey from direct coastal trading with the Europeans, and such traders were required to sell their slaves to Dahomey middle-men. Private Dahomey merchants, the *ahisinon*, received royal permission to engage in the slave trade with European merchants.

The European traders were similarly regulated by the state. Dahomey's rulers exercised control over the slave trade by charging European merchants for the privilege of trading, basing the fee on the size of the ship and on the volume of trade. Occasionally, Dahomey's kings expelled European traders they suspected were betraying the interests of the king or the state. Thus, Tegbesu (1740–1774) deported French and Portuguese directors that he suspected of disloyalty. Dahomey appointed a minister, the *yovogan*, to be in charge of the Europeans and of trade at the port of Whydah. The *yovogan* conducted trade on behalf of the king, collected customs duties from the European merchants, and was in charge of relations with the European traders in Whydah. Another office created by Dahomey in the nineteenth century and held initially by the Brazilian merchant Felix da Souza, was the *chacha*. Besides conducting his own private trade, the *chacha* directed the selling of the king's slaves, purchased imported goods for the king, and served as the representative of the European traders.

The abolition of the slave trade and slavery reduced the outlets for Dahomey's slaves in the New World. Brazil continued slave importation until the 1850s, but Dahomey, which had become dependent upon the trade, needed new markets to replace those lost to the abolition movement. Cuba provided such an outlet, but the bulk of Dahomey's slaves were now utilized domestically in Dahomey to cultivate palm products for sale in a new "legitimate" trade. In the 1890s, France declared a protectorate over Dahomey and abolished the slave trade, but domestic slavery in Dahomey persisted into the twentieth century.

—*Patience Essah*

For Further Reading
Ajayi, J. F. A., and Michael Crowder, eds. 1971. *History of West Africa*. London: Longman; Law, Robin. 1977. "Royal Monopoly and Private Enterprise in the Atlantic Trade: The Case of Dahomey." *Journal of African History* 18: 555–577; Manning, Patrick. 1982. *Slavery, Colonialism, and Economic Growth in Dahomey, 1640–1960*. Cambridge: Cambridge University Press.

DANISH AFRICA COMPANIES

Several companies formed from 1660 to 1803 during the period of the Danish slave trade in Africa and the West Indies. The first company, chartered in 1660, was the Danish Africa Company (Dansk afrikanske kompagni or Glückstadtkompagniet), and it was based in Glückstadt on the Elbe in present-day Germany, a city founded by the Danish king Christian IV. This company conducted limited trade, and its charter was revoked in 1674.

In 1671, the Danish West Indian Company (Vestindisk kompagni, later the West Indian–Guinean Company, or Vestindisk-guineisk kompagni) was chartered for the purpose of colonizing the West Indian island of St. Thomas, its surrounding islands, and if possible, parts of the North American mainland closest to those islands. The last purpose was never fulfilled. When the charter for the Danish Africa Company was revoked, the new company was also given the right to trade in Guinea. Trade was initially slow, and the king leased company rights to the Copenhagen shipowner Nic. Jansen Arf from 1684 to 1697. Arf eventually lost the trading rights, which reverted back to the company, for the West Indies in 1694 and Guinea in 1697. During the eighteenth century, the company established a West Indies–Guinea Office in Copenhagen, and its first chief was Peder Mariager. In 1754, the crown took over the company.

In 1765, the Guinean Company (Guineisk kompagni) was established. Fort Christiansborg and Fort Fredensborg, both on the Gold Coast, were leased to the company for 20 years on the conditions that they be kept in order, that the company would be responsible for the king's rights, that peace be kept with neighboring black states, and that blacks in Danish employment be protected. The company's main director was Henning Fr. Bargum, but he went bankrupt in 1774 and had to leave Denmark. The company was sold to the crown in 1776.

In 1778, the West Indian Trading Company (Vestindisk handelsselskab) was formed. It had no monopoly and by 1785 had already been taken over by the crown. Liquidated in 1816, the company had been unprofitable since the American Revolution. The Baltic Guinean Company (Østersøisk-guineisk handelsselskab) was formed in 1781, but it was active only until the prohibition of the Danish slave trade in 1803.

—*Bertil Haggman*

See also
Danish Slave Trade
For Further Reading
Feldbaek, O. 1981. "The Organisation and Structure of the Danish East India, West India, and Guinea Compa-

nies in the 17th and 18th Centuries." In *Companies and Trade: Essays on Overseas Trading Companies during the Ancien Regime*. Ed. Leonard Blussé et al. Leiden: Leiden University Press; Feldbaek, O., and O. Justesen. 1980. "Kolonierna i Asien og Afrika." In *Politikens Danmarks Historie*. Ed. S. Ellehøj and Kristof Glamann. Copenhagen: Politikens Forlag; Jørgensen, Bro, and A. A. Rasch, 1969. *Asiatiske, vestindiske og guinesiske handelskompagnier*. Copenhagen: Rigsarkivet.

DANISH SLAVE TRADE

The first Danish slave fort in West Africa was Fort Carolusburg, which had been taken from the Swedes in 1658, but it was soon lost. Soon thereafter, the king of Fetu allowed the Danes to take control of a fort at Amanfro, which became Fort Frederiksberg. The fort that would become the center of Danish activities on the Gold Coast, Fort Christiansborg, was constructed in 1661 at Osu near Accra. By then, the Danes had abandoned all trading in the western part of the Gold Coast since they were unable to compete with the British and the Dutch in that area. Instead, Danish trade was concentrated on the eastern coast toward the Volta River. New Danish forts were constructed during the eighteenth century. The new sites included Fort Fredensborg at Ningo in 1736, Fort Kongensten at Ada in 1783, and Fort Prindsensten at Keta in 1784.

The latest estimate of the number of slaves exported by the Danes from Africa to the Danish West Indies from 1660 to 1806 was made in 1992 and was based only on Danish archival sources. According to this estimate, 85,650 slaves were exported on Danish ships, 8,700 were exported officially by the Danes on non-Danish ships, and 3,500 were exported privately on non-Danish ships. Thus, 97,850 slaves were transported, but because of the incomplete sources, that figure is more an indication of the approximate level than an exact expression of volume.

The all-dominant export commodity of Danish trade on the Gold Coast was slaves, and by the 1740s, the Danish trade had become practically identical with the trade in slaves. But it was probably not a thriving business. In the early 1770s, Copenhagen traders claimed that it would take an annual export of 1,500 slaves to cover all expenses and make the trade profitable, and in reality, the approximate annual trade from 1699 to 1770 was between 250 and 300 slaves. The price of a slave rose from 1699, when the price in Rigsdaler (equal to one-sixteenth of an ounce of gold) was 30, to 1800, when it was 160.

In percentage of the total slave trade during the eighteenth century, the Danish trade reached its height in the 1780s with around 12.4 percent. It was at a low point in the 1730s and 1740s with 1.6 and 2.3 percent, respectively. From the 1730s to the 1790s, Danish guns played an important role in the trade, as in the second half of the eighteenth century, around 3,000 "Dane guns" were sold on the Gold Coast.

—*Bertil Haggman*

For Further Reading
Feldbaek, O., and O. Justesen. 1980. "Kolonierna i Asien og Afrika." In *Politikens Danmarks Historie*. Ed. S. Ellehøj and Kristof Glamann. Copenhagen: Politikens Forlag; Green-Pedersen, S. E. 1971. "The Scope and Structure of the Danish Slave Trade." *Scandinavian Economic History Review*; Hernaes, Per O. 1992. *The Danish Slave Trade from West Africa and Afro-Danish Relations on the 18th-Century Gold Coast*. Trondheim: Trondheim University.

DANISH WEST INDIES

The Danish West Indies occupied the northern portion of the Virgin Islands, extending south and east from Puerto Rico. St. Thomas (28 square miles) and St. John (20 square miles) are characterized by steeply hilly terrain, and 40 miles south is St. Croix (84 square miles). The remaining islands consist of cays totaling about 18 square miles. Although agriculture played an essential role on the main islands, the social histories of the islands are quite distinct.

In 1671, the Danish West Indian Company (DWIC) received royal permission to colonize St. Thomas. Free and indentured European settlers arrived in 1672, and 100 enslaved Africans arrived in 1673, doubling the colony's population. Although administratively Danish, most of the European colonists were Dutch, and the language that emerged was a Dutch Creole language.

The colony struggled initially, and in an attempt to increase shareholder profits, the DWIC entered, albeit on a small scale, the slave trade in 1697. Although ultimately costly in human and economic terms, the slave trade was at first profitable and also integral to agricultural expansion. During the next two decades, cotton and sugar became the largest crops on the island. Plantations increased by 60 percent, and the number of enslaved Africans increased by 450 percent. When intense agriculture exhausted the soil, St. Thomas's location and deep harbor permitted a shift to trade, and that island became a regional commercial center about 1750, shortly before the crown dissolved the DWIC and transferred its holdings. In 1764, St. Thomas was designated a free port, and because of trade, both legal and illegal, the island pros-

pered, providing economic opportunity to many, including free blacks and slave artisans. By the mid-nineteenth century, agriculture employed only 20 percent of the island's population.

In 1717, colonists and slaves from St. Thomas settled St. John, and the center of the plantation activity shifted to this island, though the new plantations were generally smaller than on St. Thomas. Larger plantations typically operated with (white) overseers or (slave) *bombas* ("drivers") who had government authorization to exploit the slave labor force. A devastating slave rebellion in 1733, when 146 men and women destroyed a quarter of the island's plantations, bears witness to the severe treatment of slaves on St. John.

With the purchase of St. Croix from the French in 1733, just as the DWIC was withdrawing from the slave trade, the center of plantation activity again shifted. On St. Croix, planters and slaves from British colonies soon outnumbered the Danes and the Dutch, and because its topography was well suited to large-scale agriculture, St. Croix emerged as a prosperous plantation economy.

An important feature distinguishing the Danish West Indies slave population from slaves in other Caribbean colonies was literacy. The Lutheran Church directed slave education, and educated free blacks provided instruction in St. Thomas's one and St. Croix's three schools. Free, compulsory, universal education began on all three islands in 1839, nearly a decade before slavery's abolition in 1848.

The social forces that resulted in state support of education in the Danish West Indies in 1790 and the abolition of Danish serfdom in 1792 also produced a curtailment of the slave trade in the Danish islands in 1802. Abolitionist sentiment grew, and in 1847, King Christian VIII declared that all children born to slave parents would be free after his birthday, and he promised full emancipation in 1859. Unwilling to wait, 8,000 St. Croix slaves gathered on July 2, 1848, to demand slavery's abolition, and after some hours of deliberation, slavery was abolished by gubernatorial fiat. A few planters responded to the bloodless revolt with violence, and three days of looting followed. The colonial government responded with arrests, five weeks of trials, and subsequent punishment of people judged guilty of crimes against the general order.

Emancipation exacerbated economic decline on St. Croix and St. John though trade on St. Thomas continued to prosper until a devastating hurricane, earthquake, and tidal wave destroyed the port's infrastructure in 1867. The area's stalled economy proved too great a drain on the resources of the Danish crown, and negotiations to sell the islands to the United States began in 1865. The purchase agreement was completed in 1917.

—*Robin Sabino*

See also
Moravian Slaves
For Further Reading
Hall, N. A. T. 1992. *Slave Society in the Danish West Indies: St. Thomas, St. John, and St. Croix.* Johns Hopkins Studies in Atlantic History and Culture. Baltimore: Johns Hopkins University Press; Olwig, Karen Fog. 1985. *Cultural Adaptation and Resistance on St. John: Three Centuries of Afro-Caribbean Life.* Gainesville: University of Florida Press; Westergaard, Waldemar. 1917. *The Danish West Indies: Under Company Rule.* New York: Macmillan.

DARFUR-EGYPT SLAVE TRADE

Trade between Egypt and the Nile region of the Sudan is of great antiquity. However with the creation of the Keira state of Darfur in the seventeenth century, a low-level and irregular trade developed into a considerable and long-term exchange of slaves and other goods. The region known as Darfur ("land of the Fur") took its name from the Fur ethnic group, who still predominate in the mountainous area around Jebel Marra in present-day western Sudan.

The early history of the region is vague, though a Fur state may have existed as early as the fifteenth century. The reign of Sulayman Solondugno (c. 1660–1680) marks the beginning of the Keira state, which saw the growth of the Fur tribal kingdom into a multiethnic empire. Instrumental in this process was a long-distance trade between Darfur and Egypt, which generated the revenue necessary to expand the authority and institutions of state in all directions. In this trade the Keira sultan himself was supreme, owning a monopoly on some goods and imposing a customs tax on others. Facilitating trade was the sultan's association with Islam: Sulayman is remembered for encouraging Islamic practices in Darfur and attracting Muslim merchants and holy men to the region.

Slaves figured prominently among the goods exported from Darfur to Egypt, though ivory, tamarind, and ostrich feathers also are mentioned in seventeenth-century accounts. The main source of slaves for the Fur was the region immediately to the south (corresponding to western Bahr el Ghazal Province), which was inhabited by a number of non-Muslim, stateless peoples collectively referred to as the Fartit.

The slave raids were large organized affairs, undertaken with the sultan's permission and led by Fur leaders. Raids could last as long as three months and penetrate as far south as the present-day Central African Republic. The number of slaves captured and exported to Egypt is difficult to determine: one estimate for the period 1750–1830 is approximately 2,000–3,000 per year, and obviously slaves were exported earlier as well (O'Fahey and Spaulding, 1974). The profitable trade in slaves enabled the sultan to acquire horses, saddles, weapons, and armor, and the constant need to procure slaves provided the impetus for the state to increase the territory under its control. At least by the nineteenth century, slaves were the staple export of Darfur, and slave labor helped run most of the organs of state.

The main link between Darfur and Egypt was a desert route known as *darb al-arba'in,* or the Forty Days Road. Beginning in the Darfur commercial center of Kobbei, it stretched north 1,117 miles through the oases of the Sahara to join the Nile just below the Egyptian town of Asyût, and from there it proceeded directly to Cairo. Allegedly a fast courier could cover the distance in 12 days, though a caravan of several hundred camels and a thousand slaves might take anywhere from 45 to 90 days to complete the journey (Walz, 1978).

Effective control of *darb al arba'in* necessitated the cooperation—willing or otherwise—of the Bedouin tribes whose territory the route passed through, and in this the Darfur sultan was successful. Actual leadership of the caravans was invested in a chief merchant *(khabir)* appointed by the sultan, who was authorized to conduct the ruler's commercial and political relations in Egypt. The size of caravans traversing *darb al-arba'in* varied considerably. Caravans of anywhere from 2,000 to 24,000 camels were noted in the late-eighteenth century, though most were on the smaller end of this spectrum. The sheer difficulty of the route accounted for its importance since, unlike the riverine routes, it generally was free of banditry. Slaves, like camels, walked the length of the route.

The height of trade along *darb al-arba'in* had been reached by the mid-nineteenth century, and after that time, Sudanese merchants of the Nubian diaspora began to monopolize trade in slaves and ivory. Slave trading continued sporadically thereafter, but dwindled in the face of new political and economic conditions in Sudan. Illicit slave trading persisted under Anglo-Egyptian rule (1899–1955), though rarely from Darfur.

—*Robert S. Kramer*

See also
Jihadiyya; Sudan
For Further Reading
O'Fahey, R. S. 1973. "Slavery and the Slave Trade in Dar Fur." *Journal of African History* 14 (1): 29–43; O'Fahey, R. S., and J. L. Spaulding. 1974. *Kingdoms of the Sudan.* London: Methuen; Walz, Terence. 1978. *Trade between Egypt and Bilad As-Sudan, 1700–1820.* Paris: Institut Francais D'Archeologie Orientale du Caire.

DE RE RUSTICA
See Columella's *De re rustica*

DEBOW, JAMES DUNWOODY BROWNSON (1820–1867)

James D. B. DeBow is noted among historians of the Old South as a proslavery advocate and editor of *DeBow's Review*—the only antebellum Southern commercial magazine. Historians consider him one of the prominent "fire-eaters," people, according to Ulrich B. Phillips, who were engaged in a "persistent advocacy of Southern independence" (Walther, 1992). Yet, DeBow was quite different from other Southern fire-eaters in that he firmly believed in the progress of commerce and industry in the South.

DeBow was quite a popular journalist both in the South and among commercial and publishing enterprises in New York and Boston. Thus, he was more informed about the political and economic issues of the nation than many of his colleagues. Since he tried to establish *DeBow's Review* for all Southerners, not just for particular groups or individuals, he was in a good position to receive and consider different opinions from diverse sections of the South. From its early days, the magazine had a "liberal" editorial policy and presented moderate viewpoints on political and economic conflicts between the South and the North and the future of the Union. By the mid-1850s, DeBow could not keep silent about the intensified sectional conflict, especially as it concerned questions of slavery and Southern states' rights. From then on, DeBow actively participated in the proslavery movement, which wanted to reopen the African slave trade, and, after Lincoln's election in 1860, he spearheaded the secession movement. DeBow later served the Confederate government as a loan agent.

DeBow was born in Charleston, South Carolina, on July 10, 1820. Educated exclusively in South Carolina, first in Charleston public schools and later at the Cokesbury Institute of the Methodist Church in Charleston, he graduated from the College of Charleston as valedictorian of his class in 1843. DeBow then read law and was admitted to the South Carolina bar in 1844. Dissatisfied with practicing law, he found a new career in journalism and remained a journalist throughout his life. At the age of 25, after serving briefly as assistant editor of the *Southern Quarterly Review,* DeBow moved to New Orleans and started his own magazine, *Commercial Review of the South West,* later to be better known as *DeBow's Review.*

He was one of the founders of the Louisiana State Historical Society in 1847, which eventually merged into the Academy of Science. In 1849, DeBow was appointed professor of political economy at the newly founded University of Louisiana; in the same year, he was appointed head of the Bureau of Statistics in Louisiana; in 1853, he became superintendent of the Seventh Census of the United States. After the Civil War, he resumed publication of *DeBow's Review,* but only until 1867.

In 1853, DeBow married Caroline Poe of Mobile, Alabama, who died in 1858. They had two children, Mary and James Dunwoody Brownson. James died as an infant; Mary died at 16. In 1860, DeBow married Martha E. Johns of Nashville, Tennessee, and this marriage produced four children. He died of pleurisy in New Jersey on February 27, 1867, at the age of 46.

A good example of a Southern intellectual who was converted to the radical proslavery ideology in the final period of sectional conflict, DeBow believed that slavery, as ordained by God, was an institution that was suitable for a naturally inferior race and an appropriate social system for the "union with whites in an unequal relation." Furthermore, there was no fundamental conflict between his ideas on slavery and the economic development of the South, as he adjusted and modified classical political economy to suit the conditions of the Old South.

DeBow's early proslavery ideas were based on biblical arguments and Enlightenment philosophy that maintained that slavery was a "natural" institution. His later proslavery ideas were influenced by the increased North-South sectional conflict and expanded to incorporate the scientific and racial arguments that defended slavery as being the best state of social organization.

DeBow believed that given its natural resources and a slave labor system under the guidance of enlightened masters, the South could regain its dominance in national politics and improve its economy based on agriculture, commerce, and manufacturing. With a strong and progressive economy, the South could defend its institutions, especially slavery, from Northern attacks. His economic ideas were basically informed by the economic ideas of merchant capital: progress and the prosperity of society were based on commodity exchanges rather than on the production process. Proslavery ideas allowed Southern intellectuals conveniently to place blacks in a barbarous stage in a linear social development and to justify their guidance and protection by civilized men and societies. Accordingly, slavery brought blacks into the modern world order and also perfected and harmonized the natural hierarchical social order. Ultimately, Southern intellectuals defended slavery as a social system that was ordained by God and justified by history as the most suitable system for an inferior and unequal race.

DeBow's economic ideas put an emphasis on the "industrial revolution" of the South and the sustainability of slavery, which resulted in his arguing for the reopening of the African slave trade. For Southern political economists, the security of the institution of slavery depended on a prosperous and strong South, which, in turn, relied on its capability to diversify its economy based on a balance of agriculture, commerce, and manufacturing. For these economists, the successful defense of slavery presupposed an adequate rate of economic growth. DeBow was aware that the single-crop agriculture of the South was inadequate to sustain the rapid growth of the South's economy in the competitive world market, so his advocacy of an "industrial revolution" in the South was a logical outcome of his economic theory.

Like other Southern political economists, however, DeBow's ideas on the promotion of manufacturing, and the diversification of surplus slave labor, were contradictory and impractical. His vision of industrialization was grounded upon a view of society as functioning like a working body or organism and the idea that men were responsible for each other. He saw only unity between capital and labor and thus saw no conflict between wage labor and slave labor in the South. He denied the existence of class conflict within the South, and for him, economic development was a precondition for a defense of slavery. The paradox of DeBow's economic ideas thus lay mainly in his commitment to the defense of slavery.

—*Thanet Aphornsuvan*

For Further Reading
Aphornsuvan, Thanet. 1990. "James D. B. DeBow and the Political Economy of the Old South." Ph.D. dissertation, History Department, SUNY-Binghamton, New York; Hall, Mark. 1982. "The Proslavery Thought of J. D. B. DeBow: A Practical Man's Guide to Economics." *Southern Studies* 21 (Spring): 97–104; Skipper, Ottis Clark. 1958. *J. D. B. DeBow: Magazinist of the Old South*. Athens: University of Georgia Press; Walther, Eric H. 1992. *The Fire-Eaters*. Baton Rouge: Louisiana State University Press.

DELANY, MARTIN R. (1812–1885)

Martin R. Delany was the son of a free mother and a slave father. Throughout his lifetime, he always claimed that he was descended from West African native chieftains. In 1822, his family moved to Chambersburg, Pennsylvania, and in 1831, Delany left Chambersburg for Pittsburgh where he spent the next 25 years of his life.

Upon his arrival in Pittsburgh he worked first as a barber while attending a school run by the Reverend Lewis Woodson, a black Methodist minister. During his time in Pittsburgh, Delany participated in the abolitionist movement, newspaper editing, moral reform, and the practice of medicine.

From 1843 to 1847, Delany edited *Mystery,* one of a few black newspapers of the period, and from late 1847 until the middle of 1849, he coedited the *North Star* with Frederick Douglass. In 1852 he published one of the most important books to be written by a free black in the nineteenth century—*The Condition, Elevation, Emigration, and Destiny of the Colored People of the United States, Politically Considered*. This is the text that established Delany's later reputation as the "father of black nationalism." During the Civil War years, Delany served as a major over "colored troops." In that capacity, he actively recruited blacks into the Union army. Later he was appointed subassistant commissioner of the Bureau for the Relief of Refugees, Freedmen, and of Abandoned Lands.

Delany's *Condition* is a compelling text for any number of reasons, not the least of which is the context that produced it. Published only two years after the passage of the Fugitive Slave Act of 1850, *The Condition* represents a direct response to the political ramifications of that law. Prior to the 1850s, moral suasion had been the primary political strategy for defeating slavery. In fact, Delany himself had been a great proponent of moral suasion. The logic was that if blacks could demonstrate—through education, industry, and thrift—that they were capable of citizenship with whites, then that fact would, over time, make possible the end of slavery. That was the popular ideology of the 1830s and 1840s. However, the passage of the Fugitive Slave Act confirmed that whites and the government had not been acting in good faith. It was not the condition of black people that kept them from being considered the equal of whites, it was race and racism.

Delany's *Condition* is a rhetorically sophisticated and politically astute response to that realization. The text outlined and argued for the tenets of emigration (which Delany had taken great pains to distinguish from colonization—a policy of the proslavery forces begun in 1817 to colonize blacks outside the United States). The book also argued for black self-determination, which was dependent on black economic independence. That aspect met with sharp opposition from the black churches, which believed in providential determinism, but the rhetorical sophistication of Delany's argument for materialism as sanctioned by God is noteworthy. Delany was aware of the complexity of the discursive terrain he was embarking on in the text. That awareness is one of the things that makes the book one of the most interesting and important documents written by a free black in the United States.

Fusing an unusual blend of black self-determination with the contemporary black emigration movement, Delany favored the concept of "a nation within a nation." He worked actively to establish an African American nation in Africa and saw this move as the cornerstone of the liberation and elevation of black people. Although the mass of blacks never adopted Delany's rather elitist ideas for racial uplift or his campaign for African emigration, twentieth-century thinkers such as Booker T. Washington and Marcus Garvey were deeply influenced by his philosophy.

Although the version of Delany as the "father of black nationalism" is still quite popular, historian Floyd Miller was among the first to take issue with it. He contends that it was actually Lewis Woodson, Delany's teacher in Pittsburgh, who was the real father of black nationalism and the source of Delany's emigrationist and nationalistic ideology. Miller demonstrates in a 1971 essay, "'The Father of Black Nationalism': Another Contender," that most of Delany's ideas about emigration and racial uplift were first published as letters by Lewis to the *Colored American* in the July 1, 1837, issue under the pseudonym "Augustine."

The years 1859–1862 saw the first publication of Delany's work of fiction, *Blake; or, The Huts of America.* The first attempt to publish the novel in serial form began in the *Anglo-African Magazine* in January–July 1859. For reasons that are unknown (though perhaps because Delany went out of the country) publication was halted after 26 chapters had been printed. It was not until 1861–1862 that the entire novel was printed in the *Weekly Anglo-African,* from November 26, 1861, until May 24, 1862. The novel differs from much of nineteenth-century African American literature in two important ways: first, it features an unapologetic black revolutionary thinker as the hero of the text; second, it features a man of unmixed African blood, "a pure Negro," as the hero and not a tragic mulatto figure as in works by William Wells Brown, Charles W. Chesnutt, and James Weldon Johnson. In many respects, Delany's hero is much like the author himself—a thinker and a man of action who was proud of his heritage.

—*Dwight A. McBride*

See also
American Colonization Society; Brown, William Wells; Douglass, Frederick; *North Star*
For Further Reading
Delany, Martin R. 1852. *The Condition, Elevation, Emigration, and Destiny of the Colored People of the United States, Politically Considered.* Philadelphia: Martin R. Delany; Griffith, Cyril F. 1975. *The African Dream: Martin R. Delany and the Emergence of Pan-African Thought.* University Park: Pennsylvania State University Press; Levine, Robert. 1997. *Martin R. Delany, Frederick Douglass, and the Politics of Representative Identity.* Chapel Hill: University of North Carolina Press; Painter, Nell Irvin. 1988. "Martin R. Delany: Elitism and Black Nationalism." In *Black Leaders of the Nineteenth Century.* Ed. Leon Litwack and August Meier. Urbana: University of Illinois Press.

DESSALINES, JEAN-JACQUES (C. 1758–1806)

A black slave turned general who led Haiti to independence in 1804, Jean-Jacques Dessalines remains a powerful symbol of that revolution's violence and of the commitment on the part of Haiti's new leaders to continue a forced plantation labor regime. Historians know little about Dessalines' life as a slave. Although some sources identify him as African, he was probably born around 1758 in the Grande Rivière Parish of the French colony of Saint Domingue. He may have spoken an African language used by the colony's many new slaves. Even though it was near one of Saint Domingue's richest sugar plains, Grande Rivière was a mountainous coffee-producing parish that tended to have more African and fewer Creole slaves than the sugar districts. Dessalines was considered the most anti-European of Haiti's early leaders. After 1794, he frequently displayed his scarred back as evidence of the slavery he had survived and as evidence of his hatred for the French. He was the only revolutionary figure to be identified with a voodoo spirit, or *lwa.* Unlike Toussaint Louverture, Dessalines was known to have used voodoo, though he did not hesitate to persecute folk religious leaders who opposed him.

As a young slave, the future emperor was named Jacques Duclos after his white owner on the Cormiers plantation. Nothing is known of his parents. As ruler of Haiti, he urged a French physician to save the life of one Victoria Montou, called Toya. A field slave who had been sold from the Cormiers plantation, perhaps like Dessalines' parents, Dessalines called her his aunt. Many coffee-growing parishes in Saint Domingue, like Grande Rivière, were home to more free people of color than whites. In the 1780s, a free black artisan who had himself once worked for a Frenchman named Des Salines purchased Jacques Duclos. The slave took the name of this second, black master and apparently learned the building trade from him.

Little is known about Dessalines' participation in the early years of the 1791 Saint Domingue slave uprising. Grande Rivière was near the rebellion's center, but by this time Dessalines' black master had moved him from the parish. Tradition links him with the slave general Biassou, though it is not until 1794, after slavery was abolished, that Dessalines appears in the historical record. The fact that he is then listed as being a battalion leader under Toussaint Louverture suggests that he was already an experienced soldier by 1794.

As a revolutionary leader and ultimately Louverture's top general, Dessalines was known for his harsh tactics against whites and the mulatto class. Those families of color who had been free and even prosperous under the slave regime threatened to become Saint Domingue's new planter class, but by 1798, Louverture and his black generals were the colony's leading force and had largely replaced French and mulatto officials. In 1799, Dessalines led an army against Saint Domingue's mulatto-controlled southern province. After taking the territory in 1800, he executed hundreds of prisoners; unreliable but widely repeated rumors suggested the death toll amounted to 10,000.

Dessalines' work as Saint Domingue's chief agricultural inspector magnified his reputation for brutality. Under a system that Louverture codified in 1801, the army received expanded authority over plantation agriculture. Slavery had officially ended, and many European planters had fled or been killed, but field-workers were required to continue their labor and share profits with both the state and the plantation managers it appointed. Although unpopular, this arrangement supplied the colony with vital foreign exchange and solidified the replacement of the white planter society with a new brown and black elite. It is said that Dessalines controlled over 30 plantations himself. Harsh disciplinary measures against workers marked his tours through the countryside, sometimes including executing those who challenged labor discipline.

In early 1802, Napoleon Bonaparte attempted to regain control of what had been France's most profitable colony and to reimpose racial slavery. With Louverture, Dessalines led the fight against France's expeditionary force. He vainly attempted to break its siege of the mountain fortress Crête-à-Pierrot and responded to mass executions of black prisoners by the French with similar measures against whites. Yet when Toussaint Louverture capitulated in May 1802, Dessalines followed, and for over a year he was a key French ally and helped repress black guerrilla bands.

In October 1803, Dessalines and other black and mulatto generals turned against the French, who had been unable to completely defeat the ex-slaves or to overcome yellow fever. Louverture died in a French prison in April 1803, and in November of that year, the military leaders elected Dessalines "governor general for life." Tradition maintains that he tore the white band from the French tricolor to create a new blue and red flag bearing the words, in French, "Liberty or death." On January 1, 1804, after expelling the French army, Dessalines proclaimed Haitian independence.

Dessalines' short tenure as Haiti's first emperor, a title he took in October 1804, was notable for his attempts to define the new nation around the awkward combination of anticolonial sentiment and forced plantation labor. He ordered the execution of Haiti's remaining French residents in 1805, while safeguarding citizens of Britain, the United States, and other allies. Haiti's constitution promulgated that same year prohibited whites from owning land but allowed certain whites to be naturalized Haitians. Attempting to bridge the deep rift between Haitians of African descent, most of whom had been colonial slaves, and those of mixed European-African ancestry, many of whom had been free under the French, the 1805 Constitution defined all Haitians as "black." Dessalines also proclaimed freedom of religion and instituted new marriage and divorce laws.

Most controversially, Dessalines retained the forced-labor system of agriculture inherited from Toussaint Louverture and French officials before him. Under this system, workers and the state each received one-quarter of the plantation profits, but corruption was widespread. The government instituted a system of plantation leases and official warehouses, but local military leaders and the mixed-race elite retained control of many colonial estates.

The emperor's attempts to reform the rural economy created the coalition that assassinated him. Dessalines revoked all land transfers made by French émigrés and instituted a process of title verification in 1805. In 1806 his army began implementing this process, and thus alienated landowners and local commanders. Simultaneously, many of Haiti's former slaves resented the emperor's support of the forced-labor system. Dessalines' own troops killed him on October 17, 1806, while he was traveling to Haiti's southern peninsula to quell a revolt there.

Dessalines was so identified with criticizing the European-centered elite that his role in establishing Haitian independence began to be officially celebrated only in the late-nineteenth century. Haiti's national anthem, the Desalinienne, was written in 1904.

—*John D. Garrigus*

See also
Louverture, Toussaint; Rigaud, André
For Further Reading
Brutus, Timoleon C. 1946–1947. *L'homme d'Airain, étude monographique sur Jean-Jacques Dessalines, fondateur de la nation haïtienne.* 2 vols. Port-au-Prince: N. A. Theodore.; Dayan, Joan. 1995. *Haiti, History, and the Gods.* Berkeley: University of California Press;

James, C. L. R. 1968. *The Black Jacobins: Toussaint L'Ouverture and the San Domingo Revolution.* New York: Random House; Trouillot, Henock. 1966. *Dessalines: ou, La tragédie post-coloniale.* Port-au-Prince: Editions "Panorama."

DEW, THOMAS RODERICK (1802–1846)

Thomas Roderick Dew was raised in a planter family in the tidewater region of Virginia, taught at the College of William and Mary from 1826 to 1846, and gained wide influence with his essays on public issues. He gained fame in the early 1830s for his essays on slavery, which proclaimed its merits and the impracticality of the Virginia General Assembly's enacting any legislation designed to bring an end to slavery in the Old Dominion.

In the 1831–1832 legislative session, the Virginia House of Delegates conducted a debate as to whether, after Nat Turner's slave uprising in Southampton County in August 1831, the state should inaugurate some program of gradual emancipation of slaves, coupled with the deportation of all black Virginians. Dismayed by the debate, Dew rushed a lengthy essay, "Abolition of Negro Slavery," to publication in the *American Quarterly Review* of September 1832. He published an expanded version, *Review of the Debate in the Virginia Legislature of 1831 and 1832,* in the same year, and this work reached a wide readership and was selected after Dew's death for inclusion in *The Pro-Slavery Argument as Maintained by the Most Distinguished Writers of the Southern States* (1852).

Dew lectured against "the crude, undigested theories of tampering legislators" *(Review of the Debate)*. Politicians' "passion for legislation" against slavery, he warned, intruded upon "dangerous and delicate business" and threatened to do "irretrievable" damage to Virginia. Dew hoped to demonstrate why no good, and much evil, would come from legislative interference.

Dew demonstrated "the impossibility of colonizing the blacks." How could deportation be financed, and where would the emigrants go? Drawing on historical analogies, such as Europeans migrating to the Caribbean or to North America, he contended that African Americans would die in droves from African diseases and they would occasion great hostilities with their neighbors. No matter how conceived, the costs of forced colonization would be too great for everyone who would be affected.

Nor could emancipation be accomplished without deportation. Virginia's slaves, whether from nature or nurture, were unfit for freedom in Virginia. They would work only under compulsion. And white Virginians, with their customs and prejudices, would not permit black freedom in their state. Dew rejected the models of the successful abandonment of slavery in Europe and the North. The North had started with few slaves, and European societies developed a middle class that gradually absorbed slaves as free people. The South had too many slaves for its middle class to absorb and, unlike European societies, had an unfree population that differed in physical appearance.

Dew saw three options, and he had rejected two of them. Having disposed of the arguments for emancipation, whether with or without deportation, he proceeded to adopt a proslavery stance—"to demonstrate . . . the complete justification of the whole southern country in a further continuance of . . . slavery." He denied that most slaves suffered from either discontent or poor treatment: "A merrier being does not exist on the face of the globe than the negro slave of the United States." For Dew, Nat Turner better symbolized why whites should desist from collective action than why they should feel an urgency to act: "But one limited massacre is recorded in Virginia history; let her liberate her slaves," and it "will be almost certain to bring down ruin and degradation on both the whites and the blacks."

Dew supported his position in various ways. He reached for a biblical justification of slavery: in the Old Testament the "Children of Israel were themselves slave-holders," and in the New Testament, though slavery in the Roman Empire was "a thousand times more cruel than slavery in our own country," Christ himself never challenged slavery. Slavery, for Dew, rather than being incompatible with republican liberty was basic to it, for slavery fostered "the perfect spirit of equality so prevalent among the whites of all the slaveholding states."

Even more important, Dew could not compromise on the sanctity of property, regardless of whether it was in slaves, and he called on "Western Virginia and the non-slave-holders of Eastern Virginia, not to be allured" by arguments that the state could interfere in property holding. Finally, for Dew, the French Revolution demonstrated why no legislature should be so wantonly foolish as to "tamper" with "the fundamental relations of society."

Then Dew veered from proslavery to antislavery. If only the legislature would leave slavery alone—and especially if it would foster improvements in the national infrastructure—then Virginia would emulate Maryland in gradually abandoning slavery through social and economic evolution. Towns would emerge in rural eastern Virginia, and plantations would become farms. Let the slave trade to the Deep South continue. Free labor would replace slave labor in Virginia, as white immigrants displaced black emigrants.

Looking far down the road, Dew could envision an all-white, free labor Virginia. Not only was a legislative emancipation scheme incapable of resulting in such an outcome, it would make things far worse for everyone rather than any better for anyone. Eventually, Dew forecast, "abolitionists will find" that this natural process was "working to their heart's content, increasing the prosperity of Virginia, and diminishing the evils of slavery without those impoverishing effects which all other schemes must necessarily have."

Dew as a political economist, a devotee of free trade but not necessarily of laissez-faire, had in mind the proper role of government, national and state, with regard to slavery. He blamed the federal government and its high tariff, not slavery, for the South's economic malaise. The federal government's current policies damaged Virginia; so would the state if it embraced an emancipation scheme. The state government should protect, not challenge, wealth invested in slaves, and its actions should foster economic growth and development through banking and transportation improvements. Subsequent proslavery theoreticians built on Dew's work, but they ignored his talk of "the evils of slavery."

—Peter Wallenstein

See also
Proslavery Argument, United States; Virginia Slavery Debate
For Further Reading
Faust, Drew Gilpin. 1979. "A Southern Stewardship: The Intellectual and the Proslavery Argument." *American Quarterly* 31 (Spring): 63–80; Freehling, William W. 1990. *The Road to Disunion: Secessionists at Bay, 1776–1854.* New York: Oxford University Press; Harrison, Lowell. 1949. "Thomas Roderick Dew: Philosopher of the Old South." *Virginia Magazine of History and Biography* 57 (October): 390–404; Stampp, Kenneth M. 1942. "An Analysis of T. R. Dew's *Review of the Debate in the Virginia Legislature.*" *Journal of Negro History* 27 (October): 380–387.

DIAS, BARTOLOMEU
(C. 1450–1500)

A Portuguese navigator, Bartolomeu Dias was the first known European to sail from the Atlantic Ocean to the Indian Ocean. In 1487, Dias was named leader of a small fleet of three caravels—one under his command; another under that of Diogo Dias, his brother; and the third in the charge of João Infante. The three were accompanied by some of Portugal's premier pilots, including Pero de Alenquer (who would later accompany Vasco da Gama to India), Álvaro Martins, and João Santiago. The expedition left Lisbon in August 1487 and returned home early in December 1488.

This voyage followed up the exploits of Diogo Cão, who earlier that decade had been the first European to see the mouth of the Congo River and had sailed as far as 22° south latitude. Dias continued down the southern African coast, swinging out to sea and going 45° south latitude before turning north and touching land near Mossel Bay about 250 miles east of the Cape of Good Hope. Eventually he reached the Great Fish River (Rio do Infante) on the southeastern coast of the Cape. Several days later, the expedition began its return, sighting the Cape of Good Hope for the first time, continuing along the west coast of Africa to the island of Príncipe in the Gulf of Guinea, and then to Mina in West Africa and on to Portugal.

The results of the voyages of both Diogo Cão and Bartolomeu Dias were made known to the world by a German cartographer best known by the Latinized version of his name, Henricus Martellus, who was living in Florence, Italy. Martellus's map, probably prepared in 1489 and engraved in 1490, was important for the geographical knowledge of the time because—thanks to Dias's voyage and in contrast to Ptolemaic cartography—the map showed that the Indian Ocean was not an inland sea.

Little else is known of Dias's life, and attempts at a more complete biography are complicated because there were many other fifteenth-century Portuguese seafarers with the same name. However, most historians agree that the Bartolomeu Dias who rounded the Cape of Good Hope accompanied Diogo de Azambuja's expedition of 1481–1482, which set up the fortress at São Jorge da Mina (St. George's), the important Portuguese commercial center for the Guinea coast and the islands of São Tomé and Príncipe.

In 1497, he accompanied Vasco da Gama as far as the Cape Verde Islands, and from there he sailed to São Jorge da Mina while da Gama continued on to India. Dias also captained one of the 13 ships of an armada headed by Pedro Álvares Cabral on the followup to da Gama's voyage to India, but after touching Brazil, his ship and 3 others of the armada were lost with all aboard in a sudden storm somewhere in the South Atlantic on May 24, 1500. Dias's grandson, Paulo Dias de Novais, after exploring the area that is now within the boundaries of Angola, was named lord-proprietor of that captaincy in 1571, in part because of the services of Dias.

—Francis A. Dutra

See also
Gama, Vasco da
For Further Reading
Albuquerque, Luís de. 1987. *Navegadores, viajantes, e*

aventureiros Portugueses: Séculos XV e XVI. Lisbon: Caminho; Diffie, Bailey W., and George D. Winius. 1977. *Foundations of the Portuguese Empire, 1415–1580.* Minneapolis: University of Minnesota Press; Fonseca, Luís Adão da. 1987. *O Essencial sôbre Bartolomeu Dias.* Lisbon: Imprensa Nacional-Casa da Moeda; Peres, Damião. 1983. *Histsbon: Imprensa Nacional-Casa da Moe.* Porto: Vertente.

DIASPORA
See African Diaspora

DISEASES AND AFRICAN SLAVERY IN THE NEW WORLD

Diseases played a pivotal role in the economic history of African slavery in the Americas as well as in the experiences of Europeans in both Africa and the New World. The trade in African peoples caused an unforeseen exchange of pathogens that changed the course of history. The Old World pathogens introduced into to the Americas by both Africans and Europeans irreversibly changed the disease environment across the various climatic and geographic regions of the New World.

Diseases evolve in specific environments and locations, and humans residing in those environments develop resistance, both innate and acquired, to pathogens native to their locale. Evolutionary biology indicates that human populations that have survived for generations and millennia in a specific disease environment will be less susceptible to the diseases that predominate in their region and more susceptible to diseases from different areas. Populations that have lived in distinct locations endowed with different climates and geographies would have developed different genetic endowments.

Diseases cull from populations those individuals whose genetic inheritance makes them susceptible to the diseases that exist in their homeland. Genes that confer a relative resistance to the pathogens of a location give humans that possess those genes a better chance of reproducing and, consequently, passing their genes on to future generations. The result is that those genes become more frequent in the population. An increased exposure to a variety of pathogens leads to a greater genetic (inborn) resistance to a larger number of diseases in the population. In addition to developing innate resistance, endemic diseases result in acquired childhood immunities in the afflicted populations. Consequently, people of different origins have disparate reactions to a given pathogen because they have different acquired and innate immunities to diseases native to their places of birth and residence.

The nature of diseases and the reasons for their different impact on different peoples were not understood during the centuries that the African slave trade and African slavery existed in the New World. Upon contact with peoples of other origins, Africans and people of African descent were less susceptible to pathogens that were "African" (endemic to Africa) and more susceptible to pathogens that were "European" (endemic to Europe). Conversely, Europeans and people of European descent were less susceptible to European pathogens and more susceptible to African ones. When people of African (European) descent were exposed to disease pathogens endemic to Europe (Africa), they experienced substantially higher rates of morbidity and mortality than did the people who were native to each of the disease environments.

A number of diseases affected the economic history of Africans and Europeans in the Americas and Europeans in Africa. The "European" diseases that played an important role are regarded today as primarily cold-weather and/or childhood diseases, such as upper-respiratory infections, tuberculosis, chicken pox, measles, mumps, pleurisy, influenza, pneumonia, and whooping cough. The "African" diseases that were important were primarily of tropical West African origin: malaria, yellow fever, dengue fever, hookworm, schistosomiasis, and other fevers and worm infections. Smallpox, which probably affected the greatest number of people, is in a class by itself.

Europeans involved in the slave trade came into contact with pathogens for which they had had little or no prior exposure. Europeans' susceptibility to pathogens from tropical West Africa (the area that supplied the vast majority of African slaves to the Americas) was so extraordinarily high that the papal ambassador to Portugal considered it a death sentence, and a violation of the concords that the papacy had with the Portuguese, if Catholic prelates were sent into exile there. Since Africa was a "white man's graveyard," direct contacts and trade in African slaves, especially in the interior of Africa, were carried on by African intermediaries, people of mixed African and European backgrounds, and the few hardy and lucky Europeans who survived the onslaught of African pathogens.

There are a number of reliable estimates for European mortality in Africa during Europe's involvement in the African slave trade. Estimates during the first years of European residence in tropical West Africa in the late-seventeenth and early-eighteenth centuries range from a low of 540 deaths per 1,000 per year to a high of 667 deaths per 1,000. The estimated mortality rate for European sailors during the loading of African slaves off the coast of Africa in the late-eighteenth century is 238 per 1,000 sailors per year; the comparable estimate for the enslaved Africans during loading is only 45.3 per 1,000 Africans. Estimates of the annual mortality rates for European troops in the British army stationed in West Africa during the early-nineteenth century range from 483 to 683 per 1,000 European troops; the comparable estimate for African troops in the British army stationed in West Africa is 32 deaths per 1,000. The reason for these mortality differences is the ethnically disparate reactions to diseases.

There are no reliable historical data for morbidity before the middle of the nineteenth century. However, present-day data combined with historical data on mortality and our knowledge of the disease environment allow some well-founded conjectures about morbidity rates in the past. Some diseases, such as malaria and hookworm, had low mortality rates but were virtually hyperendemic in Africa and parts of the New World, which means that the mortality rate would be an unrealistically low indicator of the incidence of these diseases. People were sickened by hookworm and malaria, but they were not killed by them.

The migration of Africans and Europeans to the Americas set in motion interchanges of human and nonhuman organisms that fundamentally altered the ecology of the various climatic and geographic regions of the New World. Prior to contact with the Old World, the Americas were relatively disease free; after contact, the disease environments in the various regions of the New World resembled their Old World counterparts. The imported diseases decimated the Amerindian populations, who had little resistance to Old World pathogens. Tropical America became infested with pathogens from tropical West Africa, and the temperate regions of the New World were infested with the diseases of temperate Europe. The regional specificity of pathogens also affected the patterns of settlement. The eventual greater relative numbers of Africans in the semitropical areas of the New World and the predominance of Europeans in the temperate regions were owing to the altered biological environment.

Once the diseases reached beyond a critical threshold, the New World regional environments began to change. As one traveled further north in the Northern Hemisphere or further south in the Southern Hemisphere, the disease environments increasingly became dominated by cold-weather European diseases. Further south in the Northern Hemisphere (or further north in the Southern Hemisphere), the disease environments evolved into a mixture of cold-weather European and warm-weather African diseases. In the tropics, the disease environment became "African," and, relative to Europeans, Africans lived longer and healthier lives in the tropical areas of the Americas. That fact made African labor economically more valuable than European labor in the tropics because it increased the Africans' lifetime productivity relative to that of the Europeans. Over time, Africans and their descendants became the predominant source of unskilled agricultural labor in tropical America.

Once European pathogens became endemic to the temperate regions of the Americas, Europeans lived longer and healthier lives there compared to the Africans. That increased their lifetime productivity in the temperate regions, making European labor more economically valuable than African labor in those regions. Accordingly, Europeans and their descendants became the predominant source of unskilled agricultural labor in the temperate regions. In the U.S. South, Europeans lived longer but less healthy lives than Africans. Africans were less susceptible to malaria and hookworm (both warm-weather diseases), and those diseases struck during the economically critical (for agriculture) warm-weather months. Thus, Africans were more productive and more valuable to planters in the U.S. South as summer weather prevailed longer there. The changed disease environment in the South created an environment that led to the concentration of African slavery there.

The growth of African slavery as a predominant source of labor in the U.S. South during the eighteenth century indicates that substantial differences in regional productivity between Africans and Europeans emerged during this period. Estimates of the mortality rates for Africans and African Americans (blacks) and Europeans and European-Americans (whites) indicate that blacks lived shorter and less healthy lives the further north they resided in the British mainland colonies.

In Philadelphia, estimated annual mortality rates in the eighteenth century are 67 deaths per 1,000 for blacks and 46 deaths per 1,000 for whites. In Boston, the rates are 80 deaths per 1,000 for blacks and 32 deaths per 1,000 for whites. In the summer months in Philadelphia, however, estimated annual mortality rates are 36 per 1,000 for blacks and 60 per 1,000 for whites. Mortality estimates for cold-weather diseases only are 88 per 1,000 for blacks and 47 per 1,000 for whites. For warm-weather diseases only, estimated rates are 59 deaths per 1,000 for blacks and 52 deaths per 1,000 for whites. Estimated mortality rates for troops in the British army stationed in the Caribbean during the early-nineteenth century show similar ethnic differences. Again, the reason for the differences is the disparate reactions to diseases.

A somewhat paradoxical result of African slavery is that it cursed both the enslaved Africans and the European migrants to the Americas. It was only after a significant African slave trade was established that the New World disease environment began to resemble that of the Old World. The changed environment made the U.S. South a pesthole and the New World tropics a graveyard for Europeans.

—*Philip R. P. Coelho and Robert A. McGuire*

For Further Reading
Coelho, Philip R. P., and Robert A. McGuire. 1997. "African and European Bound Labor in the British New World: The Biological Consequences of Economic Choices." *Journal of Economic History* 57 (March): 83–115; Curtin, Philip D. 1968. "Epidemiology and the Slave Trade." *Political Science Quarterly* 83: 90–216; Kiple, Kenneth F., and Virginia Himmelsteib King. 1981. *Another Dimension to the Black Diaspora.* New York: Cambridge University Press; McNeill, William H. 1977. *Plagues and Peoples.* New York: Anchor Books.

DISQUISITION ON GOVERNMENT

See Calhoun's *Disquisition on Government*

DOMESDAY BOOK
(1086)

The Domesday Book, compiled in England in 1086, was the result of an effort on the part of William I (William the Conqueror) to gather and record statistical information about the holdings of all areas under Norman rule, including such things as the amount of land and the number of laborers and slaves each landholder maintained. Although the accuracy of the Domesday Book is not sufficient enough for it to be used as statistical data, its information is useful because it shows a definite decline of slavery in England.

The officials who were sent to the various counties under Norman authority were required to question each landholder regarding his holdings during three different periods: in the time of Edward the Confessor (i.e., before William I); at the time William I conquered England (i.e., 1066); and the present time (1086). Because most holdings had transferred from Saxon to Norman hands following the victory of William the Conqueror, significant change had occurred in both ownership and method of maintenance since the time of Edward. One of the most apparent of these changes was a decrease in the number of slaves and an increase in the number of free laborers.

Occupants of each manor were recorded according to position—whether free, laborer, or slave. However, the headings the various groups appeared under are inconsistent, which presents several problems when one tries to determine exact figures. For example, in only a few areas were slaves recorded as either male, *servi,* or female, *ancillae.* Generally, all slaves, regardless of gender, were recorded as *servi.* Nor is it clear whether those recorded represented individual slaves or heads of slave households.

There is also difficulty in distinguishing between the categories of slave and laborer. Although *servi* and *ancillae* clearly refer to slaves, other terms used, like *cotarii, bordarii,* and *villani,* are not so easily understood. Their use was not consistent, which suggests that in some cases they represented slaves while in others they indicated free laborers. *Bordarii* ("smallholders") and *cotarii* ("cottagers") suggest laborers of lesser status, holding either a small piece of land or a cottage, as the names imply; *villani* was a common term for villagers or commoners. In many of the areas recorded, the number of *servi* shows a decrease while the figures for *cotarii* and *bordarii* increase, which suggests that members of those groups had once been slaves, or were descended from slaves, and in acquiring their smallholdings had risen to the level of free laborer.

The distribution of *servi* in the Domesday Book shows a distinct geographical pattern. Slaves were most prevalent in the west of England, where the Celtic tradition of slavery was strongest, and less so in the east, where areas under the Danelaw (the law in force in the part of England held by the Danes before the Norman Conquest) included the highest numbers of freemen. Although cultural practice affected the use of slaves, other factors like quality of land and economic development played a part as well. Land in the east was more suited to farming, and a more sophisticated economy also existed there, which meant that it was more profitable for landholders to hire self-sufficient laborers as they were needed than to support slaves whether they were needed or not.

The Domesday Book's inconsistencies and lack of definition of terms make it unreliable in determining exact numbers of slaves in England, but it does provide a valuable record of the decline of slavery in England at the time when the old structures of labor in use under the Saxons were being replaced by the feudal system under the Normans.

—*Elizabeth Schoales*

See also
Celts; Serfdom in Medieval Europe; Slavery in Medieval Europe; Vikings

For Further Reading
Moore, John S. 1988. "Domesday Slave." *Anglo-Norman Studies* 11: 191–220; Morris, John. 1976. *Domesday Book.* Chichester, Eng.: Phillimore; Pelteret, David A. E. 1995. *Slavery in Early Mediaeval England from the Reign of Alfred until the Twelfth Century.* Woodbridge, Eng.: Boydell Press; Wood, Michael. 1986. *Domesday: A Search for the Roots of England.* New York: BBC Books.

DOMESTIC SLAVE TRADE IN THE UNITED STATES

The domestic slave trade in the United States was the internal movement of slaves from the upper South and eastern seaboard states to the cotton- and sugar-producing regions of the old Southwest. The trade's golden age followed the abolition of the international slave trade by Britain in 1807 and by the United States in 1808 and the subsequent expansion of the cotton region following the War of 1812 between Great Britain and the United States. From the 1790s through the 1820s, there was a gradual increase of slave trading south from the Chesapeake Bay area and the Carolinas, with 40,000 to 50,000 transportations in the 1790s and 150,000 by the 1820s.

As the South's slave system expanded into the old Southwest, the domestic trade moved south and west to accommodate it. Some states, and regions within states, changed from being net importers to net exporters of slaves. Georgia, which had imported slaves until the 1830s, became a net exporter of slaves in the 1850s. The 1830s through the 1850s witnessed further expansion of the trade, averaging nearly a quarter of a million movements, or 10 percent of the upper South's slave population, each decade. Over 1 million American-born slaves were transported via the domestic trade.

The mechanisms for the domestic trade were well developed. Slave-trading firms (e.g., Franklin and Armfield) specializing in mass purchases of slaves operated throughout the South, but professional slave traders, operating independent of the trading firms, purchased either individually or in small groups most of the slaves transported in the trade. After purchasing slaves in summer and early autumn, traders usually transported them south during fall and put them on the market in early winter at New Orleans, Louisiana, or Natchez, Mississippi, the major entrepôts for trade into the old Southwest. En route to their new homes, most slaves were transported in overland coffles, some containing 300 slaves. Additionally, an active waterborne trade flourished between the eastern seaboard ports (Baltimore, Alexandria, Norfolk, Richmond, and Charleston) and along the Mississippi River and its tributaries to the New Orleans and Natchez markets.

The domestic trade was one of the most hotly debated issues of the antebellum period. Abolitionists attacked the trade and the destruction of slave families it entailed as the penultimate evil of the South's slave system. They charged that the change from tobacco to wheat cultivation in the Chesapeake Bay region had revealed the unprofitable nature of slavery and led slaveowners in the upper South to switch from plantation agriculture to slave breeding. Proslavery apologists countered that plantation owners treated their slaves paternalistically and encouraged the formation of slave families; most interregional movements of slaves resulted from planter migrations west to more fertile lands; planters sold slaves only when economic hardship required them to do so; the trade was unprofitable; and most important, slave traders were pariahs within Southern society.

Historians' examinations of the nature of the trade have challenged the abolitionists' contention that the upper South was a breeding ground for slaves. Since most slaves were sold after age eight, it was unprofitable, and thus unlikely, for slaveowners to breed their slaves solely for the purpose of selling them. However, abolitionists were correct in arguing that the trade destroyed slave families as nearly 20 percent of all slave marriages in the upper South were destroyed by it. In addition, the number of slave families sold and transported as a unit accounted for less than 2 percent of the total trade. Between 1820 and 1860, slaveowners in the upper South sold 10 percent of that region's teenage slave population to slave traders, the very age group necessary for the formation of slave families.

The proslavery defense of the domestic slave trade has not withstood the scrutiny of historical inquiry, as is demonstrated by Michael Tadman's *Speculators and Slaves* (1996). Tadman contends that the scale of the domestic slave trade destroyed black families more than any paternalistic sentiments toward encouraging families could have hoped to accomplish. The proslavery argument that most slaves were part of planter migrations is also specious; from the 1810s and 1820s on, 60 percent of the slaves transported to the lower South were sold to slave traders. In addition, slaveowners willingly speculated in the domestic slave trade. Tadman argues that only 4–5 percent of slaves sold to traders were sold out of economic necessity. He notes that from the 1830s on, the sale of slaves to traders resulted in windfall profits for the seller while profits from the resale of slaves often made traders some of the wealthiest men in their communities. As such, slave traders gained positions of influence, power, and respect within Southern society and were hardly the pariahs proslavery apologists contended they were.

Historians continue to grapple with the significance of the domestic slave trade in the United States. Several historians, including Robert Fogel and Stanley Engerman in *Time on the Cross* (1974), have discounted both the scale and the significance of the trade, but Tadman's groundbreaking work convincingly argues that the domestic slave trade was a central characteristic of the antebellum South's slave system and offers profound insight into the functioning of that system.

—*John Grenier*

See also
Breeding of Slaves; Franklin and Armfield; Paternalism
For Further Reading
Caldehead, William. 1972. "How Extensive Was the Border State Slave Trade? A New Look." *Civil War History* 18 (1): 42–55; Kotlikoff, Laurence J., and Sebastian Pinera. 1977. "The Old South's Stake in the Inter-Regional Movement of Slaves, 1850–1860." *Journal of Economic History* 37 (2): 434–450; Tadman, Michael. 1996. *Speculators and Slaves: Masters, Traders, and Slaves in the Old South.* Madison: University of Wisconsin Press; Wesley, Charles H. 1942. "Manifests of Slave Shipments along the Waterways, 1808–1864." *Journal of Negro History* 27 (2): 155–174.

DOUGLASS, FREDERICK (C. 1817–1895)

The most famous and influential former slave in the United States in the nineteenth century, Frederick Douglass rose from being a slave in Maryland to being a popular abolitionist lecturer, narrator of slavery, newspaper publisher, president of the Freedmen's Bank, and author of *Lessons of the Hour* (1892), a denunciation of lynching. The story of his confrontation with a "slave-breaker" is a classic moment in the literature of Southern slavery, but Douglass's greater importance lies in the work he did after fleeing bondage in 1838.

Neither the fame nor the power could have been predicted from Douglass's origins as Frederick Bailey, house slave. But when he learned to read, while serving in a Baltimore home, he was inspired by a dialogue in the *Columbian Orator* that denounced the injustice of owning human beings. Determined to win his freedom, even while he was a field hand and caulker who was obliged to turn over his wages to his master, the intrepid "Fred" borrowed the free papers of a black sailor and went to Massachusetts. There, he was joined by his wife, took a new name, and joined the abolitionists around William Lloyd Garrison.

Although admired, Douglass was always controversial. His assurance and intelligence angered some whites—later, he and Garrison would be estranged by political differences—and he tangled with the "holiness" militant, Sojourner Truth, on religious grounds. Outstanding among fugitive and former slaves for his literary skills and the power of his address, Douglass

Frederick Douglass

was even charged with faking the role of former slave. These attacks persuaded him to commit his life story to print as the *Narrative of the Life of Frederick Douglass, an American Slave: Written by Himself* (1845).

With the publication of the book, Douglass grew famous but endangered. He sailed to Great Britain, where his power and insights were acclaimed, to lecture in England, Ireland, and Scotland. In 1846, English friends purchased Douglass from his legal master so he could continue his campaign to establish racial justice in the United States. A year later, Douglass returned to the land of his birth and began a publishing career with the help of fellow activist, Martin Delany.

In Douglass's newspaper—first called the *North Star,* after the astronomical signpost to the free states, and later *Frederick Douglass' Paper*—the country's most famous former slave excoriated the practice of owning and trading in human beings and advocated women's rights. He also stoutly opposed the exclusion of blacks from white churches and the segregation of public schools in the United States and analyzed the theory of separate accommodations for blacks and whites. In 1855, he rewrote and expanded his life story as *My Bondage and My Freedom* to distance himself from the white "handlers" who had limited his participation in the abolitionist cause.

Too brilliant to go unnoticed, Douglass was attacked for the *Narrative*'s harsh words about the Christianity of slaveholders; his dark view of racial justice in the United States, both before and after the slaves were freed; and his second marriage, to a white woman, in 1884. Verbally gifted and tirelessly dedicated, Douglass rode out such attacks to become the century's most feted black man. His important essays include "What to the Slave Is the Fourth of July?" (1852), which has been called the greatest abolitionist address, and "The Claims of the Negro, Ethnologically Considered" (1854).

Persuaded of the need for violent resistance by passage of the Fugitive Slave Act in 1850, Douglass was privy to John Brown's plans to initiate insurrection in the slave states, and Douglass welcomed the onset of civil war and helped to recruit black troops with essays like "Men of Color, To Arms!" (1863). Two of his four children served in the famous Massachusetts Fifty-fourth Regiment, but Douglass would come to scorn the injustices that the Union army meted out to black volunteers. "No war," he demanded, in 1864, "but an Abolition war; no peace but an Abolition peace; liberty for all, Chains for none; the black man a soldier in war, a laborer in peace; a voter at the South as well as at the North; America his permanent home, and all Americans his fellow-countrymen" (Foner, 1964). In August of the same year, Douglass proposed that black federal agents infiltrate the slave states to incite the bolder slaves to revolt. Lincoln was apprized of the scheme, but it was never tried.

Douglass continued to fight for social reforms after the slaves were emancipated. In the essay "We Are Not Yet Quite Free" (1869), he informed Americans: "We have been turned out of the house of bondage, but we have not yet been fully admitted to the glorious temple of American liberty. We are still in a transition stage." He concluded, "and the future is shrouded in doubt and danger" (Foner, 1964). He defended the new rights of blacks during Reconstruction, remonstrated with Andrew Johnson for his pro-South policies, and cheered the passage of the Fifteenth Amendment, which gave black men the right to vote.

Douglass served as marshal of and recorder of deeds for the District of Columbia, minister-resident and consul-general to Haiti, and chargé d'affaires for Santo Domingo when its annexation to the United States was under discussion. In 1892, Haiti appointed him to represent the country at the Columbian Exposition in Chicago, and he used the opportunity to distribute copies of the pamphlet he cowrote with Ida B. Wells, "Why the Colored American Is Not in the World's Columbian Exposition." At the end of his life, when Douglass was asked what course young black Americans should follow, he replied: "Agitate! Agitate! Agitate!"

—*Barbara Ryan*

See also
Abolition, United States; Autobiographies; Brown, John; Delany, Martin R.; Garrison, William Lloyd; Narratives; *North Star;* Truth, Sojourner

For Further Reading
Douglass, Frederick. 1855. *My Bondage and My Freedom.* New York: Miller, Orton; Douglass, Frederick. 1845. *Narrative of the Life of Frederick Douglass, an American Slave: Written by Himself.* Boston: American Anti-Slavery Office; Foner, Philip S. 1964. *Frederick Douglass: A Biography.* New York: Citadel; Quarles, Benjamin. 1968. *Frederick Douglass.* New York: Oxford University Press.

DRED SCOTT V. SANDFORD
(1857)

Although universally condemned as the U.S. Supreme Court's worst decision, *Dred Scott v. Sandford* emerged amid deep political crisis. Renewed sectional conflict over slavery's extension had shattered the relative calm that had been won by the Compromise of 1850. With Kansas erupting into bloody conflict and South Carolina representative Preston Brooks viciously assaulting Massachusetts senator Charles Sumner, the spring of 1856 saw the slavery issue flare up once again and threaten the nation. In this political setting, the Supreme Court heard the first of two oral arguments in the Dred Scott case. In response to heightening tensions, Chief Justice Roger Taney sought to impose his own judicial solution on the problems posed by slavery's extension.

The case centered on whether a slave named Dred Scott became a freeman by residing in free territory, and whether he had standing as a Missouri citizen to make that claim in federal court. What the case ended up representing was something much different: Taney's decision came to symbolize the danger of judicial ambition exceeding its grasp and reminds us that not all constitutional conflicts are amenable to judicial resolution.

The lawsuit arose from two series of events: the travels of Dred Scott with his owner, Dr. John Emerson, and congressional efforts to prevent slavery's expansion into western territories. Buying Scott in 1833, Emerson, an assistant surgeon in the U.S. Army, took him from St. Louis, Missouri, to Fort Armstrong in Illinois, a free state. Emerson, who complained repeatedly of physical ailments and about his military postings, was later transferred to Wisconsin Territory, in what is now Minnesota. Because of the Missouri Compromise (1820), Wisconsin Territory (later called Iowa Territory) was a free state and no slavery existed there.

During his stay in that free territory, Scott married Harriet Robinson, but subsequently he followed Emerson to Louisiana and then back to Minnesota, as Emerson continued requesting transfers. Emerson married Eliza Irene Sanford in 1838 during his brief sojourn to Louisiana, and in 1840, Mrs. Emerson, along with Dred and Harriet Scott, returned to St. Louis while her husband served in Florida during the Seminole War. Emerson's duties in Florida lasted two years before he was honorably discharged. Returning north, he tried establishing a private medical practice in Iowa but died shortly after leaving the army, possibly of syphilis.

In 1846, Dred and Harriet Scott filed suit for freedom against Mrs. Emerson in state court in St. Louis, claiming that their travels and residence (on two occasions) in free territory had removed their condition of slavery. Legal precedent existed in Missouri to support their argument, and in 1850, after initial legal wrangling, a state judge declared Dred Scott (and by extension, his wife) free. But by this time Mrs. Emerson had moved to Massachusetts, leaving her affairs in the care of her brother, John F. A. Sanford. Sanford appealed the ruling to the Missouri Supreme Court, which over-

Dred Scott

turned the lower court's decision in 1852.

Shortly thereafter, Scott filed another suit, this time in federal court, against Sanford, claiming diversity jurisdiction because of Sanford's residence in New York. (The case is entitled *Dred Scott v. Sandford* because a clerk misspelled Sanford's name in the court records.) Sanford's attorneys claimed that Scott had no standing to sue in federal court; quite simply, because he was a slave he was not a Missouri citizen. The judge ruled that Scott had the necessary standing to sue, but the jury nonetheless returned a verdict against him. Scott appealed the verdict to the U.S. Supreme Court.

The issues presented before the Supreme Court were threefold: the question of Dred Scott's citizenship, the status of slaves living on free soil, and the constitutionality of federal legislation prohibiting slavery in the territories. Clearly, Justice Taney did not have to rule on all three; he could have narrowly interpreted the issues and confined his ruling to Scott's standing to sue in federal court. But Taney wanted to impose a judicial solution on this intractable political problem. Taney hoped to resolve the constitutional status of slavery in the territories by deciding the issue in favor of Southern interests, but in doing so, he solved too much and established the basic framework for the U.S. Civil War.

What, then, did Taney rule? First, he declared that blacks were not citizens of the United States, nor could states bestow U.S. citizenship on them. In a gross historical distortion, Taney claimed that blacks never had been citizens nor could they ever become citizens. According to Taney, blacks, whether free or slave, were not part of the original popular sovereignty that had created the United States. At the Founding, wrote Taney, only whites were citizens. Moreover, states could not expand their definitions of citizenship to include free blacks because naturalization was a federal responsibility. Accordingly, no black had the standing to sue, as a U.S. citizen, in federal courts.

This ruling, alone, ended Dred Scott's claim, but Taney, propelled by a need to resolve larger political issues, continued. He ruled, second, that slavery was a property right recognized by the U.S. Constitution. Therefore, Congress could not outlaw slavery in territories, nor could territories exclude slaveholders. As a consequence, the Missouri Compromise was unconstitutional, and in short, all territories were slave territories. They were, Taney ruled, the common lands of the United States and therefore their governments must recognize the property rights of all U.S. citizens, including slaveholders.

Taney's decision drew on two important factors of

American political ideology: a doctrine of racial superiority and a doctrine of limited government. The first dimension of Taney's decision is obvious, but the second merits further attention. Taney argued that Congress cannot destroy through legislative action property that is recognized as legitimate throughout much of the nation. Because congressional powers are limited, their scope cannot be exceeded without violating the Founders' first concern, the protection of liberty. A government of limited powers is a government that protects liberty, but Taney transformed that doctrine by linking it with the defense and preservation of slavery. A popular sovereignty committed to slavery at the local level necessarily meant slavery at the national level if congressional powers were as limited as Taney claimed they were. For Taney, slavery was a necessary outcome of the conjunction of popular sovereignty and congressional limitations, and that linkage soon spurred events much larger than Dred Scott or Roger Taney.

Taney's decision lit a fire in the North. It dramatically fueled the Republican Party's growth and convinced its members that slavery, in addition to being morally wrong, was an assault on the North and the cause of liberty. Rather than resolving the contradiction between slavery and liberty that lay at the heart of the country's founding, Taney's decision propelled the nation headlong into a bloody struggle to redefine the terms of that bitter compromise. In the wake of the Civil War, the nation overturned Taney's decision by ratifying the Thirteenth and Fourteenth Amendments, which ended slavery throughout the United States, explicitly created national citizenship, and provided for the equal protection of the law for all persons.

John F. A. Sanford died in an insane asylum less than two months after the decision came down, and Dred Scott was manumitted shortly thereafter. Scott lived only 16 months as a freeman before dying of tuberculosis.

—*Douglas S. Reed*

For Further Reading
Ehrlich, Walter. 1979. *They Have No Rights: Dred Scott's Struggle for Freedom*. Westport, CT: Greenwood Press; Fehrenbacher, Don E. 1978. *The Dred Scott Case*. New York: Oxford University Press.

DRUMS

African American music is multiethnic in the racial, cultural, and regional senses. Slaves from various African ethnic groups were brought to the Americas, and once enslaved in the Western Hemisphere, Europeans largely forced them to abandon their separate cultural identities and cast them into an amalgamated group that knew no cultural distinctions. Very few African traits were allowed to flourish openly, but those that survived did so in the essential, rather than the traditional, sense. Instead of speaking their traditional languages, the English the slaves spoke absorbed the rhythm and nuance of the African tongue. Elements of ritual dance combined with recreational and secular dance, and slaves played western instruments with the potency and vigor of the African style. The Africans had no choice but to use the structures afforded by their European captors. Accordingly, they synthesized (as opposed to syncretizing) a culture. Western expressive devices, like trumpets and drums, that were once old could become new, but not western, again.

Analyzing the drum's connection to slavery necessarily requires an expanded view of the instrument, which invites a broader understanding of a cultural aesthetic that overrides genres of instrumentation and defined disciplines. They took the drums away, but they could not stop the beat because Africans clapped their hands and stomped their feet; they put their hands in the air and slapped their knees, thighs, chest, heels, and mouths.

Drums signaled the 1739 Stono Uprising in South Carolina, which meant the end of the drum for Africans in the United States because that event heightened plantation owners' fears that "wild Negroes" would revolt—beating drums, dancing, and killing whites. Enticed by a desire to be free and by the open invitation of Florida's Spanish forces in a black-controlled area known as Fort Mose, the Africans acted. Nearly 100 Angolans and a few creolized Africans planned and executed the revolt they hoped would lead them to Florida. Some of them died and others were caught, but a few tasted freedom. But things would never be the same for black music as European domination, particularly by the British, meant that drums, dancing, and worship would be tightly controlled from that point on. The drum and many types of signal horns were banned.

Some writers argue that drums died in the Americas then—that the Americas have no drum culture. Obviously, this is an incorrect assumption. African Americans have consistently continued a vital drum culture that lives in languages (like Gullah), shouting, dancing, body percussion, hand clapping, juba (a dance of African origin), steppin', tambourine, call and response, work songs, and preaching. In Florida and Georgia's Maroon encampments (camps composed of fugitive black slaves) and on Sea Island plantations, Africans and their descendants hid drums and played them. At Congo Square in New Orleans, Louisiana, authorities "allowed" drums on certain occasions, and Florida's Seminole Indian camps offered another unique opportunity for musical synthesis as African and indigenous (primarily Creek) forms combined.

Concepts of pitch variation and polyrhythm are important in analyzing the development and evolution of drum culture in the United States, as these factors undergird the range of African-derived drum forms. Bessie Jones, a Sea Island musician and griot (an entertainer whose performances include tribal histories and genealogies), addressed these points in her book *Step It Down* (1987). Various practices like foot stomping, pitched hand claps, stamping the stick, tambourines, and bones all rest upon these ideas. The unique characteristic of this form of African-derived "drumming" draws its essential duality from tonal semantics—i.e., using subtle and overt intonation shifts to change meaning or feeling. That is essentially how pitch variation works. Drums are not merely rhythm or sound effects as in western music, they are the music. Pitch changes and manipulations allow musicians to create a range of sounds or moods equal to or greater than those of any tuned instrument.

Polyrhythm concerns the deliberate layering of those pitches into interlocking and/or contrasting rhythmic shapes, and rhythms are the superstructures of orchestrated patterns that move and breathe in relation to one another. Unisons (playing the same things simultaneously) are generally used as an effect rather than as the music's substance. Clearly then, the thumping of pestle in mortar, the clump of multiple axes on a tree, and the flailing of rice chaff were the plantation's drum music, especially when accompanied by rhythmic chanting and singing.

Drums live in the essence of African American sensibility through the previously mentioned forms and in contemporary musical forms such as rap, scat, and bebop. Both on plantations and in Maroon camps, drums were a form of praise, worship, and community. Even when banned, practices like the shout sprang forth, again making drums the center of the community. The shout, a circular shuffling movement supported by a "stampin' stick," hand claps, tambourine, and call and response was a culmination of all essential African American forms in lieu of the physical drum. The form developed in response to Christian worship's absence of drums, and African Americans invigorated Christian worship with it.

Drums connected African Americans to their ancestors. Worship was exhaustive, lively, and sparked with possessions by the Holy Spirit and trances. Sea Islanders' worship services were often considered vulgar, barbaric, and "too African." Their style, whether intentional or not, evoked the drum's true spirit in a new context. The shout brought together the best and most characteristic African American percussion styles. From call-and-response vocalizations to rhythmic movements, it underscored the African personality's innovative capacity and adaptability. Other forms of expression, including juba, buck dancing, and tap, owe much to the shout, either spiritually or literally, as they continue the idea of the front-line drum in a polytonal and polyrhythmic sense. From revolution to religion, drums have played and still play a central role for people and communities in the United States.

—*David Pleasant*

For Further Reading
Hartigan, Royal J. 1986. "Blood Drum Spirit: Drum Languages of West Africa, African-America, Native America, Central Java, and South India." Ph.D. dissertation, History Department, Wesleyan University, Middletown, CT; Jones, Bessie, and Bess Lomax Hawes. 1987. *Step it Down: Games, Plays, Songs, and Stories from the Afro-American Heritage*. Athens: University of Georgia Press.

DUBLIN

Vikings established the port of Dublin around A.D.1000 as a base from which to conduct raids on England, Scotland, and the European continent. Dublin was also an embarkation point for Viking longships heading west to Iceland, Greenland, and North America. Although Irish Celts who inhabited the Dublin area routinely took prisoners from neighboring provinces and parts of western Britain, it is generally believed that the organized exportation of enslaved Irish men and women began with the rise of Viking settlements. Icelandic sagas and several early Norse manuscripts repeatedly mention Irish slaves, and contemporary Irish literary and historical works like "Wars of Gaedhil with the Gall" poignantly lament losing men and women who were routinely abducted by Norse invaders.

Although the medieval transportation of Irish slaves out of Dublin is a well-documented phenomenon, the forced migration of many Irish people did not begin until the mid-seventeenth century. At that time, successive wars ravaged Ireland, and English imperial forces crushed a major uprising of Irish armies. Oliver Cromwell and his administrators were largely responsible for the mass exportation of Irish prisoners into forced servitude overseas. After Cromwell secured decisive victories throughout the British Isles, he was left with thousands of potentially dangerous prisoners, many of whom he allowed to flee to the Continent. The English sent many of the remaining prisoners to the colonies (mainly in the Caribbean) as indentured servants.

The type of bondage to which Irish political prisoners were subjected was significantly different than the "voluntary servitude" into which thousands of English and Irish men and women sold themselves later in the colonial period. Politically driven forms of indentured servitude during and after the Cromwellian conquest occupied an indefinite position between temporary bondage and permanent enslavement. Although evidence records few cases of Irish prisoners being in bondage for more than 15–20 years, these servants were clearly not laboring under similar conditions endured by "voluntary exiles" before and after. The main distinction between Irish indentured servants and African slaves was that "unlike slaves, servants were not sold as chattels" (Truxes, 1988). Irish prisoners, unlike other white bonded laborers in the West Indies, were often subjected to glaringly inhumane treatment by aristocrats of the planter class and were not given the monetary or material compensation usually provided to indentured servants when their period of servitude ended.

The Irish servant trade outlasted the Cromwellian period by nearly two centuries. Although the transportation of Irish men and women after the Protectorate's collapse and the end of the Jacobite risings was not as explicitly political an enterprise as it was during the days of open warfare, English overlords certainly did not discourage the westward movement of a people who did not share their cultural, religious, and (often) linguistic perspectives. Throughout the colonial period, the American colonies received nearly 10,000 Irish convicts. Obviously, the servant trade provided a useful way for the English to remove potentially revolutionary elements of the Irish populace.

Even before the 1707 union of the kingdoms of Ireland, England, and Scotland, oppressive legislation designed to hinder the growth of the Irish trade had been firmly established. By 1663, "Ireland was forbidden to ship anything directly to the colonies except servants, horses, and provisions" (James, 1985), and the imposition of tariffs on wool, linens, and other commodities created a greater emphasis within Dublin's trading community on exploiting the remaining unregulated resources, including human beings. Throughout the eighteenth and nineteenth centuries, thousands of Irish convicts, political prisoners, and economically desperate people from countryside were shipped out of Dublin.

Although a trade in Irish servants through Dublin was one of the mainstays of the Irish trade for centuries, there is little evidence to suggest that any significant movement of African slaves through Irish ports ever occurred. In 1767, a Cork newspaper advertised for sale "a likely negro boy about four years old, American born, and past all disorders," but such transactions were relatively rare. Yet, the relative absence of African slaves in Ireland itself did not prevent Irish merchants abroad from participating in the slave trade, and many of Dublin's Anglo-Irish and Scotch-Irish trading families, who had established themselves throughout the British Empire, conducted a thriving business in both Irish servants and African slaves. Most, however, did not rely on commerce in African slaves as their primary source of income. Generally, "Irishmen were not represented among the great West Indian slave traders" (Truxes, 1988), and most Dublin traders resorted to trafficking in African slaves only as a secondary component of their primary commerce in wool, provisions, linen, and indentured servants.

In the mid-nineteenth century, humanitarian organizations throughout the British Isles, but particularly in the Dublin metropolitan area, began agitating to end the Irish servant trade. The permanent enslavement of Africans had already been outlawed throughout the British Empire, and the continued exportation of Irish "white slaves" throughout the world (and particularly to the Caribbean) had begun to embarrass reform-minded politicians. Ironically, the decline in the transatlantic movement of Irish indentured servants was immediately followed by the Great Potato Famine (1845–1849), an unprecedented catastrophe that drove millions of starving Irish peasants overseas.

—*Kevin Brady*

See also
English Caribbean; Irish as Slaves in the Caribbean
For Further Reading
James, Francis G. 1985. "Irish Colonial Trade in the Eighteenth Century." *William and Mary Quarterly* 19 (3): 329–356; Truxes, Thomas M. 1988. *Irish American Trade, 1660–1783*. Cambridge: Cambridge University Press.

DUBOIS, SYLVIA
(C. 1768–1889)

Known for her quick tongue and aggressive behavior, Sylvia Dubois secured freedom from slavery through physical resistance, an avenue rarely available to women, and her militant stance against slavery demonstrates the multiple forms of resistance employed by slave women. Additionally, her experience in slavery suggests the dynamic relationship between African American women slaves and their mistresses.

Dubois was born a slave on New Jersey's Sourland Mountain sometime between 1768 and 1789. Her mother, Dorcas Compton, purchased her freedom with financing from Dominicus Dubois when Sylvia was two years of age, but when Compton failed to repay the loan, she and her children became Dubois's slaves. In her efforts to secure her freedom, Compton was forced to leave her children with Dubois in Great Bend, Pennsylvania, as she sought work elsewhere.

Left without her mother's protection, Sylvia suffered incredible abuse from her mistress, Mrs. Dubois, who used a variety of tools to abuse the young girl. Sylvia asserted, "She'd level me with anything she could get hold of—club, stick of wood, tongs, fire-shovel, knife, axe, hatchet, anything that was handiest" (Larison, 1988). Yet, after enduring years of torture, Sylvia maintained her will and eventually triumphed over Mrs. Dubois.

As a young girl, Sylvia determined to defend herself physically from her mistress's abuse when she became older and stronger, and Sylvia finally seized her opportunity when Mrs. Dubois struck her publicly. Sylvia recognized the advantage offered by an audience and struck her mistress in return. Both Mrs. Dubois and the onlookers were stunned by her action. Sylvia then warned the crowd against attacking her, declaring, "I smacked my fist at 'em, and told 'em to wade in if they dared and I'd thrash every devil of 'em" (Larison, 1988). Sylvia realized the crowd would be cautious of a black woman who was courageous, or insane, enough to strike her mistress in public. The fact that she was not attacked and escaped to the next town proved her surmise correct.

When Sylvia's master learned of her resistance and flight, he summoned her back to Great Bend and freed her on the condition that she take her child and leave the area. She moved to Flagtown, New Jersey, and worked until she inherited land on Sourland Mountain upon her father's death. She died on the mountain in 1889.

Although the date of Sylvia's birth is unclear, she was an expressive and articulate centenarian when she related her life story to Dr. Cornelius Wilson Larison in 1883. Larison published Sylvia's narrative in *Sylvia Dubois: A Biografy of the Slav Who Whipt Her Mistres and Gand Her Fredom* (1883).

—DoVeanna S. Fulton

For Further Reading
Larison, Cornelius Wilson. 1988. *Sylvia Dubois: A Biografy of the Slav Who Whipt Her Mistres and Gand Her Fredom*, Ed. Jared C. Lobdell. New York: Oxford University Press.

DUBOIS, WILLIAM EDWARD BURGHARDT (1868–1963)

William Edward Burghardt DuBois was the first professionally trained African American historian to examine slavery "scientifically." He devoted his life as a historian, sociologist, editor, and polemicist to explaining slavery's long-term negative influence on blacks and whites and race relations in the United States.

Raised among only a handful of blacks in western Massachusetts, as a youth W. E. B. DuBois had little firsthand contact with ex-slaves, their history, or their culture. It was when he was studying at Nashville's Fisk University in the 1880s that DuBois became familiar with and intrigued by the folk traditions of former slaves. After studying historical methods at the University of Berlin (1892–1894), he finished his doctorate at Harvard University under Albert Bushnell Hart, completing what became his landmark dissertation, *The Suppression of the African Slave-Trade to the United States of America, 1638–1870,* in 1896. The dissertation was the first volume published in the series Harvard Historical Studies.

In that study, DuBois argued that the white Founding Fathers, both northern and southern, never were committed seriously to ending the Atlantic slave trade in 1808. Driven by economic self-interest and racism, whites imported more than 250,000 Africans into the United States between the congressional prohibition on slave importations and 1862. The 1808 prohibition, DuBois noted with sarcasm, was "probably enforced as the people who made it wished it enforced." Coastal slave patrollers performed their tasks loosely, especially in the 1850s when some Southern partisans were lobbying for a reopening of the Atlantic slave trade. According to DuBois, the lax control of slave smuggling was part and parcel of white Americans' persistent "bargaining, truckling, and compromising" with slavery and its proponents.

Although DuBois exaggerated the number of Africans brought surreptitiously into the United States after 1808 and undervalued the natural rate of reproduction among slaves, his use of West African port records and other primary sources set a high standard for later studies of the transatlantic slave trade. He was also the first scholar to emphasize the broad panic Toussaint Louverture's 1791 Haitian slave revolt caused throughout the Atlantic rim. Alone among contemporary works, DuBois's pathbreaking *Suppression of the African Slave-Trade* sympathized openly with the plight of the expatriated Africans. He viewed with scorn white racism and the complicity of white officials at every level in the transatlantic slave trade.

In his many other writings, DuBois both explored particular features of American slavery and underscored slavery's direful legacy for race relations in the United States. In *The Philadelphia Negro* (1899), he remarked that the powerful, polygamous slave family, "with all its shortcomings," provided more protection for black women than "the promiscuous herding" of the U.S. slave plantation.

In an article published in *Southern Workman* in 1901, DuBois uncovered important connections between African building design and technology and the first homes of American slaves. They shared an essential form, he insisted, which meant windowless huts with woven walls and thatched roofs positioned around four posts. As "the cold brutality of slavery" increased, however, the slave cabins came to reflect the harshness of the institution.

In his classic work, *The Souls of Black Folk* (1903), DuBois analyzed the African contributions to African American slave religion. The slaves, DuBois explained, drew upon "the resources of Heathenism"—exorcism, witchcraft, Obi worship, spells, and blood sacrifices—to resist their captivity. The slave drew upon religion as a weapon to resist "the dark triumph of Evil over him." The slave preacher, according to DuBois, provided a vital cultural link between the slaves' African background, their ability to survive the hardships of slavery, and their preparation for the afterlife. The slaves, DuBois said, also drew upon their African-derived cultural forms, especially music, to withstand the horrors of enslavement.

In his popular book *The Negro* (1915), DuBois also championed the cultural achievements of past and contemporary Africans in art, industry, political organization, and religion. Three years later, DuBois attacked Ulrich B. Phillips, who then reigned as the master of slave historiography. According to DuBois, Phillips's *American Negro Slavery* (1918) was "curiously incomplete and unfortunately biased" (Smith, 1991). DuBois attacked Phillips both for his inability to treat blacks as "ordinary human beings" and for his unwillingness to see growth and change in blacks from the fifteenth to the twentieth centuries.

In later books, articles, and editorials, DuBois missed few opportunities to identify slavery as the source of the "veil" of racism that envelops society in the United States. For over six decades, DuBois eloquently and powerfully condemned slavery for denying the descendants of the slaves true freedom and justice.

—*John David Smith*

See also
Family; Housing, United States; Louverture, Toussaint; Phillips, Ulrich Bonnell

For Further Reading
Byerman, Keith E. 1994. *Seizing the Word: History, Art, and Self in the Work of W. E. B. DuBois*. Athens: University of Georgia Press; Lewis, David Levering. 1993. *W. E. B. DuBois: Biography of a Race*. New York: Henry Holt; Smith, John David. 1991. *An Old Creed for the New South: Proslavery Ideology and Historiography, 1865–1918*. Athens: University of Georgia Press; Zamir, Shamoon. 1995. *Dark Voices: W. E. B. DuBois and American Thought, 1888–1903*. Chicago: University of Chicago Press.

DUNMORE, JOHN MURRAY, FOURTH EARL OF (1730–1809)

On November 14, 1775, Virginia governor John Murray, fourth earl of Dunmore, offered freedom to slaves and indentured servants willing to desert rebel masters and join "his Majesty's troops . . . for more speedily reducing the Colony to a proper sense of their duty" (Selby, 1977). The proclamation was tactical, not humanitarian. Lord Dunmore needed soldiers and hoped to awe colonists into obedience; he did not wish to enact general emancipation.

Nonetheless, hundreds of slaves sought and obtained liberty by responding to his call. Dunmore reinforced the slaves' belief that a British victory provided the best hope for liberty. Consequently, his action galvanized slave resistance on the eve of the American Revolution and alarmed and angered slaveholders. Like no previous measure, it alienated the Southern colonies and spurred their drive for independence from Great Britain.

The decision to arm slaves itself reflected the collapse of imperial authority in Virginia, which Dunmore had exacerbated by seizing gunpowder from the public magazine in Williamsburg in April 1775 and weeks later taking refuge on a man-of-war stationed in the York River. Dunmore had exploited the colonists' fear of a slave revolt during the crisis by threatening to arm blacks and Indians if the colonists resisted British rule and by receiving on board his fleet nearly 100 escaped slaves in fall 1775.

After defeating the colonial militia at Kemp's Landing outside of Norfolk on November 14, Dunmore published his proclamation, declaring the colony in rebellion and calling upon all Virginians, including the rebels' slaves, to rally to the king's standard. Three hundred slaves joined Dunmore within a week of the proclamation; he may have recruited as many as 1,500 in succeeding months. The threat of punishment and the difficulty of reaching the flotilla from land discouraged others. Most who reached Dunmore were employed as soldiers in his Ethiopian Regiment, with many dressed in uniforms bearing the inscription, Liberty to Slaves.

The Ethiopian Regiment met a tragic end. Dunmore's defeat at Great Bridge in December 1775, where black soldiers composed nearly half of his troops, drove Dunmore to the James River, away from provisions and access to loyalists. Smallpox then decimated Dunmore's troops in spring and summer 1776 at Tucker's Point and Gwynn Island. The 300 remaining black troops went with Dunmore to New York in 1776, and some emigrated as free persons to Nova Scotia and England in 1783.

Dunmore's initiative had varied consequences. In arming slaves, the governor had acted on his own, and the controversial measure never received official approval, although slaves would figure significantly in British military strategy during the American Revolution. Commanders later granted liberty to slaves who defected from the rebels, and more than 10,000 escaped to British lines during the American Revolution. They were then employed as pioneers and military laborers, and the British honored some of the fugitives' claims to freedom at the conclusion of the war.

In 1782, after Cornwallis's surrender at Yorktown, Dunmore and British officers in South Carolina proposed to recruit 10,000 black troops for service in the low country areas of coastal Georgia and the Carolinas and the Floridas. The British government, however, would not authorize the establishment of black regulars until the Haitian Revolution and the Napoleonic Wars more than a decade later.

—*Christopher L. Brown*

For Further Reading
Frey, Sylvia. 1991. *Water from the Rock: Black Resistance in a Revolutionary Age*. Princeton, NJ: Princeton University Press; Quarles, Benjamin. 1961. *The Negro in the American Revolution*. Chapel Hill: University of North Carolina Press; Selby, John. 1977. *Dunmore*. Williamsburg: Virginia Independence Bicentennial Commission.

DURNFORD, ANDREW (1800–1859)

As the son of a white man and a free woman of color, few people in antebellum Louisiana held a position as complex as Andrew Durnford. In 1828, he purchased a large piece of property in Plaquemines Parish on a bend of the Mississippi River about 33 miles from New Orleans and built the St. Rosalie sugar plantation. St. Rosalie would become the home of Andrew; his wife Marie Charlotte Remey, a free woman of color; their children, Thomas, Rosema, and Andrew, Jr.; and more than 75 Negro slaves.

Very little is known about Durnford's early life, and most of what we do know of him is derived from letters written to his friend and mentor John McDonogh, a wealthy white businessman who held, for his time, enlightened views regarding race and slavery. McDonogh was a close friend of Thomas Durnford, Andrew's father, and when Thomas died, his friendship was extended to Andrew. Through McDonogh, Durnford remained informed of the American Colonization Society's activities and was introduced to the English

abolitionist Elliot Cresson. Durnford's letters to McDonogh are numerous and provide information about St. Rosalie's operations and insights into the psychology of a man who disliked the institution of slavery yet maintained and profited from his position as a mulatto plantation master.

Although there is every indication that Durnford was relatively humane in the treatment of his slaves, he was first and foremost a businessman, and his letters reveal the pressures of successfully operating St. Rosalie. Durnford mentions an occasion when he severely threatened his slaves in order to get them to do their duties. He also revealed anger over a runaway slave and the flogging of another. Although Durnford appears to have been conscientious in seeing to his slaves' material needs, he was not above using coercion to ensure the plantation's profitability.

Perhaps in order to come to grips with his unusual and often awkward place in society, Durnford developed an interest in philosophy. A letter to McDonogh dated January 12, 1844, provides this telling statement on Durnford's view of society: "I think society is made up of two distinct parts. On the one hand wolves and foxes, and on the other hand lambs and chickens providing food for the former. In the forest a lion recognizes another lion, tiger does not make another tiger its prey" (Whitten, 1981). Believing the abolition of slavery to be an unattainable goal in his lifetime, Durnford suppressed his idealism and used the existing system for his own benefit.

—*Mark Cave*

For Further Reading
Sterkx, H. E. 1972. *The Free Negro in Ante-Bellum Louisiana*. Cranbury, NJ: Fairleigh Dickinson University; Whitten, David O. 1981. *Andrew Durnford: A Black Sugar Planter in Antebellum Louisiana*. Natchitoches: Northwestern State University of Louisiana.

DUTCH CARIBBEAN

Two different types of slavery coexisted in the Dutch Caribbean: the harsh planter regimes of Suriname and the smaller Guiana colonies and the reputedly milder regimes of the insular colonies. In Berbice, a Dutch Guiana colony, the heavy labor to which the Africans were subjected and the brutal treatment they received caused a major slave rebellion in 1763. By contrast, the main Dutch plantation colony of Suriname, in which blacks held a large majority over whites, never experienced a single general slave rebellion. Instead, black protest took the form of marronage, the escape from Surinamese society by vast numbers of slaves who left individually or in small groups. Occasionally, the escapees joined to form permanent Maroon communities, which invited an armed response from colonial authorities. These military measures failed to have the intended effect, however, and the whites were eventually forced to recognize various Maroon settlements.

Throughout the slavery period, Suriname coped with a high death rate among its unfree population, and recently arrived Africans outnumbered seasoned slaves until the slave trade declined. Slave imports reached a high in the 1760s and 1770s, only to fall steeply thereafter because of a grave financial crisis that deprived many planters of the means to purchase slaves. Generally a rather uncommon phenomenon, manumission after 1788 was taxed to reduce the number of Africans who were withdrawn from plantation labor. After the international slave trade ended, the colonial government took some measures to alleviate the plight of the slaves. Slaves themselves also took action to enhance their leverage by organizing walkouts. At this point, a process of creolization was well under way, and it eventually led to the formation of a homogeneous Afro-Surinamese population.

Slavery was almost as marginal on the Dutch Caribbean islands (St. Martin, St. Eustatius, Saba, Aruba, Bonaire, and Curaçao) as it was fundamental in the Guianas. Only St. Martin and St. Eustatius were plantation colonies, and rather insignificant ones at that. The other islands lacked a sizable slave population, except for Curaçao, and slavery there was noted for its mildness because there were no capitalist plantations, few slaves per slaveholder, and a high degree of social control. Artisans and domestic slaves predominated. From the outset, manumission on Curaçao was much more common than it was in Suriname. A slave rebellion that broke out on the island in 1795, influenced by events in Saint Domingue, resulted in the promulgation of a decree limiting the working hours and outlining some of the slaves' rights.

Like elsewhere in the New World, slavery in the Dutch Caribbean was justified by reference to the slaves' supposed paganism. At the same time, Suriname blocked slaves' conversion to Christianity under the pretense that they were not ready for it. Underlying this policy was the sense that mass conversion would endanger the colony's very foundation. Until well into the nineteenth century, missionaries were therefore confined to working among the Maroons and the Amerindians. On Curaçao, however, the picture was quite different. Its elite showed indifference rather than resistance regarding the question of conversion, an attitude shared by the local Protestant ministers. As it was the Roman Catholic priests, who from an early date onward were allowed to preach in the colony, who showed concern for the spiritual welfare of African slaves, Catholicism was the religion most blacks and mulattoes embraced.

The Maroon wars and the 1795 rebellion on Curaçao failed to have an impact on Dutch ideas about abolition. Although Dutch Caribbean slavery was hardly profitable comparatively speaking, it was not abolished before 1863, as the lack of a viable alternative kept the local whites from making major initiatives before that date. The one exception was the island of Saint Martin, which was shared between the Netherlands and France. In the wake of the French abolition of slavery in 1848, the Dutch slaves declared themselves free, which prompted Dutch authorities to implement immediate de facto abolition.

—*Wim Klooster*

See also
Dutch West India Company
For Further Reading
Hoetink, H. 1972. "Surinam and Curaçao." In *Neither Slave nor Free: The Freedman of African Descent in the Slave Societies of the New World*. Ed. David W. Cohen and Jack P. Greene. Baltimore: Johns Hopkins University Press; Oostindie, Gert, ed. 1996. *Fifty Years Later: Antislavery, Capitalism, and Modernity in the Dutch Orbit*. Pittsburgh: University of Pittsburgh Press; Stipriaan, Alex van. 1993. *Surinaams Contrast: Roofbouw en overleven in een Caraïbische plantagekolonie, 1750–1863*. Leiden: KITLV Uitgeverij.

DUTCH EAST INDIA COMPANY

*A*lso called the Vereenigde Oostindische Compagnie, the Dutch East India Company was an immensely successful and wide-ranging concern, from both the public's and the investor's point of view, all but eclipsing its sister company in the West Indies in profitability. During its long history the company was involved in various concerns including, most notoriously, the slave trade.

Chartered in 1602, the company was drawn to the East by the promise of trade in spices, indigo, and textiles. It was able to displace Portuguese merchants, who had previously opened the region to western trade, and gained a monopoly of Dutch trade and navigation east of the Cape of Good Hope and west of the Strait of Magellan. The entry into the slave trade was more by accident than by design. Indeed, early Dutch explorers had been horrified at the Portuguese colonists' mistreatment of slaves and had written back to their country's States-General to denounce the cruelty, and the first settlers taken into the area by the company chose not to rely upon slave labor to the same extent as their predecessors had.

Dutch naval dominance in the seventeenth century enabled the tiny country to trade and conquer from the Americas to the East Indies. In this symbolic treatment of the subject, Amsterdam "receives the tribute of four continents."

The situation started to change as the East India Company expanded and gained control of territories right across the Indian Ocean, coming eventually to include the southern tip of Africa and eastern Asia. In the absence of a steady stream of incoming Dutch colonists, the company found itself facing labor shortages in its new possessions and accepted the well-tried expedient of slave labor. Company directors found that slaves not only solved the short-term labor problem but also provided the company with a new and lucrative income source to set beside the other commodities.

By the 1630s, the East India Company was firmly established in the slave trade. It exported East African slaves across the Indian Ocean to its Asian colonies and others down the African coast to settlements clustered around the Cape of Good Hope. Approximately 4,000 slaves were shipped to Cape Colony between 1652 and 1795, and many more slaves of Asian origin were brought into the colony from company ships stopping there on the return voyage from the East Indies to the Dutch Republic.

The use of slaves became so entrenched with the company that on the Coromandel coast in southeastern India, where a cheap source of free labor was readily available, Dutch merchants still often preferred to employ slaves. Batavia (now Djakarta), one of the company's most important commercial and administrative centers, was largely repopulated with slaves introduced from the Bay of Bengal after the original inhabitants had been removed or killed. Slavers particularly sought young couples with healthy children since it was believed that they would provide a stable and self-sustaining workforce. The Dutch did fear slave revolts in their territories and consequently enacted a great body of draconian legislation aimed at deterring any prospective troublemakers. The Statutes of Batavia, issued in 1642, were part of this attempt. The Dutch also sought to forbid arbitrary violence by slaveowners, but numerous eyewitness accounts suggest that they carried very little weight in practice.

Plantation slavery remained a worse fate than domestic slavery, and the company's factors in Suriname acquired a particularly bad reputation for cruelty in the eighteenth century. They were especially keen to obstruct attempts to preach Christianity among the slaves. Accordingly, African culture tended to survive the long journey between continents, more or less intact, and to become deeply entrenched in the slaves' consciousness. Slave revolts became endemic, and some slaves were able to escape into the interior. These runaways, or "bush Negroes" (Maroons) as they were known, banded together to create small settlements in jungle clearings. Occasionally the company organized punitive raids led by burghers and soldiers in order to remove those settlements, but those efforts proved to be very costly and were largely unsuccessful. Communities of ex-slaves simply moved ever farther into the jungle and continued thriving.

Dutch influence in the East and their control of the slave trade always rested on their naval dominance, and during the eighteenth century this hold slackened in response to aggressive competition from English merchants. The Fourth Anglo-Dutch War (1780–1784) hit the company hard as its traditional markets began looking elsewhere to buy raw materials, luxury goods, and slaves. The long period of warfare from 1795 to 1815 gradually weaned Dutch merchants back home, and the company itself away from the slave trade, thus causing the merchants to seek alternative income sources. Many Dutch colonies formerly administered by the Dutch East India Company fell under British influence, and Suriname itself became practically incorporated into the British Empire. Britain and the United States each passed legislation in 1807 to prevent their own ships from trading in African slaves, and that legislation also had a limiting effect on Dutch vessels and further constrained the trade. The end came in June 1814 when William I of Holland issued a royal decree forbidding Dutch participation in the slave trade.

—*John Callow*

See also
Dutch West India Company; East Africa; Portuguese Slave Trade
For Further Reading
Postma, Johannes Menne. 1990. *The Dutch in the Atlantic Slave Trade, 1660–1815*. Cambridge: Cambridge University Press.

DUTCH SLAVE TRADE

The Dutch played a significant role in the transatlantic slave trade although their rate of participation in terms of slaves carried was far behind that of Portugal, England, and France. In total, Dutch ships carried approximately 540,000 enslaved persons from Africa to various Western Hemisphere destinations. Besides transporting slaves, the Dutch also financed slaving expeditions by Scandinavian ships. The Dutch East India Company also shipped slaves from East Africa to South Africa and to colonial possessions in Indonesia, but the number of slaves transported in that traffic is insignificant when compared to the transatlantic slave trade. In the Atlantic, the chief agent of Dutch slaving activities was the Dutch West India Company (WIC), which monopolized African shipping traffic until 1730 and the transatlantic slave trade from its inception in 1621 until 1738. It also retained a partial monopoly to

Slaves arriving in sixteenth-century Jamestown, Virginia, from a Dutch vessel.

Africa's Gold Coast (Ghana) and to Suriname in the Guiana region until 1734.

The year 1619 is often considered as the beginning of the Dutch involvement in the Atlantic slave trade, because in that year the Virginian chronicler John Rolfe reported that a Dutch man-of-war had sold the colonists 20 Negroes, but that transaction must have been an isolated case of disposing of cargo from a captured Portuguese vessel. There were other incidental cases of private slave shipments by Dutch skippers, but none represented a systematic participation in the transatlantic traffic. Initially, the Dutch resisted participating in the traffic, and civil authorities rejected an effort to establish a slave market in the Dutch town of Middelburg in 1596 on the grounds that the Dutch Republic did not legally recognize slavery.

The attitude of Dutch policy makers changed after the conquest of northern Brazil in 1630 because the Brazilian sugar plantations required slave labor. During the next decade the Dutch captured several African coastal trading stations, which were needed to meet their forced labor supply. Dutch captains shipped more than 30,000 slaves to Brazil during the next two decades, and this introduction to the traffic and the lure of potential profits became the primary motivation for expanded involvement.

With the return of Brazil to Portugal in 1654, the Dutch West India Company began searching for new slave markets and found them in the Spanish-American colonies, because Spain had no access to the African continent. It was through the *asiento* trade, which the Dutch dominated from 1662 till the 1690s, that they became the chief suppliers of forced labor from Africa to Spain's American colonies. This traffic was operated mostly by way of the Dutch island depot at Curaçao but sometimes also directly to Spanish colonial ports. Besides the legal *asiento* trade, the Dutch frequently made illicit shipments of slaves to the Spanish colonies, and the Antillean island of St. Eustatius occasionally served as a slave trade depot for the illicit trade with the Spanish colonies and, during times of war, also with the French Antilles.

During the second half of the seventeenth century, the Dutch established their own small plantation settlements on the Berbice and Demerara Rivers (in present-day Guyana) and in 1667, they captured an English colony on the Suriname River. These settlements also needed slave labor as Dutch citizens showed little inclination to emigrate to tropical regions. By 1700, Suriname had become the most important of these settlements, and it attracted increased investments and slave deliveries as the eighteenth century progressed. Initially a sugar colony, Suriname also began cultivating increasing quantities of other crops like coffee, cotton, and cacao. After 1700, Suriname became the primary market in the Dutch slave trade, and approx-

imately 190,000 African slaves were landed there before 1795. After that date, the Dutch slave trade virtually ended as a result of international political tensions resulting from the French Revolution. Only a few Dutch slave ships crossed the Atlantic during the early-nineteenth century, and under British pressure, the king of the Netherlands issued a decree in 1814 that formally ended Dutch participation in the Atlantic slave traffic.

Following the example of other European nations, the Dutch moved somewhat belatedly from monopoly slave trade to free trade practices during the 1730s, which made it possible for all Dutch nationals to engage in the slave trade if they purchased a permit from the Dutch West India Company. That company retained an indirect involvement in the slave trade because it maintained trading stations on the African coast and in the West Indies. The free trade also signaled a shift to smaller slave ships and slave consignments, which resulted in faster deliveries.

The Dutch presence on the African coast was concentrated on the Gold Coast (Ghana), where they began regularly maintaining 10–12 fortified trading stations in the early-seventeenth century. The gold trade had initially attracted the Dutch to this location, but when they began to trade in slaves they obtained them primarily from the Slave Coast (the Benin Bay area) and to a lesser extent from the region north of the Congo River (Loango). After 1700, the Gold Coast also became a primary slave-producing region, and after 1730, Dutch free traders began acquiring slaves from regions west of the Gold Coast, primarily from present-day Liberia and the Ivory Coast. Unlike other nations, the Dutch Republic rarely obtained slaves in the Biafra Bay region for transatlantic shipment and never from eastern Africa, except for shipments to South Africa or to the Dutch East Indies (Indonesia). Dutch merchants purchased approximately 70 percent of their slaves in the Guinea coastal regions and the remainder from the area north of the Congo River.

The volume of the Dutch slave trade reached an early peak between 1668 and 1672, when the Dutch may well have been the dominant European participant in the traffic with average annual landings of nearly 6,000 slaves. A significant decline followed with the loss of the *asiento* trade, and similar numbers were not reached again until the 1750–1772 period. By then, the overall volume of the Atlantic slave trade had grown to such proportions that Dutch participation was less than 10 percent of the total traffic. Overall, the Dutch share in the Atlantic traffic was approximately 5 percent, making that nation a distant fourth-largest participant after Portugal, England, and France.

Slave mortality rates on Dutch ships averaged around 15 percent, similar to rates on the vessels of other European nations. Before 1740, slave death rates on Dutch ships averaged about 16 percent, but after that year the rates dropped to about 14 percent; after 1760, they were less than 14 percent, and after 1790, they dropped to less than 12 percent. Epidemics and the length of the voyage seem to have been the major reason for the deaths on Dutch slave ships. Mortality rates ranged greatly from one consignment to another. Some ships recorded no deaths during the trip while on other ships large numbers of slaves perished. The most tragic case of slave mortality was the loss of 702 slaves who drowned below decks on the shipwrecked vessel *Leusden* off the Suriname coast in 1737. Most crew members of this ship were saved, but generally slave ship crew members died at higher rates than the slaves.

The treatment of slaves aboard Dutch ships seems to have been typical for the times. Slaves were chained below decks in unbearably crowded, hot, and unhygienic conditions. There were certainly many instances of cruelty and abuse in this humiliating and deadly experience, but a slave cargo was a valuable investment so owners made careful preparations for food supplies and gave instructions about medical care and treatment to ensure that their human cargoes reached their destinations in the best salable condition. Although there are no surviving written testimonies of slaves on Dutch vessels, the slaves obviously resented their lot immensely. Many records about slave suicides and attempted suicides, refusal to eat, and some major slave revolts have been preserved. Such activities were undertaken against all odds and rarely met with success.

The profits made in the Dutch slave trade are difficult to verify because financial records are often unreliable. A careful study of the MCC free trade company records suggests that more slaving ventures incurred losses than made profits, although overall profits averaged 2.9 percent. Because of the perishable human cargo, slaving was certainly a risky business. Placed in the overall context of the Dutch economy, the slave trade and its affiliated plantation complex must have produced reasonable profits for many individuals through employment and investments or the traffic would not have been maintained for so many years.

—*Johannes Postma*

See also
The *Asiento*
For Further Reading
Postma, Johannes. 1990. *The Dutch in the Atlantic Slave Trade, 1600–1815*. New York: Cambridge University Press; Priester, L. R. 1987. *De Nederlandse houding ten aanzien van de slavenhandel en slavernij 1596–1863*. Middelburg: L. R. Priester; Unger, W. S. 1958–1960, 1965. "Bijdragen tot de geschiedenis van de Nederlandse slavenhandel." *Economisch-Historisch Jaarboek* 26, 28.

DUTCH WEST INDIA COMPANY (1621)

The West India Company (WIC) was a private company vested with wide powers by the Dutch government. Founded in 1621 as a joint-stock company, it had a monopoly of Dutch trade and navigation in Africa south of the Tropic of Cancer, in the Americas, and in the Atlantic islands. Like the Dutch East India Company, the WIC could administer justice, make treaties with foreign princes, and maintain an army. The company went bankrupt in 1674 but was immediately reestablished. It monopolized African shipping traffic until 1730 and the transatlantic slave trade until 1738. Its role in the latter had already become insignificant by 1715 when Britain acquired the *asiento* under the terms of the Treaty of Utrecht. Huge deficits made the company a liability to the Dutch Republic's States-General, and it was dissolved in 1791.

Utilizing its principal monopoly, the slave trade, the company transported African slaves to various New World destinations from New Amsterdam (New York) to Buenos Aires. In the period 1630–1651, most were shipped to Brazil; from 1658 to 1700, to Spanish America; and from 1700 to 1738, to Suriname. After losing its monopoly in 1738, the company stopped supplying slaves, but the number of African slaves shipped to the Americas from 1621 to 1738 totaled 272,000, or about half the overall number of slaves carried by all Dutch ships bound for the New World between 1621 and 1803—various smaller Dutch companies that moved into the slave trade after 1738 accounted for the other half. Although the Dutch share of the transatlantic slave trade from the sixteenth through the nineteenth centuries was no more than 5 percent, the WIC dominated that trade during two periods.

The first of those periods of domination was 1630–1654, the years of Dutch colonization of northeastern Brazil, when over 30,000 slaves were imported to work on the sugar plantations there. The colony's loss had unpleasant financial consequences for the WIC's budget, as most slaves had been sold on credit to Portuguese planters and payments were never received. The second period of domination was 1663–1688 when the WIC concluded several contracts with private traders or companies holding a monopoly under the *asiento* system but preferring to buy slaves from the Dutch. In those years, the Dutch island of Curaçao became the main slave distribution center for Spanish colonies in the Caribbean, and there was regular traffic in Africans between Curaçao and Cartagena, Portobelo, and Veracruz. In the subsequent period of 1689–1716, the WIC again signed *asiento* subcontracts but was no longer the main supplier of slaves.

The overall number of slaves shipped by the Dutch to Spanish colonies in 1658–1729 was just under 100,000, a small proportion of which was carried by others. On a more modest scale, the Dutch island of St. Eustatius had a similar function as Curaçao for the French Antilles. Although most of the slaves were reexported from Curaçao and St. Eustatius, in Suriname and other Dutch Guiana colonies, slaves were sold directly to planters.

During Dutch control of northeastern Brazil, the official position that Indian freedom should be respected served as a guiding principle, but during the short period of Dutch rule in Maranhão in the same area, Indian slavery did exist, being legitimized because of an absence of black slaves and a prior Portuguese employment of Indian slaves in the area. African slavery was introduced in other parts of Brazil.

In a move to obtain a regular flow of new African workers, a small WIC force conquered the Portuguese fort of São Jorge da Mina (Elmina) on West Africa's Gold Coast in 1637. That supply was deemed insufficient, however, and in 1641–1642 a successful attack was launched on several other Portuguese colonies in Africa, leaving the Dutch with Luanda and Benguela in Angola, São Tomé, and Fort Axim on the Gold Coast. A Portuguese attack expelled the Dutch in 1648, but São Jorge remained Dutch, and on the Gold Coast, the WIC added a series of forts and factories. By 1700 there were a dozen such forts in Dutch hands, more than any other European state. Supplies from the Slave Coast nonetheless exceeded those from the Gold Coast. Following the decline in power of the kings of Aja in Great Ardra, who had controlled the Slave Coast trade, supplies from Loango to Angola came to constitute one-quarter to one-third of Dutch slaves.

—*Wim Klooster*

See also
The *Asiento;* Dutch Caribbean; Dutch-Portuguese Wars in West Africa

For Further Reading
Boogaart, Ernst van den, and Pieter C. Emmer. 1979. "The Dutch Participation in the Atlantic Slave Trade, 1596–1650." In *The Uncommon Market: Essays in the Economic History of the Atlantic Slave Trade.* Ed. Henry A. Gemery and Jan S. Hogendorn. New York: Academic Press; Postma, Johannes Menne. 1990. *The Dutch in the Atlantic Slave Trade 1600–1815.* Cambridge: Cambridge University Press.

DUTCH-PORTUGUESE WARS IN WEST AFRICA (1620–1655)

The Dutch-Portuguese wars in West Africa from 1620 to 1655 were a series of military encounters on land and sea that were partly fought over access to African slave supplies. Although Portugal's presence on Africa's coast dated from the mid-fifteenth century, its efforts to obtain recognition of a trade monopoly from other European states had been ineffective, and the Dutch were perhaps the least impressed. Latecomers on the scene, their attempts to gain a foothold on African soil failed until they founded Fort Nassau at Moure, east of São Jorge da Mina on the Gold Coast, in 1612.

After the Dutch West India Company was chartered, the Dutch started an offensive against Spanish and Portuguese colonies throughout the world. Dutch maritime prevalence along parts of West Africa's coast generally was matched by Portuguese predominance on the mainland. The mid-1620s saw two modest Dutch attacks on Luanda, which were equally unsuccessful, as was an assault on Portuguese headquarters in West Africa at São Jorge da Mina, which left 441 Dutchmen dead. The Portuguese celebrated this Battle of Pilicada (October 25, 1625) as a major victory.

Initially concentrating on Africa's gold trade, the Dutch showed practically no interest in the slave trade prior to their conquest of Pernambuco (now Recife) in 1630 and the subsequent colonization of large parts of northeastern Brazil (1630–1654). The sugar industry, which became the economic rationale of this new colony, presented the Dutch with a labor problem, since the planned recruitment of farmhands from the Netherlands never materialized. Directors of the Dutch West India Company therefore decided to start importing African slaves. The first cargoes of Africans arrived in Pernambuco in 1636, and plans were made to conquer São Jorge da Mina in Africa in order to secure a steady flow of slave workers. A Dutch war fleet of nine ships, 800 soldiers, and 400 sailors sent from Pernambuco succeeded with the help of African allies to subdue São Jorge in August 1637. In February 1642, the Portuguese Fort Axim fell into Dutch hands as well.

Despite a peace treaty signed by Portugal and the United Provinces on June 12, 1641, hostilities in Africa were not suspended. The volume of slaves the Dutch imported through São Jorge was disappointing, which induced the company to seize Angola. In August 1641, a Dutch fleet of 21 ships captured Luanda in Angola and proceeded to occupy Benguela and the island of São Tomé, a major slave depot. Finding themselves surrounded by hostile states, Luanda's exiled citizens retreated to the fortified town of Massangano. Although Portugal's trade monopoly had not left that country with many friends in the area, it could count on military support from the Ndongo ruler Ngola Ari. The eastern Mbundu kingdom of Matamba, ruled by Queen Nzinga, allied with the Dutch and supplied prisoners of war to them as slaves.

After relations between Luanda and Massangano had seemingly normalized, the Portuguese returned to their farms on the Bay of Bengo. The Dutch then launched a surprise attack in an attempt to dispel the Portuguese from Angola once and for all. The Portuguese were defeated on several occasions in the next few years, but the Dutch reign came to a sudden end in August 1648 when a Portuguese squadron of 15 reconquered Luanda. This operation was supervised by the experienced Admiral Salvador Correia de Sá, who had been named governor and captain-general of the captaincy of Angola. The small force left behind by the Dutch surrendered rapidly to him, and the Dutch West India Company was forced to surrender all conquests in the Angola region. Peace between the Dutch and the Portuguese was formally restored after a treaty was signed between both governments in 1661.

—*Wim Klooster*

See also
Dutch West India Company

For Further Reading
Birmingham, David. 1966. *Trade and Conflict in Angola: The Mbundu and their Neighbours under the Influence of the Portuguese 1483–1790*. Oxford: Clarendon Press; Boxer, C. R. 1952. *Salvador de Sá and the Struggle for Brazil and Angola 1602–1686*. London: Athlone Press; Vogt, John. 1979. *Portuguese Rule on the Gold Coast 1469–1682*. Athens: University of Georgia Press.

EAST AFRICA

East Africa covers a vast area, stretching south from the Horn of Africa, through modern Kenya, Tanzania and Uganda, west into eastern Zaire, through Rwanda and Burundi, and encompassing northern Mozambique and Malawi in the south. Varieties of slavery may have existed in this region in prehistory, yet it was not until Muslim merchants reached Africa's eastern coast, starting in the eighth century, that slaves of East African origin are known to have been exported. An anonymous Greek classical text dating from the middle of the first century, the *Periplus of the Erythraean Sea,* states that slaves were obtained from northern Somalia, but no mention, in an otherwise detailed list of trade goods, is made of slave exports from the East African coast.

After the middle of the eighth century, slaves for the households and farms of the Persian Gulf region and Arabia were obtained from eastern Africa, and the slave trade appears to have flourished, especially in the ninth century considering the number of East African or "Zanj" slaves recorded as being employed in the marshes of southern Iraq (Mesopotamia) at the time. Zanj slaves were engaged in extracting salt, land preparation, and reclamation, and their revolt between 869 and 883 led to a decline in eastern Africa's slave trade for nearly 900 years.

In the intervening centuries, the Swahili civilization developed and flourished on the coast and offshore islands, as did numerous Iron Age societies in the interior. Local slavery occurred as did some slave export via the Indian Ocean trade, but it was not until the eighteenth and nineteenth centuries that demand for East African slaves increased dramatically. Foremost among the various reasons for this change was the development of plantation economies on the islands of Zanzibar and Pemba and in various places on the coastal mainland. Swahili and Omani planters grew export crops such as coconuts and, most important, cloves in a system that Lovejoy (1983) suggests had similarities to the slave plantation economies of the Americas.

In addition to the inspiration from the Americas, Muslim slavery systems were utilized, and Indian capital was employed in what appears to have been a multidimensional activity. The clove production peaked between the 1840s and 1870s, a fact that was reflected directly in the slave trade. Alongside the coastal trade, which supplied the plantations, slaves were also exported north to India, Persia, and Arabia, continuing the centuries-old trading pattern, and, in lesser numbers, south to the Americas.

The majority of the slaves were obtained from the East African interior, a process helped by the increased availability of firearms. Three main trade routes existed: from Lake Nyasa to Kilwa and other southern Swahili harbor towns, from Lake Tanganyika to Zanzibar and the central coast, and further north from the highland edges to Mombasa. Inhabitants of the areas where the ivory and slave trade routes passed were often directly involved in this trade, with the Yao, the Nyamwezi, and the Kamba being linked with the three routes mentioned, respectively. These indigenous merchants supplied the coast with slaves, and by the mid-nineteenth century, Arab and Swahili merchants were themselves venturing into the interior, initially competing with local groups such as the Nyamwezi, though eventually this competition settled down as each side realized it needed the other's cooperation.

Plantations were established in the interior to supply both slaves and traders with food, and slaves were siphoned off in large numbers to work on them, notable examples of such plantations include those attached to Tabora and Ujiji. Further inland, all amenities for a comfortable life were available at Swahili and Arab traders' bases, as at Nyangwe and Kasongo, which fell within the domain of Hamed bin Muhammed, better known as Tippu Tip, perhaps the best-known Swahili merchant who established a "sultanate," Utetera, on the upper Zaire (Lualaba) River.

In the late-nineteenth century, primarily because of British pressure, East African slavery declined. The Kirk-Barghash Treaty (1873) banned public slave markets in Zanzibar, the primary center of the slave trade, and in 1875, the Portuguese, operating to the south of the region under discussion, nominally freed slaves in the Mozambique area. Finally, slavery's legal status was abolished in Zanzibar in 1897, and the institution of slavery itself was abolished in 1909.

—*Timothy Insoll*

See also
Swahili

For Further Reading
Alpers, E. A. 1975. *Ivory and Slaves in East Central Africa*. London: Heinemann; Casson, L. 1989. *The Periplus Maris Erythraei*. Princeton, NJ: Princeton University Press; Lovejoy, P. E. 1983. *Transformations in Slavery*. Cambridge: Cambridge University Press; Sutton, J. E. G. 1990. *A Thousand Years of East Africa*. Nairobi: British Institute in Eastern Africa.

EAST ASIA

Chinese and Korean slavery follow the typical pattern of East Asian slavery whereas much of Japanese history developed under a feudal system in which no institution like slavery appeared except serfdom. Numerous nineteenth-century accounts suggest that the nomads in greater China had a harsh system of slavery, but more study is needed to determine if that is true or not. Elements of Confucianism and a dynastic cycle determined the basic characteristics of East Asian slavery. Confucian ideology involved a strong bureaucracy, based upon a large pool of free people, under a symbolic king or emperor. The mainstays of the nation were the commoners, who provided the bureaucrats, selected after a civil service examination, and paid the most taxes to maintain the nation's economy. Therefore, slaves usually made up a small portion of East Asia's population.

Slaves belonged to the class of people that constituted the bottom layer of the social hierarchy, normally less than 10 percent of a nation's total population. Being the hereditary outcasts—including butchers and entertainers—this class of people was ineligible to take the civil service examination. Scholar-officials remained at the top of the hierarchy, and though they composed less than 5 percent of the population, they monopolized the privileges. A massive group of commoners filled the middle position.

Two kinds of slaves lived in East Asia. Public slaves, owned by the government, worked in an office or farmed to pay the tribute tax. Some of these slaves rose high in government agencies because of their skills. Private slaves, owned by individuals, worked as domestic servants or farmed to pay tribute for their masters.

The lifestyle of the farming slaves was similar to that of free tenant farmers. Many of the farming slaves lived away from the master's residence and had an independent economy because they performed intensive agriculture on small landholdings that were scattered in different areas. In East Asia, bureaucracy was responsible for the geographical separation of the landholdings because without primogeniture (an exclusive right of inheritance belonging to the eldest son) the land was parceled out in smaller quantities. Normally,

a slave's tax burden was heavier than a commoner's, but later, the commoner's tax burden rose as high as the slave's, so that all the tenant farmers shared the same burden. The slave's legal status was slightly lower than the commoner's, but there was a bigger difference between the slaves and commoners as one group and the scholar-officials.

East Asian slaves had more opportunity to gain their freedom than their counterparts in other areas. In China and Korea, slaves and masters were of the same race, and determination of status rested on the status of the father. These two factors resulted in a unique East Asian pattern of slave heredity. If a slave man took a slave woman or a poor freewoman to be his wife and they lived on his master's property, their children became the master's property. If a slave woman became the concubine of a man of means and bore a child, it became free. However, if a slave woman married a poor freeman and they lived on her master's property, their children could be either slave or free depending on current practice.

Balancing the proper ratio of commoners and slaves was a major concern for East Asian nations, because large number of private slaves meant weak revenue collection. At the beginning of a dynasty, a nation was generally strong both economically and militarily, and a large number of taxable commoners meant that a smaller tax burden fell on each person. As the dynastic cycle progressed, corrupt officials exploited both land and slaves, and to enlarge their slaveholdings, they would manipulate slave heredity for their own expediency and make it either matrilineal or patrilineal. Therefore, the rules of slave heritage varied.

War offered another opportunity for slaves to be free if they demonstrated military valor or contributed financially. However, war also shook the social order, which helped a nation sink into the irrevocable downward cycle. The nation builders of a new dynasty in China and Korea usually freed all slaves who had been forcefully placed into servitude. With one full cycle, then, the nation recovered the delicate balance between the free and slaves.

Several particular features are worth noting with regard to East Asian slavery. By the tenth century, semislaves (e.g., serfs who lived in villages of servitude such as Puch'u and Kuanhu in China or Bugok and So in Korea) had disappeared. Japan also had such servitude prior to its feudal age. Under the Ch'in dynasty (221–206 B.C.), serfs again appeared to till the nobles' land in Manchuria and around Beijing, and there were some privileged imperial slaves who lived as bond servants as well. The domestic and international slave trades were active after Han (206 B.C.–A.D. 220) and T'ang (A.D. 168–907) times, and then the slaves were of diverse ethnic origin, including Africans and Romans. The Yuan Mongols (1279–1368) especially engaged in the trans-Eurasian slave trade with traditional Arabic merchants, and many of the ethnic minorities under Mongol rule became its victims.

Slave prices in East Asia probably equaled two or three years of wages for the hired laborer. From the 1830s on, with the European nations prohibiting both the slave trade and slavery, the former African slave traders, and opium dealers, turned to Asia. They shipped Chinese coolies, and then their Japanese and Korean counterparts, instead of African slaves to North America and Southeast Asia, and those workers suffered a modern version of semiservitude.

East Asian nations began developing slavery systems in ancient times, and by the eighth century, the well-codified T'ang laws provided an institutional guide to slavery in East Asia that lasted until emancipation. However, socioeconomic changes began taking place in the twelfth century in China and Korea, including agricultural renovation, and the ensuing population explosion and increasingly available cheap labor substantially weakened slavery.

By the sixteenth century, for instance, all the lower classes, except slaves, acquired the commoner status in Korea, and many travelers' accounts from eighteenth-century Qing China stated that no social difference existed between slaves and free laborers. Many scholar-officials still insisted on maintaining their slaveholdings, but gradual emancipation was taking place. The final blow to East Asian slavery came with the establishment of Western-style modern governments at the turn of the twentieth century in Qing China and Choson Korea.

—Hyong-In Kim

See also
Abolition, East Asia; China (Ancient, Late Imperial, Medieval); Korea

For Further Reading
Biot, M. Edward. 1849. "Memoir on the Condition of Slaves and Hired Servants in China." *Chinese Repository* 18 (7): 347–363; Ch'u, T'ung-tsu. 1961. *Law and Society in Traditional China*. Paris: Mouton; Kim, Hyong-In. 1990. "Rural Slavery in Antebellum South Carolina and Early Choson Korea." Ph.D. dissertation, Department of History, University of New Mexico; Wilbur, C. Martin. 1943. *Slavery in China during the Former Han Dynasty, 206 B.C.–A.D. 25*. Chicago: Field Museum of Natural History Press.

EGYPT, CONDITION OF SLAVES IN

There is evidence of slavery, mostly the employment of dependents acquired from other communities through purchase or capture, which spared the "host" society part of the cost of rearing the individual during his unproductive period and resulted in the estranged condition of the slave, throughout the history of Pharaonic Egypt. It seems, however, to have functioned as a complementary institution in the framework of an economy that was essentially based on the exploitation of indigenous peasant labor. Furthermore, the distinction between slavery and other forms of dependency in Egypt is not always clear-cut. Enslaved foreigners in some instances apparently shared the status and condition of certain servants to whom scholars also often apply the term "slave" but use it in a different legal sense.

The motif of the victorious campaign of the king against the enemies of Egypt, systematically concluded with the annihilation of the foe and the bringing back of captives (seqeru-'ankh) and cattle, goes back to the dawn of the Pharaonic state. Such actions are attested on dynastic items like the mace head of King Narmer (c. 3000 B.C.), the famous palette of the same king, and the Gebel Suleyman graffito of King Djer (first dynasty, c. 2920–2770 B.C.). The annals of the Palermo stone (Old Kingdom, fifth dynasty, c. 2465–2323 B.C.) record two military campaigns during the reign of Snofru (c. 2575–2551 B.C.) that resulted in the taking, respectively, of 7,000 Nubian and 1,100 Libyan captives.

No truly specific linguistic equivalent of *slave* as used here seems to have existed in the Old Kingdom (c. 2700–2300 B.C.). *Isuu* referred to workers that may have been bought but were more probably hired. *Meryt* ("dependents") was generally used for native laborers in the employment of the state, temple, or private persons and continued to be used up to the New Kingdom (c. 1560–1070 B.C.). *Bak* referred generically to individuals employed in menial labor, or servants. *Hem* (plural *hemu*), which in later times certainly designated slaves, began to be used toward the end of the Old Kingdom, but it may refer to hired employees.

The Middle Kingdom (c. 2184–1785 B.C.) provides the earliest clear evidence for slaves in the possession of private persons. Papyrus Brooklyn 35.1446 contains a list of 70 dependents, of whom 33 bear Egyptian names and the 27 adults are called *hem-nesu* and *hemet* ("king's slave" and "female slave"), the latter being the normal feminine form of the former); 45 are Asiatics, explicitly designated as such ('*aam*) and bearing northwestern Semitic names. The 8 children of the latter group have Egyptian names.

The term "king's slave" was commonly used in this period, and it is generally thought to refer to criminals, in particular escaped corvée workers (*hesebu*) who were punished with life sentences. The term has also been interpreted as alluding, instead, to the peasant class, the main labor force of the country and the class that provided most of the seasonally recruited workers (*hesebu*). Both *hesebu* and king's slaves were employed by private persons. King's slaves and Asiatics were both called *chenemu* ("associates"), and they seem to have shared the same condition, although the lowest menial jobs (agricultural tasks) seem to have been reserved to the former.

In a letter dated in the same period, the word *bak* ("servant"; plural *baku,* feminine *baket*) apparently refers to a different relationship of dependency. In the letter, one Heqanakht instructs his family to kick out the female *baket* Senen because she was causing trouble—it is legitimate to presume that she must have had a family or village to go back to. Yet it should be remarked that in the Middle Kingdom, *baku* could be inherited, as could Asiatics, and that *bak* could be synonymous with *hem.*

Campaigns resulting in the bringing back of prisoners apparently occurred only sporadically in the Middle Kingdom. Fragments of the annals of Amenemhet II (1929–1892 B.C.), however, explicitly state that 1,554 captives from a campaign in Syria were used to provide reinforcements for the city of workmen building the king's pyramid.

In the New Kingdom (c. 1560–1070 B.C.), the terminology used for dependents changed. King's slave was used only at the beginning of this period although *meryt* was still employed, especially collectively for the personnel of the temples but in some instances it is explicitly stated they were captives from Egypt's campaigns (annals of Thutmose III and tomb of Rekhmire). The most common word, however, from the beginning of the New Kingdom to the twenty-second dynasty (c. 945–745), was *hem/hemu,* which was occasionally synonymous with the more generic *bak.* *Hemu* were employed by private owners and by the state and the temples. They systematically had Egyptian names, but their origin, when it is known at all, was foreign. In the early 18th dynasty, Ahmose the son of Ebana took part in a war waged by King Ahmose I (r. 1580–1557 B.C.) against the Asiatics and was rewarded for his valor with the 19 slaves (*hemu*) he had captured personally.

New Kingdom sources record the taking of tens of thousands of captives in the campaigns of several pharaohs. In one account of the victories of Ramses III (r. 1198–1166 B.C.), the treatment of the prisoners is especially remarkable. Part of them were given as *hemu* to the temples, and the chiefs of the Meshwesh were installed in fortified settlements, branded with the name of the king, and made into *hemu*. The branding of the captives by applying the king's cartouche on the right upper arm by means of a stylus is depicted on the walls of the same king's temple at Medinet Habu on the west bank of the Nile. It seems to have been a relatively painless process, possibly closer to tattooing than branding. As the cartouche of the king appears on the right upper arm of many statues of Egyptian officials, the brand should not be seen as differentiating the *unfree* from the *free.*

An alternative means of access to slaves, not clearly described before the New Kingdom, was trade. Papyrus Cairo 65739 (early Ramses period, end of the fourteenth to early-thirteenth century B.C.) refers to a Syrian slave woman who was bought from a foreign merchant (*shuty*), and the purchase of slaves is also found in other sources, like the Adoption Papyrus and the Tomb Robberies Papyrus (both dated to the reign of Ramses XI, c. 1100–1070 B.C.). The services of a slave could also be hired, as some surviving contracts bear out.

The freeing of slaves appears in the Adoption Papyrus, in which the owner, by marrying his slave, made her and her children "free" (*nemeh*). The word *nemeh* also means "orphan" and "pauper," and the condition of being "free" it alludes to is not necessarily a viable one, for by 772–30 B.C., there were acts of self-sale and self-dedication in which freedom was voluntarily renounced to place oneself under the patronage of an institution or a private person, a condition of clientele rather than slavery. The fact that the same terms were used for slaves and clients suggests there was no clear-cut legal or ideological distinction between these different forms of dependency.

The earliest surviving contracts for the sale of slaves date from the later part of the New Kingdom (664–332 B.C.) and more specifically from the twenty-fifth to the twenty-seventh dynasties (712–404 B.C.). In several surviving papyrus documents, slaves are explicitly qualified as foreigners. The last document is especially interesting because it is rare evidence of the branding (or tattooing) of the name of a private owner on his slave (on the palm of the right hand). In this later period, use of the word *bak* totally replaced *hem.*

In the Ptolemaic period (304–30 B.C.), the Hellenistic forms of slavery, based on capture in war and the slave market, prevailed. The institution of self-dedication to the temple was still practiced.

—*Federico Poole*

For Further Reading
Berlev, Oleg. 1987. "A Social Experiment in Nubia during the Years 9–17 of Sesostris I." In *Labor in the Ancient Near East.* Ed. Marvin A. Powell. New Haven, CT: Yale University Press; Daressy, Georges. 1915. "Une stèle de l'Ancien Empire maintenant détruite." *Annales du Service des Antiquités de l'Egypte* 15: 207–208; Meillassoux, Claude. 1986. *Anthropologie de l'esclavage: Le ventre de fer et d'argent.* Paris: Presses Universitaires de France.

EGYPT, SLAVERY IN ANCIENT

The ancient Egyptian language used different words to express varying degrees of dependency that correspond to social roles like "servant," "prisoner," "serf," and "dependent," which makes it difficult to define "slavery" as an autonomous social position. Egyptians were subject to varying degrees of bondage to other peoples, of which only some compare to our modern concept of slavery.

In all periods of Egyptian history, military campaigns were the most important source for slaves. Although no Egyptian "empire" existed in Asia before the New Kingdom, military campaigns occurred before that period, and foreigners were often taken as prisoners of war and subsequently enslaved. The capture of prisoners during these campaigns imposed considerable pressure upon the local population.

In the Old Kingdom (2700–2300 B.C.), captives were mainly used as agricultural workers and served in newly founded agricultural "domains" that spread across Egypt during a period of rapid reclamation. These sites eventually produced the crop surpluses needed to feed the workers on the vast national pyramid-building projects.

In the Middle Kingdom (c. 2134–1785 B.C.), increasing foreign activity yielded numerous slaves for the Egyptian economy. A Middle Kingdom papyrus mentions both Egyptians and Asians when describing what appears to be a forced-labor camp where families of runaway slaves were imprisoned. When caught, escaped slaves faced the death sentence (Loprieno, 1992).

The New Kingdom (c. 1560–1070 B.C.) was the most flourishing period of Egyptian slavery. The imperial Egyptian state controlled large parts of what now constitutes Israel, the Sinai, Syria, and the northern Sudan. Thus, Nubia was forced to contribute slaves, and entire lists of captured Nubians from this period have been found (Sethe, 1906). Although certain numbers given in the inscriptions are exceedingly high and might be exaggerations, it is obvious that tens of thousands of slaves were imported to Egypt during the great wars of expansion.

Another important source of slaves was natural increase. Loprieno (1992) attests to the principle of slavery by birth, and as a rule, the offspring of slaves were regarded as enslaved. Slavery could also be inflicted upon native Egyptians as a form of punishment. In the New Kingdom, officials could be punished by being reduced to the status of field laborer, thus making them "serfs."

Slavery through voluntary servitude appeared only in the Late Period (1560–1070 B.C.), and was either by an act of self-sale in payment of debts (Bakir, 1952) or by so-called self-dedication, according to which people sought the protection of religious institutions. According to surviving texts, these acts were restricted to individual cases and involved a legal concept unknown before the Late Period that "forever" bound the slave to his master. Native Egyptians who sold themselves seem to have enjoyed a higher social status than foreign captives (Bakir, 1952). Evidence also suggests that the Egyptian and Ptolemaic systems of slavery became integrated during this period.

Although slaves could be owned by a community, as opposed to individual ownership, most such cases also acknowledged either private or royal ownership. Captives from military campaigns were very often distributed to the temples, and the slaves owned by temples must have been numerous, as the inscriptions mention hundreds of them throughout the eighteenth to twentieth dynasties (Sethe, 1906). Usually, temple slaves labored in agricultural production on the vast temple landholdings (Bakir, 1952) or were used for food production work, such as in the "chamber of sweets" (Sethe, 1906). Some worked as weavers in textile production.

Slaves were also used as maintenance personnel in the New Kingdom army (Loprieno, 1992), and some brave soldiers, like the famous warrior Ahmose, received captives as war booty (Sethe, 1906). Thus, slaves became an important reward serving both to strengthen the loyalty between army and king and to improve the economic basis of the warriors' households.

Domestic activities were another major area of slave labor, primarily female, and female servants were closely integrated into the master's family. Slaves were their masters' private property and could be claimed as personal property or stolen goods if they escaped (Bakir, 1952); masters could also bequeath them to next generations in documents similar to modern wills and testaments (Loprieno, 1992). Slave ownership was not restricted to social elites, as records indicate that some masters had professions like herdsman, priest, stable master, singer, merchant, or even sandal maker (Bakir, 1952). Extant documents show that private slave ownership ranged from one to ten slaves with the average being one or two.

Slave prices are only rarely mentioned and vary from two-fifths of a deben of silver to more than four deben (c. 91 grams). Compared to prices of other commodities (Bakir, 1952), it appears that slaves were not cheap. Their purchase, sale, and hiring implies at least a limited market for them, and the slave trade is only rarely mentioned before the New Kingdom. However, Egyptians acquired natives from the mysterious country of Punt (the coast of modern Somalia) through the Nubian trade. These "pygmies" were used for "exotic" entertainment at the royal court. In a famous letter, King Pepi II asked a courtier to take care of such a "dancing-dwarf" (Eichler, 1991). Some

A popular misconception. This image shows slaves building the Egyptian pyramids, but although slavery existed in Egypt at the time, the laborers on the pyramids were not slaves but corvée laborers.

New Kingdom Egyptian traders were also involved in the slave trade, but the sources are scanty and instances are restricted to individual cases, which implies that the slave market was casual and small.

Slaves could possess property, inherit possessions, and acquire legal competence. In Ptolemaic times, self-dedications show that while a slave had to surrender all property to a master, he nevertheless might acquire personal property, presumably with the master's consent (Bakir, 1952). The will of a person named Naunakhte shows that slaves did have personal property as early as the New Kingdom (Loprieno, 1992). The Wilbour papyrus, a register of landholdings that dates into the fourth year of King Ramses IV (c. 1164 B.C.), identifies some slaves as landholders. Although slaves could be owned and sold like objects, there were obvious legal and economic limitations of the master's absolute power.

The most important emancipation case appears in the "Adoption Papyrus," which tells of a barren woman who adopts children who are her husband's offspring by a female slave (Loprieno, 1992). As a result, the children and their offspring become emancipated. In the Late Period, slaves tended to have a more legally recognized status in which they held more control over their property and services and could be emancipated by their masters.

Since all historical documentation is derived from the slaveowners, it is therefore biased and incomplete. Slaves were not merely objects, but people who could own property, be emancipated, and marry freewomen. To a limited extent, they did participate in social and economic life.

Domestic servants were regarded as property, and their abuse without their master's consent was treated as an offense. It is also clear that some foreign slaves were "educated" in that they were made to adopt the Egyptian language and culture. A Middle Kingdom papyrus from Illahun mentions the education of slaves where a slave shall "be taught how to write without letting him escape" (Loprieno, 1992). As early as the Old Kingdom, Nubian people were taken to Egypt to serve as a police force and were called "peaceful Nubians," implying that they had been pacified by adopting the "real" (i.e., Egyptian) culture. Egyptians believed that even slaves could become "normal" persons if they accepted Egyptian culture, and such acceptance was often expressed by adopting an Egyptian name.

In legal documents, slaves occur as witnesses in court (Bakir, 1952) where their testimony was regarded as equal to that of a nonslave. If a slave were found guilty of theft, he faced the same punishment as ordinary Egyptians and had to replace double the value of the stolen goods (Loprieno, 1992). One final cultural aspect of slavery should be noted: the spread of foreign (especially Semitic) elements became common in the New Kingdom. Notably, the cult of Semitic gods like Baal, Reshep, Astarte, and Anat became widespread in Egypt and was supported by worship in the royal temples. Knowledge of these gods could have reached Egypt through diplomatic relations and/or the experiences of Egyptian military personnel stationed abroad. Yet it is very likely that cultural elements of the Semitic world were introduced by slaves who came with nothing but their bodies and minds to Egypt. The Old Testament still recalls for us the fate and culture of the Semitic workforce in the land of the Pharaohs, working on the "brickfields of Egypt."

—*Eckhard Eichler*

For Further Reading
Bakir, Abd el-Mohsen. 1952. *Slavery in Pharaonic Egypt.* Cairo: Imprimerie de'l IFAOC; Eichler, Eckhard. 1991. "Untersuchungen zu den Königsbriefen des Alten Reiches." In *Studien zur Altägyptischen Kultur* (18): 141–171; Eichler, Eckhard. 1993. *Untersuchungen zum Expeditionswesen des ägyptischen Alten Reiches.* Wiesbaden: Harrassowitz; Loprieno, Antonio. 1992. "Der Sklave." In *The Egyptian Man.* Ed. Sergio Donadoni. Chicago: University of Chicago Press; Sethe, Kurt. 1906. *Urkunden der 18. Dynastie.* Leipzig: Hinrichs.

ELKINS, STANLEY M. (1925–)

Born in Boston, Massachusetts, in 1925, Stanley M. Elkins earned his Ph.D. at Columbia University in 1959 and published one of the most provocative works on slavery, *Slavery: A Problem in American Institutional and Intellectual Life,* in the same year. This book stimulated debate among historians of slavery throughout the 1960s.

Influenced by the pathbreaking works of Gilberto Freyre and Frank Tannenbaum, and dissatisfied with Kenneth M. Stampp's method in *The Peculiar Institution* (1956), Elkins's book was richly comparative, analytical, and thought provoking. In his opinion, "Stampp, locked in his struggle with Ulrich Phillips," proved unable "to disengage his mind from the debate of which he, Phillips, and [James Ford] Rhodes were all a part and which they had taken over from the proslavery and antislavery debaters of ante-bellum times." Distancing himself from the old debate, Elkins looked beyond questions of slavery's morality and racial inferiority and considered what he deemed was slavery's deleterious psychological damage to African Americans. To do so, Elkins used interdisciplinary approaches, including comparative history, role psychology, and interpersonal theory.

Elkins argued that slaves in Spanish and Portuguese America experienced a milder, more "open" enslavement than those in British America. This difference resulted, he said, from the Catholic and hierarchical traditions of Latin America as contrasted with the Protestant, locally autonomous, and "unrestrained" capitalist orientation of British America. Slaves in British North America lived in a "closed" system, one in which "virtually all avenues of recourse for the slave, all lines of communication to society at large, originated and ended with the master."

So oppressive and so brutal was slavery in British America that slaves there often developed "Sambo" personalities. White Southerners defined "Sambo" as "docile but irresponsible, loyal but lazy, humble but chronically given to lying and stealing; his behavior was full of infantile silliness and his talk inflated with childish exaggeration."

In one of his more controversial statements, Elkins argued that the slaves' "Sambo" personality was analogous to behavior exhibited by Nazi concentration camp inmates during World War II. In his opinion, both slaves and death camp dwellers suffered psychic shock and became both dependent and infantilized. "The individual, consequently, for his very psychic security, had to picture his master in some way as the 'good father,' even when, as in the concentration camp, it made no sense at all. But why should it not have made sense for many a simple plantation Negro whose master did exhibit, in all the ways that could be expected, the features of the good father who was really 'good'?"

Elkins's provocative *Slavery* sparked much criticism in the 1960s, criticism that was directed at the author's method and conclusions. Though richly theoretical, suggestive, and imaginative, the book lacked thorough grounding in the day-to-day lives and variety of responses of the blacks to their enslavement. Elkins also failed to recognize that slaves might have had more than one significant person in their lives. Nor did Elkins come to grips satisfactorily with the notion that what he deemed "Samboization" might have been simple manipulation by the slaves of the system that kept them in chains. Stampp, for instance, remarked in 1952 that "there were plenty of opportunists among the Negroes who played the role assigned to them, acted the clown, and curried the favor of their masters in order to win the maximum rewards within the system" (Lane, 1971).

But it was Elkins's concentration camp analogy that drew the most fire. According to the historian John W. Blassingame, Hitler's death camps "differed significantly from the plantation." "If," he added, "some men could escape infantilism in a murderous institution like the concentration camp, it may have been possible for the slave to avoid becoming abjectly docile in a much more benign institution like the plantation" (Lane, 1971). Still other critics faulted Elkins's thesis that Latin American institutions protected the slaves from the victimization that sealed their fate in British North America.

The debate over Elkins's book ignited a spirited discourse that, according to Peter J. Parish, represents "the supreme example of a book which has exercised a profound influence, not by the persuasiveness of its arguments, but above all through the questions it raised, the massive critical response it elicited, and the new work it stimulated" (Parish, 1989). Determined to refute Elkins, many historians of the 1970s examined the various slave responses to oppression, including overt and covert resistance, community formation, familial solidarity, and folk and cultural expression, and some scholars probed the nature of slave treatment by examining other comparative systems of unfree labor. Elkins's book, then, redirected the attention of historians away from focusing on the behavior of the masters and toward studying the ways that the bondsmen and women withstood and overcame their captivity.

—*John David Smith*

See also
Comparative Slavery, Recent Developments; Freyre, Gilberto de Mello; Phillips, Ulrich Bonnell; Sambo Thesis; Stampp, Kenneth M.; Tannenbaum, Frank
For Further Reading
Gilmore, Al-Tony, ed. 1978. *Revisiting Blassingame's "The Slave Community": The Scholars Respond.* Westport, CT: Greenwood Press; Kolchin, Peter. 1993. *American Slavery, 1619–1877.* New York: Hill and Wang; Lane, Ann J., ed. 1971. *The Debate over Slavery: Stanley Elkins and His Critics.* Urbana: University of Illinois Press; Parish, Peter J. 1989. *Slavery: History and Historians.* New York: Harper and Row.

ELLISON, WILLIAM
(1790–1861)

A cotton-gin maker and Southern planter, William Ellison was born April Ellison in South Carolina of mixed racial origin. His mother was a slave and his father a white man, probably his first owner, Robert Ellison, or Ellison's son William. For the first 26 years of his life, April was a slave. Perhaps because of his parentage, he was apprenticed to a trade rather than sent to the fields, and the training he received making and repairing cotton gins served him well. During his apprenticeship, which extended over 14 years, April learned to read and write and acquired basic bookkeeping and managerial skills.

In April 1816, April Ellison appeared in the Fairfield District Courthouse with his owner to formalize his freedom, purchased with money he saved while working for the cotton-gin maker to whom he had been apprenticed. Shortly after his emancipation, Ellison moved to Stateburg, South Carolina, and established his own cotton-gin business. Within a year, Ellison had purchased the freedom of his wife and daughter; their subsequent children were born free. In 1820, April Ellison legally changed his name from April to William, symbolizing his passage from slave to freeman.

Also in 1820, William Ellison purchased the first of his many slaves. Ownership of slaves attached him and his family to the dominant class of the South and helped to preserve his family's greatest asset, their freedom. By becoming a planter and a slaveowner, William Ellison was conforming to the ways and norms of that particular era. Evidence suggests that William Ellison held his slaves, not in a more benevolent form of slavery, but to exploit them for profit just as white slaveholders did. Probably because they were of little use to his business, Ellison sold most of his slaves' female children. He employed slave hunters to recapture escaped slaves, and he never freed any of his slaves. Interestingly, all of Ellison's slaves were listed in the records as black; none were ever listed as mulatto.

When William Ellison died on December 5, 1861, he was the wealthiest free black in South Carolina and one of the wealthiest free blacks in the South. Indeed, by 1835, Ellison was prosperous enough to purchase the home of Stephen D. Miller, former governor of South Carolina. Ellison owned approximately 63 slaves, more than any other free black in the entire South exclusive of Louisiana. He had gained the respect of his white neighbors, symbolized when the Church of the Holy Cross permitted the Ellison family a pew on the main floor of the church, below the gallery where other free blacks and slaves sat behind the rows of white worshipers.

For the Ellisons, emancipation resulted in the loss of their labor supply and slave capital, and it affected them much as it did white Southern planters. The subsequent breakdown of the plantation system further affected members of the Ellison family, and they never recouped their losses or regained their prosperity or stature after the war.

—Sharon Roger Hepburn

See also
Black Slaveowners
For Further Reading
Berlin, Ira. 1974. *Slaves without Masters: The Free Negro in the Antebellum South.* New York: Pantheon Books; Johnson, Michael P., and James L. Roark. 1984. *Black Masters: A Free Family of Color in the Old South.* New York: Norton; Johnson, Michael P., and James L. Roark, eds. 1984. *No Chariot Let Down: Charleston's Free People of Color on the Eve of the Civil War.* New York: Norton; Wikramanayake, Marina. 1973. *A World in Shadow: The Free Black in Antebellum South Carolina.* Columbia: University of South Carolina Press.

ELMINA

Called Edina by its Eguafo founders, Elmina is a town located in coastal Ghana (formerly the Gold Coast) where the Benya River meets the Gulf of Guinea, and it was a principal trading port in the Atlantic trade for gold and slaves. The name derives either from the Portuguese term for the area, *Mina de Ouro* ("the gold mine") or the short form, *Mina* ("the mine"), or perhaps from the Arabic word for port, *al-Minah*.

As the southern terminus of a trade route linking the coast with the interior states, Elmina maintained vital trade ties with powerful kingdoms to the north like Denkyira and Ashanti and even farther north with the savanna states through the northern market at Begho. Elmina's strategic trade connections and the presence of gold attracted Portuguese attention in 1471, and in 1482, the Portuguese built the castle of São Jorge da Mina (St. George's), which was the headquarters of Portuguese trading in West Africa until 1637. From this fort in Elmina, Portuguese merchants vigorously promoted trade and established a complex commercial pattern involving gold and slaves. Portuguese traders exchanged manufactured goods for Gold Coast gold, traded manufactured goods for

A seventeenth-century view of Elmina Castle. Originally the Portuguese fort São Jorge da Mina, or St. George of the Mine, it was the first permanent trading station built by Europeans in Africa.

slaves in the Slave Coast, and sold the slaves for gold in the Gold Coast—the slaves being employed, among other things, in mining gold and serving as porters to carry trade items.

In 1637, the Dutch captured St. George's castle and made it their headquarters. Like the Portuguese, the Dutch conducted a profitable trade in gold and slaves at Elmina, and to promote and protect this trade, the Dutch reconstructed the castle, enhanced its defense, and augmented its capacity to hold slaves en route to the Americas. As additional security, particularly against rival European traders, the Dutch surrounded Elmina castle with several defensive fortifications—Forts St. Jago, Waakzaamheid, Beeckestyn, Schomerus, Java, and Nagtglas—and a watchtower. Fort Java was not only a fortification but also a post for recruiting Africans into the Royal Dutch East India Army. The recruits, mainly free Gold Coast men, also included slaves purchased by the Dutch, then freed on condition that they serve a military duty of 6 or 12 years in the Dutch East Indies and pay back from their salary the cost of their emancipation.

Control of trade in Elmina loomed large in local politics. At different times, the Fanti, Denkyira, and Ashanti states fought for control of Elmina's trade. Particularly prized was the Elmina Note—the Dutch agreement to pay rent on the land on which the castle stood—for possession of it entitled the holder to the rent, and most important, control of the access to trade at Elmina castle.

—*Patience Essah*

See also
Gold Coast
For Further Reading
Boahen, Adu. 1975. *Ghana: Evolution and Change in the Nineteenth and Twentieth Centuries*. London: Longman; Daaku, Kwame Yeboa. 1970. *Trade and Politics on the Gold Coast, 1600–1720: A Study of the African Reaction to European Trade*. Oxford: Oxford University Press; van Dantzig, Albert. 1980. *A Short History of the Forts and Castles of Ghana*. Accra: Sedco Publishing; Dickson, Kwamina B. 1969. *A Historical Geography of Ghana*. Cambridge: Cambridge University Press.

EMANCIPATION PROCLAMATION

Issued by Abraham Lincoln on January 1, 1863, the Emancipation Proclamation freed all slaves in territories still rebelling against the federal government of the United States. The decision to proclaim slaves of the Confederate States free took years of deliberation and debate. There were speculations from the onset of the U.S. Civil War about the possibility of emancipating slaves. Abolitionists, black and white, who supported the Republican Party's antislavery platform, envisaged the abolition of slavery, but Northern Democrats opposed such measures. Lincoln himself, despite his antislavery sentiments, was not enthused about making slavery the focus of a war he thought of as a war to protect and preserve the Union. Cautious about emancipation, he was also uncertain if executive authority gave him jurisdiction over slavery and was concerned about the loyal border states of Maryland, Kentucky, and Missouri. Lincoln, therefore, opposed and reversed decisions of Union officers who emancipated slaves flocking to their command.

When Lincoln eventually decided on emancipation, he proposed two plans. The first was for gradual emancipation with compensation to slaveowners for their property losses. The second was a plan to colonize free blacks, believing that both races could not coexist. In fall 1861, Delaware rejected Lincoln's plan for gradual emancipation with compensation. In spring 1862, he sent a resolution to Congress recommending government cooperation with and assistance to any state willing to adopt a gradual-emancipation-with-compensation plan. He pleaded unsuccessfully for the support of congressional delegates from Maryland, Delaware, West Virginia, Kentucky, and Missouri.

In April 1862, Lincoln recommended emancipation in the District of Columbia, with limited compensation and a provision for voluntary colonization of free blacks in Haiti or Liberia. This recommendation became law, and $100,000 was earmarked for colonizing Negroes of the District of Columbia. That same month, Lincoln summoned a prominent black delegation to discuss colonization. The outcome is unclear, but Lincoln indicated that the delegates seemed favorably disposed toward his plan. On June 17, 1862, Lincoln signed a bill freeing slaves who joined the Union side. Two days later, another bill abolished slavery in the territories. Between July 21 and 22, he presented the cabinet with the draft of a proposal freeing all slaves, to take effect from January 1, 1863.

Public opinion developed in favor of emancipation. White abolitionists urged Lincoln to regard emancipation as the consummation of his party's antislavery platform. Prominent black leaders, including Frederick Douglass and Martin Delany, implored him to adopt emancipation on moral, humanitarian, and military grounds, but others advised waiting for an opportune moment. The Union victory at Antietam on September 17, 1862, finally prompted Lincoln to act. Five days later, he issued a preliminary draft, suggesting the possibility of compensated emancipation with voluntary colonization. The draft proclaimed that effective January 1, 1863, "all persons held as slaves

This 1865 drawing contrasts enslaved African Americans with those who had been freed by Abraham Lincoln's Emancipation Proclamation.

within any state or, designated part of a state, the people whereof shall be in rebellion against the United States, shall be, then, thenceforward, and forever free" and pledged government support for protecting the freedom of such persons. The government also promised not to do or act in any manner that would jeopardize such persons in the exercise of their freedom.

The draft enraged many Northerners who felt that it committed the nation to a cause that was not the war's original intent, but abolitionists applauded it. The presentation of the draft prompted debates and suggestions for modification in the months ahead, and Lincoln held several deliberative and discursive sessions with his cabinet before completing the final draft on the morning of January 1, 1863. He immediately signed it into law.

Lincoln underlined the proclamation's strategic importance. He issued it "upon military necessity" because it was "a fit and necessary war measure" designed to end the rebellion. He had come to realize how vital slaves were to both the economy and the

war effort of the South. In fact, by January 1863, the Southern economy was heavily dependent on slave labor, and rebels were also tapping into slave resources to carry out noncombatant war tasks like fortification construction. Blacks in the North hailed the emancipation, celebrating with prayers, barbecues, and thanksgiving, and January 1, 1863, has since remained for blacks a defining moment in their struggle for equality. For the entire nation, the proclamation was a milestone in the tortuous journey toward obliterating the cancer of slavery and racism.

Despite the applause and celebrations it evoked, the proclamation did not free all slaves. It affected only slaves of the rebellious territories and left untouched the more than 800,000 slaves in the border states; 13 parishes of Louisiana, including the city of New Orleans; West Virginia; and 7 counties in eastern Virginia, including Norfolk and Portsmouth. The proclamation had the desired effect of crippling the South's war effort. The Confederates almost immediately lost control of their slave population, and there were mass desertions.

The proclamation transformed the war from a struggle to preserve the Union to a crusade for human freedom. It gave the Union cause a moral and humanitarian complexion, which generated worldwide support, and it established Lincoln's reputation among Negroes as "the Great Emancipator." It has since given an added significance to New Year's Day, and many blacks celebrate January 1 as a day of commemoration by reading the proclamation. Reaction to the document today is mixed. Many blacks and whites continue to view the proclamation positively as a shining example of the nation's accomplishment while others remember it differently as a living testimony to the unfulfilled national aspirations. During the 1960s, many statesmen and politicians invoked the Emancipation Proclamation as proof of the nation's commitment to freedom and equality and as a reminder of its "unfulfilled promises." Such sentiments fed the flames of the civil rights movement.

—*Tunde Adeleke*

For Further Reading
Franklin, John H., and Moss A. Alfred. 1994. *From Slavery to Freedom: A History of African Americans.* New York: McGraw Hill; Quarles, Benjamin. 1962. *Lincoln and the Negro.* New York: Oxford University Press; Wiggins, William H. 1987. *O Freedom! Afro-American Emancipation Celebrations.* Knoxville: University of Tennessee Press.

ENCOMIENDA *SYSTEM*

Many scholars argue that the Spanish *encomienda* system in the New World, a system for extracting labor and tribute in kind from conquered Indians, was the same as slavery. It was not, however, for the Spaniards did not own the Indians "commended" to their charge. The *encomienda* system developed through European concepts of patriarchy and feudal obligations and originated as a reciprocal system to reward the crown and conquistadors and to integrate Indians into Spanish society. Accordingly, the Spanish crown used local administrators to commend a group of Indians, vassals of the crown, to a particular Spaniard, the *encomendero* (the person who held the *encomienda* rights), in reward for his service.

The *encomendero* was to care for these Indians, teach them the basic Catholic tenets and how to live in a "civilized" manner, and keep them from sliding into their habitual patterns of "idleness and vice." Additionally, the *encomendero* was to pay the Indians a wage, and he had to be prepared to fight for his king when necessary. In turn, the Indians owed their *en-comendero* tribute in the form of labor and/or agricultural goods.

Encomiendas were not inheritable (although the crown amended this point to make *encomienda* grants good for one additional generation), and commended Indians could not legally be sold nor could their labors be rented out. That was the theory, but in practice, the *encomienda* system was exploitative, repressive, and isolating.

In 1499, Christopher Columbus granted the first New World *encomiendas* on Hispaniola to Francisco Roldán and other rebellious Spaniards who had illegally usurped the labor and tribute of Taino natives in various villages for several years. Columbus called the tribute grants *repartimientos,* from the Spanish verb *repartir* ("to divide"). The action was part of his futile attempt to make peace with the rebels and to re-exert control over the island and its peoples. "By what authority does the Admiral give my vassals away?" Queen Isabella asked when she heard what Columbus had done. Yet by 1503, realizing the political benefits to be gained by granting *repartimientos,* the crown had institutionalized the system under Governor Nicolás de Ovando.

The same system went by many names. In several documents from the early decades of the sixteenth century these labor grants are called *casycos,* which indicates the importance of the *caciques* ("chiefs") to the system as middlemen. The grants were normally for the labor of entire villages under a particular Taino *cacique,* whose traditional role included the authority to assign and send out work parties. The change to the word *encomienda* appears to have been made to conserve crown control and as a concession to the island's clergymen, who protested the system's brutality.

The Dominican friar Antonio de Montesinos preached a shocking sermon on Hispaniola in 1511: "Are these not men?" he asked the Spaniards about the Taino, demanding that the Indians be freed from their excessive labors in the gold mines so they could be catechized properly and converted to Catholicism (Hanke, 1949). Other Dominicans, including the persuasive Bartolomé de Las Casas, supported Montesinos's demands and called for an end to the exploitative *repartimiento* system. But instead of eliminating it, the crown instituted several changes designed to improve the treatment of commended Indians. These were the Laws of Burgos, implemented in 1513.

Among the changes, the name of the system was amended to *encomienda* to emphasize the reciprocal responsibilities that the *encomenderos* owed to the crown and to the Indians commended to their care. The Laws of Burgos did not protect Indian *naborías,* a word the Spaniards adapted from the Taino social classification for commoners. *Naboría* came to designate Indian slaves, who worked side by side with commended Indians. Indian slaves could be taken in "just wars" (such slaves included cannibals, sodomists, and Indians who did not acquiesce to the Spanish "requirement" that they accept the crown's dominion) or by *rescate* ("rescue"). *Rescate* refers to Indians who were the slaves of other Indians; they were "rescued" from a state of pagan slavery and put into one of Christian slavery, which was considered infinitely better.

From Hispaniola, the *encomienda* system spread to Cuba, Puerto Rico, and the mainland of the Americas. In locations like the Valley of Mexico, where there was a teeming indigenous population and a tributary system organized on an empire-wide basis, *encomiendas,* in combination with land grants, became streamlined routes to riches, elite status, and political power for the Spanish *encomenderos,* who placed themselves, instead of Aztec elite, at the top of the tributary pyramid. Mexico's riches were primarily in the form of agricultural tribute from commended Indians, not from mining labor as on Hispaniola, since the mineral-rich regions of northern Mexico had no settled Indian populations.

The *encomienda* played a similar role in densely populated Peru, where the Inca established and maintained an empire-wide tributary system long before the Spaniards arrived. In places like Chile, which was sparsely populated and where the Indians were not a settled people, commended Indians were used primarily to provide personal service and as laborers for building roads and bridges, quite similar to the *mita* service the Inca had imposed on their subordinates. One scholar argues that Paraguay was the only place where the *encomienda* system aided the integration of the indigenous peoples into mainstream colonial society, as the Spanish crown had intended it to do throughout the empire.

The Spanish crown attempted to check the rising power of the *encomenderos,* the New World's landed elite, by implementing New Laws (1542), which were to put an end to the *encomienda* system. Like any regulation of the system itself, enforcement of the New Laws was sporadic. *Encomenderos* played important economic, social, and political roles into the late-colonial era. Many scholars argue that *encomiendas,* combined with land grants, evolved into haciendas, the sprawling estates whose owners dominated Latin American politics into the twentieth century.

—*Lynne Guitar*

See also
Mita; Taino
For Further Reading
Arranz Márquez, Luis. 1991. *Repartimientos y encomiendas en la isla Española (El repartimiento de Albuquerque de 1514).* Santo Domingo: Fundación García-Arévalo; Hanke, Lewis. 1949. *The Spanish Struggle*

for Justice in the Conquest of America. Philadelphia: University of Pennsylvania Press; Simpson, Lesley Byrd. 1966. *The Encomienda in New Spain: The Beginning of Spanish Mexico.* Berkeley: University of California Press; Zavala, Silvio Arturo. 1973. *La Encomienda Indiana.* Mexico: Editorial Porrua.

ENGERMAN, STANLEY L. (1936–)

Stanley L. Engerman's most influential book, *Time on the Cross: The Economics of American Negro Slavery* (1974), coauthored with Robert William Fogel, ignited a crucial historical debate over the nature of slavery. In response to the first volume, critics initially wrote favorable comments. Yet the ensuing dialogue, which centered on the nature of antebellum slavery and spanned more than two decades, would call into question Fogel and Engerman's methodology, their conclusions, and even their personal intentions. The avalanche of responses came from critics in every corner of the United States and as far away as Finland, Sweden, Holland, Russia, and France.

Following the tradition of articles by Alfred Conrad and John Meyer in the late 1950s, which sparked a debate over Southern growth rates and the importance of slavery to the Southern economy based on statistical evidence, Fogel and Engerman provided a new methodological paradigm. No longer could historians intuitively interpret documents without facing serious criticism. Fogel and Engerman's statistical methods, fully explicated in their second volume, *Time on the Cross: Evidence and Methods—A Supplement* (1974), offered a more systematic approach to large bodies of quantifiable data in the hopes of producing some definitive answers to historical questions. They sought to correct previous interpretations concerning the slave economy of the antebellum South and described the 10 most common misconceptions about slavery in their prologue.

Their statistical evidence suggested that slavery had been a flexible, highly developed form of capitalism. The future of this productive, efficient, and profitable system looked bright in the eyes of slaveholders and could only have been destroyed by some event as devastating as the U.S. Civil War. Engerman and Fogel argued that slavery stimulated economic growth in the South and provided slaves with a measure of economic security not enjoyed by many free urban, industrial workers in the North. Twenty-five percent of the slaves held skilled or semiskilled jobs and received goods and food as compensation, placing them above the subsistence level. Capitalist developments made slavery ever more profitable while they simultaneously encouraged slaves to become achievement-oriented, hard workers. Moreover, the developments helped lead to relatively stable slave families headed by husbands, out of which slaves cultivated a distinctively black culture.

Critics argued from many perspectives, some even claiming that Fogel and Engerman were self-righteous racists bent on resurrecting old notions about slavery's benevolent qualities. Historians like Herbert G. Gutman chose to focus on the authors' selection and use of quantifiable data and questioned their calculations, samples, and assumptions. Gutman, in *Slavery and the Numbers Game* (1975), charged them with underrepresenting the large plantations, incorrectly calculating data, and then making erroneous assumptions based on their misinterpretation of the evidence. More generally, he insisted that they completely ignored racism and that they asked and answered the wrong historical questions. Gutman countered Fogel and Engerman's assertions of stable slave families by arguing that the families were fragile at best and not merely because of the selling of family members.

Other critics, like Richard Sutch, Paul A. David, and Peter Temin, followed suit, suggesting that Fogel and Engerman had underestimated the issues of general welfare, psychic well-being, and brutality in slave life. Some things, according to this view, could not be understood in numerical terms, and these critics recognized the limited usefulness of statistics.

Stanley Engerman and Robert Fogel, together and separately, have replied to critics in writings following *Time on the Cross,* and it is significant that historians continue to address the arguments and methodology presented in their two volumes. Yet Engerman has also made new and important contributions to slave history, including his work on the growth of the world economy and the Atlantic slave trade, with books like *The Atlantic Slave Trade* (1992) and *Race and Slavery in the Western Hemisphere* (1975), coedited with Joseph Inikori and Eugene Genovese, respectively. Additionally, Engerman has delved into the slave history of other colonies, including the West Indies in *The Lesser Antilles in the Age of European Expansion* (1996), coedited with Robert Paquette.

—*Debra Meyers*

For Further Reading
David, Paul, et al. 1976. *Reckoning with Slavery: A Critical Study in the Quantitative History of American Negro Slavery.* New York: Oxford University Press; Fogel, Robert. 1989. *Without Consent or Contract: The Rise and Fall of American Slavery.* New York: Norton; Fogel, Robert, and Stanley Engerman. 1974. *Time on the Cross: The Economics of American Negro Slavery.* Boston: Little, Brown; Fogel, Robert, and Stanley Engerman. 1974. *Time on the Cross: Evidence and Methods—A Supplement.* Boston: Little, Brown; Gutman, Herbert. 1975. *Slavery and the Numbers Game: A Critique of* Time on the Cross. Urbana: University of Illinois Press.

ENGLISH CARIBBEAN

Slavery in the Caribbean islands began shortly after Europeans established their initial sixteenth-century settlements there. Generally, the Spanish left the smaller eastern islands to the native inhabitants, which made them easy prey for the northern European powers of England, France, and Holland to seize during the seventeenth century. The English settled St. Christopher in 1624, Barbados in 1627, Nevis in 1628, and Antigua and Montserrat in 1632. What remained of the native Carib population was killed or driven off these English islands into Dominica and St. Vincent, leaving the islands free for immigration by English colonists. The English took over other islands later in the seventeenth century, including Jamaica in 1655, when an armada conquered it from the Spanish. By the early-eighteenth century, Jamaica had surpassed Barbados as England's richest colony in the Americas.

Early settlers founded mixed farming communities using free labor. The importation of sugarcane cultivation into Barbados and other Lesser Antilles islands from Dutch settlements at Pernambuco (now Recife) in Brazil during the 1640s created a demand for manual labor that drove the slave market. Following Portugal's recapture of northeastern Brazil from the Dutch in 1654, hundreds of experienced Dutch planters migrated to Caribbean islands, and sugar cultivation accelerated. The new large-scale plantation system favored using slave labor and undercut the viability of small farms worked by free labor. In Barbados, the 2,000 small farms that existed in 1640 had been consolidated into fewer than 300 large sugar plantations by 1670.

The profitability of sugar cultivation encouraged planters to maximize the amount of land devoted to cane, and the result was the nearly total elimination of vegetable and grain cultivation. Planters depended upon importing food and other necessities from England's North American colonies and from Ireland. During frequent regional wars, famines occurred among the enslaved population as ships were reluctant to risk capture in order to supply the islands.

The frequent regional wars entailed other hardships on the free and enslaved populations. Except for Barbados, every Caribbean island suffered invasion from other European powers during the seventeenth and eighteenth centuries, resulting in the seizure and resettlement of slaves and the flight of free settlers. Hard conditions also encouraged growing absenteeism among the islands' landowners, who left colonial management to hired overseers and thus caused a larger net capital drain from the settlements than occurred in the North American colonies.

The English colonists' lifestyles divided markedly between the very large island of Jamaica and the "older" islands of the eastern Caribbean. The Jamaican plantations tended to be much larger than plantations of the other islands, and Jamaica's nearly impenetrable interior mountains facilitated the growth of so-called Maroon (from the Spanish *cimarron*, "wild") communities of escaped slaves. The existence of these communities resulted in a relatively high number of runaway slaves and forced English settlers to maintain an embattled frontier mentality like that on the North American colonists' Indian frontier.

A determined British effort to subdue the Maroons resulted in the First Maroon War (1730–1739), in which Cudjo and his sister Nanny led 5,000 Maroons to victory over British forces. In the treaty ending the war, the British acknowledged the Maroons' independence in exchange for cooperation in returning future runaway slaves. A Second Maroon War (1795–1796) resulted in the capture and deportation of one Maroon community to Nova Scotia and from there to Sierra Leone in West Africa. The presence of Maroon communities engendered an ambivalence among Jamaica's black population, embodying as they did both fierce independence and limited collaboration with the imperial government.

Escape from slavery was a less viable option in the eastern Caribbean where the inhabitants developed a more settled lifestyle than in Jamaica. Numerous native slaves and an elaborate hierarchy of skills and occupations contributed to the smaller islands' less turbulent lifestyle. Each colony maintained its own law code regulating slave life, as Britain never promulgated an empire-wide code comparable to the French Code Noir of 1685. Slavery ended in the eastern Caribbean when the Emancipation Act of 1833 abolished slavery throughout the British Empire.

—*Thomas W. Krise*

See also
Abolition, British Empire; The *Asiento;* Barbados; Black Caribs; Cudjo; English Slave Trade; Jamaica; Jamaica Rebellion; Proslavery Argument, British; Sugar Cultivation and Trade; Transition from Slave Labor to Free Labor, Caribbean; Trelawney Town Maroons; West Indies

For Further Reading
Beckles, Hilary, and Verene Shepherd, eds. 1991. *Caribbean Slave Society and Economy.* New York: New Press; Bush, Barbara. 1990. *Slave Women in Caribbean Society, 1650–1838.* Kingston, Jamaica: Heinemann; Dunn, Richard S. 1972. *Sugar and Slaves: The Rise of the Planter Class in the English West Indies, 1624–1713.* Chapel Hill: University of North Carolina Press; Stinchcombe, Arthur L. 1995. *Sugar Island Slavery in the Age of Enlightenment: The Political Economy of the Caribbean World.* Princeton, NJ: Princeton University Press.

ENGLISH SLAVE TRADE

Beginning with Sir John Hawkins's illegal shipment of slaves to the Spanish West Indies in 1562, the English (and after the union of 1707, the British) trade in African slaves amounted to most of the trade during its peak in the later-eighteenth century. Of the estimated 11 million slaves transported across the Atlantic, the English slave trade accounted for half.

Transatlantic trade in enslaved Africans began early in the sixteenth century when Spanish and Portuguese New World colonists began losing the forced labor of indigenous peoples owing to overwork and the spread of Old World diseases. Africans were better able to withstand those diseases, so the Iberians expanded the African slave trade to supply their New World plantations and mines. The wealth of the colonies in the Americas eventually attracted adventurers from northern European countries, and French, Dutch, and English sailors eagerly pursued the Iberian colonies' wealth by piracy and illegal trade in slaves.

Hawkins's illicit sale of slaves to Spanish Hispaniola in 1562 initiated a long period of English incursion into the Spanish slave trade, and beginning in the early-seventeenth century, the English, French, and Dutch established colonies in the Caribbean islands and along portions of North and South America that the Spaniards and Portuguese were unable or unwilling to settle or defend. By the 1650s, the English had established thriving colonies along the North American coast, in Suriname, and in the Windward and Leeward Islands of the eastern Caribbean.

Initially, these new colonies were founded upon free and indentured white labor drawn primarily from the British Isles, but after the temporary Dutch colonies in northeastern Brazil introduced sugarcane cultivation to Barbados and other islands, the region's small farms were consolidated into larger sugar plantations, which demanded much larger numbers of laborers. In Virginia and other North American colonies, tobacco cultivation also encouraged development of large, labor-intensive plantations, although not to the same degree as in the sugar colonies.

The first Africans arrived in Virginia aboard a Dutch vessel in 1619. Initially, Dutch slave traders

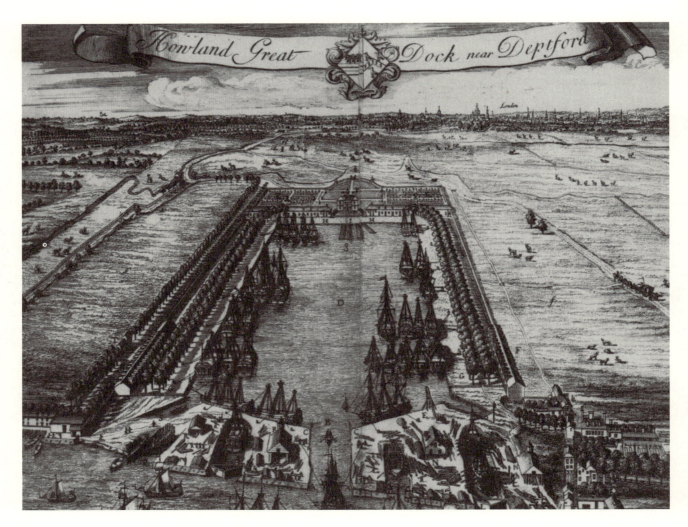

Howland Great Dock, built in 1695, was London's largest dock for over a century, producing ships for the transatlantic slave trade.

supplied most of the demand for African slaves during the 1640s through the 1670s, but increasingly, English adventurers pushed their way into the lucrative trade. In 1663, King Charles II granted a trading monopoly to the Royal Adventurers Trading to Africa, and that monopoly passed in 1672 to the Royal African Company. The monopoly lapsed in 1698, when the trade was opened to all English companies. The Treaty of Utrecht (1713), which ended the War of the Spanish Succession, granted Britain the *asiento,* or permission to sell slaves to Spanish colonies in the Americas for 30 years, thus boosting the already lucrative market for British slave traders.

During the late-eighteenth-century heyday of the British slave trade, dozens of small shipping concerns and independent slavers profited from the practice. For British traders, Jamaica represented the largest single market, absorbing more than 700,000 Africans from its conquest in 1655 until the British slave trade was abolished in 1807. The total trade to the British West Indies amounted to more than 1.6 million people. By contrast, all of English-speaking North America received fewer than 500,000 slaves during the same period. On the eve of the American Revolution, more than 150 British ships per year supplied 40,000 slaves to British and other New World colonies.

Unlike North America's colonies, which managed to reproduce much of their slave population, the Caribbean sugar colonies (with the exception of Barbados) depended upon a steady supply of African-born slaves to maintain slave populations. Exceptionally hard working conditions, the dangers attendant upon sugar factory work, the planters' preference for buying men over women, and a high death rate because of disease all contributed to the sugar colonies' inability to maintain slave populations through natural increase. The large proportion of African-born slaves in the West Indies resulted in numerous violent slave rebellions and in a better preservation of African culture in the island societies.

The English slave trade formed a vital link in the transatlantic commercial system that helped propel Britain to the position of world power it held throughout the eighteenth and nineteenth centuries. The slave trade made it possible for the sugar trade to account for more than two-thirds of the world's recorded trade in the late-eighteenth century, and profits from sugar fueled the rise of manufacturing, which further enhanced British power in the period.

Three principal factors led to the decision on the part of the British to abolish the slave trade in 1807: the loss of the North American colonies in the American Revolution, which reduced the demand for the British slave trade; the development of the European sugar beet industry after 1800, which afforded an alternate sugar supply during the British trade embargo of Napoleon Bonaparte's continental empire; and the declining value of sugar relative to other industries in the British imperial economic system, which reduced the political influence of the once-powerful "West India interest" in London. The movement to abolish the slave trade gained widespread support in two waves: the first, in the late 1780s, ended with the reactionary mood that followed in the wake of the French Revolution; the second began in the later 1790s and culminated with passage of the act of Parliament that abolished the slave trade in 1807. It would take nearly 30 years more for the British Empire to become the first power to abolish the institution of slavery.

—*Thomas W. Krise*

See also

Abolition, British Empire; The *Asiento;* English Caribbean, Slavery in the; Proslavery Argument, British; Royal African Company; Sugar Cultivation and Trade; Transition from Slave Labor to Free Labor, Caribbean; Utrecht, Treaty of; Volume of the Slave Trade; West Indies

For Further Reading

Eltis, David, and James Walvin, eds. 1981. *The Abolition of the Atlantic Slave Trade.* Madison: University of Wisconsin Press; Inikori, Joseph E., and Stanley L. Engerman, eds. 1992. *The Atlantic Slave Trade: Effects on Economies, Societies, and Peoples in Africa, the Americas, and Europe.* Durham, NC: Duke University Press; Solow, Barbara L. 1991. *Slavery and the Rise of the Atlantic System.* New York: Cambridge University Press; Walvin, James. 1992. *Black Ivory: A History of British Slavery.* London: HarperCollins.

THE ENLIGHTENMENT

The single most important philosophical development of the Enlightenment was, perhaps, that of "natural rights" discourse. In the eighteenth century, when much of learned European and American society was consumed with systematizing and structuring knowledge, the rise of empiricism, Denis Diderot's *Encyclopedia* project, and measuring and quantifying the world as a way of knowing it, it is not surprising that attention would turn to one of the most discussed, volatile, and morally important issues of the day—slavery. All of the rhetorical and philosophical force of the Enlightenment came to bear on the question of African humanity, which lay at the center of the question of slavery itself.

There had to be a way of justifying slavery that made it morally permissible. Otherwise, Charles Louis Montesquieu's prophecy would return to haunt the slave owners: "If they [African slaves] are, indeed, human, then we [whites] are not Christian" (Tiainen-Anttila, 1994). This need for moral justification made "natural rights" and Christian morality as both the language used to wage the rhetorical battle over slavery between abolitionist and proslavery advocates and the primary areas Enlightenment thinkers fought to control in their effort to legitimize and authorize their positions.

The issue of literacy was a very important issue in discussions of slavery during the Enlightenment. Proslavery advocates argued that Africans were suited to be slaves because they could not reason. The visible sign of reason during the Enlightenment, as Henry Louis Gates, Jr., (1987) has argued, was the ability to read and to write (especially creatively). Since blacks were unable to produce poets and artists, they were not considered to be of the same variety of humanity as whites. Of course, the literary accomplishments of figures like Phillis Wheatley, Jupiter Hammon, and George Moses Horton flew in the face of such racist claims and went far to demonstrate that Africans shared the same "natural rights" as whites.

Hence, any consideration of the Enlightenment and slavery must necessarily take into account the circulation and influence of the language of "natural rights" and "natural laws" in the eighteenth and nineteenth centuries. Robert M. Cover, in *Justice Accused: Antislavery and the Judicial Process* (1975), analyzes the ways in which the judicial and political discourses of the period (particularly the decisions of judges sitting on the bench) aided and abetted the system of slavery. He begins his analysis with a discussion of "natural law" and "natural rights." These concepts have sources as disparate as Thomas Hobbes's *Leviathan* (1651), Montesquieu's *The Spirit of the Laws* (1752), Jean-Jacques Rousseau's *Discourse on Inequality* (1761) and *The Social Contract* (1762), Thomas Paine's *Rights of Man* (1791–1792), and Thomas Jefferson's *Notes on the State of Virginia* (1781–1782) among others.

Concomitant with the rise of natural rights philosophy and rhetoric is the development of the "master-slave dialectic." The dominant articulations of this idea can be traced most usefully, perhaps, through the philosophy of Hobbes's *Leviathan,* Georg Wilhelm Freidrich Hegel's *Phenomenology of Spirit* (1807), Karl Marx's *Grundrisse* (1850), and Friedrich Wilhelm Nietzsche's *Beyond Good and Evil* (1885). Each of these works provided a discussion of the relationship between master and slave that influenced the intellectual and public debates surrounding slavery well into the nineteenth century.

Similarly, since the primary progenitors of these discourses of natural rights that influenced social and political thought in Britain and the United States were French (primarily Montesquieu and Rousseau), it is important to remember that these discourses also animated the discussions of French slavery and colonialism. The support that American intellectuals like Thomas Jefferson, Benjamin Franklin, and Thomas Paine offered the French Revolution is well documented.

Jefferson, for example, spent much time in France; in fact, he was there in 1787 when the U.S. Constitution was drafted. He was greatly influenced not only by John Locke's philosophy of knowledge (especially his *Essay Concerning Human Understanding* [1690]) but also by the natural rights philosophies of Montesquieu and Rousseau.

Thomas Paine was involved in revolutionary activity in the United States, France, and England. In fact, it was in 1775 in London that he met Benjamin Franklin, whose letters of introduction allowed Paine to go to Philadelphia where he worked as a journalist. It was during that time that he wrote his attack on U.S. slavery, "African Slavery in America" (1775) and the anonymously published *Common Sense* (1776), which encouraged American colonists to declare independence from Britain. *Common Sense* was enormously successful in both the United States and France. While back in London in 1791, Paine joined the pamphlet war over the French Revolution with his *Rights of Man* (1792), written in response to Edmund Burke's conservative *Reflections on the Revolution in France* (1790).

Such transatlantic concern and writing led to the political debate between the recently defeated British and the Americans over the rights of man, with Burke and Paine squaring off as the representative interlocutors. This kind of political and intellectual cross-fertilization again demonstrates the need believe that the triangular relationship among the three nations framed the political and moral philosophical discourses that gave rise to the Enlightenment and later ushered in romanticism. In light of such compelling evidence, the connections between slavery and the Enlightenment are undeniable.

—*Dwight A. McBride*

See also
French Declaration of the Rights of Man and Citizen; Hobbes, Thomas; Locke, John; Marxism; Montesquieu, Charles Louis de Secondat; *Notes on Virginia* by Thomas Jefferson; Racism; Romanticism and Abolitionism; Wheatley, Phillis
For Further Reading
Gates, Henry L., Jr. 1987. *Figures in Black: Words, Signs, and the "Racial" Self.* New York: Oxford University Press; Hume, David. 1987. "Of National Characters." In *Essays: Moral, Political, and Literary.* Indianapolis, IN: Liberty Classics; Pieterse, Jan Nederveen. 1992. *White on Black: Images of African and Blacks in Western Popular Culture.* New Haven, CT: Yale University Press; Tiainen-Anttila, Kaija. 1994. *The Problem of Humanity: Blacks in the European Enlightenment.* Helsinki: Finnish Historical Society.

ENRIQUILLO

The Taino *cacique* ("chieftain") Guarocuya, better known as Enriquillo (a diminutive form of his baptismal name, Enrique), was a grandnephew of the great *cacica* ("chieftainess") Anacaona and one of the first native children in the New World to be converted to Catholicism. The friars taught Enriquillo to read and write Castilian and to act "civilized." His achievements did not prevent his being assigned as a laborer to a Spaniard named Francisco de Valenzuela of San Juan de la Maguana in 1514, during the last great division of Hispaniola's Indians, and then passed on to Francisco's son and heir, Andrés.

Enriquillo cooperated with the Spaniards, ordering his people to mine gold and grow food for them, until 1519 when Andrés seized not only Enriquillo's prized mare but also his wife, Mencía, to whom he had been married in a sanctified Catholic ceremony. Enriquillo went to the town's leading Spaniard, Pedro de Vadillo, to demand justice, but Vadillo reprimanded him for speaking out against Andrés. Furious, Enriquillo consulted the church fathers in the capital, and they approached the royal Audiencia (governmental council) with Enriquillo's demands for justice. Although the Spanish officials in the capital sympathized with the *cacique* and ordered Mencía's release, Enriquillo was forced to take their letter back to Vadillo, who threatened to jail him or put him in the stocks if he pursued the issue. Enriquillo gathered up Mencía and the rest of his people and led them to the desolate lands called Bahoruco, and from there he staged successful raids against the Spaniards for the next 13 years. As his fame spread, rebellious Indians and African slaves joined him.

Over the years, numerous heavily armed bands of

Spaniards were sent to dislodge Enriquillo, but they had no success until the 1533 expedition of Captain Francisco de Barrionuevo, who bore promises of a pardon and liberty for all from King Charles V—and who took along the Dominican friar Bartolomé de Las Casas to convince the *cacique* of the sincerity of the offer. (Las Casas described Enriquillo as "grave and strict," neither handsome nor ugly, tall, with a well-proportioned body [Las Casas, 1988].) Enriquillo reconciled with the king and agreed, henceforth, to return runaway slaves to Spanish officials. Later a group of escaped African slaves attacked the town of Azua, where Enriquillo was buried in 1535, to retaliate for his actions against black slaves.

Bahoruco remained a refuge for rebellious *cimarrones* ("runaway slaves") until the late-nineteenth century. Today, there is a monumental sculpture dedicated to Enriquillo on the main road to Bahoruco, and the large salt lake in the region is known as Lago Enriquillo. The region is still considered unruly, for it is a center of voodoo.

—*Lynne Guitar*

For Further Reading
Jesús Galván, Manuel de. 1989. *Enriquillo*. Dominican Republic: Ediciones de Taller; Las Casas, Bartolomé de. 1988. *Historia de las Indias*. Madrid: Alianza; Oviedo y Valdés, Gonzálo Fernández de. 1959. *Historia general de las Indias*. Madrid: Ediciones Atlas; Peña Batlle, Manuel Arturo. 1948. *La rebelión de Bahoruco*. Ciudad Trujillo: Impresora Dominicana.

ENTREPOTS

The last glimpse enslaved Africans had of Africa's shore was frequently the entrepôt (transshipment center) from which they were shipped. The Atlantic slave trade in Africa was organized around a series of trade entrepôts, which were primarily located along Africa's coasts although some were located several miles inland. The trade ports generally corresponded to one of several models: African towns that became important in the slave trade, European trade posts where towns were originally not present but developed outside the walls, and trading posts where no significant indigenous settlement developed. The most common entrepôts were those where the establishment of a European trading outpost, perhaps adjacent to a minor fishing village, led to the development of a major town.

Elmina ("the mine") was Africa's first major trade entrepôt. Founded by the Portuguese in 1482, the town was originally established as a storehouse and trading establishment for acquiring gold from mines

Slaves bound to a shed in an entrepôt on the coast of Africa awaiting European traders.

in the Ghanaian forest and as a way station for trade bound for India. Elmina became a significant influence on the Gold Coast, first as the Portuguese headquarters and after 1637, as the Dutch headquarters. The Gold Coast enjoyed the greatest density of European trading posts, as each nation attempted to control the greatest possible coastal trade, and because the region had many favorable anchorages and political divisions, numerous opportunities were available.

By the mid-seventeenth century, slave entrepôts existed along the coast of West Africa from the mouth of the Senegal River, around the west coast—including the islands of São Tomé and Príncipe—to Angola. On the eastern coast, Swahili entrepôts existed from Somalia south to Tanzania, where they were supplanted by Portuguese posts in Mozambique. Most were located on the western coast, and of them, Gorée Island near Dakar, forts at the mouth of and along the Gambia River, Bunce Island in Sierra Leone, major forts along the Gold Coast, and Savi, Ouidah, Grand Popo, Keta, and Porto Novo along the Slave Coast were particularly important. Beyond the Slave Coast, British trading posts existed in the Niger Delta region with centers at Calabar, Lagos, Benin, and Bonny. South of the Zaire River, the Portuguese held greater sway, basing much of their Angolan trade in Luanda and Benguela.

In contrast to most of the western coast, where at best individual European nations enjoyed trade monopolies with small coastal states and relatively small numbers of Europeans generally staffed trading establishments, the Angolan trade was nearly exclusively Portuguese at both Luanda and Benguela. A large European presence, as much as 10 percent, and a similar proportion of people of Creole origin characterized this region. North of Angola, the British, French, and occasionally the Portuguese vied for trade in the lower Zaire River at Cabinda, Molembo, and Luango. After the British and French ceased slave trading along the Gold and Slave Coasts in the early-nineteenth century, the Angolan region became increasingly important as a source for the illegal trade to the Caribbean and Brazil (legal trade until 1830, illegal thereafter).

—*Kenneth G. Kelly*

See also
Gold Coast; Slave Coast
For Further Reading
van Dantzig, Albert. 1980. *A Short History of the Forts and Castles of Ghana.* Accra: Sedco; DeCorse, Christopher R. 1992. "Culture Contact, Continuity, and Change on the Gold Coast: AD 1400–1900." *African Archaeological Review* 10: 163–196; Kelly, Kenneth G. 1997. "The Archaeology of African-European Interaction: Investigating the Social Roles of Trade, Traders, and the Use of Space in the Seventeenth and Eighteenth Century Hueda Kingdom, Republic of Bénin." *World Archaeology* 28 (3): 351; Lawrence, A. W. 1963. *Trade Castles and Forts of West Africa.* London: Jonathan Cape.

EPICTETUS
(C. 55–C. 135)

Antiquity's most famous slave philosopher turned teacher, Epictetus had a consuming passion for freedom, which he believed was attainable only by assiduously living according to the tenets of Stoicism. Born in Hierapolis in Phrygia, he was the slave, by either birth or sale, of a man named Epaphroditus, possibly a freedman of Nero. Epictetus became lame early in life, from either the brutality of his master or rheumatism. He was educated by the great Stoic teacher Musonius Rufus and later manumitted. Epictetus taught in Rome until the philosophers were banished by Domitian in either A.D. 89 or 92 and then founded his own Stoic school at Nicopolis in Epirus and taught there the rest of his life. Among his many students was Flavius Arrianus, who collected Epictetus's *Discourses* in eight books (four of which survive) and a compendium, his famous handbook the *Encheiridion*.

Epictetus believed that all human beings have Zeus as their father and so all who are masters and slaves by human law are truly brothers by nature. Accordingly, he held that the lowly, earthly laws permitting the buying and selling of human beings are miserable laws of the dead, not the laws of the gods. He criticized as unacceptable to the gods the behavior of the master who explodes in anger at his slave for not perfectly obeying his commands (*Discourses* 1.13.1–5). Epictetus called such an intolerant, unforgiving master a "slave," a person of debased character. He thought

that the man who has put his own slave in chains on a mere whim is punished by his own wrongdoing; it is the nature of humans to do good and be kind and helpful to one another, so the man who is mean to his slave fares badly when he acts thoughtlessly or unfeelingly (4.1.120–122). Moreover, Epictetus did not regard physical labor as ignoble. He maintained that in contrast to the indolent, pampered life of the wealthy, slaves, manual laborers, and genuine philosophers (like Socrates) live the life of healthy men (3.26.23).

Epictetus's overriding concern was not with political reform, much less the abolition of slavery or any other institution. Instead, his mission was to teach how Stoicism liberates our true inner selves from a desire for things "not up to us." The human body, he argued, is a slave of fever, gout, dysentery, tyrants, fire, iron, and everything that is stronger than it, so freedom lies, not in the body, but in the power of assent (3.22.40–42). Assent, unlike the body, is "up to us" since it cannot be constrained by anyone or anything else.

Epictetus believed that when we hate and fear pain, hardship, illness, loss of property, bad reputation, disfranchisement, exile, imprisonment, and death, and when we love comfort, health, possessions, wealth, familiar places, the pleasant favors of a sweetheart, public office, and fame, then it must be that those who control these things are masters over us. Real freedom, he believed, is achieved, not by manumission, but through eradicating desire for externals and being averse only to the things up to us that are contrary to nature, namely irrational, vicious beliefs, judgments, and choices.

—*William O. Stephens*

See also
Roman Empire; Stoicism

EPISCOPAL CHURCH

The history of the American Episcopal Church and slavery is ambivalent at best. Although some church leaders denounced the institution and fought for its abolition, others remained silent as many wealthy slaveholders, who were dependent on the economic status quo, were Anglican or Episcopalian. The church took virtually no stand on the issue at the national level.

The history of slaves and the Anglican Church began in the early colonial era. Most black Christians in America were Anglicans because most slaveowners in the middle and southern colonies belonged to the Church of England and church leaders viewed captive peoples as fertile ground for missionary work. The Society for the Propagation of the Gospel in Foreign

Parts, established in England in 1701, made a concerted effort to convert slaves. Although enabling many slaves to learn to read and write, to acquire instruction in catechism, and to marry in the church, blacks were usually segregated into slave galleries or even separate buildings during worship services. Religious instruction was almost always under the control of a white priest or bishop.

After the American Revolution, the Church of England in the United States was reorganized and became the American Episcopal Church in 1787. Instructing and evangelizing slaves became prominent issues from this time on until the Civil War. Taking a paternalistic stance, slaveowners felt it their Christian duty to provide religious instruction, arguing that Christianized blacks were more honest, truthful, moral, well behaved, and devoted to their masters than those who were not so instructed. Slaveowners believed that providing religious instruction to slaves would convince Northerners that the slave system was not so evil after all and argued that the effect of the black preacher—who often acquired influence independent of the slaveowner—must be minimized by "proper" religious teaching. Slaveholders who argued against providing religious instruction feared that separate black churches, though necessary in places where white church buildings were overcrowded, might incite insurrection. They also feared that slaves could misinterpret the gospel message itself—"freedom in Jesus" might be interpreted as political freedom and opposition to slavery.

Abolitionist forces in the United States pressured Christian leaders, including Episcopal slaveholders, to dismantle the system. Although few U.S. bishops were on this side of the issue—a Bishop Onderdonk of New York did address the Episcopal Convention in 1843 in powerful antislavery language—several Church of England bishops did speak out, and their abolitionist sermons were distributed widely in North America. Some of these bishops included the Right Reverend William Fleetwood of St. Asaph speaking in 1711; William Warburton, bishop of Gloucester, in 1776; and Bishop Thomas Burgess of Salisbury in 1789 and 1806.

Meanwhile, many blacks sought to establish themselves as Africans within the church. Absalom Jones, born a Delaware slave, eventually bought his own freedom and became a leader of Philadelphia's free black community, the largest urban community of former slaves in the postrevolutionary period. Jones became the first minister of St. Thomas's African Episcopal Church in 1794 and, with his ordination to the priesthood in 1804, the first black Episcopal priest.

In Jones, the Episcopal Church found one of its few eloquent spokesmen against slavery. In 1797, he helped organize the first petition of African Americans against slavery, the slave trade, and the Fugitive Slave Act of 1793. From the pulpit, he preached pride and self-respect to blacks, especially newly enfranchised males. Jones taught in schools established by the Pennsylvania Abolition Society and helped found the Society for the Suppression of Vice and Immorality.

During the Civil War, Southern bishops formed a group that was welcomed back into the national church fold at the war's end, and Southern black Episcopalians had the unfortunate choice of acquiescing to this arrangement or leaving the church. Most left and became aligned with Methodist or Baptist congregations. By this time, blacks had already been leaving the Episcopal Church fairly steadily for several reasons: exclusion from membership, the ministry, and convention proceedings; the church's rejection of African and evangelical traditions; and literacy requirements related to the Episcopal/Anglican liturgy and catechism.

The Episcopal Church in the United States today—through the Union of Black Episcopalians; the publication in 1981 of the official hymnal supplement, *Lift Every Voice and Sing: A Collection of Afro-American Spirituals and Other Songs;* the 1994 Bishops' Pastoral against Racism; and other efforts—is working to correct some of the mistakes from its slaveholding past.

—*Valerie Abrahamsen*

For Further Reading
Bennett, Robert A. 1974. "Black Episcopalians: A History from the Colonial Period to the Present." *Historical Magazine of the Protestant Episcopal Church* 43 (September 3): 231–245; Edwards, Lillie Johnson. 1996. "Episcopalians." In *Encyclopedia of African-American Culture and History*. Ed. Jack Salzman, David Lionel Smith, and Cornel West. New York: Macmillan; Hayden, J. Carleton. 1971. "Conversion and Control: Dilemma of Episcopalians in Providing for the Religious Instruction of Slaves, Charleston, South Carolina, 1845–1860." *Historical Magazine of the Protestant Episcopal Church* 40 (June 2): 143–171; Jay, William. 1853. "Introductory Remarks to the Reproof of the American Church Contained in the Recent History of the Protestant Episcopal Church in America, by the Bishop of Oxford." In *Miscellaneous Writings on Slavery*. Boston: John P. Jewett.

EQUIANO, OLAUDAH (1745–1797)

The most important and widely published author of African descent in the English-speaking world of the eighteenth century, and founder of the genre of the slave narrative, Olaudah Equiano argued in newspapers and his autobiography for the abolition of the transatlantic slave trade and slavery. Born in 1745 in what is now southeastern Nigeria and kidnapped into slavery around the age of 11, Equiano was taken to the West Indies for a few days before being taken on to Virginia and sold to a local planter. Michael Henry Pascal, an officer in the British Royal Navy, soon bought him, renamed him Gustavus Vassa, and took him to London. Equiano served under Pascal in the Seven Years War (1756–1763), but Pascal reneged on his promise of freedom and sold Equiano into West Indian slavery at the end of 1762. Equiano purchased his freedom in 1766.

After obtaining freedom, he remained in the employ of his former master, the Quaker Robert King, for a year and made several trading trips for him to Georgia and Pennsylvania. Between 1767 and 1773, Equiano was based in London, worked on commercial vessels sailing to the Mediterranean and the West Indies, and commented on all the versions of slavery, white and black, that he observed. After joining an expedition to the Arctic seeking a Northeast Passage in 1773, he returned to London where he embraced Methodism.

Again becoming restless, in 1775–1776 he helped his friend and a former employer, Dr. Charles Irving, in a short-lived attempt to establish a plantation in Central America, with Equiano acting as buyer and driver (overseer) of the black slaves. After returning to London in 1777, he published hostile newspaper reviews of proslavery books and argued for racial intermarriage (Equiano married an Englishwoman, Susanna Cullen, in 1792). He became increasingly involved with Thomas Clarkson, Quobna Ottobah Cugoano, James Ramsay, Granville Sharp, and others in efforts to help his fellow blacks, with a project to resettle black poor in Sierra Leone, and with the drive to abolish the African slave trade.

Equiano's *The Interesting Narrative of the Life of Olaudah Equiano, or Gustavus Vassa, the African. Written by Himself* (1789) is a spiritual autobiography, captivity narrative, travel book, adventure tale, slavery narrative, economic treatise, apologia, and argument against the transatlantic slave trade. The author supervised the publication and distribution of nine British editions between 1789 and 1794, and during his lifetime, unauthorized editions and translations appeared in Holland (1790), New York (1791), Germany (1792), and Russia (1794). Part of the book's great popularity can be attributed to the timing of its initial publication at the height of Britain's movement to abolish the slave trade. Equiano's was the only account by a former slave of slavery in Africa; about the voyage to the New World, or the Middle Passage; as well as about slavery in the West Indies, North America, the Mediterranean, the Middle East, and Britain. His first reviewers quickly acknowledged the signifi-

cance of the *Narrative*, which greatly influenced the development of the nineteenth-century African American slave narrative. Equiano died on March 31, 1797.
—*Vincent Carretta*

See also
Abolition, British Empire; Clarkson, Thomas; Cugoano, Quobna Ottobah; Middle Passage; Ramsay, James; Sharp, Granville; Sierra Leone
For Further Reading
Costanzo, Angelo. 1987. *Surprizing Narrative: Olaudah Equiano and the Beginnings of Black Autobiography.* New York: Greenwood Press; Equiano, Olaudah. 1995. *Olaudah Equiano: The Interesting Narrative and Other Writings.* New York: Penguin.

EUGENE IV, PAPAL BULLS OF

Although Christianity had won many converts in the Canary Islands by the early 1430s, the question of the ownership of the islands remained a constant source of friction between Portugal and the Kingdom of Castile. Without any recognized European overlordship, the inhabitants of the islands had been forced to endure periodic slave raids, and concerned that the enslaving of newly converted Christians would impede the spread of the faith on the islands, Pope Eugene IV (1431–1447) promulgated the bull Creator Omnium on December 17, 1434.

In this bull, Eugene excommunicated anyone who took converted natives from the Canary Islands to sell as slaves, and the sentence was to stand until the slaves had been restored to their liberty and possessions. However, the pope offered no protection to any natives who chose not to convert. Although canon law allowed unbaptized prisoners of war to be enslaved, by denying those inhabitants of the Canary Islands who did not convert protection from the Holy See, Eugene effectively modified the policy; now conversion, not a state of war, was the only effective guarantee against enslavement.

As Portuguese soldiers continued to pillage the islands through 1435, Eugene issued a general edict prohibiting anyone from waging war or capturing slaves in the Canaries. King Duarte of Portugal protested, and Eugene tempered his response on September 15, 1436, with the bull Romanus Pontifex, ceding to the Portuguese crown the right to conquer all parts of the Canaries as yet unconverted; the Christian inhabitants were to be left under the protection of the general edict. Amounting to the right to wage a legitimate war against an unbaptized people, implicit in the bull was the right to enslave captives. It was, therefore, a step toward transplanting the legal notion of just war, forged in the context of the struggle between Christianity and Islam in the Crusades, to a region beyond the confines of the Mediterranean.

Eugene also took similar steps with respect to Africa. When the first cargo of slaves arrived in Lisbon in 1441, Prince Henry of Portugal petitioned the pope to elevate the status of Henry's raids along the West African coast to the level of a crusade. Within the context of crusading law, such a move would legitimize enslaving captives. Eugene responded with *Illius qui* on December 19, 1442, which granted full remission of sins to all who participated in military expeditions against the Saracens.

A month later, Eugene added to these provisions by granting spiritual jurisdiction over all the lands to the south, whether they were known or not, to the Order of Christ. As Henry was, in effect, the Grand Master of the Order of Christ, the bull bestowed on him the rights the order's predecessor, the Knights Templar, had previously had in the Levant at the height of the Crusades.

Thus, Pope Eugene's bulls went some way to transferring the notion of crusading, as developed in the Levant in the twelfth century, to non-Muslim regions. By so doing, they allowed the Portuguese, and those Europeans who came after them, to view the act of enslaving Africans as dealing a blow for Christendom.

—*Richard Raiswell*

See also
Medieval Slavery; Papal Bull of June 18, 1452
For Further Reading
De Witte, C. M. 1953–1954. "Les bulles pontificales et l'expansion Portuguese au XVe siecle." *Revue d'Histoire Ecclesiastique* 48: 683–718, 49: 438–461.

EUNUCHS

Eunuchs, castrated male slaves, were employed in various Old World empires from antiquity through the early-twentieth century. Many ancient Asian empires chose eunuchs from their prisoners of war. In China, poorer indigenous families might offer young sons to the palace, hopeful that they would prosper. In the Islamic empires, eunuchs were typically slaves imported from outside the Islamic domains, much like the uncastrated military slaves, or mamluks. The populations from which eunuchs were purchased varied according to availability and perhaps constitutional fortitude. The Abbasid empire (750–1258), centered in Iraq, employed European people known in Arabic as *Šaqàliba* (possibly Slavs) as eunuchs. The Mamluk sultanate, which ruled Egypt and Syria from 1250 to 1517, and the Ottomans exploited various neighboring populations: Greeks, Armenians, Circassians, Indians, and Africans.

In most of these civilizations, eunuchs were castrated before puberty began by specially designated practitioners. Since castration violated Muslim law, eunuchs destined for Islamic lands were occasionally castrated by non-Muslims outside Islamic territory. Castration could entail removing only the testicles, or it could mean removing the entire genitalia, as was the case for Chinese eunuchs and African eunuchs in the Ottoman Empire. In the latter method, the threat of death from blood loss or infection was proportionately greater, and even if the eunuch survived, he often suffered painful complications, most commonly urinary tract infections. Nonetheless, many eunuchs lived to quite advanced ages: some Chinese and Ottoman eunuchs died in their nineties.

The practice of employing eunuchs as guardians of palace inner sanctums, where the ruler and the palace women lived, dates at least to Achaemenid Persia (538–331 B.C.) and seems to have been common in several ancient Asian empires. It was common in the Chinese, Roman, Byzantine, and virtually all Islamic empires. The notion that castration before puberty attenuated a young man's sexual drive, thereby rendering him little threat to palace women, was at least partially responsible for this phenomenon. Castration also ensured that the eunuch could never be bound by family ties; instead, his sole loyalty would be to the ruler who had castrated him, and any wealth he accumulated reverted to the ruler on his death. The premium placed on absolute loyalty to the ruler explains why in the Islamic world, eunuchs were typically imported from abroad.

Still puzzling is the displacement of white eunuchs by black African eunuchs as Ottoman imperial harem guards beginning in the late-sixteenth century. European observers attributed this change to what they regarded as the Africans' physical unattractiveness, which reduced the risk of dalliances with harem women. In fact, availability probably played a role, as Russian encroachment on the Caucasus threatened the supply of slaves in that area. Additionally, the greater natural immunity of Africans, owing to Africa's dense disease pool, rendered them more likely than Caucasian slaves to survive castration.

Palace eunuchs could form a vast hierarchy, numbering as many as several thousand. In numerous Asian empires, the chief of these eunuchs formed a power alliance with the ruler's mother, who headed the hierarchy of palace women with whom the eunuch had daily contact. In empires like the Chinese and later the Ottoman, where princes were raised within the palace's inner sanctum, a prince's mother and the chief eunuch were typically the two greatest influences on his upbringing. When an inordinately young or mentally deficient prince gained the throne, his mother and the chief eunuch could find themselves virtually running the empire.

A number of empires employed eunuchs in military positions. The eunuch's lack of conflicting ties and consequent unquestioned loyalty to the ruler probably constituted the largest reason for this phenomenon. In the Mamluk sultanate, a eunuch with the title *muqad-dam* oversaw the training of new mamluks. Eunuchs were particularly visible as admirals, notably in the Byzantine, Ming, and Ottoman empires and the Fatimid empire, which ruled Egypt and Syria from 969 to 1171. The Chinese admiral Cheng Ho (Zhenghe), whose pioneering expeditions in the early-fifteenth century extended as far as the Red Sea, was a Muslim eunuch, as were several sixteenth-century Ottoman admirals, notably Süleyman Pasha, who fought the Portuguese in the Indian Ocean. By the late-seventeenth century, eunuchs had virtually disappeared from the Ottoman military cadre.

The last use of eunuch slaves was as guardians of the prophet Muhammad's tomb in Medina, a practice introduced by the Mamluk sultans and continued under the Ottomans. The Saudi government allowed the practice to lapse in the twentieth century.

—*Jane Hathaway*

See also
Mamluks; *Šaqàliba*

For Further Reading
Anderson, Mary M. 1990. *Hidden Power: The Palace Eunuchs of Imperial China.* Buffalo, NY: Prometheus Books; Marmon, Shaun E. 1995. *Eunuchs and Sacred Boundaries in Islamic Society.* Oxford: Oxford University Press; Penzer, Norman. 1936. *The Harem.* London: George G. Harrap; Tsai, Shih-shan Henry. 1996. *The Eunuchs in the Ming Dynasty.* New York: State University of New York Press.

FACTORS

Along Africa's coast, factors functioned as agents or divisional directors of commercial enterprises, and the word has often been used to refer to European merchants resident on the coast or to Euroafrican or African merchants acting as agents of larger European-based commercial firms. Before 1700, most factors were of Spanish, Portuguese, or Euroafrican ancestry, the last being called *lançados* or *crioulos*. Africans employed as factors' subagents were called *grumettas*.

After 1700, increasing commercial interest from organized monopoly groups and companies in northern Europe and the United States brought English, French, and U.S. traders to the coast of West Africa, where they established residence and built trading facilities. Newly arrived factors almost always had to endure a traumatic adjustment to local customs, diseases, and other conditions. If they survived, they became "seasoned" and might expect to enjoy economic success. The factors generally established liaisons with African wives and produced large numbers of offspring who conducted the enterprise with relatives and indigenous ethnic groups. Factors thus became significant agents of change in African society as they produced people who served as brokers between two world systems, European and African.

The factor's physical plant, a factory, generally consisted of a trading station, living quarters, storage facilities for goods, and repair facilities for visiting shippers. During the height of the slave trade, factories also needed a corral or barracoon where factors kept their salable slaves. Essentially, factors were intermediaries between African sellers/buyers and European/American sellers/buyers. Factors traded products of European or American origin (or goods transported to the coast in European/American vessels) for slaves or commodities such as gold, hides, ivory, skins, camwood (an African hardwood used as a dyewood), dyes, and gum.

Factors regularly warehoused commodities for quick sale to both merchants from the interior and ship captains who plied the coast searching for slaves or commodities. Factors might settle in only one place along the coast or cluster factories into convenient bulking centers where shippers might find slaves or commodities in large quantities. The arrangement between the factor (stranger) and the indigenous ruler (landlord) was known as the landlord-stranger relationship, and it stipulated expected rents, taxes and customs, and obligations of the factor to the landlord and the types of protection a factor could expect in return.

Factors served an important role in the economics of the slave trade, but as the trade declined in the nineteenth century, so too did their influence.

—*Bruce L. Mouser*

See also
Barracoons; Branding of Slaves; Bulking Centers; English Slave Trade; Guinea Company; Portuguese Slave Trade; Royal Adventurers; Royal African Company
For Further Reading
Barry, Boubacar. 1988. *Le Senegambie du XVe au XIXe siècle*. Paris: Harmattan; Brooks, George E. 1970. *Yankee Traders, Old Coasters, and African Middlemen*. Boston: Boston University Press; Curtin, Philip D. 1975. *Economic Change in Precolonial Africa*. Madison: University of Wisconsin Press; Rodney, Walter. 1970. *A History of the Upper Guinea Coast, 1545 to 1800*. Oxford: Clarendon Press.

FAMILY

Wherever they were enslaved, slaves established kinship bonds and constructed families, often struggling against tremendous odds to do so. These families varied greatly in structure, size, stability, and autonomy, and they were always insecure. Every definition of slavery stresses that slaves were outsiders, marginal people—thus lack of social recognition for kinship relations was a constituent element of slavery.

No system of slavery recognized slave marriages as being fully equivalent legally to marriages of free people or gave slaves comparable rights over their children as free people had over theirs. Yet many slaves considered themselves married (some lived with husbands or wives for more than 20 years), raised children, worked together on provision grounds (gardens that slaves maintained for their private use) when they were not working on plantation crops, and bequeathed land to

A slave family in the nineteenth-century southern United States is broken up as the young daughter is sold away from her parents.

their children when they died. Studying the slave family is interesting precisely because it involves people forming and maintaining kinship relations in situations where the material functions served by kinship—organizing production and reproduction—were absent or had to be contested.

Masters almost universally tried to subsume their slaves within their own kin relationships, thus preventing the establishment of autonomous slave families. Even in the southern part of the United States, where arguably the strongest slave families existed, masters referred to plantation residents as "my family, white and black." The ability of slaves to establish families distinct from their masters' families correlated with the extent to which slaves formed a separate strata of society.

Many slave societies incorporated slaves into the master's family, as inferior and less powerful members, and many African and Islamic slave systems ac-

quired female slaves specifically for the purpose of being wives or concubines of the master, who would also have a free wife. The slave family in such circumstances could establish a slave lineage, and people who became free over time would still be considered part of that lineage. This situation produced an ongoing stigma for members of that branch, which continues today in parts of Africa.

In contrast, in large-scale slave systems in which slaves were largely used to produce agricultural commodities, as in Rome and especially in the Americas, slaves were not integrated into a master's family even as subordinate members, despite a master's use of the family idiom. In these societies, slaves established their own family groups, and slave communities developed their own kinship rules and rituals.

Research on slave families and kinship relations has been one of the most important areas in the study of slavery in the Americas in the last 30 years, and that research has led to a dramatic revision of the slave family's historiography. Earlier interpretations, in which slaves were believed to have been utterly stripped of kin, have been superseded by more empirically grounded work that indicates the resilience of family relationships among slaves. Still, we should not forget that even in societies in which slaves formed a specific stratum or class, the slave population usually had an extremely "unbalanced" sex ratio, and if cultural values define family as the group established by a male-female couple, that ratio, along with the ever-present risk of sale, meant that for many slaves family formation was impossible. Many male slaves in Bahia, Brazil, for instance, lived without female partners.

Research on same-gender kinship and sexual relationships among slaves in such situations might reveal homoerotic relationships, including relationships the slaves considered to constitute kin ties. Such research has hardly begun and has been held back by the assumption that the discovery of such relationships among slave men would contribute to the denial of slave (or black) men's manhood, but we do know that many slaves constructed kinlike fraternal relationships with other slaves who had crossed the Atlantic aboard the same ship.

Family formation was undoubtedly strongest in the United States, the only slave society in the Americas and one of the few in history in which the slave population naturally reproduced. This is one reason for the richness of the scholarship on the slave family in the United States, and the field was also stimulated by the controversy surrounding the 1965 Moynihan Report, "The Negro Family." In this report, it was argued that the roots of contemporary problems of black poverty lay in the "disorganization" of black family life under slavery. The report, and the scholarship that responded to it, were published in the context of an increasingly militant Black Power movement, in which the reassertion of black masculinity was a prominent theme. This political context explains much of the passion surrounding discussions of the slave family in the late 1960s and 1970s.

The Moynihan Report was part of the dominant paradigm in slavery studies of the early 1960s, a paradigm (exemplified by Stanley Elkins's *Slavery: A Problem in American Institutional and Intellectual Life* [1959]) that saw slavery as having severely and lastingly damaged black family relationships. Elkins argued that the harshness of slavery in the United States, and especially the slaves' lack of relationships with anyone but their masters, had produced "Sambo" personalities—people who were childlike and solely dependent emotionally upon their master. Elkins argued that the slave family did not exist beyond the mother-child dyad, but later scholars noted that he had not studied plantation records for evidence of slave family

formation. Once they began to do so, a very different picture of the slave family emerged.

More significantly, Herbert Gutman's pathbreaking *The Black Family in Slavery and Freedom* (1976), explicitly written in response to the Moynihan Report, reconstructed the kinship groups of hundreds of slaves (although from a limited number of plantations) and demonstrated that most of those slaves had lived in stable households headed by both a male and a female. Overturning earlier scholars' belief that slave fathers played little role in their children's lives, Gutman demonstrated the frequency with which children were named for their fathers. He also showed that slaves had different normative values than whites, including an acceptance of women bearing one child before settling down permanently with a male partner and hostility to marriage between cousins in a region of the United States where the practice was not uncommon among wealthy whites.

Scholars of other periods in U.S. history as well as Brazilianists and Caribbeanists have adopted Gutman's methodology, and in the United States, an intricate portrait of an evolving family structure has developed. This work shows, unsurprisingly, that slave family life was most stable in regions and at periods when plantations were large and slaves constituted a high proportion of the population. Even in areas of small-scale slaveholding, though, family ties among slaves created links across farms and plantations. Kinship relations among slaves owned by different masters were the most likely to be disrupted by sale or migration.

The most significant challenge to the work of Gutman and his followers comes from feminist historians who have questioned his replacement of Elkins's and Moynihan's isolated and emasculated slave with a patriarchal slave culture. Scholars like Deborah Gray White argue that Gutman's project was flawed because it accepted the assumption that female-headed households, or families in which women have power, are inherently problematic. These scholars argue that the lack of institutional power available to enslaved men did lead to marital relationships among slaves that were relatively more egalitarian than white marriages of the same period. Rather than construing this fact as a negative sign of "matriarchy," they recognize it as something valuable in the African American experience. Although slave women were less subordinate with respect to their own husbands, they were hardly powerful in relation to their masters, and thus only with extreme and bitter irony could they be considered "matriarchs."

The "slave family" included relationships that extended beyond blood ties. In Brazil and Spanish America, slaves adopted the Catholic institution of godparents and used it to interpose another individual between themselves and their master. Slaves asked people of higher status, often free people, to be their children's godparents, which established not only a relationship between child and godparent but also a relationship of *compadrazgo* ("copaternity") in Spanish) (or *compadrinho* in Portuguese) between themselves and the godparent. This relationship was very important in terms of mutual aid and often created significant connections between the free black and slave communities. The discovery that slaves almost never asked their masters to act as godparents is significant, as it shows that slaves could call on free people other than their masters and could thus avoid increased dependence upon their masters.

Evidence about the slave family in the slave societies of antiquity is sparse, and scholars of this period have reached much more tentative conclusions than those who work on the Americas. Slaves on Roman latifundia (estates) probably rarely formed lasting families since few women were present. Nevertheless, there is evidence that some slaves were married—although their marriages were not legally recognized.

—Diana Paton

See also
Gender
For Further Reading
Bradley, K. R. 1987. *Slaves and Masters in the Roman Empire: A Study in Social Control.* New York: Oxford University Press; Elkins, Stanley M. 1976. *Slavery: A Problem in American Institutional and Intellectual Life.* Chicago: University of Chicago Press; Gutman, Herbert G. 1976. *The Black Family in Slavery and Freedom, 1750–1925.* New York: Pantheon; White, Deborah Gray. 1985. *Ar'n't I a Woman?: Female Slaves in the Plantation South.* New York: Norton.

FEDERAL WRITERS PROJECT
See Works Progress Administration Interviews

FEDON'S REBELLION

Fédon's Rebellion was the French-backed armed rebellion of Grenadian slaves, Francophone free people of color, and whites led by the free colored planter Julien Fédon between March 1795 and July 1796. After a brief period of toleration immediately following Grenada's secession to the British in 1763, the island's French population had struggled under mounting legal restrictions on their language, religion, and right to hold public office. Free colored Francophones had suffered additional constraints that barred them from voting, holding any civil or military office, or acquiring more land. Matters had only worsened in 1793 after France had declared war on Britain and the staunch Protestant Ninian Home had become lieutenant governor.

Fédon and other free colored settlers began plotting a revolt throughout 1794 and sought help from radical French (Jacobin) agents working in the Caribbean. In February 1795, Fédon became commandant-general of Grenada for the revolutionary army, and on March 1, he captured three of the island's settlements in a surprise attack. There were several bloody engagements throughout the year, during which time most Anglophone whites fled to the capital, St. George's, while many of the island's slaves joined the rebels in the hope of attaining freedom. By January 1796, Fédon's forces controlled all of Grenada except the capital.

After the arrival of massive reinforcements, the British were able finally to capture Fédon's camp (near his estate at Belvidere) in June, though not Fédon himself, who escaped and whose subsequent fate remains a mystery. The British imposed summary executions on most of the blacks caught while rebel free coloreds faced show trials before their executions. Many of the rebel whites and some of the free colored officers were deported to non-British territories along the Honduran coast. Rooting out all of the remaining insurgents took nearly another year. In all, the revolt involved 150 whites and free coloreds and over 7,000 slaves (roughly half the island's total).

The rebellion caused an estimated £2.5 million damage to property and undermined any British hopes that Grenada would become a major sugar producer. In fact, the island largely reverted to small-scale plantations and peasant agriculture after the uprising. The material devastation, coupled with the psychological shock of the rebellion, led many whites to leave the island.

For British imperial authorities, Fédon's Rebellion was the most serious challenge to their control of the West Indian islands during the wars with France, and the uprising nearly became a Grenadian version of the Haitian Revolution. Indeed, like Toussaint Louverture, Fédon used the ideas of the French Revolution to ally all blacks, both slave and free, on a single island against a major European imperial power, and consequently, Fédon became a symbol of resistance and unity.

—Jeff Pardue

See also
French Declaration of the Rights of Man and Citizen; Louverture, Toussaint
For Further Reading
Cox, Edward. 1982. "Fédon's Rebellion 1795–96: Causes and Consequences." *Journal of Negro History* 67: 7–20; Craton, Michael. 1982. *Testing the Chains:*

Resistance to Slavery in the British West Indies. Ithaca, NY: Cornell University Press; Devas, Raymond P. 1974. *A History of the Island of Grenada, 1498–1796*. St. George's, Grenada: Carenage Press.

FIFTEENTH AMENDMENT

The Fifteenth Amendment to the U.S. Constitution, ratified in 1870, represents one portion of the unprecedented legislation passed by the radicals in Congress during the Reconstruction period guaranteeing every male citizen the right to vote. Many people consider this amendment the culmination of the work begun by the radicals with the Fourteenth Amendment, which focuses on establishing equal civil and political rights for freedmen by limiting the authority of state governments with the threat of federal intervention. Congress thought it necessary to initiate the later legislation because, at least in part, they saw the political advantage of ensuring the black male suffrage that the Fourteenth Amendment had merely encouraged.

In 1868, when Republican Ulysses S. Grant garnered 3 million popular votes compared to Democrat (and former New York governor) Horatio Seymour's 2.7 million, it became clear just how valuable the Republican black vote could be. Republican leaders recognized that black suffrage had won them several states, and they had lost others when states denied freedmen the right to vote. Most Southern states, under federal pressure during Reconstruction, ratified the new amendment quickly, as did the Northern states.

The Fifteenth Amendment further abridged states' rights, a process begun by the Fourteenth Amendment, by prohibiting disenfranchisement based on "race, color, or previous condition of servitude" with the threat of federal enforcement if states chose to ignore the new provisions. With this amendment (supplemented by the Enforcement Acts of 1870 and 1871), Congress sought to prevent states from encroaching upon the federal rights of black men, but it did nothing to prevent individuals, like Ku Klux Klan members, from injuring, killing, or destroying the property of black Americans. To address that problem, Congress passed an unprecedented act in April 1871, aimed at Klan members, that called for placing individuals under federal jurisdiction if a state failed to punish their criminal acts of terrorism.

With the ratification of the Fifteenth Amendment, many reformers, like William Lloyd Garrison and members of the American Anti-Slavery Society, felt their job was done. Having grown weary of Reconstruction in general and believing they had accomplished their goals by ensuring the black man's political participation, and thus his ability to protect himself against exploitation, Americans turned their attention to other issues.

Ex-Confederate leaders gained political power during the 1870s, and Democratic "redeemers" sought to reestablish white supremacy in the South. Their success meant a dramatic decline in black rights. Property qualifications, poll taxes, and literacy tests, not specifically prohibited in the Fifteenth Amendment, effectively disenfranchised Southern black men. Subsequently, Southern states passed Jim Crow laws, which stripped the freedmen of their right to vote while legalizing racial segregation, and thus effectively nullifying the Fifteenth Amendment.

—*Debra Meyers*

See also
Fourteenth Amendment
For Further Reading
Foner, Eric. 1989. *Reconstruction: America's Unfinished Revolution, 1863–1877*. New York: Harper and Row; Fridlington, Robert. 1995. *The Reconstruction Court, 1864–1888*. Danbury, CT: Grolier; Wesley, Charles. 1970. *The Fifteenth Amendment and Black America, 1870–1970*. Washington, DC: Associated Publishers.

FILIBUSTERS

The U.S. acquisition of the vast Southwest after the Mexican War (1846–1848) led many expansionists to advocate the conquest or liberation of other foreign territories, and the idea was directly related to the slavery issue. During the 1850s, thousands of citizens openly defied the Neutrality Act of 1818 by participating in several private military expeditions against Mexico and other Central American or Caribbean nations. These adventurers were popularly known as "filibusters," a term derived from the Dutch *vrijbuiter* ("freebooter"), which was first applied to Caribbean buccaneers.

The major filibustering expeditions of the era were Narciso Lopez's forays against Cuba in 1850–1851 and William Walker's invasions of Mexico, Nicaragua, and Honduras between 1853 and 1860. Motivated by the aggressive spirit of manifest destiny and the lure of adventure, many filibusters were also influenced by the rising controversy over slavery, as many Southern expansionists believed that the acquisition of new territory would maintain the political balance of power between slave and free states.

The conspiracy of Mexican War hero and former Mississippi governor, John A. Quitman, to invade Cuba between 1853 and 1855 was largely influenced by Southern fears that Spain planned to abolish slavery on the island. In 1853, Juan de la Pezuela, a known abolitionist, was appointed captain-general of Cuba. He issued orders freeing all Africans imported illegally from the United States since 1835, permitting marriage between black women and white men, and allowing freedmen to serve in the militia.

Pezuela's measures alarmed Southern expansionists, who dreamed of bringing Cuba into the Union as a new slave territory. Furthermore, the island's proximity to the Gulf Coast states led many Southerners to regard Cuban emancipation as a direct threat to Southern society and institutions. Many were convinced that news of Cuban events would spark slave rebellions throughout the South.

Backed by Cuban associates of the ill-fated Narciso Lopez, Quitman, an ardent advocate of Cuban annexation, was preparing to lead a major invasion of the island at the time of Pezuela's appointment. The Mississippian regarded the possible emergence of what he called a "Negro" or racially mixed "mongrel empire" in the Caribbean a serious threat to the "whole social fabric of the Southern states" (May, 1985). Motivated by the desire to prevent the "Africanization" of Cuba, leading Southerners helped Quitman gather men, arms, and ships for the expedition.

Besides widespread Southern support, Quitman apparently obtained assurances from members of President Franklin Pierce's cabinet that the administration would not intervene to thwart his invasion plans, and Pezuela's seizure of a U.S. vessel in early 1854 produced a crisis that might have assured government support of Quitman's enterprise. However, the filibuster chief continued to delay, explaining to his Cuban backers that he would not move until he had sufficient men, an armed ship, and adequate funds.

Although the reasons are not entirely clear, spring 1854 saw a shift in official policy that boded ill for Quitman's venture. One factor might have been a desire to avoid the overwhelming criticism that could result from government support of a proslavery invasion of Cuba. Whatever the true motive, the Pierce administration decided to withdraw support for filibustering and to acquire Cuba by purchase.

Instructing his minister in Madrid to offer $130 million to the Spanish government for the island, Pierce blocked efforts in the U.S. Senate to repeal the neutrality laws. He also issued a proclamation warning that the government would prosecute any violators. Quitman protested what he regarded to be a violation of his understanding with the administration, and he continued to prepare for the invasion.

In June 1854, a federal grand jury in New Orleans compelled Quitman to enter a recognizance in the sum of $3,000 to observe the neutrality laws for nine months. Quitman promptly postponed his expedition until spring 1855, but the delay only worsened his prospects. In early 1855, Spanish authorities arrested over 100 of the filibuster's Cuban supporters, thus destroying all hopes of revolutionary support on the island.

In early spring 1855, President Pierce met personally with Quitman in Washington, D.C., and offered convincing evidence that Cuba was virtually invulnerable to attack. This factor, coupled with the knowledge that Cuba's new captain-general did not share Pezuela's zeal for emancipation, led the filibuster to disband his private army on March 15. Although Quitman formerly severed ties with his Cuban backers on April 30, he continued to support other filibustering schemes, including William Walker's Nicaraguan venture.

The abortive Quitman expedition was followed by another failed filibuster venture, the plot of the Knights of the Golden Circle, a secret proslavery society in the United States, to invade Mexico in 1859–1860, before the outbreak of the U.S. Civil War brought an end to large-scale filibustering activities. Although filibustering cannot be regarded solely as a manifestation of Southern expansionism, the expeditions of Lopez, Walker, and others received widespread support in the South, particularly among people who advocated the annexation of additional slave territory. Besides being regarded by the international community as a symbol of U.S. imperialism, filibustering also contributed to the sectional discord that led to the Civil War.

—*James M. Prichard*

See also
Lopez, Narciso; Quitman, John; Walker, William
For Further Reading
Brown, Charles H. 1980. *Agents of Manifest Destiny: The Lives and Times of the Filibusters*. Chapel Hill: University of North Carolina Press; May, Robert E. 1985. *John A. Quitman: Old Southern Crusader*. Baton Rouge: Louisiana State University Press; May, Robert E. 1973. *The Southern Dream of a Caribbean Empire 1854–1861*. Baton Rouge: Louisiana State University Press.

FINLEY, MOSES
(1912–1986)

One of the twentieth century's most important and influential historians of classical antiquity, Moses Finley had an enormous impact on the study of slavery in ancient Greece and Rome. As a researcher in the late 1930s for Columbia

University's International Institute for Social Research, Finley was influenced by Marxist theory and more importantly by Weberian sociological analysis categories. This experience, combined with earlier training in law, prepared Finley for his groundbreaking work on ancient Mediterranean slavery. He produced most of his voluminous scholarship in Great Britain, where he was professor of ancient history at Cambridge from 1970 until his retirement. He was knighted in 1979.

An early work, *Studies in Land and Credit in Ancient Athens* (1952), reveals Finley's long-standing interest in land, labor, and law in preindustrial societies. Although detailed philological investigation appears in his early writings, Finley's mature work largely consists of historical generalizations based on sociological typologies and comparisons of preindustrial societies at a similar stage of economic and technological development with the economies and societies of ancient Greece and Rome. These methodologies were founded upon a mastery of the primary sources and an insistence upon the historical contingencies of human societies.

Finley's work represented a radical departure from earlier, traditional studies in ancient history, as earlier scholars wrote as if they were insulated from contemporary social problems and concerns. Finley viewed history as a dialectic between past and present and was committed by the historian's obligation to act. Consequently, he departed from the philological minutiae that are the province of many classical scholars toward interdisciplinary, holistic analyses of the Greco-Roman world. These analyses were informed by broad reading in historical, legal, sociological, and anthropological literature.

In his work on Greek and Roman slavery, Finley rejected mere description and insisted on identifying the function of political institutions and social practices in classical civilization. His most important historical generalizations on classical slavery include the observation that in practice, there was no clear-cut dichotomy of the free and the servile but rather a spectrum of statuses between free and unfree; the idea, which rejected the Marxist analytical tool of class in favor of the Weberian notion of status, being that slaves defined the free in social hierarchies and this social function probably was of greater importance than the slave's economic function.

He also recognized the related conceptions of a Greco-Roman nonproductive mentality that was uninterested in technological progress and its possible consequences, the rejection of economically inefficient slave labor, and the startling conviction that chattel slavery was a prerequisite for the development of Greek democracy.

—*Craige Champion*

For Further Reading
Finley, Moses. 1973. *The Ancient Economy.* London: Chatto and Windus; Finley, Moses. 1980. *Ancient Slavery and Modern Ideology.* New York: Viking; Finley, Moses. 1981. *Economy and Society in Ancient Greece.* New York: Viking; Finley, Moses. 1960. *Slavery in Classical Antiquity: Views and Controversies.* Cambridge: Heffer.

FITZHUGH, GEORGE (1806–1881)

One of the most vociferous, and certainly one of the most radical, proslavery Southern polemicists in the United States, George Fitzhugh married nearly Marxist critiques of European and Northern capitalism to an impassioned defense of a feudal style of patriarchy in two major antebellum books, *Sociology for the South; or The Failure of Free Society* (1854) and *Cannibals All! or, Slaves without Masters* (1857).

In these books, and numerous articles in the *Richmond Examiner* and *De Bow's Review,* Fitzhugh characterized the capitalism of Europe and the Northern part of the United States as a form of slavery in which, unlike Southern plantation society, the industrialist had no motive to care for his labor force's well-being. Fitzhugh rejected the notion of human equality and liberty advanced by John Locke and Thomas Jefferson and argued that ancient slave patriarchies like Rome and Greece were more compassionate than the so-called modern democracies. Western society had declined, he suggested, after post-Luther philosophers had extended the Protestant Reformation's ideas to promote notions of individualism and personal liberty.

Heavily influenced by Thomas Carlyle's philosophical attack on economic liberalism, Fitzhugh believed that competition spawned by the emerging capitalist order resulted in wealth for few and misery for many. Humans are by nature social creatures, like ants and bees, and all people are not created equal. In an unequal world, he argued, to require "inferior" individuals such as women, children, African Americans, and poor whites to compete with "superior" white male elites was cruel. In an industrial society, the inferior and incompetent were slaves to capital rather than to human masters. Unlike the well-fed plantation slave, industrial workers were left to starve and were denied civilizing contact with Christian masters.

Fitzhugh suggested Northern capitalism was ultimately doomed and, anticipating Frederick Jackson Turner's "frontier thesis," contended that only the open frontier and the opportunity it gave white industrial workers to escape wage slavery and become landholders suppressed class violence north of the Mason-Dixon line. Fitzhugh's writings provoked a storm of protest in the North, and quotes were taken from his books out of context to suggest that he favored the enslavement of white industrial workers and the poor.

Despite his fondness for the master-slave relationship, Fitzhugh never suggested the extension of slavery to white laborers in the United States. In fact, he called for mass education among the South's working class and poor whites as a way of winning nonslaveholders' loyalty to plantation elites. Nevertheless, Fitzhugh's writings provided fodder for abolitionists, who warned of Southern slaveholders' plotting to enslave Northern workers, and his rhetoric proved influential. Abraham Lincoln, in particular, was inflamed by Fitzhugh's prediction in *Sociology for the South* that slavery would later be "everywhere abolished" or "everywhere re-instituted," and a more famous restatement of this idea appeared in Lincoln's 1858 "house divided" speech.

Fitzhugh was largely self-taught and his reading tastes not always sophisticated, but he was widely exposed to French and English socialist thought, and occasionally his wording suggests that he had read Karl Marx. His writings exhibit some understanding of Marxist theories on surplus value, and some ringing phrases in *Cannibals All,* such as when Fitzhugh described the industrial poor as "continually forging new chains for themselves," sound as if they were lifted directly from the *Communist Manifesto* (published nine years earlier in 1848). Other aspects of Fitzhugh's economic analysis foreshadowed twentieth-century leftist thought.

His description of the handicaps agricultural regions like the antebellum South suffer in world trade, and the damaging effects of unequal exchange on an agricultural economy when competing with industrial centers, are reminiscent of the arguments of dependency theorists like Arghiri Emmanuel, Immanuel Wallerstein, Fernando Cardoso, and Enzo Faletto. Despite his flirtation with socialism, Fitzhugh neither conceded the extent to which African American slaves were exploited nor fully acknowledged that the plantation culture he so vigorously defended might have played a part in the region's economic dependency.

Fitzhugh has typically been portrayed as a Southern anomaly. He vigorously attacked Jefferson's ideas of human equality, which are enshrined in the Declaration of Independence, and he asserted that the American Revolution was no battle for human liberty but merely a struggle of local elites to achieve political independence. He bitterly denounced free trade, laissez faire, and the liberal economic thought of classical economists like Adam Smith while praising pre-Reformation feudalism.

Those notions may have placed Fitzhugh outside the mainstream of Southern thought, and planters must have winced when Fitzhugh declared plantation slavery as the "beau ideal of communism" or when he bitterly depicted the "vampire capitalist class" of Europe and the Northern portion of the United States. Yet, Mitchell Snay's research suggests that Fitzhugh was less iconoclastic than has traditionally been suggested. Snay argues that Fitzhugh's depiction of man as naturally social, his argument that patriarchy produces a harmonious society of mutual obligations, and his view of the master-slave relationship paralleling that of God and humanity all reflect ideas common among antebellum Southern clergy.

Ironically, despite his vociferous defense of Southern planters, Fitzhugh's family had lost its farm at auction in 1825, and for much of his career, Fitzhugh was a mediocre lawyer depending largely on the property of his wife, Mary Brockebrough, in Virginia's Caroline County. Despite his relatively humble status, he became perhaps the most famous propagandist for the planter class. For all his occasional prescience, however, Fitzhugh's writings are highly repetitive and disorganized, symptomatic of his lack of formal schooling. "We are no regular built scholar," as Fitzhugh acknowledged in *Cannibals All!* (Fitzhugh, 1960), and even his supporters were forced to acknowledge his intellectual eccentricity. If Fitzhugh's ideology was not exactly embraced by Southern elites, he was seized upon as a spokesman for Southern ideology, and in the North, he symbolized the threat that attitude posed to the working class throughout the Union.

—*Michael Phillips*

See also
Jefferson, Thomas; Locke, John; Marxism
For Further Reading
Fitzhugh, George. 1960. *Cannibals All! or Slaves without Masters.* Cambridge, MA: Belknap Press; Perskey, Joseph. 1992. "Unequal Exchange and Dependency Theory in George Fitzhugh." *History of Political Economy* 24:1 (Spring): 117–128; Snay, Mitchell. 1989. "American Thought and Southern Distinctiveness: The Southern Clergy and the Sanctification of Slaves." *Civil War History* 35:4 (December): 311–328; Wish, Harvey, ed. 1960. *Antebellum: Writings of George Fitzhugh and Hinton Rowan Helper on Slavery.* New York: Capricorn Books.

FOLKTALES

Folktales are among the most significant bodies of material depicting the autonomy slaves carved for themselves within the context of their own enslavement. The existence of so many folktales shows that the institution of slavery did not destroy the slaves' capacity for creativity, nor did it completely break their will and render them docile, dependent children, completely devoid of any culture apart from that of the whites who held them in bondage. Folktales constitute an important mass of evidence that historians of slavery marshal to discredit Stanley Elkins's Sambo thesis. Products of African cultural heritage and the unique circumstances of enslavement in the Western Hemisphere, the folktales African slaves told on weekend evenings in the U.S. South, the Caribbean, and South America offered slaves survival strategies for daily life and helped to assure their survival as a people.

African slaves' animal tales contained survival strategies for coping with daily life in slavery. One of these tales advised slaves against talking too much in the presence of whites. Most involved a slave's encounter with an animal who could speak. Once the slave hears the animal speak, he rushes to inform his master of the unbelievable occurrence and to encourage him to return with him to hear the talking animal. The master consents to go, but warns the slave that he will be whipped if his claim is false. When master and slave arrive in the animal's presence, the animal remains silent, and the slave is whipped for lying to his master. After the master leaves, the animal tells the slave that he talks too much and should refrain from telling whites everything he knows.

In the animal tales, the animal's admonitions frequently derive from personal experience. For instance, in another animal tale a skeleton head warns a slave that its own mouth brought it to its present resting place and admonishes the slave to keep his mouth shut lest he suffer the same fate. Nevertheless, the slave tells his master that he found a talking skeleton head. Upon their return to the skeleton head, master and slave hear nothing, whereupon the master kills the slave for lying. Following the master's departure, the skeleton head reminds the dead slave that it had warned him that its mouth (i.e., talking too much) had brought it there and that it would bring the slave there, too. Though the particular kind of animal contained in tales varied, they offered slaves similar advice: do not talk too much in the presence of whites.

Animal-trickster tales, as opposed to animal tales, also served as a survival mechanism for slaves in their daily lives, because they provided slaves with emotional release. Most animal-trickster tales involve two animals, one of which is physically strong and possesses considerable power and authority. The other animal is weaker physically yet has the capacity to outwit the stronger opponent and usually emerges on top at the conclusion of their encounters.

In one of these tales, a wolf—the stronger animal—maneuvers a rabbit into a hollow tree and then sets the tree afire. Ultimately, the rabbit outsmarts the wolf: he escapes through a hole in the rear of the tree, convinces the wolf that there is food in it and in all the other trees in the area, and tricks the wolf into entering another tree in search of food. The tree the wolf selects, of course, contains no food and also lacks an escape hole. Consequently, the weak-but-cunning rabbit turns the tables on his stronger opponent: he sets the tree afire, and the wolf burns to death. Animal-trickster tales provided slaves with symbolic ways to reverse actual power relationships in their own lives by subverting symbolically the authority owners exercised over them. Accordingly, slaves enjoyed an emotional release from the everyday rigors of their lives.

Many animal-trickster tales highlighted the slaves' value system and worldview, particularly when they illustrated the trickster's resort to cunning and deceit in acquiring food from a stronger animal. In one tale, the rabbit trickster and a wolf own a butter tree together. Gradually, the rabbit sneaks nibbles of butter until the tree is completely gone. All the while, the rabbit denies that he ate any butter, smears some on the sleeping wolf's mouth, and quickly accuses the wolf of having eaten the butter. This tale and others like it showed slaves that trickery and deceit are acceptable behaviors when one is forced to survive in a world in which the power distribution is wholly arbitrary and others hold most of the power; such was the world as seen through the slaves' eyes. Actually, slaves developed a value system that frowned upon theft from other slaves but accepted, even celebrated, slaves who took food and other articles from their master. Judging by the frequent disappearance of food from masters' and overseers' pantries in all slave societies, most slaves learned well the lessons imparted by rabbit/wolf tales and others like them.

Slaves also told slave-trickster tales. In these, the trickster is not an animal but a slave, usually named John. His role in these tales is that of a slave in an ongoing battle of wits with his master, and from John's exploits, slaves learned much about the potential, and the danger, of deceptive activities.

In one tale, John dupes his master into believing that John has special powers. He does this by secretly hiding things from his master and then finding them, or by apparently predicting the future after secretly listening to his master's intentions. John so impresses his master that he gains a high-status position on the plantation. Ultimately, the master brags about John's powers to other slaveowners, who, doubting the veracity of his claims, place bets that they can demonstrate that John possesses no special powers whatsoever. Shortly afterward, the dubious slaveowners hide something in a barrel and bring John forward to identify what they have hidden. As he approaches the barrel, John assumes that he is about to be caught at his trickery and declares that his master has finally caught the coon. Yet John's careful choice of words saves him from the brink, for the slaveowners then reveal the raccoon they had hidden in the barrel. As a result, John's master wins the bet and gives John a handsome reward. The tale not only illustrates the danger inherent in playing the trickster role but also conveys the importance of skillful words in the presence of whites, a talent important for all slaves to develop.

Slave-trickster tales frequently contained the theme of food acquisition, much like the animal-trickster tales. One tale involves a slave's theft of his master's chicken. While the slave is cooking the chicken, the master appears at his cabin and is informed that possum is being cooked. The master immediately invites himself to linger and share some of the possum, whereupon the slave tells him that he had spat in the pot. The master, quite taken aback, asks the slave to explain. The slave then declares proudly that slaves always spit in the gravy in order to tenderize the meat—and then quickly offers his master a generous portion. The disgusted master runs from the cabin, never discovering the chicken. Like the animal-trickster tales, slave-trickster tales show that the manner in which food was obtained was as important as its possession—and taught slaves how to survive.

Sometimes, slaves told jokes and stories to their masters, and many of these tales offered slaves a chance to laugh in their white masters' faces—and get away with it. One slave who went to France with his master blatantly poked fun at the French; in other instances, slaves told derogatory jokes about the Irish, to which their masters responded with roars of laughter. In these cases, the slaves knew that their masters made fun of the French and Irish themselves, so they assumed their tales would be appreciated. More important, slaves knew that the French and the Irish were white and that slaves were not permitted to poke fun at any white people. When they did so and got away with it, slaves gained, through their own laughter, a brief respite that went a long way toward helping in their ultimate survival of enslavement.

—*John J. Zaborney*

See also
Anansi Stories; Elkins, Stanley M.; Sambo Thesis; Trickster
For Further Reading
Genovese, Eugene D. 1974. *Roll, Jordan, Roll: The World the Slaves Made*. New York: Vintage Books; Joyner, Charles. 1984. *Down by the Riverside: A South Carolina Slave Community*. Urbana: University of Illinois Press; Levine, Lawrence W. 1977. *Black Culture and Black Consciousness: Afro-American Folk Thought from Slavery to Freedom*. Oxford: Oxford University Press.

FORT CAROLUSBURG

Although the Swedish slave trade was not as massive as that of other European powers, Sweden developed a network of forts along the West African coast to conduct its enterprise. The Swedish Africa Company began building Fort Carolusburg at Cape Coast (Cabo Corso) in what is now Ghana in 1652, and the fort later became known as Cape Coast Castle. Isaac Mivilla, the company's main representative, supervised the fort's construction. Little is known about Mivilla, but he is believed to have been Swiss, born in Basel. He took over the company's affairs in Africa in 1652, succeeding one Henrich Carlof. Three company ships—*Christina, Johannesburg*, and *Norrköping*—had left Stade in one of Sweden's German provinces, Bremen Verden, in December 1651 with the building materials, and the construction had been approved by the local government of the Futu state. Slaves laborers were used, and the construction lasted until 1656.

There is only one contemporary description of Fort Carolusburg (Lawrence, 1963). It was strongly built with thick walls and two gates, one larger than the other. Toward the sea there were two gun batteries. (According to the local population, the site was supposed to have been protected by a large holy stone.) Inside were the quarters for company officers and a large hall for council meetings. Some of the company's slaves also lived in the fort. After being captured by the British in 1665, the fort was extended and rebuilt.

—*Bertil Haggman*

For Further Reading
Lawrence, Arnold Walter. 1963. *Trade Castles and Forts of West Africa*. London: J. Cape; Müller, Wilhelm Johann. 1968. *Die Africanische auf der Guneischen Gold Cust gelegene Landschafft Fetu*. Hamburg: Graz.

FORTEN, CHARLOTTE (1837–1914)

Charlotte Forten was active in U.S. abolitionist, women's rights, intellectual, and art circles from the antebellum years through the post-Reconstruction period. As a diarist, her record of the thought and activities of Northern free blacks of the antebellum and post-Reconstruction periods contributes significantly to an understanding of the evolution of free black ideologies and culture.

Forten was part of the fourth generation of a prominent, free black family in Philadelphia, Pennsylvania, and as a link between slave and free, maintained by the

Charlotte Forten

Fortens' antislavery activity based upon an antebellum free black philosophy of racial "uplift" and self-help, Charlotte provided an important model for blacks of the period and her story is still important for the telling of African American history. Forten attended a private girls' school in Salem, Massachusetts, because her father objected to Philadelphia's racially segregated schools. While in Massachusetts, she witnessed the capture of a runaway slave, who was then returned to slavery, and this event, along with the example of her family's activism, encouraged her own participation in antislavery and other social reform movements. At the age of 17, Forten joined the Salem Anti-Slavery Society.

Her grandfather (James Forten) had made a fortune as a sail maker and as an entrepreneur by patenting a device used on sailing vessels. Her father, Robert Forten, was less successful as a businessman but a model of social activism and belonged to both local and national abolitionist societies. Many of Charlotte Forten's associates and models were white, including *Liberator* publisher William Lloyd Garrison and Theodore Parker. Although Forten began teaching at Salem Normal School, her delicate health forced her to curtail many physical activities. A meticulous recorder of contemporary events in her diaries, Forten

also tried writing poetry, and although most literary critics have found her poetry to be merely adequate, Garrison published her poems, which contained antislavery messages, in the *Liberator*.

In 1862, during the Civil War, Forten traveled to South Carolina's Sea Islands to teach freed children, and her memoirs of her experiences there were published in the *Atlantic Monthly*. Her essays convey both her sincerity and her dedication to the cause of black freedom while they also reveal the confusion of a sheltered black daughter from a privileged background when confronted with blacks whose life experiences were so different from her own.

In 1878, Forten married Francis J. Grimké, the son of a slave woman named Nancy Weston and her white slaveowner. Although disowned by their Southern relatives, Francis Grimké and his brother had been taken in by their father's sister, Angelina Grimké Weld, a Northern aunt who was prominent in antislavery circles. Francis J. Grimké earned degrees in law and theology before taking a pulpit in Washington, D.C. He and Charlotte Forten had only one child, who died in 1880. Forten herself died in 1914.

—Dale Edwyna Smith

For Further Reading
Billington, Ray Allen. 1953. *The Journal of Charlotte L. Forten*. New York: Collier; Hine, Darlene Clark, Elsa Barkley Brown, and Rosalyn Terborg-Penn, eds. 1993. *Black Women in America, An Historical Encyclopedia*. Brooklyn: Carlson; Sterling, Dorothy, ed. 1984. *We Are Your Sisters. Black Women in the Nineteenth Century*. New York: Norton; Stevenson, Brenda, ed. 1988. *The Journals of Charlotte Forten Grimké*. New York: Oxford University Press.

FORTEN, JAMES, SR. (1766–1842)

Noted for his work as an abolitionist and a sail maker, James Forten was one of the eighteenth century's most distinguished African American leaders and the grandfather of the abolitionist Charlotte Forten. Born in Philadelphia the son of Thomas and Sarah Forten, James was a mulatto whose ancestors had been free for at least two generations. In 1773, when Forten was seven years old, his father died. James briefly attended a local school for Philadelphia's free blacks established by Anthony Benezet, a Quaker abolitionist and philanthropist, but in 1775, Forten left school to go to work in a local grocery store to help support his family.

In 1781, Forten became a powder boy on the *Royal*

Louis, a vessel commanded by Stephen Decatur. During the American Revolution, when the British vessel *Amphion* captured the *Royal Louis,* Forten anticipated being sold into slavery. Instead, his future was altered when he was sent to Great Britain where he met many prominent abolitionists, including Granville Sharp. After a seven-month imprisonment, Forten returned to the United States and became an apprentice to Robert Bridges, a prominent sail maker in Philadelphia.

In 1786, Forten became a supervisor, and when Bridges died 12 years later, Forten took ownership of the firm. The business flourished, and by 1832, Forten had acquired a fortune of about $100,000, which made him one of Philadelphia's wealthiest African Americans. With his newly found resources, Forten was able to maintain a large country home and a city dwelling for his wife and family of eight children.

Forten; Richard Allen, pastor of the African Methodist Episcopal Church; and Absalom Jones, founder of the African Episcopal Church, gradually became prominent leaders within Philadelphia's African American community. In 1797, they organized the city's first African-American Masonic Lodge, and during the War of 1812, they recruited nearly 2,500 African Americans to build fortifications around Philadelphia to protect the city after the British had burned parts of Washington, D.C.

During the early-nineteenth century, Forten, Allen, and Jones began directing their attention toward ending slavery. In 1800, they petitioned Congress to pass a law to end slavery through gradual emancipation, and in 1817, the three created a public forum to protest creation of the American Colonization Society, which intended to send many free black Americans back to Africa. In 1830, Forten, Allen, and Jones sponsored the first national convention to focus on the problem of colonization within the interracial abolition movement.

Forten's success as an abolitionist and entrepreneur made him one of the country's outstanding African American pioneers. His leadership skills, the respect he gained within Philadelphia's African American community, and the number of people who attended his funeral on February 22, 1842, all illustrate the wide acclaim of this exceptional African American.

—*Eric R. Jackson*

See also
Allen, Richard; Jones, Absalom; Sharp, Granville
For Further Reading
Billington, Ray Allen. 1953. *The Journal of Charlotte L. Forten.* New York: Collier; Douty, Esther M. 1968. *Forten the Sailmaker: Pioneer Champion of Negro Rights.* Chicago: Rand McNally; Feldman, Lynne B., and John N. Ingham, eds. 1994. *African American Business Leaders: A Biographical Dictionary.* Westport, CT: Greenwood.

FOSTER, ABIGAIL KELLEY (1811–1873)

Better known as Abby Kelley, Abigail Foster was an extraordinarily effective lecturer, fund-raiser, and organizer for women's rights, nonresistance, and antislavery. She was notorious both for her radical abolitionism and for her willingness to speak before "promiscuous assemblies" of men and women. Only Maria Stewart and Sarah and Angelina Grimké preceded her on the lecture platform. Like Angelina Grimké, Kelley married a prominent abolitionist, but unlike Grimké she did not let marriage or motherhood stop her antislavery work. The emancipation of the slaves and the end of racial prejudice came first, and Kelley endured years of misogynist attacks, illness, and frequent separation from her husband, Stephen Symonds Foster, and her daughter to achieve these goals—without accepting any pay.

Kelley's deep belief in women's equality brought her to the center of the 1840 split in the abolitionist movement when the followers of William Lloyd Garrison broke with the "new organization" abolitionists led by Lewis Tappan and Amos Phelps over the role of women in the American Anti-Slavery Society and other philosophical and strategic differences. When Kelley, a Garrisonian, was elected to an important committee at the 1840 convention and insisted on speaking, the Tappanites and Garrisonians separated. Kelley had begun lecturing in 1838 and was becoming well known, but the fight within the American Anti-Slavery Society brought her to new prominence. In particular, she inspired women to become abolitionists and cultivated a number of young women to travel the antislavery lecture circuit, most prominent among them being Lucy Stone, Susan B. Anthony, Sallie Hollie, and Sarah Redmond, the sister of Charles Redmond.

Kelley was an organization woman, fiercely promoting Garrison's radical brand of antislavery and the Massachusetts and American Anti-Slavery Societies. For 20 years she lectured, raised money, and planned lecture and propaganda campaigns throughout New England, Pennsylvania, New York, and the Midwest. She also helped found Ohio's *Anti-Slavery Bugle.* Other abolitionist leaders relied on her abilities as a shrewd organizer and administrator. In an 1859 meeting of the New England Anti-Slavery Society, Garrison accused Kelley of fraudulently obtaining funds for the abolitionist movement. Kelley broke with Garrison, who refused to apologize, and withdrew from her prominent role in abolitionist organizations. Their disagreements continued during the Civil War and after, for Kelley was skeptical of Lincoln and the Republican Party's commitment to emancipation and to the civil rights of the freed slaves. After the Fifteenth Amendment was ratified in 1870, Kelley turned her attention to the issues of temperance and women's rights.

—*Andrea M. Atkin*

See also
Anthony, Susan Brownell; Garrison, William Lloyd; Stone, Lucy
For Further Reading
Pease, Jane H. 1969. "The Freshness of Fanaticism: Abby Kelley Foster." Ph.D. dissertation, Department of History, University of Rochester, Rochester, New York; Sterling, Dorothy. 1991. *Ahead of Her Time: Abby Kelley and the Politics of Anti-Slavery*. New York: W. W. Norton.

FOURTEENTH AMENDMENT

The U.S. Constitution's Fourteenth Amendment, ratified by three-fourths of the states in 1868, represented a radical move on the part of Congress during the Reconstruction period. Submitted to the states for approval in 1866, this amendment significantly reduced state powers, attacked the Southern black codes, defined citizenship, and granted considerable political rights to freedmen. After its passage, states could no longer legally enforce laws like the black codes that stood in opposition to federal legislation.

Reacting to Reconstruction, the Southern states had instituted black codes in an effort to control the labor of the freed blacks. The legal restrictions placed upon ex-slaves differed from state to state, but all essentially denied the freedmen the rights mandated by the first eight amendments to the Constitution, which included their rights to free speech, bear arms, obtain a trial by an impartial jury, protection against cruel or unusual punishment, and unwarranted search and seizure. Moreover, the black codes regulated the relationships between white landowners and black laborers, limiting the workers' ability to rent land in certain areas and to negotiate wages. The codes and the punishments meted out for their violation, like whipping and forced labor, essentially permitted slavery to continue in the South after emancipation. With the passage of the Fourteenth Amendment, states could be prevented from enforcing black codes by the federal government if states chose to "deprive any person of life, liberty, or property, without due process of law."

The first clause declares that everyone "born or naturalized in the United States, and subject to the jurisdiction thereof, are citizens of the United States." Congress believed that by admitting freedmen into the political community as citizens with rights, the ex-slaves could protect and defend themselves from exploitation. Besides legally defining citizenship, the Fourteenth Amendment stipulated that the right to suffrage was reserved for men 21 years old or older.

However, the freedman's political rights were not assured. By basing a state's congressional representation upon the number of enfranchised men, the second clause encouraged, but did not require, states to grant freedmen the right to vote. The final three clauses attempted to conclude some of the issues Congress had been grappling with during Reconstruction. Hoping to fill the U.S. House of Representatives with loyal unionists, clause three barred ex-Confederate leaders from holding state or national offices unless two-thirds of each house of Congress voted to grant a pardon. The fourth repudiated the Confederate debt, and the fifth empowered Congress to enforce the amendment's provisions with any legislation it found necessary.

Congress initiated the Fourteenth Amendment for at least three reasons: its members wanted to guarantee ex-slaves equality before the law at the federal level, and they sought to secure black Republican support, even as they legally defined the right to vote for males. The amendment failed in its mission to enable the freedmen to defend themselves against white Southern Democrats, and therefore the Republican-dominated Congress began the ratification process of the Fifteenth Amendment, which would, at least for a time, bar states from preventing black males from voting.

—*Debra Meyers*

See also
Fifteenth Amendment
For Further Reading
Antieau, Chester James. 1997. *The Intended Significance of the Fourteenth Amendment*. Buffalo, NY: W. S. Hein; Nelson, William Edward. 1995. *The Fourteenth Amendment: From Political Principle to Judicial Doctrine*. Cambridge, MA: Harvard University Press; Perry, Michael. 1994. *The Constitution in the Courts: Law or Politics?* New York: Oxford University Press.

FOX-GENOVESE, ELIZABETH (1941–)

Elénore Raoul Professor of the Humanities, professor of history, director of women's studies at Emory University in Atlanta, Georgia, and the author of several books, Elizabeth Fox-Genovese is among the most prolific writers on slavery and on women in the Southern United States. She studied at Bryn Mawr College and at Harvard, where she completed her Ph.D. in 1974, studying social and economic changes in eighteenth-century France. As an assistant professor at the University of Rochester from 1973 to 1976, she became involved in the Marxist debate on merchant capitalism and the role of slavery in the transition from feudalism to capitalism. From a Marxist perspective, she and her husband, Eugene D. Genovese, published a series of articles on European slave economies, on the origins of Western capitalism, and on the economic and social relations in slaveholding societies in the United States.

Fox-Genovese participated in the vigorous academic debate following the publication of Robert Fogel and Stanley Engerman's *Time on the Cross* (1974), which portrayed Southern slavery as a successful rational and capitalist system. She criticized the book's analysis of slavery as a simple matter of economics and suggested instead that one should see the peculiar institution as a paternalistic, precapitalist economic and social system, one that was based essentially on personal relations and should be analyzed with research tools taken from psychology, anthropology, sociology, and economics.

Her own interests became increasingly focused on gender aspects and women's history. In her book *Within the Plantation Household* (1988), she discussed issues of gender, race, and class in the antebellum South. Drawing on women's diaries, letters, and memoirs and on WPA Federal Writers Project interviews, she reconstructed the lives of Southern black and white women, lives that revolved around a system of household labor. In her meticulous description of Southern women based on psychological and anthropological analysis, class and race rather than gender were the dominant categories defining women's identity and behavior within the system, which differed fundamentally from life in the North. In a more recent study on feminism and individualism in the United States (*Feminism Is Not the Story of My Life* [1996]), she argues that the lives of African American women are still defined by the experience of slavery and racial discrimination.

—*Raingard Eßer*

See also
Gender

For Further Reading
Fox-Genovese, Elizabeth. 1991. *Feminism without Illusions*. Chapel Hill: University of North Carolina Press; Fox-Genovese, Elizabeth. 1976. *Origins of Physiocracy*. Ithaca, NY: Cornell University Press; Fox-Genovese, Elizabeth. 1988. *Within the Plantation Household*. Chapel Hill: University of North Carolina Press; Fox-Genovese, Elizabeth, and Eugene D. Genovese. 1983. *Fruits of Merchant Capital*. New York: Oxford University Press.

FRANKLIN AND ARMFIELD

Franklin and Armfield was a major slave-trading firm created by the partnership of Isaac Franklin and John Armfield, his nephew by marriage, on February 28, 1828. The company engaged in a long-distance domestic slave trade, with Franklin's offices in Natchez, Mississippi, and Armfield's in Alexandria, Virginia. A junior partner, Rice C. Ballard, later joined the firm.

The partnership enjoyed a favorable reputation in a commercial area frowned upon even by advocates of slavery. Abolitionist E. A. Andrews reported that Virginia slaves, aware of their impending sale, often requested to be sold to Franklin and Armfield. The firm's positive image derived from two perceptions. First, Franklin and Armfield appeared to treat their subjects humanely. According to all reports, their slaves appeared healthy, well-groomed, and well-fed. Second, the firm had a reputation for preserving families. Although the firm cultivated this reputation, it is clear that when profitable, families were separated by sale and by purchase.

Franklin and Armfield transported slaves to Natchez overland via coffles and by sea on coastal brigs. The firm sent one annual coffle, of 100 or more slaves, in late summer when travel conditions were best for walking. More frequently, they shipped the slaves by sea. The partners owned several brigs, including the *Uncas*, the *United States*, the *Tribune*, and the *Isaac Franklin*, each of which could transport 150 slaves. Such a capacity allowed the firm to ship slaves belonging to migrating planters and other traders for additional profit.

The ships unloaded at New Orleans, where a few slaves were sold, and the remaining slaves went to Natchez by steamboat. At the apex of the firm's operation in the early 1830s, Franklin and Armfield sent a boatload of slaves every two weeks. Contemporary estimates that the firm sold 1,000–1,200 slaves annually in Mississippi are probably accurate. The firm's income reportedly rose from $33,000 in 1829 to $500,000 in 1834.

Franklin and Armfield was the largest of the slave-trading firms in Natchez, but not the only one. Although observers attributed responsibility for most of the slaves in Mississippi to Isaac Franklin, at least 30 other slave traders were operating in Natchez by the 1830s. Nonetheless, Franklin and Armfield was the dominant and most influential firm in the area. Indicative of its influence is that after the firm relocated its Natchez stockade outside of town in 1834, the new stockade, Forks in the Road, became the chief Natchez slave market for the remainder of the antebellum period.

The partnership's charter expired in November 1841, but owing to a Mississippi legislative ban on the importation of slaves as merchandise, Franklin and Armfield had ceased operations in 1837. Isaac Franklin retired from the trade and became a respected planter in Tennessee. John Armfield continued in the trade, managed Franklin's operations in Louisiana, and oversaw the firm's remaining affairs into the 1840s.

—*David J. Libby*

See also
Domestic Slave Trade in the United States
For Further Reading
Andrews, E. A. 1836. *Slavery and the Domestic Slave-Trade in the United States*. Baltimore: Light and Stearns; Bancroft, Frederick. 1931. *Slave-Trading in the Old South*. Baltimore: J. H. Furst; Stephenson, Wendell. 1938. *Isaac Franklin: Slave Trader and Planter of the Old South*. Baton Rouge: Louisiana State University Press; Tadman, Michael. 1989. *Speculators and Slaves: Masters, Traders, and Slaves in the Old South*. Madison: University of Wisconsin Press.

FREE BIRTH, LAW OF (1871)

With the effective termination of the international slave trade in 1850, domestic slavery in Brazil came under increasing pressure. Foreign criticism—mainly from the United States and Great Britain, the example of the U.S. Civil War, and measures in Spain's remaining New World colonies all persuaded thinking Brazilians that a gradualist approach to the end of slavery was desirable. By 1870, Brazil was the only nation in the Americas that still allowed slavery.

In 1871, the Visconde do Rio Branco, Jose María da Silva Paranhos (1819–1880), was summoned by Emperor Dom Pedro II to form a cabinet to deal with the issue. Silva Paranhos had earlier distinguished himself in various government positions and particularly in diplomatic activities during the Triple Alliance War (1864–1870) with Paraguay. Earlier, the visconde, as a leader of the Conservative Party, had seen no justification for changing the slavery system, but experience abroad, internal pressure, and the emperor's desire persuaded him to adopt a new attitude. In four years as prime minister (1871–1875), his greatest accomplishment was the passage of the Law of Free Birth, also known as the Rio Branco Law.

In September 1871, the Brazilian government enacted the law that freed all future children born to slave mothers. Debate in Parliament over the issue had lasted for five tempestuous months and had attracted great press attention. Opposition to reform came mainly from coffee growers in the south of Brazil. They, and other opponents, emphasized that any changes to the labor system would damage the empire's agricultural economy and endanger property rights. Silva Paranhos and his supporters advanced the benefits of a free labor system, as well as the obvious moral and religious arguments. The prime minister was an extremely skilled politician and used his powers (supported firmly by the emperor) to isolate and triumph over the recalcitrant planters.

Under the provisions of the Rio Branco Law, children now born to slave mothers were free. Masters of the mothers had to care for the children until they were 8 years old, and in return for that expense, masters had either the right to the labor of the children until the age of 21 or compensation from an imperial fund. The law also created an emancipation fund to be used for the annual manumission of slaves throughout the empire, as well as giving, for the first time, slaves the legal right to gifts and inheritances. With that money, a slave could buy his freedom when he had a sum of money equal to his value. All state-owned slaves were immediately freed, and a national registry of slaves was to be compiled. Those slaves not registered by masters were considered free within one year of the special registration. To ensure public order, the government placed under its supervision all people who gained freedom and required them to acquire employment.

The Law of Free Birth can rightly be judged a compromise to satisfy critics of Brazilian slavery while at the same time guarding the immediate economic interests of slaveowners. Furthermore, execution of this law was erratic at best. It did, however, offer hope of eventual emancipation to an increasingly restive labor force. Ardent abolitionists considered it an unsatisfactory half-measure while resentment against the imperial government and the emperor rose within the politically and socially important planter class. Half-measure or not, the Rio Branco Law was still a watershed in the Brazilian march to the full abolition of slavery in 1888.

—*Jerry W. Cooney*

See also
Abolition, Latin America; Brazilian Anti-Slavery Society
For Further Reading
Conrad, Robert. 1972. *The Destruction of Brazilian Slavery, 1850–1888*. Berkeley: University of California Press; Nabuco, Joaquim. 1975. *Um estadista do império*. Rio de Janeiro: Editora Nova Aguilar; Taunay, Alfredo d'Escragnolle. 1930. *O visconde do Rio Branco, gloria do Brasil da humandade*. 2d ed. São Paulo: Weiszflog Trmãos.

FREE PERSONS OF COLOR

All slave societies in the Americas contained free persons of color, individuals occupying an intermediate social place between slave and free. The position these persons occupied varied widely from colony to colony, and it is difficult to generalize. Major variables included the identity of the European colonizer, the level of development of the plantation complex, and the proportion of whites in the colony's population. These factors affected the extent to which and under what conditions the colonial society in question would accept free persons of color as citizens with rights to own property, hold public office, take advantage of public services, use the court system, and otherwise participate in society alongside whites.

Spanish and Portuguese colonizers were generally readier to accord some attributes of citizenship to free people of color than were other European colonizers. In the 1940s, the historian Frank Tannenbaum attributed this tendency to the influence of universal Catholic values and the lengthy apprenticeship that Iberians had had as a result of the Reconquista (711–1492; period when the Muslims were removed from the Iberian Peninsula) in learning how to coexist with subject African populations. No Iberian society accepted free people of color as full equals of whites, but Portuguese and Spanish mulattoes advanced in colonial society as plantation owners, government officials, and planters.

The French were less ready to allow such people full participation in colonial society. Most public offices were barred to them, and various humiliating regulations limited their participation in certain professions, prohibited any display of symbols of wealth on their part, and denied them access to education; some regulations required deferential signs from any free person of color to any white. Yet, their economic activities were unrestricted, so in the great French plantation colony of Saint Domingue (modern Haiti), free people of color were large land- and slaveholders, sometimes achieving success equal to that of wealthy white planters.

The English and Dutch were the least welcoming to their free colored populations. Even in Jamaica's plantation heartland, free people of color were prohibited from owning more than tiny plots of land, and social restrictions included residential segregation and legally imposed deference toward whites.

In places where the plantation complex was not highly developed, free people of color were often almost indistinguishable socially from their white neighbors. This was true, for example, in Cuba before the great sugar boom in the early-nineteenth century.

There, they constituted a majority of the peasantry, and their social position seemed very similar to that of white peasants living alongside them. In Britain's colony of the Cayman Islands, relatively harmonious and egalitarian social relationships seem to have existed between free people of color and whites from the earliest days despite the British tradition of repression of any colored population.

As the plantation complex strengthened its grip on any colony, social, occupational, and economic restrictions on free persons of color seemingly deepened. For example, in colonial French Saint Domingue, a host of new regulations between the 1750s and 1780s removed such people from the colonial militia officer corps (1751), forbade them to work as doctors (1764), required that they furnish proof of their free status before executing notarial acts (1773), forbade them to "affect" the dress or hairstyles of whites (1779), and required special "deference" to all whites (1776, 1783). During the 1750s, coffee-growing had resulted in the colonization of Saint Domingue's mountains, and at the same time, sugar plantations finished their conquest of the valleys. As the number of slaves grew, whites began to feel threatened, and as free people of color took advantage of the economic boom to get ahead, whites began to fear their competition.

High numbers of whites in a plantation society contributed to poor treatment for free people of color. The latter often were part of the small-artisan, small-farmer, and lower-managerial class in plantation society, but when large numbers of poor whites were available, the two groups often found themselves competing for these jobs. Simple racism meant that society would react to this "unseemly" competition by progressively excluding free people of color from occupations and legal rights they might have enjoyed in the absence of significant numbers of poor whites. This fact helps to explain differences between Jamaica's free people of color and those in the Southern part of the United States.

There were several avenues by which a person of color might become free. Running away was the most direct method. Every plantation colony at some point in its history harbored a runaway slave community in some remote area, but these settlements were always under siege and their life expectancy, like that of their inhabitants, was short. More runaways quietly fit into colonial society as free people. Colonial administrations continually fought this practice, but in many colonies, slaves with some resources could find ways to live as free people in a faraway town or on a patch of poor land near their old plantation. Many such incompletely free persons were living as free with their masters' tacit agreement, as many masters permitted slaves to live off the plantation and to keep the fruits of their labor for a fee or as a reward for services.

Formal manumission was common, but difficult, as most colonies charged a significant tax or otherwise restricted the practice. Manumitting more than a small percentage of any master's workforce was typically prohibited, and most colonies required that some socially acceptable reason—for example, wet-nursing the master's children, loyal militia service, or reporting slave resistance plots—exist before manumission was approved. Sometimes, if the motive was persuasive enough or the master influential enough, the government might free a slave tax free and perhaps even grant a pension or reward as an example of proper behavior to others. Regulations did not stop masters from selling freedom to their slaves who had acquired property, but they did limit the procedure and make it more expensive.

Some colonies, like Cuba, formalized the practice of self-purchase, such as the *coartación* system, which permitted slaves to request that their master fix a price and permit them to work for their freedom. Other places, like Brazil's Minas Gerais, maintained the same kind of practice informally, but so commonly as to be a cornerstone of society.

One important reason for manumission was the existence of a family relationship between master and slave. Particularly in Catholic Iberian and French colonies, custom obliged the white father of a mixed-race slave to free at least the child if not the mother as well. This practice was particularly marked in plantation colonies with low white-female populations and where it was consequently socially acceptable for white slaveowners to establish households with female slave concubines. In places like British North America where there was a large white-female population, this "mulatto escape hatch" was less available to mixed-race children of slaves.

Generally, women were more likely to be freed than men. Women could provide sexual services to white masters, who often had no other sexual outlet and thus might be disposed to be grateful, but this is not the only reason for the gender imbalance in manumissions. Women had dominated retail marketing in most of the African societies from which the slaves had been taken, and this tradition persisted in the New World. The opportunity to sell services, surplus production from provision grounds, and misappropriated plantation property gave female slaves preferential access to the resources needed for purchasing freedom. Conversely, men who achieved success in a slave society were promoted to choice work assignments, such as overseer or technical specialist, which thus increased their value and made it more difficult for them to achieve manumission through self-purchase.

The most common way to become a free person of color was to be born to the status. Free people of color formed the only segment of the population of most plantation colonies (with the notable exception of North America) that increased naturally. Free people of color who were born in the colony were less subject to the tropical diseases that slew nearly half of all new white and African immigrants, and their population, although somewhat overloaded with women, was closer to attaining a natural balance than either the white or the slave groups. Families tended to be stable, even those formed between white men and free women of color, and fertility rates were high.

Free persons of color filled a number of societal roles, from humble artisan or peasant to great slaveholding plantation owner, depending upon what the society in which they lived would allow. In all slave societies they were an important intermediate class, either as subalterns of the white master class—overseers, rural policemen, slave catchers, militiamen, small agriculturists supplying the plantations—or at least as living examples to the slaves of the rewards that might possible as a result of faithful service.

—Stewart King

See also
Black Slaveowners; *Coartación*; Manumission Laws; Palmares
For Further Reading
Cohen, David, and Jack Greene. 1972. *Neither Slave nor Free*. Baltimore: Johns Hopkins University Press.

FREE SOIL PARTY

The Free Soil Party's significance far outshines its brief existence on the antebellum political scene. As the first antislavery party to attract widespread support from members of the major parties, the Free Soil Party ushered in a new era of sectionalism and set the stage for the political crises of the 1850s.

Officially christened in Buffalo in August 1848, the national Free Soil Party was an amalgam of disgruntled Democrats, Northern Whigs, and Liberty Party men. Advocating a broad array of (mostly Democratic) reforms like free homesteads and cheap postage, the party's fundamental issue was the restriction of slavery. The extension of slavery had become the nation's preeminent political issue as a result of the Mexican War (1846–1848), when the acquisition of vast new western territories forced Americans to consider the future of the "peculiar institution." Northerners believed that extending slavery into the West would threaten the development of that region as a haven for family-sized farms while Southerners generally advocated opening the territories to slave labor. The issue crystallized when the Wilmot Proviso, which was introduced in Congress in 1846, attempted to bar slavery from territories gained during the Mexican War.

Although the Wilmot Proviso never passed in the Senate, the slavery issue remained at the center of national politics as the 1848 election approached. In 1847, the South Carolina Democrat and slaveholder John C. Calhoun formulated a strong "Southern rights" position, which affirmed the constitutional right of slaveowners to take their human chattel into any territory. This direct challenge to the Wilmot Proviso convinced many Northern Whigs and Democrats that slaveholders intended to spread the institution throughout the new territories.

The antislavery Liberty Party, which had attracted few voters in 1840 and 1844, responded to Calhoun by endorsing the Wilmot Proviso and nominating former Democratic congressman John P. Hale of New Hampshire for the presidency. The Democrats, severely split over the slavery extension issue, attempted to prevent a formal rift by excluding the issue from that party's platform. That was too much for an antislavery faction of New York Democrats (and Martin Van Buren supporters) known as Barnburners, and they walked out of the convention, vowing to adhere to the Wilmot Proviso. Similarly, a part of the Whig Party known as Conscience Whigs bolted their party when it nominated the slaveholding Mexican War general Zachary Taylor for president. Under the brilliant coalition-building abilities of Ohio Liberty Party men Salmon P. Chase and Gamaliel Bailey, Conscience Whigs and Barnburners combined with the Liberty Party to form a new, broad-based antislavery party.

Thousands of Northerners streamed into Buffalo for the Free Soil convention, which nominated former president Martin Van Buren and ex-Whig Charles Francis Adams (the son and grandson of presidents) on a platform of "No more slave states and no more slave territories." During the 1848 campaign, both major parties tried to bury the slavery issue, but pressure from the many Free Soil papers that sprang up across the North kept it in the national spotlight. On election day, the Free Soil Party polled 14 percent of the Northern vote (most of it coming from former Democrats) and essentially threw the election to Taylor and the Whigs. Still, the Free Soil Party had increased the number of antislavery votes from 62,300 in 1844 to 291,263 in 1848.

Although the party won no electoral votes in 1848, the Free Soil Party did make significant gains. Nine Free Soil congressmen were sent to Washington from states like New York, Massachusetts, Ohio, and Indiana, and political realignments secured the election of two famous Free Soil senators—Salmon P. Chase in Ohio and Charles Sumner in Massachusetts. Also, the 1848 election reflected a restructuring of U.S. politics at national, state, and local levels. Insurgencies at each level severely damaged both major parties and encouraged the development of a far-reaching national political realignment in the 1850s and 1860s, as Northerners, fearing slavery's expansion, abandoned their old parties in growing numbers and thus presaged the new Republican coalition in the North.

In 1852, the Free Soil Party became the Free Democratic Party and nominated John P. Hale for the presidency. It polled fewer votes than in 1848, and with the Kansas-Nebraska Act (1854), most former Free Soil adherents entered the new Republican Party. Former Free Soil leaders like Chase, Sumner, and Preston King helped launch the new party at every level and founded its large and enduring radical wing.

—*Jonathan Earle*

See also
Barnburners; Wilmot Proviso
For Further Reading
Blue, Frederick J. 1973. *The Free Soilers: Third Party Politics, 1848–54.* Urbana: University of Illinois Press; Mayfield, John. 1979. *Rehearsal for Republicanism: Free Soil and the Politics of Antislavery.* Port Washington, NY: Kennikat Press; Rayback, Joseph G. 1971. *Free Soil: The Election of 1848.* Lexington: University Press of Kentucky.

FREEDMEN'S AID SOCIETIES

Freedmen's aid societies were private charitable associations, active during the Civil War and the immediate postwar years, that provided both short-term welfare and educational opportunities for ex-slaves. These organizations influenced government policy regarding emancipated African Americans and laid the foundation for public education in the South, thereby contributing significantly to the reconstruction of Southern society.

The issue of Northern welfare assistance to freed slaves arose as Union armies began occupying portions of the Confederate states. By March 1862, reports concerning the impoverished conditions of ex-slaves prompted the formation of the first freedmen's aid societies in Boston, New York, and Philadelphia. These societies' organizational objectives included not only the distribution of food, clothing, and medicine but also the deployment of teachers to bring literacy and Northern values to the freedmen. Union victories in 1863 and 1864 swelled the ranks of needy freedmen, which encouraged the expansion of the early societies and the formation of new, regional societies based in Cincinnati and Chicago. Denominational societies also came into existence. Cooperation among

The Pennsylvania branch of the American Freedmen's and Union Commission sponsored this school on St. Helena Island, off the South Carolina coast.

these regional and denominational societies became more effective after the formation of the umbrella American Freedmen's Aid Commission (AFAC) under the leadership of James Miller McKim in late 1865.

Leaders of the societies quickly understood the practical and ideological importance of involving the federal government directly in welfare assistance for Southern blacks. In November 1863, officers of the regional societies initiated a lobbying campaign to influence Congress to establish a federal agency to aid emancipated slaves. This campaign culminated in the founding of the Freedmen's Bureau in March 1865. Moreover, lobbying by the societies was critical in gaining congressional support to expand the bureau's functions to include maintaining educational facilities for freedmen.

The societies and the bureau worked closely during 1865 and 1866 to offer a primary education to Southern blacks. The societies were responsible for the recruitment, salaries, and supervision of teachers while the bureau provided facilities. This joint effort resulted in the operation of 975 schools by the end of 1866, with 1,400 teachers serving 90,000 pupils. These teachers, mainly white, unmarried Northern women,

were also the principal agents for the distribution of clothing and food to communities of freedmen.

Despite their successes, the societies declined after 1867 as controversies sapped Northern enthusiasm for their projects. The societies were eventually forced to defend their efforts from criticism by Frederick Douglass and others that such welfare paternalism would only encourage retention of negative views toward the freedmen. Critics also grew more numerous because of the contentious efforts of McKim to fuse the AFAC with Lyman Abbott's American Union Commission, an organization providing relief to white Unionist refugees (Southerners with Unionist sympathies). The American Freedmen's and Union Commission (AFUC), which became operational in May 1866, split freedmen's relief ranks because of fears that whites would receive disproportionate benefits as a result of the new organization.

The most serious controversy occurred when the influential American Missionary Association (AMA) called on AFUC teachers to combine evangelicalism with their teaching duties. AMA pressure fractured the AFUC, whose leadership remained committed to secular, nonevangelical education. This controversy prompted the denominational and western regional societies to withdraw from the AFUC and turn to support of the AMA during 1867 and 1868. The resulting drop in membership, combined with the advent of an independent Southern educational movement, led to the disbanding of the AFUC in 1869.

—David L. Ferch

For Further Reading
Bentley, George. 1955. A *History of the Freedmen's Bureau.* Philadelphia: University of Pennsylvania Press; McPherson, James. 1964. *The Struggle for Equality: Abolitionists and the Negro in the Civil War and Reconstruction.* Princeton, NJ: Princeton University Press; Morris, Robert. 1981. *Reading, 'Riting, and Reconstruction: The Education of Freedmen in the South, 1861–1870.* Chicago: University of Chicago Press.

FRENCH CARIBBEAN

The first French colonists in the Caribbean arrived at St. Kitts in 1627, the first Africans arrived there two years later, and by the 1780s, 40,000 slaves a year were being imported into the French colonies. Toward the end of the seventeenth century, in order to regulate relationships between masters and slaves, the French government issued the famous Code Noir. These legal regulations were relatively humane regarding the treatment of slaves; unfortunately, many of the provisions were more honored in the breach than in the observance.

The small islands of Martinique and Guadeloupe served French colonizers in the same way that Barbados served the English, as places to refine techniques and amass capital before attempting the larger challenge of the Greater Antilles. Saint Domingue (modern Haiti) contained by far the largest slave population in the Antilles among either French or English colonies: when the Saint Domingue Revolution began in 1791, there were about 465,000 slaves in that colony and about 180,000 in French Guiana, Martinique, and Guadeloupe combined.

Most, but by no means all, slaves worked the fields of moderately sized plantations, and the average slaveholding unit contained about 100 slaves. These plantations were much larger than those in the United States but smaller than those of Jamaica or Cuba at the height of their colonial development. The largest plantations grew sugar, but coffee and indigo were also important crops in Saint Domingue. As in other plantation societies, French field slaves worked in gangs, overseen mostly by commanders, boss slaves, or technical experts (professional managers, sugar refiners and millers), who might be whites, free blacks,

An eighteenth-century engraving of slaves at work on a plantation in the French West Indies.

or even valuable and pampered slaves. French Caribbean gang labor differed little from patterns seen throughout the plantation complex.

Feeding the slaves sufficiently was difficult. Land was much more profitable when devoted to the production of primary crops, so food crops were often neglected. Slaves in the French Caribbean usually received small plots of second-rate plantation land to be used as provision grounds, and slaves were encouraged to cultivate food crops on them for private consumption on their Sundays and other days off. Slaves who managed to produce surpluses on their provision grounds could sell the leftovers. Some slaves owned chickens or pigs, which fed on scraps and residue from the cane fields. The slaves' diet consisted mostly of manioc, maize, and rice supplemented by occasional bits of meat. Malnutrition, especially among children, was common. Slave housing in the French colonies differed from common Caribbean patterns in that the structures were smaller and barracks-type housing was rare. Families were also more likely to live together than in some other colonies.

Despite the colonial government's occasional laws and statements favoring family life, slave birthrates were low. Moreover, slaves did not live long, especially the new African arrivals. The colonies were unfamiliar disease environments that killed about half of all new immigrants of any color during their initial years in a colony. Additionally, many new slaves had difficulty adjusting to the changed living conditions and committed suicide.

Slave society was internally stratified. At the bottom were the African imports, the *bossales* (newly arrived, unacculturated slaves). Both masters and slaves considered the native-born slaves superior to African-born ones, but both types of slaves aspired to high-status work assignments. Domestic slaves were more valuable and ranked higher in the slave hierarchy, but slaves particularly sought jobs as skilled tradespeople or foremen. These individuals were at the top of slave society and were the white plantation manager's subalterns. Boss slaves were almost exclusively men, but many domestics and some technical specialists were women.

A significant minority of the slaves did not work on plantations as cities harbored large slave populations, mostly working as domestics, skilled workmen, or laborers. Many small farms existed in the countryside, too small to be plantations and often owned by free people of color, and these farms employed one or two slaves who performed a broad range of tasks, often working alongside their masters. Finally, significant numbers of slaves received the right to work on their own account, sometimes in exchange for regular payments to their masters.

—*Stewart R. King*

See also
Code Noir; Comparative Slavery in the Americas; Haitian Revolution; Société des Amis des Noirs
For Further Reading
Carolyn Fick. 1990. *The Making of Haiti: The Haitian Revolution from Below.* Knoxville: University of Tennessee Press.

FRENCH DECLARATION OF THE RIGHTS OF MAN AND CITIZEN

The Declaration of the Rights of Man and Citizen was the most celebrated and influential document of the French Revolution. The National Assembly adopted it on August 26, 1789, as a preamble to a new French constitution, and the declaration was a statement of the general principles that formed the basis of the new constitution. The purpose of the document was to proclaim "the natural, inalienable, and sacred rights of man," and the first of its 17 articles asserted: "Men are born and remain free and equal in rights. Social distinctions may be based only on common utility" (Hunt, 1996).

The second article asserted that the purpose of government was "the preservation of the natural and imprescriptible rights of man. These rights are liberty, property, security, and resistance to oppression." The third article declared, "The principle of all sovereignty rests essentially in the nation," which rejected the monarchist notion that sovereignty rested in the king. The sixth article affirmed: "The law is the expression of the general will. All citizens have the right to take part, in person or by their representatives, in its formation."

The last article stated, "Property being an inviolable and sacred right, no one may be deprived of it except when public necessity, certified by law, obviously requires it, and on the condition of a just compensation in advance." Obviously, this affirmation was very important to the relatively affluent men who were members of the National Assembly.

Even after adopting the Declaration of the Rights of Man and Citizen, the delegates continued to debate which categories of people should be included among the men whose rights were proclaimed in the declaration. A constitutional distinction was made between "active" and "passive" citizens. All citizens had the same civil rights, like freedom of religion and equal protection of their property rights, but to be an "active" citizen with the right to vote and hold public office, one had to be a male citizen over the age of 25 who paid a tax equal to three days' pay. About half of all Frenchmen qualified.

Just as the American Declaration of Independence spoke of "inalienable rights" such as "life, liberty, and the pursuit of happiness" yet condoned slavery, most of the delegates who voted for the French Declaration of the Rights of Man also acquiesced in allowing slavery to continue in the French Caribbean colonies. Since slavery was illegal in France itself, slavery in the colonies seemed peripheral to the urgent political and constitutional issues at home.

However, a small minority within the National Assembly advocated the abolition of slavery. They belonged to the Société des Amis des Noirs, which included revolutionary luminaries such as the marquis de Lafayette; Emmanuel-Joseph Sieyès; Marie-Jean Caritat, the marquis de Condorcet; Jacques-Pierre Brissot de Warville; and Honoré-Gabriel Riqueti, comte de Mirabeau.

Just as slaveowners in the United States had enormous economic and political power, so too did the French colonial interests. On the eve of the French Revolution, trade between France and its Caribbean plantations accounted for 30–50 percent of France's total trade, and about 12 percent of the French population earned its living in colonial trade. Furthermore, 10 percent of the members of the National Assembly owned colonial property.

France's wealthiest Caribbean colony was Saint Domingue (modern Haiti), where there were about 465,000 slaves, 30,000 whites, and 27,000 free blacks (a category that included both blacks and mulattoes). The situation was complicated because free blacks owned about 25 percent of the slaves and over 30 percent of plantation lands.

At the beginning of the French Revolution, white plantation owners from Saint Domingue sent representatives to Paris to ask for seats in the new National Assembly. Vincent Ogé, a mulatto plantation owner and lawyer, led a delegation of mulatto plantation owners to Paris. These mulattoes hoped to be included in the Saint Domingue delegation, but the whites refused to include them. This exclusion enabled the Société des Amis des Noirs to convince the National Assembly to grant only 6 seats to the Saint Domingue whites instead of the 37 they had sought.

On August 20, 1789, while the National Assembly was debating the wording of the Declaration of the Rights of Man, the white delegates from Saint Domingue joined with sympathetic French delegates to form the Club Massaic in an attempt to combat the influence of the Société des Amis des Noirs. They shared the fear that if mulattoes were granted equality with whites, that would imply that the principle "all men are born and remain free and equal in rights" would take priority over the property rights of slaveowners.

In September, about a month after the approval of the Declaration of the Rights of Man, mulatto delegates appeared before the National Assembly to demand representation on the grounds that they were also men of property, though they made clear their intention to retain their ownership of slaves. The assembly avoided a decision by referring the issue back to the colony.

In October 1789, the royal governor of Saint Domingue reported that many slaves were familiar with the events in France and that there was a serious risk of a slave insurrection at any time. In spring and summer 1790, there were a few acts of racially motivated murder by both blacks and whites. In October, 1790, Vincent Ogé, embittered by the failure of the leaders of the French Revolution to help his cause, returned to Saint Domingue and led a revolt by mulattoes against the whites. The French troops and the local white militia defeated the rebels, and Ogé was executed. In August 1791, about 30,000 slaves rose up and emancipated themselves in the only successful slave revolt in modern history. In 1794, the French government belatedly decreed the abolition of slavery in all French colonies.

—*Richard W. Sanders*

See also
Haitian Revolution; Ogé, Jacques Vincent; Société des Amis des Noirs
For Further Reading
Blackburn, Robin. 1991. "Anti-Slavery and the French Revolution." *History Today* 41: 19–25; Hunt, Lynn. 1996. *The French Revolution and Human Rights: A Brief Documentary History*. New York: St. Martin's; James, C. L. R. 1963. *The Black Jacobins*. New York: Vintage Press; Ott, Thomas O. 1973. *The Haitian Revolution, 1789–1804*. Knoxville: University of Tennessee Press.

FRENCH ROYAL AFRICA COMPANY

The Royal Africa Company was a mercantilist enterprise established to trade slaves and other commodities to the islands of the French Caribbean. French colonists first settled the islands of the Caribbean in the early-seventeenth century. The first to arrive were pirates and privateers, who attacked Spanish, English, and Portuguese holdings in the hope of attaining personal enrichment while also advancing French military interests. By mid-century, the government of Louis XIV had taken these colonies into a formalized French empire. France gained legal title to its last major colony in the Caribbean, Saint Domingue (now Haiti), in 1689, but by that time the French government had already been shaping the colonial economy to its liking for decades.

Cardinal Armand Richelieu, and Jean-Baptiste Colbert, his loyal subordinate and eventual successor as principal minister of Louis XIV's government, laid out the basic lines of France's relationship with its Caribbean colonies as early as 1664. In that year, the French crown took direct possession of the colonies from their private owners and put them under the jurisdiction of the Compagnie des Indes Occidentales, or West Indies Company. The sole purpose of the company was to bring wealth to mainland France. It was to do so through the exclusive privilege of French merchants to trade in the colony and through a prohibition on taking precious metals into the colonies. The company, and its many successor entities, were financially unsuccessful, but their mercantilist principle remained the cornerstone of French policy in the Antilles until the French Revolution.

Colbert's policy was that the Antilles would produce plantation crops using slave labor, and to perform this task, the colonists needed slave imports. An assortment of companies was created to respond to this demand, the most notorious being the Compagnie des Indes, or John Law's company, which was succeeded by the Royal Africa Company.

The companies held monopolies on slave trading to the French Caribbean colonies. However, most of the actual trading in France was done by smaller investors, who paid the company for the privilege of infringing on its monopoly. French slave traders, both the large company and the smaller operators, were unable to supply all the slaves the rapidly growing sugar and coffee industries in the French Caribbean demanded, so the colonists turned to foreign merchants in defiance of the exclusive mercantilist arrangement. Philip Curtin (1975) estimates that at least 15 percent of the slaves imported into the French Caribbean colonies were smuggled in in defiance of mercantilist regulations. This smuggling led to a greater diversity in the slave populations of the French colonies and also strengthened English merchants at the expense of the French slave traders.

—*Stewart R. King*

See also
French Caribbean
For Further Reading
Curtin, Philip. 1975. *Economic Change in Pre-Colonial Africa: Senegambia in the Era of the Slave Trade*. Madison: University of Wisconsin Press; Stein, Robert Louis. 1979. *The French Slave Trade in the Eighteenth Century: An Old Regime Business*. Madison: University of Wisconsin Press.

FRENCH SLAVE TRADE

Most of the Indians who inhabited the Caribbean islands died from disease, conflict, or overwork as a result of enslavement within a few years after the area was occupied by Europeans, including the French. Lacking a native source of slaves, the Europeans then turned to Africa for a steady labor supply. Although there were some African slaves in the French Antilles before the introduction of sugarcane, the rise of the sugar plantation system made slavery a central component of French colonial life. As the European demand for sugar and coffee increased, the slave trade grew proportionately. By the late-seventeenth century, slave labor was crucial to the economies of the Caribbean islands.

The French slave trade expanded considerably following the signing of the Treaty of Utrecht (1713), which ended the War of the Spanish Succession. In the 80 years following the signing, the French sent more than 3,000 ships to Africa to trade for slaves. These ships transported an estimated 1.25 million captives and delivered more than 1 million of them to the French Antilles; nearly 150,000 died in French ships, either along the African coast or while crossing the Atlantic.

A slaving triangle operated between France, Africa, and the Antilles, and although a typical voyage lasted 15–18 months, many were longer. In France, a slave ship was loaded at a key port with cargo to be used as barter in Africa. After a voyage of 2–3 months, the ship arrived off the west coast of Africa, where the French captain used his cargo to barter for slaves brought to an established trading site by African merchants. After 3–4 months in Africa, the ship sailed for the Antilles, where the French captain sold the captured slaves to colonial merchants, or directly to slaveowners, in exchange for sugar, coffee, or other commodities. After anytime from 1 month to nearly a year, the ship made the 2-month return voyage to France, where the colonial commodities were sold to buyers from all over Europe.

The French also colonized the Mascarene Islands of Mauritius and Réunion in the Indian Ocean. For those colonies, they developed an East African slave trade in the eighteenth century, obtaining captives from Madagascar or Mozambique to be slaves in the two island colonies.

Revolts by captives aboard ship were common, especially when slavers were still in sight of Africa. Most uprisings were routinely suppressed, but one of the rare successful revolts occurred on the *Diamant* in September 1774 off the coast of Corisco, a small island near the Gabon coast. In this instance, the captain and crew were forced to abandon the ship to the captives.

Besides the Antilles, the French slave trade also operated elsewhere in the Americas. On the Louisiana plantations, the greater proportion of the slaves were from Africa; in Canada, most were Indians. French presence figured prominently in the fur trade, with the coureurs de bois, or trappers, trading with the Indians for furs and other goods they could take to settlements in French or English colonies. The trade included Indian slaves, obtained from tribes who had captured them in war. If slaves were in short supply, the coureurs de bois would sometimes incite tribes to war so that captives might become available for sale.

The French employed Indian slaves as guides and interpreters, agricultural laborers, and domestics; in Canada, a shortage of white women gave rise to a steady traffic in female slaves. Indians slaves were also used as bribes or rewards to gain the goodwill or alliance of various tribes. French missionaries pressured the monarchy to end the trade in Indian slaves, with limited success. Eventually, many of the Indian tribes from which the French drew their slaves, weakened by contact with whites, withdrew and joined with more distant tribes, which made it more difficult for whites to obtain them as slaves.

The French Revolution temporarily ended French involvement in the trade in African slaves. Napoleon subsequently reinstated slavery and legalized the trade in 1802 in an attempt to restore the old colonial system, but abolished it again in 1815 under British pressure. Although the slave trade was outlawed in 1815, it continued until the revolutionary government in France finally ended it in 1848.

—*Patricia A. Kilroe*

See also
Amerindian Slavery, Plains; French Royal Africa Company

For Further Reading
Daget, Serge. 1990. *La traite des noirs. Bastilles négrières et velléités abolitionnistes.* Nantes: Ouest France Université; Lauber, Almon Wheeler. 1969. *Indian Slavery in Colonial Times within the Present Limits of the United States.* New York: AMS Press; Peabody, Sue. 1996. *"There Are No Slaves in France": The Political Culture of Race and Slavery in the Ancien Régime.* New York: Oxford University Press; Stein, Robert Louis. 1979. *The French Slave Trade in the Eighteenth Century: An Old Regime Business.* Madison: University of Wisconsin Press.

FREYRE, GILBERTO DE MELLO (1900–1987)

In his 1933 classic *Casa grande e senzala* (published in English as *The Masters and the Slaves*), social historian Gilberto Freyre refuted many assumptions of Brazilian historiography.

Following decades of scientific racism, which had characterized Brazil's large African population as a hindrance to national development and blamed high levels of miscegenation for supposed racial degeneracy, Freyre launched a nationalist defense against traditional thinking with regard to eugenics, or the manipulation of the hereditary qualities of a race.

Freyre contended that African slaves had contributed not only brawn to the Brazilian economy but also agricultural knowledge and highly developed skills in metalwork and cattle raising. Africans had also provided Brazil with its distinctive music and its healthiest cuisine. Sexual union between Africans and Portuguese settlers, he contended, had allowed colonizers to be successful in their attempt to establish a vital tropical colony. Subduing the hostile environment, he suggested, had begun with the slave women's seduction by their sexually prolific masters, with the Brazilian mulatto representing the new conquering race.

Published in English in 1946, *Casa grande e senzala* shaped comparative slavery studies among historians like Frank Tannenbaum and Stanley Elkins. They accepted Freyre's contention that slavery was more benign in Latin American Catholic nations than in the Protestant North because of a theology that stressed universal brotherhood and depicted slavery as an earthly misfortune, one that was not reflective of the slave's value in God's eyes. Freyre describes the Portuguese as a people virtually without race consciousness who were more preoccupied with religious compliance than with race and ethnicity. Slaves who accepted Catholicism experienced a social tolerance that included relaxed sexual liaisons between the races. Unlike the Protestant North, there was no inherent link between race and servitude, and Freyre argued that racial democracy flourished under the plantation aristocracy. Afro-Brazilians, and especially mulattoes, played active roles in the church (including the priesthood), held social leadership positions, and enjoyed a relatively congenial racial climate.

Freyre's happy gloss on slavery in Brazil may stem from his background as the child of a planter family in the sugar plantation–dominated world of Pernambuco (now Recife) on Brazil's northeastern coast. Freyre wrote frequently of his sexual initiation with a mulatto woman and of hearing childhood tales of preemancipation life. Freyre was further molded by two sojourns in the United States. Having been converted by Baptist missionaries in Brazil, Freyre traveled to Waco, Texas, at the age of 18 to study at Baylor University. While he was there, the lynching of a black man horrified him and spurred him to ponder the profoundly different race relations in his homeland and the United States.

His interest in race and comparative slavery deepened while working on his master's degree at Columbia University in New York. Later he recalled his horror, after years away from Brazil, at seeing mixed-race Brazilian sailors, men Freyre then saw as representing racial degeneracy. He was soon influenced by anthropologist Franz Boas, who attributed racial differences to environment and culture, and Freyre came to the conclusion that the alleged disabilities of blacks and Indians were caused partly by factors such as education, nutrition, and syphilis rather than mere genetics.

Freyre never completely escaped his generation's racism. He characterized the culture of Brazil's Indian population as "inferior" to that of African slaves, and he stereotyped the slaves as happy, singing Negroes. Freyre never considered that a gulf may have existed between Catholic doctrine on universal brotherhood and actual practice on Brazilian plantations, and he overlooked the fact that Protestant churches in the U.S. South often acknowledged the slave's humanity and that miscegenation was also commonplace in the United States. He also neglected evidence of brutality, such as the high slave mortality rate in Brazil. Freyre's work reads as a reactionary apologia for Brazil's departed patriarchal monarch, written in reaction to the republican chaos of the 1920s and 1930s.

Despite these shortcomings, Freyre's eclectic use of cultural materials, then so shocking, paved the way for later, more sophisticated social history. His discussion of sexuality also marks the first serious exploration of Brazilian gender oppression. Later books have further explored race relations and the conflict between plantation patriarchy and urban modernity in Brazil, but no other work has had the global influence enjoyed by *Casa grande e senzala*. So profound was Freyre's impact on Brazilian scholarship, disseminated through *Casa grande* and 62 other books, that some people suggest that the country's historiography can be divided into pre-Freyre and post-Freyre eras.

—*Michael Phillips*

See also

Elkins, Stanley M.; Tannenbaum, Frank

For Further Reading

Freyre, Gilberto. 1966. *The Masters and the Slaves: A Study in the Development of Brazilian Civilization.* New York: Alfred A. Knopf; Hennessey, Alistair. 1989. "Reshaping the Brazilian Past." *Times Literary Supplement*, July 14–20, 763–764; Needell, Jeffrey D. 1995. "Identity, Race, Gender, and Modernity in the Origin of Gilberto Freyre's *Oeuvre*." *American Historical Review* 100:1 (February): 51–77; Skidmore, Thomas E. 1990. "Racial Ideas and Social Policy in Brazil, 1870–1940." In *The Idea of Race in Latin America*. Ed. Richard Graham. Austin: University of Texas Press.

FUGITIVE SLAVE ACT OF 1850

The Fugitive Slave Act passed by the U.S. Congress in 1850 allowed slaveowners from states and territories that permitted slavery to pursue and capture slaves who had escaped to states and territories where slavery was prohibited. It gave teeth to the older Fugitive Slave Act of 1793 by giving federal marshals full authority to enforce the law and reward those who aided in capturing fugitive slaves and punish those involved in their escape. The law tested the resolve of Northern states in upholding the constitutional right of Southern states to retain a practice that, to many people, was abhorrent and evil.

The Missouri Compromise of 1820 set the stage for future conflict by admitting Maine to the Union as a free state, admitting Missouri as a slave state, and confining slavery to areas south of 36° 30' north latitude in territory west of the Mississippi River. The states that were dependent upon slavery were forever fearful that the number of states in which slavery was outlawed would outnumber those where it was not and were insistent that a balance be maintained when territories were admitted into the Union as states. Additionally, they felt that slaveholding citizens under their jurisdiction had a right to carry the practice with them into federal territories if they chose to migrate there. By the 1840s, the pace with which territories were being admitted into the Union as states had increased, and some Southern states, with South Carolina in the lead, were threatening to secede from the Union because of what they considered was undue Northern influence in limiting their constitutional right to uphold and even extend the institution of slavery into federal territories.

In 1850, Senator Henry Clay of Kentucky presented to Congress a bill that offered a sweeping compromise to assuage the forces of North and South. California was to be admitted to the Union as a non-slave state; the slave trade, though not slavery itself, was to be abolished in the District of Columbia; the boundary dispute between Texas and the territory of New Mexico was to be settled in favor of New Mexico—but Texas, which had become a state in 1845, would receive compensation in the form of the assumption of its public debt by the federal government. Also, the Wilmot Proviso, which had proposed that slavery would never be allowed in territories acquired from Mexico, was to be overlooked, and the issue of slavery was not to be considered in organizing the territories of New Mexico and Utah. Finally, the Fugitive Slave Act of 1793 was to be enforced by placing the extradition of escaped slaves into the hands of federal marshals.

After this omnibus legislation was defeated in spring 1850, Senator Stephen A. Douglas of Illinois

A political cartoon depicting the Fugitive Slave Act of 1850.

led the fight to have each provision passed as a separate piece of legislation, and the passage of the Fugitive Slave Act in late September 1850 was a victory for Southern slaveholding interests. The South had a strong argument in the U.S. Constitution (Article 4, sec. 2, par. 3) to justify the correctness of its position, and now federal officers could be called upon to press claims on escaped slaves.

Although Southerners may have felt victorious, the Fugitive Slave Act, in reality, did little to help their cause. Northern abolitionists were furious, and several celebrated cases surrounding the capture of fugitive slaves helped to galvanize sentiment for their movement. Several Northern states enacted personal liberty laws to protect slaves who had legitimately won their freedom and to counteract the eroding effects that enforcement of the Fugitive Slave Act had upon civil liberties. The very popular Daniel Webster of Massachusetts was ostracized in his own state after he supported the Fugitive Slave Act when it was enacted, and Harriet Beecher Stowe published *Uncle Tom's Cabin* (1852), which further inflamed Northern passions against the South.

Led by Harriet Tubman, Josiah Henson, Levi Coffin, Thomas and Muriel Hayden, and many others, participants in the Underground Railroad and members of vigilance committees intensified the effort to aid in the rescue of escaped slaves. Despite the efforts of Presidents Millard Fillmore, Franklin Pierce, and James Buchanan to uphold the law and the zeal of Attorney General Caleb Cushing and Chief Justice Roger B. Taney to enforce it, relatively few escaped slaves were actually returned to slavery, and few rescuers were actually tried and prosecuted.

The Fugitive Slave Act (1850) made life miserable for "passengers" aboard the Underground Railroad and struck fear in the hearts of blacks in the United States, slave and free. The cases of Anthony Burns and Ellen and William Craft, the murders in Christiana, Pennsylvania, and several other episodes involving the apprehension and extradition of escaped slaves only widened the gulf between North and South and made the Fugitive Slave Act of 1850, along with the Dred Scott decision of the Supreme Court in 1857, one of the darkest spots in the history of civil liberties in the United States.

—*Terrence M. Vaughan*

See also
Burns, Anthony; Christiana Riot; Craft, William and Ellen; Personal Liberty Laws; Underground Railroad
For Further Reading
Campbell, Stanley W. 1968. *The Slave Catchers: Enforcement of the Fugitive Slave Law, 1850–1860.* Chapel Hill: University of North Carolina Press; Gara, Larry. 1961. *The Liberty Line: The Legend of the Underground Railroad.* Lexington: University of Kentucky Press; Nye, Russell B. 1963. *Fettered Freedom: Civil Liberties and the Slave Controversy, 1830–1860.* East Lansing: Michigan State University Press; Pease, Jane H., and William H. 1975. *The Fugitive Slave Law and Anthony Burns: A Problem of Law Enforcement.* Philadelphia: J. B. Lippincott.

FUGITIVE SLAVE ACTS, STATE

Beginning with Virginia in 1660 and continuing until the U.S. Civil War, colonial assemblies and state legislatures in the U.S. South passed hundreds of fugitive slave acts to aid in the orderly and effective recovery of runaway bondsmen, especially those within their jurisdictions. These statutes established procedures for the capture and return of escaped slaves and mandated punishments for runaways and people who encouraged and assisted them in their escape. Historians of slavery in the United States have usually concerned themselves with the federal fugitive slave acts of 1793 and 1850; "almost completely missing," as Philip Schwarz has noted, "is an understanding of slave states' laws concerning runaways and fugitives, the first line of defense on which owners relied" (Schwarz, 1996). But state acts were an omnipresent, and often important, element in the effort to control slave behavior.

Fugitive slave acts in the colonial South defined runaways as outlaws in rebellion against their masters. Outlawry mandated harsh punishments, ranging from whipping, maiming, cropping of ears or noses, and branding with an R on the cheek to permitting pursuers to kill fugitive slaves on sight. A 1705 Virginia law authorized justices of the peace to issue proclamations against runaways and directed sheriffs to raise forces to track them. Under the law, if a fugitive failed to surrender, he or she could be killed by any white. If captured alive, runaways could be maimed or dismembered as punishment for their flight. Similar statutes were drafted in Maryland, North Carolina, and South Carolina.

By the late-eighteenth century, most Southern states had ended outlawry and its harsher punishments. What remained were statutes outlining a legal procedure for the recovery of fugitive slaves. Most antebellum state acts stated that individuals capturing runaways should deliver them to a justice of the peace, who would then have the slave jailed. If the owner were known, he or she could immediately claim the slave. If the owner were unknown, the slave's capture would be advertised in local newspapers. If not claimed after a specified period of time, the slave could be sold. Some of these statutes provided that slaves could be hired out until claimed or sold.

State fugitive slave acts were a moderately effective means of protecting the economic interests of Southern slaveholders, but many barriers worked against their complete enforcement. One was the problem of recovering fugitive slaves beyond state lines. Southern state legislatures responded in several ways. They pressed for federal fugitive slave acts; they tightened their control of state boundaries—Virginia even created a system of inspection commissioners in 1856 to search for runaways on every boat leaving one of the state's ports; and they set substantial compensation amounts and mileage allowances for individuals apprehending and returning fugitives from other states, including Northern states.

A second barrier was those whites (especially Quakers) and free blacks who helped or encouraged slaves to escape. All of the state statutes provided punishments for harboring fugitives. Slaves were to be whipped; all free persons—whether black or white—received fines or imprisonment. Only one state, Texas, actually defined the offense of harboring as the "act of maintaining and concealing a runaway slave; a person so harboring having knowledge of the fact that the slave is a runaway."

A related offense was to entice slaves to run away from their masters (also called inveigling). An 1816 Georgia law prescribed a year in prison and sale as a slave for life for any free black found guilty of this crime. By mid-century, it was also a serious criminal offense for whites in most Southern states. Mississippi and Kentucky, for example, mandated 2–20 years in prison for anyone found guilty of slave enticement. Although enforcement varied, many Southerners were punished for violating state fugitive slave acts. An 1860 list of inmates of the Virginia Penitentiary listed 15 whites and free blacks who were serving sentences for encouraging or participating in slave escapes.

The onset of the Civil War further hampered the enforcement of state fugitive slave acts as Southern slaves fled by the thousands to the safety of Union lines. Even so, Confederate state and local courts continued to prosecute violations of these laws throughout the conflict. Such efforts, while strenuous, proved fruitless in stopping the flood of runaways from Southern cities and plantations. State acts concerning fugitive slaves were effectively nullified in 1865 by the passage of the Thirteenth Amendment.

—*Roy E. Finkenbine*

See also
Fugitive Slave Act of 1850
For Further Reading
Morris, Thomas D. 1996. *Southern Slavery and the Law, 1619–1860.* Chapel Hill: University of North Carolina Press; Schwarz, Philip J. 1996. *Slave Laws in Virginia.* Athens: University of Georgia Press.

GALLEY SLAVERY

Galley slavery is the use of forced, captive labor to propel a specific genre of oar-driven vessels, and the practice first appeared on the cusp of the Middle Ages and the Renaissance in the Mediterranean. In terms of the relationship between ships and slaves, galley slavery represents a unique occurrence in which the slave played an active role in the propulsion of the vessel rather than the passive role of cargo.

During the Crusades, certain orders of knights and Islamic factions frequently raided each other's settlements, took captives, and forced them to the oars of large galleys and other physical labor while awaiting their ransom. Later, convicted prisoners, or *forzati*, were sentenced to "the galleys" in the Mediterranean well into the eighteenth century. Nations used the threat of the galleys to control both political and religious dissent, and the institution of galley slavery endured as a psychological weapon among and within nations long after the tactical usefulness of the type of vessel involved had begun to wane.

The use of servile labor to row galleys had an economical basis as a then-practical and acceptable solution in adapting the oared warship to rapidly advancing weapons technology. The introduction of heavy iron guns and their subsequent naval application challenged the traditional concept of the galley. The oared warship had been developed to serve in coastal confrontations, and the tactical strength of the galley lay in its ability to maneuver swiftly, independent of the wind; consequently, light construction was a necessity. The oared warships in the ancient Mediterranean were powered by oarsmen who propelled the vessel so that its primary weapon, the ram, was brought to bear on their opponents. The introduction of effective incendiary and missile weapons during the medieval period helped to effect the galley's transformation into a waterborne fighting machine that conducted engagements as if on land. It was during the Fatamid period (969–1171) that the first distinctions were drawn between sailors and combatants.

Iron guns demanded that the galley be larger and more heavily constructed, which demanded a larger complement of oarsmen, collectively known as the *cirumi*. By the time of the later Crusades, Muslim forces and some Christian factions, like the Knights of St. John, used captive labor to meet the need for additional oarsmen to power these vessels. The fundamental form of the galley remained constant after the mid-thirteenth century, but the use of slaves rather than free oarsmen, captives, or prisoners prompted a change in the configuration of the oars. In the sixteenth century, there was a shift from the traditional rowing scheme of one man per oar to a system that placed many men on one oar. That change reflected the implementation of galley slavery, not only because it made for a more efficient arrangement for chaining the men, but more important, because it increased the assurance that a given oar would be pulled when needed despite an individual's noncompliance.

Western nations depended more upon *forzati* as galley slaves, which proved to be a significant factor in the Battle of Lepanto between the Christians and the Ottomans in 1571, the last major naval engagement between galleys and the first in which a vessel was sunk by gunfire. During the battle, the Christians at the oars of the Turkish galleys were able to free themselves with fallen weapons and turned against their masters. Certain Christian vessels freed the *forzati* from their oars to reinforce their lines at crucial moments. At the battle's end, an estimated 15,000 Christian slaves were liberated. The long literary tradition of the galley slave has its roots at Lepanto: a young army man on a Venetian galley, Miguel de Cervantes, would later write the novel *Don Quixote de la Mancha*, which includes a biting commentary on the institution.

The deep-hulled sailing ship proved itself to be the most effective vessel for mounting iron guns, but the shallow-draft galley operated by forced labor would endure in the Mediterranean for centuries. Galleys were used on a seasonal basis by the major powers in the theater, including Spain, the Italian maritime powers, the Ottoman Empire, the Barbary States, and France.

The notorious Corps de Galères of King Louis XIV (r. 1643–1715) was one of the last and largest coastal fleets, and those galleys were armed with the finest bronze ordnance and manned by a diverse crew, including a significant component of "infidel" prisoners of war (the only ones actually called "slaves"), hardened violent criminals, and men imprisoned for political and religious dissidence. For using the last group of men, Louis suffered a barrage of negative press from Protestant England but received favor from the Vatican. Despite the grandeur of the Corps de Galères, its galleys were no match for a single broadside of a ship of the line. As the eighteenth century began, galley slavery had become a potent psychological factor of a political and symbolic weapon that was all but tactically obsolete.

—*David A. Johnson*

For Further Reading
Bamford, Paul. 1973. *Fighting Ships and Prisons: The Mediterranean Galleys of France in the Age of King Louis XIV.* St. Paul: University of Minnesota Press; Clissold, S. 1977. *The Barbary Slaves.* Totowa, NJ: Rowman and Littlefield; Guilmartin, John. 1980. *Gunpowder and Galleys: Changing Technology and Mediterranean Warfare at Sea in the Sixteenth Century.* Cambridge: Cambridge University Press; *A Narrative of the Adventures of Lewis Marott, Pilot-Royal of the Galleys of France.* 1677. London: Edward Brewster.

GAMA, VASCO DA
(C. 1469–1524)

The Portuguese explorer and discoverer of the maritime route to India, Vasco da Gama, was born in Sines, a fishing town in southeastern Portugal, the son of Estêvão da Gama, a member of the household of Prince Fernando, master of the Order of Santiago. Little is known about Vasco's early career, except that he had been a *fidalgo* (one who is reliable/trustworthy) in the household of King John II (r. 1481–1495) and was a knight and commander in the Order of Santiago when he was named to lead an expedition of four ships, including a caravel and a supply ship, to discover a maritime route to India. The sixteenth-century chronicler Damião de Gois described him as "an unmarried man of the right age to bear up under the strains of such a voyage" (in *Urbis olisiponis descripto* [1533]).

Two of the ships, *São Gabriel* and *São Rafael,* captained by Vasco da Gama and his brother Paulo da Gama, respectively, were constructed especially for the voyage. The caravel *Berrio* was captained by Nicolau Coelho. The pilots included such experienced seafarers as Pero de Alenquer, Pero Escobar, João de Coimbra, and Afonso Gonçalves. There were 150–170 men on the expedition at the start; only about one-third returned to Portugal alive.

The small fleet left Lisbon on July 8, 1497, rendezvoused at the Cape Verde Islands, and left there on August 3. Da Gama spent the next three months out of sight of land—the longest known such voyage up to that time—before anchoring on November 8 in the Bay of Santa Helena, approximately 100 miles north of the Cape of Good Hope. After verifying the location of the cape, he rounded it on November 22.

After breaking up the supply ship and redistributing the supplies at Angra de São Brás, da Gama continued north up the east coast of Africa, reaching the farthest point traveled by Bartolomeu Dias in 1488 by late November and arriving at what is now known as Natal in South Africa on Christmas Day. Further up the coast, he met hostile receptions at Mozambique (March) and Mombasa (April) but was aided at Malindi. With the assistance of a pilot from India, da Gama sailed from Malindi across the Indian Ocean. The voyage took 27 days (23 of them spent out of sight of land).

Arriving a short distance north of Calicut on the southwestern coast of India on May 20, 1498, da Gama made his way to Calicut. Shortly thereafter, he met the area's Hindu leader *(samorim)* and presented him with a letter from the Portuguese monarch, King Manuel I (r. 1495–1521) in an attempt to negotiate a trade agreement. But relations with the *samorim* deteriorated, and on August 29, 1498, after three months at Calicut, da Gama began the difficult voyage home.

First, however, he worked his way north and careened his ships on Angediva Island south of Goa. After another three months at sea—this time in the Indian Ocean—da Gama reached the Somali coast but was unable to land at hostile Mogadishu. Sailing south, da Gama's expedition was once again well received at Malindi. After five days there, he continued on but was forced to abandon and destroy the *São Rafael* (after transferring men and supplies) because of a shortage of manpower. Da Gama stopped again at Angra de São Brás for provisions and then rounded the Cape of Good Hope, arriving near the Cape Verde Islands 27 days later. After reaching the island of Santiago, da Gama turned over the command of the *São Gabriel* to one João de Sá, rented a caravel, and with his dying brother Paulo sailed to the island of Terceira in the Azores.

Da Gama arrived in Lisbon in late-August or early-September 1499, seven to eight weeks after the first of the two surviving ships, the *Berrio*. He was lavishly rewarded by King Manuel, given the title of dom, named admiral of the Indian Seas, granted valuable emoluments, and promised the title of count.

In February 1502, da Gama again left Lisbon as leader of the fourth Portuguese expedition to India. This time he sailed with 20 ships (15 under his command and 5 under that of his brother Estêvão da Gama) and visited Sofala, Mozambique, and Kilwa (all on the eastern coast of Africa) en route. In India, da Gama avenged the massacre of some Portuguese in

Calicut during the visit of Pedro Alvares Cabral a year or so earlier and established a *feitoria*, or trading post, at Cochin. He departed from India on December 28, 1502, and reached Lisbon on September 1, 1503.

About 1507, da Gama transferred to the Order of Christ, and in 1519 he was created the first count of Vidigueira. In 1524, he made a third voyage to India, this time as viceroy, ordered by King John III (r. 1521–1557) to restore royal authority there. Sailing from Lisbon on April 9, 1524, with 14 ships (2 were lost en route), da Gama reached India on September 5 of that year. He died at Cochin on December 24 or 25, 1524.

—*Francis A. Dutra*

See also
Dias, Bartolomeu
For Further Reading
Albuquerque, Luís de. 1983. *Os descobrimentos Portugueses*. Lisbon: Publicações Alfa; Aragão, Augusto C. Teixeira de. 1898. *Vasco da Gama e a vidigueira. Estudo historico*. Lisbon: Imprensa Nacional; Peres, Damião. 1983. *História dos descobrimentos Portugueses*. Porto, Portugal: Vertente; Ravenstein, E. G., ed. 1898. *A Journal of the First Voyage of Vasco da Gama, 1497–1499*. London: Hakluyt Society.

GARDENS, SLAVE

Historically, masters have often allotted slaves and serfs small plots of land to cultivate, but it is difficult to trace this concept's early history. In the neo-Babylonian period, at least some slaves had gardens—even large fields and farms—and clay tablets record that Babylonian slaves raised dates, barley, wheat, chickpeas, lentils, garlic, onions, herbs, sesame, flax, and mustard in gardens and fields. But the large size of some of these enterprises means that they were a *peculium* type of business, one that is given into a slave's trust with the proceeds partly going to allow the slave to purchase freedom. In Babylonia, some slaves owned land that they could either rent or employ other slaves to work.

Romans associated the custom with *servi casati* ("hutted slaves"), who had a house and a small plot to grow their own food, as opposed to slaves kept in *cellae* ("cells") or *ergastulae*. The hutted slaves could presumably also sell produce for cash, to accumulate the money needed to buy their freedom. The Roman scholar Varro recommended that slaves be given women, huts, and land to make them less likely to escape. This type of slavery is sometimes seen as a step in the evolution of serfdom, which Pierre Dockes (1982) disputes. Yet he does liken the condition of hutted slaves to that of West Indian slaves, with each family having a hut and garden plot. Late-Roman and early-medieval hutted slaves in England worked both by the gang system and the task system. The *Rectitudines singularum personam* allotted Anglo-Saxon slaves a strip of land to grow vegetables as part of their yearly allowance, which also included beasts and measures of honey.

Slaves in Africa also had similar plots, and the custom persisted in the West Indies where larger islands had space enough for slaves to plant "provision grounds." One interdisciplinary study of Galways plantation on Montserrat yielded evidence of a large array of "economic plants" ranging from almond to thyme, and Lydia Pulsipher's study (1994) of Galways identifies three types of slave gardens: plantation-managed common grounds, where staple crops were grown to ensure that slaves were fed as the law required; remote mountain and ravine lands, where slaves grew produce and tree crops for "truck" (barter or cash sale at Sunday markets), usually illegally and clandestinely; and house gardens, including fruit trees and kitchen herbs. Slaves in Jamaica, Montserrat, and South Carolina developed complex "proto-peasant economies" based on their gardens' proceeds and the raising of animals like chickens and pigs.

The gardens and the traditional Sunday markets were an important part of the economy in most slave societies of the Americas. In the United States, law and custom prevented slaves from profiting too much from the "truck patches," and often they were forbidden to keep animals. In many places they were forbidden to sell produce to anyone but their owner, who was thereby assured of a constant supply of fresh produce, eggs, and the like. Crops included yams, sweet potatoes, okra, chili peppers, and sesame seeds. Charles Ball's narrative, one of the best nineteenth-century accounts, explains the crucial role of slave gardens as supplements to the diet, which was often dangerously low in green vegetables.

After emancipation, freedmen in the West Indies relied on their garden plots for necessities and scorned the "apprentice" wage system planned by the British government, which they saw as being similar to slavery. Large numbers of dislocated freedmen in the United States after the Civil War often squatted on deserted plantation land and planted small garden plots similar to the provision grounds they had tended before the war. Masters in many slave societies have regarded slave gardens as one way to reduce expenditures for rations, and slaves have seen them as a means to support families and make small sums of money.

—*Jim Comer*

See also
Peculium

For Further Reading

Danadamaev, Muhammad. 1984. *Slavery in Babylonia*. DeKalb: Northern Illinois University Press; Dockes, Pierre. 1982. *Medieval Slavery and Liberation*. Chicago: University of Chicago Press; Pulsipher, Lydia Mihelic. 1994. "Landscapes and Ideational Roles of Caribbean Slave Gardens." In *The Archaeology of Garden and Field*. Ed. Naomi Miller. Philadelphia: University of Pennsylvania Press; Varro. *Agriculture*. Quoted in Thomas Wiedemann. 1981. *Greek and Roman Slavery*. Baltimore: Johns Hopkins University Press.

GARNET, HENRY HIGHLAND (1815–1882)

A noted fugitive slave, abolitionist, clergyman, diplomat, and political activist, Henry Highland Garnet was one of the nineteenth century's most elusive and provocative African American leaders. His grandfather was a leader in West Africa's once powerful Mandingo empire, and Henry was the son of George and Henny (Henrietta) Garnet, who later changed her name to Elizabeth.

He was born a slave on a plantation in New Market, Kent County, Maryland, but when he was nine, his family, assisted by Quakers, escaped and moved to Pennsylvania. In 1826, the family moved to New York, and Garnet entered the famous African Free School #1. Later, Garnet enrolled in the Noyes Academy in New Canaan, New Hampshire, a school that was constructed during the height of intense racial agitation. In summer 1835, a mob of nearly 300 men, with perhaps 100 oxen, tore the building apart, leaving it in ruins.

Garnet continued his education at Oneida Theological Institute, near Utica, New York. There, under the tutelage of Rev. Theodore S. Wright, a Presbyterian minister, Garnet developed his intellectual skills and obtained his spiritual framework. His friendship with Wright greatly influenced Garnet's later career as an abolitionist and a minister.

Completing his theological training in 1840, Garnet moved to Troy, New York, where he became the minister of a local African American Presbyterian church, and he rapidly developed into an ardent abolitionist for the American Anti-Slavery Society. In 1843, Garnet delivered a speech in which he called for African slaves to rebel against their masters at a national convention of free black Americans in Buffalo, New York. This speech frightened the audience greatly, and many attending the convention refused to support Garnet's radical ideas. Frederick Douglass, a prominent leader in the African American community and Garnet's chief critic, was in attendance. Douglass disagreed with several major points in the speech and disapproved of Garnet's call for African slaves to use violence to end slavery.

The convention signaled the beginning of Garnet's decline as a prominent African American abolitionist and stimulated Douglass's rise as the new African American abolitionist leader. Still, Garnet did not give up his antislavery efforts entirely and even traveled overseas to promote the cause. In August 1850, he delivered an emotional speech as a delegate to the World Peace Congress, in Frankfurt, Germany, and in 1851, he gave several antislavery speeches to abolitionist organizations in England and Scotland.

As his abolitionist status declined, however, Garnet began devoting most of his energy to spreading the gospel. From 1843 to 1848 he was the minister of the Liberty Street Presbyterian Church in Troy, New York; in 1852, the United Presbyterian Church of Scotland sent him to Jamaica to spread Christianity; and in 1853, he became pastor of Jamaica's Stirling Presbyterian Church. A few years later, upon the death of Reverend Wright, Garnet returned to the United States to become the new pastor of New York's Shiloh Presbyterian Church.

During the Civil War, Garnet demanded that President Abraham Lincoln enlist the service of African Americans in the Union army, and he continued expressing this viewpoint despite the 1863 New York City race riot, which threatened his own safety. In 1864, Garnet moved to Washington, D.C., to become the pastor of the Fifteenth Street Presbyterian Church, and on several occasions his sermons attracted enormous biracial audiences. Having this pulpit encouraged Garnet to reactivate his antislavery message, and he traveled throughout the northeastern part of the United States to deliver inspirational sermons to battle-weary African American troops serving in the Union army. On February 12, 1865, Garnet delivered a sermon in the U.S. House of Representatives to celebrate the passage of the Thirteenth Amendment.

After the Civil War, Garnet held an administrative position with the Freedmen's Relief Association. This privately funded association, which was separate from the government-sponsored Freedmen's Bureau, sought to build schools and shelters in local African American communities in the United States. These facilities were designed to help African Americans adjust to their new status as free men and women.

In Washington, D.C., alone, the Freedmen's Relief Association had built 4 schools and 12 shelters by late 1865, and Garnet played an active role in developing one of these—the African Civilization Society School. Eventually, he became dissatisfied with the association's position on the role of African American teachers and withdrew his support.

Disillusioned by declining race relations within the United States, Garnet began to express an interest in Africa in the later years of his life. He had opposed colonization vigorously throughout the antebellum and Civil War years, but gradually, his views began to change. Undoubtedly, his change of heart stemmed partly from continuing racial problems within United States and partly from the inability of African Americans to move up the socioeconomic ladder during the Reconstruction era.

In 1881, President James Garfield appointed Garnet the minister and counsel general to Liberia, and in January 1882, Liberian President Edward Wilmot Blyden sponsored a dinner to honor Garnet. Many high-ranking government officials attended the celebration, and Garnet praised the many achievements of the Liberian people in the speech he gave at the ceremony. Following this event, his health declined, and on February 13, 1882, Garnet died in his sleep.

—Eric R. Jackson

See also
Abolition, United States; Liberia

For Further Reading
Brewer, W. M. 1928. "Henry Highland Garnet." *Journal of Negro History* 13 (1): 36–52; Pasternak, Martin B. 1995. *Rise Now and Fly to Arms: The Life of Henry Highland Garnet.* New York: Garland; Schor, Joel. 1977. *Henry Highland Garnet: A Voice of Black Radicalism in the Nineteenth Century.* Westport, CT: Greenwood; Stuckey, Sterling. 1988. "A Last Stern Struggle: Henry Highland Garnet and Liberation Theory." In *Black Leaders of the Nineteenth Century.* Ed. Leon Litwack and August Meier. Urbana: University of Illinois Press.

GARRETT, THOMAS (1789–1871)

An ardent abolitionist, Thomas Garrett made major contributions to the antislavery cause in the United States through his work with fugitive slaves. Tradition traces his concern for slaves to 1813 when kidnappers attempted to sell a female servant from the family home in Pennsylvania into slavery. The incident led Garrett to a prolonged period of volunteer service on behalf of escaping slaves, and building on his Quaker family's antislavery sentiment, Garrett provided skilled leadership, time, and money to the efforts of the abolition movement's Underground Railroad.

Although most Quakers held moderate antislavery views, Garrett allied with William Lloyd Garrison and his confrontational approach to the issue. After 1822,

Garrett lived and worked in Delaware, a border state whose population held mixed views on slavery. He asserted that there was as much antislavery sentiment in Delaware as in Boston, but only a few citizens were willing to join Garrett in his work with fugitives. He organized a small group of accomplices who provided food, transportation, and temporary shelter to escaping slaves, an endeavor so successful that it later contributed to the legend of a nationally organized network of Underground Railroad operatives.

Garrett claimed to have assisted 2,700 men and women to escape slavery. He worked closely with William Still, the African American chairman of the Philadelphia Vigilance Committee, which was an arm of the Pennsylvania Anti-Slavery Society. On several occasions Harriet Tubman escorted escaped slaves to Garrett's home, though he himself neither entered Southern states nor enticed slaves to leave their masters. Garrett's commitment to nonviolence did not prevent his advising fugitives to join the Union army. To one friend he wrote, "Am I naughty, being a professed non-resistant, to advise this poor fellow to serve Father Abraham?" (McGowan, 1977).

As a successful businessman, Garrett was largely immune from public criticism and physical attack, but not entirely. On one occasion he was nearly thrown from a train while trying to keep a woman from being sold into slavery. In 1848, Garrett and a coworker, John Hunn, were sued for damages for helping several slaves to escape. Roger B. Taney was one of two judges who heard the case, and both defendants were found liable for $54,000 in damages. An often-repeated story suggests Garrett's total impoverishment as a result, but actual court records show a compromise settlement of $1,500, enough to reduce Garrett's resources seriously but not enough to impoverish him. In 1860, the Maryland legislature proposed offering a $10,000 reward for Garrett's arrest, though the action was largely symbolic.

Following emancipation, Garrett worked for civil rights, woman suffrage, and temperance. After ratification of the Fifteenth Amendment to the Constitution, African Americans drove Garrett through Wilmington's streets in an open carriage under a banner that proclaimed, "Our Moses." Upon learning of Garrett's death, William Lloyd Garrison observed, "His rightful place is conspicuously among the benefactors, saviors, martyrs of the human race" (McGowan, 1977).

—Larry Gara

See also
Still, William; Tubman, Harriet; Underground Railroad
For Further Reading
Drake, Thomas E. 1938. "Thomas Garrett Quaker Abolitionist." In *Friends in Wilmington, 1738–1938.*

Ed. Edward P. Bartlett. Wilmington, OH: Clinton County Historical Society; McGowan, James A. 1977. *Station Master on the Underground Railroad: The Life and Letters of Thomas Garrett.* Moylan, PA: Whimsie Press; Still, William. 1883. *The Under-Ground Railroad.* Philadelphia: William Still.

GARRISON, WILLIAM LLOYD (1805–1879)

William Lloyd Garrison

William Lloyd Garrison was the most significant U.S. champion of immediate abolitionism. Born into poverty, Garrison had a lifelong empathy with the disadvantaged and oppressed. He was apprenticed to a printer at 13 and worked at various reform newspapers in New England until 1829 when he became coeditor of the newspaper *Genius of Universal Emancipation* in Baltimore, Maryland. Garrison's fervid antislavery editorials roused the anger of the local elite, and in January 1830, Garrison was jailed for libeling a slave trader. His plight caught the attention of philanthropist Arthur Tappan, who bailed him out of jail and provided partial financial support for Garrison to start a new antislavery paper, the *Liberator,* on January 1, 1831.

In the *Liberator,* Garrison abandoned the gradualist approach of most earlier opponents of slavery and embraced the new doctrine of abolitionism. Denying that slavery was a social and an economic problem of such great complexity that it might take years to abolish, Garrison said slavery was a matter of personal morality that could be remedied on an individual basis instantly. Slavery wrongfully denied blacks certain rights, and slaveholders should be asked to free their slaves immediately in the same way that they would be asked to immediately stop any other immoral action. Slaveholders should not be financially compensated for abandoning sin. The effort to colonize manumitted slaves in Africa reflected white prejudice and should be abandoned. Garrison proposed that blacks be given the same civil and political rights as white citizens of the United States.

The *Liberator* spoke to a generation of antislavery activists who were unhappy with the moral compromises involved in the old gradualist approach to emancipation. Soon after the *Liberator* began publication, abolitionism burst onto the scene with a suddenness that shocked Americans and alarmed slaveholders. Garrison played the leading role in galvanizing and organizing the new immediatists. Garrison's pamphlet, *Thoughts on African Colonization* (1832), rallied antislavery forces against the American Colonization Society, and he helped found the New England Anti-Slavery Society in 1832 and the American Anti-Slavery Society (AAS) in 1833.

Garrison endorsed several other controversial reforms that affected the antislavery movement. Embracing the doctrine of nonresistance, Garrison rejected the use of violence and coercive force and argued that many human relationships were, like slavery, based on violent coercion. Garrison believed that the power of religious denominations to compel adherence to creeds was a kind of slavery, and by the late 1830s, he had rejected organized religion.

Garrison also believed that government was an example of coercive force. Rejecting the moral authority of governments, Garrison argued that Christians needed no law but the higher law of God, and he refused on principle to vote. Understanding that most abolitionists would not follow his nonresistant principles, Garrison continued to speak out in the *Liberator* on political issues, telling others how to exercise the franchise if they believed in voting. Nevertheless, Garrison argued it was tactically wrong for abolitionists to concentrate their reform activities on the political world. The role of the abolitionist was, not to organize political parties, but to practice moral suasion, holding forth the standard of right and exhorting others to follow it.

Garrison applied his beliefs about human equality to gender relationships and encouraged the efforts of abolitionist women such as Sarah and Angelina Grimké to carve out a public role for themselves in the abolitionist movement. Such actions shocked the conventional morality of the nineteenth century and helped split the American Anti-Slavery Society in 1840. Members of the society argued about whether women should be able to vote and hold office within the AAS and whether abolitionists should organize a political party to accomplish their goals.

Ultimately, Garrison himself became an issue. Some abolitionists believed potential supporters were driven off by his positions on nonresistance and women's rights and by his increasingly unorthodox religious ideas and harsh denunciations of opponents. When Garrisonian abolitionists emerged with a majority from the society's convention in 1840, Garrison's opponents, led by Arthur and Lewis Tappan and James G. Birney, left the AAS and formed a rival organization, the American and Foreign Anti-Slavery Society.

While other abolitionists worked in the 1840s and 1850s to end slavery through political parties and religious organizations, Garrison played the roles of prophet and agitator. He remained a lonely voice crying out for truth and justice as he saw it and urging others to follow him. In 1843, Garrison proclaimed the U.S. Constitution a "Covenant with Death, an Agreement with Hell" (*Liberator*, March 17, 1843). Arguing that the Constitution protected slavery, Garrison urged Northerners to secede from the Union. Believing that slavery could not survive without the support of the federal government, Garrison believed that the disruption of the Union would strike a death blow to slavery.

The outbreak of the U.S. Civil War caused a change in Garrison's views and public standing. Heartened by the North's stand against the South, Garrison believed Northerners had been converted to antislavery, and he supported the effort to preserve the Union. Abraham Lincoln's decision to issue the Emancipation Proclamation prompted Garrison to violate his no-voting principle by casting a ballot for Lincoln's reelection in 1864. During the war, Garrison was transformed in the public's mind from crank to hero. At the end of the fighting, he was the government's guest of honor at the ceremony raising the U.S. flag over Fort Sumter. Believing his abolitionist work was largely done, Garrison ceased publication of the *Liberator* in 1865. Until his death, Garrison continued to lecture occasionally and to write essays for the *New York Independent* newspaper on various social reforms, including the rights of freed people.

—*Harold D. Tallant*

See also
Abolition, United States; American Colonization Society; The *Liberator*

For Further Reading
Kraditor, Aileen S. 1969. *Means and Ends in American Abolitionism: Garrison and His Critics on Strategy and Tactics, 1834–1850*. New York: Pantheon Books; Merrill, Walter M. 1963. *Against Wind and Tide: A Biography of William Lloyd Garrison*. Cambridge, MA: Harvard University Press; Stewart, James Brewer. 1992. *William Lloyd Garrison and the Challenge of Emancipation*. Arlington Heights, IL: Harlan Davidson; Thomas, John L. 1963. *The Liberator: William Lloyd Garrison*. Boston: Little, Brown and Company.

GEECHEE

The word Geechee (also spelled Geechie) is thought to be derived from an island in the Sierra Leone region of West Africa called "Kissee" or "Kissi" but pronounced "gee chee." The Gizzis, Kizzis, or Giggis were captured from the forest belt along Africa's windward coast (modern-day Sierra Leone and Liberia) and heavily populated the Sea Islands of Georgia. (Some Georgia residents have mistakenly believed that the name derived from the Ogeechee River, which empties into the Atlantic Ocean near Savannah.) The word Gullah is thought to be derived from the Gola peoples of the same region of Africa. Both Geechee and Gullah share many linguistic influences with the Fula, Mende, upper Guinea coast, and Gambia River areas.

The word has sometimes been used to describe the people of the Georgia Sea Islands who speak the Gullah language and share similar traditions, and often the words Gullah and Geechee are used interchangeably when speaking of Sea Islanders. There are approximately 125,000 speakers of Geechee and Gullah in the coastal region from Jacksonville, Florida, to Jacksonville, North Carolina, with smaller clusters in urban areas like New York City and other parts of the world.

The Geechee linguistic patterns and associated culture persist today although scholars have predicted their demise for the past century. The Geechee culture, like the Gullah, represents an important link between African American and African peoples who speak similarly; use like words and names; have common folktales, music, and food patterns; and create comparable crafts.

Geechee is also an English dialect spoken in the Southern part of the United States that is closely related to or stems from the Gullah language. African Americans who spoke this or any similar dialect were called "Geechee" derogatorily. In common parlance, to be called "Geechee" meant that you were a backward, ignorant, country, African American Southerner who ate rice every day.

—*Marquetta L. Goodwine*

See also
Gullah; Sea Islands
For Further Reading
Creel, Margaret Washington. 1988. *A Peculiar People: Slave Religion and Community-Culture among the Gullahs.* New York: New York University Press; Goodwine, Marquetta L. 1995. *Gullah/Geechee: The Survival of Africa's Seed in the Winds of the Diaspora.* Vol. 1, *St. Helena's Serenity.* New York: Kinship Publications; Montgomery, Michael, ed. 1994. *The Crucible of Carolina: Essays in the Development of Gullah Language and Culture.* Athens: University of Georgia Press; Turner, Lorenzo Dow. 1974. *Africanisms in the Gullah Dialect.* Ann Arbor: University of Michigan Press.

GENDER

Slavery inevitably involves a contradiction between the slaveholder's desire to reduce a human being to a thing without will and the practical impossibility of achieving this desire. Gender, a structuring principle of social relations in all societies, is one of the most fundamental ways that human beings have historically marked themselves as human. Accordingly, conflicts over slaveowners' efforts to reduce their slaves to a nonhuman status have often appeared in discussions about the extent to which masters recognized and acknowledged that their slaves were of different genders when they became enslaved.

The attempt to dehumanize and disempower slaves usually led slaveowners to attempt a partial "degendering" of slaves. Slave men were denied access to the privileges of manhood, most commonly and significantly by refusing them social recognition—and thus social support in exercising power—of their roles of husband and father, but also by forcing them to perform tasks that were considered "women's work" and occasionally by castrating them to create eunuchs. Enslaved men have also been subjected to sexual exploitation, being forced in classical antiquity, and probably in other slave societies, to engage in the "passive" and "unmanly" role in male-male intercourse.

Because women have almost always been considered as being lower on the human scale, the symbolic necessity to degender them when enslaved was generally less pressing. The powerlessness marked by their femininity has often been reinforced through sexual abuse and enforced reproduction. Nevertheless, in slave societies, where a woman's freedom from labor was a mark of privileged class status, female slaves provided much of the labor that allowed slaveowning women to attain ladyhood while the slaves themselves were denied the moral status of "woman."

Despite efforts at degendering, slaveowners never treated their slaves as absolutely ungendered. Even in slave societies where masters most nearly treated slaves as interchangeable units of capital, like the Caribbean sugar colonies, gender conventions of the masters' world led them to classify slaves by sex and to utilize male and female slaves differently. In most slave societies, including ancient Greece and Rome and most African slave systems, male and female slaves performed different types of work according to the gender division of labor governing unbonded people. In republican and imperial Rome, male slaves worked mainly on latifundia (large estates) and in the mines while women were domestic workers, prostitutes, concubines, urban traders, and artisans.

The plantation slave systems of the Americas constitute the major exception to the rule. There, some women worked alongside men in sugar, cotton, and coffee fields, doing work that was defined, and which defined them, as unfeminine. However, even in the Americas, a gender division of labor governed other work assignments, with skilled sugar-making tasks and most supervisory work assigned to men while women occupied positions of cook, nanny, and maid.

Since slave populations have, with few exceptions, been reproduced through external recruitment rather than natural reproduction, the divergent uses made of men and women slaves created significant imbalances in the sex ratio among slave populations. The earliest slaves, recruited from war captives, were usually women; a result of the exclusive assignment of military activity to men by most societies throughout history. In ancient Greece, most slaves (who constituted a relatively small proportion of the population) apparently were women, but by the time classical Greece and Rome became economically dependent on slavery, a high proportion of the slaves were men performing agricultural work.

In African slave systems, slaves were mostly always women, not because their primary function was reproductive, but because African societies made much greater use of women's labor than of men's and thus women slaves were more useful. Slavery in the Islamic world was also primarily a female phenomenon, although men occupied some high-status slave positions, and most female slaves were concubines and menial domestic workers, living demonstrations of the importance and wealth of powerful men.

Men outnumbered women slaves throughout the

This European representation of an African slave family emphasizes female fecundity, an increasingly important concern to New World slaveowners once the outlawing of the slave trade in the nineteenth century removed that means of replenishing the slave population.

Africa and the Islamic world, the children of a slave woman and her master were free and incorporated into the master's lineage, often as rulers or advisers to rulers. In these societies, slave women tended to have less autonomy in socializing their children. In matters not affecting the economic and social functions of slaves, slave communities could develop gendered practices that diverged substantially from those of their masters. For example, in the U.S. South and Brazil, the slaves' norms governing sexual relationships differed significantly from those of the white population.

The slaves' gender conventions could lead to some of the most intense daily struggles between slaveowners and slaves, and such struggles fell along two major axes: first, situations in which slaves demanded to be treated according to gender conventions that they shared with their masters and, second, situations in which slaves struggled to be allowed to live according to their own gender conventions. The complaints of women slaves about being stripped naked for punishment or of being abused by overseers, who called them "bitch" or "whore," fell into the first category. Struggles of this type appealed to abolitionists, who found slavery's distortion of "proper" gender relations to be one of its most horrible aspects. Abolitionists were far less sympathetic to struggles of the second type, which included efforts by enslaved African women to be allowed to nurse their babies for longer than Europeans considered normal or the practice of polygyny (having more than one wife or mate at a time) by African and African American slaves in many parts of the Americas. Most abolitionists considered those efforts to indicate either the corruption of slaves by slavery or the lesser level of civilization reached by Africans.

How has the subordination of women been related, historically and logically, to the institution of slavery? Many slave societies have been strongly patriarchal, manifesting intense gender and generational hierarchies within the free population and between masters and slaves. The slave societies of fifth-century Athens, classical Rome, the antebellum U.S. South, the medieval Islamic empire, and Brazil as both colony and empire all shared this characteristic. This similarity was not mere coincidence but generated by the relations of honor, dishonor, and dependency built into slavery—the honor and respect paid the master through the accumulation of people dependent upon and subordinate to him (or occasionally her). Slaves, through their own dishonor and powerlessness, increased the master's honor and power. Free wives and children, if sufficiently subordinated, fulfilled a similar function. In those societies in which the honor-producing function of slavery was most completely subordinated to the economic goal of commodity production, like the Caribbean sugar islands, gender hierarchy among the free population was far less extreme.

Americas, with the exception of the U.S. South after the mid-eighteenth century, where the only naturally reproducing slave population in the hemisphere produced a roughly even sex ratio. Although women were used for fieldwork, American slaveowners preferred purchasing men, believing (probably wrongly) that they were stronger and more effective workers. The predominance of men in the transatlantic slave trade also resulted from the African and Islamic preferences for female slaves, which created a surplus of men available for the Atlantic slave trade.

The gender aspects of slave life and culture should not be understood as the mechanical effect of sex ratios or merely the result of the slaveowners' efforts. Enslaved people brought their own gender conventions and meanings with them to their enslavement and endeavored to reproduce those conventions. In societies where the children were also enslaved, slave women usually socialized their children into masculine and feminine roles. In some slave societies, particularly in

The connection between slavery and women's subordination was made by many living in slave societies. Aristotle argued that those he considered to be natural slaves were subordinate to their masters as wives were subordinate to their husbands. Analogies between the status of wives and the status of slaves built upon each other through time, and in the nineteenth century such analogies were utilized by abolitionists and proslavery theorists with similar intensity. Many of the former, especially those who were women, became feminists through their experience in the struggle against slavery while many defenders of slavery pointed to the inevitable disruption in gender relations that would result if slavery were destabilized.

The fact that free women in slave societies lived in a situation of subordination structured and reinforced by slavery should not lead us to imagine a natural alliance between those free women and the slaves whose labor directly generated their wealth. Evidence from the U.S. South and Brazil suggests that mistresses could be even harsher in their daily interactions with slaves than were their husbands. Slaveowning women, in all but a few cases, actively supported slavery and performed the tasks necessary to sustain it on a daily basis.

—*Diana Paton*

See also
Concubinage; Eunuchs; Prostitution; Women and the Antislavery Movement
For Further Reading
Morrissey, Marietta. 1989. *Slave Women in the New World: Gender Stratification in the Caribbean.* Lawrence: University Press of Kansas; Patterson, Orlando. 1991. *Freedom: Freedom in the Making of Western Culture.* New York: Basic Books; Robertson, Claire C., and Martin A. Klein, eds. 1983. *Women and Slavery in Africa.* Madison: University of Wisconsin Press; White, Deborah Gray. 1985. *Ar'n't I a Woman?: Female Slaves in the Plantation South.* New York: Norton.

GENERAL ABOLITION BILL (1807)

The General Abolition Bill, which became law in 1807, ended the slave trade within the British Empire. Although slavery as an institution remained legal in British territory until 1833, the General Abolition Bill marked the first major victory for antislavery forces within Britain and ended nearly 30 years of legislative battles over banning the trade. The bill also began the process that eventually resulted in slavery's abolition within the

empire and Britain's attempts to suppress the African slave trade worldwide.

The British abolitionist movement had become a powerful political force by the 1780s, but equally powerful economic interests fought to retain the slave trade. West Indian planters and merchants involved in the trade waged a vigorous parliamentary defense of the system through numerous debates on the subject. Planters argued that three-fifths of the West Indian economy relied on slavery and that eliminating the source of new labor would ruin the colonial economy and cause sugar shortages within Great Britain. Simultaneously, merchants involved in transporting slaves argued the trade's economic importance. By the 1780s, Britain had 14 slave factories on the West African coast and was the largest slave supplier to the Western Hemisphere. Traders also argued that if Britain unilaterally abolished involvement in the slave trade, other nations would take its place.

Nonetheless, public opinion began to turn against the slave trade. Upon establishment of the Society for Effecting the Abolition of the Slave Trade (1787), various British antislavery trade elements coordinated their efforts and in 1789, the society launched regular mass campaigns to mobilize public opinion against the trade.

Parliamentarians like William Wilberforce, Charles Fox, and Henry Thornton formed a House of Commons coalition that initiated a series of bills which ultimately culminated in the 1807 act. In 1788, Parliament passed a measure officially limiting the number of slaves that could be transported on a single ship (although enforcement of this law was ineffectual). A 1789 Privy Council report on the slave trade containing vivid reports of slavery's brutality further galvanized Parliament's antislavery forces. In spring 1791, supporters introduced a bill to end the slave trade, but the House of Commons defeated it by a vote of 163 to 88.

In 1792, abolitionists passed a bill, by a vote of 230 to 85, calling for the gradual abolition of the trade. The House of Commons fixed the targeted abolition date as 1796, but the more conservative House of Lords blocked the measure's implementation and with the outbreak of war with France, abolition of the trade became secondary to the war effort. Wilberforce shepherded another abolition bill through the House of Commons in 1796. This bill shared the fate of the earlier abolition measure when it also fell in the House of Lords, although the cabinet passed an Order in Council prohibiting Britain from establishing slavery in those colonies acquired as a result of the Napoleonic Wars.

Not until 1804 would Wilberforce introduce another abolition bill, and this measure failed in the House of Commons by a vote of 77 to 70. Prime Minister William Pitt, who wanted to forestall debate over the ban until conclusion of the war with France, died in 1806. His government was replaced by a coalition led by Charles Fox and another abolitionist, William Grenville. A measure replacing the Order in Council ban against the spread of slavery into new colonies with a parliamentary decree passed both houses with overwhelming support. Additionally, Parliament passed a law prohibiting ships from engaging in the slave trade unless they were presently employed in the trade.

The success of these measures led abolitionists to realize that at Parliament's new session in 1807 they could succeed in passing legislation to end the trade completely. Consequently, it was important to craft the potential bill as effectively as possible. The measure that became law as the General Abolition Bill not only prohibited the slave trade but also contained measures to suppress the trade and contemplated the fate of freed slaves. British subjects engaged in the trade would be fined £100 for each slave bought, sold, or transported, and British ships used in the trade would be confiscated by the government. Insurance companies issuing contracts on ships or property used in the trade would also be penalized. The bill also established a bounty system that paid commissions to British soldiers and sailors for captured slave ships and for each freed slave. Freed slaves became crown wards, and eventually measures were taken to resettle those former slaves, who could not be returned to their point of capture, in crown colonies like Sierra Leone.

On January 2, 1807, Grenville introduced the General Abolition Bill to the House of Lords, where it carried on a vote of 100 to 36. In the House of Commons, the bill passed on a vote of 283 to 16, and the king gave his assent to the measure on March 25. The bill took effect on January 1, 1808.

Upon implementing the ban, Britain immediately dispatched two ships to begin patrolling West Africa's coast to intercept slave traders. In 1811, Parliament strengthened the ban equating involvement in the slave trade with piracy, and when the Napoleonic Wars ended in 1815, the antislavery squadron was increased in size dramatically. Although these measures produced a dramatic decrease in overt British participation in the trade, most slave traders shifted their ships' flags to those of nations still permitting the trade. Only after prolonged diplomatic and military efforts were the British able to suppress the trade successfully in the late-nineteenth century.

—*Tom Lansford*

See also
Closing of the African Slave Trade; Sierra Leone; Wilberforce, William

For Further Reading
Coupland, Reginald. 1964. *The British Anti-Slavery Movement*. New York: Barnes and Noble; Donnan, Elizabeth, ed. 1931. *Documents Illustrative of the History of the Slave Trade to America*. Washington, D.C.: Carnegie; Inikori, Joseph, and Stanley Engerman, eds. 1992. *The Atlantic Slave Trade: Effects on Economies, Societies, and Peoples in Africa, the Americas, and Europe*. Durham, NC: Duke University Press; Miers, Suzanne. 1975. *Britain and the Ending of the Slave Trade*. New York: Longman.

GENOVESE, EUGENE (1930–)

*P*rominent historian and author of numerous monographs, Eugene Genovese more than any other historian has used Marxian theory to analyze slavery in the United States and the antebellum South. With Herbert Aptheker and Raimondo Luraghi, Genovese argues that the slave labor system was the Old South's distinguishing feature. Slavery retarded capitalism's development, created a powerful class of planter elite, and inevitably led to the U.S. Civil War. "Slavery," Genovese wrote in his first work, "gave the South a social system and a civilization with a distinct class structure, political community, economy, ideology, and a set of psychological patterns and . . . as a result, the South increasingly grew away from the rest of the nation and from the rapidly developing sections of the world" (in *The Political Economy of Slavery* [1961]).

A graduate of Brooklyn College and Columbia University, where he earned a Ph.D. under the supervision of Richard B. Morris, Genovese almost single-handedly challenged much of the accepted wisdom on the antebellum South. Whereas historians had increasingly focused on the similarities between North and South, arguing that the Civil War had been the ghastly mistake of a "blundering generation," Genovese elaborated the striking contrasts between the two sections of the country. In his pathbreaking book *The Political Economy of Slavery: Studies in the Economy and Society of the Slave South* (1961), Genovese explored how "slavery gave the South a special way of life" that made it a distinct section of the nation. Borrowing from the so-called Hegelian Marxism of Antonio Gramsci, Genovese explained Southern planter control over both black slaves and the white yeomanry as being a result of cultural hegemony. The yeomanry "went against its apparent collective interests" in large measure because the planter class disguised its domination behind a mask of race solidarity. Some whites might have nothing but freedom, but they were not slaves.

Genovese's conviction that slavery proved the great distinguishing characteristic of the Old South led him to undertake focused studies on both slaves and slave-owners. In *Roll, Jordan, Roll: The World the Slaves Made* (1972), he asserts that slaves "laid the foundations for a separate black national culture while enormously enriching American culture as a whole." In this pioneering work, the author incisively demonstrates how slaves often imaginatively responded to an odious and oppressive system. With a mixture of accommodation and resistance, including petty theft and arson, slaves succeeded in maintaining at least some measure of human dignity in the face of great hardship while simultaneously establishing autonomous black cultural institutions. Meticulously researched, *Roll, Jordan, Roll* offers an extraordinarily detailed panorama of black, religious, linguistic, and familial cultural formations. Genovese concludes that for all its African roots, "separate black national culture has always been American."

Of all his work, Genovese's examination of the planter class has drawn the most criticism. Although his development of the notion of planter "paternalism," a precapitalist, protective stance toward slaves, has gained wide acceptance, Genovese's generous view of the paternalistic slaveowner has also engendered much skepticism. In works remarkably reminiscent of Ulrich B. Phillips in the early-twentieth century, Genovese has offered a surprisingly sympathetic portrait of the anticapitalist, patrician planter class. More remarkably still, Genovese later maintained his admiration for the planter elite while simultaneously renouncing his former Marxist convictions.

Spanning four decades, the work of Eugene Genovese has contributed enormously to the understanding of the antebellum South. By documenting in rich detail the remarkable, uniquely American, and deeply complex development of masters and slaves, slavery and freedom, Genovese has forcefully demonstrated the centrality of slavery to the history of the U.S. South.

—*Peter S. Field*

See also
Aptheker, Herbert; Fox-Genovese, Elizabeth; Phillips, Ulrich Bonnell

For Further Reading
Aptheker, Herbert. 1943. *American Negro Slave Revolts.* New York: Columbia University Press; Frederickson, George. 1981. *White Supremacy: A Comparative Study in American and South African History.* New York: Oxford University Press; Luraghi, Raimondo. 1978. *The Rise and Fall of the Plantation South.* New York: New Viewpoints; Morgan, Edmund. 1975. *American Slavery, American Freedom: The Ordeal of Colonial Virginia.* New York: Norton.

GEORGIA

In 1732, King George II chartered the British colony of Georgia and put it under the direction of a group of British gentlemen, the Georgia trustees. The trustees hoped that their colony would provide a haven for Britain's unemployed and Europe's persecuted Protestants and that they could settle in towns and produce luxury commodities, like silk and wine, for a British market. Prohibiting African slavery was essential to the trustees' plan, for they believed that slavery would jeopardize the colony's safety by making slaves an internal threat and making slave masters both lazy and ungovernable.

The prohibition on slavery caused immediate controversy. In 1735, several Lowland Scots petitioned the trustees to allow slavery, arguing that white servants were more expensive, performed less labor, and were more unsuited to Georgia's climate than African slaves. Despite or perhaps because of proslavery agitation, the trustees secured royal approval for an act that officially prohibited colonists from keeping African slaves within the colony, although the act remained silent about the enslavement of Native Americans.

Official policies notwithstanding, proslavery sentiment continued to grow. In 1738, most of Savannah's white men signed a petition asking the trustees to allow slaves. However, counterpetitions from German and Highland Scottish colonists defended the prohibition, and the trustees remained adamant. Unsuccessful, the proslavery faction retreated to South Carolina—but also sent an agent to London to influence the British Parliament against the trustees.

The agent, Thomas Stephens, circulated a number of proslavery pamphlets, one of which argued that slaves were "as essentially necessary to the cultivation of Georgia, as axes, hoes, or any other utensil of agriculture" (Wood, 1984). Although Stephens's effort was ineffective, a loss of interest in Georgia on the part of the trustees weakened enforcement of their policies during the 1740s, and by 1747, Georgia magistrates were overlooking the ban on slavery. In 1750, the trustees repealed the prohibition on slavery, and they surrendered their charter in 1752.

After the withdrawal of the trustees from the colony's affairs, Georgia adopted South Carolina's slave code almost entirely. The number of slaves in the colony grew from about 600, 14 percent of the total population, in 1752 to 15,000, or 50 percent of the total population, in 1775. Many Georgia slaves arrived with their masters from South Carolina, and some came from the West Indies, but they were not imported directly from Africa until 1766. Georgia's dependence on South Carolina for slaves ensured that Georgia would inherit the unique culture of Afro-Carolinians, meaning task labor, a relatively high level of slave autonomy, and a Creole language, Gullah. Rice and indigo cultivation, mostly along the coast, dominated Georgia slavery.

The British occupation of Savannah during the American Revolution dramatically affected slavery in Georgia. Early promises of freedom for slaves who joined the British turned the conflict into a violent civil war. Some slaves became British supporters, and all slaves became potential plunder for patriot and loyalist bands. During the war, approximately 10,000 slaves died, escaped, or were captured by the British. Those who remained enjoyed an unprecedented level of autonomy. With their masters either absent from home or unwilling to grow crops without a market, the slaves were free to grow provisions and cotton for themselves.

After peace in 1783, Georgia's rice planters were eager to modernize their production methods but faced a severe labor shortage. They imported many slaves from Africa and from other states, and Georgia's slave population reached 20,000 in 1787 and nearly 30,000 by 1790. White immigrants also flooded into Georgia, bringing or buying additional slaves, to grow tobacco and provision crops on farms and small plantations in the up-country.

After Eli Whitney introduced the cotton gin in 1793, short-staple cotton cultivation in the piedmont supplemented rice cultivation in the low country. Plantations in the up-country varied greatly in size and in patterns of slave management. Although planter control over cotton-field workers increased with time, slaves continued an independent production of provisions for market in both rice and cotton.

The Civil War brought emancipation to Georgia's slaves. Gen. William T. Sherman's march from Atlanta to Savannah in late 1864 drew many slaves to the Union lines and freedom. Sherman granted freed people exclusive possession of the Savannah low country and proposed that 40 acres be allotted to each family. On the ashes of the wealthiest plantation region in the United States, these freedmen and women began constructing a society of free families on small farms, after 120 years of slavery in Georgia.

—*Gary L. Hewitt*

See also
Oglethorpe, James Edward
For Further Reading
Mohr, Clarence L. 1986. *On the Threshold of Freedom: Masters and Slaves in Civil War Georgia*. Athens: University of Georgia Press; Reidy, Joseph P. 1992. *From Slavery to Agrarian Capitalism in the Cotton Plantation South: Central Georgia, 1800–1880*. Chapel Hill: University of North Carolina Press; Smith, Julia Floyd. 1985. *Slavery and Rice Culture in Low Country Georgia, 1750–1860*. Knoxville: University of Tennessee Press; Wood, Betty. 1984. *Slavery in Colonial Georgia, 1730–1775*. Athens: University of Georgia Press.

GEORGIA CODE
(1861)

Georgia was the first jurisdiction in the United States to codify the common law. Although Dakota Territory (1866), California (1872), and Montana (1895) later adopted codes, and other states (notably Massachusetts and New York) debated codification proposals, the Georgia Code (1861) represents the only systematic attempt to incorporate slavery into the legal framework of a common law jurisdiction. (Louisiana based its code on the French civil law system rather than common law.)

In December 1858, the Georgia legislature created a three-member commission with a broad mandate to compile all laws of the state, whether based on statute or common law, into a code covering political organization, private law, penal law, and rules of procedure. The commissioners began preparing a code "which should embody the great fundamental principles of our jurisprudence, from whatever source derived, together with such Legislative enactments of the State as the wants and circumstances of our people had from time to time shown to be necessary and proper."

Thomas R. R. Cobb, a leading Athens attorney and University of Georgia law professor, drafted the code's private and penal law sections. Having written *A Historical Sketch of Slavery from the Earliest Period* (1858) and a digest of Georgia's common law, Cobb was well suited to integrate slavery into private law. He was also a prominent member of the Confederate Constitutional Convention, served as a brigadier general in the Confederate army, and died in the Battle of Fredericksburg. David Irwin and Richard H. Clark, the other commissioners, were primarily responsible for the remaining portions of the code.

The Georgia legislature passed the code on December 19, 1860, to take effect on January 1, 1862. Georgia's secession in 1861 required an extensive revision of the code and accounts for the code's name. Irwin revised the code again in 1867 to take into account the end of the Confederacy and of slavery. Comparing the 1861 and 1867 versions of the code shows the effect of the end of slavery on private law.

The foundation of the code's view of slavery is its classification of all persons into five categories: citizens, residents who are not citizens, aliens, slaves, and free persons of color. The code defined a slave as "one over whose person, liberty, labor and property another has legal control." The code made slavery the default status of blacks: all "negros and mulattos" were "prima facie slaves" and required to prove their free status if they claimed they were not slaves. Slaves could not legally hold property or make contracts independent of their masters. Slaves were a form of chattel property, and the rules governing such property applied to them "except where the nature of the property requires a modification of the ordinary rule." The "state of slavery" did not eliminate the natural right to life and limbs.

The code's provisions concerning free persons of color contained an implicit justification of slavery based on an assumption of the mental inferiority of blacks. An extensive set of laws governed free persons of color, requiring that they have legal guardians, restricting their ability to make contracts, and requiring their registration with the county in which they resided. The only legal difference between a free person of color and a slave was that the former was "entitled to the free use of his liberty, labor and property, except so far as he is restrained by law." All laws concerning slaves also applied to free persons of color unless specifically exempted.

Although free persons of color over age 20 could sell themselves into slavery, the code barred manumission within Georgia except by legislative act. (Masters could send slaves out of state to be freed.) Provisions in wills and other agreements that attempted to free a deceased's slaves were void, and title to the slaves concerned passed as if the provisions were not present.

The code contained comprehensive provisions for the direct regulation of slavery. It also provided detailed rules governing private law areas such as contracts for the hiring of slaves, the treatment of slaves during life tenancies, will provisions concerning slaves, gifts of slaves, and torts (wrongful acts) committed by slaves. Because of its systematic approach to private law based on common law, the Georgia Code offers a unique opportunity to study slavery's effect on private law.

—*Andrew P. Morriss*

For Further Reading
The Code of the State of Georgia. 1861. Prepared by R. H. Clark, T. R. R. Cobb, and D. Irwin; *The Code of the State of Georgia.* 1867. Revised and corrected by David Irwin; Morriss, Andrew P. 1995. "'This State Will Soon Have Plenty of Laws'—Lessons from One Hundred Years of Codification in Montana." *Montana Law Review* 56:3 59–450; Smith, Marion. 1930. "The First Codification of the Substantive Common Law." *Tulane Law Review* 4: 178–189.

GERMAN COAST UPRISING
(1811)

*I*n January 1811, the worst nightmare of Louisiana's planter class became reality. A massive slave revolt occurred in St. Charles and St. John the Baptist Parishes, an area located about 40 miles upriver from New Orleans. The region was known as the German Coast because of its initial European settlers. Estimates of the number of slaves involved in the revolt vary from 150 to perhaps 500, but regardless of the number, the event caused widespread panic in the Territory of Orleans and warranted worldwide attention.

On the evening of January 8, slaves on Manual Andry's Woodlawn plantation attacked Andry and his son, killing the latter and wounding Andry. The slaves then began marching downriver, pillaging, burning buildings, and recruiting more slaves as they went. White residents in the region were terrified. Many sought refuge in New Orleans while others hid in the woods as the mob approached their homes. Only two white people were killed, Andry's son and Jean-Francois Trepagnier, who was killed while confronting the mob at his plantation. The beginning of the revolt seemed well planned, with leaders on horseback directing its movement, but organization deteriorated as the revolt grew. Evidence suggests one primary leader—Charles Deslondes, a mulatto slave, possibly of Saint Domingue origin, who was temporarily in the service of Andry.

After surviving the attack on his plantation, Manual Andry notified U.S. authorities of the insurrection and within 25 hours had organized a militia of nearly 80 men and set out after the slaves. The governor of the Territory of Orleans, William C. C. Claiborne, was informed, and he immediately dispatched Gen. Wade Hampton, commander in chief of the U.S. troops in the southern division, who was by coincidence visiting New Orleans at the time. An additional force of 200 regular soldiers was sent from Baton Rouge under the command of Maj. Homer Virgil Milton. The forces led by Andry, Hampton, and Milton converged on the slaves on the morning of January 11 near Francois Bernard Bernoudi's plantation. The result was more a massacre than a battle. Armed only with cane knives, axes, and a few small arms, the slaves were no match for the well-armed militia that surrounded them. Estimates regarding casualties vary, but at least 60 slaves were killed and countless others wounded.

On the afternoon of January 13, the trial began for the slaves who were captured. Held at the nearby Destrehan plantation, the proceedings were directed by St. Charles Parish judge Pierre Bauchet St. Martin. For the next two days the court listened to testimony from

30 of the accused. Twenty-one were found guilty and were sentenced to death. As a brutal example to others who might disturb the social order, their corpses were beheaded and the heads placed on posts along the German Coast.

From the trial testimony it is difficult to ascertain a specific cause for the insurrection other than the slaves' obvious hatred of the system that held them captive. Perhaps the idea of rebellion had been imported to the region in 1809 when more than 9,000 refugees from Saint Domingue settled in Louisiana. They had been expelled from Cuba in reaction to the war between France and Spain and had witnessed the successful Saint Domingue slave revolt in 1791. Among the 9,000 refugees were 3,000 slaves and over 3,000 free people of color. In addition, some evidence suggests that the leaders of the rebellion had been influenced by runaway slaves, often referred to as "outlyers," who lived by their own means on the fringes of the plantations.

In response to the insurrection, the territorial legislature completely reorganized the militia, something Governor Claiborne had been urging since 1806, in the hope that it would be more responsive to internal threats. To strengthen security in the territory further, the federal government stationed a regular-army regiment at New Orleans and sent three gunboats to add to the existing naval force in the region. Perhaps the revolt's most important outcome was that it intensified the state of tension brought about by the slave economy and raised doubts in the minds of many people as to whether or not that type of economy could be maintained.

—*Mark Cave*

For Further Reading
Dormon, John H. 1977. "The Persistent Specter: Slave Rebellion in Territorial Louisiana." *Louisiana History* 18: 389–404; Rodriguez, Junius Peter, Jr. 1992. "Ripe for Revolt: Louisiana and the Tradition of Slave Insurrection, 1803–1865." Ph.D. dissertation, Department of History, Auburn University, Auburn, Alabama.

GHANA, KINGDOM OF

Situated on the bend of the upper Niger River, the Kingdom of Ghana at its peak stretched west to the Senegal River, south to the gold-producing region of Bambuk, and as far north as the Berber trading center of Awdaghost. Founded by the Soninke (Sarakolle) branch of the Mandingo people of West Africa, ancient Ghana's exact beginnings are unknown, but it probably existed by the fifth century A.D., and descriptions of ancient Ghana began appearing in Muslim scholarly writing by the eighth century. The Arab geographer, al-Fazari, writing in the eighth century, described the kingdom of Ghana as "the land of gold" (Levtzion, 1973). Ancient Ghana had reached its peak by the eleventh century and lasted until its conquest and incorporation into the Kingdom of Mali during the early-thirteenth century.

Ghana's capital, Kumbi Saleh, was divided into two sections: one, a Muslim and commercial town and the other, lying six miles away, the royal town where the king and his subjects lived. The Muslim traders, mostly Berbers from North Africa, brought not only trade but also the Islamic faith to the Kingdom of Ghana.

The kingdom was a major commercial center in the trans-Saharan trade. Indeed, ancient Ghana's rise to power and fame in West Africa's savanna belt is largely credited to the critical role it played in that trade. Strategically located between the Sahara and North Africa to the north and the gold-bearing region south of the savanna, the Kingdom of Ghana enjoyed the enviable role of middleman in the lucrative trans-Saharan trade. Trans-Saharan trade routes linked the kingdom with traders from North Africa, and trade routes to the south brought Ghana's merchants into contact with the gold-producing region of West Africa. Ghana's rulers profited from taxes levied on trade items entering and leaving the kingdom.

Gold remained the primary commodity in this trade from Ghana, but slaves, destined for faraway markets in North Africa and elsewhere, were also sold. Ancient Ghana obtained slaves through purchase and by raiding neighboring peoples and states. The Arab scholar al-Idrisi, writing in the twelfth century, confirmed that "the people of Barisa, Silla, Takrur and Ghana raid the country of the Lamlam, capture its inhabitants, and bring them to their own countries, where they sell them to merchants who come there. The latter export them to other countries" (Levtzion, 1973).

Domestic slavery was also practiced in the Kingdom of Ghana, with slaves employed in various occupations, including service in the royal household and as porters in the trans-Saharan trade. The scholar al-Bakri described a court scene in which the king of Ghana had standing behind him "ten slaves carrying shields and swords mounted with gold and wearing costly garments" (Oliver and Fagan, 1975).

In 1076, the Kingdom of Ghana was invaded by the Almoravids, a Muslim group seeking to impose true Islam in Ghana but also to recapture the commercial city of Awdaghost, and the Almoravid invasion marked the beginning of the decline of the kingdom. Ghana's tributary states took advantage of the invasion to sever ties, which weakened the kingdom, and although Ghana subsequently regained possession of the kingdom from the Almoravids, it remained a much weaker state. In 1203, Sumanguru Kante of the Soso state (a former tributary state of ancient Ghana) conquered Ghana and sacked Kumbi Saleh, which precipitated an exodus of merchants and scholars from Ghana. Soso rule over ancient Ghana was short-lived, as in 1235, Sundiata conquered Sumanguru's kingdom and incorporated it, along with the remainder of ancient Ghana, into the rising Kingdom of Mali.

—*Patience Essah*

For Further Reading
Ajayi, J. F. A., and Michael Crowder, eds. 1971. *History of West Africa.* London: Longman; Levtzion, Nehemiah. 1973. *Ancient Ghana and Mali.* London: Methuen; Oliver, Ronald, and Brian M. Fagan. 1975. *Africa in the Iron Age: c. 500 B.C. to A.D. 1400.* Cambridge: Cambridge University Press.

GHULAMS

*G*hulām (Arabic plural, *ghilmān*) is an Arabic word literally meaning "youth." In practice, *ghulāms* were elite slaves recruited from non-Muslim populations, not unlike *mamluks* or *devsirme* recruits in the Ottoman Empire. In fact, the term *ghulām* was often virtually synonymous with *mamluk.*

The Abbasid empire, which ruled the Islamic heartland from Baghdad from 750 to 1258, first institutionalized this type of elite slavery in the eighth century. Abbasid elite slaves were known variously as *mamluks* and *ghulāms,* although the former term was more commonly applied to them. Notwithstanding, the procedure for recruiting *mamluks* and *ghulāms* was similar: young men and boys were purchased from neighboring non-Muslim territories—in the Abbasid case, the central Asian steppe—brought to the capital; converted to Islam; given a religious, military, and literary education; and ultimately manumitted, whereupon they could attain high court positions. The rationale for this practice was that nonnative slaves would be bound by no family or community ties and would be loyal solely to the ruler who had enslaved them.

The polity best known for erecting a *ghulām,* as opposed to a *mamluk,* institution was that of the Seljuks of Rum, a Turkic people who migrated from the central Asian steppe into Iran and Iraq early in the eleventh century. The main Seljuk force occupied Baghdad in 1055 and established the so-called Great Seljuk sultanate, which continued to recognize the Abbasid caliph as spiritual leader. As the Great Seljuk state disintegrated early in the twelfth century, a Seljuk offshoot established the sultanate of Rum in central and eastern Anatolia, with its capital at Konya. The Rum sultanate survived until the Mongol invasions of the thirteenth century, which reduced it to political insignificance.

From the outset, the Rum Seljuks staffed their armies and palace bureaucracy with *ghulāms.* The key distinction of the *ghulām* in this society was youth: as the name implies, *ghulāms* were enslaved while still relatively young boys; a *mamluk,* in contrast, was often a mature adult. In this sense, the Seljuk *ghulām* institution resembled the Ottoman *devsirme* more closely than the *mamluk* system. It has been suggested that the Seljuks occasionally employed a version of the *devsirme* by enslaving young boys from non-Muslim populations under their rule, primarily Greeks in former Byzantine territory, even though such a practice technically violated Muslim law. This Seljuk practice may even have offered a model for the Ottoman *devsirme.*

Several manumitted *ghulāms* became prominent courtiers and military commanders of the Rum Seljuk state. Many of them were also adept in belles lettres, the religious sciences, and mysticism, and later in life, these *ghulāms* endowed some of the sultanate's great religious institutions. The architect of the İnce Minare *madrasa,* a Muslim academy in Konya, was originally a Greek *ghulām,* as was Celaleddin Karatay, a Seljuk courtier who ultimately adopted the life of an ascetic mystic, or *sūfī.* He became a follower of the great thirteenth-century mystics Umar al-Suhrawardi and Celaleddin Rumi. Karatay likewise built a *madrasa* in Konya; it is now a ceramics museum, and Karatay is entombed there in a simple coffin topped with a green *sūfī* turban.

Although female elite slavery in the Rum sultanate has received far less scrutiny than the parallel institution in Ottoman, Mamluk, or even Abbasid societies, it appears that the Seljuks recruited slave girls through much the same process by which they recruited *ghulāms;* hence, these slave girls might be termed *ghulāmas.* Apart from the fact that they received no military training, their conversion and education appear to have been similar to that of their male counterparts.

Like Ottoman slave women, the Seljuk *ghulāmas* could acquire wealth and prestige through concubinage and marriage alliances. Since the Seljuk sultans never abandoned the custom of marrying the daughters of neighboring rulers, Seljuk concubines never achieved the political leverage of Ottoman concubines. That difference may explain the lack of charitable institutions founded by Seljuk *ghulāmas;* indeed, monuments founded by the royal women in general tended to be tombs.

In recent decades, historians have begun to reappraise the influence of Seljuk institutions on other Middle Eastern polities. The influence of the Rum Seljuks' *ghulām* institution now appears to have been profound. Although the *ghulām* system's influence on the Ottoman *devsirme* remains open to debate, there is virtually no question that the system served as a key model for the *mamluk* institutions of the Ayyubid and Mamluk states in Egypt and Syria.

—Jane Hathaway

See also
Janissaries
For Further Reading
Ayalon, David. 1977. "The Muslim City and the *Mamluk* Military Aristocracy." In *Studies on the Mamluks of Egypt*. Ed. David Ayalon. London: Variorum Reprints; Bates, Ülkü. 1978. "Women as Patrons of Architecture in Turkey." In *Women in the Muslim World*. Ed. Lois Beck and Nikki R. Keddie. Cambridge, MA: Harvard University Press; Cahen, Claude. 1968. *Pre-Ottoman Turkey: A General Survey of the Material and Spiritual Culture and History, c. 1071–1330.* Trans. J. Jones-Williams. New York: Taplinger; Vryonis, Speros, Jr. 1971. *The Decline of Medieval Hellenism in Asia Minor and the Process of Islamization from the Eleventh through the Fifteenth Centuries.* Berkeley: University of California Press.

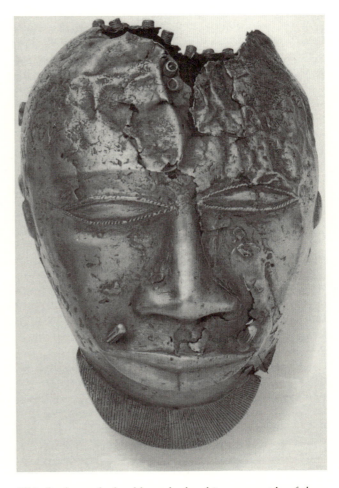

This finely worked gold trophy head is an example of the artifacts that led Europeans to label the region the Gold Coast.

GOLD COAST

The Gold Coast originally described the coastal region of modern Ghana (approximately, from Half Assini to the Volta River), but later the name was applied to the colony that became the Republic of Ghana. Portuguese explorers, believing they had discovered the gold-producing area of West Africa, referred to this stretch of coast as *Mina de Ouro* ("the gold mine") or *Costa da mina,* from which the English adaptation, Gold Coast, was derived.

Known foremost for gold, the people of the Gold Coast also engaged in slavery and the slave trade, and domestic slavery and the sale of slaves into the trans-Saharan trade predate the arrival of Europeans in the Gold Coast. Two other slave trades, a regional trade in slaves and the slave trade to the New World, arose in the region after the Portuguese arrived in 1471.

Drawn to the area by gold, the Portuguese initiated a new slave trade pattern to the Gold Coast. Because of the high demand for gold and the shortage of labor to work in the mines, Portuguese traders imported slaves from the Slave Coast to the east and sold the slaves for gold in the Gold Coast, where they were employed in mining gold and in carrying trade items or were sold into the domestic or trans-Saharan trade system.

The Portuguese monopoly of the Atlantic trade on the Gold Coast ended in the seventeenth century when French, British, Dutch, Brandenburger, Danish, and Swedish companies entered the trade on the Gold Coast. These companies dotted the coastline with castles and forts to provide residence for company agents, to store trade goods, to confine slaves en route to the New World, and to defend against attacks from local states and from rival European traders. Ultimately, these companies built more castles and forts in the Gold Coast region than anywhere else in Africa.

The New World's sugar revolution and the consequent sharp demand for slave labor altered the gold trade in the Gold Coast, and by the early-eighteenth century, the Gold Coast had been transformed into a slave coast: the gold trade was in decline, and slaves had become the prime commodity. This period in Gold Coast history coincided with the rise and expansion of the Ashanti empire. The Ashanti wars, intended largely for state building and defense, supplied war captives who were sold into the Atlantic slave trade system.

The people of the Gold Coast actively participated in the trans-Saharan trade, exchanging primarily gold but also slaves and kola nuts for products from the savanna and from across the Sahara. Early Portuguese accounts confirm that Mandingo merchants traded in Elmina for gold and slaves. The Mandingo traders obtained the slaves from both the locals and from the Portuguese, who by now, were importing slaves from the Slave Coast into the Gold Coast for sale.

Domestic slavery in the Gold Coast varied, ranging from slaves who served for life to those whose enslavement was temporary. Title to some slaves was nontransferable, but other slaves could be sold. There were slaves dedicated to shrines or owned by a state, others were privately owned. Slaves were employed in households, some worked on farms and in the gold mines, and others served in the forts and castles to facilitate the selling of slaves across the Atlantic.

The abolition of the slave trade and British enforcement of that policy reduced Gold Coast slave exports to the Americas, but domestic slavery continued unabated. Domestic slavery in the region survived into the twentieth century, with slave markets like Salaga reaching their peak long after the abolition of the Atlantic slave trade. When Britain established the Protectorate of the Gold Coast in 1874 (covering the southern portion of the Gold Coast), it issued two ordinances abolishing slavery and the slave trade in the colony. However, the acts provided no immediate universal emancipation, and existing slaves had to seek freedom by appealing to the authorities or by escaping. A similar policy of abolishing slavery without actively liberating the slaves was initiated in the northern territories in the 1890s and in Ashanti areas in 1901.

—*Patience Essah*

See also
Elmina
For Further Reading
Boahen, A. Adu. 1975. *Ghana: Evolution and Change in the Nineteenth and Twentieth Centuries.* London: Longman; Daaku, Kwame Yeboa. 1970. *Trade and Politics on the Gold Coast, 1600–1720: A Study of the African Reaction to European Trade.* Oxford: Oxford University Press; Fynn, John Kofi. 1971. *Asante and Its Neighbours, 1700–1807.* London: Longman; Reynolds, Edward. 1974. *Trade and Economic Change on the Gold Coast, 1807–1874.* London: Longman.

GOLDEN LAW
See Lei Aurea

GOREE ISLAND

Gorée is a small island measuring approximately 65 acres located in the Atlantic Ocean two miles west of Senegal's capital city, Dakar. From the late-fifteenth century until 1848, when France abolished slavery on the island, nearly 20 million slaves were taken to Gorée Island for shipment across the Atlantic. During that period, Gorée was successively the property of the Portuguese, Dutch, British, and French. Although many other slaves were also transported from other West African ports, Gorée's location as Africa's westernmost point made it an important entrepôt for the slave trade industry.

The Portuguese explorer Dinís Dias first claimed the uninhabited island in 1444, uninhabited because African tribes had previously deemed the land unsuitable for farming. European settlers were drawn to Gorée's curved coastline, which could serve as a shipping dock and a natural fortress to guard against ocean currents. Portuguese colonists soon established a network from Gorée and the Cape Verde Islands to supply the shipping trade with slaves, ambergris, beeswax, hides, grain, fuel, and fresh water.

During an era of European wars, Gorée had various owners. The Dutch claimed it for the longest period, from 1602 to 1779, and it was then alternately owned by Britain and France until the Vienna Treaty (1815) gave France exclusive ownership. Slave trading was outlawed in 1848.

Slaves were transported to Gorée from many west and central African tribes: Yoruba from Nigeria; Fulani from Senegal; and Mandinka from Mali. The island had 118 slave houses, one of the most infamous being La Maison des Esclaves (House of the Slaves). Built by the Dutch in 1776, the Senegalese government has restored this slave house and reopened it as a museum.

The small two-story house held as many as 400 slaves for periods of three or four months. There is a courtyard with numerous doors leading to small, dark, and damp cells in which up to 30 people were chained to the walls in an area no larger than the average bedroom. Men and women were separated. Some rooms were used for breeding, and others were used for fattening children so they would garner a high sale price. One large cell contained about 40 women who served as cooks and concubines.

When slave ships arrived at Gorée, slaves were weighed, inspected, and sold. Families and tribes were

An eighteenth-century view of the island of Gorée, off the coast of Senegal.

usually separated for departure to different western ports. Slaves were branded with a company emblem or a registration number in place of names. The slave's last exit before boarding, called "the door of no return," was a 200-foot-long bridge leading directly onto the ship. Those jumping from the pier rather than boarding found shark-infested waters. Of the 20 million slaves taken to Gorée, it is estimated that 6 million perished there.

During the French occupation, women impregnated by traders were set free to live on Gorée while their mulatto children received French citizenship. These women, known as *signares*, came to make up a wealthy and privileged class—owning slaves, managing businesses, and becoming mistresses to French and British dignitaries.

Gorée was named a Senegalese historic site in 1944 and in 1984 was declared an international historic site by UNESCO. Senegal gained independence from France in 1960, and today, only a 20-minute ferry ride from downtown Dakar, Gorée now contains the former homes, schools, and summer residences of French officials.

—*Anthony Todman*

See also
Africa; Ships

For Further Reading

Barboza, Steven. 1988. "The Doorway of No Return—Gorée." *American Visions* 3 (3): 6–9; Clark, Andrew Francis, and Lucie Colvin Phillips. 1994. *Historical Dictionary of Senegal.* Metuchen, NJ: Scarecrow Press; Moore, Shelley. 1986. "Gorée." *Crisis* 93 (6): 18–21, 56; Ndiaye, Joseph. 1989. *The Slave Trade at Gorée Island and Its History.* Gorée, Senegal: Ndiaye.

GORTYN, LAW CODE OF

Sometimes called the queen of inscriptions, the Cretan law code of Gortyn provides important evidence for the development of early Greek law. The probable date of this prose inscription is 480–460 B.C., but it preserves earlier legislation, some perhaps as old as the seventh century B.C. Discovered piecemeal from 1857 to 1884, the Gortyn Code consists of 600 lines in 12 columns inscribed on stone. Its provisions concern regulations and the administration of justice in matters of property, marriage, and kinship. Each provision is a third-person conditional statement, which supports other evidence suggesting that in ancient Greece formal procedural law preceded written statutory law and developed from voluntary submission of private disputes to third-party arbitration.

Crete stood at the vanguard of Greek written law codes, and classical Greeks had great respect for Cretan law. In Greek mythology, the Cretans Minos and Rhadamanthys, inspired by Zeus, sat as judges in the underworld, and the early lawgivers Zaleucus of Locris and Lycurgus of Sparta allegedly visited and learned much from Crete.

Gortyn society illustrates Moses Finley's conception of a "spectrum of statuses" between free and unfree in ancient Greece (Finley, 1982). Gortyn's social structure consisted of a ruling class, free persons excluded from political rights, serfs, debt-bondsmen, and chattel slaves, and the code's scale of fines reinforced the social hierarchy. For example, the fine for raping a free woman was 50 or more times that for raping a slave woman. A smaller body of evidence was required to convict a slave than a free person, and in some cases, only the free counted as competent witnesses.

The code reveals a society in transition to a money economy. The development of exchange values led to the introduction of chattel slavery as an alternative source of dependent labor to patriarchal serfdom. Masters usurped the rights of serf husbands over their children, and if the husband's master rejected a child, the choice devolved upon the wife's master. Serfs had marriage rights (free women could marry unfree men whose children under certain conditions would be free), had rights of possession, and could inherit masters' estates in default of clansmen. Gortyn's patriarchal serfs therefore enjoyed several rights and benefits that their chattel counterparts in Athens of the later-fifth century B.C. lacked.

—*Craige Champion*

See also
Aristotle's *Politics*; Finley, Moses; Greece; Plato's *Laws*; Solon

For Further Reading
Finley, Moses. 1982. "The Servile Statuses of Ancient Greece." In *Economy and Society in Ancient Greece*. Ed. Brent D. Shaw and Richard P. Saller. New York: Viking; Gragarin, Michael. 1986. *Early Greek Law*. Berkeley: University of California Press; Gragarin, Michael. 1995. "The First Law of the Gortyn Code Revisited." *Greek Roman and Byzantine Studies* 36 (Spring): 7–15; Willetts, Ronald. 1967. *The Law Code of Gortyn*. Berlin: de Gruyter.

GRACCHUS, GAIUS SEMPRONIUS (151–121 B.C.)

Brother of the murdered controversial tribune of the plebeians, Tiberius Gracchus, Gaius was both an accessory to Tiberius's land redistribution reforms and an instigator of greater and further-reaching proposals designed to ease the burden and suffering of the poor and dispossessed in Roman Italy, many of whom had been affected by the rapid expansion of slave labor. After his brother's death in 133 B.C., Gaius continued with the work of the agrarian commission, and epigraphic evidence indicates that he oversaw large redistributions of land. Plutarch provides a charismatic and ebullient characterization of the younger of the Gracchi, and further information appears in the works of Appian and several other Roman writers.

Gaius began his career with the traditional military service and returned from Sardinia after his election as tribune of the plebs, or plebeians, in 123 B.C. He immediately implemented a large program of well-conceived reforms, though the exact order of these measures is unclear. From the sources it is evident that the his brother's experience led Gaius to formulate a plan to undermine the authority of the Senate by vitalizing the political strength of the wealthy entrepreneurial class, the *equates*. One of the more significant reforms was the *lex Acilia,* which gave control of the jury courts to the *equates.*

While enriching the *equates,* Gaius simultaneously ensured that the urban poor in Rome, most of whom had previously been farmers but had been dispossessed by the arrival of thousands of slaves from the East, were offered grain at reasonable prices. He created employment opportunities for many of his supporters by beginning a large program of public works and road building. Additionally, he reestablished the agrarian commission, which had been temporarily halted in 129, and provided finance and land grants for new colonies—at Tarentum in Italy and on the site of the former city of Carthage overseas.

Gaius's second tribunate (122 B.C.) aroused the full hostility of the Senate. His concern for the urban poor seems to have expanded to include the wider impoverishment and disenfranchisement of the natives of the entire peninsula, and his most extraordinary measure was to offer Roman citizenship to Latins and Latin status to the Italians. This offer was opposed by his fellow tribune, Livius Drusus, and when Gaius sought a third term in office, a riot occurred. In response, the consul of 121 B.C., Lucius Opimius, obtained a decree from the Senate to restore order and rescue the state from anarchy. Gaius was slain in the struggle.

The violent struggle between the rich and poor in Rome continued after Gaius's death, but the reforms of his brief tribunate were some of the more startling responses to the arrival of hundreds of thousands of slaves from Greece, Asia Minor, and elsewhere.

—*Benjamin N. Lawrance*

See also
Gracchus, Tiberius Sempronius; Latifundia; Lex Poetelia Papiria; Roman Empire; Roman Law; Roman Republic
For Further Reading
Brunt, Peter A. 1971. *Social Conflicts in the Roman Republic*. London: Chatto and Windus; Scullard, Howard H. 1963. *From the Gracchi to Nero*. London: Methuen; Stockton, David. 1979. *The Gracchi*. Oxford: Oxford University Press.

GRACCHUS, TIBERIUS SEMPRONIUS (163–133 B.C.)

Son of the famous censor of the same name and Cornelia, daughter of Africanus, Tiberius Sempronius Gracchus was a tribune of the plebs and the people's champion; in attempting widespread land reform to reduce the slave-based *latifundia*, he brought civil crisis to Rome. Tiberius was educated by Greek philosophers and was well-versed in the ideals of democracy and reform. The Greek biographer Plutarch has left a vivid and striking portrait of the passion that gripped Tiberius during his travels through Italy before he embarked on a political career in Rome. Other sources include Appian's history of the Roman civil wars, passing comments by other Roman historians and orators, and an ever-increasing amount of epigraphic data.

Tiberius's career, like that of most politicians in the late republic, began in the army. Under Scipio Aemilianus he fought at Carthage and later in the Numantine War (137–133 B.C.), which marked the end of organized resistance to Rome in Spain. According to

Tiberius's brother, Gaius, Tiberius first became concerned about the welfare of dispossessed farmers, who were reduced to penury in the cities, when he observed vast tracts of *latifundia*, or landed estates, worked by slaves in Etruria in central Italy.

Tiberius's agrarian law *(lex agraria)* was designed as a mechanism whereby large tracts of public land *(ager publicus)* could be taken from the wealthy and made available to poor tenants. He based his legislation on an earlier law that limited the size of estates and attempted to curry favor with factions in the Senate by creating additional revenue from rent derived from this redistribution. One of Tiberius's main concerns was that the backbone of the army, the yeoman farmer, was quickly being displaced by slave-based agriculture, which underpinned the encroachment of senatorial estates.

A board of three was to oversee the redistribution of land. This board, in the fashion characteristic of Roman nepotism, consisted of Tiberius himself, his brother, and his father-in-law, Appius Claudius. The *lex agraria* dismayed the senators, and they attempted to block its financing. Overturning the authority of the Senate in financial and foreign matters, Tiberius went before the people with a plebiscite designed to divert funds from a bequest given by the king of Pergamum, which led the Senate to persuade Octavius, a fellow tribune, to veto the land law. Tiberius subsequently insisted on deposing the senatorial puppet.

In seeking reelection, Tiberius made some senators fear that he was aiming at despotism. A violent battle ensued between the senators, led by Tiberius's cousin Scipio Nasica and Tiberius's supporters. Tiberius was killed and his body thrown into the Tiber. Although many of his colleagues were executed, the triumvirate that had been created to oversee the redistribution of land to the dispossessed continued successfully.

—*Benjamin N. Lawrance*

See also
Gracchus, Gaius Sempronius; *Latifundia*; Lex Poetelia Papiria; Roman Empire; Roman Law; Roman Republic
For Further Reading
Carcopino, Jerome. 1967. *Daily Life in Ancient Rome*. Paris: Les Belles Lettres; Scullard, Howard H. 1963. *From the Gracchi to Nero*. London: Methuen; Stockton, David. 1979. *The Gracchi*. Oxford: Oxford University Press.

GREAT TREK

The Great Trek was the 1830s migration of Dutch-speaking pastoralist farmers (Boers) away from the British Cape Colony into the interior of southern Africa. This migration ultimately resulted in the establishment of the Afrikaner republics of Orange Free State and Transvaal that later came into conflict with the British Empire in the Great Boer War (1899–1901) and were incorporated into a newly united South Africa in 1910. During the centenary celebrations of the 1930s, the Great Trek was used symbolically to mobilize the Afrikaner nationalist movement that came to power in 1948 and subsequently implemented apartheid.

Dutch-speaking pastoral farmers had regularly migrated in search of better land and water supplies ever since they had established the colonial settlement at Cape Town in the seventeenth century. In the 1830s, a number of more concerted and premeditated emigrations occurred among about 15,000 Dutch-speaking colonists from the Cape Colony's eastern districts. With them went almost 7,000 servants, many of them slaves, whose presence has been steadfastly ignored in the many portrayals of the trek.

Some historians explain the Great Trek as a patriotic Afrikaner nationalist reaction against the British takeover of the Cape Colony in 1795 (finally confirmed in 1814), but the eastern Cape Colony pastoralists also objected to policies of the Dutch East India Company, with which they felt no close affiliation, and there was little sign of dissatisfaction with British administration before the late 1820s. Other explanations focus on the devastating impact of Xhosa attacks on eastern Cape Colony districts in 1834–1835 and the uncertain future many pastoralist settlers felt, although some parties of trekker emigrants had already left the colony before these events occurred.

Recent research shows that most of the trekkers were reacting against a more general deterioration in their economic position. Many were poor farmers who lacked the capital to benefit from the commercial wool farming that was developing in the region. Specific government policies in the late 1820s worsened their situation, such as the demand that land rent be paid in cash, the devaluation of the local currency against sterling, and changes in the land tenure system. Many leaders of trekker emigrant groups were deeply in debt by the early 1830s.

That economic distress explains the trekkers' opposition to changes taking place in Cape Colony labor policies and legislation in the late 1820s and 1830s. In 1828, Ordinance 50 freed the indigenous Khoi from their previous obligation to enter indentured labor contracts, thus enabling more of them to enter wage employment with commercial farmers and a few to acquire their own land. The undercapitalized white pastoralists found it difficult to retain labor under such circumstances, and the abolition of slavery in 1834 was the last straw for many poor white farmers. Many of those leaving the colony complained that the government had no right to deprive them of slave property.

During the years of apprenticeship (1834–1838), when ex-slave apprentices were still obliged to work for their former owners, a number of trekkers left the colony and illegally took their servants and apprentices with them. Some of the latter escaped and returned to the Cape Colony where they were freed, but many others remained as bonded servants in the new trekker republics. Yet an expedition sent by the Cape Colony government in 1839 found that some apprentices did not wish to return to a colony in which freedom was not accompanied by land or status.

Although slavery itself was not legalized, trekkers and their descendants perpetuated indenture and other forms of bonded labor. Moreover, many trekkers who had been adversely affected economically by emancipation of the Khoi and slaves articulated their opposition in racial terms, arguing that such actions were "contrary to the . . . natural distinction of law and colour" (Peires, 1989), and the trekker republics permitted only whites to have full political and landholding rights. In 1910, the new Union of South Africa perpetuated this racial exclusivity when it failed to extend the Cape Colony's multiracial franchise to the rest of the country. Although segregation and apartheid have much more complex causes, the association of the Great Trek with the preservation of white exclusivity gave a powerful impetus to the Afrikaner nationalist movement in the 1930s and 1940s.

—*Nigel Worden*

See also
Apartheid; Cape Colony
For Further Reading
Eldredge, Elizabeth, and Fred Morton, eds. 1994. *Slavery in South Africa: Captive Labor on the Dutch Frontier*. Boulder, CO: Westview Press and Pietermaritzburg, South Africa: University of Natal Press; Peires, Jeff. 1989. "The British and the Cape, 1814–1834." In *The Shaping of South African Society, 1652–1840*. Ed. Richard Elphick and Hermann Giliomee. Cape Town: Maskew Miller Longman; Van der Merwe, Pieter. 1995. *The Migrant Farmer in the History of the Cape Colony, 1657–1842*. Trans. from Afrikaans by Roger Beck. Athens: Ohio University Press; Venter, C. 1991. "Die Voortrekkers en die ingeboekte Slawe wat die Groot Trek meegemaak het." *Historia* 39 (1): 14–29.

GREECE

E
vidence for the existence of slavery in Greece appears in Mycenaean palace documents of 1500–1200 B.C. and in Homer and other written and archaeological sources from the

archaic period (800–500 B.C.) onward. By the classical period (450–330 B.C.), chattel slavery was widespread, and the impact of slavery can be detected in most aspects of Greek lifestyle, culture, and industry. But while the evidence does not allow the preclusion of slavery from any aspect of Greek life, it was concentrated in the classical and Hellenistic periods and particularly in Athens, Delos, and Delphi.

A Greek slave was a person who could be bought and sold as an object, and the Bronze Age word for slave appears frequently on Mycenaean Linear B tablets (Linear B was the alphabet/script used by the Mycenaeans). The collapse of palace societies led to aristocratic kingdoms, and it is likely that slavery persisted throughout. Many words were used for slaves in the archaic period. In Homer, *dmoes* are often war booty, and more often female; men were often slaughtered on the battlefield. Anyone could be enslaved in this period; Briseis and Chryseis, both Homeric (fictional) women of high rank, were enslaved. The *Odyssey* provides evidence for slave occupations: females could be nurses, personal servants, and kitchen hands while men were generally farm laborers. The source of slavery was not the besieging of towns but simple plundering expeditions. In the epics, slaves often dine with their masters and share in household experiences.

Chattel slavery became more widespread in the archaic period. Hesiod's work mentions small numbers of slaves, and traditionally, farmers owned a few and worked alongside them in the fields. There was marginal status differentiation: it is not always clear if people were free or enslaved. Slaves *(douloi)* appear in the lyric poetry of the time, in Herodotus's description of the seventh and sixth centuries B.C., and in the poetry of the Athenian lawgiver Solon.

Slavery was prominent in the *poleis* (city-states) of Athens, Delos, and Delphi. Evidence from Athens suggests that slaves composed approximately one-third of the population, but all calculations are problematic and based on fragmentary evidence. The early historian Athenaeus gives the fantastic figure of 400,000 Athenian slaves in the fourth century B.C., but the orator and statesman Hyperides (338 B.C.) gives the number of 150,000. It is generally accepted that most households would probably have one to three slaves, and Aristophanes' plays support this probability. Thus, the estimate of 100,000 for Athens in about 340 B.C. is not improbable. That figure is comparable to the percentage of slaves in the antebellum U.S. South, but perhaps the Greek slaves were more evenly distributed.

The rising dependence on slavery has been viewed as inseparable from the rise of liberty in the Greek *polis* (city-state). Moses Finley (1980) portrayed slavery in Athens as advancing in a similar way to slavery in Chios. Thucydides claimed there were huge numbers of slaves in Chios at the end of the fifth century, and an early-sixth-century-B.C. inscription suggests that democracy was making an early start in Chios, which meant that more people were free to participate in government structures. It may be that Chians and Athenians needed leisure time to pursue democracy and thus became dependent on chattel slavery. This advancement spread over the centuries until most of Greece was socioeconomically reliant on chattel slavery. At the same time it is unwise to consider Greek slaves to be a "class." The experience of slavery was highly individualistic and should be investigated in terms of status and orders.

The theory of natural slavery was popular in classical Greece, and it stemmed from the idea that all foreigners ("barbarians") were inferior. For instance, in Aeschylus's *Persians*, only the king was truly free in Persia. Anyone under such a king was inferior and lacked independence, though Hippocrates argued that easterners were naturally inferior because a less varied climate produced inferior personalities. Slavishness is a joke in Aristophanes' and Menander's comedies, but the main proponent of the "natural slave" argument was Aristotle. The *Politics* argues for the natural slave: he who uses his mind instead of his body is a freeman. Those who do not are natural slaves and can fairly be enslaved by others.

Athenian slaves had a complex legal position. Athenians recognized slaves as human but also as possessions to be bought, sold, or given away. As a possession, an Athenian slave could not own other things. Although allowed savings, slaves could spend them only with their master's consent. Generally, slaves were privately owned, but there were a number of public slaves *(demosioi)*. A slave family had no legal protection and could be willfully dispersed. Anthropologically, a slave was an uprooted nonperson to be counted among possessions.

Slaves were permitted rights of sorts. Their identity was recognized as part of the household and within that, as part of the master's authority. If born in Greece, a slave could become an initiate into religious rights. Slaves were given some economic freedom to act as go-betweens for their masters. Although slaves could not sue, they could seek representation though another citizen. Damages done by a slave were ultimately the master's responsibility.

Manumission was widespread in Greece, and evidence for it dates from the mid-sixth century B.C. Inscriptions were erected to celebrate liberty, many of them in important religious centers; over 900 inscriptions at Delphi exist from the first and second centuries B.C. alone. To ensure that the new status was not revoked, manumission was done in public, such as at a religious festival, at a play, or in a court. This display was banned in some parts of Greece because of public outcry. Xenophon and Aristotle regarded manumission as a form of social control, one that became more common from fourth century B.C. onward. Manumission often included financial compensation to the master. This money might be the slave's own savings or from an *eranos,* an association that pooled money for this purpose.

Two types of manumission existed, religious and civil. The granting of religious freedom is considered the more ancient and involved consecrating a slave to a deity. For example, the Hellenistic Delphi (330–140 B.C.) witnessed many resales of slaves to deities, principally to Apollo. A slave would entrust the purchase of his freedom to a priest and give him money to effect it. Civil manumission occurred when a deity was not involved and might be expressed in the will of the former owner. If the freedman wanted the state to record the event, he was obliged to pay a sum. A "mixed" manumission meant a slave, freed by his master, was then put under the protection of a deity.

Freedom gave a former slave the right to go where he or she pleased, with fines imposed on the master or family for any attempt at reenslavement. In practice, however, the slave was tied to the former master or the master's heir. This person gave the slave legal redress, and other obligations included funerary duty. Yet the law provided for the slave to be released from this state, too, by paying a higher price. The freedman was obliged to help his or her master in every way, subject to corporeal punishment, and in extreme cases, if duties were unfulfilled, reenslavement.

The question arises as to whether these people were indeed free? Although they had legal and property rights, and their children were born free, there were considerable restrictions. It is generally accepted that they were between slavery and freedom and that duties to the heir and the obligation to the master were examples of conditional manumission.

Slavery did not exist throughout Greek history in the same form. Each *polis* had its own legal statutes for slavery, and the laws from Athens are the most accessible and may be broadly representative. Homeric slavery differed from that of the classical period, and that in turn differed from slavery in the Hellenistic period. Greater exposure to slavery in the *poleis* led to tighter legal mechanisms to protect the position of citizens. There were forms of slavery that are best described as being between slavery and freedom. Yvon Garlan (1988) argues that this was true for the Helots of Sparta, the *penestai* of Thessaly, and the *clarotai* and *mnoitai* of classical Crete. All of these types of slave seem to have performed a kind of "communal servitude" within their respective societies.

The practice of slavery was deeply entrenched by the classical period. The utopian realms in Plato's *Laws* and *Republic* contain slaves, as do the anarchic societies of Aristophanes. In the mythical and prehistoric Herodotean worlds, slavery might be absent, but Aristotle's idea that an automaton might one day replace slaves is the closest Greek theorists came to envisioning universal abolition.

Slavery was a necessity in Greece. It allowed the rich leisure time to pursue philosophy, sports, music, and politics. Slavery developed its own hierarchy in accordance with this necessity, with harborside prostitutes at the bottom and bankers and elite pedagogues at the top. This status differentiation meant that slave revolts were uncommon and unsuccessful. Sparta was sometimes afflicted by internal strife and there were uprisings during extended periods of war, but it is impossible to calculate their impact.

—*Benjamin N. Lawrance*

See also

Aristotle's *Politics;* Art, Ancient; Epictetus; Helots; Hesiod's *Works and Days;* Homer's Theory; *Perioeci;* Second Messenian War; Solon; Theognis of Megara's *Theognidea*

For Further Reading

Austin, M., and P. Vidal-Naquet. 1977. *Economic and Social History of Greece.* Berkeley: University of California Press; De Ste. Croix, Geoffrey E. M. 1981. *The Class Struggle in the Ancient Greek World.* Ithaca, NY: Cornell University Press; Finley, Moses. 1980. *Ancient Slavery and Modern Ideology.* New York: Penguin Books; Garlan, Yvon. 1988. *Slavery in Ancient Greece.* Ithaca, NY: Cornell University Press.

GREGOIRE, ABBE HENRI (1750–1831)

The fiery bishop of Blois who campaigned for Jewish and African rights during the French Revolution, Abbé Henri-Baptiste Grégoire used a selective blend of Christian humanism and Enlightenment rhetoric to support his arguments. He believed that all men were equal before God and hoped that exposure to French culture would overcome slavery's debilitating effects upon Africans on their home continent and in the Caribbean. He worked closely with British abolitionists, particularly Thomas Clarkson and Zachary Macaulay, and somehow managed to survive the many twists and turns of power politics during the turbulent periods of revolution and restoration in France.

Abbé Grégoire was known for his lobbying efforts on behalf of the Jews until 1789 when he joined the National Assembly's Credentials Committee. When this group selected the mulatto delegation over the white planters to represent the colonies in the National

Assembly, the previously ignored issues of slavery and abolition suddenly came to the forefront. Grégoire, influenced by Clarkson and the Société des Amis des Noirs, published a pamphlet in December 1789 entitled *Mémoire en faveur des gens de couleur* (Memorandum on behalf of colored people), and in it he outlined the case for enfranchising mulattoes and free blacks. Grégoire argued that slavery was a temporary institution, an unnatural human state, and that religion and culture could overcome its effects to create good citizens. Grégoire suggested that socioeconomic conditions and not race determined a person's ability. It was an explosive issue and one that preoccupied Grégoire for the rest of his life.

Grégoire had tremendous prestige in France during this time. He became president of the National Assembly in January 1791 and fought to extend the limited enfranchisement of mulattoes granted under a May 15 law. For his efforts, the planters in Saint Domingue (today, Haiti) burned him in effigy in August 1791. Upon becoming bishop of Blois in October 1791, Grégoire left Paris for his new post and attempted to extend abolitionist sentiment in the country without compromising his neutrality as a priest. He enthusiastically supported the republic in 1792 but was disturbed by the factionalism of his old friends, the Jacobins.

In August 1794, Grégoire joined a committee that was charged with studying the uprisings in the French West Indies and, not surprisingly, came out supporting full enfranchisement for mulattoes and free blacks as the antidote. His interest in Caribbean affairs began to decline after the National Convention granted limited religious toleration in France in February 1795; at that time, Grégoire turned his attention to the reorganized Constitutional Church.

Abbé Henri-Baptiste Grégoire was a significant figure in the history of abolition in France and the West Indies. He argued for the enfranchisement of free blacks and mulattoes and tried to persuade fellow citizens that environment and opportunity created good citizens, not race or skin color. His many essays examined the history, cause, and effects of slavery upon the Africans and suggested methods for overcoming their current debility. Henri Christophe and Jean-Pierre Boyer consulted Abbé Grégoire for advice on governing the newly independent state of Haiti, and he always remained optimistic that Haiti would serve as a model for former slaveholding colonies. Through his legislation and writing, Abbé Grégoire imbued the cause of abolition with tones of Christian piety and enlightened reason.

—*Karen Racine*

For Further Reading
Certeau, Michel de. 1975. *Une politique de la langue: La Révolution française et les patois: L'enquête de Grégoire.* Paris: Gallimard; Ezran, Maurice. 1992. *L'Abbé Grégoire, defenseur des juifs et des noirs: Révolution et tolérance.* Paris: Editions L'Harmittan; Necheles, Ruth. 1971. *The Abbé Grégoire 1787–1831: Odyssey of an Egalitarian.* Westport CT: Greenwood.

GREGORY I (SAINT)

Saint Gregory I (also called Gregory the Great, 540–604) influenced several areas in both church and secular society through his writings and works. Although his views on slavery generally adhered to the views of his time, in both his letters and treatises he wrote frequently concerning the issue of slavery and its rights and obligations.

Church doctrine on slavery stemmed from the biblical letters of Paul, who wrote as a member of society under Roman law, which accepted slavery as integral and necessary. His writings illustrate the conflict for emerging Christian people, who not only saw slavery as unavoidable but also saw it as unacceptable in a religion that believed all people were created equal.

The Roman civil law Paul wrote under eventually ended, but the acceptance of slavery did not. Although the Roman Empire officially became Christian in the fourth century, the church did little toward eliminating slavery. Rather, it held to the tradition established by Paul, and Gregory demonstrated this tradition in his *Pastoral Rule* (A.D. 591). In the chapter on admonishing slaves and masters, Gregory states that although master and slave are created equal, slaves must keep in mind their lower state and obey their master. His writing gives no indication of Christian disapproval of slavery, retaining the contradiction found in Paul of people being equal and yet compelled to live within a hierarchy.

However, Gregory was not oblivious to the contradiction that arose from supporting slavery while representing a religion that espoused equality. In a deed of manumission in 595, Gregory granted freedom to two Roman slaves. Addressing another common theme of the day, he referred to the law of nature as opposed to the law of the people. In this deed of manumission, Gregory stated that slavery and its inequality were results of the laws of people, not of the laws of nature. This deed was eventually incorporated into church common law.

Gregory echoed the deed in several letters in which he addressed the issue of giving manumission to slaves, particularly those who were intended for the church. He encouraged those to whom he wrote to free their slaves, who would then be trained for monastic life. Gregory particularly supported this practice when a slave showed a definite inclination to convert to Christianity.

Gregory's stand did not differ greatly from that of previous and succeeding church leaders, who occasionally encouraged the freeing of slaves but within the context of the church. Both before and after Gregory, letters from the church imploring masters to free their slaves most often occurred as part of a request to give up all worldly goods, slaves included. Requests also were made with respect to the hope of converting newly freed slaves to Christianity or of acquiring new monastic members. Gregory's writings followed this tradition and the continuing conflict of existing Christian traditions concerning slavery, that of acceptance of the status quo and that of a desire to promote equality.

—Elizabeth Schoales

See also

The Bible; Manumission Laws; Paul (Saint); Roman Law; Slavery in Medieval Europe

For Further Reading

Colgrave, Bertram. 1968. *The Earliest Life of Gregory the Great by an Anonymous Monk of Whitby.* Lawrence: University of Kansas Press; Davis, Henry. 1950. Gregory I. *Pastoral Care.* Trans. Henry Davis. Baltimore: Newman Press; Maxwell, John Francis. 1975. *Slavery and the Catholic Church: The History of Catholic Teaching Concerning the Moral Legitimacy of the Institution of Slavery.* London: Barry Rose Publishers.

GREGORY OF NAZIANZUS (C. 330–C. 390)

It is chiefly through the writings of Gregory of Nazianzus that we gain much information about his family's background and that of his friend, Basil the Great. Often recognized for his work on the Trinity, Gregory wrote no theological or political treatises but concentrated instead on domestic observations and everyday people, including slavery. In A.D. 17, Emperor Tiberius made Cappadocia a Roman province, and since three centuries of Greek influence had preceded the Roman conquest, the fathers of the early Christian church worked with a diverse population. When Romans conquered Greek territories, the entire city-state became enslaved to the empire, and Cappadocia became known for its many slaves, along with Crete and Caria.

After leaving Cappadocian Caesarea, Basil and Gregory separated for a time. Basil continued studying rhetoric in Constantinople while Gregory traveled to the Christian school in Palestinian Caesarea. He and Basil met again in Athens where they immersed themselves in an encyclopedic, classical education. It was there that the two men also planned for a monastic life, a life that Gregory would embrace while Basil seemed compelled to minister in a more public fashion. For several years, Basil and Gregory conducted their joint monastic enterprise in Pontus, but the tension between a contemplative life and a public life forever tormented them. Basil became bishop of Caesarea, but Gregory's sense of obligation toward his aging parents prevented him from making the final break to the monastery.

Gregory's words concerning slavery appear in poetic form. In the autobiographical *Concerning His Own Affairs*, Gregory confessed that he missed his devoted slaves, who were separated from him by an ancient tyranny, and pitied the slaves in Cappadocia, who carried the burden of being both freeman and slave. Still in poetic language, Gregory suggested that the lower classes might improve their lives by fleeing such persecutors as the Egyptians and the Assyrians. He used his own experiences to encourage others.

In his correspondence and in his sermons, Gregory seemed to understand enslavement as oppressive, but he upheld the need for a hierarchy for the sake of good order and as a way for the experienced to teach the young. In his funeral oration for Basil, he extolled his friend as one who never won people by enslavement but by example. Yet elsewhere in the oration, he recognized the value of the ecclesiastical hierarchy, especially if all bishops were like Basil. Gregory, then, encouraged people to flee a tyrannical ruler but to obey the benevolent ruler. There is nothing to suggest the overthrow of the class structure. He admired Basil for his work with the sick and the poor and seemed to applaud the equal treatment of human beings within their respective social groups.

When Gregory died, he left all he had to the poor of Nazianzus, and in his will, he requested the freedom of two female virgin slaves should they desire freedom. Gregory seemed to attack the concept of slavery throughout his letters, sermons, and memoirs, whereas Basil attacked social injustice. Neither attacked the institution of slavery but were concerned about the general mistreatment of human beings and the threat of disunity in both church and state.

—Judith T. Wozniak

For Further Reading

Defarri, Roy Joseph, et al., eds. 1951–1987. *The Fathers of the Church.* 70 vols. Washington, DC: Catholic University of America Press; Farrar, F. W. 1907. *Lives of the Fathers: Sketches of Church History in Biography.* London: Adam and Charles Black.

GRIMKE, ANGELINA (1805–1879)

As a Southern woman who became a leader of the abolitionist movement, Angelina Grimké attracted widespread notoriety by agitating publicly against slavery before mixed audiences of men and women, thus bringing into question traditional views of women's roles. Angelina was born into a prominent South Carolina slaveholding family. In 1829 she followed the lead of her elder sister Sarah, who wanted a more intellectually active life than that traditionally available to upper-class Southern women, and moved to Philadelphia and converted to Quakerism.

Over the next six years, Angelina Grimké became interested in the abolitionist movement by reading William Lloyd Garrison's *Liberator* and attending meetings of the Philadelphia Female Anti-Slavery Society. In 1835, she wrote Garrison a letter praising his adherence to the principle of immediate emancipation and referring briefly to her own experience with slavery in the South. Garrison published the letter in the *Liberator,* and as a consequence, Grimké received and accepted invitations to speak before women's discussion groups. She also wrote the pamphlet *An Appeal to the Christian Women of the South* (1836), which implored Southern women to use their influence upon men to end slavery. Although well received among abolitionists, the work caused an uproar in the South where U.S. postmasters judged it seditious and destroyed copies of it.

A passionate and animated speaker, Grimké drew large crowds to her public lectures. In 1836, she and her sister began acting as unofficial agents for the American Anti-Slavery Society, traveling throughout New York and New England raising funds and boosting society membership. Grimké's nine-month speaking tour in 1837 broke attendance records, but she also attracted criticism from those within the society who did not like women challenging traditional gender roles by speaking before mixed audiences. She was criticized for her position that it was as important to end Northern prejudice as it was to end Southern slavery. Early in 1838, Grimké gained further notice when she gave evidence to a committee of the Massachusetts legislature about the horrors of slavery, as she was the first woman ever to testify before a legislative body in the United States.

On May 14, 1838, Grimké married fellow abolitionist Theodore Dwight Weld, and the marriage marked the end of her active involvement with the abolitionist cause. Her last significant contribution to the movement was a book, which she jointly authored with Weld and her sister, entitled *American Slavery as It Is* (1839). In this compilation of Southern newspaper editorials and runaway notices, the authors hoped that the slaveholders' cruelty would speak for itself, and, indeed, the book became one of the antislavery movement's most influential works.

Although Grimké's involvement with the abolitionist movement was brief (1835–1839), she played a significant role in two ways. First, she had personal knowledge of slavery's cruelty, which made many New Englanders sympathetic to the antislavery cause. Second, her success as a public speaker heightened tensions within the abolitionist movement regarding women's proper roles and civil rights for blacks. Her stance on these two issues brought into question traditional notions of gender and race, sparked a series of controversies that contributed to a split in the abolitionist movement, and thus altered the course of the antislavery effort in the United States.

—Elizabeth Dubrulle

See also
An Appeal to the Christian Women of the South; Garrison, William Lloyd; Grimké, Sarah Moore; The *Liberator*; Weld, Theodore Dwight

For Further Reading
Barnes, Gilbert H., and Dwight L. Dumond, eds. 1934. *Letters of Theodore Dwight Weld, Angelina Grimké Weld, and Sarah Grimké, 1822–1844.* New York: D. Appleton; Ceplair, Larry, ed. 1989. *The Public Years of Sarah and Angelina Grimké: Selected Writings, 1835–1839.* New York: Columbia University Press; Lerner, Gerda. 1967. *The Grimké Sisters from South Carolina: Rebels against Slavery.* Boston: Houghton Mifflin; Lumpkin, Katharine Du Pre. 1974. *The Emancipation of Angelina Grimké.* Chapel Hill: University of North Carolina Press.

GRIMKE, SARAH MOORE (1792–1873)

Intelligent, pious, dedicated to justice, and withal a determined lecturer and essayist, Sarah Moore Grimké was a strong foe of Southern slavery and a fearless proponent of women's rights. Born to a wealthy South Carolina slaveholding family, Sarah could have enjoyed an unusually leisured life. Yet like many other Southern women, she abhorred the use of slaves and had trouble reconciling her principles with the culture of her home state. Formally educated in the scant manner thought appropriate for young ladies of good families, Sarah read widely in her father's library. She was denied her wish to study law, and for years, she tried to satisfy her restless mind in a giddy social whirl.

In 1817, she experienced a religious conversion and joined the Presbyterian Church; in 1820, after reading John Woolman's memoirs, she became a Quaker. A year later, Sarah moved to Philadelphia. She returned to Charleston in 1827 and persuaded her sister Angelina to join her in the Quaker faith. In 1829, the Grimké sisters joined forces in Pennsylvania, and after 1831, Sarah never returned to the slaveholding states.

In Philadelphia, fellow religionists did not appreciate the Grimké sisters' participation in abolitionist activities. Relations grew more difficult when the pair moved to New York to be trained as activists and worse yet when Sarah and Angelina took to the lecture halls. As Southerners familiar with, and disgusted by, slavery's daily realities, both women were valuable additions to the antislavery cause.

Because Angelina made more speeches and was judged the better orator, Sarah's contributions to abolition have been deemed less significant than her advocacy of women's rights. Sarah herself always held that her abolitionism and support for women's rights were inseparable, as both were predicated on a scriptural view of the moral responsibilities of women. She wrote an antislavery statement called *An Epistle to the Clergy of the Southern States* (1836), and a year later, she cowrote the "Letter to Clarkson," which answered a call for advice as to what nonslaveholders could do to bring an end to slavery. In 1839, Sarah edited the antislavery compendium, *American Slavery as It Is,* along with her sister Angelina and new brother-in-law, Theodore Weld.

After that project, Sarah Grimké's participation in antislavery activities waned despite importunings when abolitionists in the United States quarreled over the question of the role of women in the movement to free the slaves. In addition to teaching in progressive schools, she wrote on women's rights and translated a biography of Joan of Arc. In 1868, she and Angelina acknowledged and befriended two nephews who were mulattoes. An ardent supporter of woman suffrage, Sarah lived to vote in a local election.

—*Barbara Ryan*

See also
Grimké, Angelina; Weld, Theodore Dwight; Women and the Antislavery Movement
For Further Reading
Birney, Catherine H. 1885. *The Grimké Sisters.* Boston: Lee and Shepard; Ceplair, Larry, ed. 1989. *The Public Years of Sarah and Angelina Grimké: Selected Writings, 1835–1839.* New York: Columbia University Press; Lerner, Gerda. 1967. *The Grimké Sisters from South Carolina: Rebels against Slavery.* Boston: Houghton Mifflin.

GRINNELL, JOSIAH B. (1821–1891)

An early Republican Party founder, Josiah B. Grinnell was also an abolitionist and western settler and developer. Born in New Haven, Vermont, he graduated from Oneida Institute (1843) and Auburn Theological Seminary (1846). Employed briefly at an integrated church in Union Village, New York, Grinnell left New York in 1851 to found the first Congregational Church in Washington, D.C. There, Grinnell made the mistake of preaching an abolition sermon, reportedly the first of its kind in the nation's capital, and when he persisted, he was forced to leave Washington for the safety of New York City. A chronic throat problem led Grinnell to refocus his career, and in 1854, he followed journalist Horace Greeley's advice to "go west." He and two business associates purchased 5,000 acres in central Iowa's Poweshiek County and founded the town of Grinnell. Two years later, Iowa College relocated from Davenport to Grinnell, and, in 1909, the institution was renamed Grinnell College.

Grinnell was active in Iowa and local affairs and was a prime mover in founding the state's Republican Party at Iowa City in 1856. Elected to the Iowa Senate in 1856 (serving one term until 1860), he became a major voice in the free school movement. He likewise favored temperance and prohibition and soon became Iowa's most recognized abolitionist. In February 1859, Grinnell hosted John Brown in his home as Brown escorted a group of fugitive slaves to Canada. According to legend, Brown penned part of his Virginia Proclamation while under Grinnell's roof.

In 1860, Grinnell represented Iowa at the Republican National Convention in Chicago, which nominated Abraham Lincoln for the presidency, and Grinnell's rise in national politics culminated with his election to two terms in Congress (1863–1867). An energetic supporter of Lincoln, Grinnell advocated using black troops in the Union army and supported a high protective tariff. He also supported the president's use of war powers, including the detention of wartime opponents.

Grinnell's visibility as an abolitionist meant he was held in good standing by Iowa Republicans but distrusted by the state's Democrats. He opposed Andrew Johnson's Reconstruction plan and voted against readmitting the Southern states to the Union until they granted blacks the vote. Thus began Grinnell's decline as a public figure. He lost the Republican renomination for a third congressional term to William Loughride, a proponent of radical Reconstruction, and his final stand was in favor of his old friend Horace Greeley for president in 1872. Seemingly, without the abolitionist cause, Grinnell's influence in the party disappeared.

—*Boyd Childress*

For Further Reading
Payne, Charles Edward. 1938. *Josiah B. Grinnell*. Iowa City: State Historical Society of Iowa.

GROTIUS, HUGO
(1583–1645)

Hugo Grotius

Hugo Grotius was a diplomat, lawyer, and writer versed in the classical traditions of Renaissance Europe and the religious traditions of moderate Dutch Protestantism, and like many of his contemporaries, he had mixed views about slaveholding. He represented Dutch commercial interests committed to principles of free trade against Portugal and Spain, and although twentieth-century writers find his principles archaic in many respects, Grotius still is generally considered the founder of modern international law, especially as it relates to principles of just war and the conduct of belligerents.

As a writer, Grotius is best known for *De jure praedae,* written from 1604 to 1606 but not published until 1868; *Mare librum* (1609); and *De jure belli ac pacis* (1625). All three works were derivative in many respects and expressed no startlingly new or original ideas, but *Mare librum* and *De jure belli ac pacis* have exerted lasting influence in determining freedom of the seas and the laws of war. These books represent the theoretical side of the work of a practicing diplomat, lawyer, and politician, and they should be seen in a context similar to the political writings of John Milton during the English civil war. As a diplomat, Grotius held real power from 1613 to 1618.

There are some passages very favorable to slaveholding in *De jure praedae,* but slavery is viewed less favorably in Grotius's other published writings. When examining his view of slavery, modern readers should be careful to remember that slavery was acceptable to most seventeenth-century Europeans, especially when the enslaved were non-Christian and non-European.

In *De jure belli ac pacis,* Grotius defined slavery thus: "That is complete slavery which owes lifelong service in return for nourishment and other necessaries of life; and if the condition is accepted within natural limits it contains no element of undue severity." Grotius used classical examples to show slavery as a natural and perhaps just refuge for the weak, who might voluntarily sell themselves into slavery for material benefit. However, Grotius also wrote: "By nature at any rate, that is apart from a human act, or in the primitive condition of nature, no human beings are slaves, as we have said elsewhere. In this sense, it is correct to accept what was said by the jurists, that slavery is contrary to nature."

Grotius did not see slavery as an unequivocal right offering the slaveowner unlimited power over the slave, and he believed that slaves should not be executed except for crimes. In addition, despite noting apostolic writings urging slaves to return to their masters, Grotius recognized that slaves who were severely maltreated should have the right to flee.

To place further limits on the power of masters, Grotius stated that slaves did not have to honor commands that were contrary to the law of God. He quoted the apostle Paul in declaring that slaves should receive some recompense for their work. He also repeated Seneca's statement that "we are not able to give all orders nor are slaves compelled to render obedience to all commands. They will not carry out orders against the State: they will not set their hands to a crime."

Grotius's legal training helped him categorize 160 types of incomplete slavery, including temporary slavery, conditional slavery, and slavery for certain purposes. He also discussed the status of apprentices and Roman freedmen as forms of temporary slavery. In addition, Grotius mentioned the status of serfs and Jews subjected to servitude for seven years or until a year of Jubilee (a year of emancipation that occurred every 50 years) as forms of temporary slavery.

For Grotius, slavery was, not the racial issue that it would later become in the United States, but a theoretical issue he generally treated by using well-known classical writers and New Testament quotations to buttress his opinions. Grotius cited classical examples to justify the enslavement of prisoners of war, who could lose their formerly free status and become slaves when brought within enemy lines. All children who were born after the enslavement of their parents became slaves since slavery was a heritable status.

Grotius took two major positions that were later advocated by slaveowners in the United States. Although he recognized that the status of both parents could be considered in determining the status of a child, Grotius supported a system in which the status of the mother determined the status of the child, which meant that a child of a slave mother and a freeman was born into slavery. Grotius also stressed that the children of slaves were expensive to raise and that masters needed to be compensated for the expense of raising slave children.

Many modern readers would find Grotius's views of slavery abhorrent. However, they should be seen as the worldview of someone looking back to classical antiquity and the New Testament and not as the view of one actively participating in the enslavement of non-European peoples. Grotius was more sympathetic to the rights of indigenous people in newly discovered lands than most of his contemporaries, and he had no contact with African slaves.

—Susan A. Stussy

For Further Reading
Bull, Hedley; Benedict Kingsbury; and Adam Roberts, eds. 1992. *Hugo Grotius and International Relations.* Oxford: Clarendon Press; Grotius, Hugo. 1925. *The Law of War and Peace, De jure belli ac pacis, libri tres.* Indianapolis, IN: Bobbs Merrill.

GUERRERO, VINCENTE (1783?–1831)

Vincente Guerrero was a Mexican soldier, an independence leader, and the president who abolished slavery in the Mexican republic in 1829. Born in Tixtla in southern Mexico, Guerrero eventually became a beloved hero of Mexican independence. His adherence to José María Morelos's liberal ideals, his forceful arguments on behalf of the underclass, and his military prowess earned him the respect of all classes, but most especially the Indians of southern Mexico.

Born a mestizo, or person of mixed Indian and European descent, Guerrero was rumored to have some African blood, which earned him the nickname "El Negro." He received no formal education, but his occupation as a mule driver allowed him to learn much from the people he encountered during his travels. He enlisted in José María Morelos's army in December 1810 and quickly rose through the ranks because of his natural military ability and his devotion to the cause of independence. When royalists executed Morelos in 1815, Guerrero assumed command of the southern forces. Popular with both the soldiers and the local populace, Guerrero managed to keep the independence movement alive even as it suffered reverses. In 1821, he joined his former adversary Agustín de Iturbide in the Plan de Iguala, which called for union, defense of Catholicism, and a limited constitutional monarchy.

Guerrero managed to survive the stormy and factious politics that enveloped Mexico in the 1820s. He and Nicolás Bravo opposed Iturbide when he declared the empire and participated in the government that succeeded it. In February 1823, Guerrero joined the executive council and held that position for several years despite repeated pleas of ill health. In 1827, President Guadalupe Victoria sent Guerrero to suppress a revolt in Veracruz.

Guerrero lost the presidential election to Manuel Gómez Pedraza in April 1829, but a complicated series of events, including armed intervention by Antonio López de Santa Anna, sent Gómez Pedraza into exile and installed Guerrero in office. As Mexico's second president, Guerrero attempted to address the nation's rampant banditry and financial disasters. He also pledged to respect property rights while stressing the legality of his seizure of power.

Guerrero's presidency is most noted for Mexico's abolition of slavery on September 15, 1829, when he decreed slaves free and promised that owners would be indemnified in some form when treasury funds permitted. Guerrero's emancipation decree raised the threat of revolt among Texas's Anglo-American settlers, who viewed abolition as an assault on their property and rights, and under pressure, Guerrero signed another decree in December exempting Texas from abolition. But the settlers remained uneasy, and partially because of these events, Santa Anna, Anastasio Bustamante, and other conservatives overthrew Guerrero in December 1829 and later ordered him shot. Today, Guerrero remains a popular hero of Mexican independence and has given his name to one of Mexico's federal states.

—Karen Racine

For Further Reading
Áviles Fábila, René. 1957. *Vicente Guerrero, el insurgente ciudadano*. Mexico, City: Sociedad de Amigos del Libro Mexicano; Fuentes Díaz, Vicente. 1989. *Revaloración del General Vicente Guerrero: Consumador de la independencia*. Chilpancingo, Mexico: Gobierno del Estado de Guerrero; Harrell, Eugene Wilson. 1976. "Vicente Guerrero and the Birth of Modern Mexico." Unpublished thesis, Department of History, Tulane University, New Orleans; Sprague, William. 1939. *Vicente Guerrero—Mexican Liberator*. Chicago: R. R. Donnelley and Sons.

GUINEA COMPANY

Chartered in 1618, the Company of Adventurers Trading to Gynney and Bynney, more commonly called the Guinea Company, represented England's first significant effort to develop trade with West Africa, a trade that eventually included slaves. Tudor and Stuart monarchs commonly used monopoly charters as they sought expansion of foreign trade, and in 1552, with the Cathay Company, the monarchy began using such charters to open trade routes to the Far East, Russia, the Mediterranean, and North America.

Initially, the Guinea Company concentrated its efforts on Africa's windward coast between the Gambia and Sherbro Rivers, and investors hoped to profit from gold, hides, redwood, and ivory. Some shipments of redwood in the 1620s and gold in the 1630s did produce profits—for example, one ship returned to England in 1636 with a cargo worth about £30,000—but the successes were infrequent.

Although Portuguese merchants had pursued the African slave trade for several generations, the Guinea Company eschewed it in the early 1620s. Richard Jobson, an early company ship captain, had an opportunity to purchase slaves from a native merchant in 1620 but declined, explaining that his company refused to deal in human commodities. Despite Jobson's reservations, the company could not resist the potential profits and began buying slaves and selling them in the colonies in the early 1630s.

When the Guinea Company reorganized in 1631, it extended its operations to the Bight of Benin and constructed England's first permanent African trading station at Kormantine on the Gold Coast. Spurred by the rapid development of sugar-producing colonies in the English West Indies, which were desperate for labor, the company had several ships trading along the Slave Coast by the early 1640s.

The capture of several of the company's slaving ships, notably one in 1651 carrying 200 slaves, contributed significantly to the Guinea Company's ultimate demise. Competition with foreign rivals, particularly the Dutch and French, and numerous English interlopers also played a part, and repeated appeals to English courts failed to stop that country's interference in the lucrative slave trade. Neither further reorganization nor a shift in the roster of officers could save the company, and by the late 1650s, company prospects were so bleak that its leadership decided to sell the remaining time of its monopoly to the English East India Company.

Although the Guinea Company failed to supply the labor needs of the English colonies in the West Indies, its collapse did not prevent Charles II from attempting to meet the demand with other monopoly companies. He issued a charter to the Company of Royal Adventurers in 1663 and another to the Royal African Company nine years later. Like the Guinea Company, neither could satisfy the growing colonial demand for slaves at reasonable prices. Planters in the Caribbean, and later in the Chesapeake Bay colonies, preferred individual slave traders over monopoly companies, believing that the former offered more reliable supplies at lower prices.

—*Larry Gragg*

For Further Reading
Blake, J. W. 1949. "The Farm of the Guinea Trade." In *Essays in British and Irish History*. Ed. H. A. Cronne, T. W. Moody, and D. B. Quinn. London: Frederick Muller; Marti, Evelin. 1929. "The English Slave Trade and the African Settlements." In *The Cambridge History of the British Empire*. Ed. J. Holland Rose, A. P. Newton, and E. A. Benians. Cambridge: Cambridge University Press; Porter, R. 1968. "The Crispe Family and the African Trade in the Seventeenth Century." *Journal of African History* 9 (1): 57–77; Zook, George F. 1919. "The Company of the Royal Adventurers Trading to Africa." *Journal of Negro History* 4 (2): 134–231.

GULLAH

There are various explanations for the meaning of the word Gullah as it applies to the people of African descent who dwell in the coastal islands of the Atlantic Ocean off South Carolina, Georgia, and Florida. Given that during the time of chattel slavery the people who populated this area, generally known as the Sea Islands, were predominately from Africa's western coast (some directly and others by way of the Caribbean islands), it is believed that the word derives from the Gola, Vai,

Gala, or Gallian peoples of what is now Sierra Leone. The presence of an island called Gola in western Africa supports this theory, and additionally, there was also a tribe of Golas or Goulahs in the neighboring Liberian hinterland. Some people believe the word is a shortened version of Angola. Numerous Africans brought from the area that is now the country of Angola were named Gullah to denote their origin, which is why names like Gullah Jack and Gullah Mary appear in some plantation accounts and stories.

Gullah is in essence the African American version of the Krio (pronounced Creole) language that is still spoken in Sierra Leone. For decades, linguists and others thought that Sea Islanders spoke corrupted English or a dialect of English. However, it has now been proved that Gullah is a language with its own lexicon and grammatical structure and was derived from the amalgamation of several African languages and a sprinkling of Old English.

Since the African islanders were isolated from the Europeans on the mainland, the Gullah language and culture synthesized and developed. The Gullah culture still retains Africanisms in its language, traditions, and day-to-day activities, and thus it is a distinct African American culture.

Some of the Sea Islanders of South Carolina and Georgia joined forces with the indigenous or Native American peoples on the islands and became part of the Seminole Nation. Many eventually migrated to northern Florida and settled the islands and swamplands there. After continued pursuit by groups of Europeans (and later Americans) who wanted to recapture and reenslave them, the Seminoles and Afro-Seminoles migrated west even before the Trail of Tears forced movement in 1838–1839. The Afro-Seminoles who remain in in the United States speak the least "Anglified" version of Gullah but call their language Seminole.

—*Marquetta L. Goodwine*

See also
Creole Languages; Geechee; Sea Islands
For Further Reading
Creel, Margaret Washington. 1988. *A Peculiar People: Slave Religion and Community-Culture among the Gullahs.* New York: New York University Press; Goodwine, Marquetta L. 1995. *Gullah/Geechee: The Survival of Africa's Seed in the Winds of the Diaspora.* Vol. 1, *St. Helena's Serenity.* New York: Kinship Publications; Montgomery, Michael, ed. 1994. *The Crucible of Carolina: Essays in the Development of Gullah Language and Culture.* Athens: University of Georgia Press; Turner, Lorenzo Dow. 1974. *Africanisms in the Gullah Dialect.* Ann Arbor: University of Michigan Press.

GULLAH JACK

Gullah Jack, who was also known as Cooter Jack and Jack Pritchard, was born in Africa in the town of McChoolay Mooreema and spoke an Angolan language. One Zephaniah Kingsley purchased him as a prisoner of war at Zanguebar (later Zanzibar) on Africa's eastern coast and took him to the Florida Sea Islands early in the nineteenth century.

Gullah Jack was allowed to take a bag aboard ship, and he always retained it. As a priest, conjurer, witch doctor, medicine man, and sorcerer, he carried his necessary implements in this bag. His knowledge and use of herbal medicine and magical traditions made some people respect him and call him intelligent and charismatic while others feared and stood in awe of him.

Numerous accounts describe Gullah Jack as a small man, possessed "of tiny limbs, which look grotesque despite his small frame" with "enormous black whiskers" (Freehling, 1965). He had an animated manner and a changing countenance, and because of his demeanor, he was sometimes called diabolical, artful, cruel, and bloody.

Approximately 40 people escaped or were taken in 1812 during a Seminole raid and attack on Kingsley's plantation. Gullah Jack was among this group and somehow ended up in Charleston, South Carolina, in 1821, when one Paul Pritchard purchased him. As a slave in Charleston, he was a member of the same AME congregation that Denmark Vesey attended, and just after Christmas 1821, Vesey recruited Gullah Jack to be a lieutenant in the uprising that he planned for Charleston and nearby islands. Vesey chose Gullah Jack because he represented an Angolan company called the Gullah Company, or Gullah Society, and also because people believed that Gullah Jack was "a man who could not be killed" and who "had a charm to lead his people" (Freehling, 1965).

Gullah Jack summoned African gods and fused African and European religious forms. He even provided those participating in the Vesey conspiracy with charms to prevent injury in battle and to injure anyone who betrayed them. But betrayal did come, and the authorities captured Vesey and others involved. A total of 131 people were put on trial as conspirators. The authorities captured Gullah Jack on July 5, 1822, condemned him to death on July 9, and hanged him three days later.

The people who testified against Gullah Jack stated that he had intended to implement the plans that Vesey, he, and others had developed despite Vesey's arrest. Testimony from Gullah Jack's trial mentions that he requested an extension of his life for one or two weeks. We will never know if he wanted this time to complete what the conspirators had begun or if he feared death.

—*Marquetta L. Goodwine*

See also
Vesey, Denmark
For Further Reading
Freehling, William W. 1965. *Prelude to Civil War: The Nullification Controversy in South Carolina, 1816–1836.* New York: Oxford University Press; Lofton, John. 1964. *Insurrection in South Carolina: The Turbulent World of Denmark Vesey.* Yellow Springs, OH: Antioch Press; Pearson, Edward A. 1992. "From Stono to Vesey: Slavery, Resistance, and Ideology in South Carolina, 1739–1822." Ph.D. dissertation, Department of History, University of Wisconsin-Madison; Starobin, Robert S. 1970. *Denmark Vesey: The Slave Conspiracy of 1822.* Englewood Cliffs, NJ: Prentice-Hall.

GYPSY SLAVERY
See **Rom Slavery**

HAITIAN REVOLUTION
(1791–1804)

The Haitian (or Saint Domingue) Revolution of 1791 to 1804 was the most important event in the history of eighteenth-century Atlantic slavery. The only successful slave uprising in the Western Hemisphere, it forced France to abolish slavery in its most profitable plantation colony and led directly to the establishment of the second independent nation in the Americas. The existence of a self-governing black state in the Caribbean generated great pride for African Americans throughout the hemisphere and was an object of enormous concern for anyone who profited from black slavery. For Haiti's ex-slaves, the revolution meant more than substituting French planters for black- and brown-skinned masters. Defying their leaders' attempts to resurrect colonial-era plantations in the nineteenth century, Haiti's people established their own Afrocreole peasant agriculture in districts that once supplied Europe with much of its sugar and coffee.

From the 1660s to 1804, Haiti was the French colony of Saint Domingue. In the mid-seventeenth century French governors coopted the pirates and hunters living in the western third of Spanish Hispaniola, and by the time Spain formally acknowledged this French possession in 1697, the buccaneers had turned to planting. An accelerating slave trade after 1720 allowed Saint Domingue, by mid-century, to produce more sugar than all other French colonies combined, even surpassing its British rival Jamaica. The end of the Seven Years War (1756–1763) further intensified both plantation production and the slave trade that made it possible.

Rapid growth accelerated the tensions generated by the sugar plantation society. With nearly 800 sugar estates, and thousands of smaller indigo and coffee estates, slavery in the French colony took various forms. In 1789, there were nearly 500,000 slaves in Saint Domingue, and annual slave imports reached 30,000; about half of these workers were African-born. In contrast, the colony had only about 30,000 whites, many of them born in France. After 1763, European immigration rose dramatically, but many newcomers did not become wealthy planters as they had dreamed.

The colony's third social group was a free population of African or mixed European-African descent, nearly as numerous as the whites in 1789. Racial intermarriage and concubinage had been common in the colony since the seventeenth century, but after the Seven Years War, French colonists paid increasing attention to racial categories, even reclassifying some wealthy families as "mulatto" or "quadroon" (categories of mixed blood). Despite increased racism, royal officials relied on free men of color for local militia service and granted freedom papers for faithful service in slave patrols.

Revolutionary events in France in 1789 raised expectations among colonial whites and free people of color. Wealthy planters hoped to be freed from French commercial restrictions, and poor immigrants hoped to overturn the power of royal officials and powerful families. Free men of color, especially the handful who had been eliminated from elite society in the racial distinctiveness that followed the French and Indian War after 1763, pushed for full French citizenship.

Colonial whites could contain these expectations initially, but in Paris a coalition of wealthy men of color and French abolitionists brought the question of mulatto citizenship before the new National Assembly. In Saint Domingue, men of color clashed with whites in October and November 1790 after Vincent Ogé, an unofficial Paris representative, returned to the island claiming that the French Revolution had enfranchised his class. Whites captured and brutally executed Ogé, but on May 15, 1791, the French National Assembly ruled that all financially qualified men born of free fathers and mothers would be considered full citizens in the colonies. Whites refused to apply the decree, and by July and August 1791, whites and free men of color were battling in the district behind Port-au-Prince.

Amid this confusion, slaves rose up against their masters in the densely settled plains and hills of the colony's northern province. On Sunday August 14, 1791, members of the mostly Creole slave elite from about 100 plantations gathered on a sugar estate to plan the revolt. One week later, in the woods of another plantation, a second and more African group of slaves celebrated a religious ritual. The following day the revolt broke out, sweeping through seven parishes in a week with the number of rebels growing from 1,500 to as many as 40,000 within a month.

The capture of Toussaint Louverture by the general of the French expedition.

The slave revolt did not end the violence between whites and free men of color, but it accelerated white recognition of the latter group's civil rights. Though many whites blamed mulattoes for rousing the slaves, the free colored militia was a vital tool against the rebels. Moreover, the image of brown colonial citizen-soldiers grew more and more palatable to France itself as that country moved toward war. On April 4, 1792, the French National Assembly extended citizenship to all free men of color.

Meanwhile, in much of Saint Domingue the rebel slaves remained unchecked. The January 1793 execution of Louis XVI brought Great Britain and Spain into war with France, and in neighboring Santo Domingo, Spanish officials supported the ex-slave armies of the black generals Jean-François and Biassou. As this counterrevolutionary alliance came to control much of northern Saint Domingue, white French colonists began to turn against the new French Republic. Léger Félicité Sonthonax, a Jacobin commissioner sent out from Paris, offered freedom to slaves who joined the revolutionary army. By late September 1793, he extended this decree into an outright abolition of slavery, confirming what the slaves themselves had already accomplished. White counterrevolutionary planters appealed to Jamaica for help, and British troops won control of key ports and plantation districts in Saint Domingue's South and West Provinces.

On February 4, 1794, the Revolutionary Convention in Paris confirmed Sonthonax's abolition of slavery, and two months later, Toussaint Louverture shifted his allegiance from the Spanish to the French, thus turning the tide of battle in Saint Domingue's North Province. In July 1795, the Treaty of Bayle ended Spanish control and gave France official control of the entire island. In the isolated South Province, the mulatto general André Rigaud, already successful in repressing rebel slaves, began pushing the British back into the coastal cities. Though he did not challenge the abolition of slavery, Rigaud established a military work regime for ex-slaves that made his territory the most orderly and profitable in the colony by 1796.

Although the mulatto class and its experienced, island-born soldiers won favor with Jacobin commissioners in 1792 and 1793, the French agents sent to govern the colony suspected Rigaud of aiming to establish his own independent republic, and they turned increasingly to Toussaint Louverture. More than a winning general, Louverture commanded the ex-slaves' loyalty, and that group constituted nearly 90 percent of Saint Domingue's population.

Born in the colony, and literate and free before the revolution occurred, Louverture was expert at manipulating the French military and political figures sent from Paris. Urging some to retire to France for more fruitful political work and threatening others with peasant and army revolts, by 1798 Louverture ruled Saint Domingue. Ignoring his French superior, General Gabriel Marie Hédouville, Louverture negotiated the final withdrawal of British troops from the island and agreed to allow counterrevolutionary whites and blacks to fight under his command. He secured favorable commercial and political arrangements with the British and the United States, again sidestepping the French Republic's policies.

With this external support, in July 1799 Louverture's general Jean-Jacques Dessalines attacked the mulatto southern peninsula, leading 45,000 troops to victory over Rigaud's army of 15,000 in August 1800. By the end of the year, Louverture's troops occupied Spanish Santo Domingo, despite orders from Paris, and in 1801, a "central assembly" of Louverture supporters named him governor general for life. He established new, stricter regulations governing agricultural labor in an attempt to resurrect Saint Domingue's sugar and coffee exports.

The rise of this astute general and revolutionary politician in Saint Domingue coincided, unfortunately for Louverture, with the rise of Napoleon Bonaparte in France. After signing the Treaty of Amiens (1802) with the British, Bonaparte planned to make Saint Domingue the launch pad for a Latin American campaign. In the same year, a massive French expedition under the command of the French general Charles-Victor-Emmanuel Leclerc landed in the colony with orders to reestablish plantation slavery. After accepting Louverture's resignation, Leclerc arrested him for conspiracy and sent him to France where he died the following year.

The French invasion and Louverture's arrest provoked a fierce colonial war. Local black insurgent leaders fighting the reimposition of slavery recognized Louverture's lieutenant Dessalines as their chief in May 1803. Their guerrilla tactics and experience in colonial warfare, combined with the devastating effect of yellow fever on European soldiers and the collapse of the Peace of Amiens in 1803, forced the French to evacuate the colony before the end of the year. On January 1, 1804, Dessalines proclaimed the colony's independence, renaming it Haiti.

Fierce popular nationalism and France's distractions under Napoleon allowed the new country to survive numerous intrigues and division into two separate polities from 1806 to 1820. Ostracized by other American states, Haiti was linked to slave revolts from South Carolina to Bahia, Brazil. Nevertheless, brown and black soldiers enforced plantation labor requirements in the new nation until the 1830s. In Haiti's third decade of independence, the laborers began abandoning the large estates to work on their own peasant holdings. Although not as dramatic as the slave uprising of August 1791, this flight closed the long history of slavery in this part of Hispaniola.

—*John D. Garrigus*

See also
Dessalines, Jean-Jacques; Louverture, Toussaint; Raimond, Julien; Raynal, Abbé Guillaume-Thomas-François; Rigaud, André

For Further Reading
Geggus, David P. 1989. "The Haitian Revolution." In *The Modern Caribbean*. Ed. Franklin W. Knight and Colin A. Palmer. Chapel Hill: University of North Carolina Press; Geggus, David P. 1989. "Racial Equality, Slavery, and Colonial Secession during the Constituent Assembly." *American Historical Review* 94 (December): 1290–1309; James, C. L. R. 1968. *The Black Jacobins: Toussaint L'Ouverture and the San Domingo Revolution*. New York: Random House; Pluchon, Pierre. 1989. *Toussaint Louverture: Un révolutionnaire noir d'Ancien Régime*. Paris: Fayard.

HALE, EDWARD EVERETT (1822–1909)

Edward Everett Hale was a prominent nineteenth-century American minister and writer who was an active abolitionist and cofounder of the New England Freedmen's Aid Society. Hale was born in Boston on April 3, 1822, to a family with deep roots in Massachusetts society and history. Hale's father was the owner and editor of the *Boston Daily Advertiser*, his maternal uncle was the prominent orator/statesman, Edward Everett, and his paternal great-uncle was the revolutionary spy and martyr, Nathan Hale.

Hale graduated from Harvard in 1839 intending to become a teacher. After three years of teaching in several New England schools, however, he followed a new calling into the ministry. As a Unitarian minister, Hale served for a decade at the Church of the Unity in Worcester, Massachusetts. In 1856, he accepted a position as minister at the larger South Congregational Church in Boston where he served for 45 years, from 1856 to 1901. Throughout his ministry, Hale worked first for the abolition of slavery and after emancipation, for the social and economic improvement of freed slaves.

On February 7, 1862, Hale, along with fellow abolitionists and social activists Charles Bernard, William Cullen Bryant, Samuel Cabot, and William Lloyd Garrison, founded the New England Freedmen's Aid Society in Boston to promote education among free African Americans. The society raised funds to support schools throughout the region for native free blacks and for newly freed slaves, both children and adults, male and female.

Hale was a prolific writer, novelist, and biographer. His most successful literary work was the short story, "The Man Without a Country," which he published in 1863. That story's central character, a U.S. naval officer, curses his native land and announces his desire never to set foot again on U.S. soil. As punishment for betraying his country, he is condemned to spend the rest of his life aboard U.S. naval vessels, within sight of the United States but never being allowed to land. The story was widely reprinted and became a sentimental favorite during the years of post–Civil War patriotism that gripped late-nineteenth-century readers.

In 1903, Hale was appointed chaplain of the U.S. Senate, a position he held until his death on June 10, 1909, in Roxbury, Massachusetts.

—*Frederick J. Simonelli*

For Further Reading
Adams, John R. 1977. *Edward Everett Hale*. Boston: Twayne Publishers.

HAM, CURSE OF

A primary argument of the proslavery contingent in the western world has been that the Bible justifies the enslavement of blacks. Slavery's advocates, following Benjamin of Tudeal, the twelfth-century author of *The Itinerary of Benjamin of Tudella*, claimed that Noah, the biblical father of all subsequent humanity, cursed his son Ham with both blackness and the condition of slavery for looking at him drunk and naked and exposing him to his other sons, Shem and Japheth. The most important thing to realize about the curse is that it never existed. Ham was not cursed, and his erroneous association with black slavery does not appear in the Hebrew Bible.

Instead, when Noah learned what his youngest son had "done to him" (suggesting that he was upset about more than Ham's indiscretion of seeing and mocking), Noah cursed Canaan. Why Noah was upset with Canaan, we are never told, but biblical scholars are of two minds about the passage. Those desiring a consistent text insist that Ham was the culprit. They assert that Canaan was Ham's son, so cursing Canaan indirectly cursed Ham. Conversely, those preferring to see the Scriptures as a composite text argue that there must have been a tradition according to which Canaan was Noah's youngest son. Ham is usually identified as the second of three children—Shem, Ham, and Japheth—and the text declares that Noah cursed his youngest son (but not Japheth) for a misdeed. That youngest son must have been Canaan, the supporters of a composite text argue.

Whatever one makes of such arguments, this much is certain: since the curse of being a "servant of servants" was placed on Canaan, eponymous ancestor of the Semitic Canaanites, who occupied the territory of Israel before their cousins the Hebrews, any attempts to justify the enslavement of blacks by referring to a curse of Canaan are without foundation. If geography can be trusted, Ham's African, and therefore darker-skinned, sons were Cush (Ethiopia), Put (Libya), and Mizraim (Egypt), and they, like their father, Ham (sometimes associated with Egypt in his own right), were not cursed.

Egypt is key to the issue. Jews, revolted by their experience as slaves there, abhor slavery—for anyone. Their Bible, while recognizing that a person may for one reason or another be indentured, requires that slaves be freed after seven years (Exodus 21:2). But that tradition notwithstanding, slavery became a standard feature of both the Christian and the Muslim worlds, which nevertheless professed to embrace the Hebrew Scriptures as their own. In short, groups that benefited by slavery either hypocritically or blindly used the nonbiblical phrase Curse of Ham in an attempt to excuse their abuse of humanity.

The Hebrew Bible text cited contains neither the phrase nor the concept Curse of Ham and actually forbids lifetime slavery, the abuse many people have embraced. These facts notwithstanding, a sufficient number of hypocrites, careless readers, or nonreaders have existed over the centuries to perpetuate the myth.

—*Albert Wachtel*

See also
Christianity
For Further Reading
Friedman, David Noel, ed. 1992. *Anchor Bible Dictionary*. New York: Doubleday; Grant, Frederic C., and H. H. Rowley, eds. 1963. *Dictionary of the Bible*. New York: Scribners; Speiser, E. A., ed. 1964. *The Anchor Bible*. Garden City: Doubleday.

HAMMOND, JAMES HENRY (1807–1864)

James Henry Hammond, governor of South Carolina, U.S. senator, and states' rights advocate, was born at Stoney Point in the Newberry District of South Carolina. He was the son of Elisha Hammond, a Massachusetts native, and Catherine Fox Spann of Edgefield District, South Carolina. Throughout his public career, slavery and the

James Henry Hammond

sectional politics that it engendered influenced his views on national policy.

Hammond attended South Carolina College and graduated in 1825. After a brief career as a teacher, he read law in Columbia, South Carolina, and was admitted to the bar in 1828. Hammond built a successful legal practice in Columbia and entered politics as a nullification supporter. In 1830, he established a newspaper, the *Southern Times*, in which he upheld South Carolina's stand on nullification and states' rights. He also called for a convention to consider the state's course of action in the nullification crisis.

On June 23, 1831, Hammond married Catherine E. Fitzsimmons, daughter of Charles Fitzsimmons, a wealthy Charleston, South Carolina, merchant. The couple moved to their cotton plantation at Silver Bluff on the Savannah River. Hammond's love of the land and his devotion to agricultural pursuits eclipsed his participation in politics for a time, although he ran unsuccessfully for a seat in South Carolina's nullification convention in 1832, and when the danger of armed conflict became a possibility, Hammond urged his state to prepare for war. He became a colonel of a volunteer regiment and offered a part of his cotton crop and the use of his slaves to defend South Carolina. After the immediate danger of conflict was over, Hammond still advocated military preparedness for his state.

Following the nullification crisis, Hammond gave his full support to the eventual secession of the Southern states from the Union and became an ardent supporter of Southern nationalism. He also supported the institution of slavery and proposed the death penalty for abolitionists.

In 1836, owing to ill health, Hammond left to travel in Europe, and when he returned, he devoted his energies to his plantation. However, in 1840 he ran unsuccessfully for governor of South Carolina. When he was elected to the office in 1842, Hammond served two terms. While governor, he supported public education, had an agricultural survey made of the state, reformed the Bank of South Carolina, and established military academies in Columbia (the Arsenal) and Charleston (the Citadel).

In 1842, Hammond again advised the secession of the Southern states from the Union. When the South did not secede, Hammond again turned his interests to politics by considering a run for the U.S. Senate, but that ambition was thwarted by the threat of disclosure of a sexual liaison with a young girl. Nevertheless, Hammond continued to maintain a high profile in South Carolina politics. In 1850, he supported the Nashville Convention and attended as a delegate. Disgusted by the lack of action by the South on secession, Hammond returned to South Carolina and pursued his agricultural interests. In 1855, he established a plantation at Redcliffe, where he lived the rest of his life.

In 1857, Hammond attained election to the U.S. Senate. He became convinced that the South could eventually control the destiny of the Union, and on March 4, 1858, on the floor of the Senate, Hammond gave his famous "King Cotton" speech. In it he stated that no power on earth dare make war on cotton, "Cotton is king." Although Hammond had supported the secession of the South from the Union, he did not participate in politics after the formation of the Confederacy. Instead, he frequently criticized the leadership of Jefferson Davis and the Confederate Congress. By 1864, Hammond could see the end of Southern independence and the defeat of the Confederacy. Exhausted and ill, he died at his beloved Redcliffe.

—*Ron D. Bryant*

For Further Reading
Bleser, Carol K. 1987. *The Hammonds of Redcliffe*. Oxford: Oxford University Press; Faust, Drew Gilpin. 1986. *A Sacred Circle: The Dilemma of the Intellectual in the Old South, 1840–1860*. Philadelphia: University of Pennsylvania Press; Merritt, Elizabeth. 1923. *James Henry Hammond, 1807–1864*. Baltimore: Johns Hopkins University Press.

HAMMURABI, CODE OF

The Code of Hammurabi is an extensive collection of nearly 300 laws compiled by the sixth monarch of Babylon's First Dynasty, Hammurabi (r. 1792–1750 B.C.), who consolidated most of Mesopotamia politically during his reign. Like the Hittite laws, the Code of Hammurabi was not a true code but a combination of diverse traditions combined by a recently unified polity, and thus it was not an innovation of new legislation. The code is in the tradition of older but not well-preserved legal collections stemming from Mesopotamia, and the collection's internal arrangement followed a conceptual pattern that is not always apparent to the modern scholar.

The laws were surrounded by a poetic prologue and epilogue, both of which were propagandistic in nature. The laws themselves were constructed in a conditional fashion, with a protasis and an apodosis (in other words, "if this shall happen, then this shall happen"). It is not certain how the laws were enforced in society, as the code's prices, fines, and penalties do not always correspond with other textual information from this period and existing court records never cite the code as the rationale for a particular decision.

The code divided society into three categories: *awīlum* (literally, "man"), the nobility or upper class; *mushkēnum*, a vague term representing a class of people dependent upon the state; and *wardum*, slaves. Slavery was part of the Old Babylonian socioeconomic system (c. 2000–1600 B.C.) and was thus regulated in the code. Assisting another person's slave to escape or providing refuge for fugitive slaves was punishable by death (#15–16). Like other classes, slaves had rights, and like laws in the Torah, a free person could be sold into slavery if he could not pay his debts (#53–54). Further, unpaid obligations often resulted in the debtor's wife and/or children being sent as slaves to the creditor's house, but for a maximum of three years (#117). They were then released back to the debtor, but if a slave were given as collateral for an obligation, the creditor could foreclose if the debt was not paid on time. Creditors were then allowed to sell the slave, who could not be reclaimed by the debtor.

The code was sensitive to class issues. Like the Hittite laws, marriage upgraded both male and female slaves to free status if they married a free person. Moreover, if a man claimed a handmaiden's sons as his own, they would share equally in his inheritance (#170). And they gained free status (without inheritance) even if he did not claim them as his own (#171). Similarly, children of an upgraded male slave could not be claimed by the man's former master (#175). As marriage was considered a partnership, what a free woman and a former male slave acquired in their marriage was divided among their children (#176). Alternatively, husbands were permitted to sell dishonest or wasteful wives into slavery (#141).

As in the Hittite laws, society's lower orders merited smaller compensations or penalties. The penalty for striking a man's slave was half the price of striking another *awīlum* (#198–199), and the slave who struck a freeborn person was mutilated while an *awīlum* was charged 10 shekels for the same crime (#204–205). A female slave's fetus also had a lower value ascribed to it. If a female slave was struck causing her to miscarry, the penalty was merely 2 shekels of silver compared to 15 shekels (half a mina) of silver for a freewoman who was caused to miscarry (#212–214).

Slaves played a major role in the Old Babylonian economy, and thus slave ownership was a matter of legal safekeeping. One who marked a slave with a wrong identification had his hand amputated, and anyone causing a brander to mark a slave incorrectly was killed (#226–227). The code made distinctions between native born and alien slaves. A native Babylonian slave who went into exile was given his freedom upon returning home, but if an alien was returned back to Babylonia, his owner could repossess him or her (#280–281). As in other ancient Near Eastern societies, the institution of slavery was taken for granted and therefore was not condemned.

—*Mark W. Chavalas*

For Further Reading

Deimel, A. 1930. *Codex Hammurabi.* Rome: Pontifical Biblical Institute; Driver, G., and J. Miles. 1952–1955. *The Babylonian Laws.* 2 vols. Oxford: Clarendon Press; Gordon, C. 1963. *Hammurapi's Code: Quaint or Forward Looking?* New York: Holt, Rinehart, and Winston; Wiseman, D. 1962. "The Laws of Hammurabi Again." *Journal of Semitic Studies* 7: 161–172.

HARPERS FERRY RAID

Harpers Ferry, the scene of radical abolitionist John Brown's 1859 raid for initiating armed slave insurrection, was established as the second federal armory and arsenal in 1794. Strategically situated at the confluence of the Potomac and Shenandoah Rivers in northern Virginia, it was also well supplied with raw materials and near Washington, D.C., and Baltimore, Maryland. The reasons for Brown's selection of the place were threefold. It offered easy access to the heart of the slave South down the Appalachian range, it was lightly defended with civilian rather than military troops, and most important, it was well-stocked with arms and munitions.

In 1859, there were approximately 100,000 arms for potential distribution to slaves and free blacks who wished to revolt.

Brown conceived of the raid on Harpers Ferry during the mid-1850s, but it was not until late-winter 1858 that he secured anonymous financial backing from a group of six men. By 1859, Brown had also collected a band of 21 followers, which included former slaves, free blacks, and radical whites. The youngest follower, 20-year-old William H. Leeman explained the nature of the plan in a letter to his mother: "We are now all privately gathered in a slave state, where we are determined to strike for freedom, incite the slaves to rebellion, and establish a free government." On July 3, Brown and his two sons arrived at Harpers Ferry and rented a farmhouse seven miles distant across the Maryland border. The next three months were spent planning and waiting.

The raid began on Sunday, October 16, 1859, in the late evening. The 22 revolutionaries left their rented farm and marched by stealth to Harpers Ferry, where they quickly occupied the lightly defended armory, arsenal, and bridge. Brown then ordered sorties into the surrounding countryside to capture hostages and free slaves. He liberated 10 slaves and seized three hostages, including Col. Lewis W. Washington, the great-grandnephew of George Washington. The colonel's sword was also captured, and Brown believed both were important symbols of a past successful revolution against tyranny. This first phase of the campaign was an unmitigated success.

Then problems began. Rather than seizing as many weapons as possible and taking to the hills, Brown and his followers waited in the armory for an expected uprising by slaves and dissident whites. Some of Brown's men came across Heyward Shepherd, a free black baggage porter who panicked when confronted and was shot. Shepherd was tended by Dr. John Starry, who had been awakened by the gunfire, and after treating the wounded man, Starry was released. He immediately went to Charles Town, capital of Jefferson County, Virginia (now West Virginia), and alerted the garrison. Soon, the local militia was en route for Harpers Ferry. Brown's final error was when he failed to stall an eastward-bound train traveling through Harpers Ferry. The conductor telegraphed news of the raid, and authorities in Washington, D.C., were alerted. Federal marines under the command of Lt. Col. Robert E. Lee, seconded by Lt. J. E. B. Stuart, were soon on their way to Harpers Ferry as well.

During the early morning hours of Tuesday, October 18, federal troops demanded the surrender of the insurgents. Brown, barricaded in the engine house of the armory, refused. The marines stormed the firehouse, using a ladder as a battering ram, and marine lieutenant Israel Greene entered the building and

Federal troops entering the arsenal at Harpers Ferry and capturing John Brown.

slashed Brown across the head and neck with his saber. Two raiders were bayoneted and killed; two others were captured; no hostages were harmed. The final death toll reached 15 with 10 of Brown's raiders either killed or mortally wounded, including his two sons; four townsfolk, including the mayor, and one marine also died. Thirty-six hours after it had begun, the raid on Harpers Ferry ended in dismal defeat.

Brown was taken to Charles Town and tried by the circuit court in session under Virginia law, not by federal law, and he was indicted for treason even though he was not a Virginia citizen. The trial began on October 27, 1859, and lasted three days. Its result was a foregone conclusion. The jury found him guilty, and on November 2, Judge Richard Parker sentenced him to the gallows.

Exactly one month later, John Brown was hanged. Six days later his corpse was transferred to the family farm in North Elba near Lake Placid in upstate New York. Shields Green and John Anthony Copeland shared the gallows with Brown, and their remains were subsequently dissected by Winchester College medical students. Dangerfield Newby and Lewis Sheridan Leary, who had been killed during the raid, were also buried at North Elba. Anderson moved to Canada,

contracted tuberculosis, returned to the United States, and died in Washington, D.C., in late 1872.

The historical significance of the Harpers Ferry raid is profound. Most immediately, it served as the opening shot of the impending Civil War in the United States. Brown's raid also revealed that the issue of slavery was the underlying reality of the sectional crisis between the South and North—as the *Richmond Enquirer* eloquently put it in the October 25, 1859, issue, "The Harper's Ferry invasion advanced the cause of Disunion more than any other event." Furthermore, the episode suggested that a decades-long sectional crisis could only be resolved through armed struggle. Finally, it planted the popular image of John Brown as a freedom fighter in African American history.

—*Jeffrey R. Kerr-Ritchie*

See also
Brown, John

For Further Reading
DuBois, William E. B. 1909. *John Brown*. Philadelphia: G. W. Jacobs; Finkelman, Paul, ed. 1995. *His Soul Goes Marching On: Responses to John Brown and the Harpers Ferry Raid*. Charlottesville: University of Virginia Press; Oates, Stephen B. 1970. *To Purge This Land with Blood: A Biography of John Brown*. New

York: Harper and Row; Perdue, Charles L., et al. 1976. *Weevils in the Wheat: Interviews with Virginia Ex-Slaves.* Charlottesville: University of Virginia Press.

HARRIS, JOEL CHANDLER (1848–1908)

Until recently, historical scholars have given scant attention to slavery's folklore and dialect, but slave songs and oral traditions help to chronicle slavery from the slave's perspective. Joel Chandler Harris spent his adolescence living on a plantation, and his literary works offer both sympathy for the slavery tradition and a humanistic concern for black people. This combination resulted in the nostalgic, yet controversial, writings known as the Uncle Remus tales.

Born on December 9, 1848, in Eatonton, Georgia, Harris was the illegitimate son of an Irish laborer and a village seamstress. He was a very shy youth who used practical jokes and humor to seek acceptance. He and his mother lived among rural poor white farmers, and he grew to appreciate Southern culture and traditions.

Harris took a job working as an apprentice typesetter for plantation owner Joseph Addison Turner in 1862. Turner's publication, *Countryman*, was possibly the first weekly newspaper issued from a plantation. During this time, Harris called Turnworld plantation home, and he spent his evenings in the slave quarters absorbing the slaves' folklore, tales, and dialogue. Turner allowed him to publish some of the anecdotes in the paper.

Soon, however, in 1864, General Sherman's Civil War conquest of the area meant that it would be a struggle just to keep the Turnworld plantation going. The plantation had been ransacked, the slaves had fled, and the *Countryman* ceased publication in 1866. At age 17, Harris moved to Macon, Georgia, and began a typesetting job at the *Telegraph*. During the next decade he held various positions as typesetter, book reviewer, associate editor, and staff writer for several Georgia and Louisiana newspapers.

In 1876, Harris became associate editor of the *Atlanta Constitution*, and it was there that he wrote sketches in an Afro-American dialect about slavery's folklore. These works were critically acclaimed for their accuracy and entertainment value, and by 1879, they included the Uncle Remus character as Harris recounted slave tales that he heard as a youth at Turnworld.

The Uncle Remus tales followed a particular scenario. Uncle Remus, a former slave, is depicted as a bear standing in front of a hearth and cooking as a young white child listens to his stories, tales involving the protagonist Brer Rabbit and his nemesis Brer Fox. Brer Fox is constantly trying to catch Brer Rabbit, but when the fox is thwarted, the scene always returns to a cabin.

Uncle Remus is an affectionate Negro narrator who speaks of the adventures of bears, rabbits, and foxes. Harris made certain that readers understood that these tales were only entertainment and that animals could not face the same moral judgments or dilemmas as humans. He also introduced a positive black literary character.

Commercial success and the newspaper column's popularity led Harris to publish a collection of 10 Uncle Remus books. Many are deemed classics and are still widely read today. Harris has been praised for his attention to detail and literary mastery of the plantation slave culture, but he has also been ridiculed for the social and political agenda that the tales represent.

—Anthony Todman

See also
Folktales

For Further Reading
Fluche, Michael. 1975. "Joel Chandler Harris and the Folklore of Slavery." *Journal of American Studies* 9 (December): 347–363; Harris, Julia Collier. 1918. *The Life and Letters of Joel Chandler Harris.* New York: Houghton Mifflin; Jones, Alfred Haworth. 1983. "Joel Chandler Harris: Tales of Uncle Remus." *American History Illustrated* 18 (3): 34–39; Trotsky, Susan M., and Donna Olendorf, eds. 1992. *Contemporary Authors,* vol. 137. Detroit: Gale Research.

THE HAUSA

Sources estimate that the nineteenth-century slave population of the Sokoto caliphate in Africa ranged between 1 million and 2.5 million (Lovejoy and Hogendorn, 1993). The Sokoto caliphate comprised 30 emirates and their subdivisions, including a number of Hausa states, and stretched from present-day Burkina Faso in the west to Cameroon in the east. The caliphate's rise was accompanied by the spread of slavery through war, slave raids, and tribute from conquered areas.

Slavery itself was not a new phenomenon in Nigeria. Arab records first refer to the trans-Saharan slave trade in the ninth century, and within 300 years, references to the slave trade in the Sudan were common. The slave trade was part of the everyday commerce linking the Sudanic region, including the Hausa states, with North Africa and the Guinea Coast, but the establishment of Hausa-Fulani power led to the expansion and increasing importance of the slave trade in northern Nigeria.

With the rise of Fulani jihads (holy wars) in the early-nineteenth century, the merger of the town Fulani with the Hausa states, and intermarriage with the ruling Hausa, there emerged a powerful Hausa-Fulani ruling class, and this Islamic class had no hesitancy about enslaving the pagan peoples over whom they held dominion. Thus, when British, French, and German imperialists entered the area in the late-nineteenth and early-twentieth centuries, slavery was a thriving enterprise, complete with slave raiding and trading.

Indeed, the Sokoto caliphate had ties with various types of slavery. As a Muslim state, it had characteristics of slavery found in other Islamic areas, and it supplied African slaves to the Ottoman Empire and present-day Arabia. It also was involved in the transatlantic slave trade, and being centered in Africa, it had connections with non-Islamic slavery and modifications to the institution. Only during the nineteenth century did a significant proportion of either the Fulani or the Hausa become Muslim, and regional slavery certainly predated that process.

The slow elimination of slavery among the Hausa demonstrates just how deeply their political, social, and economic systems were tied to the institution. Not only were personal prestige and wealth tied to slaves, but a ruler's power often depended on the loyalty of slave officials. The British, who used slavery's elimination as justification for conquering and ruling northern Nigeria, found it expedient to go slow in actually eliminating the institution as opposed to the slave trade. Although the international and transatlantic trade ended in the nineteenth century, the trade within Africa continued into the twentieth, and it was not until the eve of World War II that slavery was abolished, at least in name, in Nigeria.

—*Frank A. Salamone*

For Further Reading
July, Robert W. 1992. *A History of the African People.* Prospect Heights, IL: Waveland Press; Lovejoy, Paul E., and Jan S. Hogendorn. 1993. *The Slow Death of Slavery: The Course of Abolition in Northern Nigeria.* Cambridge: Cambridge University Press; Lugard, Lord Frederick. 1933. "Slavery in All Its Forms." *Africa* 6: 1–14; Oliver, Roland, and J. D. Fage. 1990. *A Short History of Africa.* New York: Penguin Books.

HAWKINS, JOHN
(1532–1595)

Sir John Hawkins, Elizabethan rear admiral, merchant, and privateer, has the dubious distinction of being responsible for the first recorded case of English involvement in the Atlantic slave trade. As the son of one William Hawkins, he was born into mercantile and naval circles, and he married a secretary of the navy's daughter. After 1555, Hawkins participated in trade to the Canary Islands, a stopover point in the Atlantic trade, where he learned from Spanish contacts that a New World labor shortage combined with the limited nature of the Portuguese slave trade provided a market for an illicit slave trade. Since French ships had been ignoring the Portuguese and Spanish trade monopolies on African and West Indian trade for some time and London merchants connected to Hawkins had begun funding trading expeditions to the Gold Coast in the 1550s, the opportunity seemed like a golden one.

In 1562, Hawkins used his London connections for funds and set sail from England with three ships. Stopping at the Canaries he secured a Spanish pilot for American waters and continued to Sierra Leone. There, he gathered approximately 300 slaves, which the Portuguese later claimed he took by force from their ships, and sailed to Hispaniola where—with the illegal connivance of local Spanish authorities—he sold the slaves and other English goods for a great profit. His success meant that his next expedition attracted noble patronage and the queen lent him a large warship. He sailed in 1564, collected slaves by trade and raids along Guinea's coast, and again sold them in Hispaniola and on the mainland.

Hawkins returned to England in 1565 with massive profits, but Spanish complaints meant he would not sail again himself again until 1567 when he left with a fleet of six ships. In Sierra Leone, Hawkins participated in local wars, assaulted coastal towns, and intercepted Portuguese vessels until he had amassed 500 slaves and other cargo. Sailing to Dominica he sold most of his cargo through a mixture of forced trade and guile, but upon arriving in Mexico, his fleet became trapped when a heavily guarded Spanish treasure fleet appeared. A battle ensued, despite Hawkins's attempts at peacemaking, and only Hawkins's ship and two others survived. Hawkins continued to have a glittering naval career, but his involvement in slave trading ended with this voyage.

The success of Hawkins's maritime expeditions inspired many contemporaries, but successors like Drake, animated by the hostility to Spain created by Hawkins's defeat, turned to violent privateering rather than to smuggling slaves. Nevertheless, in the long term Hawkins's exploits were vital in fueling English mercantile and imperial ambitions that resulted in the creation of an overseas empire in which the slave trade eventually played an unquestioned and profitable part.

—*Gwilym Games*

See also
Portuguese Slave Trade
For Further Reading
Andrews, Kenneth. 1984. *Trade, Plunder, and Settlement: Maritime Enterprise and the Foundation of the British Empire.* Cambridge: Cambridge University Press; Williamson, James A. 1927. *Sir John Hawkins.* Oxford: Oxford University Press.

HAYNES, LEMUEL (1753–1833)

A noted Revolutionary War veteran, abolitionist, and clergyman, Lemuel Haynes was one of the eighteenth century's most enigmatic African Americans. Born a mulatto of African and Scottish descent, Lemuel was the slave of John Haynes of Hartford, Connecticut, until the age of five months when he was indentured to Deacon David Rose of Granville, Massachusetts.

In 1774, when his tenure ended at age 21, Haynes remained with the Rose family, although he left twice. He joined Gen. George Washington's army during the attack on Boston in 1775, and in fall 1776, he served in a garrison regiment during a battle at Fort Ticonderoga. These experiences made a deep impression on Haynes's political consciousness. After returning from the battle in Boston in April 1775, Haynes composed a ballad titled "The Battle of Lexington," in which he incorporated the revolutionary and patriotic sentiment that was sweeping many of the colonies. In this lyrical ballad, Haynes argued that the American colonies were no longer the land of freedom and equality but had become a place where corruption and political savagery, stimulated by George III and Parliament, thrived.

In 1776, perhaps after returning from Fort Ticonderoga, Haynes wrote a pointed critique of slavery in an essay titled "Liberty Further Extended." His work contained three main arguments. First, based upon his interpretation of the Declaration of Independence, Haynes urged his fellow revolutionaries to consider the broader implications of the independence struggle. Second, he proclaimed that the principles of freedom and liberty should be applied to all colonial citizens. Third, drawing closely on the arguments of early anti-slavery writers like Samuel Hopkins and Anthony Benezet, Haynes argued that slaveowners must liberate their African slaves to free themselves from the inherent corruption and sin of slavery.

After the American Revolution, Haynes devoted the rest of his life to spreading the gospel. In 1785, he was ordained by the Association of Ministers in Litchfield County, Connecticut, and moved to Torrington, Connecticut, to become the minister there. From 1788 to 1818, he served as pastor of West Parish Congregational Church of West Rutland, Vermont. For six months, Haynes then traveled throughout Vermont spreading Christianity, but in late 1818, he obtained a position as minister at a small church in Manchester, Vermont, for three years. In 1822, Haynes moved again when he became minister at the Granville Congregational Church in New York where he remained until his death on September 28, 1833.

—*Eric R. Jackson*

For Further Reading
Cooley, Timothy Mather. 1837. *Sketches of the Life and Character of the Reverend Lemuel Haynes, A.M., for Many Years Pastor of a Church in Rutland, Vermont, and Late in Granville, New York.* New York: Negro University Press; Newman, Richard, ed. 1990. *Black Preacher to White America: The Collected Writings of Lemuel Haynes, 1774–1833.* Brooklyn: Carlson Publishing; Roberts, Rita. 1994. "Patriotism and Political Criticism: The Evolution of Political Consciousness in the Mind of a Black Revolutionary Soldier." *Eighteenth Century Studies* 27 (Summer): 569–588; Saillant, John. 1994. "Lemuel Haynes' Black Republicanism and the American Republican Tradition, 1775–1820." *Journal of the Early Republic* 14 (3): 293–324.

HAYNE-WEBSTER DEBATE

The Hayne-Webster debate of 1830 consisted of several speeches in the U.S. Senate between Robert Hayne of South Carolina and Daniel Webster of Massachusetts focusing on whether the United States was one country or many. Although the Senate discussion formally centered on a resolution concerning western lands, a part of it, consisting of two speeches each by Hayne and Webster, has become known as the Hayne-Webster debate.

The debate focused more on the issue of what the United States was—whether it was one nation united under the Constitution or merely a group of sovereign states united by a treaty called the Constitution. The second of Webster's replies guaranteed for all time that Webster would be seen as one of the greatest defenders of the U.S. Constitution. The debate was widely covered in the newspapers of the time, and 100,000 copies of Webster's second speech were reprinted in pamphlet form.

The debate was more than just between Webster and Hayne, however. It truly was between the people in the South who promoted nullification (whether or not a state had the right to nullify federal law), including John C. Calhoun, vice-president at the time of the debate, and people who believed in a strong Union and a (relatively) strong role for the federal government, with that role including the sponsorship of internal improvements and the use of tariffs to promote domestic industry. This group included Webster from Massachusetts and Henry Clay of Kentucky.

In Hayne's first speech, on January 19, 1830, he addressed westerners who disliked the federal government's ownership of land in their states. He attacked such control of the land as transferring state funds to the federal government and suggested that states should be able to control all land within their boundaries. He cited the tariff (although not referring to it by name) and land sales as "taxation" that should cease.

Webster replied on January 20 by arguing that the land policy had been successful in most areas, recalling that Ohio had moved from wilderness to having a population of a million in only 35 years. He also cited the need to pay off the national debt, and the conditions under which the land was transferred to the federal government, as reasons why the land could not be given back to the states. Throughout he noted the value of the Union. He mostly avoided the question of the tariff, but did laud New England as a great friend of the West. Webster also praised the Northwest Ordinance, noting its banning of slavery, and claimed that New England would always be a friend of the West.

Hayne's second speech, delivered the next day, mixed wit, Shakespeare, ridicule, and attack. He cited Webster's participation in the supposed "corrupt bargain" that had elected John Quincy Adams president in 1825 and accused Webster of inconsistency regarding the public lands and the American system. He also attacked the Federalists (Webster had been a member) for their role in the Hartford Convention, a meeting during the War of 1812 at which New England Federalists who were disenchanted with the war had met and discussed disunion. However, he also bit on Webster's bait, defending slavery, and claimed that slaveholders defended freedom more than any other group. He defended nullification, contrasting it with the evil, in his view, of the Hartford Convention and closed with the claim that the actions South Carolina took in resisting the tariff were the only way to actually preserve the Union.

Webster responded, on January 26–27 (in the interim, the Senate had been adjourned), with what has been called one of the greatest speeches in U.S. history. He spoke for six hours on two days. Webster first answered some of Hayne's barbs with some of his own, even noting errors in Hayne's references to Shakespeare. Webster defended his and New England's consistency on the public lands issue and the tariff and also answered the charge regarding the corrupt bargain. He accused the South of inconsistency on the tariff, implying that Calhoun had changed his opinion. Webster directly attacked the nullification doctrine, describing it as unconstitutional, and contrasted it with New England's earlier actions, which he described as constitutional.

Webster then suggested that the actions of South Carolina to resist the tariff would lead to civil war and a weak union. Throughout he noted how the government was one of constitutionally restricted powers, made by the people, responsible to it, and restricted by the Supreme Court rather than by the states. Webster closed by arguing that the United States should not have "Liberty first and Union afterwards," but "Liberty and Union, now and for ever, one and inseparable."

—*Scott A. Merriman*

See also
Calhoun, John C.; Webster, Daniel
For Further Reading
Baxter, Maurice. 1984. *One and Inseparable: Daniel Webster and the Union.* Cambridge, MA: Harvard University Press; Smith, Craig R. 1989. *Defender of the Union: The Oratory of Daniel Webster.* New York: Greenwood.

HELOTS

Helots was the appellation given to servile populations of some Greek city-states who were not technically privately owned slaves and is usually associated with peoples subjugated by Sparta. The class consisted of descendants of the original inhabitants of Laconia and most of the Messenian population, which Sparta conquered in the eighth century B.C. It may also have included descendants of Spartans who, because they had refused to fight in the First Messenian War (735 B.C.), became Helots. Their status remained vague—somewhere between freedom and slavery—but probably resembled that of serfs. Their services belonged to the Spartan *polis* (city-state) rather than to individuals, but the state apportioned them to individual Spartans, who could neither sell nor emancipate them (a power the state reserved for itself).

Living in their own dwellings on the land they tilled or in villages, the Helots owed their masters and the *polis* various services. Each Helot provided his master with an allotment of barley, fruit, vegetables, oil, and wine from the plot of land *(kleros)* he cultivated. The amount was fixed at an early time and could not be changed. Whatever surplus the Helot produced beyond this quota remained his own. Besides cultivating the land, Helots attended their masters at mealtimes and performed other menial services. They and their wives had to mourn their masters when they died, although this regulation may have referred to enforced attendance at the funerals of Spartan kings—a gesture of allegiance and humiliation. The state also demanded their labor on public works. In war, Helots were skirmishers, carriers of heavy equipment, servants to their masters, aides to the wounded, and heavy infantry in emergencies.

The Spartan system offered a degree of hope to Helots. The state sometimes rewarded those who distinguished themselves in battle with freedom, and they became part of a class known as *neodamodeis* ("new citizens") and garrisoned the borders or served as hoplites (heavily armed infantry soldiers), but lacked the franchise or right to vote. Another class, the *mothones* or *mothakes*, consisted in part of the children of Spartan fathers and Helot mothers. They lacked political rights but were personally free and took part in Spartan training, and some acquitted themselves with great distinction in the military and attained full citizenship. The state also rewarded Helots who had provided special services by placing them in one of several intermediary categories whose privileges and duties remain uncertain. These included the *aphetai* ("liberated ones"), the *adespotoi* ("those without masters"), the *erukteres* ("policemen"), and the *desposionautai* (associated with the navy).

Unlike chattel slaves owned by other Greeks, Helots were homogeneous and kept their own language, customs, and social organization. They also maintained family and community relations, occupied their original homes and lands, could own and accumulate property, were not supervised by a taskmaster, and were themselves never considered as property. Thus, after Sparta's defeat at the Battle of Leuctra (371 B.C.), Thebes granted Messenian Helots their freedom, which the entire Greek world recognized.

Nevertheless, ancient literary sources suggest that Spartan treatment of the Helots was oppressive and abusive. The Helots had to wear distinctive clothing—a badge of their degradation—and they could be forced to intoxicate themselves and perform indecent dances, supposedly to demonstrate to the Spartans the beastliness and disgrace of such practices. They were liable to annual whippings to remind them of their unfree status and even to murder by young Spartans acting as secret police—the *cryptia (krypteia)*—who sought out those suspected of sedition or rebellion. To make such executions legal, the ephors (group of five leaders/council members who governed Sparta) annually made a ritualistic declaration of war on the Helots.

Moreover, Thucydides related an incident in his *History of the Peloponnesian War* in which the Spartans called for Helot warriors who believed "they had most distinguished themselves against the enemy" to come forward so they might receive freedom. The Spartans reasoned that those who responded "would be the most high spirited and most apt to revolt." Some 2,000 Helots took advantage of the offer, and soon the Spartans executed them in a secret manner.

The persistent threat of a Helot uprising helped mold much of Sparta's history and policy until well into the fourth century B.C. The Spartans never ventured into the countryside without their spears, and at home they bolted their doors to provide an extra measure of protection. Their obsession with security was well-founded. There were several major Helot rebellions, which although suppressed, forced the Spartans to be in a constant state of readiness.

—*Charles H. McArver, Jr.*

For Further Reading
Austin, M. M., and P. Vidal-Naquet. 1977. *Economic and Social History of Ancient Greece.* Berkeley: University of California Press; Bury, J. B., and Russell Meiggs. 1975. *A History of Greece to the Death of Alexander the Great.* New York: St. Martin's; Cartledge, P. A. 1979. *Sparta and Lakonia.* London: Routledge; Finley, Moses I. 1981. *Economy and Society in Ancient Greece.* New York: Viking Press.

HELPER, HINTON ROWAN (1829–1909)

Best known for writing the antislavery tract *The Impending Crisis of the South and How to Meet It* (1857), Hinton Rowan Helper became the leading white Southern abolitionist in the United States. Born into a nonslaveholding family in western North Carolina's Rowan County, Helper received a minimal formal education and was indentured as an apprentice to a store clerk. Earning little money as an apprentice, Helper chafed at his lot and occasionally stole from his master. When his indenture expired in 1850, he left the South to pursue potential opportunities elsewhere.

Helper journeyed to New York and California, believing that the free states offered better chances for advancement to an ambitious but poor young man. After experiencing financial disappointments, Helper turned to writing, the career that made him famous. He published *The Land of Gold: Reality versus Fiction*, an exposé of some difficult encounters in California. The book was a modest commercial success, and its diatribes against nonwhites exhibited the vehement racism that characterized all of Helper's writings.

Despite his disappointments in seeking his fortune outside the South, Helper concluded that the North was more prosperous than the South because slavery damaged the Southern economy. He became an abolitionist, and unlike antislavery moderates, who wished to confine slavery within its existing limits and only stop its expansion into new territories, Helper favored an immediate abolition of slavery.

In 1857, Helper sought a publisher for his abolitionist book, *The Impending Crisis of the South and How to Meet It*. Southern presses were out of the question because the book contained incendiary passages calling for the overthrow of slaveowners, and his rhetoric was so extreme that he had difficulty finding even a Northern publisher. Finally, Helper agreed to secure a book agent as a hedge against possible financial loss, and the book was published in the North.

Helper dedicated *The Impending Crisis* to "Nonslaveholding Whites of the South." The impassioned, angry book included elaborate statistical measures of economic and population growth indicators to show that slave states were rapidly falling behind their free state counterparts. Helper's contempt for "aristocratic" slaveholders resonated throughout the book, and he posited that slavery did not produce profits because it exhausted the soil and impoverished nonslaveholders by degrading manual labor. Having little hope that the master class would change its way of life, and wishing instead for a political revolt of nonslaveholding whites against an economic system that denied job opportunities readily available to Northern workers, Helper demanded that nonslaveholding whites must be organized for independent political action. Although he asked for immediate abolition of slavery, Helper hated slaves even more than their owners. He saw abolition as a historic opportunity to remove African Americans from the South, and advocated removing African Americans to Central America or Africa.

Book sales were slow at first, despite glowing reviews in various Northern newspapers. Antislavery editor Horace Greeley summed up Northern Republicans' hopes that Helper, speaking for white nonslaveholders, represented the beginning of a Southern antislavery movement. Helper's Southern origins certainly gave him greater authority to speak against slavery: if a Northern abolitionist had written the book, it would have been of little consequence.

In 1858, Helper negotiated with the Republican Party to improve the sales and influence of *The Impending Crisis* by circulating a free compendium edition of 100,000 copies to the public. Republicans, eager to advance Helper's thesis that slavery damaged the economy and harmed the South's "poor whites," underwrote the costs of the venture, and Helper promoted sales and financing of the 200-page compendium by writing a circular advertising the book. This notice carried the signatures of prominent Republicans, including 68 of the 92 Republicans in the U.S. House of Representatives.

Republican promotion of *The Impending Crisis* brought increased publicity and controversy for the book. Southern newspapers railed against Northern politicians for promoting a book the former viewed as dangerous, since it called for the overthrow of their social system. Even though Helper had not addressed his book to slaves, Southern slaveholders argued that any book promoting abolition encouraged sedition by blacks. The book had little circulation in the South, and in Helper's home state of North Carolina, circulation of the book was a felony.

Few of the congressional Republicans who endorsed *The Impending Crisis* had read it, and they mistakenly promoted a book that was much more militant than their party's policies in both rhetoric and policy prescription. Republicans who claimed to have no desire of interfering with slavery where it existed were attacked by Southerners for endorsing a book calling for the immediate overthrow of slavery.

The book became central to congressional debate beginning in 1859. Ohio congressman John Sherman was among the Republicans who had endorsed Helper's book, and his nomination to be Speaker of the House ran into a roadblock placed by Southern Congressmen who viewed his recent action as proof that he was an abolitionist. Sherman opposed immediate action against slavery in states where it existed and disowned the book, declaring that he had never read it. Nevertheless, his previous approval of *The Impending Crisis* lost him the position of Speaker of the House. The House deadlocked on the matter, with a majority supporting Sherman but unable to gain the two-thirds vote necessary to appoint a Speaker. Debate raged about Helper and Sherman, and after a month's controversy, Sherman withdrew his candidacy for Speaker of the House in January 1860.

Southern opinion makers, editorialists, and politicians viewed the Republicans' cooperation with Helper a major grievance: some argued it justified secession. Leading Southerners worried that a Republican administration entering the White House would use its influence to promote Helperism—Southern abolitionism based on the nonslaveholders' interests. Helper symbolized Southern anxiety about class conflict between whites.

In fact, most antebellum nonslaveholders never adopted Helper's radical abolitionism, and Republicans, who had hoped that Helper represented the tip of an antislavery iceberg, were disappointed as most nonslaveholders remained loyal to the proslavery Confederacy. Although few white Southerners adopted Helper's radical sentiments, his work touched on central issues that divided whites in the South politically. Since Andrew Jackson's presidency two decades earlier, conflict between elite planters and plain farmers had been central to Southern politics. Helper's solution to Southern problems was atypical, but the class resentment of slaveholders' privilege that he exposed was widespread among the so-called poor whites.

Following publication of *The Impending Crisis*, Helper faded from public view. He served briefly as a diplomat in Argentina and also published several additional racist tracts. The people who knew him only as an abolitionist were surprised by the vicious language he used against blacks. Helper epitomized a glaring flaw in antislavery politics in the United States—that even people who opposed chattel bondage often despised slavery's victims.

—*Wallace Hettle*

For Further Reading
Bailey, Hugh C. 1965. *Hinton Rowan Helper, Abolitionist-Racist*. Tuscaloosa: University of Alabama Press; Crenshaw, Ollinger. 1942. "The Speakership Contest of 1859–60." *Mississippi Valley Historical Review* 29: 323–338; Helper, Hinton R. 1968. *The Impending Crisis of the South and How to Meet It*. Ed. George Frederickson. Cambridge, MA: Harvard University Press.

HEMINGS, SALLY (1773–1835)

One of Thomas Jefferson's slaves most of her life, Sally Hemings gained notoriety when a political opponent charged that she was also Jefferson's mistress. Sally was born to Betty Hemings, a slave woman alleged to be a concubine of her owner, John Wayles, and when that wealthy slave-trading Virginia planter died a year later, Sally became part of the estate of Thomas Jefferson, who had married Wayles's daughter Martha in 1772. Sally's first duties quite probably included caring for Jefferson's daughter Mary, often called Polly.

In 1787, five years after Martha Jefferson's death, Sally accompanied nine-year-old Polly to Paris where her father was serving as the U.S. minister to France. While there, Sally received a modest wage from Jefferson because the French did not permit slavery.

Upon Jefferson's return to Virginia in 1789, Sally became a house slave at his home in Virginia, Monticello. Over the next two decades, Sally had six children, four of whom survived to adulthood. After Jefferson's death in 1826, his daughter Martha freed Sally, who lived with her sons Eston and Madison in Charlottesville, Virginia, until her death nine years later.

In 1802, Sally became famous as the subject of a rumor promoted by a frustrated office seeker, James T. Callender. Angry because he had failed to secure a government appointment during Jefferson's first term, Callender published a story in a Richmond, Virginia, newspaper charging that Jefferson was the father of Sally's children. Based upon gossip gathered in the neighborhood around Monticello, the story spread quickly as other newspapers reprinted the allegations, sometimes in scurrilous verse. Although his friends and political associates denied the story and condemned Callender, Jefferson remained forever silent on the matter.

After a time, interest in the story flagged until Sally's son Madison granted an interview 70 years later to the *Pike County Republican*, an Ohio newspaper. In it, the 68-year-old man, who had been freed in Jefferson's will and subsequently had moved to Ohio, contended that his mother became Jefferson's mistress while they were in Paris and that although Sally wished to remain in France, where she would have been free, Jefferson promised to free any children she should have if she returned to the United States with him.

Most historians acknowledge the possibility of a relationship between Sally Hemings and Thomas Jefferson, but only two, Fawn Brodie and Page Smith, have found the circumstantial evidence persuasive. Because the question cannot be resolved absolutely, Hemings's relationship with Jefferson will remain controversial, but the possibility that he had a liaison with one of his slaves adds another dimension to the intriguing study of a man who remained a slaveowner while being widely known as a bitter opponent of slavery.

—*Larry Gragg*

See also
Jefferson, Thomas
For Further Reading
Brodie, Fawn. 1974. *Thomas Jefferson: An Intimate History*. New York: W. W. Norton; Cunningham, Noble. 1987. *In Pursuit of Reason: The Life of Thomas Jefferson*. Baton Rouge: Louisiana State University Press; Dabney, Virginius. 1981. *The Jefferson Scandals: A Rebuttal*. New York: Dodd, Mead; Smith, Page. 1976. *Jefferson: A Revealing Biography*. New York: American Heritage.

HERMOSA CASE
(1840)

Litigation involving the U.S. slaver *Hermosa* occupied admiralty courts for nearly 15 years. On October 19, 1840, the schooner *Hermosa*, commanded by a Captain Chattin, wrecked on one of the Abaco islands in the Bahamas. Bound for New Orleans from Richmond, Virginia, the *Hermosa* carried a cargo of 38 slaves. Wreckers escorted the ship into Nassau, where Chattin refused to allow the slaves to disembark the ship or to have contact with anyone on the wharf. Instead, he met with the U.S. consul to arrange for another ship to deliver his cargo. While the two were attempting to make arrangements, uniformed magistrates, armed and backed by British troops with muskets and bayonets, forcibly removed the *Hermosa*'s slaves. After hurried proceedings before a Nassau magistrate, the slaves were freed, despite protests from the captain and the U.S. consul.

The *Hermosa* case was one in a series of instances involving the removal of slaves from U.S. ships by the British. Despite different circumstances, there were similarities between this case and the *Encomium*, *Comet*, *Enterprize*, and *Creole* cases. Each focused upon a parliamentary act of August 28, 1833, which abolished slavery. In the *Comet* and *Encomium* cases, the British paid indemnities because the incidents occurred before abolition, but the other three occurred after the parliamentary act became effective. Britain's position concerning the *Hermosa* was to deny liability, claiming instead that the slaves had become free when they entered British jurisdiction. The Americans countered that the *Hermosa* had committed no illegality and had only sought aid. Like the other cases, that of the *Hermosa* became entangled in international arbitration for years.

The *Hermosa*'s owner, H. N. Templeman, persisted in his claims for compensation for the 38 slaves, as did the U.S. government, but it took years before the case was resolved. The *Hermosa*, *Enterprize*, and *Creole* cases were considered together, and a commission of claims was established to hear arguments. Meeting in London, the commission included Nathaniel L. Upham, representing the United States, and Edward Hornby of Great Britain. The commission operated under articles that established an umpire for cases in which the two commissioners were at odds. The *Hermosa* claim was presented on March 14, 1854, the commissioners heard arguments on May 23–25, and further papers were filed on June 19.

The *Hermosa*, *Enterprize*, and *Creole* claims were submitted to the umpire on September 26, 1854. The umpire was Joshua Bates, a prominent London banker and partner in the Baring Brothers banking firm. Bates conducted hearings from October 19 to October 21, 1854, with John A. Thomas representing the United States and James Hannen defending the British position. Bates announced his ruling in the *Hermosa* case on January 15, 1855, and ruled in favor of the United States, awarding $8,000 each to the two U.S. firms Templeman had transferred the claims to.

—*Boyd Childress*

For Further Reading
United States Congress, Senate. 1856. Senate Executive Document 103, 34th Congress, 1st Session. *Report of the Decisions of the Commissioner of Claims under the Convention of February 8, 1833, between the United States and Great Britain, Transmitted to the Senate by the President of the United States, August 11, 1856.* Washington, DC: Nicholson.

HESIOD'S WORKS AND DAYS

Hesiod wrote after the completion of the Homeric epics, but not much later, perhaps in the eighth century B.C., and his work gives us a better understanding of slavery in ancient Greece. What is known about him comes from biographical details in *Works and Days (Erga kai hemerai)*. He was born in Ascra in Boeotia, where his father had a farm that Hesiod and his brother Perses jointly inherited, which caused a painful legal battle between them. *Works and Days* concerns Hesiod's experience working the land, and he was the first Greek poet to write about a practical subject rather than myth and legend.

The poem *Works and Days* is a mixture of ethical maxims, agricultural advice, and descriptions of peasant life. It gives a realistic picture of primitive rural conditions and the tasks of each season. Its 828 hexameters form a loosely linked series of themes, including the myths of Pandora and the five ages of man—golden, silver, bronze, heroic, and iron—as a means of explaining mankind's harsh and toilsome contemporary condition. Hesiod comments extensively upon the necessity of labor but makes little or no distinction between the free worker and the slave. His attitude to slavery is similar to that shown in Homer: there are few slaves, most are captives of war or born to such foreigners in bondage, and their position in households fortunate enough to own them is almost indistinguishable from that of a paid servant.

Hesiod grew up in poverty and never prospered, so he mentions slaves as too expensive to buy and costly in food, clothing, and shelter, which their owner must provide. Hesiod implies that slaves are protected by their status from many of the anxieties and responsibilities of paid free workers. In his account, slaves are traded comparatively rarely, and he does not write of slaves as commodities. Moreover, since Hesiod expresses the belief that laboring to survive is the destiny of all men in the age of iron, slaves have no worse a fate than that decreed by the gods for the writer himself. He depicts slave and free farmhands working together, and his horticultural instructions are given to both equally. He places emphasis upon the need for right conduct and mutual respect between individuals, regardless of status, and upon the demands of shared labor uniting slaves and freemen in a common purpose.

Hesiod's particular situation and social environment may have shaped his views to some extent, but in his era slavery had not become the widespread institution that it was for later Greeks. By the mid-seventh century B.C. onward, slavery was accepted as the essential means by which free citizens could be liberated from the tyranny of manual labor. Complete Greek commercial and social dependence upon slaves developed over the two centuries after Hesiod set out the principles of the work ethic, which he regarded as binding upon freemen and slaves alike.

He defined the universal burden of hard work as being the result of a decline in the human condition brought about by oppression and injustice, which have caused resources to be unevenly distributed in society. In *Works and Days,* slavery is only one symptom of lamentable political and economic inequality, and slaves as human beings are the equals of their free companions in labor.

—*Lindy J. Rawling*

See also
Homer's Theory; Theognis of Megara's *Theognidea*
For Further Reading
Bowra, C. M. 1935. *Ancient Greek Literature.* Oxford: Oxford University Press; Holden, A. 1974. *Greek Pastoral Poetry.* London: Penguin; Lesky, A. 1961. *A History of Greek Literature.* London: London University Press; Rose, H. J. 1934. *A Handbook of Greek Literature.* London: London University Press.

HIGGINSON, THOMAS WENTWORTH (1823–1911)

A Unitarian minister, radical abolitionist, disunionist, social reformer, orator, and writer, Thomas Wentworth Higginson was the consummate nineteenth-century intellectual whose ideas and theories compelled him to a life of militant social activism. In the years following his graduation from Harvard College in 1841, Higginson was intrigued by the possibility of study at Harvard's Divinity School yet doubted his vocation for the ministry. Through his increasing involvement in several social reform movements, including temperance, antislavery, and women's rights, he discovered his immense attraction to the social activism of liberal Unitarian clergymen Theodore Parker and William Henry Channing. Thus inspired, he enrolled in Harvard Divinity School to prepare for a ministry in which he would lead his congregants, or, as he once wrote, "take hold and shake them up a little" and exhort them to follow him in missions of committed social reform (Edelstein, 1968).

Higginson served as pastor of the First Religious Society in Newburyport, Massachusetts, from 1847 to 1849 and as minister of the Free Church in Worcester, Massachusetts, from 1851 to 1861. He used the pulpit to refine and promulgate his radical abolitionism and disunionism, which completely alienated his congregation in Newburyport. In 1850, he made an unsuccessful bid for Congress as a Free Soil Party candidate but eventually withdrew from that party's politics because of a deeper personal commitment to the principles of disunionism, believing that dissolution of the Union was the only way to extract slavery permanently from the lives and consciousness of Northerners.

Higginson was actively involved in the effort to maintain the liberty of Boston's fugitive slaves. In 1851, he conceived a plan to free the fugitive slave Thomas Sims, who was incarcerated in Boston, and although the plot failed and Sims was returned to slavery, the incident confirmed for Higginson the necessity of concerted militant action against a government responsible for upholding the evil institution of slaveholding. In 1854, Higginson and several other abolitionists devised a plan to free the fugitive Anthony Burns. This attempt also failed and resulted in Higginson's arrest and a facial wound. Higginson found that the more he engaged in "forcible resistance," the more convinced he became of its necessity and the more he sought its opportunities. As he noted in his journal, "I can only make life worth living for, by becoming a revolutionist" (Edelstein, 1968).

Higginson's personal writings from the 1850s display the beliefs and theories that led to his conviction that violence was essential to the eradication of slavery. Despite his obvious moral outrage against slaveholding, his militancy did not solely derive from his morality. Journals and letters reveal his obsession with a heroic, romantic ideal in which men prove their courage, their manliness, and the power of their moral fortitude through militant, armed action.

Following the passage of the Kansas-Nebraska Act (1854), Higginson became the New England agent for the Massachusetts Kansas Committee, the militant branch of the New England Emigrant Aid Society, an organization that actively supported the settlement of free-state emigrants in Kansas. In that capacity, Higginson made two trips to Kansas and also purchased arms and ammunition to help free-state settlers defend their settlements against attacks by proslavery forces.

In 1857, Higginson became one of the group of six abolitionists, all members of the Massachusetts Kansas Committee, who collaborated to provide John Brown with funds to stop proslavery forces in Kansas and who helped subsidize John Brown's raid on Harpers Ferry. The "secret six"—which besides Higginson included Samuel Gridley Howe, Theodore Parker, Frank Sanborn, Gerrit Smith, and George Luther Stearns—provided funding, arms, and other supplies Brown required to execute his plan.

One scholar has argued that Higginson played a pivotal role in producing the "rationale for violence" that persuaded the group members who were most reluctant to accept militant action. Higginson fervently believed that participation in an insurrection would prepare enslaved African Americans to assume independent lives in a democratic society. Higginson also favored Brown's plan because he was convinced of the need to destroy the belief among Northerners that all slaves were docile and submissive (Rossbach, 1982).

Unlike his five coconspirators, once Higginson decided to support Brown's plan, he did not equivocate. He detested his collaborators' ambivalence, and from the earliest days of the group's collaboration, Higginson judged his colleagues' inability to support their moral imperatives with vigorous militancy as evidence of their moral and physical cowardice.

After the raid's failure and Brown's capture, Higginson's colleagues panicked and frantically destroyed evidence of their involvement. Higginson neither destroyed his records nor denied his role but instead dedicated himself to raising money for Brown's defense and developing a plot to free Brown from captivity. Although these efforts were unsuccessful, Higginson was not as disturbed by those failures as he was by the failure of Brown's raid to trigger a massive slave insurrection that would break Southern slaveowners. From this point on, Higginson realized that only unified action by Northern whites could destroy slavery.

Higginson welcomed the outbreak of hostilities that began the U.S. Civil War. In November 1861, the governor of Massachusetts authorized him to raise a regiment, which he filled by August 1862. In November 1862, Higginson eagerly accepted an appointment as colonel of the first all-black regiment in the Union army, the First South Carolina Volunteers, which was composed entirely of freed slaves. He enthusiastically trained the recruits, then sought skirmishes with the enemy as a means of giving his men the opportunity to exercise, display, and prove their valor. In 1864, persistent ill health brought on by a leg wound and malaria forced Higginson to resign his post and return to civilian life.

Although Higginson became briefly involved in supporting radical reconstruction after the war, including full citizenship and enfranchisement for freedmen, he soon recognized that his decades of radical militancy had passed. He wrote to Ralph Waldo Emerson of his new longing to be "an artist . . . lured by the joy of expression itself" (Edelstein, 1968). By 1867, African American concerns no longer captivated him. He devoted himself to writing, prolifically producing essays, literary criticism, fiction, and the memoir *Army Life in a Black Regiment* (1870). He remained an ardent supporter of women's rights and woman suffrage, and with fellow former abolitionists Lucy Stone and Henry Blackwell, he edited *The Woman's Journal* from 1870 to 1884.

—*Judith E. Harper*

See also
Brown, John; Burns, Anthony; Harpers Ferry Raid
For Further Reading
Edelstein, Tilden G. 1968. *Strange Enthusiasm: A Life of Thomas Wentworth Higginson.* New Haven, CT: Yale University Press; Howe, Marc A. DeWolfe. 1932. "Thomas Wentworth Higginson." In *Dictionary of American Biography.* Ed. Dumas Malone. New York: Charles Scribner's and Sons; Renehan, Edward J., Jr. 1995. *The Secret Six: The True Tale of the Men Who Conspired with John Brown.* New York: Crown; Rossbach, Jeffrey. 1982. *Ambivalent Conspirators: John Brown, the Secret Six, and a Theory of Slave Violence.* Philadelphia: University of Pennsylvania Press.

HIRING OF SLAVES

Slave hiring was a practice whereby slaves were temporarily rented, or otherwise temporarily transferred, between persons for various reasons. Many hired slaves labored in urban centers or helped with internal improvements. Less noted by historians are hired field hands and slaves hired out for their personal upkeep, particularly those in poor health or of very young or advanced age. Hired slaves' terms of service ranged from one day to one year, sometimes longer. Although agreements did vary, most stipulated that the hirer assumed the expenses of food, clothing, and taxes. Slaves hired out for their upkeep constituted the most common exception to these arrangements. Frequently, owners of very young, very old, or infirm slaves paid another person

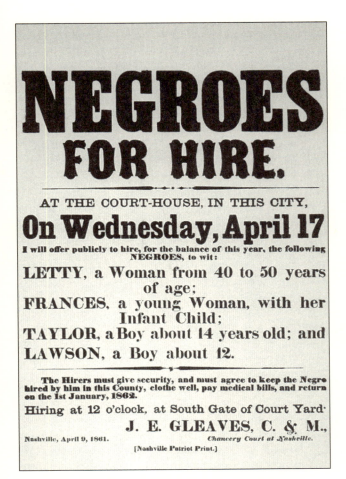

NEGROES FOR HIRE.

AT THE COURT-HOUSE, IN THIS CITY,

On Wednesday, April 17

I will offer publicly to hire, for the balance of this year, the following NEGROES, to wit:

LETTY, a Woman from 40 to 50 years of age;
FRANCES, a young Woman, with her Infant Child;
TAYLOR, a Boy about 14 years old; and
LAWSON, a Boy about 12.

The Hirers must give security, and must agree to keep the Negro hired by him in this County, clothe well, pay medical bills, and return on the 1st January, 1862.

Hiring at 12 o'clock, at South Gate of Court Yard·

J. E. GLEAVES, C. & M.,

Nashville, April 9, 1861.   *Chancery Court at Nashville.*

[Nashville Patriot Print.]

A poster advertising specific slaves for hire, with a disclaimer that they must be returned to their owner by a particular date.

to feed and clothe them, or transferred the slave in exchange for food and clothing.

To varying degrees, slave hiring occurred nearly everywhere African slavery existed in the Western Hemisphere. It evolved as an institutional modification, reflecting slavery's flexibility in changing economic circumstances, and became most prevalent in areas characterized by diversified agriculture and urbanization. In the late-eighteenth-century U.S. South, for instance, planters in Virginia's tidewater and northern piedmont regions began shifting from labor-intensive tobacco to mixed agriculture, including wheat and other small-grain crops. Slave hiring became widespread in those areas and remained so through the Civil War. The practice was even more ubiquitous in the larger cities, where diversified economies demanded flexible employment of slave labor. In Richmond and Petersburg, Virginia; Atlanta, Georgia; and St. Louis, Missouri, for example, hired slaves worked as factory hands, house servants, carriage drivers, dock workers, and many other forms of service.

Similarly, in sixteenth-century Peru, slave hiring was widespread in urban and rural areas. Free persons rented slaves in Peru, as did the Spanish government, which rented slaves to work in shipyards and on fortifications. As in the United States, Peruvian slave hiring served the purpose of providing a more flexible employment of slave labor.

Although there has not been much scholarly investigation of the practice, slave hiring is a subject of considerable debate among historians. The main point of contention is the impact of the practice on both hired slaves and the institution of slavery. The debate turns chiefly on whether one is talking about slave hiring in an urban or a rural milieu. Historians of urban slave hiring stress that in some cases, being hired out conferred special advantages upon the affected slave. These historians show that urban tobacco-factory workers and carriage drivers, for instance, were often hired slaves and predominantly male. These workers enjoyed relative freedom of movement between their homes and work sites, and bargaining for privileges was another benefit they received.

Recent research on rural slave hiring, however, shows that the experiences of these hired slaves—both women and men, agricultural and industrial—differed radically from those of their male, urban counterparts. With no need to find their own room and board away from the work site, rural hired slaves did not enjoy freedom of movement any more than slaves living and working on their owner's farm or plantation. Furthermore, much of the evidence shows that slaves rented out in rural areas were generally unsuccessful in attempts to manipulate the relationship among themselves, renters, and owners to their own advantage. Finally, slaves rented out in rural areas usually did not choose their own hirer but were rented to the highest bidder at public hirings.

Other factors applicable to both urban and rural settings must also be considered. In both city and countryside, slave hiring frequently separated slave children from their mothers once children were considered old enough to work for a prospective renter. For this reason, slave hiring was a particular type of slave trading, one that often entailed the rupture of a slave's ties with family and friends. Additionally, the prospect of owners' lawsuits did not always deter hirers from beating or otherwise abusing hired slaves mercilessly. Since slave hirers lacked interest in the long-term welfare of the slaves they rented, many were probably even more likely to shoot or whip the hired slaves in their charge.

The effect of slave hiring on slavery's long-term viability is also a matter of debate. Some historians contend that freedom of movement and other aspects of city hiring were symptomatic of a fundamental incompatibility of slavery and an urban environment.

Other scholars believe that slave hiring afforded slavery new vitality in regions characterized by mixed agriculture and urbanization because the practice permitted slaveowners temporarily to divert their surplus labor elsewhere. In 1850s Virginia, for instance, rapidly advancing hire rates and a growing demand for slave labor in other areas of the state combined to induce many slaveowners to hire out surplus slaves rather than sell them to areas further south. Ultimately, many lower-class whites, including nonslaveowners and tenants, hired these slaves and acquired a stake in the institution of slavery. Thus, these historians maintain, slave hiring afforded slavery the flexibility it required to survive in diversified economies.

—*John J. Zaborney*

See also
Peru

For Further Reading
Klein, Herbert S. 1986. *African Slavery in Latin America and the Caribbean.* Oxford: Oxford University Press; Stampp, Kenneth M. 1956. *The Peculiar Institution: Slavery in the Ante-Bellum South.* New York: Vintage Books; Wade, Richard C. 1964. *Slavery in the Cities: The South, 1820–1860.* Oxford: Oxford University Press; Zaborney, John J. 1997. "'They Are Out for Their Victuals and Clothes': Slave Hiring and Slave Family and Friendship Ties in Rural, Nineteenth-Century Virginia." In *New Directions in the African-American History of Virginia.* Ed. John Saillant. New York: Garland.

HISPANIOLA SLAVE REVOLT (1521)

Spaniards on Hispaniola complained about *ladinos,* slaves of African descent who had been born in Spain or had spent enough time there to become Christian, speak Castilian, and have "civilized" manners, saying the *ladinos* encouraged the native Indians to escape with them. Therefore, *bozales,* African slaves coming directly from Africa, were the slaves of choice, ostensibly because they were more docile. But in 1521, a group of *bozales* belonging to the island's governor, Diego Colón (son and heir of Christopher Columbus), planned, organized, and conducted Hispaniola's first major African slave rebellion.

The rebellion began on an *ingenio* ("sugarcane plantation") owned by Colón near Azua, about 60 miles from the capital, Santo Domingo. The 20 or so slaves who planned the uprising were mainly Wolofs, Africans from the West African region of the Senegal and Gambia Rivers. They planned well. The initial up-

rising occurred on Christmas Day 1521, a time when most Spaniards were celebrating and therefore off guard. Gonzálo Fernández de Oviedo y Valdés, the official chronicler of the Indies, wrote that the year was 1522, but the document labeled Patronato 295, No. 104, at the Archivo General de Indias in Seville, Spain, reveals that the year was 1521.

The 20 or so slaves who instigated the affair gathered more of the *ingenio*'s slaves to their cause, and about 40 of them headed for Azua, the center of the island's sugar industry, planning to augment their numbers by recruiting slaves from the many *ingenios* in the region. They stopped along the way to gather provisions from the ample storehouses on a cattle ranch owned by Melchior de Castro, who controlled the island's mining operations. According to later Spanish reports, the rebels killed several Spaniards on their way to de Castro's; killed another during the raid; took more than a dozen captives, including at least 1 African and 12 Indian slaves; and burned whatever they did not steal. Cristóbal Lebrón, who was visiting his own *ingenio* near Azua, sent to Santo Domingo for help.

In Santo Domingo, Colón gathered a small troop of horsemen and foot soldiers and rushed to crush the rebellion. Colón ordered his troops, led by de Castro and Francisco Dávila, to follow and apprehend the rebel slaves while he spent the night along the Nizao River awaiting more help. Twelve horsemen found the rebels about daybreak. They slashed their way through the rebels not once but twice, using Toledo swords against stones, sticks, and *dados* ("lightweight lances"), killing six of the Africans and wounding many others before the rebels broke and ran. De Castro, too, was wounded. Spanish troops retreated to a nearby *ingenio* belonging to Alonso de Zuazo, where they were joined by Colón and more Spanish horsemen. Colón sent the troops after the rebels again, this time under the command of Capt. Pedro Ortiz de Matienzo.

The uprising was suppressed within a week. Colón ordered that captured rebels be hanged on gallows built along the road as a warning to other slaves with similar thoughts. After that Christmas Day, Spanish settlers on Hispaniola "transferred to Wolofs all the vices and defects that at the beginning had been attributed to *ladinos*" (Deive, 1989).

—*Lynne Guitar*

For Further Reading
Cassá, Roberto, and Genaro Rodríguez Morel. 1993. "Consideraciones alternativas acerca de las rebeliones de esclavos en Santo Domingo." *Anuario de la Escuela de Estudios Hispanoamericanos* 50 (1): 103–131; Deive, Carlos Esteban. 1989. *Los Guerrilleros Negros: Esclavos fugitivos y cimarrones en Santo Domingo.*

Santo Domingo: Fundación Cultural Dominicana;
Oviedo y Valdés, Gonzálo Fernández de. 1959. *Historia
general de las Indias*. Madrid: Ediciones Atlas.

HISTORIOGRAPHY, AFRICAN

Much of the early writing on slavery in Africa was done by travelers, explorers, navigators, and geographers from the Christian and Muslim worlds. With the development of the abolition movement, slavery in Africa became the subject of a debate between proslavery and antislavery thinkers. Defenders of slavery like John Norris and Archibald Dalziel pictured Africa as a savage continent and suggested that slaves were being taken to a better life. In the nineteenth century, there was an increasing European presence in Africa and the penetration of the interior by explorers and missionaries, and explorers like Mungo Park, David Livingstone, Louis-Gustav Binger, and Gustav Nachtigal provided European readers with detailed descriptions of the slave trade, the havoc caused by slave raiders, and the treatment of slaves within Africa. Missionaries wrote and lectured about the horrors of the trade, and imperialists used antislavery to justify their conquest of Africa.

With the beginning of the colonial period, the literature on slavery suddenly dried up. Once slave raiding had ended within Africa and the slave trade was under control, colonial regimes treated slavery as something that was finished. Very little was written about slavery or its heritage. Even the missionaries in Africa turned to other concerns once there were no longer refugees to be housed and dying slave children to be saved.

The first anthropologists generally studied small-scale societies in which slavery had never been important. They saw no long lines of slaves, and if they wrote anything about it, they depicted African slavery as a benign institution. To be sure, there were exceptions. Robert Rattray described slavery among the Akan of Ghana (Gold Coast), and Horace Miner did so for Timbuktu. French novelists Oswald Durand and Robert Arnaud, both colonial administrators, described slavery in the Fouta Djallon district of Guinea, Reginald Coupland wrote about abolition and the East African slave trade, and E. W. Bovill wrote about the trans-Saharan trade.

This curtain of silence was lifted only when colonial rule ended and the first professional historians of Africa appeared. New universities in Africa attracted young professionals, and the former home countries began to train African scholars. A Nigerian historian, K. O. Dike, published a thesis, *Trade and Politics in the Niger Delta* (1956), in which he described slavery

in the delta and the area's role in the struggle for control of the trade with the interior. In the 1960s, Africa was discovered by U.S. scholars, who were often influenced by the civil rights struggle in the United States and the resultant reevaluation of that country's past. As Americans produced major works on slavery, students of African history looked to the African roots of African Americans. Finally, there was a new group of French scholars who were not beholden to colonial rulers. Influenced by the publication of Marx's early writings, they broke away from both colonial and communist conventional beliefs.

Members of all of those groups were struck by the importance of slavery and the slave trade to any understanding of African history. The first descriptive work came from anthropologists like M. G. Smith, who recognized the importance of slavery in his study of Zaria in northern Nigeria, and the new research produced three heated debates. The first was provoked by Philip Curtin in *The African Slave Trade: A Census* (1969), which provided a detailed synthesis of previous work on the demography of the slave trade.

Early attention focused on Curtin's downward revision of the number of slaves taken from Africa from 15 million to 9–10 million, and that revision was attacked unfairly as an apology for European involvement in the slave trade. Subsequent research has revised the numbers upward again to between 11 and 12 million. The numbers debate shifted attention away from Curtin's major contribution, which was to show where slaves came from, where they went, how they reproduced themselves, and when and where the trade grew. The most rigorous of Curtin's critics is the Nigerian economic historian, Joseph Inikori.

The second debate was provoked by the Guyanese historian Walter Rodney. In *History of the Upper Guinea Coast* (1970) and a series of articles, Rodney argued that the slave trade contributed to depopulation, to the increased use of slaves within Africa, to the development of more predatory political systems, and to a greater gap between the rich and the poor. John Fage, Rodney's most important critic, questioned whether the export of slaves led to serious depopulation and argued that the trade contributed to political centralization and economic growth. The most rigorous contribution to the population studies is Patrick Manning's *Slavery and African Life* (1990), which argues that the export of human beings slowed down the rate of population growth and for a long period led to no growth at all. A slight change in some of Manning's estimates would, in fact, produce a picture of decline.

The third debate was stimulated by the publication of two major collections: Claude Meillassoux's *L'esclavage en Afrique précoloniale* (1975) and *Slavery in Africa* (1977), edited by Suzanne Miers and Igor Kopytoff. Both works consist of a series of original articles. Between them, they establish the importance of slavery, but they present very different analyses. Both see slavery within a range of coerced relationships, and both stress a process of incorporation. Meillassoux, however, places more stress on violence—on the arbitrary nature of the master's authority—and the chattel nature of slavery. Miers and Kopytoff present a more benign view, one that sees slavery as one of a series of relationships, like marriage and parentage, which involve rights in persons. More important, Miers and Kopytoff argue that the slave gradually ceased to be alien and that there was a transition from slavery to kinship.

Since then, Paul Lovejoy has published a history of slavery in Africa, *Transformations in Slavery* (1983), and Meillassoux has pulled his ideas together in his *Anthropology of Slavery* (1991). There has been a series of important monographs, the most important being Frederic Cooper's studies of slavery and emancipation in East Africa and a study of the end of slavery in northern Nigeria by Paul Lovejoy and Jan Hogendorn. Robin Law has published several major studies of the slave trade in West Africa; Suzanne Miers and Richard Roberts have published a collection of papers on the end of slavery; and with the work of Robert Shell, Julian Cobbing, Nigel Worden, and Elizabeth Eldridge, there has been a flowering of South African slave studies.

—*Martin A. Klein*

For Further Reading
Curtin, Philip. 1969. *The Atlantic Slave Trade: A Census*. Madison: University of Wisconsin Press; Lovejoy, Paul. 1983. *Transformations in Slavery*. Cambridge: Cambridge University Press; Manning, Patrick. 1990. *Slavery and African Life: Occidental, Oriental, and African Slave Trades*. Cambridge: Cambridge University Press; Rodney, Walter. 1970. *History of the Upper Guinea Coast*. Oxford: Clarendon.

HISTORIOGRAPHY, GENERAL

Slavery has existed in almost all parts of the world, but writing on slavery focuses on classical antiquity and the Americas. The only important works that consider the full range of forms of slavery are H. I. Nieboer, *Slavery as an Industrial System* (1910) and Orlando Patterson, *Slavery and Social Death* (1982). Slavery has existed since early times, but the institution was unquestioned until recent centuries and was rarely the subject of historical analysis. Modern concern began with the Enlightenment and the antislavery movement, both of which

produced literature that was moral and polemical rather than historical.

Historical questions first developed in the study of classical antiquity, the first major history being Henri Wallon, *Histoire de l'esclavage dans l'antiquité* (1847). Classicists were concerned with three debates: whether ancient Greece and Rome relied on slave labor and whether doing so diminished their accomplishments; why slavery persisted after the development of Christianity; and whether there were stages of economic growth. Friedrich Engels in *Anti-Dühring* and *The Origin of the Family* (1902) suggested evolution through four modes of production: from primitive communism to slavery, feudalism, and capitalism. Doctrinaire application of this model operated as a straitjacket on Marxist scholarship, and its rejection influenced many scholars, most strikingly Moses Finley, who rooted classical research in a broadly cross-cultural understanding of servitude. The work of Keith Hopkins, Geoffrey E. M. De Ste. Croix, and Yvon Garlan has also been important.

The literature produced by the debate on abolition includes important autobiographies—for example, those of Olaudah Equiano and Frederick Douglass—as well as fiction, travel literature, and descriptive accounts, but there was little serious history until the publication of W. E. B. DuBois, *The Suppression of the African Slave Trade* (1896) and Ulrich Phillips, *American Negro Slavery* (1918), the latter study marked by a sympathetic view of Southern society and a belief in white supremacy.

Reevaluation of the role of slavery in modern history began with Eric Williams, *Capitalism and Slavery* (1944), in which he made four arguments: first, slavery was an economic phenomenon and racism was the result, not the cause; second, slave economies were a major source of capital for the Industrial Revolution; third, abolition came when slave economies were declining in profitability; and fourth, abolition was driven more by economic interests than by philanthropy. Each of these arguments provoked debate. Carl Degler and Winthrop Jordan questioned the notion that slavery itself caused racism, Roger Anstey argued that the slave economies were but a minor contributor to the Industrial Revolution, Seymour Drescher and David Eltis argued that the West Indies were not in decline, and Howard Temperley and David Brion Davis argued that the attack on slavery was more owing to ideology than to economic interest.

A second debate was provoked by Frank Tannenbaum's *Slave and Citizen* (1946), in which he argued that in Spanish and Portuguese America, legal codes, the Catholic approach to slaves, and royal intervention mitigated the harshness of slavery. This theory has not stood up well, but it stimulated much comparative study. A third debate was provoked by Stanley Elkins,

Slavery (1959), who argued, using the analogy of the Nazi concentration camp, that the slave plantation in the United States was a total institution and resulted in the infantilization of slaves. A fourth seminal work of this early period, Kenneth Stampp's *The Peculiar Institution* (1956), was less controversial in depicting American slavery as harsh, coercive, and inefficient.

Increasing interest in slavery was influenced by the civil rights movement, which forced a reevaluation of African American history and a reconsideration of the role of slavery in it. Stampp and Elkins opened the floodgates to a tremendous outpouring of historical scholarship. David Brion Davis's *The Problem of Slavery in Western Culture* (1966) was the first of a series of magisterial works that dealt with thought about slavery in the Western world. Peter Wood described the development of slavery on the rice lands of South Carolina; Edmund Morgan described the transition from white indenture to black slavery in Virginia, linking the process to a development of the ideal of freedom for whites; and Winthrop Jordan linked the growth of racism and slavery.

The first works treated slavery primarily as something that was forced on the slaves, but they were written in a period when African Americans were claiming their past and historians everywhere were writing the history of the powerless. John Blassingame, *The Slave Community* (1972), re-created the life of the slave quarter. Herbert Gutman looked at *The Black Family* (1976) and stressed the way slaves constructed their own family life. Lawrence Levine drew attention to African roots in his study of African American folk culture, *Black Culture and Black Consciousness* (1977), as did Sterling Stuckey in *Slave Culture* (1987) and Albert Raboteau in *Slave Religion* (1978).

The subtlest and most richly textured picture of slavery came from Eugene Genovese. One of his earlier works was entitled *The World the Slaveholders Made* (1969), and his most important work, *Roll, Jordan, Roll* (1974), was subtitled *The World the Slaves Made*. Using the ideas of Antonio Gramsci on hegemony, Genovese described a balance between accommodation and resistance, between coercion and persuasion, and depicted the ways slaves struggled to shape their world.

The most controversial book of the 1970s was Robert Fogel and Stanley Engerman's *Time on the Cross* (1974), which used cliometrics ("number crunching") to depict slavery as mild, more efficient than Northern labor systems, and profitable. Attacks from Richard Sutch, Herbert Gutman, Gavin Wright, and others sharpened our understanding of slave economies. Numerous local studies, among them outstanding works by Barbara Fields, Charles Joyner, and William Harris, sharpened the picture of different kinds of slavery. Deborah Gray White explored female slaves, and a series of productive comparative studies

appeared. The United States was compared by Carl Degler to Brazil, by George Frederickson to South Africa, and by Peter Kolchin to Russia.

More than anywhere else, most of today's Caribbean societies were born in slavery, and historians have explored the painful conditions of their struggle for independence. Elsa Goveia described development of slavery on the Leeward Islands, and Richard Dunn and Hilary Beckles wrote about Barbados. Edward Kamau Brathwaite wrote about Jamaica, Barry Higman wrote about demography, and Barbara Bush wrote about women.

Brazil, too, was shaped by slavery, and it received more slaves than any other country in the Americas. Gilberto Freyre, *Masters and Slaves* (1933), gave slavery and African culture a central place in Brazilian historiography. During the 1950s and 1960s, a series of works explored different slave systems in Brazil, described slave life and culture there, and depicted the impact of slavery on the economy, polity, and society of that country. Particularly important has been the work of Katia Mattoso, Jacob Gorender, and Fernando Henrique Cardoso. Also important is Stuart Schwartz, *Sugar Plantations in the Formation of Brazilian Society: Bahia, 1550–1835* (1985).

Philip Curtin's conception of a South Atlantic system builds on the work of Charles Verlinden on the development of plantation system. Two major efforts to deal with Verlinden's seminal work are Joseph Miller's magisterial *Way of Death* (1988), the most successful effort to see a trade system as a whole, and John Thornton's provocative *Africa and Africans in the Making of the Atlantic World, 1400–1680* (1992), which looks both the African and the American experience within slavery. Curtin's study of slave trade demography, *The African Slave Trade: A Census* (1969), has provoked debate on the demographic impact. His most effective critic has been Joseph Inikori, but the most substantial revision of his estimates is in David Eltis, *Economic Growth and the Ending of the Transatlantic Slave Trade* (1987).

The study of slavery within Africa was stimulated by a quest for African origins by people in the United States and by a new generation of scholars who recognized the role of slavery in shaping modern Africa. In 1975, Curtin provided a seminal study of Senegambia (the basin of the Senegal and Gambia Rivers) during the era of the slave trade. In that same year, Claude Meillassoux published a collection of articles by French scholars, many of them Marxists who had been inspired by a new reading of Marx. Two years later, Suzanne Miers and Igor Kopytoff brought out a rival collection. The debate between the two schools has been productive.

The most important subsequent work is by Frederick Cooper, whose *Plantation Slavery on the Coast of*

East Africa (1977) resembles the work of Genovese in that it recognizes the way a complex interaction of slave and master shaped a slave system. Also important have been Paul Lovejoy's synthesis, *Transformations in Slavery* (1983), and studies by Robert Harms, Jean-Pierre Olivier de Sardan, and Richard Roberts.

There were also slave systems in Eastern Europe and Asia, but in those areas, slaves were not racially distinct or, if distinct, were usually absorbed into the dominant population. The study of slave systems in those areas is therefore less important to an understanding of modern society. There has, however, been a smattering of work, some of it outstanding. Particularly interesting is the delineation by C. Martin Wilbur of a system in Han China in which slaves were not a source of productive labor but of people who served the elite: eunuchs, servants, and concubines. The literature on Asia also describes systems in which debt and poverty were more important sources of slaves than warfare. The work of James Watson on China and that of Anthony Reid and James Warren on Southeast Asia have been important.

The Indian subcontinent is unique in that the slave systems there operated within and were shaped by caste. The most important work dealing with India is summed up in a collection edited by Utsa Patnaik and Manjari Dingwaney, but the most provocative work is that of the postmodernist Gyan Prakash, who argues that the imposition of alien categories of analysis has shaped the perceptions and policies of colonial powers.

—*Martin A. Klein*

See also
Historiography (African, United States)
For Further Reading
Fogel, Robert, and Stanley Engerman. 1974. *Time on the Cross: the Economics of American Negro Slavery.* Boston: Little, Brown; Nieboer, H. I. 1910. *Slavery as an Industrial System.* The Hague: M. Nijhoff; Patterson, Orlando. 1982. *Slavery and Social Death.* Cambridge, MA: Harvard University Press; Williams, Eric. 1944. *Capitalism and Slavery.* Chapel Hill: University of North Carolina Press.

HISTORIOGRAPHY, ISLAMIC

After the seventh-century expansion of Islam, early Muslim scholars were faced with various nations, creeds, and cultures requiring integration and synthesis of several religious interpretations. The ninth century was a dynamic period of intellectual formulation, with seminal debates between Muslim and non-Muslim communities abounding.

Each group delved into its opponents' dogma and history and attempted to justify the private and communal faiths of their respective community to the outside world.

For Muslim scholars, and later scholars of Islam, discovering the preponderance of Islamic revelation in historical thought was a primary research goal. The questions they shared in their writings were, What defined this new historiography and new religion? and What unique features did it enjoy that other faiths did not have? Muslim writers often embellished and invented the history of the Muslim *'ummah* ("community") during its initial years, primarily in an effort to ingratiate themselves with influential and generous patrons. Many patrons lacked legitimate credentials to rule the political factions that proliferated during that period, and the ongoing need to have public images enhanced and unflattering realities altered, in a usually cautious *'ummah,* was important. The fact that that situation did exist casts a serious shadow on larger events framing the historicity of precise episodes.

With consolidation and expansion of Islamic civilization through conquest and voluntary conversion, Umayyad and Abbasid Caliphate Muslim scholars made extensive use of the Qur'an; Prophet Muhammad's *hadiths* ("sayings"); and the complex interpretation of the concepts of *j'ihad* ("struggle"), *ijtih'ad* ("innovation"), *'ijm'a* ("consensus"), *wuj'ub* ("obligation"), and *ahl al-hal-wa'l-'aqd* (elders of the *'ummah* who loose and bind). They used each to justify the religious and moral guidance that *'ummah* members sought of their elders, which later included the roles played by the principles of *jabr* (preordained actions of Allah), and *qad'ar* (human responsibility for actions freely undertaken in Allah's preordained world) in their lives.

Therefore, within Islam's early troubled history, the authors created perfect interpretative circles. In historiography, these interpretations, up to the recent past, developed an endless pattern of repetition. By re-creating new truths, the scholars made total use of an earlier truth that had been proclaimed. The Muslim *'ummah* and widespread civilizations for centuries remained conservative bastions for such views.

As trade grew, men and goods moved throughout the Islamic world from Spain to Egypt, western India, and China. Ideas traveled the wide expanse of the empire as Egyptians, Syrians, Chinese, Indians, and Persians brilliantly contributed to the expanding civilization's humanities, arts, and sciences. Religious studies and intellectual activity flourished. By the seventeenth century, Ottoman bureaucrats and writers trained in the "palace" system rather than the *medrese*, or religious school, and an unusual view of the interrelation of religion and politics had emerged.

Those men saw their duties as preserving state integrity and promoting Islam, and the concept of *din-u-devlet* ("religion and state") expressed this Muslim idea. The state became an essential viable entity, primarily for religious preservation, and in its need to maintain religion's flourishing status, the state acquired priority over it. Muslim writers and legalists subtly wove this concept into Ottoman culture, and it can be detected in the controversy surrounding using secular law codes and the Muslim scholars' tendency to support bureaucrats who abrogated significant portions of the sultan's criminal law prerogative. The specter of further state control over histories and studies being written crystallized with the Ottoman government's gradual control over the "learned institution," the *ilmiye* (hierarchy of religious men of learning), whose more influential *ulema* (leading religious scholars) became part of the ruling official class and depended upon state remuneration.

In the twentieth century and with Kemal Atatürk's secularism—abolishing the caliphate, eliminating Islam as the state religion, and adopting the Swiss civil code and Latin alphabet in 1924 for the new Turkish state—a new breed of Muslim scholars and writers began emerging. As Atatürk dismantled the former Ottoman edifice of an Islamic state, thinkers such as Muhammed Rashid Rida and the *ulema* of al-Azhar (Islam's oldest religious institution of higher learning) became more vocal in predictions regarding the perceived impossibility of resurrecting the caliphate. Adherents of militant Islam increased their efforts to assert Islamic values in the face of Western inroads, and Muhammed Rashid Rida was the founding theoretician of the Islamic state whose ideas continued in doctrines of later fundamentalists.

Rashid Rida was influential in shaping the activist ideology of Muslims in Egypt and elsewhere in the Sunni-Muslim world, and his thesis provided a starting point for a change in the concept that the modern Islamic state was formulated from its earlier spiritual character to give it a totally political nature. He believed the *sunna* ("precedent" or "tradition") bound all Muslims, becoming the ultimate *ijti'had*. Rashid Rida and other *mujt'ahid* ("innovative") Muslim thinkers supported the Sunni jurists' methods of discourse and analysis. Reaching into Islamic history, Rashid Rida relied heavily on the *hadiths* of Muhammad and long-neglected *'ijm'a*, to make his case, but he minimized dependence on the Qur'an for interpretation for the Muslim faithful. Basing his arguments on extensive quotations from writings of former Muslim scholars, legalists, and writers, he created the impression that they had based their arguments on a legalistic interpretation; by quoting from past authoritative sources, he hoped to establish a primary line of defense against orthodox attacks.

Rida later turned against the *ulema*, castigating their corruption and subservient ways with the rulers. He believed that an important cause for the serious "deviations" of some caliphates, which evolved into institutions serving the basest tyrants and despots, was the legitimation that earlier *ulema* and other scholars conferred upon them. According to Rida, the individuals and elite charged with duties of preserving the system's justness were the primary detractors of its abuses. The scholars and the *ulema* gave an air of divine providence that applied not only to the defunct institution of the caliphate but also to new secular institutions seeking support for their ideologies. Such ingrained practices would regenerate self-appointed guardians of the system or the inherent *truth* of institutions, and accusations of heresy would be hurled at all actual or potential rivals.

Rashid Rida's *ijti'had*'s opened the gate for modern *ijti'had*'s by numerous twentieth-century *ulema* and other scholars. Muslims falling within that diverse milieu have included Ayatollah Ruhollah Khomeini and his concept of *wilayat-ifaqih* ("government of the Islamic jurist"); Ali Shar'iati and his more "religious" and secular approach to Muslim sociology; 'Umar Abd al-Rahman, an extremist Egyptian Muslim cleric who was given a life sentence in the United States for his violent politics; and Naguib Mahfouz, the Egyptian who won the 1988 Nobel Prize for Literature and whose secular approach to Muslim society is evidenced in books such as *The Children of Gebalaawi* and *Midaq Alley*.

Discourse within the Islamic world in the late-twentieth century has maintained a furious pace that has not yet abated. Postcolonial realities and numerous attempts to reconstruct the Muslim voice in the global postmodern discourse have occurred in the regular pattern of Islamic history. Issues including male oppression of women, complex negotiation of power, class inequality, and some officially nonsanctioned instances of slavery in Muslim societies are gradually appearing on the literary shelves of both Western and non-Western markets. Muslim historiography now occupies its rightful place in the ongoing discourse—among the twentieth-century forces of capitalism, socialism, imperialism, nationalism, totalitarianism, anti-imperialism, liberalism, racism, antiracism, feminism, religion, and secularism—but the path traveled since its earliest days of formulation has been arduous. Still, its diverse and proven literary and historical resilience enriches the body of global discourse.

—*Talaat Shehata*

For Further Reading
Abu-Lughod, Ibrahim. 1963. *Arab Rediscovery of Europe*. Princeton, NJ: Princeton University Press; Hourani, Albert. 1970. *Arabic Thought in the Liberal*

For Further Reading
Abu-Lughod, Ibrahim. 1963. *Arab Rediscovery of Europe*. Princeton, NJ: Princeton University Press; Hourani, Albert. 1970. *Arabic Thought in the Liberal Age, 1798–1939*. Oxford: Oxford University Press; Rosenthal, Franz. 1952. *A History of Muslim Historiography*. Leiden: E. J. Brill.

HISTORIOGRAPHY, LATIN AMERICAN

The annals of African slavery in Latin America might be considered as a recent history. With the exception of Cuba and Brazil, the institution of colonial slavery and African influence in national societies are similar to the national histories. Gonzalo Aguirre Beltrán's anthropological work *La población negra en México: Estudio etnohistórico* (The Negro population in Mexico: An ethnohistorical study) (Mexico City: Fondo de Cultura Económica, 1989), initially published in the early 1940s, opened a regional debate that culminated with interpretations including, not only general population movements, such as Claudio Sánchez Albornoz's *La población de América Latina desde los tiempos precolombinos al año 2000* (The population of Latin America from precolumbian time to the year 2000) (Madrid: Alianza, 1977), but also regional histories dedicated to African slavery, such as Rolando Mellafe's *Breve historia de la esclavitud en América Latina* (Brief history of slavery in Latin America) (Mexico City: Secretaría de Educación Pública, 1973) and Herbert Klein's *African Slavery in Latin America and the Caribbean* (New York: Oxford University Press, 1973).

A theoretical debate on slavery arose and paralleled the avenue of interpretation just mentioned. Eric Williams's work *Capitalism and Slavery* (London: Andre Deutsch, 1975) inspired works by other historians like Eugene Genovese's *Esclavitud y capitalismo* (Capitalism and slavery) (Barcelona: Ariel, 1971) and Octavio Ianni's work with the same title (Mexico City: Siglo Veintiuno, 1976). Some followers of this school of interpretation gave special attention to the problem of rebellion, such as Richard Price in *Maroon Societies: Rebel Slave Communities in the Americas* (Baltimore: Johns Hopkins University Press, 1996).

Décio Freitas's *Palmares a Guerra dos Escravos* (Palmares: The War of the Slaves) (Pôrto Alegre, Brazil: Editora Movimiento, 1973) specifically addressed Palmares and other Brazilian *quilombos* (settlements founded by runaway slaves). Clovis Moura's work, *Rebelioes de senzala, quilombos, insurreiçoes, guerrilhas* (Slaves rebels, maroons, insurrections, guerrillas) (São Paulo: Livraria Editora Ciencias Humanas,

1983), contains an excellent bibliography on this subject, and Rafael Duharte's *Rebelda esclava en el Caribe* (Rebel slaves in the Caribbean) (Mexico City: Gobierno del Estado de Veracruz, 1992) addresses the Cuban experience with a chapter dedicated to urban Maroons (runaway slaves).

The abolition debate has become the focus of attention for many scholars. It has also gained international support, giving rise to both general and particular interpretations. Two of the recent works to address this issue generally for Latin America are Hebe Clementi's *Abolición de la esclavitud en América Latina* (Abolition of slavery in Latin America) (Buenos Aires: Pleyade, 1974) and Leslie B. Rout's *The African Experience in Spanish America* (Cambridge: Cambridge University Press, 1976).

Recent studies devoted to specific national or regional experiences include Robert Conrad, *The Destruction of the Brazilian Slavery 1850–1888* (Berkeley: University of California Press, 1972); Rebecca Scott, *Slave Emancipation in Cuba: The Transition to Free Labor, 1860–1899* (Princeton, NJ: Princeton University Press, 1985); and John Lombardi, *The Decline and Abolition of Negro Slavery in Venezuela 1820–1854* (Westport, CT: Greenwood, 1971). Some of the main ideas regarding the transition from slavery to free labor are found in Manuel Moreno Fraginals, Frank Moya Pons, and Stanley Engerman's *Between Slavery and Free Labor: The Spanish Speaking Caribbean in the Nineteenth Century* (Baltimore: Johns Hopkins University Press, 1985).

Several books about plantation slavery have been published in which slaves are placed within their productive milieu. Those books show planters' concerns about the profitability of slave labor, but that was never the main concern. Some of the most important of these studies include Stuart B. Schwartz, *Sugar Plantations in the Formation of Brazilian Society: Bahia, 1550–1835* (Cambridge: Cambridge University Press, 1985); Manuel Moreno Fraginals, *The Sugar Mill: The Socioeconomic Complex of Sugar in Cuba, 1760–1860* (New York: Monthly Review Press, 1976); and Crespo Horacio, *Historia del Azticar en México* (History of the Aztec in Mexico) (Mexico City: Fondo de Cultura Económica, 1988).

Since the 1970s, interest in slavery and in African cultures studied in their surroundings has generated numerous studies. Marta B. Goldberg addressed Argentina's experience in "Los Negros de Buenos Aires" in Luz M. Martinez Montiel's *Presencia Africana en Sudamérica* (The African presence in South America) (Mexico City: Consejo Nacional para la Cultura y las Artes, 1995), and Bolivian slavery is the topic of Alberto Crespo's *Esclavos negros en Bolivia* (Negro slavery in Bolivia) (La Paz: Academia Nacional de Ciencias de Bolivia, 1977). George Reid Andrews' *The*

Afro-Argentines of Buenos Aires is considered the standard study of slavery in the River Plate region.

Brazilian slavery is addressed in Gilberto Freyre, *Casa grande y senzala* (published in English as *The Masters and the Slaves*) (Brasília: Universidade de Brasilia, 1963); Jacob Gorender, *O Escravismo Colonial* (Colonial slavery) (São Paulo: Atica, 1980); and Katia Queiros Mattoso, *To Be a Slave in Brazil, 1550–1888* (New Brunswick, NJ: Rutgers University Press, 1986). Rolando Mellafe's *La introducción de la esclavitud negra en Chile: Tráfico y rutas* (Introduction of Negro slavery in Chile: Trade routes) (Santiago, Chile: Editorial Universitaria, 1984) is one of the best works on Chilean slavery.

The Colombian experience is addressed in W. F. Sharp, *Slavery on the Spanish Frontier: The Colombian Chocó 1680–1810* (Norman: Oklahoma University Press, 1978); Jaime Jaramillo Uribe, *Ensayos sobre historia social Colombiana* (Essays on the social history of Columbia) (Bogotá: Universidad Nacional de Colombia, 1968); and Nina S. De Friedmann, "Presencia Africana en Colombia" (African presence in Colombia) in Luz M. Martinez, *Presencia Africana en Sudamérica* (Mexico City: Consejo Nacional para la Cultura y las Artes, 1995). Significant works on Cuban slavery include Fernando Ortiz's *Los Negros esclavos* (Negro slaves) (Havana: Ciencias Sociales, 1975), Aimes Hubert's *The History of Slavery in Cuba 1522–1868* (New York: Octagon Books, 1907), Franklin Knight's *Slave Society in Cuba during the Nineteenth Century* (Madison: University of Wisconsin Press, 1970), and Kenneth F. Kiple's *Blacks in Colonial Cuba* (Gainesville: University Presses of Florida, 1976).

Several works worthy of note on Mexican slavery include Gonzalo Aguirre Beltrán's work mentioned earlier and his *El Negro esclavo en Nueva España* (The Negro slave in New Spain) (Mexico City: Fondo de Cultura Económica, 1994). Adriana Naveda Chávez de Hita's *Esclavos negros en las haciendas Azucareras de Córdoba, Veracruz, 1690–1830* (Negro slaves on the sugar haciendas of Córdoba, Veracruz) (Mexico City: Centro de Investigaciones Históricas, 1987) and Colin Palmer's *Slaves of the White God: Blacks in Mexico, 1570–1650* (Cambridge, MA: Harvard University Press, 1976) further explore the topic of Mexican slavery.

Peruvian slavery is assessed in Frederick Bowser's *The African Slave in Colonial Peru, 1524–1650* (Stanford, CA: Stanford University Press, 1974); Luis M. Díaz Soler evaluates slavery in Puerto Rico in his *Historia de la esclavitud negra en Puerto Rico* (History of Negro slavery in Puerto Rico) (Rio Piedras: Universidad de Puerto Rico, 1969); and slavery in the Dominican Republic is the topic of Carlos Deive's *La esclavitud negra en Santo Domingo, 1492–1844* (Negro slavery in Santo Domingo) (Santo Domingo: Museo del Hombre Dominicano, 1980). Ildefonso Pereda Valdés evaluates

Uruguayan slavery in *Negros esclavos y negros libres; Esquema de una sociedad esclavista y aporte del negroa en nuestra formación nacional* (Negro slaves and free Negroes) (Montevideo: Gaceta Comercial, 1941).

Research on urban slavery has found a new field of study in the subjects of abolition and rebellion. Typical of these studies are Mary Karasch's *Slave Life in Rio de Janeiro, 1808–1850* (Princeton, NJ: Princeton University Press, 1986) and Pedro Deschamps's *Los cimarrones urbanos* (Urban *cimarrones*) (Havana: Editorial de Ciencias Sociales, 1983). Arturo Morales Carrin's *Auge y decadencia de la trata negrera en Puerto Rico (1820–1860)* is another classic study of slavery in Puerto Rico.

—*Juan M. de la Serna*

HISTORIOGRAPHY, U.S.

The history and meaning of slavery in the United States has been studied intensely because the African American past is so linked to slavery. Essentially, scholars are not simply debating a historical issue, they are making insights into modern race relations, and some of the more significant authors and works of slavery in the United States are discussed here.

Born a Southerner, Ulrich B. Phillips revered the Southern planter class and wrote the first scholarly Southern work on slavery, *American Negro Slavery* in 1918. The work is the result of the most extensive research on the topic at that time, and Phillips was extremely selective in his sources, utilizing only records from large plantations, favorable traveler's commentaries, and white accounts to draw his picture of slavery.

Phillips's work is a justification for slavery, and he asserted that "concession when accompanied with geniality and not indulged so far as to cause demoralization would make plantation life not only tolerable but charming" (Phillips, 1918). Phillips utilized a racist approach, common to the time he was writing, when he described slaves as "impulsive and inconstant, sociable and amorous, voluble, dilatory, and negligent, but robust, amiable, obedient and contented, they have been the world's premium slaves." Other contemporary authors viewed slavery from similar racist perspectives. For example, the historian Harry H. Johnson argued in *The Negro in the New World* (1910) that "the Negro should be regarded as a sub-species of the perfect human type [and] inferior in mental development and capacity to the peoples in Europe and their descendants in America."

Phillips introduced his arguments by describing African life as being so dismal that the reader was ex-

Phillips wrote, "Every plantation of the standard southern type was, in fact, a school constantly training and controlling pupils who were in a backward state of civilization" (Phillips, 1918). Furthermore, slavery conversely helped to develop civilization in places where it was nonexistent: "Where population is scant and money little used it [slavery] is almost a necessity in the conduct of large undertakings, and therefore, more or less essential in the advancement of civilization."

Phillips developed the notion of paternalistic, caring masters, claiming that owners cared for slaves not only because they were valuable property but also because masters on the whole were a kind lot. In return, the vast majority of slaves loved their masters as they loved their own fathers. To complete this paternalistic picture, Phillips claimed that owning slaves was generally an unprofitable venture and planters owned slaves out of a sense of responsibility to the Negroes. He wrote, "Thus while the slaves had a guarantee of their sustenance, their proprietors, themselves the guarantors, had a guarantee of nothing" (Phillips, 1918).

During the liberal historical revisionism of the 1950s, authors attacked these earlier, racist attitudes and concentrated instead upon the slaves' victimization. Kenneth M. Stampp used the same sources as Phillips, and a similar format, but reached vastly different conclusions in *The Peculiar Institution* (1956). Stampp refuted Phillips's racial justification of slavery writing, "I have assumed that the slaves were merely ordinary human beings, that innately Negroes are, after all, only white men with black skins, nothing more, nothing less" (Stampp, 1956).

Stampp dismissed the theory that slaves were kept out of a sense of responsibility, contending instead that slavery was maintained primarily for economic reasons. Slaves were relatively inexpensive, cheaper to maintain than paying wages to free laborers, and could be quite profitable. Stampp proposed a second reason for owning slaves when he argued that "no other profession gave a Southerner such dignity and importance as the cultivation of the soil with slave labor. The ownership of slaves . . . had become a fashionable taste, a social passion" (Stampp, 1956).

Although Phillips used travelers' accounts to show paternalistic slavery, Stampp produced much contradictory evidence. He presented a long list of runaways and attempted escapes and showed myriad ways slaves resisted their masters. For example: "A Kentucky slave made himself unserviceable by downing medicines from his master's dispensary. A slave woman was treated as an invalid because of the swelling of her arms, until it was discovered that she produced this condition by thrusting her arms periodically into a beehive" (Stampp, 1956). To show slav-ery's harshness, Stampp devoted an entire chapter to the ways in which slaves were kept fearful and noted that "the only principle in which slavery could be maintained, reported a group of Charlestonians, was the principle of fear." If slaves were happy in a paternalistic institution, as Phillips had maintained, there would be no need to maintain fear.

Beginning in the late 1950s, many authors initiated comparative studies that recognized the differences between Latin and North American slavery. In these works, scholars illustrated the totality of North American slavery in its brutality and racism. Frank Tannenbaum noted: "He still remained a Negro, and as a Negro, according to the prevailing belief, he carried all the imputation of the slave inside him. The distinction had been drawn in absolute terms, not merely between the slave and the free man, but between the Negro and the white man" (*Slave and Citizen* [1946]).

Stanley Elkins was influenced by Tannenbaum's theories and took some of them a step further. Elkins's *Slavery: A Problem in American Institutional and Intellectual Life* (1959), studied the effects of this brutal institution on slaves. Elkins disputed Phillips's idea that the slave personality came from Africa, claiming instead that it developed while in bondage, since "much of his [the slave's] past has been annihilated [in transport]; nearly every prior connection has been severed" (Elkins, 1959). Once in bondage, North American slaves lived in a harsh and controlled system, a system that forced them to become connected and dependent on their masters. Elkins theorized that "Sambo, the typical plantation slave, was docile but irresponsible, loyal but lazy, humble but chronically given to lying and stealing. . . . His relationship with his master was one of utter dependence and childlike attachment: it was the very childlike quality that was the key to his being."

The Moynihan Report was the result of a special study commissioned by the Johnson administration in 1965 to study why there are so many dysfunctional modern black families. The report drew heavily upon Elkins's work, especially his conception of helpless slave personalities, which would seem to make the creation of strong black families impossible.

In the New Left historiography since the 1960s, scholars have refused to accept earlier victimization theories and believed that such arguments created a new kind of racism. Instead, these authors have focused less on the institution of slavery and more on the responses of the slaves themselves. Prominent works by such authors include John W. Blassingame's *The Slave Community* (1972) and Herbert Gutman's *The Black Family in Slavery and Freedom, 1750–1925* (1976).

Blassingame drew the darkest picture of slavery, noting that "when angry, masters frequently kicked, slapped, cuffed, or boxed the ears of domestic servants, sometimes flogged pregnant women, and often punished slaves so cruelly that it took them weeks to recover." Despite this violence, slaves retained their individuality, neither depending upon their masters nor identifying with them. The reason for this independence, Blassingame theorized, was the presence of slave families, an entity largely overlooked by earlier authors.

The family provided the slave a place to express himself and his culture, giving him an identity apart from the white world and master. Blassingame suggested that "the secular songs told of the slave's loves, work, floggings, and expressed his moods and the reality of his oppression . . . he sang of the proud defiance of the runaway, the courage of the black rebels, the stupidity of the patrollers" (Blassingame, 1972). Folktales served a similar purpose, as although "primarily a means of entertainment, the tales also represented the distillation of folk wisdom and were used as an instructional device to teach young slaves how to survive."

Gutman utilized census figures to highlight the black family's importance, concluding that the family had survived slavery and remained strong well after emancipation. He demonstrated that "more than three-fourths of the households contained either a father or a husband . . . [in conflict with] conventional assertions that slavery had shattered the immediate slave family and made the two-parent household uncommon among poor, rural blacks fresh to legal freedom" (Gutman, 1976). These kinship patterns were allowed to survive and flourish because the master was unaware of them.

Blassingame claimed that slave quarters were where the slave culture and family units thrived. Although the quarters were quite dismal, they were free of white influence and "were so rarely under the constant surveillance of their masters that there the black man faced no obstacles in exercising authority in his family" (Blassingame, 1972).

More recent works on slavery in the United States discuss the social organization and cultural self-determination of slaves. For instance, Michael Conniff and Thomas Davis argue that "creation of a strong cultural setting gave Africans and their descendants the psychological, spiritual, economic, and cultural resources they needed to face the challenges of the emancipation era and beyond" (Conniff and Davis, 1994).

—*Matt C. Bischoff*

For Further Reading
Blassingame, John W. 1972. *The Slave Community.* New York: Oxford University Press; Conniff, Michael L., and Thomas J. Davis. 1994. *Africans in the Americas: A History of the Black Diaspora.* New York: St. Martin's; Elkins, Stanley M. 1959. *Slavery: A Problem in American Institutional and Intellectual Life.* Chicago: University of Chicago Press; Gutman, Herbert. 1976. *The Black Family in Slavery and Freedom, 1750–1925.* New York: Pantheon; Phillips, Ulrich B. 1918. *American Negro Slavery.* Gloucester, MA: D. Appleton and Company; Stampp, Kenneth M. 1956. *The Peculiar Institution.* New York: Random House.

HITTITE CODE

An understanding of Hittite slavery comes almost exclusively from the Hittite law code. This collection consists of about 200 edicts compiled in cuneiform at Hattusha, the Hittite capital in Anatolia, circa 1650 B.C. (although references to earlier pre-Hittite laws do exist). In addition, an abridged version written three centuries later contains some modifications. The laws were divided into two series: the first 100 after the beginning words of the first law, "if a man," and the second 100 after "if a vine."

The Hittite Code is not a law code in the strict sense of the term, since not every type of legal case is represented. It is more a collection of cases that were originally precedents, not unlike other ancient Near Eastern law codes. One group of laws was especially related to runaway slaves (Laws 19–24), and numerous other laws pertained to slaves and other social classes. The laws are constructed in a conditional format (if . . . then), not unlike collections from Israel and Mesopotamia.

As in other ancient Near Eastern societies, Hittite slaves were commodities that could be bought and sold. Runaway slaves were returned to their master, even if they had crossed national boundaries. Slaves could be married to free persons (Laws 31–36), although if a marriage were dissolved, children remaining with the slave parent were to be considered slaves. If a slave took a wife, she condescended to his social level as long as they were married. These laws suggest that apparently a Hittite slave could have his own wealth in order to be able to pay the bride price. In fact, if the bride's parents paid the bride price, they relinquished the right to redeem their daughter.

Thus, the legal system recognized the slaves' rights and responsibilities. In fact, district governors were ordered not to pay less attention to cases concerning slaves and others less fortunate. A slave paid half the amount a free person paid as reparation for crimes, and only received half as much in reparation, but slaves suffered corporal punishment for a series of offenses, including the loss of nose and ears (Law 95). If a slave committed a crime requiring payment, it was paid by the master (Laws 95, 99). If the master refused, the slave was given to the injured party.

Some slaves were literate (both male and female); debt-slavery existed in Hittite Anatolia; a Hurrian-Hittite bilingual text encouraged rulers to proclaim a general release from debt slavery, not unlike the Hebrew Bible's Jubilee Year. As in other ancient Near Eastern societies, the king's subjects were called his slaves, creating a large chasm between the royal family and the rest of the population. The king also was considered a slave of his deity.

—*Mark W. Chavalas*

For Further Reading
Güterbock, H. G. 1970. "Bermerkungen zu den Ausdrücken ellum, wardum und asirum in hethitischen Texten." In *Gesellschaftklassen im alten Zweistromland und in angrenzenden Gebeiten.* Munich: Verlag der bayerischen Akademie der Wissenschaften; Hoffner, H. 1995. "Hittite Laws." In *Law Collections from Mesopotamia and Asia Minor.* Ed. M. Roth. Atlanta, GA: Scholars Press; Hoffner, H. Forthcoming. *The Hittite Laws: A New Edition.* Leiden: E. J. Brill; Neufeld, E. 1951. *The Hittite Laws.* London: Luzac and Company.

HOBBES, THOMAS
(1588–1679)

The English philosopher and political theorist Thomas Hobbes's famous studies of power and politics, *Elements of Law* (1640), *De Cive* (1641), and *Leviathan* (1651), became the core texts of seventeenth-century political theory. Once considered subversive, Hobbes's works were publicly burned and condemned as being one of the causes of the Great Fire of London. Writing against the backdrop of the English Civil War, Hobbes sought ways of achieving political stability in a world of apparent disorder. The ideas he formulated to achieve this end—ideas concerning the nature of human rights and the need to subordinate, where necessary, these rights to ensure social order—had dramatic implications for many Europeans in their intellectual justification of slavery.

Hobbes sought to demonstrate ways in which people could move from a prepolitical state of nature, where there is no community, only a group of individuals with conflicting interests, to a structured and well-ordered civil society. For Hobbes, the state of nature was one of complete liberty, but he did not feel that was desirable. He equated liberty with an absence

of law, which he believed gave individuals the right to kill each other at will. In a world of equals, aggressive behavior would never allow a single, dominant ruler to emerge. Life would, therefore, become uniformly miserable, brief and insecure, as numerous warlords engaged in a never-ending struggle for power. To end this chaotic situation, and to save them from themselves, Hobbes believed that people sacrificed some of their basic human rights to achieve lasting stability. In *Leviathan,* he suggested how this can be done through surrendering popular power to one man or a single assembly, who alone would be sovereign.

Hobbes did not accept that people are born with natural or inviolable rights. Instead, he viewed liberty as a commodity, like any other, that can be passed or traded at will to the advantage of society as a whole. Just as individuals can sell themselves into servitude, so, too, can a whole nation. Once the right to self-government has been surrendered, as part of the contract—or covenant—with the sovereign, it cannot be reclaimed. Hobbes also thought that the covenant could remain valid even if consent were not freely given, but coerced by the stronger party. Initially, Hobbes suggested that individuals retained some rights, to feed and clothe themselves and to self-defense if abused by their master, but in his later writings he claimed that absolutely everything was surrendered in such a transaction, the sovereign was absolute and controlled every aspect of his subjects' lives.

Hobbes explored the nature of political legitimacy and considered the rights of conquerors and the conquered. He believed that there was neither justice nor injustice in a state of war; victory and the achievement of stability was all that really mattered. Consequently, conquerors were seen as having rights and powers over their new subjects while the people were granted no residual rights of resistance. Yet the conqueror could only become sovereign if the defeated population consented to his rule, which was achieved by establishing a covenant—as before—between the victor and the vanquished. Until this new covenant was made, members of the defeated party remained slaves. Although they could serve their new master to avoid death or injury, since there was no covenant between them, slaves were not compelled to obedience. Quoting Leviticus (25: 39–55), Hobbes maintained that slaves were under no obligation at all and could break their bonds and escape, or even kill their master if acting in a just cause.

The situation all changed once the covenant had been concluded, the defeated ceased to be slaves and became servants instead. Hobbes chose this term carefully, not only to highlight their subordination and change in status, but also to appeal to the Old Testament's authority, which often refers to subject peoples as being their sovereign's servants. The idea of likening the relationship between ruler and ruled to that of a master and his domestic servant, with duties and obligations on either side, was one that had particular resonance for a seventeenth-century audience. The sovereign could be seen fulfilling his half of the covenant by sparing the life of the defeated party while the subjects fulfilled their half of the covenant by obeying their lord. If the servant is captured by a new invader, the covenant lapses, and he or she is free to begin the cycle again, concluding a fresh covenant with the new conqueror. Hobbes therefore perceived one master, or source of strong authority, to be as good as another.

Thus, the Leviathan of the sovereign state can be seen to remove effectively both the motivation and the right of a people to rebel against their ruler. Both sides are seen to gain from the arrangement. But Hobbes's work, stressing time and again the central overriding importance of order over individual rights, could easily be adopted as a justification for colonial conquest and the system of slavery itself. Although Hobbes's writings were primarily intended as a blueprint for future English or European government, they made many dangerous assumptions about the nature and value of other societies. It was too easy for Europeans casting covetous eyes toward Africa and the East to equate the people of remote or newly discovered lands with those "unfortunate" individuals still existing in a state of nature, supposedly unable or unwilling to control their own self-destructive urges. Thus dehumanized, they appeared open to conquest and exploitation, with the system of slavery, which denied them human rights, designed to appear as a progressive and even beneficial force.

—*John Callow*

For Further Reading
Hobbes, Thomas. 1985. *Leviathan*. New York: Penguin Classics; Sommerville, Johann. 1992. *Thomas Hobbes: Political Ideas in Historical Context*. London: Macmillan; Warrender, Howard. 1957. *The Political Philosophy of Thomas Hobbes*. London: Oxford University Press.

HOMER'S THEORY

Although Homer (c. eighth century B.C.) did not theorize directly about slavery in his writings, the interactions among characters in his works exemplify what Aristotle called the conventional ancient Greek view that people conquered in battle deserved to be taken as slaves. In the *Iliad*, it is clear that all Trojans, regardless of social class, will ei-

Homer

ther be slaughtered or enslaved. The women taken as slaves by the Achaean leaders are part of the spoils of war, and the most deserving men earn a right to the greater spoils. This principle is contradicted only when a higher principle is violated. The right to seize slaves is, like other human rights, given by the gods. Although triumphant warriors had this right, they would be punished if they exhibited hubris, exaggerated pride leading to disrespect for the gods' laws. For example, in the *Iliad*, when Agamemnon refuses to allow Chryses, a priest of Apollo, to ransom his daughter, who was taken as a battle trophy, Apollo visits a pestilence on the Achaean troops, forcing Agamemnon to surrender her.

Homer's *Odyssey* shows how slaves should behave. The slaves represented by Homer are expected to endure their slavery and remain true to their master's interests; those who do not, deserve to be tortured and killed. The *Odyssey* presents two contrasting views of slaves after Odysseus, in disguise as a beggar, reaches his home of Ithaka: those loyal to their master, and those who are disloyal. The former are represented by Eumaios, the swineherd who offers shelter to Odysseus, and Eurykleia, the nursemaid who recognizes her former charge through his disguise but keeps his identity secret. The disloyal slaves are represented by the women who submit to the sexual advances of

Penelope's suitors and the goatherd Melanthios. After Odysseus defeats the suitors, his son, Telemachos, hangs the disloyal maidservants. Melanthios, who sided with the suitors and insulted Odysseus when he was disguised as a beggar, is mutilated by being castrated and having his ears, nose, hands, and feet severed and fed to the dogs.

Ancient Greeks considered Homer's works to be highly authoritative sources on social mores and the gods' laws. Plato and Aristotle argued against the commonly held view that people conquered in battle should be enslaved—Plato because he believed that Greeks should not enslave fellow Greeks, and Aristotle because he believed that defeat in battle did not necessarily indicate the inferiority natural to the slave—but ancient Greeks and Romans continued to believe that victory in battle brought with it the right to take slaves.

—*Mary Ellen Cummings*

See also
Aristotle's *Politics;* Greece; Plato's *Laws*
For Further Reading
Lattimore, Richmond, trans. 1967. *The Iliad of Homer.* Chicago: University of Chicago Press; Lattimore, Richmond, trans. 1991. *The Odyssey of Homer.* New York: Harper Perennial.

HOUSING, UNITED STATES

The structures inhabited by slaves in the United States, known as slave quarters, served as the slaves' primary social environment. The size, shape, and appearance of these quarters varied over time and space, but the family and community functions that the quarters fostered remained more constant.

In their quarters, slaves learned the slave community's rules and values and shared secrets for surviving the slave system. The quarters were the one part of the plantation not under the white family's constant supervision. Thus, in their quarters, American slaves both learned and conveyed their unique culture. Separate and usually impermanent slave housing existed almost from the beginning of slavery, and the housing marked the separation in the South of blacks' and whites' worlds. Whereas white planters and masters largely dominated the South's fields, kitchens, and other work environments, slaves found an arena of autonomy and solidarity in their quarters.

In the eighteenth century, there was a shift from temporary wood structures to more permanent brick ones, which signaled an increasing commitment on the part of whites to the slave system and economy. In the seventeenth century, separate quarters were not always common, and the small black population often lived in the same house as the white master and his family. During the late-seventeenth- and early-eighteenth-century boom years, planters found slave labor to be the most profitable way to tend the South's cash crops and legally sanctioned slavery for the first time. White masters then separated themselves from their legal and perceived cultural inferiors, and in the years between 1680 and 1720, separate housing for servants and slaves emerged. Once they could live more independently, slaves could begin to develop the material goods, family traditions, and community values that crystallized into a new African American culture. As the eighteenth century progressed and slaves became an increasing presence on the land, slave quarters were gradually constructed more soundly and with more durable materials.

The form of the slave quarters varied among Southern regions. Single-family log cabins, multiple-family duplexes, and large barracks for male slaves were all forms of slave housing. Generally of wood frame construction with stick-and-mud or brick chimneys, the structures rested on the ground, on buried wooden posts, or sometimes on brick foundations. In the upper South, quarters tended to include more European architectural elements like 18-foot rooms and post construction. By contrast, quarters in the lower South showed a greater African influence, including clay walls and thatched roofs. The lower South's continued commitment to the African slave trade and the resultant black majority in many areas of that region explain the difference.

Most slave quarters included an unusual element, a root cellar. Root cellars were underground storage areas that slaves dug into the floor of their quarters, often near the hearth. Slaves used these pits for root preservation, food storage, garbage disposal, and as hiding places for personal or stolen goods. The proliferation of these cellars meant that the ground beneath and around the quarters tended to be strewn with broken pottery, glass, animal bones, and other debris. By the late-eighteenth century, a reform movement had begun among planters to lift quarters off the ground and place them on pier supports to allow for better ventilation and get the slaves off the damp and trash-covered ground.

Quarters for field slaves were always built some distance from the "big house," usually in a circular or straight-line pattern. House servants resided closer to or even inside the main house—either in a small closet under a stairwell, an attic room, or a loft over a kitchen dependency. In urban areas, slaves resided in narrow brick tenements that were located behind the master's house and often surrounded by tall brick

This reconstructed log cabin at the Booker T. Washington National Monument is representative of much slave housing. Washington inhabited such a house as a young slave boy at the Burroughs plantation in the foothills of the Blue Ridge Mountains.

walls. These quarters were generally windowless one-room dwellings with fireplaces and dirt floors. Overcrowding, poor sanitation, lack of ventilation, shoddy furniture, and a lack of privacy characterized the condition of slave life in slave quarters.

—Laura Croghan Kamoie

See also
Plantation Archaeology
For Further Reading
Singleton, Theresa A., ed. 1985. *The Archaeology of Slavery and Plantation Life.* Orlando, FL: Academic Press; Sobel, Mechal. 1987. *The World They Made Together: Black and White Values in Eighteenth-Century Virginia.* Princeton, NJ: Princeton University Press; Vlach, John Michael. 1993. *Back of the Big House: The Architecture of Plantation Slavery.* Chapel Hill: Univer-

sity of North Carolina Press; Wade, Richard C. 1964. *Slavery in the Cities: The South, 1820–1860.* London: Oxford University Press.

HOWE, JULIA WARD (1819–1910)

A poet, author, and abolitionist, Julia Ward Howe is best known for writing "Battle Hymn of the Republic," the rallying song for the North during the U.S. Civil War. Born and raised in New York City, she moved to Boston in 1843 upon marrying Dr. Samuel Gridley Howe, head of the

Perkins Institute for the Blind and an ardent abolitionist. Unhappy in her new surroundings and prohibited by her husband from participating in public reform work, she attended lectures; privately studied foreign languages, religion, and philosophy; and wrote poetry and drama while maintaining a household with children.

In the 1850s, while embarking upon a literary career, Howe became a convert to abolitionism. Having been raised in a family that feared abolitionism as a threat to society, she now became thoroughly convinced that it was a just and necessary cause. Although she supported ending slavery, she did not believe in racial equality. She thought that freed slaves would have to be trained, educated, and "refined by white culture" in order to be more than "the laziest of brutes." Her derogatory comments about blacks, published in her book *A Trip to Cuba* (1860), drew public criticism from fellow abolitionist William Lloyd Garrison.

Howe wrote the "Battle Hymn of the Republic" on November 19, 1861, while in Washington, D.C., with her husband to distribute supplies to Massachusetts regiments. Seeing Union troops return from the battlefield and personally witnessing President Lincoln's sadness over the war deeply affected her. She wrote the poem as her personal contribution to the Union cause, and upon returning to Boston, she submitted it to the *Atlantic Monthly* for publication. The magazine's editor, James T. Fields, gave the poem its title and published it on the cover page of the February 1862 issue. In April 1862, Oliver Ditson and Company published sheet music, which set the poem to the tune of "John Brown's Body," a song already popular among Union troops. Not long after its publication, regiments throughout the North were singing the new "Battle Hymn of the Republic."

In the work, Howe used biblical imagery from both the Old and the New Testaments to depict a powerful, wrathful God marching alongside Union troops to the battlefield. She depicted a God who "sounded forth the trumpet that shall never call retreat" and "loosed the fateful lightning of His terrible swift sword." God marched with the Union to preserve truth and justice and "crush the serpent [symbol of the South] with his heel." In the last of the song's five verses, Howe gave the Union the emotional boost it needed to legitimize and continue the war by proclaiming it a crusade to end slavery. Referring to Christ, she wrote, "As he died to make men holy, let us die to make men free, While God is marching on." The "Battle Hymn of the Republic" remained popular even after the Civil War and was a serious contender for the national anthem until 1931 when "The Star-Spangled Banner" was chosen instead.

—*Mary Jo Miles*

See also
Abolition, United States; Garrison, William Lloyd
For Further Reading
Clifford, Deborah Pickman. 1979. *Mine Eyes Have Seen the Glory*. Boston: Little, Brown and Company; Grant, Mary H. 1994. *Private Woman, Public Person: An Account of the Life of Julia Ward Howe from 1819 to 1868*. Brooklyn: Carlson; Ream, Debbie Williams. 1993. "Mine Eyes Have Seen the Glory." *American History Illustrated* 27 (1): 60–64.

IAROSLAV THE WISE
(FL.1016–1054)

Foremost among the early rulers of Kievan Russia, Grand Prince Iaroslav Vladimirovich codified and issued the first Russian law code, which, among other matters, outlined certain aspects regarding the legal position of slaves in his principality. Iaroslav issued his law code under the title *Russkaia Pravda* (Russian justice) between 1016 and the 1030s. Sometimes known as the Short Pravda, it was later added to by his sons until a revised and enlarged version, the Expanded Pravda, appeared in the mid-twelfth century.

Only 3 of the 18 sections or articles of the Short Pravda relate specifically to slavery. Article 11 states that if a slave runs away from a foreign merchant and is concealed by a third party, then that party must give up the slave within three days or else be liable for a monetary fine. Since Iaroslav made no similar provision in cases where the aggrieved slaveowner was a native Russian, the article appears to have been designed as a safeguard for non-Russian buyers whose newly bought slaves escaped before their master could return to his homeland.

In Article 17, Iaroslav imposed a penalty on the owner of any slave who struck a freeman and who afterward hid "in his master's house." Should the owner fail to present the slave, he was to pay a fine, and the victim of the assault would be allowed to "beat the slave wherever he finds him." The use of later terminology in this article has led to suggestions that it may be an interpolation into the manuscript of Iaroslav's Pravda, not part of the original work.

The only complex slave legislation in Iaroslav's Pravda is Article 16, which relates to runaway slaves who are sold over and over to successive new owners while still technically at large. In cases in which the original owner recognizes the slave and wishes the slave returned, Iaroslav decreed that responsibility for compensation lay with whomsoever was the fourth party in the dispute. In other words, the owner who is the third master since the slave ran away becomes liable to reimburse the person to whom he sold the slave with an appropriate compensatory fee, and the slave is returned to the original owner.

Prior to Iaroslav's time, slavery in Kievan Russia was not regulated by formal legislation, despite the major role the international slave trade played in the development of the Russian state. The brevity of Iaroslav's Pravda reduced its overall usefulness as a law code and must have rendered its statutes of limited value to slaves and slaveowners alike. Being in essence a means whereby fines or compensations for a range of offenses could be codified, the Pravda barely addressed the myriad legal questions that slavery engendered in practice. It would therefore seem likely that a much more extensive corpus of unwritten "common" law must have existed to deal with the myriad legal problems for which Iaroslav's legislation was plainly inadequate.

—*Tim Clarkson*

For Further Reading
Dmytryshyn, Basil. 1973. *Medieval Russia: A Sourcebook*. Hinsdale, IL: Dryden; Vernadsky, George. 1965. *Medieval Russian Laws*. New York: Octagon.

THE IBO

The Aro, an elite religious clan of eastern Nigeria's Ibo people, sacrificed slaves to the oracle Aro Chukwu before proceeding to the coast for business. The oracle was understood to be the voice of Chuckwu, the supreme deity, and Aro control of the oracle entailed great religious and judicial authority and power. Through this control, the Aro were able to centralize their scattered colonies into a formidable mercantile network, as they were able to protect goods and services through people's fear and respect for the oracle that was the final court of appeal in judicial cases.

The oracle levied fines in terms of slaves, thereby enabling the Aro to increase their wealth and power, and they exploited their position and built an enormous slave-trading network. Because of their location, the Aro were able to acquire slaves from throughout Ibo territory and monopolize the slave trade, sending the slaves to ports in the Niger Delta and the Cross River

Anglican missionaries visit an Ibo village in 1853. The British considered that spreading Christianity in Africa would help stamp out the slave trade.

regions. Depletion of eastern Nigeria's Ibibio region appears to have been the result of Aro expansion into the area and the clan's enslavement of large numbers of the native people for the transatlantic slave trade.

The Ibo also supplied many slaves from their heavily populated interior to surrounding peoples in the Brass River and old Calabar regions. These peoples, like the Ijo and Efik, had developed what is called a "house system" in which "houses" consisted of a family of freeborn members and their slaves. These powerful houses formed a type of oligarchy, but an internal form of democracy existed since freemen and slaves alike elected household heads. In some houses, skilled slaves even rose to become household heads.

Generally, domestic slavery in the Ibo heartland, or the Biafran interior, was as frequent as anywhere else along the West African coast. As would be expected, the highest proportion of slaves was found around commercial centers like those in the Niger Delta and along the northern frontier. Slaves worked in the palm tree trade, and control of this commodity among the Ibo remained in individual hands or small-scale units in contrast to the situation among the Yoruba. The situation paralleled that described in Lovejoy's (1983) early stage of slavery in kinship-based societies.

Although most palm oil in the Ibo area came from small, family farms, Aro communities continued to dominate the area. Their palm oil was generally produced on plantations, and some Aro owned thousands of slaves, hired overseers, and in other ways differed little from plantation owners elsewhere. Ironically, slavery's spread in the Ibo region was related to Britain's desire to increase legitimate trade. As demand for agricultural products increased, the use of slaves in agriculture grew to meet the new demands of trade.

—*Frank A. Salamone*

For Further Reading
Herskovits, Melville J. 1958. *The Myth of the Negro Past*. Boston: Beacon Press; July, Robert W. 1992. *A History of the African People*. Prospect Heights, IL: Waveland Press; Lovejoy, Paul E. 1983. *Transformations in Slavery*. Cambridge: Cambridge University Press; Oliver, Roland, and J. D. Fage. 1990. *A Short History of Africa*. New York: Penguin Books.

IBRAHIMA, ABDUAL-RAHAHMAN (1762–1829)

Abdual-Rahahman Ibrahima was a Fulani prince of the ruling family of Timbo in present-day Guinea. His biographical account reminds us that many African captives who were made slaves and transported across the Atlantic were Muslim. The presence of Muslim slaves in colonial America is unquestioned, but what is needed is a judicious estimate of their number. Current investigation reveals that from "ten to fifteen percent of the total trade in humans taken from Africa to North America between 1731–1867 were Muslims" (Austin, 1996).

Captured, sold, transported, and then enslaved in America, Abdual's personal narrative asserts that he managed a slave plantation shortly after his arrival in Natchez, Mississippi, late in 1788. He spent the next 40 years as a slave overseer, a tradesman, and later, a spokesman for the abolitionist movement. In serving the abolitionists' cause, he traveled extensively in the United States, witnessing the plight of his fellow Africans in captivity and seeking redress for their sufferings.

The Fulani were among several West African groups who were known for producing fervent Islamic scholars with proselytizing religious appeal. These groups disseminated Islam via itinerant preachers who visited the urban trade centers and countryside of western Sudan. Abdual's father, Maudo the Great, led a successful jihad against non-Muslims to liberate his people in the nineteenth century, and Abdual himself received instruction in Islamic jurisprudence and military science at an early age.

In 1788, his father gave him 2,000 soldiers and orders to seize the lucrative trade monopolized by rival groups on the coast of West Africa. After defeating his opponents, Abdual set them free before returning to Timbo, but the opposing commander, disgruntled by his defeat, ambushed and captured Abdual and several warriors. Abdual was marched to the coast, sold as a slave, and put on board a ship bound for Dominica and then New Orleans and Natchez.

One day, his account informs us, while selling goods in a marketplace for his master in Mississippi, Abdual recognized a white man he had known in Timbo and recalled that he had saved this man's life. The man, John Cox, also remembered and tried unsuccessfully to gain Abdual's freedom. Educated and literate, the slave's eloquence attracted many sympathizers, and they did finally succeed in assisting him in his struggle. With the help of a journalist named Andrew Marschal, Abdual's plight received prominent attention in the media, which facilitated his subsequent release. He was so popular that even Southern antebellum newspapers wrote extensively about his cause. Secretary of State Henry Clay, compelled to act, insipidly offered to employ "the Moor" as an Arabic interpreter for the federal government. Abdual won the praise of notables in the South and the North; even President John Quincy Adams was impressed by his abilities.

Abdual was finally emancipated. His wife was later freed and his children, too, although their liberation took more time. This remarkable human being survived slavery, won freedom for himself and his family, and eventually returned to his homeland. However, after only five months in Africa, he took ill and died before he could see his hometown of Timbo again—or his wife and children when they arrived later. Having been compelled to convert to Christianity to appease his master while he was a slave, he reembraced Islam before he died.

—Au'Ra Muhammad Abdullah Ilahi

See also
Muslim Slaves in the Americas

For Further Reading
Austin, Allen D., ed. 1996. *African Muslims in Antebellum America: Proud Exiles*. New York: Routledge; Clarke, Peter B. 1982. *West Africa and Islam: A Study of Religious Development from the 8th to the 20th Century*. London: Edward Arnold; Curtin, Philip D. 1968. *Africa Remembered: Narratives by West Africans from the Era of the Slave Trade*. Madison: University of Wisconsin Press; Kolchin, Peter. 1993. *American Slavery, 1619–1877*. New York: Hill and Wang.

IDEOLOGY OF WARTIME FORCED LABOR

Heinrich Himmler, the German leader who was in charge of establishing the concentration camps in Nazi Germany and the areas controlled by that regime, said: "Whether other nations live in prosperity or starve interests me only in so far as we need them as slaves for our culture" (Homze, 1967). By 1944, 7 million foreign civilians and prisoners of war labored for Germany, and 3 million slaves had died in concentration camps. The Nazis followed a policy of exterminating Jews and other "undesirables" by working them to death while denying them adequate food, clothing, shelter, and sanitary facilities. At the Nuremberg war crimes trials, prosecutors considered all forced laborers as slaves, but on closer examination, historians question applying that label to all foreign workers and prisoners of war.

The Nazis in charge of the concentration camps followed the philosophy that enemies of the state did not deserve to live. Jews constituted a high proportion of this population, but most Jews were not enemies of the state. Political prisoners and others whom the Nazis disliked (e.g., homosexuals) were also condemned to the camps, including "partisans," or individuals unlucky enough to live in areas near partisan operations, who were gathered up by the army and sentenced to slave labor. Anyone defying the Nazis could become a concentration camp slave.

The system dehumanized the slaves by reducing them to a number and encouraging them to fight and betray one another for enough food to survive. Inmates wore numbered clothing, tattoos, and color-coded triangles. Political prisoners wore red triangles; homosexuals, pink; saboteurs, black; gypsies, brown; and common criminals, green. Inside each triangle, there was a letter designating the prisoner's nationality: P for Pole, U for Ukrainian. Jews wore the yellow star of David. "Race" largely determined a prisoner's status, and prisoners were told to enslave one another according to each "race's" position in the Nazi hierarchy. The Nazis purposefully murdered the slaves by working them beyond endurance, beating them constantly, and killing them for small and imagined infractions.

Jews and political prisoners were the first Nazi slaves, but they were not important to industry until late in the war when reverses on the eastern front created a shortage of foreign workers. Poland's capture resulted in labor recruitment that followed a long-standing habit of employing Poles as agricultural laborers, but at first, their status was unclear. Were they slave or free? When an influx of Russian workers followed the invasion of the Soviet Union, the German government clarified the position of the *Untermenschen* ("inferior races"). Fearing any mixing of *Untermenschen* and Germans, the Nazis housed the eastern workers in barbed-wire enclosed compounds, compelled them to wear a badge reading *Ost* ("east") on their clothes, and hung any such worker who had sexual relations with a German woman. They received pay and some medical care but were also beaten like slaves.

After the failure of the invasion of Russia, Adolph Hitler appointed Fritz Sauckel to administer Germany's manpower resources, and he carried out four "actions" that were designed to force all available labor within the command of the Third Reich to work. Foreign workers, he said "must be fed, sheltered and treated in such a way as to exploit them to the highest possible extent at the lowest conceivable . . . expenditure" (Homze, 1967).

Initially, recruitment produced the needed laborers from German-occupied Europe, but when that failed the Germans resorted to force. In areas to the east, they kidnapped individuals leaving church or the cin-

ema, took parents hostage, and burned entire villages to force men and women to work in Germany. In the last years of the war, the eastern workers' newborn babies were placed by force in "care facilities" where they often died of neglect. In the western theater, the Germans relied on the occupation governments to collect workers but resorted to intimidation when necessary. The "actions" increased resistance, and the later drives failed. By 1945, one in five workers was non-German, and Sauckel was working to mitigate their harsh treatment and to improve their living conditions to encourage productivity.

Nazis forced prisoners of war to work in violation of Article 27 of the Geneva Convention, which limited the work of prisoners to jobs not contributing to the war effort. The Nazis treated western prisoners of war reasonably but contended that the USSR had not signed the Geneva Convention and that Russians were therefore not protected by its provisions. Most Russian prisoners died of mistreatment and starvation in prisoner-of-war camps and were never enslaved. "Asiatic" or "Mongol" Russians were not sent to Germany, but by May 1944, 875,000 non-Asiatic Russians were working for the Germans for wages that were a fraction of those paid to British and American prisoners. Some British prisoners worked on farms and even ate at the table with their employers while Russians mined coal and lived in deplorable conditions.

Some Germans sympathized when slaves were marched through their towns and passed them food in defiance of the guards. Most Germans were indifferent, however, and accepted slavery as the natural order. Still, generalizations are difficult. The Nazi government was confused and working at cross-purposes. Even as the need for slave labor increased, the German government continued to work slaves to death and the army starved Russian prisoners of war. Unquestionably, Jews and Slavs suffered more because German ideology condemned them as *Untermenschen*. Whether individuals considered themselves to be slaves depended on local conditions and the attitude of the Germans controlling their lives.

Germany's dependence on slave labor grew as the war neared its end. The Nazis, for example, even used slaves to build the rockets they hoped would save them from defeat. The needed technicians were found among the slaves, and they provided the scientists with a skilled labor force. When some of the slaves sabotaged the rockets they were helping to build, the Germans combined space age technology with ancient brutality by hanging the saboteurs on cranes in the underground tunnels of the rocket factories.

—*Dennis J. Mitchell*

See also
Nazism

For Further Reading
Herbert, Ulrich. 1990. *A History of Foreign Labor in Germany, 1880–1980*. Ann Arbor: University of Michigan Press; Homze, Edward L. 1967. *Foreign Labor in Nazi Germany*. Princeton, NJ: Princeton University Press; Milward, Alan S. 1977. *War, Economy, and Society, 1939–1945*. Berkeley: University of California Press; Piszkiewicz, Dennis. 1995. *The Nazi Rocketeers: Dreams of Space and Crimes of War*. Westport, CT: Praeger.

ILLEGAL SLAVE TRADE

The illegal slave trade in the modern era involved two aspects: the smuggling of slaves to avoid paying taxes and customs duties and the smuggling of slaves in violation of international laws prohibiting the slave trade. Because of the nature of the illegal slave trade, little information exists on the number of slaves traded illegally.

Smuggling slaves to avoid paying customs and tax duties on them was an integral part of the slave trade, and throughout the period of that trade, Dutch, English, French, Danish, Swedish, and Genoese smugglers supplied, at varying times, French, English, Portuguese, and Spanish colonies with illegal slaves. Obviously, those slaves were unrecorded in customs-house ledgers. For example, in the eighteenth century, the Spanish *asiento* (which licensed foreigners to trade slaves in the American viceroyalties) contributed to slave smuggling, as quality standards and duty payments required by the Spanish government were often too high to allow for substantial profits on the sale of slaves. Indeed, the *asiento* was used more for the illicit sale of goods other than slaves, but the illicit cargoes often contained untaxed slaves. Additionally, the failure of official *asiento* holders meet the demand for slaves often led to a market for smuggled slaves. Thus, the illegal slave trade was profitable in most periods, albeit difficult to estimate.

The second aspect of the illegal slave trade, the smuggling of slaves in violation of international laws prohibiting the trade, meant, of course, that the illegal trade's practitioners strove to keep their dealings secret. Legal abolition began with the Dutch in 1805, and Great Britain and the United States prohibited engagement in the international slave trade in 1807. Following the Vienna Treaty (1815), all European maritime powers, often under British diplomatic pressure, passed piecemeal abolition acts.

In 1817, the British established a naval squadron off Africa's western coast to suppress the slave trade, and the United States followed suit. Great Britain and the United States also established a court to enforce their agreement, but formal abolition rarely meant an end to the trade. Neither Spain, Portugal, nor France took effective measures to enforce legislation, so much of the history of the illegal slave trade centers on efforts of the British and U.S. naval squadrons to suppress the trade. In 1845, a British House of Commons report suggested that although most nations had agreed to abolish the trade, an illegal trade remained active; the report also listed 2,313 known slavers.

Exact figures for the number of slaves illegally smuggled into the New World after 1808 are unavailable. Indeed, only estimates and educated guesses are possible. For example, the African American historian W. E. B. DuBois argued that the nonenforcement by the United States of its international agreement with Britain implied high levels of imports to the United States after 1808, and he estimated the number of those illegal imports to be 250,000. Recent scholarship has suggested that DuBois's figures were too high and that the correct figure (still only an educated guess) was more like 1,000 illegal imports per year until 1860.

Because it is nearly impossible to determine the total number of slaves illegally smuggled into the New World, students of the illegal slave trade have concentrated on specific cases in which illegal slave traders were caught (for example, the *Wanderer* case of 1859) and on records of both the antislavery squadrons and the courts. As those data suggest, the illegal slave trade constituted a significant part of the overall slave trade.

—*John Grenier*

See also
Abolition (British Empire, United States); African Squadron; The *Asiento;* Closing of the African Slave Trade; The *Wanderer*

For Further Reading
Curtin, Philip D. 1969. *The Atlantic Slave Trade: A Census*. Madison: University of Wisconsin Press; Daget, Serge. 1979. "British Repression of the Illegal French Slave Trade: Some Considerations." In *The Uncommon Market: Essays in the Economic History of the Atlantic Slave Trade*. Ed. Henry A. Gemery and Jan S. Hogendorn. New York: Academic Press; Drake, Frederick C. 1970. "Secret History of the Slave Trade to Cuba Written by an American Naval Officer, 1861." *Journal of Negro History* 55: 218–235; Emmer, Pieter. 1981. "Abolition of the Abolished: The Illegal Dutch Slave Trade and the Mixed Courts." In *Abolition of the Atlantic Slave Trade*. Ed. James Walvin and David Eltis. Madison: University of Wisconsin Press.

IMMEDIATISM

Immediatism was a word used among abolitionists in England and the United States beginning in the late 1820s to define their stance toward emancipation and to distinguish themselves from a gradualist approach to abolition. Immediatists advocated the immediate and unconditional abolition of slavery; they fervently believed that sin must never be compromised, and therefore they refused to resort to such intermediate agencies as the closing of the slave trade, colonization, and apprenticeship as gradual remedies for the evil. The shift from gradual to immediate emancipation signaled a fundamental transformation in reformers' worldviews and was a major turning point in intellectual history.

The doctrine of immediatism had its roots in the natural rights philosophy of the Enlightenment and in Quaker theology. Abolitionists in the eighteenth century theoretically believed that slaves had a right to their immediate freedom, and many Quakers, viewing slavery as an embodiment of worldly sin that corrupted masters and slaves alike, concluded that the evil must be immediately cast off to escape moral contamination.

But while immediatism was latent in the origins of antislavery thought, most eighteenth-century abolitionists advocated gradual abolition. Despite their understanding of slavery as a horrible sin that needed to be eliminated, their stance toward emancipation was detached and indirect. They sought gradual and cautious measures that retained Enlightenment attitudes toward linear progress and history; natural law and property rights; and a stable, orderly, and hierarchical universe. Consequently, British and U.S. reformers focused on the abolition of the slave trade as an indirect means toward emancipation. Gradualists in the United States also embraced the American Colonization Society, which was organized in 1816 as a way to rid the country of both the stain of slavery and blacks without upsetting the social order or natural rights doctrine.

Slaveholders, however, continually sought to block the path to gradual emancipation, and when reformers concluded that indirect means did not accomplish their morally urgent objectives, a crisis resulted that led to immediatist views. In 1824, the British Quaker Elizabeth Heyrick gave one of the most eloquent early pleas for immediate emancipation. Antislavery efforts, she said, were a "holy war" against the very powers of darkness that precluded any compromise with the sin. By 1830, many prominent British abolitionists had converted to immediatism, and the following year, the British Anti-Slavery Society officially embraced immediate emancipation.

Similarly, by the 1820s many abolitionists in the United States had concluded that the American Colonization Society was founded on racist principles and not interested in ending slavery, and reformers increasingly viewed gradualism as ineffectual. William Lloyd Garrison, the most persistent U.S. immediatist, rejected colonization in 1829 and two years later began publishing the *Liberator*. In 1833, the American Anti-Slavery Society was organized on the doctrine of immediate abolition.

In one sense, the turn to immediatism reflected a shift in strategy, but in a much more fundamental sense, it represented a conversion experience in the reformer and a shift from Enlightenment to romantic worldviews. Immediatists became "born again," free from the fetters of original sin and ready to make the world holy. They defined themselves as outsiders and stood apart from what they considered to be the vague and insincere policies of gradualists. Immediatism was at once their religion and their "sacred vocation"; it defined who they were and shaped everything they did.

In contrast to Enlightenment thought, immediatists affirmed a sharp break with the past, a profound leap that transcended the previous limits of history and progress. They understood that emancipation was a root-and-branch operation that would severely disrupt prevailing conventions, order, and stability. Their worldview "was essentially romantic," in the words of David Davis, "for instead of cautiously manipulating the external forces of nature, [they] sought to create a new epoch of history by liberating the inner moral forces of human nature" (Davis, 1986).

—*John Stauffer*

See also
Abolition (British Empire, United States); American Colonization Society; The Enlightenment; Garrison, William Lloyd; Romanticism and Abolitionism; Second Great Awakening

For Further Reading
Davis, David Brion. 1986. "The Emergence of Immediatism in British and American Antislavery Thought." In *From Homicide to Slavery: Studies in American Culture*. Ed. David Brion Davis. New York: Oxford University Press; Loveland, Anne C. 1966. "Evangelicalism and 'Immediate Emancipation' in American Antislavery Thought." *Journal of Southern History* 32 (2): 172–188; Scott, Donald M. 1979. "Abolition as a Sacred Vocation." In *Antislavery Reconsidered: New Perspectives on the Abolitionists*. Ed. Lewis Perry and Michael Fellman. Baton Rouge: Louisiana State University Press.

INDENTURED SERVANTS

Indentured servitude was a widespread system of bound labor in British colonial America, and it foreshadowed many later aspects of slavery. Servants signed articles of indenture in Britain that bound them to serve a master without pay for a period ranging from about three to seven years. Accordingly, masters paid their passage to America and gave them "freedom dues" of goods and sometimes land when their indenture ended. Fully established in Virginia by the 1620s, indentured servitude provided tobacco planters cheap labor and created a profitable sideline for merchants in importing servants, encouraged by the headright of 50 acres per person brought into the colony. Essentially the same system was adopted with great success and profit in the English West Indies and all British North American settlements. Estimates suggest that 60 percent of seventeenth-century British emigrants to America crossed as servants, most of them going to plantation colonies.

The system developed by adapting to American conditions existing elements of the English labor system, like apprenticeship and hiring unmarried agricultural laborers to supply labor demands to grow cash crops. There were several significant changes in the newer system. First, servant contracts or indentures were far longer and more formal than in England, where for agricultural labor, verbal one-year agreements were often used. The extended period resulted from planters' needs for a long-term workforce and the considerable investment they made by paying for a servant's migration. Second, masters could sell a servant's contract, a practice that had become illegal in England although it had applied to apprentices' contracts in the medieval period. Transferable contracts evolved because servants were bound in England by an agent, who sometimes engaged them under false pretenses, or even kidnapped them, and then sold to masters on arrival in America.

Servants who arrived early in Virginia and the West Indies, particularly the Irish ones, seemed to have faced far-harder work regimens and harsher treatment than was normal in Britain, combined with heavy mortality from disease. Court records reveal that in response, servants frequently escaped, or disobeyed, and a complex law code evolved to handle servant problems, including restricting their movement by issuing passes for any allowed travel and severe punishments, including extensions of time in service. The "custom of the country" also regulated the length of service and the amount of freedom dues for servants arriving without a written contract. Whereas in the early period the difference between bound English servants and African slaves was not always clear, particularly in the Chesapeake Bay area, the development of this later legislation clearly defined the two groups by guaranteeing servants legal protection from abuse and rights, like testifying in court, that were denied to slaves.

In many early colonies, when their time of service was over, servants who had survived gained land and might do well for themselves, but through time, giving land to ex-servants became uncommon and freed servants had to find waged work or move to frontier areas. This change resulted in a discontented class of poor white ex-servants who threatened rebellion in Barbados in the 1640s and backed Bacon's Rebellion in Virginia in 1676, but ironically, as the slave population grew larger these poor whites became vital allies for planters against the danger of slave rebellion.

Throughout the colonial period, the type and number of servants recruited and their destinations and length of service varied considerably. In the Northern colonies, no crops were profitable enough to warrant serious investment in servants for agricultural work. In the Southern colonies, indentured servants were initially generally cheaper than slaves, but as the demand grew, prices for servants sometimes rose because the number of migrating servants was limited, especially if British wages rose, whereas slave prices remained constant.

In the West Indies, where the monoculture started changing from tobacco to sugar in the 1640s, slaves increasingly seemed the cheaper option for agricultural labor, particularly as the islands were already on transatlantic slave routes. There was still a demand for skilled white artisans and servants to act as overseers, but by the mid-eighteenth century, native-born slaves were being trained to fill skilled positions. This development caused much contemporary complaint but occurred because the short contracts needed to attract servants to a region famed for poor conditions and having no free land were too expensive in comparison. A similar move from servant to slave labor occurred in the Chesapeake Bay area over a longer period of time, as there it was not until the early-eighteenth century that the shift from servant to slave agricultural labor occurred because of shortages in the supply of servants.

During the seventeenth century, most plantation servants were young, single, male, and British, but in the eighteenth century, a traffic in German servants arose, and they provided skilled labor in New York and Philadelphia. These servants, traveling in families, were transported under the redemption system, according to which migrants promised to pay for their passage within about two weeks of arrival and if the fare remained unpaid, they were sold into servitude, with families sometimes being split up. This trade acquired an evil reputation because the ships were overcrowded, had insufficient rations, and mortality rates of 25 percent were common. This trade disappeared as an increasing urban underclass in the colonies made cheap wage labor possible.

By the time of the American Revolution, indentured servitude had grown uncommon, having been replaced by slavery or wage labor, but clearly it had played a paramount role in making British America an economic success and in populating the new colonies. Revolutionary ideas about liberty may have made the idea of keeping bound white servants distinctly unfashionable, but the social and economic patterns that surrounded indentured servitude remained ingrained in the plantation colonies, and in the increasingly stratified Northern cities, the patterns were merely transferred to a new labor system.

—*Gwilym Games*

See also
Apprenticeship; English Caribbean; Irish as Slaves in the Caribbean

For Further Reading
Morris, Richard B. 1946. *Government and Labor in Early America.* New York: Columbia University Press; Sallinger, Sharon. 1987. *To Serve Well and Faithfully: Labor and Indentured Servants in Pennsylvania.* Cambridge: Cambridge University Press; Smith, Abbot Emerson. 1947. *Colonists in Bondage: White Servitude and Convict Labor in America, 1607–1776.* Gloucester, MA: Peter Smith.

INDONESIA

In the Indonesian archipelago, indigenous slavery, other systems of bondage and serfdom, and colonial slavery under Dutch rule existed together until well into the nineteenth century. Indigenous slavery often is characterized as a "personal-based" system in a traditional social hierarchy whereas the Dutch East India Company–introduced institutional slave system was more impersonal.

There is no absolute dichotomy between indigenous and colonial slavery, however—both systems shared similar characteristics despite some differences between them. Indigenous and colonial slave traders both had several ways of supplying the slave market, such as to be born of one or two slave parents, to be a debtor, to be a convicted criminal, to be a prisoner of war or the victim of a raid under the pretense of war. Where slaves were needed and natural reproduction was insufficient, slave imports had to meet the shortages. In both systems, it was possible for a slave to be manumitted and sometimes to have certain rights.

Indigenous slavery consisted of various labor relations and several gradations of dependency to an employer or master. There were bondsmen, debtors, slaves, and prisoners who worked on the land or in the households. This variety of indigenous relations and systems had existed for centuries before the Portuguese and then the Dutch settled the area. Slaves were recruited and introduced to several areas of the archipelago, and the circumstances in which slaves and other dependent people found themselves could vary, as did the status of slaves. For instance, it made a difference if slaves were treated by Islamic religious law *(shari'a)* or by customary law *(adat)*.

Colonial slavery was predominantly an urban phenomenon. In the colonial urban centers, slaves were to be found in the households of whites, the harbors, and other places in town. Slave women could be used for sexual services, or they might become concubines since the Dutch colonial society was predominantly a male one. Work on the land was done by peasants—only on the Banda Islands in the Moluccas did the Dutch use slaves on the spice plantations. If available, peasant labor often proved to be cheaper than slave imports, but this "free" labor was not obtained without some form of coercion. In the nineteenth century, the Dutch administration introduced a labor system on Java that was known as the Cultivation System *(Cultuurstelsel).* Under this system, which lasted from 1830 until about 1870, land and labor were exploited for the benefit of the Dutch treasury.

In the seventeenth century, the Dutch made a distinction between prisoners of war, who had no rights at all and did the hardest physical work, and work slaves, who fared somewhat better and had some rights. These slaves, mostly skilled workers, came mainly from India until the 1660s. After 1660, there was a new slave category, the so-called kuli slaves who came from the Indonesian islands of Bali, Celebes (the southern part), Banda, and Timor. They did unskilled work in the town and harbor.

From the end of the seventeenth century on, the number of slaves increased, especially the household and kuli slaves, and the distinction between the categories became blurred. At the same time, new ordinances were issued that distinguished people on the basis of their place of origin, which meant that some people, like the Javanese, could not be enslaved, and others could. The stereotype that the Buginese of Malaysia and the Makassarese from Celebes were dangerous and violent peoples could prevent them from being enslaved, as an ordinance in 1665 showed, but this image was also used in the nineteenth century as an argument to prevent the abolition of slavery.

In the nineteenth century, the problem of abolition became a general one both in Indonesia and in the mother country. Not only did the Dutch abolish the slave trade in 1818, but they also decreed that all slaves in both the East and the West Indies should be registered and taxes paid for every slave. For political reasons, indigenous slaveowners in the Indonesian archipelago often were exempted from these new rules and regulations, as the colonial administration was afraid that indigenous rulers would take these rules as attacks on the indigenous slave system.

Before the Dutch government abolished slavery in all Dutch colonies in 1863, there had been successful and unsuccessful attempts to abolish colonial slavery in the Indonesian archipelago, whether for individual cases or in general. For centuries, individual slaves were manumitted by their indigenous or colonial masters, and the reasons for manumission could vary. To avoid further costs a slaveowner might free sick or old slaves; female slaves who were pregnant or had given birth to a child of their master could be set free; sometimes slaves could purchase their freedom; or slaves could be freed by the government if their master was found to be too cruel.

—*Angelie Sens*

For Further Reading
Knaap, Gerrit J. 1996. "Slavery and the Dutch in Southeast Asia." In *Fifty Years Later: Antislavery, Capitalism, and Modernity in the Dutch Orbit*. Ed. Gert Oostindie. Pittsburgh: University of Pittsburgh Press; Reid, Anthony, ed. 1983. *Slavery, Bondage, and Dependency in Southeast Asia*. New York: St. Martin's.

INFANTICIDE

Cultural definitions of infanticide are highly variable, which means that defining it is problematic. The *Oxford English Dictionary* offers these definitions: (1) One who kills an infant. (2) The crime of murdering an infant after its birth, perpetrated by or with the consent of its parents, especially the mother. (3) The killing of infants, especially the custom of killing newborn infants, which prevails among savages, and was common in the ancient world.

Infanticide, which usually occurs immediately after birth, has been practiced on every continent by many ethnic groups at every level of cultural complexity and goes back to prehistoric times. Archaeological evidence for child sacrifice dates back to Jericho in 7000 B.C. Infanticide is not currently legally sanctioned by any society, though it is still practiced in some societies. Infanticide is a practice that bears moral weight relative to the cultural belief system within which it is embedded.

Cultural practices that are widely distributed, both temporally and geographically, tend to have practical functions perpetuating their existence. No single factor can account for infanticide in all societies, and it has served different functions, including eliminating defective children, motherless infants, multiple births, and illegitimate children; interbirth spacing; regulating future adult sex ratios; and population control. Suffocation, abandonment, drowning, and exposure are common methods used to commit infanticide. It is rarely practiced to express violence or cruelty but usually occurs for economic or demographic reasons. The practice of infanticide among slave populations had additional dimensions.

The African slave trade that Europeans conducted totally dehumanized and depersonalized the slave. For female slaves, race rather than sex determined their fate. A slave woman's qualities as a laborer often superseded her reproductive role in determining her value. Furthermore, her reproductive role was reduced to an economic one, and a pregnant slave female's status was as childbearer rather than mother. Slave narratives indicate that slave populations practiced infanticide, and many motives are responsible for its occurrence.

A female slave's life consisted of many harsh realities. A woman born into slavery could expect to be subjected to harsh labor conditions, violence, and exploitation throughout her lifetime. Laws in the U.S. South did not recognize the rape of an enslaved woman as a crime, and sexual abuse of female slaves was common. Any child borne by a slave became the master's property and could be sold away from the mother at any time. Slave narratives record mothers' committing infanticide for many reasons. Many did so to free their children from a life of bondage; one woman killed her newborn to prevent her master from selling him as he had sold her three previous children; yet another woman killed her child to end its suffering caused by the continual abuse of her mistress. The last woman claimed that the master was the father of her child and that that was the cause of the abuse; if true, the situation was not uncommon.

Illegitimacy and infanticide have had a strong association throughout history. Because slave marriages were not legally recognized, technically all slave children were illegitimate. Cross-culturally, the illegitimate class that most often falls victim to infanticide is made up of biracial children. Infanticide was one method to handle unwanted pregnancies resulting from sexual abuse by the master, and it was also a form of passive resistance by which the female slave exercised control over her body and the body of her child.

Another aspect of infanticide is that it may not always be intentional. Because of the minimum or nonexistent medical care given to slaves and the lack of a mother's attention to her child necessitated by her commitments as a slave, many children died of neglect. Some slave mothers served as wet nurses and were nursing their masters' children at the same time as their own. Slave mothers were sometimes forced to wean their own children to benefit the masters' children, and some slave children died from a resultant lack of nutrition. The living conditions of slaves were often poor, and small children often slept with the mother. The mother might accidentally roll over onto her child and smother it in her sleep—however, she might also commit this act intentionally.

Because infanticide is difficult to detect and prove, the act often went undetected and unpunished. But if a slaveholder suspected infanticide, the slave would be punished harshly and sometimes fatally. It was an issue of economics for the slaveholder—infanticide meant a loss of property, but for slave women it meant much more. Infanticide among slave populations was not an act committed by women with no maternal feelings for their children but rather a compassionate act of freedom or resistance or a means of self-survival.

—*Lori Lee*

See also
Family; Gender; Narratives
For Further Reading
Kellet, R. J. 1992. "Infanticide and Child Destruction—The Historical, Legal, and Pathological Aspects." *Forensic Science International* 53: 1–28; Meillassoux, Claude. 1991. *The Anthropology of Slavery: The Womb of Iron and Gold.* Chicago: University of Chicago Press; White, Deborah. 1985. *Ar'n't I a Woman: Female Slaves in the Plantation South.* New York: Norton; Williamson, Laila. 1978. "Infanticide: An Anthropological Analysis." In *Infanticide and the Value of Life.* Ed. Marvin Kohl. New York: Prometheus Books.

IRELAND, SCOTLAND, AND WALES, RAIDS ON

Throughout the early-medieval period, between the fifth and eleventh centuries, Celtic areas of the British Isles were subjected to slave-raiding activity from various external states. The raids' frequency and severity increased during the Viking period and were not eradicated until long after the Norman conquests of the eleventh and twelfth centuries.

Documentary sources for slavery and the slave trade around the British Isles at the beginning of the early-medieval period are scarce. The collapse of Roman rule in mainland Britain undoubtedly heralded an increase in lawlessness, banditry, and piracy, but it also resulted in the disappearance of a coin-based economy in favor of trade in movable goods. Human beings, like cattle, represented an easily movable source of material wealth and could be readily transported across the Irish Sea and along navigable rivers by small bands of raiders.

Saint Patrick, himself a victim of an Irish slave raid on Britain in the fifth century, bemoaned the abduction by British slavers of young male and female members of his newly evangelized Irish Christian congregation. In a strongly worded letter to the British king Coroticus, Patrick accused the raiders not only of kidnap but also of selling young Irish Christian captives to the barbaric Picts, whom he denounced as apostates.

A wider slave trade that centered on the Irish Sea and linked England, Scotland, Ireland, and Wales with countries further afield became evident during the Viking period, especially in the years following the establishment of permanent Scandinavian trading centers and other settlements. Contemporary sources show clearly that the prime object of many Viking raids on Wales was to capture potential slaves. In the ninth century, Dublin began emerging as a major slave market where captives were brought from raids not only on mainland Britain but also elsewhere in Ireland. The Icelandic Laxdaela saga includes a story about the Irish princess Melkorka who, after being captured in a raid, was sold in a Norwegian market and transported to Iceland as a slave. The tale may be apocryphal, but it is consistent with historical references to Irish slaves being sold in Scandinavian markets.

In 870, Vikings besieged and captured the stronghold of Alt Clut (modern Dumbarton) in Scotland and took most of the site's inhabitants. These unfortunates may have been among the multitude that Olafr the White and Ivarr the Boneless took to the Dublin slave market in 871. References to other Scottish raids are perhaps concealed in the sources by the Vikings' tendency to call the Scots "Irish," and attacks are sometimes only identifiable as attacks on Scotland when the captives are named as Picts, Strathclyde Britons, or, as in the case of a noble's daughter captured near her Hebridean home, fellow-Scandinavians.

There are documented cases of slaves captured in raids being freed by ransom. One Welsh slave in the Irish province of Munster received help from no less a personage than the bishop of Armagh, who in 913 sought to ransom the slave. Later that century, Prince Maredudd of North Wales paid the Viking raider Godfrey one penny in ransom for each of 2,000 Welshmen taken in a raid on Anglesey. This instance illustrates the effect of large-scale slave raiding upon a single region, for Maredudd desperately needed to get the captives back to his area of Wales to keep his own armed forces up to strength.

An Irishman and his wife are recorded as having

been sold at Corbridge in northern England sometime around the year 1000. The captors of this couple were most probably Danes, operating perhaps from an English base. Vikings from Ireland, employed as mercenaries by a Welsh prince, were found seeking slaves on the Anglo-Welsh border in 1098, but they departed angrily when the Norman earl of Chester offered them a collection of lame and elderly people.

Inferences drawn from the Domesday Book survey of about 1086 imply that Welshmen captured on the English border in Herefordshire and Worcestershire as late as the eleventh century were often exported abroad as slaves. They were perhaps traded from Bristol, which served as a major slave port in Anglo-Saxon times and slaves were sent from there to various countries, including Ireland. Other Welshmen who were sent to Ireland as slaves were probably sent from Chester, at least until the English trade declined after the Norman Conquest in 1066. Viking raids still continued, with the Church of St. Gwynllyw in Wales being plundered for captives as late as 1087, although by that time the Viking age, and with it the great era of Scandinavian slave raids, was already drawing to a close.

—*Tim Clarkson*

See also
Celts
For Further Reading
Bromberg, E. I. 1942. "Wales and the Medieval Slave Trade." *Speculum* 17: 263–269; Charles, B. G. 1934. *Old Norse Relations with Wales.* Cardiff: University of Wales Press; Holm, P. 1986. "The Slave Trade of Dublin: 9th to 12th Centuries." *Peritia* 5: 317–345; Pelteret, David. 1995. *Slavery in Early Medieval England.* Woodbridge, Eng.: Boydell.

IRISH AS SLAVES IN THE CARIBBEAN

Toward the mid-seventeenth century, several powerful Irish Catholic families managed forcibly to overturn the military and colonial enterprises England had been working to solidify since the twelfth century. Oliver Cromwell's government responded to this assertion of native Irish power by driving the Irish from their home counties into the relatively barren and inhospitable province of Connaught.

Many uprooted peasants were forced to wander the countryside, attempting to survive by any means. Cromwell also took many Irish and Scottish Highland prisoners in battle. Although he allowed many prisoners to go into exile on the Continent, Cromwell was still left with numerous potentially hostile soldiers who posed a real threat to his government. To relieve the intense political pressure created by this unruly mass, Cromwell instituted a forced-labor system, which provided English Caribbean planters with a massive influx of white indentured servants.

One of the chief objectives of Cromwell's transportation policy was to undermine Ireland's Gaelic Catholic culture, which had flourished for many centuries despite English attempts to eradicate it. Cromwell accomplished his goal by instituting wholesale deportations of Irish Catholic peasants who were not linked to antigovernment activities. In 1654, Parliament gave Cromwell a free hand to banish "undesirables" at will, and Cromwell's forces made sweeps of the Irish countryside, randomly arresting Catholic peasants and immediately placing them on ships bound for the West Indies. Throughout Ireland, guardians of native culture—Catholic priests, teachers, and Gaelic bards—were assembled and transported. English authorities in the Caribbean anticipated the potential effect the arrival of these leaders of the old Irish order might have on the Irish already resisting servitude in the West Indies and consequently treated the exiled Irish intelligentsia particularly harshly. Records suggest that priests may have been routinely tortured and executed soon after arriving.

In 1648, the first Irish political prisoners arrived in Barbados, and 12,000 political prisoners had been shipped there by 1655. Although indentured servants (Irish included) had been going to Barbados since 1627, these new arrivals were the first to be taken there involuntarily. Irish prisoners arriving in the Caribbean during this period compensated for a serious labor shortage caused by the English planters' inaccessibility to African slaves. The Dutch and Portuguese dominated the slave trade in the early-seventeenth century, and most white landowners in Barbados and neighboring islands were unable to purchase African slaves because they were English colonists.

Most of the Irish who were coerced into Caribbean servitude were not in the strictest sense, slaves. Although there were incidents when the normal terms of servitude were grievously violated, nothing like lifelong servitude was expected of the Irish. Still, the structure of the indenture system in the islands was brutally oppressive. Overlords typically worked white servants to exhaustion, as generally, "planters conceived the contractual agreement with servants as a major capital investment in labor which had to be fully exploited" (Beckles, 1986). There was no "paternalistic moral responsibility" reigning in the white Caribbean planters' behavior. Irish indentured servants, like African slaves, were commodities that industrious landowners intended to exploit.

Irish and Scottish Highlanders, who constituted most of the Caribbean servant population, were commonly called "redlegs" by the islands' white and black inhabitants. Throughout the Caribbean, the term eventually became a slur, often directed at poor whites. It may have originally described the unusual Irish or Highland dress prisoners may have worn during their initial servitude, or it might have derived from the reddish hue that white flesh takes when exposed to the blistering Caribbean sun.

In the late-seventeenth and early-eighteenth centuries, the white population of many eastern Caribbean islands began declining. By this time, many Irish prisoners had been released from their indenture, and their position in the Caribbean economy was being replaced by African slaves. Free whites remaining on the islands began finding themselves economically redundant and soon became a permanent white underclass. Those Irish with the resources booked passage to Jamaica or the American colonies where conditions for greater social mobility existed. Many of the Irish who remained in the Caribbean intermarried with black neighbors and became practically indistinguishable from the Afro-Caribbean population.

Today, remnants of "redleg" culture still survive in parts of the Caribbean. To begin with, the place-names of many island villages reflect the Irish ancestry of local citizens. Montserrat alone has a Galway, a Kinsale, and a Cork Hill. On Barbados, a region that housed Scottish Highland prisoners is still called "Scotland." Montserrat, St. Kitts, Barbados, Nevis, and other islands have substantial white and biracial populations that claim direct descent from the seventeenth-century Irish and Highland prisoners exiled by Cromwell. Several Caribbean islands celebrate St. Patrick's Day, and a hybridized Afro-Irish or "black Irish" culture has developed. Sadly, many descendants of the Irish exile community remain identifiably white, living with a deep sense of racial and cultural alienation. These poor Caucasians find themselves "belonging neither to the white 4 percent of population, of which they statistically form a part, nor the black 91 percent of the population, to the lowest echelons of which they are nearest in economic and class terms" (Sheppard, 1977).

—*Kevin Brady*

See also
Dublin; English Caribbean
For Further Reading
Beckles, Hilary. 1986. "'Black Men in White Skins': The Formation of a White Proletariat in West Indian Society." *Journal of Imperial and Commonwealth History* 15 (October): 5–21; Sheppard, Jill. 1977. *The "Redlegs" of Barbados: Their Origins and History.* Millwood, NY: KTO Press; Smith, Abbot Emerson. 1947. *Colonists in Bondage: White Servitude and Convict Labor in America, 1607–1776.* Chapel Hill: University of North Carolina Press.

ISIDORE OF SEVILLE
(A.D. 560–636)

Isidore, bishop of Seville, preserved and compiled works of literature, science, philosophy, languages, and history. His three major works are *Historiae Gothorum, Historia vel Origo Gothorum,* and *Chronica Gallica.* From his philosophical commentaries it is clear that Isidore was an abolitionist, and as a Christian and a leader of the early church, he had strong instincts against the institution of slavery and trade in people for profit.

Although he criticized abuse of slaves and urged manumission, he accepted the Visigoth customs of serfdom and feudal retainership. He recorded that the distinction between slave and free was only that the former had been prisoners of war or conquest and had not yet been integrated into the Visigoth society.

He mentioned freemen being punished by years in bondage for offenses against a liege lord that did not merit death. Since the Visigoths had developed their laws and customs as migrating tribes of nomadic habit, this kind of penal servitude was practical and did not waste manpower. Such bondsmen were released at the end of their sentences and returned to free status with no further penalty. If they fought for their tribe as bondsmen and showed courage, they could win early release. In other cases, transition from slave to freeman was a matter of time and circumstance rather than fixed practice or legal requirement.

The freeman, whatever his origin, was equal to a native-born Visigoth and had, therefore, to be trusted to be loyal to his community and to take up arms to defend it like any other free citizen. Once he had the confidence of his neighbors, he could make the transition to freeman by common consent, swearing an oath of allegiance to his former owner. By so doing, he became a retainer, obligated to serve his liege lord but with all the rights of a freeman, including a share in any newly acquired lands available to his tribe.

Where kingdoms were established as they were in Visigothic France and Spain, the king could command slaves or serfs or higher orders of feudal retainers to work on construction projects for his own needs. He could deploy such slave and vassal labor to public works for the good of the kingdom, whether defensive walls, roadways, harbors, or buildings, either secular or religious. The serf laborer was usually responsible for farming and crafts; the retainer for personal or military service to his liege lord.

The two types of workers were unfree in the sense that they could make no decisions about where they lived or whom they served, and they inherited the obligations of their feudal position from generation to generation. They were not owned, as such, nor could they be sold. Their upward mobility was achieved by showing bravery on the battlefield, or by other conspicuous service, and being raised to the ranks of the free as a reward for service.

Isidore of Seville saw no need to question the feudal system upon which Visigothic society was dependent, but he did believe that outright ownership of slaves as commodities was unacceptable and contrary to Christian teaching. His was one of the most influential voices raised against slavery in medieval Christendom, and his writings hastened its decline and demise in Christian kingdoms.

—*Lindy J. Rawling*

See also
Serfdom in Medieval Europe; Slavery in Medieval Europe
For Further Reading
James, E., ed. 1980. *Visigothic Spain.* Oxford: Oxford University Press; Laistner, M. 1957. *Thought and Letters in Western Europe* A.D. *500–1000.* London: London University Press; Thompson, E. A. 1969. *The Goths in Spain.* Oxford: Oxford University Press; Wolfram, H. 1988. *The History of the Goths.* Berkeley: University of California Press.

ISLAM

See **Abolition, Islamic World; Historiography, Islamic; The Qur'an; Women and Slavery in Islam**

ISOCRATES
(436–338 B.C.)

The Athenian orator Isocrates wrote a rhetorical exercise known as the "Archidamus" about 366 B.C. In form it is a speech by the Spartan prince Archidamus addressed to Sparta and its allies at the point when the victorious city-state of Thebes demanded, as the price of peace, that Sparta free the city of Messene, which Sparta had ruled for over 400 years. For at least a century, the Messenians had been reduced to the rank of Helots, state serfs tied to agricultural labor. The "speech" defends the Spartan position of intransigence and urges refusal of the Theban demand. Isocrates sent a copy to Archidamus, but it was probably never delivered, nor perhaps was it meant to be.

Antagonistic to Theban imperialism, Isocrates rhetorically defended Sparta's right to autonomy and freedom, which meant its right to continue enslaving Messenians and other Helots. His own voice is disguised, but Isocrates certainly accepted slavery, and in his "Trapeziticus," he insisted on the right to torture a slave for judicial testimony. In "Archidamus," Isocrates has the prince trace Sparta's historic domination of Messene, explaining that the gods Heracles and Apollo willed it, Spartan arms won it, and Messenian leaders themselves surrendered the people to slavery. Thus, the Spartans should do all in their power "to prevent this territory, which our fathers left to us, from becoming the possession of our slaves."

Fears of slave autonomy are reiterated as the statement declares, "The worst fate that threatens us is not that we will be robbed of our land contrary to justice, but that we shall see our slaves made masters of it." Isocrates argues that outside observers "would see our slaves bringing from the land which our fathers bequeathed to us first fruits of the harvest and sacrifices greater than our own, and would hear from their lips such taunts as you would expect from men who were once subjected to the strictest bondage but now have a treaty with their masters on terms of equality. How keenly each one of us would smart under these insults no man alive could set forth in words." It would be "better to suffer annihilation rather than derision."

From the beginning, Spartans had based their society upon the continued subjection and labor of Helots, which both forced and freed the true ethnic Spartans to pursue development of a military culture second to none among the Greeks. Each year the city-state's magistrates (ephors) ritually declared war on the Helots, legitimizing official harassment and even persecution of potential troublemakers. Military defeat by the Thebans at Leuctra (371 B.C.) was galling enough, but allowing "the helots to settle on our borders and allow Messene to flourish undisturbed" truly struck a blow at Spartan civic dignity. In the end, the Thebans successfully detached Messene, and Sparta never regained its previous position of hegemony in the Greek world.

—*Joseph P. Byrne*

See also
Greece; Helots
For Further Reading
Van Hook, Larue, trans. 1945. *Isocrates.* Cambridge, MA: Harvard University Press.

IVORY COAST

Located on Africa's western coast between Liberia and Ghana, the Ivory Coast did not develop into a major colonial external-slave-trading area. Lacking natural harbors, having a coastline protected by either rocks or sandbars, and possessing dangerous Gulf of Guinea currents, the region was ill-adapted for slave-trading operations. Nonetheless, slavery persisted in the territory's interior regions well into the twentieth century. The first Europeans to attempt establishing a presence in the Ivory Coast were the French, who eventually incorporated the territory's numerous chiefdoms into a French colony.

In 1637, French missionaries attempted to settle an outpost at Assinie, but this effort quickly failed. A more substantive settlement, including factories (trading posts), was later established at the site, and there the French bought slaves, gold, and rubber for export from local chiefdoms. The small scale of the trade rendered the colony unprofitable to the French crown, however, and that unprofitability, combined with Dutch naval attacks, caused France to abandon the colony in 1704. France also established a major slave factory at Grand Bassam in the territory's eastern corner, but this settlement also failed and was abandoned in 1707.

Throughout the eighteenth century, the Ivory Coast slave trade was relatively minor when compared with that of neighboring territories. Individual British, French, and Dutch slavers occasionally stopped along the coast to purchase slaves, but the trade never reached the level of other West African territories. Along much of the Ivory Coast's coastline a series of shallow lagoons separated the sea from the land, which made it nearly impossible for deep-draft vessels to approach the shore for trading with indigenous populations. During the 1700s, a significant trading center developed around Grand Lahou where the natives traded slaves, ivory, and rubber for manufactured goods. In 1787, France negotiated a series of treaties with local chiefs that allowed the establishment of French factories, including slave factories, at Grand Lahou, but the advent of the French Revolution shifted resources for developing those factories elsewhere and the treaty obligations went unfulfilled.

There was then only minor European interest in the Ivory Coast until 1838 when France reestablished the Grand Bassam trading post. Subsequently in 1842, in conjunction with British efforts to suppress the West African slave trade, France stationed a naval squadron off the Ivory Coast to interdict slavers. The squadron's commander, Capt. Edouard Bouët-Willaumez, was also instructed to negotiate treaties with native chiefs to support French naval activities and open the territory for trade. Bouët-Willaumez initially signed such treaties with local chiefs at Grand Bassam and Assinie, but by 1852 he had extended French influence over virtually all coastal areas of the Ivory Coast. France used this foothold to move into the Ivory Coast's interior, hoping to gain access to the Ashanti gold mines, forestall British influence in the region, and suppress indigenous tribes. This French colonization ended the Ivory Coast's small, external slave trade.

Although the region's external slave trade was relatively minor and largely suppressed by the 1840s, an immense internal slave trade continued among interior tribes until the early years of the twentieth century. Much of the persistence of the Ivory Coast's interior slave trade was attributed to the short-lived empire established by Samory Touré, a leader of the Mandingo peoples. During its height, from 1880 to 1900, Touré's empire stretched across parts of present-day Ivory Coast, Mali, Guinea, and Burkina Faso. Touré traded large numbers of subjugated tribal men and women to forest tribes in exchange for ivory, which was sold to finance his wars of conquest. A colonial war ensued as the French moved northward and Touré's empire moved south. Eventually, the French defeated Touré and captured most of his empire, and with his defeat, France was able to suppress the majority of the internal Ivory Coast slave trade. Still, slaves were bought and sold even as late as 1904 in heavily colonized areas like Grand Lahou and Jacqueville even though slavery was illegal in the French colony.

—Tom Lansford

See also
French Royal Africa Company; French Slave Trade
For Further Reading
Mundt, Robert. 1987. *Historical Dictionary of the Ivory Coast*. Metuchen, NJ: Scarecrow Press; Stein, Robert Louis. 1979. *The French Slave Trade in the Eighteenth Century*. Madison: University of Wisconsin; Wieskel, Timothy. 1980. *French Colonial Rule and the Baule Peoples*. New York: Oxford.

JACOBS, HARRIET ANN (1813–1897)

Born a slave in Edenton, North Carolina, Harriet Jacobs underwent severe trials before escaping to the North and publishing her narrative about the sexual vulnerability of slave women. Though attacks on Southern masters' concubinage and even rape had been standard abolitionist fodder for years, Jacobs's *Incidents in the Life of a Slave Girl* (1861) revealed horrors that strengthened the antislavery cause. The book was also remarkable for its portrait of free and enslaved blacks working together and the indication that Southern white women also suffered from slavery.

Born to comparative comfort, since her grandmother had a small business and was free, Jacobs was taught to read and write by a mistress whom she recalled with a sense of love betrayed. This woman's decision to will Harriet to a three-year-old niece put the young slave girl into the hands of the toddler's father. James Norcom harassed Jacobs to the extent that the slave girl felt trapped by impossible ideals of virtue and chastity. Though Jacobs foiled Norcom's designs by taking a white lover, with whom she had two children, this desperate expedient did not free her from her mistress's father's power.

Forced to hide in her grandmother's garret to elude Norcom, Jacobs finally escaped to Philadelphia in 1842 with the help of her grandmother and uncle. Aided by abolitionists, she joined her daughter in Brooklyn, but was forced to flee to Boston when Norcom put slave catchers on her trail. After supporting herself and her children as a seamstress, Jacobs returned to the job of nursemaid in a New York family. Later, she moved to Rochester, New York, where her brother was an active abolitionist, but she remained unsettled because of Norcom's relentless pursuit. In 1852, Jacobs was purchased and freed by Cornelia Willis, whom she served in New York.

Jacobs asked Harriet Beecher Stowe to write the story of her life, but Stowe refused. Determined to make her experiences known, Jacobs decided to write her own book and practiced with shorter antislavery pieces, signed "Linda," which appeared in New York's reformist *Tribune*. In 1859, Jacobs arranged for the publication of her manuscript with a Boston firm. Their request for a preface from Maria Child led to one final editing and the decision that the characters' identities should be disguised. Thus, Jacobs's autobiography is told as the story of Linda Brent. Favorably received, *Incidents in the Life of a Slave Girl* was republished in England as *The Deeper Wrong* (1862), and portions of the book appeared in Child's *Freedmen's Book* (1865).

During the Civil War, Jacobs did relief work among former slaves in Washington, D.C., and then taught and nursed in Alexandria, Virginia. After the war, Jacobs and her daughter traveled to Southern cities carrying relief supplies. In 1868, the two women sailed to England to try to raise funds for a Savannah orphanage and home for the aged, but Jacobs later advised against building either because of Southern racist agitation. In 1897, she was buried in Massachusetts near her brother John.

—*Barbara Ryan*

See also
Child, Lydia Maria; Narratives; Stowe, Harriet Beecher
For Further Reading
Yellin, Jean Fagan, ed. 1987. *Incidents in the Life of a Slave Girl*. Cambridge, MA: Harvard University Press.

JAJA (JACK ANNA PEPPLE), KING OF OPOBO (C. 1821–1891)

Jaja (also known as Jack Anna Pepple) was a slave who, through resourcefulness and trading acumen, became a late-nineteenth-century king in the Niger Delta. Born in the West African Igbo village of Amaigbo, he was captured by slave raiders when he was 12. Bought and sold many times, he served several masters before finally arriving in Bonny, a coastal delta city-state. Stiff competition for controlling the trades in slaves and palm oil characterized the politics of all the delta city-states at the time, and ability rather than birth or social status counted most. Jaja's intelligence, hard work, and trading ability persuaded one master to make him the head of a trading canoe, and by 1860, Jaja, though still technically a slave, had become one of the richest trader slaves and slaveowners in the Niger Delta. Jaja's growing wealth was pleasing to his master, because rich slaves meant rich masters.

By the time Alali, the erstwhile ruler of Bonny and head of the Anna Pepple House (or family) died in 1861, it was clear that no one among the leading chiefs and traders had the personality, respectability, qualities of leadership, and command of men and resources to succeed him except Jaja, and though still a slave, he became chief of the Anna Pepple House in 1863. Challenged by another wealthy trader slave of the leading rival house of Bonny who was supported by 14 of the 18 principal chiefs of Bonny, Jaja withdrew with his followers eastward to establish a new settlement, Opobo, where he became king in 1869.

Opobo's strategic location at the mouth of the Imo River and near the palm oil–producing region of Igboland proved decisive in attracting European traders to Opobo, ruining Bonny, and establishing Jaja as the Niger Delta's wealthiest trader and most powerful ruler. In January 1873, Britain's Queen Victoria reached an agreement with Jaja and recognized him as king of Opobo.

In the 1880s, however, the British and other European nations scrambled to establish African colonies, which produced a clash with Jaja who relentlessly resisted British imperialism. In 1887, a British consul, Henry Hamilton Johnston, resorted to a highly reprehensible stratagem. He tricked and kidnapped Jaja and deported him to the Gold Coast, where after an illegal trial, he was exiled to the West Indies. Permitted to return home, he died en route in July 1891. His body was brought home where his people gave him a royal state burial.

A bronze monument commemorating Jaja's memory stands today at the center of Opobo, and he continues to be remembered in African history as one of the most astute statesman and illustrious heroes and defenders of African independence in the nineteenth century. Jaja's story demonstrates the nature, varieties, mobility, and dynamism of the slave experience in Africa.

—*Funso Afolayan*

See also
Africa; Slave Coast
For Further Reading
Alagoa, E. J. 1970. *Jaja of Opobo, the Slave Who Became a King*. London: Longman; Anene, J. C. 1966. *Southern Nigeria in Transition, 1885–1906*. London: Cambridge University Press.

JAMAICA

First colonized by the Spanish, Jamaica in the seventeenth century was a Caribbean way station and a haven for buccaneers. English forces captured the island in 1655–1660, and Jamaica's new governors wasted no time in granting patents to most of the arable land, much of it in large parcels. Eventually this policy promoted large-scale slaveholding, but Jamaica did not immediately become a major sugar producer. A series of European wars and the fact that Jamaica was located far to the west of the major trade routes through the Leeward Islands meant that Jamaica's growth was retarded during much of the seventeenth century. Nevertheless, by 1713, Jamaica rivaled Britain's other sugar islands, and its population of 55,000 slaves was constantly being augmented by newly captured Africans. Jamaica became the dominant British sugar colony of the eighteenth century, the standard by which others were measured.

Jamaica's slave population multiplied from 9,000 in 1670 to 300,000 in 1809, despite the fact that slave deaths consistently outnumbered births. This growth was fueled by the continuing importation of many Africans, ensuring that Jamaican society would remain heavily African even into the nineteenth century. On the Price family's Worthy Park plantation, for instance, Africans still constituted nearly one-third of the people living there in 1820. Not surprisingly, distinctly African cultural forms were readily apparent in funeral, magic/religious, and naming practices as well as in linguistic patterns, music, dress, and forms of resistance.

With the slave trade suppressed after 1807, fresh infusions of African culture nearly ceased, and the population became increasingly Creole (native born). By the time slaves were emancipated in 1834, most of them remembered stories of Africa but not Africa itself. Their evolving synthesis of African and European cultural forms became increasingly tailored to Jamaican circumstances. Societal creolization, in which slaves became enmeshed in an increasingly dense and localized web of social and kinship relations, was matched by cultural creolization, in which a diverse array of African peoples became synthesized into a uniquely Jamaican society.

Changing resistance patterns paralleled the creolization process. Forms of active resistance marked Jamaican slavery from beginning to end, much more so than in Barbados and the Leeward Islands. The high ratio of blacks to whites (8 to 1 in 1713 compared to 3 to 1 in other British sugar islands), together with the potential for creating autonomous Maroon communities (settlements composed of fugitive black slaves and their descendants) in Jamaica's rugged

This illustration from R. C. Dallas's The History of the Maroons *(London, 1803) shows Europeans on a foray into the wild to battle the Maroons, escaped slaves who had established independent communities.*

mountains, made it plausible that a well-planned rebellion might succeed.

Throughout the mid-eighteenth century, Africans led the major rebellions, and in the slave rebellions and Maroon wars discernable patterns of African ethnic participation, leadership, and even distinctly African military strategies emerged. Less confrontational resistance patterns predominated in the late-eighteenth and early-nineteenth centuries, as the increasingly Creole slaves largely confined themselves to work slowdowns and other attacks on productivity. The final decades of slavery brought a renewed tendency toward direct, violent resistance, but it was led by highly acculturated, native-born artisans and religious men who capitalized on their intimate knowledge of Anglo-Jamaican society.

During the period of slavery, newly established plantations included more Africans than Creoles, more young adults than children or the aged, and more men than women, but societal creolization gradually brought a more nearly balanced age and sex structure to slave communities. Work was unevenly distributed by age and sex. Large plantations included several labor gangs, organized mainly by age, with different workloads expected of each group. Women formed most of even the hardest-worked gangs, partly because African women outlived men and partly because men were more likely to be assigned to a skilled occupation in sugar production.

For men and women alike, work became both a necessity and a battleground between slaves and masters. Masters kept expenses low and expectations high, and for slaves, a concession once won assumed a lawlike force of custom. Independent food production by and for slaves, a common Jamaican practice, generated as much conflict as gang labor. Jamaica's mountainous terrain provided ecological niches that were better suited to gardening than to cane cultivation, and planters found it economical to allot time and space for slaves to supply their own dietary needs in such locations, particularly after the American Revolution affected major sources of food rations. By slavery's final years, few measures sparked as much resistance as a planter's attempt to alter such arrangements, which had come to provide not only food but also a material basis for independence.

—*James D. Rice*

See also
Comparative Slavery in the Americas; English Caribbean; Sugar Cultivation and Trade; Tacky's Rebellion; Trelawney Town Maroons; West Indies
For Further Reading
Brathwaite, Edward. 1971. *The Development of Creole Society in Jamaica, 1770–1820*. Oxford: Clarendon Press; Craton, Michael. 1978. *Searching for the Invisible Man: Slaves and Plantation Life in Jamaica*. Cam-bridge, MA: Harvard University Press; Mullin, Michael. 1992. *Africa in America: Slave Acculturation and Resistance in the American South and the British Caribbean, 1736–1831*. Urbana: University of Illinois Press; Turner, Mary. 1982. *The Disintegration of Jamaican Slave Society, 1787–1834*. Urbana: University of Illinois Press.

JAMAICA REBELLION (1831)

Known as the Jamaica Rebellion, Christmas Rebellion, the Baptist War, the Native Baptist War, and Samuel Sharpe's Rebellion, the revolt that erupted in western Jamaica in December 1831 was one of the largest slave revolts ever to occur in the British West Indies, and it played a major role in hastening the abolition of slavery by the British. Like other rebellions in the last years of British colonial slavery, this revolt was led by slaves born in the West Indies, mobilized slaves as slaves rather than as members of a particular African national or ethnic group, and articulated the outright abolition of slavery as a goal.

Beginning on December 27, 1831, in the sugar-producing parish of St. James, the rebellion spread rapidly to estates in at least seven other parishes and involved thousands of slaves. Dashing the rebels' hopes that British forces would refuse to suppress them, the governor dispatched two companies of the 84th regiment to Montego Bay, and these troops contained the uprising within two weeks. Besides those killed in the fighting, at least 300 slaves were executed after conviction in military and slave courts, a figure that stands in sharp contrast to the lack of violence with which the rebels confronted civilian whites.

Samuel Sharpe, the rebellion's most significant leader, was an urban slave from Montego Bay and a religious leader in both missionary and independent black Baptist churches. The rebellion's planning occurred at meetings of enslaved Baptist leaders, with Christianity, in particular the injunction that "no man can serve two masters," providing the guiding rebel ideology. Several conflicts in which slaves were harshly punished for insisting on their right to worship in nonconformist churches had made religion and religious freedom inflammatory issues in Jamaica by 1830.

When abolition became a central issue in British politics, Jamaican planters were outraged and held protest meetings across the island. These meetings revealed to the slaves the real likelihood that they could become legally free, but the meetings also demonstrated the depth of the division between Jamaican planters and the British government. In a pattern familiar from earlier large nineteenth-century slave rebellions in British colonies, including Demerara (1823) and Barbados (1816), the ensuing rumors of the actual abolition of slavery, which Sharpe and the other leaders encouraged, provided the rebellion's spark.

In a jailhouse interview before his execution, Sharpe revealed that what became an armed rebellion was planned as a massive general strike. Sharpe had hoped that slaves would simply refuse to return to work after the Christmas break until their freedom was acknowledged, but although groups of slaves in several areas did strike, there was insufficient organization for this tactic to work on a grand scale. The rebellion mostly took the form of groups of slaves armed with their work tools, plus the occasional firearm, setting fire to the sugar works on their plantations and engaging in battle with the white militia and later the British military. The extent of their military preparedness is measurable since the militia was unable to win a convincing victory over the rebels, although the army suppressed the rebellion within a few days.

When the rebellion was reported in Britain, much of its impact came from narratives of the brutality of the revolt's suppression. As was true in most slave rebellions, the planters did far more than was necessary simply to restore order, instead embarking on a theatrical power display. Thus, authorities erected a gibbet in Montego Bay's central square from which tens of slaves were hung, usually following extremely peremptory trials. Many rebel slaves were returned to their home estates for execution before their families and friends.

Planters, unwilling to attribute independent thought and organization to their slaves, blamed missionaries, especially Baptist ones, for inciting the rebellion. As a result, white mobs attacked and burned Baptist and Methodist chapels throughout much of 1832, Christian slaves were prevented from attending services, and missionaries were arrested and imprisoned for sedition.

Ultimately, the rebellion contributed significantly to the hastening of abolition. During several parliamentary inquiries into West Indian slavery in the early 1830s, a key underlying question was, Can slavery be safely maintained indefinitely, or will slaves always rebel in the end? The 1831 rebellion was a significant reason why answers to that question overwhelmingly stressed the likelihood of revolt.

—Diana Paton

See also
Abolition, British Empire
For Further Reading
Craton, Michael. 1982. *Testing the Chains: Resistance to Slavery in the British West Indies*. Ithaca, NY: Cornell University Press; Genovese, Eugene. 1980. *From Rebellion to Revolution: Afro-American Slave Revolts in the Making of the Modern World*. Baton Rouge: Louisiana State University Press; Turner, Mary. 1982. *Slaves and Missionaries: The Disintegration of Jamaican Slave Society, 1787–1834*. Urbana: University of Illinois Press.

JANISSARIES

Janissaries were the Ottoman Empire's premier body of infantry from the late-fourteenth century until they were abolished in 1826. The name derives from the Turkish *yeni çeri*, or "new soldiers," and the creation of the Janissary corps appears to have preceded the institution of the *devsirme*, the Ottoman impressment of non-Muslim boys from Balkan and Anatolian territories under Ottoman control. By the late-fourteenth century, the future sultan Murad I (r. 1362–1389), grandson of the dynasty's founder Osman I (r. 1281–1324), was employing Byzantine prisoners of war as soldiers. This practice was justified as an extension of the *penjik*, a one-fifth tax levied on Christian peasants by Muslim landlords. Murad established a corps of "new soldiers" to complement the Anatolian overlords, whose armies had previously been the principal group the Ottomans relied on for defense.

In the early-fifteenth century, the Ottomans extended the levy to include the regular "gathering" *(devsirme)* of boys from among their own Christian subjects, who under Muslim law should have enjoyed protection *(dhimma)*. The rationale for the extension was that slaves removed from their natal homes and forbidden to marry would have no loyalty to anyone but the sultan who had recruited them. This policy accounted for the Janissaries' legendary discipline, which, among other things, allowed the Ottomans to introduce firearms and cannon into the corps beginning in the mid-fifteenth century, and the tight square of rifle-bearing Janissaries around the sultan or grand vizier became the centerpiece of Ottoman battlefield formation.

The genesis of the Janissaries has been obfuscated by myths linking the corps to the thirteenth-century Anatolian mystical *(sufi)* leader Hājjī Bektash, who is supposed to have aided Osman. The Janissaries' distinctive headgear—a tall white cap rising roughly a foot above the head and then falling down over the shoulders—is said to have derived from Hājjī Bektash's sleeve. In fact, the Janissaries were strongly connected to the Bektashi *sufi* order established by Hājjī Bektash's disciples in the fourteenth century, and key

A group of Janissaries wearing their distinctive headgear. The Ottoman Empire's premier body of infantry, the Janissaries became a force in their own right despite their slave status.

the capital and various Ottoman provinces where they were stationed by marrying local women, entering trades, and acquiring urban, and eventually rural, tax farms. Janissary officers recruited their own clients and even purchased their own slaves. In 1553, the Janissaries threatened to revolt when Sultan Süleyman I (r. 1520–1566) had crown prince Mustafa executed. In 1622, they deposed and murdered Sultan Osman II (r. 1618–1622) because he had attempted to replace them with mercenaries.

The growing unreliability of Janissaries as a fighting force obliged the sultan and provincial governors to recruit auxiliary forces by various means, such as purchasing military slaves *(mamluks)* from the Caucasus, hiring mercenaries from among the peasantry, and exploiting Turkoman and Arab tribesmen. Finally, at the end of the eighteenth century, the reforming sultan Selim III (r. 1789–1807) formed an entirely new corps of professional soldiers that was designed to gradually replace the Janissaries. Selim's deposition delayed the execution of his plan and impressed upon his successor, Mahmud II (r. 1808–1839), the necessity of abolishing the Janissaries if real change were to be effected. This Mahmud did in 1826, initiating a brutal campaign to hunt down and eliminate Janissary holdouts. Today, only a modernized version of the Janissary band *(mehter)* survives as a museum piece, performing at Istanbul's Military Museum and various festivals.

—*Jane Hathaway*

For Further Reading
Palmer, J. A. B. 1953. "The Origin of the Janissaries." *Bulletin of the John Rylands Library* 35: 448–481; Uzunçarsili, I. H. 1943. *Osmanll Devleti Teskilatindan Kapukulu Ocaklarl.* Ankara: Türk Tarih Kurumu; Wittek, Paul. 1958. "Devshirme and Sharī'a." *Bulletin of the School of Oriental and African Studies* 17: 271–278; Zygulski, Zdzislaw, Jr. 1992. *Ottoman Art in the Service of the Empire.* New York: New York University Press.

features of Janissary spiritual culture—reverence for an early Muslim caliph; the image of that caliph's sword, Dhū'l-Fiqār, on Janissary battle flags; battle songs; and the Janissary battle prayer, known as the *gülbang*—all show Bektashi influence. Nonetheless, there is no evidence that the corps or any precursor of it existed during Hājjī Bektash's lifetime.

The Janissaries should, in any event, not be automatically identified with the *devsirme. Devsirme* recruits performed other functions, notably those of palace pages, from very early on; moreover, nonslaves managed to infiltrate the Janissary ranks. During the seventeenth century, the *devsirme* was levied more and more sporadically until it was finally abandoned early in the eighteenth century.

Imperial Janissaries were literally and symbolically incorporated into the sultan's household. Beginning in the late-fifteenth century, they ate and mustered in the second court of Topkapl Palace in Istanbul, and household, specifically kitchen, terminology was employed to describe their ranks and functions. The most famous example of the latter is that Janissaries signaled a rebellion by overturning their soup cauldrons, thus indicating that they rejected the sultan's food and, therefore, their place in his household.

Rebellions became more and more frequent beginning in the sixteenth century, as Janissaries became a separate locus of power with vested interests. Belying their original purpose, Janissaries forged local ties in

JASPER, JOHN (1812–1901)

John Jasper was a slave preacher whose sermon "De Sun Do Move" became the basis for his subsequent prominence as a pastor in Richmond, Virginia. He was born a slave on a plantation in Fluvanna County, Virginia. His mother, Nina, was a house slave while Philip, his father, was a field slave who also preached. Philip's death two months after his son's birth left Nina in charge of raising the family. Jasper was eventually sold to Samuel Hargrove, who put him to work as a stemmer in his Richmond tobacco factory. While there, Jasper married fellow slave Elvy Weadon.

In July 1837, Jasper experienced an epiphany and converted to Christianity. He subsequently joined Richmond's First Baptist Church and began preaching regularly. Like many fellow slaves, he taught himself to read by reading the Bible, the slave's primer. About this time, Jasper left Weadon and married Candus Jordan, and they had nine children. In 1839, he began becoming notable as a slave preacher for his funeral orations in Richmond and its hinterland.

During the Civil War, Jasper preached in hospitals to wounded Confederate soldiers. After emancipation in 1866, he moved with his congregation to the northern part of Richmond and helped found the Sixth Mount Zion Church, where he preached until his death.

Jasper's historical significance may be best appreciated through several facets of his slave preaching. First, he was an old-style preacher thundering fire and brimstone from the pulpit, and this preaching style was in great contrast to the more measured tones of his theologically trained contemporaries who often despised such folk ways. Second, he preached in the dialect of poor rural folk and new migrants to Richmond, who made up most of his congregation, and in this way, he acted as a conduit to link life and religion, the countryside and the town. Jasper's first biographer recalled one inspirational sermon: "He painted scene after scene. He lifted the people to the sun and sank them down to despair. He plucked them out of hard places and filled them with shouting" (Hatcher, 1908).

Third, he was a consummate performer, histrionic, and stylish. William Hatcher recalled his first sighting of Jasper: "He circled around the pulpit with his ankle in his hand; and laughed and sang and shouted and acted about a dozen characters within the space of three minutes. . . . He was a theatre within himself, with the stage crowded with actors" (Hatcher, 1908). Finally, in his hands, the Bible became a liberation text in which contemporary events like slavery and emancipation were directly explained by the Old Testament.

These aspects of Jasper's preaching were reflected in his most famous sermon, "De Sun Do Move," which asserted that the earth was flat and the sun revolved around it. Jasper delivered this sermon an estimated 250 times, much to the chagrin of many of his contemporary ministers who thought the content, style, and popularity outlandish. Their dislike was clearly fueled by class tensions among Richmond's black elite, and the organic nature of the sermon is perhaps most strongly suggested by its failure to rouse much excitement when Jasper temporarily toured Northern states.

Jasper was an important figure in Afro-Virginia history, and it is interesting to compare his life and work with that other famous slave preacher, Nat Turner of Southampton County. He was also remembered: former slave Allen Wilson fondly recalled Jasper's old sermons decades later.

—*Jeffrey R. Kerr-Ritchie*

See also
Turner, Nat
For Further Reading
Brawley, Benjamin. 1937. *Negro Builders and Heroes.* Chapel Hill: University of North Carolina Press; Hatcher, William E. 1908. *John Jasper: The Unmatched Negro Philosopher and Preacher.* New York: F. H. Revell; James, Isaac. 1954. *"The Sun Do Move": The Story of the Life of John Jasper.* Richmond, VA: Whittet and Shepperson; Perdue, Charles L., et al. 1976. *Weevils in the Wheat: Interviews with Virginia Ex-Slaves.* Charlottesville: University of Virginia Press.

JEFFERSON, THOMAS (1743–1826)

As one of the most recognized figures in early U.S. history, Thomas Jefferson advocated the emancipation of slaves, an end of the slave trade, and a prohibition on the spread of slavery in acquired territories of the United States. No figure was more enigmatic in his views on slavery than Jefferson, who was truly trapped by the institution in both public and private life. Influenced by Enlightenment ideas, Jefferson clearly recognized slavery's moral wrong, yet when he was governor of Virginia and president for two terms, he did nothing to encourage an end to the institution. Writing in 1820, Jefferson lamented, "We have the wolf by the ears," and concluded that slavery was evil but the South could not live without it. He saw on one side the concept of justice; on the other, self-preservation.

Born on April 13, 1743, in Shadwell, Virginia, Jefferson was educated at the College of William and Mary and studied law under George Wythe, Virginia's leading legal mind of the era. Jefferson was a significant figure in the nation's history after 1775: he wrote the Declaration of Independence, served as a minister to France, was secretary of state, was vice-president (1797–1801), and served as president (1801–1809). All aspects of Jefferson's public career suggest an opposition to slavery. His authorship of the Declaration of Independence included the concept of all men being equal; his Virginia Statute of Religious Freedom (1786) implied a sense of freedom of, at least, religion, and in *Notes on the State of Virginia* (written in 1781–1782), the only book he ever wrote, Jefferson stated his opposition to slavery. Historically, he believed all slaves should be freed, yet he found emancipation incompatible with his practical actions.

Despite his political stance on slavery, Jefferson's personal actions have been questioned for nearly two centuries. Jefferson was a slaveholder—at one time, he owned more than 100 slaves. He often considered freeing his slaves and allowing them to become tenants on his property, but financial problems kept him from doing so as he apparently put personal economics above his social philosophy. Additionally, Jefferson believed that blacks were intellectually inferior and also believed that the negative impact of slavery on whites was far more significant than the consequences of society supporting an enslaved race. Jefferson, a complex man, was just as puzzling in his attitudes on race and social relations.

During Jefferson's first term as president, *Richmond Recorder* newspaperman James Callender rumored that Jefferson had fathered a mulatto child by one of his slaves, Sally Hemings. Callender's attack was clearly politically motivated and lacked an accurate basis, but the charges, ironically, were protected by Jefferson's own insistence on freedom of the press. In *Thomas Jefferson, an Intimate History* (1974), Fawn Brodie explored Jefferson's involvement with Hemings, the historical importance of that association, and his interest in other women. Brodie's evidence is circumstantial, however, leaving history and historians to make a final decision.

Jefferson's stance on slavery was confused by a draft he prepared in 1784 proposing the abolition of slavery to the west, in the new region of the nation gained during the American Revolution. The Articles of Confederation committee met in Annapolis in 1784 to decide the future of that territory, and as chair of a committee assigned to establish a governmental system and land policy, Jefferson wrote a draft that became the ordinance of 1784 (which never went into effect).

In his proposal, slavery (and involuntary servitude) were prohibited in all territories of the United States—North and South. His plans included the areas that became Alabama, Mississippi, and Tennessee, but only one Southern representative supported Jefferson. Ironically, the antislavery provision lost by one vote, that of an absent New Jersey delegate. The Northwest Ordinance (1787) did ban slavery in a portion of the expanding nation, but in areas south of the Ohio River, slavery could exist. Although Jefferson had no connection with the Northwest Ordinance, his ideas from the ordinance of 1784 did influence the later legislation. From the perspective of Southern interests, the decision to allow slavery to spread was clearly economic.

As president, Jefferson's dichotomy on slavery persisted. Most historians agree Jefferson's two major accomplishments as president were the Louisiana Purchase (1803) and the abolition of the slave trade (1808). The contradiction lies in Jefferson's fight to abolish trade in human beings yet allowing human bondage to expand into land purchased from France. He envisioned the northern half of the Louisiana territory as a huge Indian reservation, yet critics, citing his earlier view of the nation as an "empire of liberty," instead saw an "empire of slavery" when the administration took no action on slavery in the vast region. In the 1780s, Jefferson favored limits on the spread of slavery, but he had become resigned to the fact that slavery was an economic necessity for Southerners.

Jefferson's second term featured an end to the foreign slave trade, which had been the object of national scorn for years. In 1787, antislavery forces had pushed for a constitutional ban on importing slaves, but an odd alliance of Southern slave interests and New England shippers, who profited from the slave trade, had combined to recognize a moratorium on federal interference with the slave trade for 20 years.

In 1794, a federal law was enacted to prohibit ships' access to any U.S. port when the cargo was slaves. By 1799, all states had banned importing slaves, but the cumulative impact of the legislation was ineffective. Smuggling was widespread and in 1803, South Carolina bent to the planters' economic needs and rescinded earlier acts. Over the next five years, an estimated 40,000 slaves were imported through South Carolina's various ports. But in March 1807, Congress passed an act that totally abolished the slave trade after January 1, 1808. Jefferson supported the legislation, but it reflected national sentiment and preference more than the president's leadership. Ironically, the foreign slave trade continued after 1808, but in total number such illegal smuggling was not excessive (estimates vary, but the total was fewer than 60,000). Instead, slaveowners turned to natural reproduction to increase their slave numbers.

Jefferson's views on slavery survived his death in 1826. From 1829 to 1832, the Virginia legislature wrestled with the issue, but emancipation was not forthcoming even though Jefferson had advocated freeing the slaves. Nat Turner's Rebellion (1831) was a defining reason for the outcome of the debate, but even a captured Nat Turner wondered, If all men were created equal, why then was he not free? Critics have continued to address the crucial question: Why did the father of democracy, the author of his nation's independence document, not free his slaves?

—*Boyd Childress*

See also
Notes on Virginia, by Thomas Jefferson
For Further Reading
Brodie, Fawn. 1974. *Thomas Jefferson, an Intimate History*. New York: Norton; Jefferson, Thomas. 1950–.

The Papers of Thomas Jefferson. 20 vols. Ed. Julian P. Boyd. Princeton, NJ: Princeton University Press; Miller, John C. 1977. *The Wolf by the Ears: Thomas Jefferson and Slavery.* New York: Norton.

JENNISON, NATHANIEL
See Commonwealth v. Jennison

JIHADIYYA

Jihadiyya (singular, *jihadi*) refers to slave soldiers impressed into military service in the Nile region of the Sudan during the nineteenth century, the name deriving from an Arabic word *(jihad)* meaning "to struggle on behalf of the faith." The use of slave soldiers in the Nile Valley is an ancient practice dating back to Pharaonic Egypt. By the seventeenth century, the Sudanic states of Sinnar and Darfur were employing slave soldiers to expand their boundaries, collect taxes, and buttress the sultan's authority.

The Turco-Egyptian conquest of Nilotic Sudan (1820–1822) had as its express purpose the acquisition of slaves to serve as soldiers in the new modern army envisioned by the Egyptian ruler, Muhammad Ali. An exceptionally high mortality rate among the slaves doomed this enterprise to failure: perhaps most died en route to Egypt as a consequence of arduous marches and harsh treatment, and those who did reach Cairo quickly succumbed to disease. By 1824, Muhammad Ali was forced to abandon his idea of a Sudanese slave army, though his provincial administration at Khartoum continued to acquire slaves to serve the Turco-Egyptian regime in the Sudan. Branded with the Arabic letter *jim* (for *jihadiyya*), these slaves were organized into regular military units and garrisoned throughout the state, which by 1874 covered most of the territory of present-day Sudan.

The number of Sudanese taken as *jihadiyya* is difficult to estimate: roughly 5,000–9,000 were garrisoned in an average year, though since many died or deserted, significantly fewer actively served. Better known is their place of origin. Virtually all came from the remote upper Blue Nile, Nuba Mountains, or Bahr el Ghazal region, territories historically on the fringe of centralized states that had supplied the earlier sultanates with their slaves. *Jihadiyya* were obtained for the state in organized raids, often conducted by private slave armies of large trading companies, though individual Sudanese also surrendered domestic slaves to the state in lieu of taxes.

As with slave soldiers everywhere, the status of the *jihadiyya* was paradoxical: they were stripped of autonomy and most liberties, but they were armed with guns and often possessed their own personal servants. When paid regularly and commanded effectively, they evinced a high degree of professionalism and esprit de corps; when not, they frequently deserted.

As career soldiers, *jihadiyya* were expected to serve for life, taking up noncombative duties when too old to fight. However, throughout their careers, *jihadiyya* frequently were employed in noncombative roles, helping to collect taxes or working in hospitals and arsenals and even in shops in the capital. Generally poor conditions prevailed, partly because of the corruption of the regime, leading to a high attrition rate among *jihadiyya* and the constant need to replace them. In a financial sense, they were "the bottomless pit of the Sudan administration" (Prunier, 1992).

Egypt's official policy to repress the slave trade (1869) had little effect on the *jihadiyya* other than to disguise the acquisition of them. Slaves confiscated from dealers were directly impressed into the army, and ultimately, the same dealers were hired to supply the army with soldiers. With the coming of the Mahdist period (1881–1898), little about the institution or use of *jihadiyya* changed. The Mahdi and his successor Khalifa Abdullahi eagerly sought the services of these professional soldiers and valued them as an important state asset.

Although Mahdist ideology preached the social integration of all believers, the *jihadiyya* remained as apart from other Sudanese as their garrison was from the rest of the capital of Omdurman. Some *jihadiyya* remained Mahdist loyalists until the very end; others deserted to the Anglo-Egyptian army, whose cause they next served as willingly as they had the previous regime(s).

Britain's antislavery stance to the contrary, the Anglo-Egyptian regime (1899–1955) continued to employ *jihadiyya* taken from the Mahdists and even recruited its own. As members of the King's African Rifles, these soldiers served throughout British East Africa, and their descendants have played important roles as professional soldiers in colonial and postcolonial armies.

—*Robert S. Kramer*

See also
Darfur-Egypt Slave Trade; Sudan
For Further Reading
Hill, Richard. 1959. *Egypt in the Sudan, 1820–1881.* London: Oxford University Press; Holt, Peter. 1970. *The Mahdist State in the Sudan, 1881–1898.* Oxford: Clarendon Press; Johnson, Douglas. 1988. "Sudanese Military Slavery from the 18th to the 20th Century." In *Slavery and Other Forms of Unfree Labour.* Ed. Leonie Archer. London: Routledge; Prunier, Gerard. 1992.

"Military Slavery in the Sudan during the Turkiyya."
In *The Human Commodity: Perspectives on the Trans-Saharan Slave Trade*. Ed. Elizabeth Savage. London: Frank Cass.

JOHNSON, ANTHONY
(FL. 1621–1669)

First called Antonio, Anthony Johnson arrived in Jamestown, Virginia, in 1621 as a Negro indentured servant. Like the Africans who been brought to the same area in 1619 by a Dutch captain, Antonio had a 4-to-7-year contract and was sold to the English colonists. His contract was purchased again, and altogether, Antonio spent 20 years laboring on a Jamestown plantation. Virginia had not yet enacted slave statutes, and Antonio was treated like an indentured servant.

During the early 1640s, Antonio, his African wife, Mary, and their four children gained their freedom. At this time, Antonio changed his name to Anthony and adopted Johnson as a surname to indicate his new status. By 1650, Johnson had acquired 250 acres of land, some cattle, and like many of the white planters he owned the labor of black indentured servants. Slowly, however, the Virginia courts and legislature began establishing the foundation for the lifetime servitude of black indentured servants, in other words, slavery. Despite the increasingly circumscribed status for Virginia's colonial blacks, Anthony Johnson, perhaps with assistance from a white benefactor, retained his property and livelihood.

During the mid-1660s, however, the changing nature of Virginia society and perhaps pressure from white neighbors forced Johnson and most of his family into moving to the Eastern Shore of Maryland. There, Johnson leased 300 acres of land and tried to reestablish his economic success. Johnson still retained the labor of several blacks, including one—Casor—who had once sued to gain his freedom in a Virginia court and lost. African-born Anthony Johnson died in 1669, leaving two sons, Richard and John.

Richard Johnson inherited 50 acres of property in Virginia, but a white planter challenged the will. Virginia's codes had by now not only legalized slavery but also denied land ownership to free blacks. Thus, Richard Johnson could not enjoy the freedom and economic success of his father. Whereas Anthony Johnson had achieved a degree of socioeconomic status, emerging Virginia slavery effectively negated the transmission of material wealth on the part of blacks. Anthony Johnson's case illustrates another point concerning early colonial America: the free black ownership of black slaves, an anomaly that would only increase in the evolving young republic.

—*Jackie R. Booker*

See also
Durnford, Andrew; Indentured Servants
For Further Reading
Burnham, Philip. 1993. "Selling Poor Steven: The Struggles and Torments of a Forgotten Class in Antebellum America: Black Slaveowners." *American Heritage* 44(1): 90–97; Nash, Gary B., et al. 1994. *The American People: Creating a Nation and a Society.* New York: HarperCollins.

JONES, ABSALOM
(1746–1818)

Absalom Jones was the first African American to be ordained a priest by the Episcopal Church in the United States. He was born into slavery near Seaford in Sussex County, Delaware, and moved to Philadelphia to work in his master's retail business. Working nights, he raised money to buy his freedom and that of his wife. He was active in St. George Methodist Church, one of that new denomination's first parishes. Friction between the two races led to a disagreement in 1787, after which the congregation split along racial lines.

In 1787, Jones was a cofounder with Richard Allen of the Free African Society, one of the first black self-improvement organizations. The society became the nucleus of independent African religious bodies. Allen had also been born a slave in the colonies and had been freed. He remained a Methodist and eventually became the first bishop of the African Methodist Episcopal Church.

Jones led the congregation that became St. Thomas Church, which affiliated with the Episcopal Church in 1794. He was ordained a deacon in 1794 and a priest in 1804. For his sake, the Episcopalians waived the requirement of literacy in Greek and Latin, but they did not permit the African congregation to participate in diocesan deliberations. In addition to his parish work, Jones helped establish African community organizations, including an insurance company, a Masonic lodge, and an antislavery society. He was opposed to the colonization movement and organized antislavery petitions to be presented to state and national legislatures.

—*Edward F. Heite*

See also
African Methodist Episcopal Church; Allen, Richard

For Further Reading
George, Carol V. R. 1973. *Segregated Sabbaths:
Richard Allen and the Emergence of Independent Black
Churches, 1760–1840*. New York: Oxford University
Press; Munroe, John A. 1979. *History of Delaware*.
Newark: University of Delaware Press.

JONES V. VAN ZANDT
(1847)

The *Jones v. Van Zandt* case tested the constitutionality of the federal Fugitive Slave Act of 1793. John Van Zandt of Ohio, known for his support of abolition and actively involved in the Underground Railroad, was accused of helping a runaway slave escape his master, Wharton Jones. The Supreme Court upheld the constitutionality of the 1793 act and ordered Van Zandt to pay the slaveowner for his lost slave, plus the costs of his recapture and a $500 penalty.

Van Zandt had been driving his wagon in Ohio when he encountered several black men walking along the road. He offered them a ride, which they accepted. A few hours later two slave catchers confronted the party and claimed the men were runaways. All of the men were recaptured except for one, who made his escape. Van Zandt claimed that he did not know they were runaways: he had encountered them walking along the road, in daylight, in the free state of Ohio. They had not urged him to make his wagon go faster once they were riding in it but proceeded rather slowly, as if they were unhurried about reaching their destination. Nothing about them suggested that they were fugitives. Van Zandt put forward the argument that since he could not have known that the men were runaways he should not be charged for aiding their escape.

Van Zandt made various other legal arguments to oppose the Fugitive Slave Act and to challenge the federal government's role of assisting in the recapture of runaways. Van Zandt's lawyer, Salmon P. Chase, argued that slavery was unlawful because it conflicted with the Declaration of Independence and violated aspects of the Bill of Rights, especially the Fifth Amendment. Most important, Chase contended that the federal government had no power to support slavery or to assist in the recapture of fugitive slaves (attacking the fugitive slave clause of the Constitution, found in Article 4). The Supreme Court rejected all of Chase's arguments in the opinion written by Levi Woodbury. Perhaps seeking political prestige and elective office in 1852 with the support of Southern slaveholders, Woodbury called the fugitive slave clause one of the

Constitution's "sacred compromises," one that could not be subverted or undone. Only three years later, Congress revised the 1793 act and replaced it with even harsher provisions in the Fugitive Slave Act of 1850.

Jones v. Van Zandt (46 U.S. 215 [1847]) was one of a series of slavery cases decided by the Supreme Court in the decades before the Civil War in which the justices supported slavery and rejected any argument attacking that institution. As in *Prigg v. Pennsylvania* (1842), *Dred Scott v. Sandford* (1857), and *Ableman v. Booth* (1859), the Supreme Court solidly defended slaveowners' rights to recapture runaways and made many Northerners uneasy about how far the Supreme Court would go to defend slavery from legal challenges.

—*Sally E. Hadden*

See also
Ableman v. Booth; Abolition, United States; *Dred Scott v. Sandford*; *Prigg v. Pennsylvania*; Underground Railroad; U.S. Constitution

For Further Reading
Cover, Robert. 1975. *Justice Accused: Antislavery and the Judicial Process*. New Haven, CT: Yale University Press; Finkelman, Paul. 1985. *Slavery in the Courtroom: An Annotated Bibliography of American Cases*. Washington, DC: Library of Congress; Swisher, Carl. 1974. *History of the Supreme Court of the United States: The Taney Period, 1836–1864*. New York: Macmillan; Wiecek, William E. 1978. "Slavery and Abolition before the United States Supreme Court, 1820–1860." *Journal of American History* 65: 34–59.

JONKONNU *(JOHN CANOE)*

Jonkonnu (in English, John Canoe) designates a mummery tradition first noted among Jamaican slaves in the latter-eighteenth century. A dance processional with carnival variants in Bermuda, Nassau, Nevis, St. Kitts, St. Vincent, Tortola, Guyana, and North Carolina, it also persists among the never-enslaved Afro-Amerindian Black Carib (Garifuna) of Belize, Guatemala, and Honduras. Deported by the British from St. Vincent to Caribbean Central America in 1797, the Garifuna have sustained a variation (known in the Garifuna language as *Wanáragua*) involving elaborately masked and costumed stilt-walkers, singers, dancers with cowry leg rattles, and percussionists playing various handmade drums, jawbone rasps, and turtle shells.

Jonkonnu was a key folk element of the year's-end celebration. Released from work on Christmas Eve, slaves took to the streets for a week-long bacchanal that included a studied mockery of European music, dance, and theater forms in a symbolic inversion of the power relations inscribed in slavery. Planter Edward Long, resident in Jamaica during the 1750s and 1760s, was first among many to describe *Jonkonnu*, reportedly named to honor one John Conny, an influential African overseer of three European trading forts on the Ghana coast in the 1720s whose reputation apparently was well known to many Jamaican slaves of the era.

Preemancipation accounts describe slaves converging on the Jamaican towns during the Christmas holiday to visit, frolic, and see *Jonkonnu*. Especially tall, imposing men performed in arresting masks and inventive costumes topped with ox horns or huge head-dresses in the form of ships or model houses, sometimes with boar tusks to accentuate the mouth fiercely. Masqueraders often wielded wooden swords, and crowds of euphoric women trailed the energetic dancers, singing and dispensing anisette to the men in the procession.

The threatening masked figures advanced from one master's house to the next, dancing vigorously until the proprietor sent them off with a small gratuity. Street routines might also include mimes, informal companies of players irreverently enacting scenes from the English folk theater, and musicians playing "fife-and-drum" or "boom-and-chime" music, usually on handmade instruments. Echoing colonial reporters' observations, *Jonkonnu* performers today say they perform for the pleasure of dancing, the immediate personal gratification of money and drink, and the prestige their dancing skill brings.

In its various manifestations, *Jonkonnu* illustrates the process whereby African, Amerindian, and European folk cultures engendered the hybrid aesthetic and cultural forms that arose through western expansion in the Caribbean and the enforced interaction of diverse peoples from three continents under conditions of inequality. The African cultural influences evident in the history and current practice of *Jonkonnu* from Honduras to North Carolina must be seen more broadly against slave society's abiding endurance of social repression and material deprivation. In its historical genesis, and in various local settings, *Jonkonnu* has constituted a creative ritual response, an opportunistic application of sundry expressive repertoires carried from Africa or adopted in the Americas, in an affirmative effort to render meaningful the structural brutality of slavery and its social legacy in the culturally multiple New World milieu.

—*Michael C. Stone*

See also
Black Caribs
For Further Reading
Bettelheim, Judith. 1988. "Jonkonnu and Other Christmas Masquerades." In *Caribbean Festival Arts*. Ed.

John W. Nunley and Judith Bettelheim. Seattle: University of Washington Press; Dirks, Robert. 1987. *The Black Saturnalia: Conflict and Its Ritual Expression on British West Indian Slave Plantations*. Gainesville: University of Florida Press; Kerns, Virginia. 1983. *Women and the Ancestors: Black Carib Kinship and Ritual*. Urbana: University of Illinois Press; Long, Edward. 1972. *The History of Jamaica*. New York: Arno Press.

JUDAISM AND THE ANTEBELLUM SOUTH

There is no American Jewish history," wrote historian Lloyd Gartner, "that does not include assimilation" (Gartner, 1981). Defining assimilation, not as the end of Jewish identity nor its diffusion, but rather as a social process whereby a minority assumes the majority's values and practices, Gartner accurately describes the Jewish experience in the United States before the Civil War. Not surprisingly, from the mid-eighteenth century, their first century of Southern existence, Jews had constituted an insignificant part of the population and economy in the U.S. South. Different in religion and ethnicity, Jews were a highly vulnerable minority in an increasingly clearly defined aristocratic region. Some Southern Jews, particularly those in urban areas like Charleston, Savannah, and New Orleans, actively sought entrance into the mythical Southern aristocracy by erroneously claiming ancestry from Spanish and Portuguese noble Jews, the Sephardim. This status, they hoped, would merit admission into the planter class of Southern gentility and thereby afford them complete social and economic acceptance by their Christian peers.

Most Southern Jews tended to eschew rural areas and for a variety of reasons felt safer in urban areas, where they could engage in fellowship and find support within a visible Jewish community. If they desired to practice their religion actively, they could only accomplish that in urban areas where other Jews resided, not in sparsely populated rural areas. Furthermore, most immigrant Jews arrived in the United States virtually poverty-stricken, which made it highly unlikely they would achieve aristocratic status in the xenophobic South. Thus, the average Southern Jew was likely to be a small trader eking out a marginal existence in an occupation that ranked considerably low on the Old South's social scale. He considered himself fortunate to pay his bills and perhaps eventually own a small business, above which a few rooms would provide a home to him and his family. In all likelihood, he lacked enough capital to purchase a slave even if he determined a need for one. Yet, to survive in a potentially hostile environment he could not, or would not, become a vocal critic of the institution of slavery.

Some Southern Jews, though, did successfully climb the socioeconomic ladder through careers as merchants or professionals. In general, these Jews did indeed conform to prevailing patterns of slave ownership, with some of them even growing wealthy from the plantation economy. Wanting to participate as equals in the slave-based South, almost all Jewish residents acclimated themselves to Southern values. True, their acceptance of slavery was hastened by the fear that opposing white Southerners would unleash a firestorm of anti-Semitic prejudice; still, some Southern Jews assuaged any moral compunctions they might have had about owning slaves. "The institution of slavery as it existed in the South was not so great a wrong as people believed," reflected Aaron Hirsch of Mississippi following the Civil War. "The Negroes were brought here in a savage state," he mused, "they captured and ate each other in their African home. Here they were instructed to work, were civilized and got religion, and were perfectly happy" (Korn, 1973).

No proslavery Southerner was more direct than Savannah Jewish leader Solomon Cohen who wrote before the war, "I believe that the institution of slavery [is] refining and civilizing to the whites—giving them an elevation of sentiment and dignity of manners only attainable in societies under the restraining influence of a privileged class—and at the same time the only human institution that could elevate the Negro from barbarianism and develop the small amount of intellect with which he is endowed" (Korn, 1973). For Jews like Cohen, who could afford to purchase slaves and who believed they needed their labor, participation in the buying, trading, owning, and selling of slaves was expected. Like their Christian peers, some Jews, especially those in Southern urban areas, owned slaves as status symbols. In accepting Southern society for what it was, Jewish residents also conformed to the dominant proslavery ideology.

For instance, no Southern Jews were abolitionists—nor were many white Southern Christians. No Southern Jewish intellectual questioned the injustice of slavery, and in many ways, through their writings, men such as Texas newspaper editor Jacob De Cordova, South Carolina political essayist Isaac Harby, and Virginia journalist Samuel Mordecai contributed to the formation and dissemination of the proslavery doctrine.

A few Jews even became prominent slaveowning planters in the Old South. Judah P. Benjamin, master of the New Orleans plantation Bellechase and its 140 slaves, was virtually an icon of the Southern gentleman and plantation owner; Maj. Raphael J. Moses owned a plantation with approximately 50 slaves near Columbus, Georgia; South Carolinians Nathan Nathans, Isaiah Moses, Mordecai Cohen, Isaac Lyons, Barnet Cohen, and Chapman Levy all maintained sizable slave holdings; and various members of the Mordecai family owned Virginia and North Carolina plantations. Yet it must be remembered that as successful as these Jewish Southerners were by Southern standards, they represented a very tiny percentage of the 20,000 Jews residing in the antebellum South who could, or would, ever aspire to own a slave. (About 5,000 Jews owned one or more slaves—about 1.25 percent of all the slaveowners in the antebellum South.)

For those Jews who did own slaves, the records demonstrate that they were not significantly different from other masters in their treatment of their bondsmen. Southern Jews were just as likely, or unlikely, to manumit their slaves, and if their last wills and testaments are indicative, Jews occasionally regarded their slaves as chattel, to be retained if possible or to be sold if the situation warranted. Incidents of cruel, sadistic, or violent Jewish slaveowners are rare, in part because such episodes generally occurred in the rural South where few Jews resided.

Being Jewish did not play any significant role in the relationship between slaves and Jews, just as Christianity and ethnicity did not for others in the Old South. Most Southern Jews, if asked about their attitudes toward slavery per se, would have been very comfortable quoting the Talmud and saying that "the law of the land is the law," but then again, so would the Christians. For antebellum Jews, as well as their non-Jewish counterparts, a peaceful, if not profitable, life in the moonlight and among the magnolias meant regarding slavery as part of the law they were bound to uphold and follow.

The Jews of the Old South were neither the victors nor the vanquished. Slavery played a more prominent role in the lives of antebellum Southern Jews than the Jews themselves played in the emergence and maintenance of slavery. The historical rise and fall of slavery in the United States would not have been affected at all had there been no Jews living in the South, and whatever minuscule part the Jews played in the historical drama would have been more than compensated for by other non-Jewish whites.

It cannot be denied that Jews benefited, as did every other Southern white, from the existence and labor of black slaves, but Southern Jews, like Southerners in general, hovered between myth and reality. As Abraham Peck has written: "The Jews assumed a certain distance from the racial question but made every effort to see that religious and economic freedoms were not harmed by an overt distaste for the system . . . and a too visible reaction against the entire oppressive nature of southern society. This was in keeping, after all, with the notion that Southern gentlemen—both Jew and Christian—were required to maintain a proper and correct attitude at all times. This was to be the proper response even if their make-believe could not hide the growing inequalities around them" (Peck, 1987). In the South, much of whose history has been shrouded in myth, the Jews were neither mythmakers nor mythbreakers.

—*Jason H. Silverman*

For Further Reading
Gartner, Lloyd P. 1981. "Assimilation and American Jews." In *Jewish Assimilation in Modern Times*. Ed. Bela Vago. Boulder, CO: Westview Press; Korn, Bertram Wallace. 1973. "Jews and Negro Slavery in the Old South." In *Jews in the South*. Ed. Leonard Dinnerstein and Mary Dale Palsson. Baton Rouge: Louisiana State University Press; Peck, Abraham J. 1987. "'That Other Peculiar Institution': Jews and Judaism in the Nineteenth Century South." *Modern Judaism* 7: 99–114; Silverman, Jason H. 1992. "Ashley Wilkes Revisited: The Immigrant as Slaveowner in the Old South." *Journal of Confederate History* 7: 123–135; Silverman, Jason H. 1997. "'The Law of the Land Is the Law': Antebellum Jews, Slavery, and the Old South." In *Struggles in the Promised Land: Towards a History of Black-Jewish Relations in America*. Ed. Cornel West and Jack Salzman. New York: Oxford University Press.

JUNETEENTH

Juneteenth, a hybrid of the words June and nineteenth, was first recognized and celebrated on June 19, 1865, when Gen. Gordon Granger and a regiment of Union army soldiers sailed into Galveston Bay, Texas, with a proclamation that freed approximately 200,000 slaves. The celebration, originally limited to the southwestern part of the United States, has been sporadically observed since the 1940s. It is now a Texas state holiday, and African Americans throughout the country commemorate it with parades, concerts, and other cultural observances.

Juneteenth's origins relate historically to the period in 1863 when President Lincoln issued the Emancipation Proclamation, but this decree was not official or totally enforced until the Civil War ended in April 1865. Texas was not notified of the news until June 19, and a number of legendary stories attempt to account for the delay in notifying the people of Texas about the end of slavery. One story describes the odyssey of a soldier Lincoln sent traveling by mule who went to Oklahoma and Arkansas before arriving in Texas, but that story negates accounts of Granger's

arrival in Galveston Bay. Many people believe that the troops waited until slaveowners had presided over planting the cotton crop before moving to enforce the Emancipation Proclamation in Texas.

Although rooted in Texas, the spread of the celebration of Juneteenth in the 1800s parallels migrations of former slaves to the country's western and northern regions as the people took cultural observances and traditions with them. Early celebrations usually occurred in rural locations not subject to segregation laws, but as the event became popular, Houston's segregated parks gradually waived their rules for this special occasion, and eventually 10 acres of land near Houston were purchased in 1872. In 1898, a community organization was chartered that bought land to establish Booker T. Washington Park in Mexia, located near Waco, to be a permanent location for celebrating the holiday. Juneteenth's established customs include ceasing all work activities, donning elaborate costumes to symbolize the shedding of slavery's rags, digging a barbecue pit as slaves used to, and holding a grand picnic with musical entertainment.

Juneteenth celebrations declined during the Great Depression and in the years following World War II. In 1979, Houston representative Al Edwards proposed legislation making June 19 an official Texas state holiday, and the bill passed and became law on January 1, 1980. This initiative, combined with a climate for increased cultural pride and ethnic identification, has helped to resurrect Juneteenth, and it is currently celebrated across the country.

—*Anthony Todman*

See also
Emancipation Proclamation
For Further Reading
Belkin, Lisa. 1989. "Freedoms Are Renewed in Recalling Deliverance." *New York Times*, June 19; Pemberton, Doris Hollis. 1983. *Juneteenth at Comanche Crossing*. Austin, TX: Eakin Publications; Thomas, Karen M. 1992. "Juneteenth Remembers Slavery, Celebrates Freedom." *Chicago Tribune*, June 18, final edition; Wiggins, William H. 1993. "Juneteenth: Tracking the Progress of an Emancipation Celebration." *American Visions* 8:3 (June/July): 28–31.

JUSTINIAN, LAWS OF

Among the achievements of Justinian I's rule over the Byzantine Empire (r. 527–565) was his major revision and codification of Roman law. Aided by legal experts, Justinian succeeded in drawing together the diverse, disordered strands of classical law into a single, cohesive text.

This mosaic in the church of San Vitale in Ravenna, Italy, depicts Justinian I with his attendants.

The process of revision and compilation codified the numerous laws relating to slavery and provided an opportunity to amend much antiquated legislation.

Justinian grouped the law codes into two main collections, the Codices and the Institutes, and these were supplemented by a third collection, the Digests, comprising the opinions of earlier Roman jurists, and by Justinian's own new legislation, the Novels. The entire corpus is known collectively as the Justinian Code or Corpus Juris Civilis.

Justinian followed earlier Roman lawmakers in his fundamental view of slavery, acknowledging it as an unnatural state of human existence that arose from the *Iuris Gentium,* the "law of nations," rather than being a feature of natural law. The Roman mind defined slavery essentially as an institution produced by warfare, with all slaves broadly labeled prisoners of war. The Justinian Code retained this principle and the notion of a slave as an item of property rather than as a being possessing rights. Yet the code does not state directly that a slave is not a human being or is devoid of personality, despite retaining the ancient idea that a slave is a *res* or object.

One example of Justinian's acknowledgment of traditional notions of slaves as property was his codification of the legal position of runaway slaves. Roman law had customarily considered the fugitive as an item of his owner's property who had "stolen" himself from his owner. Justinian retained this view but amended the legislation in cases where two slaves had persuaded each other to run away by changing the earlier law—which rather curiously considered each slave guilty of "stealing" his accomplice—to state that the act of encouragement to flee was not by itself an act of theft.

Despite such legislation, which clearly regarded the slave as a commodity rather than as a human individual, there are numerous examples of Justinian's capacity to remove earlier slave laws that to modern, egalitarian eyes might seem harsh or draconian. For instance, he made a fundamental change in the position of those slaves seeking their freedom through the judicial process. Previous Roman law had required that such slaves communicate their pleas and cases via an intermediary, known as an *adsertor*. Justinian amended the law to allow slaves to plead their cases for freedom directly and on their own behalf. Similarly, he abolished an ancient law that had decreed that a freewoman who consorted with a slave without the consent of the latter's owner would, upon discovery, be enslaved along with any children born of the union. Another fundamental tenet of classical law that Justinian amended was immunity from prosecution for any owner who killed his slave in the process of legitimate chastisement for an offense committed by the slave. Justinian not only declared that such slayings should henceforth be treated as murder but also limited an owner's authority to inflict severe punishment.

The code still retained many old laws that to modern eyes might seem cruel. Thus, the evidence of slaves in judicial cases continued to be deemed inadmissible unless it was extracted by torture. Moreover, any slave freed by a humane owner in an attempt to preserve the slave from the threat of judicial torture would still be tortured if evidence was required for legal purposes.

Justinian legislated not only for slaves and slave-owners but also for individuals involved in the slave trade. One of his laws codified the position of slave dealers in cases where slaves kept on the dealer's premises prior to delivery to new owners escaped. The dealer was relieved of any charge of breach of duty, unless of course a formal commitment to guarantee security and delivery had been promised to the new owner. The new law is interesting because it shows that although slave dealing was generally viewed as one of the less-pleasant occupations, Justinian felt that the trade, like any other, deserved legal recognition.

The Justinian Code was produced at a time when slavery was still a dominant force in the European economy. Its importance long outlasted the lifetime of its maker, for it provided medieval states with a means by which their own rather limited slave systems might be administered, and it remained the key legislative guide until the resurgence of large-scale European slave trading at the close of the Middle Ages and the rise of individual national legal systems.

—*Tim Clarkson*

See also
Byzantine *Ecloga*
For Further Reading
Buckland, W. W. 1970. *The Roman Law of Slavery.* London: Cambridge University Press; Wiedemann, Thomas, ed. 1988. *Greek and Roman Slavery.* London: Routledge.

KECKLEY, ELIZABETH
(C. 1818–1907)

Born a slave in Virginia, Elizabeth Keckley earned the money to buy her freedom and eventually became a successful dressmaker in Washington, D.C. Her skills were so much admired that the fashionable Mary Todd Lincoln hired Keckley frequently, and soon the former slave was a Lincoln family friend and confidante. After Abraham Lincoln had been killed and his widow had returned to Illinois, Keckley published an autobiographical narrative that recounted scenes from the Lincolns' private life. Keckley blamed the resultant scandal on her editor's unauthorized decision to print Mrs. Lincoln's personal letters, yet it was the dressmaker who took the brunt of Robert Lincoln's anger when he had *Behind the Scenes; or, Thirty Years a Slave and Four Years in the White House* (1868) suppressed.

No one could have foreseen this scandal when as a young slave Keckley labored as a bondwoman or when she was forced to be a white man's concubine. Yet this woman's talents appeared early enough that one master set her to earning, with her needle, the money to support his entire family. After she was taken to St. Louis, the enterprising seamstress negotiated an agreement to work herself out of slavery, and equipped with a ready needle and loans from appreciative clients, Keckley was able to purchase her own and her son's freedom in 1855. Five years later, the loans repaid, Keckley moved to the nation's capital and became the modiste of dress-conscious ladies' choice. It was in this setting that Keckley met Mary Lincoln and became a White House intimate.

No one questioned Keckley's right to compose a narrative of slavery, or even to describe her life as a freewoman during the Civil War. It was because *Behind the Scenes* revealed inside knowledge of Mary Lincoln's staggering debts and provided details on the "old clothes" sale which titillated gossipmongers that Keckley's memoirs caused a scandal, one its author apparently did not foresee. Soon, Mary Lincoln's "dearest Lizzie" was persona non grata amid former friends, and though Keckley spent the rest of her life working as a dressmaker and teaching sewing, she did not write again.

Acquaintances from Keckley's final days recalled her as dignified and ladylike. Often, she would recall the days in which she was Mary Lincoln's friend. She contended that her editor was to blame for the narrative's infelicities, and indeed, James Redpath may have had a grudge against Lincoln's widow. But it is also possible that Keckley overestimated the friendship that Mary Lincoln felt for the black woman. In *Behind the Scenes,* Keckley claimed that bonds of affection could exist between slaveholders and their slaves; she did not note that such sentiments rested on unequal relations to social power.

—*Barbara Ryan*

See also
Narratives
For Further Reading
Keckley, Elizabeth. 1868. *Behind the Scenes; or, Thirty Years a Slave and Four Years in the White House.* New York: G. W. Carleton; Washington, John E. 1942. *They Knew Lincoln.* New York: E. P. Dutton.

KEMBLE, FRANCES ANNE
(1809–1893)

Frances Anne Kemble was a famous English actress who was also well known for the publication of her antislavery book, *Journal of a Residence on a Georgian Plantation in 1838–1839* (1863). Frances Anne (Fanny) and her father, Charles Kemble, both accomplished Shakespearean actors, toured the United States from 1832 through 1834, and during the tour she met and eventually married Pierce Mease Butler, a wealthy Philadelphia resident. At the time of their wedding, Fanny was unaware of the source of Butler's wealth—plantation lands and slaves located in coastal Georgia.

Headstrong and opinionated, Fanny Butler strongly opposed slavery. Believing she could persuade her husband of slavery's evils, she openly condemned his "living in idleness from the unpaid labor of others" and sought "to bring him to a realization of the sins of slaveholding" (Kemble, 1863). Pierce Butler reluctantly assented to his wife's suggestion that they both visit the Georgia plantations as Christian "missionaries," and in late December 1838, the Butler family arrived in Darien, Georgia. Nearby was Butler's Island, the family's rice plantation of nearly 2,000 acres, and there was another property in the vicinity, a 1,700-acre tract on St. Simons Island called Hampton Point where Sea Island cotton was cultivated. The two plantations combined had a slave population of several hundred.

Already convinced of the degrading nature of slavery when she arrived in Georgia, Fanny Butler's negative opinions were not only confirmed but strengthened. During this sojourn in the South she kept a diary, which she subsequently expanded and eventually published as the *Journal of a Residence*. Her chronicle reveals a particular concern for slave women as she recounted in great detail how pregnant slaves were overworked and even whipped. Laboring in the fields until delivery, female slaves were allowed only a short period to recover from childbirth. Fanny Butler condemned medical care on the plantations as barbaric. Not surprisingly, miscarriages, stillbirths, and infant mortality rates were shockingly high.

Slave dwellings were regarded as "filthy and wretched in the extreme," and the children were depicted as having "incrustations of dirt on their hands, feet, and faces." During her months in Georgia, Fanny Butler did what she could to improve sanitary conditions in the slave infirmary and slave dwellings. Her journal also gives details regarding slave music, funerals, food and its preparation, plus other customs.

Considered to be quite an indictment of slavery, the *Journal* was published in England in 1863. Since the Butlers were divorced by this time, Frances Kemble had been persuaded by friends that publication would help the antislavery cause of Union forces during the U.S. Civil War. The *Journal* was actually published too late to have any substantial effect upon Britain's foreign policy regarding the Confederacy—government opinion already having shifted from its previous pro-Southern views. Nevertheless, the book gave a firsthand and very thorough account of slavery.

—Mary Ellen Wilson

For Further Reading
Bell, Malcolm. 1987. *Major Butler's Legacy: Five Generations of a Slaveholding Family*. Athens: University of Georgia Press; Driver, Leota S. 1969. *Fanny Kemble*. New York: Negro Universities Press; Kemble, Frances Anne. 1863. *Journal of a Residence on a Georgian Plantation in 1838–1839*. New York: Harper and Brothers; Scott, John Anthony. 1961. "On the Authenticity of Fanny Kemble's *Journal of a Residence on a Georgian Plantation in 1838–1839*." *Journal of Negro History* 46: 233–242.

KIM HAK-SUN
(1924–)

The first Korean to give public testimony of her life as a "comfort woman," Kim Hak-sun was 67 years old when she finally found a public forum to air her deep-seated *han* ("remorseful anger"), which she had kept pent-up for half a century. "Comfort women" refers to those women who were forced into sexual slavery by the Japanese military from 1937 to 1945, and until she came forth, there were no stories of these women in the history books of either Korea or Japan. Kim's life story underlines the intersection of gender, class, and ethnicity that was embedded in the tragic lives of numerous former comfort women, most of whom came from poor families in rural areas of colonial Korea.

Kim was 17 when she was abducted in 1941 by Japanese soldiers and forced to become a comfort woman (Kim, 1995). Kept in a small house located near a military unit outside of Beijing, she was given a Japanese name, Aiko, as were the other four Korean women in the house. After about two months, the military unit relocated to a more remote place, and the soldiers moved the women with them. There she met a Korean man who helped her escape and eventually became her husband.

Kim gave birth to a daughter and a son in China before the family returned to Korea after the end of World War II. Their daughter died of cholera upon their arrival in Korea; her husband, who used to mistreat her for having been a comfort woman, died of an accident in 1953; a few years later, her son died of a heart attack while swimming in the sea. Losing her will to live, Kim tried to commit suicide and led an aimless life, drinking and smoking her life away, until 1981 when she began to work as a maid and began to save some money.

In 1987, failing health forced her quit her job, and she began living in a rented room. She then came to know Yi Maeng-hi, a Korean victim of the atomic bombs dropped in Japan in August 1945. Kim wanted to vent her grudge against Japan by testifying in public about her life as a comfort woman, but she did not know where to go until she heard from Yi about the Korean Church Women United (KCWU), a group whose leadership actively supports Korean atomic bomb victims and helped found the Korean Council for the Women Drafted for Military Sexual Slavery by Japan in 1990 (Soh, 1996). Kim testified at the KCWU office in August 1991 and filed a lawsuit against the Japanese government for crimes against humanity in December 1991.

After filing suit, Kim made several appearances at conferences in Korea and abroad to give testimony about her life as a comfort women and to advocate the need to teach about the comfort women in history classes. What Kim wants most from the Japanese government is a formal letter of apology, not monetary reparation, as the Korean government now provides the survivors with a monthly stipend. It is expected that it will take the supreme court in Japan between 10 and 20 years to reach a judgment on Kim's lawsuit (Totsuka, 1995).

—*Chunghee Sarah Soh*

See also
Comfort Women; Korean Council; Sexual Slavery, Japanese Military; Yun Chông-ok

For Further Reading
Kim, Hak-sun. 1995. "Bitter Memories I Am Loath to Recall." In *True Stories of the Korean Comfort Women.* Ed. Keith Howard. London: Cassell; Soh, Chunghee Sarah. 1996. "The Korean 'Comfort Women' Movement for Redress: From a Bilateral Compensation to a Human Rights Issue." *Asian Survey* 36 (December): 1226–1240; Totsuka, Etsuro. 1995. "Military Sexual Slavery by Japan and Issues in Law." In *True Stories of the Korean Comfort Women.* Ed. Keith Howard. London: Cassell.

KNIGHTS OF THE GOLDEN CIRCLE

A colorful example of antebellum Southern expansionism, the Knights of the Golden Circle was a secret filibustering society that sought to extend U.S. control—and slavery—throughout the lands bordering the Gulf of Mexico. Founded, according to some sources, on July 4, 1854, in Lexington, Kentucky, the organization was the brainchild of Virginia-born George W. L. Bickley (1819–1867), a physician, scholar, and journalist from Cincinnati, Ohio. A self-proclaimed crusader for "Southern rights," Bickley planned to achieve sectional equality with the North by carving new slave states from territory seized in Mexico, Central America, and the Caribbean.

Little is known of the organization's activities immediately after its formation, but the outbreak of civil war in Mexico spurred Bickley to action in spring 1859. During a convention held in White Sulphur Springs, Virginia, on August 8, Bickley announced that Mexico would be the first field of operations. In early 1860, he ordered his followers to rendezvous in Texas and prepare for active operations.

Bickley was probably encouraged because both President James Buchanan and Governor Sam Houston of Texas openly advocated U.S. intervention for the purpose of restoring order in Mexico. However, Houston, a staunch unionist, was unwilling to support Bickley's efforts to extend slavery south of the Rio Grande. He refused to sanction Bickley's invasion and on March 21, 1860, issued a proclamation against the Knights' activities.

Houston's proclamation, coupled with Bickley's failure to arrive with promised reinforcements, led Bickley's Texas followers to abandon the enterprise. Charging their leader with betrayal, the Texas Knights of the Golden Circle met in New Orleans in early April and expelled him from the organization. He retaliated by summoning a grand convention at Raleigh, North Carolina, on May 7, where he was reinstated as president of the national organization.

Bickley immediately resumed efforts to lead his followers into Mexico, and on July 18, in an open letter published in the Richmond, Virginia, *Daily Whig,* he urged fellow Knights to rendezvous at Fort Ewen, Texas, on September 15. Claiming that Mexico's liberal faction would welcome the Knights as allies and colonizers, Bickley predicted that the conservatives' defeat would pave the way for the "Americanization" of the strife-torn nation. Published in newspapers throughout the South, Bickley's address assured Southerners that the acquisition of Mexico would prevent the North from reducing the slave states to "vassalage." He further promised that the abolitionists would be silenced, the South's free black population would vanish, and cotton production would soar.

Arriving in Texas on October 10, "General" Bickley established his headquarters in San Antonio and began recruiting activities throughout the state. However, the secession movement that swept the South after Abraham Lincoln's presidential victory led Bickley to abandon the Mexican venture. He announced to his followers that, henceforth, promoting secession, not filibustering, would be the society's mission.

Leaving Texas in late 1860, Bickley spent spring and summer 1861 in a futile effort to promote secession in the crucial border state of Kentucky. He eventually established a recruiting camp across the state line in Clarksville, Tennessee, but disbanded his volunteers in late-summer 1861 after a dispute with Confederate leaders in that state. Bickley later attempted to organize a mounted command in Virginia before securing a place as a rebel surgeon.

Deserting the Confederate cause in 1863, Bickley was arrested by Union military authorities in July as he attempted to return to his former home in Cincinnati, Ohio. The former filibuster chief was charged with spying and kept under close confinement until his release on October 14, 1865. He reportedly died a "broken man" in Baltimore on August 3, 1867.

Often confused with a similarly named secret antiwar society that existed in the North during the war,

Bickley's Knights of the Golden Circle was a separate organization that arose from the sectional discord and expansionism that characterized the 1850s. Far from being a man of action, like William Walker, Bickley, regarded by many as a fraud, never saw the fulfillment of his grandiose scheme. Nevertheless, many Northerners regarded Bickley's organization as symbolic of the South's determination to preserve and extend slavery, and in this respect, the organization contributed significantly to the sectional misunderstanding that led to war.

—*James M. Prichard*

For Further Reading
Bridges, C. A. 1941. "The Knights of the Golden Circle: A Filibustering Fantasy." *Southwestern Historical Quarterly* 44 (January): 287–302; Crenshaw, Ollinger. 1941. "The Knights of the Golden Circle: The Career of George Bickley." *American Historical Review* 47 (October): 23–50; May, Robert E. 1973. *The Southern Dream of a Caribbean Empire 1854–1861*. Baton Rouge: Louisiana State University Press.

KOREA

Slavery has existed in Korea since the time of its tribal states before the Christian era began. Criminals, prisoners of war, and conquered tribes generally fell into servitude. The law of Kochoson especially punished thieves, making them slaves of those they had robbed.

From the first century B.C. to the seventh century, each of the three kingdoms on the peninsula was a typical ancient nation with a centralized monarch based upon an aristocracy. In this period, slavery undoubtedly developed fully. For instance, records from one of the kingdoms, the Kingdom of Silla, show some cases of large slaveholding and even the custom of burying slaves alive for the king's funeral. A strict class division placed people into eight different groups, and the bottom layer must have included slaves, although records fail to show clearly the range of their rights and duties.

When the Kingdom of Silla unified the peninsula in 669, the class system began to weaken, and it is likely that so, too, did the institution of slavery. Such a trend had already begun, probably around the time when the infusion of Confucian ideology among Korean nobles started, and in trying to establish elites based more upon character than by blood or wealth, the ideology certainly worked to dilute class distinctions among the people. After the Koryo dynasty was established in 935, traditional Korea had only three layered social hierarchies: the nobles (including royal families), commoners, and the lowborn (in other words, the mean people to whom slaves belonged).

In 956, the Koryo freed slaves on a large scale—freeing all slaves who were impressed to servitude unfairly was the tradition in East Asia whenever any new dynasty emerged. There is no information about slavery in the middle Koryo period, but at the end of the dynasty, the slave population rose suddenly and substantially. The paradigm of a dynastic cycle and the factors that increased agricultural productivity explain this unusual transition.

At the end of the Koryo dynasty, even as the government exposed corruption and inertia, the economy prospered because improved farming technology doubled land productivity. In the expanded arable land, commercial agriculture began producing foodstuffs, and as large manors appeared, the nobles impressed commoners to servitude on them. Thus, the number of slaves swelled, and many slave rebellions broke out. Only in this period, did Korea experience slave rebellions. Decades ago, pointing to this large slave population, Japanese scholars believed that traditional Korean society was similar to an ancient slave state. However, the large number of slaves was unique to this period in Korea's history.

The new dynasty of Choson, established in 1392, freed many of the slaves owned by the large landlords. Choson courts occasionally debated the issue of the status of children born of parents who were a free person and a slave, because that status was closely related to the matter of balancing the population ratio between commoners and slaves. Slave concubines' children fathered by scholar-officials were always free, although they were barred from taking government posts. The status of children born of slaves and commoners followed diverse patterns, usually because of the ownership of their residence or because the relevant laws changed from time to time. Therefore, the widespread belief that the children born of parents of mixed status always inherited the lower, slave, status is wrong.

The period of Choson rule is the source of most of the records on slavery, and the records indicate that two kinds of public and private slaves lived in Korea and that they worked mostly as farmworkers and sometimes as domestic servants and artisans. Some of them exhibited great talent in invention and painting. The size of their population was never large, presumably 10 percent of the total population on average, but it could rise up to one-third of the total, as it did at the end of the Koryo period.

More free farmers than slaves engaged in farming. The big difference between slaves and commoners was that slaves had to pay a heavier tribute tax while commoners paid a military tax, which sometimes rose as high as the slaves' tax burden. The law treated slaves slightly worse than commoners, but the big gulf lay between rights and duties of these two groups and those of the scholar-officials.

When the population increased early in the Choson period, the ratio of the land to population became smaller, and the growing economy offered more opportunity for landless people to be hired, which encouraged slaves to run away. The problem of escaped slaves became rampant after the late-sixteenth century when the Choson dynasty began its downward cycle, and there was less distinction between the slaves and commoners as the living conditions of the former improved and those of the latter worsened.

A policy of gradual emancipation began in 1775 when King Yongjo reduced the tax on the slaves so that it was equal to that of the commoners, an idea that had arisen decades earlier. Thus, economically, slaves would no longer be different from the commoners. In 1801, the royal family and the central government freed all of their agricultural slaves, and slaves of other government agencies were then freed individually. In 1886, by limiting servitude to one generation, the Choson abolished hereditary slavery. Finally, in 1895, under the influence of Japan, which planned to modernize Korea first and then annex it after the Sino-Japanese War, the Choson court abolished slavery entirely. Uncompensated emancipation ensued, and former slaves worked for their former masters as hired laborers.

—*Hyong-In Kim*

See also
Abolition, East Asia; East Asia
For Further Reading
Hiraki, Minoru. 1982. *Choson huki nobiche yonku* (A study of slavery in the later Choson). Seoul: Chisik Sanopsa; Hong, Seung-ki. 1983. *Koryoeui kuijoksa-hoewa nobi* (Aristocratic society of Koryo and slaves). Seoul: Iljokak; Kim, Hyong-In. 1990. "Rural Slavery in Antebellum South Carolina and Early Choson Korea." Ph.D. dissertation, Department of History, University of New Mexico; Salem, Ellen. 1978. "Slavery in Medieval Korea." Ph.D. dissertation, Department of History, Columbia University.

KOREAN COUNCIL

The Korean Council for the Women Drafted for Military Sexual Slavery by Japan (the Korean Council hereafter) is a coalition of 36 women's organizations formed on November 16, 1990, in Korea under the leadership of Professor Yun Chông-ok. The council's goals are to uncover the truth about the so-called comfort women

for the Japanese troops before and during World War II and to help redress the violation of these women's human rights by seeking an official apology and compensation from the Japanese government.

A group of Korean women's organizations began publicly raising the issues concerning the suffering of the Korean people during the Japanese colonial rule in general and the reparation for comfort women in particular on major diplomatic occasions in 1989. On January 7, 1989, for example, they staged a demonstration march in Seoul to protest against the Korean government's plan to send an emissary to the funeral of Emperor Hirohito, the symbol of Japanese imperialism and colonial rule in Korea from 1910 to 1945. The formal establishment of the Korean Council was partly in response to the continued denial of state responsibility by Japan, as exemplified by the statement given by a Japanese government spokesperson in June 1990 in which he reiterated the official position that the "comfort stations" were run by private entrepreneurs and not by the government.

After Kim Hak-sun came forth to give public testimony as a former comfort woman in August 1991, the Korean Council established a hotline so that other former comfort women could register formally. It is primarily because of the courage of former comfort women to speak out and the feminist activism of the dedicated leaders and members of the Korean Council that the silenced issue of Japanese military sexual slavery before and during World War II came to the attention of the international community.

Because neither the government of Korea nor that of Japan responded positively to resolve the problem of the comfort women, Professor Lee Hyo-chae of the Korean Council submitted a petition dated March 4, 1992, to the United Nations Human Rights Commission in which she requested that the commission investigate the Japanese atrocities committed against Korean women during the war and that they help pressure Japan to pay compensation to individual women who had filed suit in Japan. The UN commission responded by placing the issue on the official agenda for its August 1992 meeting in Geneva, where delegates from the Korean Council and one former comfort woman testified.

After extensive investigation, Radhika Coomaraswamy, the UN special investigator on violence against women, concluded in a report presented on February 6, 1996, that Japan must admit its legal responsibility, identify and punish those responsible for sexual slavery during the war, compensate the victims, apologize to the survivors in writing, and teach this hidden chapter in Japanese history classrooms.

It is remarkable that the UN recommendations resemble so closely the demands that the Korean Council has made consistently since its inception in 1990.

The official response of Japan to the mounting pressure from the international community was to deal with the compensation issue on a nongovernmental level by establishing the Asian Women's Fund to disburse a lump sum of "atonement money" raised by public donation. The Korean Council and the women's organizations in other Asian countries have denounced the plan for sidestepping state responsibility on the part of the Japanese government.

The Korean Council contributed to the forging of a transnational feminist and human rights activist group among the affected Asian countries, including Japan, by hosting the first Asian conference on the comfort women issue in Seoul, South Korea, on August 10–11, 1992. The second conference of the Asian Solidarity Forum was held in Tokyo in 1993, and the third in Seoul in 1995. Also, since January 1992, the Korean Council has instituted a weekly Wednesday noon rally in front of the Japanese embassy in Seoul. At these events a small group of elderly survivors of the Japanese military sexual slavery, Korean Council staff members, and several other supporters shout in unison slogans such as Apologize! Punish! and Compensate!

The Korean Council, in collaboration with the Research Association on the Women Drafted for Military Sexual Slavery by Japan, has published the testimony of Korean survivors of Japanese military sexual slavery in Korea and China. The council also helped raise approximately $250,000 nationwide between December 1992 and June 1993, and the money was distributed among the survivors in July 1993. The Korean legislature passed a special act to help support the survivors, and the Korean government disbursed a sum of 5 million wôn (US $6,250) to each survivor in August 1993 and pays a monthly stipend.

The remarkable success of the feminist political activism of the Korean Council in making the problem of the comfort women a universal moral issue of women's human rights is owing in part to the dramatic transformations in the national and international political structures since the late 1980s, i.e., the democracy movement and the restoration of civilian government in Korea and the collapse of the Cold War world order in the international community (Soh, 1996).

—*Chunghee Sarah Soh*

See also
Kim Hak-sun; Sexual Slavery, Japanese Military; Yun Chông-ok

For Further Reading
Howard, Keith, ed. 1995. *True Stories of the Korean Comfort Women.* London: Cassell; Soh, Chunghee Sarah. 1996. "The Korean 'Comfort Women' Movement for Redress: From a Bilateral Compensation to a Human Rights Issue." *Asian Survey* 36 (December): 1226–1240.

5/01